A HISTORY OF EUROPE
H. G. Koenigsberger & Asa Briggs

Medieval Europe 400–1500   H. G. Koenigsberger

Early Modern Europe 1500–1789   H. G. Koenigsberger

Modern Europe 1789–1989   Asa Briggs & Patricia Clavin

Frontispiece The decapitated monument of Alexander III, Moscow, January 1918. Heads will roll: the statue which stood in the centre of Moscow was toppled by workers to mark the beginning of the new communist order. The scene was recreated in S. M. Eisenstein's film *Days of October* and repeated with the fall of communism over 80 years later. (See p. 411).

A HISTORY OF EUROPE
H. G. Koenigsberger & Asa Briggs

MODERN EUROPE 1789–1989

ASA BRIGGS & PATRICIA CLAVIN

Longman

An imprint of **Pearson Education**

Harlow, England · London · New York · Reading, Massachusetts · San Francisco
Toronto · Don Mills, Ontario · Sydney · Tokyo · Singapore · Hong Kong · Seoul
Taipei · Cape Town · Madrid · Mexico City · Amsterdam · Munich · Paris · Milan

Pearson Education Limited
Edinburgh Gate
Harlow
Essex CM20 2JE
England

and Associated Companies throughout the world

Visit us on the World Wide Web at:
http://www.pearsoneduc.com

First published 1997

ISBN 0 582 49406 0 CSD
ISBN 0 582 49405 2 PPR

British Library Cataloguing-in-Publication Data

A catalogue record for this book is
available from the British Library

Library of Congress Cataloging-in-Publication Data

Briggs, Asa, 1921-
    Modern Europe 1789–1989 / Asa Briggs & Patricia Clavin.
        p.   cm. — (A History of Europe)
    Includes bibliographical references and index.
    ISBN 0-582-49406-0. — ISBN 0-582-49405-2 (pbk.)
    1. Europe—History—1989–1900.   2. Europe—History—20th century.
I. Clavin, Patricia.   II. Title   III. Series: Koenigsberger, H. G.
(Helmut Georg) History of Europe.
D299.B696   1996
940.2'8—dc20   96-10174
                                                      CIP

Set by 7R
Produced by Pearson Education Asia (Pte) Ltd.
Printed in Singapore (COS)

10 9 8 7 6 5 4 3
04 03 02 01 00

Contents

List of Maps

List of Plates

Preface

This volume is a sequel to Helli Koenigsberger's *Medieval Europe* and *Early Modern Europe*. The three volumes were originally planned as a set by Koenigsberger and myself, and I wrote drafts of my own chapters before *Early Modern Europe* appeared. Little survives in this book, however, in the form that it was originally drafted, for since the original scheme was devised, Europe, west and east, has changed greatly, and historical scholarship has advanced on many fronts.

Much, for example, of a 'revisionist' kind has been written on national histories, including British history, while much that is new has been written about 'the idea of Europe', its origins and how it has been expressed intellectually and culturally in diverse forms during different periods of history. Such writing bears directly on leading questions in recent European history – on developments within the European Community and on the disintegration of communist power – and the fact that it is largely unfamiliar to politicians engaged in current debate about European identity and national identity (unity in diversity?) is one good reason for historians to seek to provide works of synthesis that stretch deep below the political surface into society and culture.

It is dangerous to see everything in the past as leading up inexorably to the present (nation states within the European Community), just as it was unwise for nineteenth-century historians dealing with English (not British) history to see the past leading up triumphantly to Victorian constitutional government. Whatever the version of European history, Britain figures, as it must do, within Europe and not apart from it, even when a sharp division is drawn between Britain and 'continental Europe' as it still is in newspaper headlines. And what British politicians, writers, artists and travellers have themselves said and felt about 'Europe' in the past adds depth as well as variety to current commentary.

There is a further, less topical, reason for concentrating on the period covered in this book within the whole span of European history. It is a strategic period in that it was only after the French Revolution that what Pim de Boer has called 'a distinct, self-reflective idea of a Europe with a history and meaning of its own' took shape. It was during this period also that the new phenomenon of the nation state was at the centre both of events and of the study of history, a study which was based largely on newly opened national archives. Nation building became a major theme.

More recently, increasing attention has been paid to local and to regional history, and while this book concentrates on the map of states, including old empires and new nation states and the boundaries that separated them, it draws attention also to the map of 'regions' within states and to the regions which cross the boundaries of states. Unevenness of regional development and the potency of regional thrust in particular parts of Europe enliven all aspects of European history, including economic and political as much as cultural history.

Narrative and analysis, national, local or regional, are strengthened when they rest on evidence 'from below'; and for the historian this applies alike in the case of the study of business and labour (economics), of social groupings (sociology) and of perceptions and motives (psychology). The evidence takes different forms, and during the last half of this century, historians have broadened their range of evidence to draw on 'folklore', 'popular culture', music, art, and, not least, language, far more than most of their predecessors did in the nineteenth century. Everything, including ephemera, is grist to their mill. Their own social backgrounds are more varied too, and they approach the past in the light of their own experience as well as of their historical researches.

It remains impossible to separate out at any point the 'facts' of geography, a subject which was itself transformed during the same period as history, from historical facts, not least because 'the facts' of geography were themselves transformed as a result of unprecedented population growth, urbanization, industrialization, innovative technology and new communications patterns in the nineteenth and through into the twentieth century. At the same time it is impossible to trace the evolution of 'the idea of Europe', the role of the nation state, or the sense of region without taking account also of the 'fundamental facts' of geography (rivers, mountains, lakes, seas, oceans) and of the agencies of change, particularly new communications devices that affected both the physical and built environment and human perceptions of distance and time. Out of geography there emerged in the period covered in this book both geopolitics and a new kind of social and cultural geography, often based on the region.

This book is a work of synthesis, pulling together different strands, and in every chapter it draws, inevitably selectively, on the work of historians of different periods, different ages and different persuasions. Sometimes they have belonged to distinct 'historical schools', more recently to 'research teams'. They have argued with each other – history, like current politics, develops through controversy – and there has seldom been full consensus. Relatively little attention is paid in this book, however, to arguments between historians, for example about the French Revolution, the character of the Italian *Risorgimento* or the origins of the First or Second World Wars. This is not only because limitations of length demand a rigorous choice of what to put in and what to leave out, but because historians often focus so sharply on their own debates that their definitions of what constitute historical problems get in the way of elucidating history itself. They also rely heavily on their own terminology, some of it forged in the heat of controversy but copied cold; and this can be forbidding to a reader who is not and never intends to be a professional historian.

Footnotes have been deliberately kept to a minimum, but the bibliography, itself highly selective, contains not only the names of books and their authors on whom our own text depends, but books and authors to whom the reader should turn in order to pursue studies independently. Some books reach conclusions different from our own. The illustrations are not a luxurious extra. They seek to provide important evidence in themselves. So, too, do the maps.

I have been fortunate in preparing this new book to have as a co-author Patricia Clavin of the University of Keele. We have each written sections of the final text, but we have discussed these fully at different stages of research and writing. The final result, therefore, is a joint work. Only this preface is entirely my own. The book will doubtless demand further revisions in the light of future changes. Europe, enriched but burdened by its past, is still in the making.

We would like to express our thanks to our editor, Stephanie Cooke. We are also deeply grateful to Andrew McLennan for his dedication – and patience – while this book was being written. We owe a great debt to him.

ASA BRIGGS April 1995

Acknowledgements

The publishers would like to thank the following for granting permission to reproduce illustrative material: The David King Collection for frontispiece and figs 6.7, 7.3, 8.6, 9.5 and 10.4; Jean-Loup Charmat (Paris) for fig. 1.1; Topham Picture Source for figs 1.2, 3.6, 4.3, 6.2, 6.4, 6.5, 7.2, 7.6, 8.1, 9.2, 9.3, 9.8, 10.1 and 12.6; The Mary Evans Picture Library for figs 1.3, 2.2, 3.1, 3.4, 3.5, 4.2, 4.4, 5.5, 5.6, 6.3, 6.6 and 8.4; The Hulton Deutsch Collected Ltd for figs 1.4, 1.6, 1.7, 2.1, 2.3, 2.4, 2.5, 2.6, 3.2, 3.3, 3.7, 4.1, 4.5, 5.4, 6.1, 7.1, 7.4, 7.5, 8.5, 9.1, 9.4, 10.2, 10.3, 10.5, 11.1, 12.3 and 12.4; The Bridgeman Art Library for figs 1.5 and 5.2; J Allan Cash Ltd for fig. 5.1; The Art Institute of Chicago for fig. 5.3; Constable Publishers for Map 7.3 taken from *August 1914* by Barbara W. Tuchman; By permission of The British Library/The Evening Standard 22/6/33 for fig. 8.2; Popperfoto for figs 8.3, 9.7, 10.6, 11.2, 11.4, 11.5 and 12.5; E. T. Archive for fig. 9.6; R. Bossu/Sygma for fig. 10.7; Punch for fig. 11.3; Greenpeace Communications Ltd for fig. 12.1; The Science Photo Library for fig. 12.2.

Chapter **1**

Revolution and Empire: Experience and Impact, 1789–1815

Change and revolution: old and new

There was so much change, most of it unprecedented, during the second half of the eighteenth century that both then and since most people have regarded this period in human history as the great divide between past and present. This, they have said, was the true beginning of 'modern times'. Looking backwards, the French nobleman, Alexis de Tocqueville, one of the shrewdest of political and social commentators, could 'find no parallel' in history. 'The past [had] ceased to throw its light upon the future.'

In the late-twentieth century, after the world has experienced further bursts of unprecedented change, much of it packed into the last 30 years, such a view of late-eighteenth-century change can be challenged. With the help of hindsight we can now identify continuities in thought, behaviour and institutions. The past did influence the future. We have also introduced the terms 'post-modern' and 'post-industrial' into our vocabulary to widen the perspectives. Yet the word 'revolution' still carries with it dramatic force. And this is true whether it is applied to late-eighteenth-century politics and society in France, in population by far the largest state in Europe (27 million in 1789, seven million more than in 1700), or to industrialization in Britain, a country with a third the population of France but with an unprecedented burst of economic growth in the last decades of the eighteenth century.

The word 'revolution' has been applied also to what happened in America following the American Declaration of Independence in 1776 (the year of Adam Smith's *Wealth of Nations* and of a large new James Watt steam engine, named not inappropriately 'Parliament Engine'). During the American War Frenchmen, including members of the French nobility, fought the British on American soil. The winning of American independence, a victory in which France shared, although at burdening financial cost, in effect bankruptcy, humiliated Britain, but it did not hold back striking industrial growth. As for the American political changes, some American historians have claimed that 'in the modern sense of the word it was hardly a revolution at all'.[1] There was, however, a new republic, and with it a commitment of the American people to the 'pursuit of happiness'. There was also the authority of a written constitution, drafted at Philadelphia in 1787.

Historians can learn much from changes in the meaning of words, indeed from the history of language as a whole. Originally the word 'revolution' had been an astronomical term applied to the regular round of the stars in their courses; and even after it came to be employed in political discussion during the seventeenth century it was usually implied that as a result of revolution the proper order of things, perverted by men in power, would be restored. You would move back to where you began. It was de Tocqueville again who wrote of the beginning of the French Revolution in 1789 that 'one might have believed that the aim of the coming revolution was not the overthrow of the old regime but its restoration'. Nonetheless, after 1789 the word 'revolution' never meant quite the same again.

Whatever continuities there were between pre-revolutionary Europe and Europe after 1789 there was a very special sense of newness. Maximilien-Isidore Robespierre, revolutionary of revolutionaries, wrote to his brother in the summer of 1789 that France had produced 'in a few days greater events than the whole previous history of mankind', while across the Channel the leader of the English Whigs, Charles James Fox, described the fall of the Bastille as 'much the greatest event that ever happened in the history of the world'. In the new world of industry the pioneering English potter Josiah Wedgwood believed that 'the wonderful revolution' had 'thrown the world off its hinges', and in the old world of the Muses poets as different as William Blake and Samuel Taylor Coleridge joined in the chorus, along with Johann Wolfgang Goethe and Friedrich von Schiller in Germany. For William Wordsworth, aged 19, this was

> . . . a time when Europe was rejoiced,
> France standing on the top of golden hours
> And human nature seeming born again.

What could be newer than that?

The leading ideological opponent of the Revolution, Edmund Burke, clearly appreciated the newness of what had happened as much as the revolutionaries themselves and those who sympathized with them. As early as 1790 he described the Revolution as a 'novelty', a deliberate break with history, not its culmination. For him it had nothing in common, therefore, with the 'glorious' English Revolution of 1688, the centenary of which had been celebrated in London just before the French revolutionary cycle began. Nor had it much in common, he believed, with the American Revolution. Unlike foreign sympathizers with the French Revolution, many of whom changed their minds about it later in the light of future events,

Plate 1.1 The Republican Calendar, 1793–94. The calendar is adorned by the Goddess of Liberty. Belonging to no particular group or place, Liberty symbolized the abstract, highly prized, quality of reason. By 1792 she had become the pre-eminent symbol of the revolution.

Burke from the start saw pattern in the novelty: revolution was a cycle, not a sequence. It began with anti-absolutist abstractions and it would end with revolutionary absolutism and war.

The Revolution hinged (Wedgwood's word) on far more than the fate of a well-intentioned king, Louis XVI, who had ascended the throne of France in 1774. Yet it was only after the creation of a new French republic in September 1792 and the guillotining of the King on 21 January 1793 that revolutionary novelty was fully and self-consciously proclaimed to the world in a new republican calendar which was adopted by the National Convention on 5 October 1793, two weeks before the execution of Queen Marie Antoinette. Year I was now stated to have begun on 22 September 1792, and in future within each year the months were to be redivided also. There were still to be 12 of them, but they were now all to be of thirty days.

Their 'republican' names, originally designated as 'first', 'second' and so on, like the names of streets in the grid pattern of American cities, were subsequently chosen by a specially appointed Commission neither from history nor from myth but from nature, nature as peasants, not as the *bourgeoisie*, were thought to understand it. The first, *Vendémiaire*, was the month of the vintage, the last, *Fructidor*, the month of fruit. The second, *Brumaire*, was the month of mist. *Germinal* was the month of seeding, *Floréal* the month of blossom, and *Thermidor*, the tenth month, the month of heat. Each month was divided into three *décades*, each of ten days. The Christian Sunday totally disappeared, as did Christian holy days. A new cult of Reason, grounded in eighteenth-century philosophy, displaced Christianity. The five days left over after the reorganization of the months were republican festival days dedicated to Virtue, Talent, Labour, Ideas (Opinions) and Rewards. In leap years the extra day, now to be the last day of the year, was to be Revolution Day.

The calendar itself lasted only until 1805, ten years before the fall of Napoleon and the restoration (for so it was called) of the Bourbons. France had not begun anew. Nor had Christianity disappeared. Nor, however, had industrialization disposed of an older order in Britain, despite the fact that British industrialists, like French revolutionaries, were fascinated by the concept of 'newness' and charged the word 'invention' with magnetic force. Matthew Boulton, James Watt's partner, took pride in dealing in 'novelties' before he sold power; and Birmingham, his city, which had no counterpart in France, was later said to represent, as other new industrial cities did, a system of life constructed according to 'wholly new principles'.

Industrialization introduced a new sense of time also, even if it did not require a new calendar. The lives of the workers, who included children, were now regulated by the factory hooter. Work started early and went on late. Monday was called Saint Monday because it was a day when, in face of tough discipline, as tough as that in Napoleon's armies, workers might take a day off. In a further phase of industrialization there were to be battles between employers and workers about hours as well as wages. More generally 'time frameworks' were to change too. Fast coaches introduced 'time tables' before the age of the railway and the use of standard railway time. Foreigners often complained of the English mania for 'saving time'.

Most critics of what came to be called 'the industrial revolution' objected to the power of the machine and the monotonous routines of industrial labour, while critics of the French Revolution believed that what was happening throughout the revolutionary sequence or cycle that ended in Napoleon's defeat at Waterloo in 1815 could better be explained in terms of nature than of history – or, as later critics were to do, of theatre. They compared it with a storm or more dramatically with a torrent or a stream of lava, and it was with relief, therefore, if with premature confidence, that the *Quarterly Review* in London in 1814 could claim that 'the volcano is now extinguished; and we may approach the crater with perfect security'. That was before the final historical twist when Napoleon escaped from the island of Elba and lived to fight again.

In this respect political change in France was completely different from the economic and industrial change in Britain to which the label 'industrial revolution' was first attached by a French economist of the 1820s, Adolphe Blanqui. Comparing the social and political changes that had happened in France during the 1780s and 1790s with the social and economic changes that took place in Britain, he could point to Georges Jacques Danton on one side of the Channel and Watt on the other. A French historian of a later generation, Paul Mantoux, writing in 1906, spoke of what happened in Britain in the late-eighteenth century as 'one of the most important moments in modern history, the consequences of which have affected the whole civilized world and are still transforming it and shaping it under our eyes'.[2]

Blanqui, the brother of a committed political revolutionary, was living at a time when most knowledgeable Europeans were arguing that it was the economic strength of Britain, based on the exploitation of coal and iron, the invention of new machinery and the harnessing of new forms of power, that had accounted for victory in the long wars against the French Revolution and Napoleon which had lasted with short breaks from 1793 to 1815. Some Englishmen disagreed. They attributed success not to industrial – or financial – strength but to 'moral strength', to Protestantism, or, in Burkean language, to the excellence of an institutional 'inheritance' of parliamentary monarchy and the rule of law. Two systems were thus being compared – the British, which appealed to history, and the French, which in the course of revolution had tried to dispose of it. Yet even within this interpretation, which purported to explain why 'free born Englishmen' had not staged a political revolution, it was relevant to ask why there had been no industrial revolution in France.

Many reasons were found. The French social system, it was argued, was more rigid, despite the development of new wealth in the eighteenth century, much of it derived from the Caribbean as was much new British wealth; it permitted the creation of new noblemen, but it did not favour *entrepreneurs*. Capital was easily diverted from 'useful' projects to 'luxuries'. Income was spent conspicuously, not productively. Quality was preferred to quantity. Unlettered English mechanics produced machines: French artisans used their ingenuity in producing gadgets, like mechanical toys. The really large French textiles factory, which had been in existence for nearly a hundred years, produced tapestries. Manchester dealt in cotton: Lyons in silk. Wedgwood's 'Etruria', centre of the Potteries, was a very different place from Sèvres, home of French porcelain, as he himself recognized. English workmen were more adaptable and more mobile: Scottish workmen were more thrifty and ambitious. Protestants accounted for only 2 to 3 per cent of the French population, and Protestant exiles from France had stimulated British industry. British raw materials were more accessible – coal was conveniently located near the seaports: iron could be imported as well as smelted at home. And if roads were better in France, Britain had twice as many canals in 1800 – after a canal boom which anticipated the railway boom (not then to be shared by France) a generation later.

Industrialization, like political revolution, is best explained in terms of complex interactions, most of them at the regional level, rather than lists of causes and effects. In fact, while most eighteenth-century British industrialization was highly regionalized, leaving large parts of the country untouched, the French economy in the 1780s included more industrial elements in it than the first historians of the industrial revolution, including their own, suggested. There were *entrepreneurs* in France, and there were several substantial plants, including a spinning factory at Nantes that employed 4,000 workers. At Chaillot, near Paris, steam engines were being produced. There were small industrial regions in the east, like that round Mulhouse. If French coal production was only 10 per cent of that in Britain, cast iron production was actually greater in France than in Britain during the 1780s.

There was, however, one other critical economic difference. While both countries had already benefited from what came to be called (misleadingly) 'commercial revolutions', based on sugar and slaves, which increased the wealth of both countries in the eighteenth century, France, unlike Britain, underwent no 'agricultural revolution', an equally misleading term yet a convenient label for significant improvements in farming, the most important branch of economic activity in both countries. British improvements involved more effective use of land; new techniques of food production, widely publicized; systematic rotation of crops; the use of winter crops for fodder; expansion of cereal production, crucial for a growing population of men, women, children – and horses; and more careful breeding and rearing of bigger and better livestock.

In summarizing and extolling their own achievements in industry as well as in agriculture the British preferred before and after the French Revolution to use the older word 'improvement', a fashionable word in the eighteenth century on both sides of the Atlantic, to the word 'revolution'; and it was not until the 1880s, just before the centenary of the French Revolution was celebrated (the Eiffel Tower was its monument), that the term 'industrial revolution' passed into general currency in Britain.[3] By then it had become obvious that there could be no reversibility in industrial change. You could no more go back from an industrial society to a pre-industrial society than you could control the movements of the stars. It was easier, indeed, to attempt political restoration after a revolution than to set the clock back economically.

By the year 1889 the French Revolution and the British industrial revolution, separate in their origins, seemed to some commentators to be directly related to each other in their consequences. Factories and barricades were part of the same stage sets. The members of a new industrial 'proletariat' (in reality a divided labour force) were thought of as carriers of continuing revolution. Particularly in the judgement of socialists, like the German-born Karl Marx, the *bourgeois* revolution against feudalism as he saw it, which had been staged in France in 1789, would be followed, as industrialization extended, by proletarian revolutions that would destroy capitalism and (ultimately) usher in a 'classless society'. Such kinds of interpretation, which were to influence French thought and action more than British, were to be challenged in the late-twentieth century in the light not only of experience but of a deeper study of the nature of the two revolutions themselves. Yet there were significant similarities about both revolutions.

First, each carried with it a universal message, relevant for more than one country and for more than one time. Universalism was part of the rhetoric of the French Revolution, as revolutionaries in Paris in 1789 appealed to 'fellow citizens' throughout Europe to join them in throwing off their chains – with considerable success at first, even in Britain. The Declaration of the Rights of Man and Citizen of the summer of 1789 was a declaration of human rights, not just a charter for Frenchmen. It was not only France which was separating itself from the past, the world was being invited to separate itself too. Tom Paine, Burke's most effective and best-selling critic, was made a citizen of France and represented Calais in its National Assembly.

There was universalism too in the 'industrial revolution' which could not be confined to Britain. Steam power was as universal as the power of ideas, and it could be written of Watt's steam engine:

> Engine of Watt! unrivall'd in thy sway.
> Compared with thine what is the tyrant's power?
> His might destroys, while thine creates and saves,
> Thy triumphs live, like fruit and flowers.

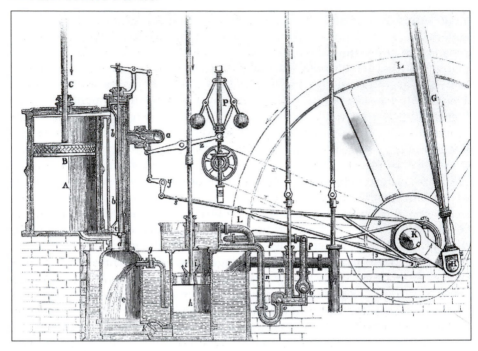

Plate 1.2 Working parts of Watt's double acting engine. James Watt and his company, working out of his purpose-built foundry in Soho, Birmingham, designed massive steam engines, like this one, which were both more efficient and more powerful. His invention, popularized through his partnership with businessman Matthew Boulton, made steam engines the main source of motive power in factories. Yet, even the gigantic collective power of Watt's engine was to be eclipsed by the turbine, already in use by the 1880s, and the electric generator.

Not everyone, of course, found steam power so beneficent. There were, indeed, alternative universalist verses written in which it was steam – and machinery – that figured as tyrants. The really 'ruthless king' was served by 'a priesthood' who were 'turning blood to gold'.

Second, each revolution carried with it a sense of being 'unfinished'. This was obvious in relation to the industrial revolution, for it was inherently unlikely that techniques invented by Englishmen during the last decades of the eighteenth century would remain 'up-to-date'. The hand-made would become standardized: steam would give way to electricity. Prometheus had been unbound.[4] It was unlikely too that parts of the world with far greater natural resources at their disposal than Britain – America and Germany, for example – would allow Britain to maintain an industrial lead based on priority in invention.

The 'unfinished' element in the French Revolution was rather more complex. There were Frenchmen who would have liked to 'finish' the revolution at one particular point – 1789, before the fall of the Bastille, a great symbolic event; 1791, when the first revolutionary programme, including the overthrow of 'feudalism', was complete; 1795, after the exhaustion of 'the Terror' during which revolutionaries fought revolutionaries; or 1799, before the accession to full power of Napoleon. Yet there were others who wanted revolution to continue much further, even to become a 'permanent revolution'. For the mid-nineteenth-century French socialist Pierre Josèphe Proudhon, who coined the phrase 'all property is theft', there was 'only one revolution, selfsame and perpetual'. It was seeking to achieve not only political freedom but economic equality.

A very different writer, the German philosopher of history Georg Wilhelm Friedrich Hegel, was deeply impressed by the French Revolution as a manifestation of the human spirit. 'World history', he began his lectures in the University of Berlin in the 1820s, was 'nothing else but the development of human freedom', and the French Revolution was a triumph of right. 'Never since the sun has stood in the heaven and the planets moved about it', he added, using an astronomical analogy, 'had it been seen that man relies on his head, that is on thought, and builds reality correspondingly.' Such a philosophy was to culminate in a belief in historical necessity. For Marx also there was necessity in the outcome, although he substituted materialism for idealism in his own post-Hegelian analysis as he brought the industrial revolution as well as the French Revolution into the human story.

Such views did not go unassailed. Just as the French revolutionaries never won a unanimous vote of confidence, nor did the philosophies of Hegel or Marx. What both men did – in the welter and aftermath of revolution – was to turn history into a key subject, in Marx's case into a call for political action. When their influence seemed to have come to an end two centuries after the destruction of the Bastille it seemed to some observers that history itself had come to an end (see below, pp. 449ff).

Long-term: short-term

Looking backwards rather than forwards, continuities are plain enough. The cult of freedom and the sense of citizenship predated the French Revolution. The exploitation of steam power did not start with Watt, who had taken out his first patent for a steam engine twenty years before the fall of the Bastille. An 'atmospheric' engine had been produced in the 1680s, and a steam pump in 1698. Watt's most talented predecessor, Thomas Newcomen, who died in 1729, had invented an engine in 1712 which pumped water from the tin mines of Cornwall: Watt's achievement was to make steam power move machines. A process for smelting iron ore with coke had been devised by Abraham Darby at Coalbrookdale in 1709.

Both things and ideas have pedigrees; and great events, like those between 1776 and 1815, were not complete in themselves on either side of the Channel. Likewise, when what appeared to be new language was used, it was often not for the first time. There had been talk even of 'revolution', particularly a revolution in government, in France and other countries of Europe long before 1789, particularly in the decade before Louis XVI became King of France in 1774. The historian Albert Sorel, who wrote a magisterial, if dated, eight-volume history of *Europe and the French Revolution*, published between 1885 and 1904, quoted one interesting specific example of the use of the word in 1751 – used with fear rather than with hope – when the writer remarked gloomily that he was 'very far from thinking that we are entering upon an age of reason: indeed, it would not take much to convince me that Europe is threatened by some catastrophic revolution'.

Trust in reason had been the core belief of the eighteenth-century 'Enlightenment', a term which, unlike the term 'industrial revolution', was used at the time by contemporaries; and the spokesmen of the Enlightenment, the *philosophes*, constituted a republic long before the establishment through revolution of a French republic, one and indivisible, in 1792. Although they were no more of one mind than the revolutionaries were to be, they shared a common outlook – unwillingness to take accepted principles for granted; interest in exploring the fields of what we would eventually separate out as politics, law, criminology, economics, administration, sociology, psychology and religion; hostility to ignorance and to superstition, which they identified with the Church; and the will (and ability) to circulate information and knowledge. The fact that the most famous (and the wittiest) of the *philosophes*, François-Marie Arouet Voltaire, talked not of a republic but of his own church, consisting of 'brothers' and 'faithful', was a testimony to its power.

In questioning 'authority' the *philosophes* freely used abstract nouns like 'reason', 'freedom', 'happiness', 'utility' and 'progress'. Nonetheless, they were equally interested in practical policies that were being pursued or might be pursued by rulers or their governments, an interest expressed in one of their great collective achievements, an 18-volume *Encyclopédie*, the first volume of which appeared in 1751. 'Everything must be examined', its editors, Denis Diderot and Jean le Rond d'Alembert, wrote. 'Everything must be shaken up without exception and without circumspection.' The full title of the work was *Encyclopédie ou Dictionaire Raisonné*.

The work covered almost every aspect of human thought and action, including 'technology', a new word of the late-eighteenth century, as was the word 'industry' in its modern sense. Hitherto it had been used to describe a human quality, hard work. Now it came to describe a branch (later the word 'sector' would be used) of the economy. The word 'constitution' was taking on a new significance also. Voltaire wrote the article on 'Men of Letters' (*Gens de Lettres*) in the *Encyclopédie*; and it was 'men of letters', for Voltaire a new nobility, who did much to develop a new vocabulary, with d'Alembert appointed Perpetual Secretary of the prestigious French Academy, guardian of the French language, in 1772.

The idea of an *Encyclopédie* had been suggested to the French by an earlier English encyclopedia, and throughout the century literary and philosophical communications between France and England (and later with Scotland) were of great importance in changing people's minds and in widening their horizons. There was a cosmopolitanism about most *philosophes*, and Edinburgh and Geneva were centres of Enlightenment thought. Voltaire had stayed in England as a young man; the Baron de Montesquieu, the most reflective of the *philosophes*, took the unwritten British constitution as his model; the French Physiocrats, who were anxiously concerned with the economic fortunes of eighteenth-century France, joined the Scottish philosopher Adam Smith in sharply criticizing the 'system of mercantilism' which in Smith's phrase could be traced back to 'Mr. Colbert, a famous minister of Louis XIV'.

Neither the Physiocrats nor Smith, whose *Inquiry into the Nature and Causes of the Wealth of Nations* was to have immense influence in shaping debates on what came to be called economic policy, clearly foresaw the revolutionary outcome of their own century, including the industrial revolution. They looked at society from above, not from below. So, too, did the French *philosophes*, most of whom put their trust in rulers rather than people as promoters of change. Diderot claimed in 1770 that 'the happiest government would be that of a just and enlightened despot'; and even Jean-Jacques Rousseau, who stands out on his own and whose theory of the 'general will' was to provide a justification of popular power, left a place for a legislator. The earlier *philosophes* were as famous for their correspondence – in French – with 'enlightened' monarchs as for their pamphlets and books. Even Jeremy Bentham, the British utilitarian philosopher, who considered 'the greatest happiness of the greatest number' to be the criterion of government, put his trust first in princes and corresponded with Catherine II (deemed 'the great') of Russia. And if Bentham lived long enough – until 1832 – to demand (and to witness) major political changes in Britain, Catherine lived just long enough – until 1795 – to be able to condemn the French Revolution.

The *philosophes*, concerned as they were with prejudice and tolerance, and with 'progress' and 'civilization', were at pains to distinguish between an 'age of Enlightenment' and an 'enlightened age', recognizing that, however enlightened they themselves might be as individuals, they were surrounded by a darkness which was only slowly being dispersed. A French observer noted in 1750 how people living a hundred miles from Paris could be a century away from it in 'their modes of thinking and acting'. It was not surprising, therefore, that most of the *philosophes* believed that change would come from above, though they knew too that the kind of 'reason' that even the most 'enlightened' of monarchs would choose to follow would be 'reason of state' (*raison d'état*) which it was for them (and not for *philosophes*) to define.

The other and very different forces, economic and psychological, that influenced not 'the great' but 'little people' (*les petits*), a high proportion of whom were illiterate, included hunger, contempt and rage. The dark side of the Paris scene – and the contrasts within it – was unforgettably depicted in the pages of Nicolas Restif de la Bretonne's *Les Nuits de Paris*, published between 1788 and 1794. They described 'all the actual facts' which Restif had witnessed on nightly tours around the great city, 'the assemblage of luxury, commerce, mud, the Opera, girls, imprudence, urbanity, debauchery, courtesy, swindling, and all the advantages and abuse of city life'. Not surprisingly, Restif was described in high literary circles as 'the Rousseau of the gutter'.

The pursuit of self-interest, like social curiosity, was a force that could be understood on both sides of the Channel. Members of what the British called 'the middle ranks of society' and what the French called the *bourgeoisie* could be stirred by aspiration and ambition that might lead them either into economic or political activity. Lawyers could be as aspiring as merchants. They could easily be shocked too by scandals in high places, vividly described in *libelles* circulated underground and in pamphlets printed and sold openly in London's Paternoster Row. They had a more immediate and potent influence than the ideas of the *philosophes*.

'The' Revolution

Restif, who vividly described the trial of Louis XVI and the guillotining of Marie Antoinette, was as disturbed as Burke was by the bloodiness of the revolutionary sequence which began ironically not with the revolt of the poor but with the revolt of the nobility.

The origins of the French Revolution – and it goes down to history as *the* Revolution – are to be found before 1789 in the impulses, often contradictory, and in the conflicts, often bitter, within an 'old regime' which was facing what were proving to be intractable financial difficulties. (France's Controller General of Finances, the Baron de Turgot, had warned King Louis XVI before France entered the American War that 'the first gunshot would drive the state into bankruptcy'.)

The general financial and economic position in 1788 and 1789 was worse. Bad harvests in 1787 and 1788 raised the price of bread, in some places doubling it, while urban unemployment rose. The poor were on the brink of starvation. Grievances multiplied. Agriculture accounted for three-quarters of the French national product, and when it languished, the country was under stress. The weather had its own drama on the eve of the Revolution. A storm which swept across France on 13 July 1788 carried with it hailstones big enough to kill men and animals as well as to destroy crops.

The timing of the sequence of political events that led up to the Revolution, many with their own drama and, unlike the weather, with their own rhetoric, was directly related to France's complex financial problems, and these ranged from accounting procedures in peace and war, to tax distribution and collection (all taxes were 'farmed out' to collectors, the most lucrative form of farming) and to powers of borrowing and public credit. Lawyers, an important element in France's vocal *bourgeoisie*, were at the centre of the economic and political argument as they were to be after the Revolution began. Nonetheless, the discontents of the poor, including poor peasants, could not be left out of the social and political equations. Arthur Young, England's indefatigable spokesman of agricultural improvement, who travelled extensively in France, stated at the time that the financial 'deficit would not have produced the Revolution had it not been for the price of bread'.

Between 1787 and 1789 one step led to another, through a series of moves and counter-moves that later proved to have been an escalation. The first was the failure in 1787 of an attempt by the King's *Comptrolleur-Général* to raise revenue through a nominated 'Assembly of Notables'. The aristocrats present there would not support a radical proposal to introduce a tax on all landowners irrespective of rank, and in May 1787 the Chamber was dismissed. Privilege had proved entrenched and unbudgeable even though the financial crisis continued and would, indeed, be bound to continue until tax burdens were reallotted. As one of the King's previous financial advisers, the Swiss banker Jacques Necker, had fully appreciated before being dismissed in 1781, it was 'a real monstrosity in the eyes of reason', the eighteenth-century litmus test, that sections of the aristocracy (nobility) avoided taxation, that the clergy (the leaders of which, archbishops and bishops, were appointed by the King) were exempt, and that heavy indirect taxation (including a tax on salt) fell on the poor.

As a result of the *impasse* in 1787 and of further (but not new) constitutional conflicts between the King's ministers and the *Parlement* of Paris, and other provincial *Parlements*, ancient bodies with legal powers and privileges which they conceived of as checks on absolute government, no alternative was found to summoning the Estates-General in 1789. This also was an ancient body, representative, not legal, consisting of three separate Estates – clergy, nobility and commonalty – and it had not met since 1614. Archbishop de Brienne, now the King's Principal Minister (a title not used since 1726), who had wrestled with the *Parlements*, summoned the Estates in August 1788 in the same week as the bankrupt French Treasury suspended all payments. By the end of the month Necker, a Protestant who was given no grand title like Brienne's, agreed to serve again temporarily, and Brienne resigned.

The *Parlement* of Paris decreed that when the Estates-General met they should follow all the ancient formalized rituals of state, just as Louis XVI had followed all the sacred coronation rituals when he was crowned at Reims Cathedral. Before they met, however, political developments had taken place which made the rituals seem archaic. The *Parlements* themselves in their constitutional struggles with Louis XVI's ministers had already been driven to using new language – 'citizens' for 'subjects', for example, and even the term 'the rights of man': they had claimed to be 'guardians of the people's liberties'. Now between August 1788 and May 1789 speakers (and writers) in a vigorous public debate drew on a variety of sources, new as well as old, in order to focus on fundamental questions concerning privileges, rights and constitutions.

No fewer than 752 pamphlets and other printed papers were published between September and December 1788, and 2,639 during the first four months of 1789. Opinions counted as much as interests. So too did violence which was generated not by the debate but by popular discontent, much of it peasant discontent. There were riots in places as far apart as Rennes in Brittany and Grenoble in Dauphiné. Thenceforth an interplay of opinion, interest and violence was to be at the heart of the story.

The spring elections for the Estates-General confirmed what was already clear – that neither the nobility nor the *Parlements* would be in any position themselves to dictate the future course of events. Every man on the tax rolls and over the age of 25 had the right to vote; and while nobles elected nobles and clergy elected clergy, the Third Estate, granted double the representation of the other two Estates, 648 deputies, was in direct contact with by far the largest constituencies. The various representatives of each Estate collected from their constituents written declarations of grievances, *cahiers des doléances*, which contained both general points, some based on precedent, some on recent political writing, and very specific grievances which multiplied during the months before the Estates-General met. The chosen representatives of the Third Estate were not occupationally or socially representative of the constituencies they served: they included 166 lawyers, 85 merchants, and 278 men holding various kinds of government post.

In Paris itself, where a far broader section of the population than this was to play an active and controversial role in the unfolding of events, there were two days of rioting in the Faubourg St Antoine in April 1789 (with 25 deaths and three subsequent executions). In this case the enemy was not the King, but local politicians and manufacturers who favoured lower wage scales. Workers from the same *faubourg* were to play a leading part in the destruction of the Bastille, one of Paris's ancient state prisons, only a few months later.

This was to be remembered as a more portentous event than the opening on 5 May 1789 in pomp and ceremony of the Estates-General, preceded by a religious service of dedication. Yet it was immediately after the opening, which started with a dull speech by Necker (the King dropped off to sleep), that the Third Estate at once asserted its special role. It conceived of itself not in traditional terms as an Estate of the realm but rather as the voice of the nation, and it refused to sit alone or to vote separately. Its claim had been advanced in speeches and in print before the

Estates-General met, notably in one of the most widely read and discussed pamphlets of the period, *What is the Third Estate?* Its author, a clergyman, the Abbé Sièyes, the son of a postal employee, was to play one of the biggest parts in the forcing of political events later in the year. 'Today', Sièyes wrote in his pamphlet, 'the Third Estate is everything, the nobility but a word.'

Just how language, verbal and visual, is related to action is one of the most fascinating issues raised by events between 1789 and 1795. In 1788 a memorandum from the municipal officers of Nantes had already stated simply that 'the Third Estate cultivates the fields, constructs and mans the vessels of commerce, sustains and directs manufactures, nourishes and vivifies the kingdom. It is time that a great people count for something.' Later spoken language was to become far more declamatory. To what extent declamation registered was itself a matter of debate. Jean-Josèphe Mounier, one of the speakers in the debates of May 1789 about constitutional rights, asked once 'What do words matter when they do not change things?', to which an Assemblyman of different persuasion replied tersely, 'Ideas are clarified when words are explained'. Later revolution-aries believed instead that words would carry their greatest force when they were designed not to clarify or to explain, but to inspire and to move men to action.

Talks in May (with spectators present) led to no agreement, and on 10 June the Third Estate deliberately forced the pace when it carried by 493 votes to 41 a motion proposed by Sièyes that if the other two Estates did not agree to assemble together it would proceed alone. A further motion, declaring itself a 'National Assembly', was carried a week later by 491 votes to 89, and two days after that the clergy decided by a narrow majority to join the Assembly. And now came the first of what were to be recalled later as the *beaux moments* in a drawn-out revolutionary sequence. On 20 June, when the members of the Assembly reached their hall of meeting they found the doors locked and guarded by soldiers, and posters on the wall announcing an unscheduled 'royal session' for the next week. Instead of leaving quietly they adjourned to an adjoining tennis court (where 'royal tennis' was played), and all but one of them took a solemn oath not to disperse until 'the constitution of the realm had been established and strengthened on solid foundations'.

The will of the members was tested when at the postponed 'royal session' the King insisted in what was otherwise a conciliatory speech that the Estates should continue to meet separately and that they should now withdraw to their separate meeting places. The Tennis Court oath stood firm. In a phrase of the Comte de Mirabeau, who had been a member of the Society of Thirty, a small group of noblemen (and others) who were opposed to privilege, nothing but bayonets would now force the National Assembly to move. They were not used. Instead, on 27 June, after much argument behind the scenes, Louis wrote to the Presidents of the first two

Estates ordering them to join the National Assembly. When he and the Queen appeared on a balcony they were cheered by the crowds. Arthur Young believed that the revolution was now over.

Instead it was beginning, and Paris, not Versailles, soon became the place of action. Dissension at court, movements of royal troops round the city and the dismissal of Necker on 11 July – he was ordered to leave the country – suggested that the will of the people was being imperilled and that the National Assembly, which four days earlier had changed its name to National Constituent Assembly, would be dissolved. And these ominous moves came at the end of a week when the Assembly had been discussing not the constitution but the price of bread. There was an immediate *furore* in what was already a restless and unruly Paris when the news reached there. A 'citizens' militia' had already been formed to protect property, but it was not able to 'contain the people's fury'. As one of its members stated, 'it was not the moment to reason with them'. He was right.

To understand the changing position of the King and the subsequent dispositions of the revolutionary leaders, it is essential to study the attitudes and reactions of people whose names have not passed into the history books. Such a study has revolutionized the historiography of the French Revolution. In the beginning historians used general terms, like 'the people': now they consider particular people in particular places. Named or unnamed, it was people without power, not the members of the National Assembly, who now pushed the Revolution further forward by storming and destroying the Bastille on 14 July. Eighty-three lives were lost, among them that of its aristocratic commander who had tried to blow it up rather than hand over the keys. He was spat upon and beaten up as he was marched through the streets before being brutally killed. His severed head was then carried on a pike through the crowds.

There had been only seven prisoners inside the Bastille at the time – Louis XVI himself had wanted to pull it down in 1784 – but the scale of the disturbance – and its character – proved (and there was more than symbolism in this) both that violence was endemic and that the King could no longer rely on his own troops. On 15 July the Duc de la Rochefoucauld-Liancourt is said to have told him, 'Sire, this is not a riot but a revolution'. He had found the right word. What was happening now was new. The King gave orders that his troops surrounding Paris should disperse. And three days later, in what was another symbolic event, he met representatives of a new Paris municipal government (with a mayor, a new title) and accepted from them a tricolour cockade.

There were some cries of 'Our king, our father', but Louis XVI himself was silent. He recalled Necker and confirmed the appointment of the Marquis de la Lafayette as commander of the citizens' militia, now called the National Guard. Lafayette, an aristocrat, had been one of the French heroes of the American War, and had named his first son, born in 1780, George Washington. He had sent a piece of the stone from the demolished

Plate 1.3 The Taking of the Bastille, 14 July 1789. The drawing seeks to capture the violence at an early and critical point in the revolutionary sequence. It shows:

1. M. de Launay, the prison Governor, taken prisoner by a grenadier
2. The white flag treacherously hung out by the Governor
3. M.'de Launay's house on fire
4. The prison kitchens on fire

Note the drawbridges (5, 6) which played an important part in the story.

Bastille across the Atlantic to Washington. Already, however, he (and Washington) were well aware that the French Revolution was following a different course from the American. In 1791, still only 31 years old, Lafayette was to counsel Louis XVI to leave Paris for Rouen and raise the royal banners there, and a year later he was to flee from France himself when the monarchy was overthrown and to be imprisoned in an Austrian gaol. That was round the corner.

The physical demolition of the Bastille by the crowds was to be followed by a burst of demolition of old institutions by the National Assembly, a positive achievement, not a symbolic act, the most important of all the achievements of the Revolution. Yet it was achieved against a background of physical violence outside as well as inside Paris. Thus, on 19 July the manor house of an unpopular landlord at Quincey in Franche Comté was destroyed in a huge explosion. Peasant disturbances, creating what Georges Lefebvre, one of the greatest French historians of the Revolution, identified as *la Grand Peur* (the great fear), now reached their peak. In the midst of panic, however, there was hope. The peasants had been aroused by a belief that their condition would be radically altered, and afraid as they now were that they were going to be cheated by the nobility, they moved to take the law into their own hands, often, at first, to shouts of 'Long Live the King!'

It was in an atmosphere of exalted enthusiasm that on 4 August 1789 the Assembly decreed 'the entire abolition of the feudal system' and with it the structure of local and provincial administration, on lines that had not been discussed when the Estates-General was called. Old scores were now settled. Privileges were renounced, sometimes with abandon. The full implications of what was done took time to work out, although the first codification followed a week later. The 'peasant revolution' did not treat all peasants alike. Some were able to buy land at low prices and, once freed from the burdens of feudal dues and tithes, went on to prosper, often becoming politically conservative in the process. Others remained landless, poor and dissatisfied.

No government could ignore the peasants, although government was subject to more immediate pressures from inside Paris, where events moved more speedily than events in Versailles. They were driven mainly not by the poorest of the poor, but by 'the little people' – artisans, small manufacturers, retail shopkeepers, cafe keepers, barbers and small booksellers. The defiant word most commonly used to describe them, *sans culottes*, referred to clothes: the *sans culottes* wore the long trousers of the working man instead of the knee breeches of the aristocrat. What brought revolutionary *sans culottes* together was not their occupation or their income, but revolutionary activism: they had a sense of fraternity and of solidarity, the solidarity of citizenship that had been positively set out in the Declaration of the Rights of Man and the Citizen which was adopted by the National Assembly on 27 August. 'Men are born free and remain equal in rights' read Article I. 'Social distinctions may be based only upon general usefulness.' The source of 'all sovereignty resides essentially in the nation' read Article III. Nine of the seventeen Articles referred to 'the rule of law'.

The language was clear, but while it was being enunciated the most urgent question for most Parisians was still the price of bread, and this was demonstrated on 5 October 1789 when insurgents, caring little for the rule of law, stormed the *Hotel de Ville* and a large crowd of women, who assembled at markets, marched through rain from Paris to Versailles asking for food. They also demanded that the King, who had hitherto been unwilling, should give his unqualified support to everything that had been so far decreed in the name of the Revolution since 17 July. He did, after more court discussion, and on the following day, accompanied by Lafayette, who had arrived with 20,000 National Guardsmen, and wagons containing wheat and flour, he and his family moved in the wake of the crowds in mud and rain from the seclusion of Versailles to the Tuileries Palace in Paris which Louis XIV had abandoned a century before. A hundred members of the National Assembly, many of them shaken by what had happened, moved with them to a turbulent city which was brightly illuminated for the occasion, ready to welcome 'the baker, the baker's wife and the baker's boy'.

The subsequent unfolding of the French Revolution involved far more than the fate of a king. It is a revolution, therefore, which in all its stages requires to be studied in detail. There were marked social and ideological differences in Paris, a city honeycombed with 'popular clubs', eagerly discussing revolutionary goals and tactics, forming revolutionary patrols, and carrying out other revolutionary tasks. Sizeable groups of activists believed that government had a duty to regulate prices, particularly the price of bread. Their political economy was their own from the start, very different from that of Smith or the Physiocrats and calculated to alarm *bourgeois* revolutionaries both in the Assembly and in the French provinces.

There were also important regional differences from the start. In some regions, where the Revolution had little initial hold, dedicated revolutionaries tightened their sense of mission after October 1789, and that added to the violence. From now onwards, there was, in fact, more than one revolution, while counter-revolutions themselves quickly became an integral part of the pattern. There were new regional boundaries also, for in 1789 *départements* took the place of the old provinces. Federation was the order of the day. A *Fête de la Fédération* was held in 1790 on the anniversary of the destruction of the Bastille.

Insurrectionary politics depended on more than constitutional debate, but it was the results of debate which made violence inevitable. The abolition of feudalism had won widespread acclaim. The next key decision of the National Assembly in November 1789 to expropriate Church property (along with Crown lands) did not. The reason for taking it was primarily financial: inevitably the Assembly had to concern itself with finance as the King's ministers had been forced to concern themselves before 1788. The situation had deteriorated, indeed, for even those who had previously paid taxes were doing their best to evade them. Confiscated Church property was to provide security for a new revolutionary currency in paper money, *assignats*, first introduced in December 1789.

Further decisions, bound to perpetuate division inside France, were taken in February 1790, when the contemplative Church orders were abolished, and in July 1790 when a 'Civil Constitution of the Clergy' was promulgated. Parish priests were now to be elected by citizens gathered in local assemblies, and bishops by electors in departments. They were all to become paid officials of the state, and no papal messages could be circulated in France except with the permission of the government. In November the clergy were further required to take an oath. All who refused were to be dismissed and replaced. Large numbers of bishops and clergy, including members of the National Assembly, refused to accept the oath, and the Pope condemned it on 13 April 1791.

The numbers who refused to take it varied, however, according to region. In the Vendeé in the west, in Brittany, in Normandy, in Flanders and in Alsace, fewer than one in five accepted it: in the Var the percentage accepting was 96. The first signs of counter-revolution had been conspiracies: the newest signs now were mass uprisings with a popular base. Emigrés had already left France – the first of them, led by the Comte d'Artois, the King's brother, as early as July 1789 – and had prepared for civil war and foreign invasion in the name of the royal family and the aristocracy. Now the civil war acquired a genuine momentum within France itself as the counter-revolution was strengthened at the base. In many places – and the regional pattern varied in this too – the counter-revolutionaries formed their own National Guards.

The flight of the King from his Parisian palace to Varennes, near the French frontier, on 21 June 1791 – he and his wife travelled in disguise – brought this phase of the Revolution to a climax; and as he was led back to Paris as a prisoner on the evening of 25 June 1791 he is said to have muttered 'There is no longer a king in France'. What then seemed to him to be fragile connecting threads between the present and the past of France had been finally cut. It was a climax for the French people also. They now had to choose (if under duress) whether or not they favoured the Revolution. The Constituent Assembly imputed the King's flight to conspirators who had misled him, but there were large-scale demonstrations of militant Parisians, roused by a militant press, demanding a new form of republican government. Lafayette succeeded in putting the first big demonstration down, and at the Champs de Mars around 50 people were killed and others wounded on 17 July, but emigration from France continued on a bigger scale and on 13 September the King reluctantly accepted a new unicameral constitution which curtailed all his powers.

Protracted discussions going back to 1789 – and earlier – about what kind of a constitution France should adopt, some of them carried on inside committees, had involved debate about what links there could be between past and future. What was a constitution? Was there an 'old constitution' to restore or should a new constitution be devised? Should the preparation of a constitution precede or follow the drafting of a bill of rights? What should be the position of the monarch? Now the answers to such key questions, some of which had never been put to the vote, seemed to have settled themselves; and the Constituent Assembly was replaced by a new Legislative Assembly, chosen on a restricted franchise, in elections held at the end of August 1791.

Half of its members were lawyers. It was within this body that distinct political groupings, not yet political parties, emerged, one of them a *Girondin* group led by Jacques Pierre Brissot, another a *Jacobin* group, named after a Paris club with over a thousand members and over a thousand affiliated societies. The name 'Girondin' referred to the department of the Gironde in south-west France from which many of its members came. Whatever their allegiances, the delegates to the Convention had to pay attention to the very varied views of their own constituents. There were large numbers of Frenchmen who detested the breakdown of order and the extremism of the social and political views which they could hear expressed around them in Paris. They were as suspicious of Paris as the *sans culottes* of Paris were suspicious of bankers or big businessmen.

By vetoing two important decrees of the Assembly, however, as the new constitution permitted him to do, Louis showed that he was still not a cipher. He even gained a measure of initiative as news arrived that *emigrés* armies were massing in Germany near the French frontier, and he was loudly cheered on 14 December 1791 when he told the Assembly that he had issued an ultimatum to the Prince-Archbishop of Trier telling him that France would declare war unless all *emigré* activity was prohibited in his territory. The Prince-Archbishop obeyed. So, too, did the Elector of Mainz.

There was nothing revolutionary about this ultimatum, for in the eighteenth century it had been taken for granted that war, the organized use of armed force by one state against another, was justifiable in terms of *raison d'état*. Nonetheless, when the Comte de Vergennes, Louis XVI's last foreign minister before the Revolution, signed a commercial treaty with Britain in 1786 and a treaty with Russia in 1787, he had stated categorically, 'it is no longer the time for conquests' ('*Ce n'est plus le temps de conquêtes*') and the National Assembly had made a 'Declaration of Peace to the World' in August 1791 at a time when a few foreign enemies of the Revolution, like Gustavus II of Sweden (soon to be assassinated, not by a revolutionary but by a nobleman) were already preaching a crusade.

Revolution, war and 'the terror'

Once begun, war, a new element in the revolutionary situation, further revolutionized the revolution. In a phrase of Friedrich Engels, Marx's friend and collaborator, all the subsequent 'pulsations' of the Revolution depended upon it. Yet more than revolution was affected. The role of the state was to be affected too. As James Madison said across the Atlantic, 'war is the matter of executive aggrandizement', and this too was to follow in France. Inflation was already a problem before the war began. The value of the *assignat* in 1793 was a quarter of what it had been two years before.

War enthusiasm had been stirred in France in 1791, and it intensified after the Austrian Emperor Leopold announced that troops would march if

Mainz and Trier were forced to capitulate. On 25 January 1792 Louis was told to inform his royal brother-in-law that war with the Habsburg Empire would ensue unless he declared his peaceful intentions. When Louis responded less toughly in his note than the Assembly wished there was yet another crisis and threats were made to impeach both him and the Queen. Again Louis changed his mind, dismissed his now unpopular ministers, and on 20 April formed a new government, which was nominated by the Girondins, and declared war on the King of Hungary and Bohemia. Leopold had died on 1 March, and his successor, Franz, had not yet been made Holy Roman Emperor.

Brissot and his Girondin group believed that war might unify France and even preserve constitutional monarchy, and the declaration received a rapturous welcome in some revolutionary circles. Only seven deputies in the Assembly voted against it. 'Here is the crisis of the universe', one patriot proclaimed, 'God [had] disentangled the primitive chaos.' Now 'free men are Gods on earth' and a 'holy war' would be embarked upon by 'free men' and 'patriots'.

Unfortunately for Brissot, a war that was begun with such eloquent words and such mixed motives was to prove disastrous for himself and for his group and, not least, for the King. After initial defeats in which the French armies did not behave like the 'armed missionaries' that active citizens wished them to be (although one French general suspected of treason was murdered by his own troops), foreign armies entered France, and on 18 May all foreigners in France were placed under surveillance. Girondin ministers were dismissed, and on 20 June an angry group entered the royal apartments in the Tuileries.

Louis at this point held his own and donned the red cap of liberty to drink the health of the nation. But the anti-revolutionary leader, the Duke of Brunswick, issued a manifesto on 25 July 1792 threatening the direst of consequences if the royal family were harmed. It quickened revolutionary resolve, and the Tuileries Palace was stormed again on 10 August. This time, 400 people were killed in the bloodiest of the revolutionary *journées* and the King's Swiss Guard was massacred. At the end of the struggle the members of the royal family were transported as prisoners to the Temple.

At this point in the Revolution a Paris Commune, seeking vengeance, was more in charge of events than the Legislative Assembly and after the fall of Languy to the Prussian Army and later Verdun, only 200 miles from Paris, in September 1792, a panicky crowd broke into the prisons of Paris and killed over a thousand 'enemies of the Revolution'. In the same month, after a citizen army had been hastily mobilized, the news arrived on 20 September of the first French victory at Valmy, and two days later the republic was proclaimed. The King, long since resigned to his fate, was interrogated (after a bitter debate as to whether he needed to be) and with the barest majority in favour, one, was guillotined in what is now Paris's Place de la Concorde on 21 January 1793.

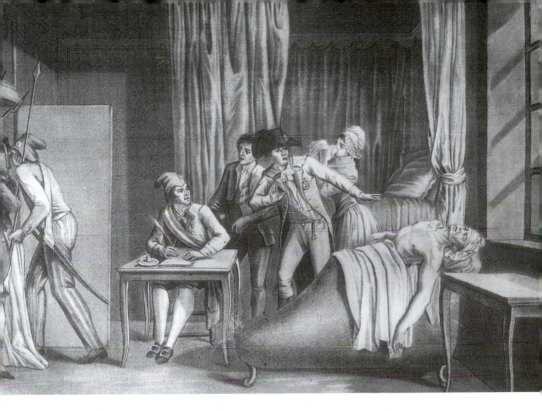

Plate 1.4 The assassination of Marat, July 1793. Among the hundreds of newspapers and broadsheets published in revolutionary France, the broadsheet *Ami du Peuple* of Jean-Paul Marat, a physician by training, won particular notoriety. He was alleged to have played a large part in inciting the September Massacres, earning him the undying hatred of the Girondins who fiercely attacked him when he was elected a deputy in Paris. The victim of a painful skin condition, he was murdered in his medicinal bath by Charlotte Corday, a noble woman with links to the Girondins, whom we glimpse being led away. Thereafter, as the rhetoric of Catholicism shaped worship of the new revolution, the 'sacred heart of Marat' attracted a cult following; he became one of the 'saints' of the Revolution.

The republic was proclaimed by a new National Convention which had been elected in the heat of the summer and which first met on the very day of Valmy. Like the Legislative Assembly, it was primarily *bourgeois* in its composition, with lawyers still predominating, and it included among its 749 deputies 200 who had belonged to the former body. There were also among them 83 members of the former Constituent Assembly. It was a young body, however, and it included a number of ex-nobles at one end of the social spectrum and artisans at the other. Within it political groupings were tightened. Confronting the Girondins were the *Montagnards*, the Mountain, so called because its members sat on the upper tiers of the Chamber. Again they were not political parties, and there was a group of Paris deputies who often worked closely together. Members independent of both groups were called 'The Plain'.

It was the experience of revolution, including the 'September massacres' and the guillotining of the King and later the Queen, that seemed to underscore Burke's prophecies concerning revolution, as did the increasing association of revolutionary politics with war. Now in 1793 there was no peace inside France itself. A revolution which had begun with revolutionaries fighting 'enemies of the people' continued, as later revolutions were to do, with revolutionaries fighting with each other. Some early enthusiasts for the Revolution, like Burke's bitter critic, Paine, who had been chosen as a member of the new Convention, were now to spend time in gaol. (Paine spent his time there writing *The Age of Reason.*) Others were to go to the guillotine. Whether or not the first phase of the Revolution had fully succeeded in its purpose of providing 'liberty' – and it certainly broke many chains – the mood of the latest phase, which was to worsen throughout 1793 and 1794, made a mockery of 'fraternity'. Useful measures that were passed, like the introduction of the metric system of weights and measures or, in a different field, the prohibition of imprisonment for debt, were overshadowed by revolutionary events.

The war, which went through many twists and turns, had its own logic too, as relentless as that of the Revolution itself. Men had to be mobilized, resources had to be found. The first war news was good after Valmy, and subsequent victories took French armies into Belgium, Germany and, in the south, Nice. One city seized was Frankfurt. On 16 November 1792 the River Scheldt was declared open to all nations and three days later France offered support to any people rising against its government.

Britain was alienated by the first of these moves and the French Ambassador was asked to leave London. In reply France declared war against Britain and the United Provinces on 1 February 1793. France now faced not a combination of Austria and Prussia but a 'First Coalition', which included Britain, bound by a cluster of alliances, Russia and Spain; and the tide of war seemed to have turned again when in March 1793 Austrian troops entered the southern Netherlands and the French General Dumouriez was defeated decisively at Neerwinden. In the following month Spanish troops besieged Perpignan, and in August the British Navy, unopposed, took over Toulon. This was because Toulon, like many other cities, had joined in large-scale royalist rebellion, particularly fierce in the Catholic Vendée region where there was bloody guerrilla war. There was treachery too at the front. After his defeat, Dumouriez asked for an armistice and tried to march his troops back to Paris to liberate the Queen and declare the Dauphin Louis XVII. When they refused, he defected to the Austrians. Lafayette too crossed the lines.

In such circumstances 'terror' became an inevitable part of the continuing revolutionary sequence. So also did tightened organization. It was in the most difficult month, March 1793, that a Revolutionary Tribunal was created and that zealous *représentants-en-mission* were dispatched to each of the armies with orders to mobilize the nation for war. To turn all

Frenchmen as rapidly as possible into soldiers meant that *élan* now counted for more than discipline. The new French national anthem, a hymn to brotherhood and war, first sung in the Rhineland, caught the mood: '*Aux armes, citoyens!*' Yet citizens needed food as well as arms, and in Paris rising food prices led the Paris Commune to decide to fix the price of bread by subsidizing grocers.

Every move in war mobilization had a political dimension to it, beginning in April with the setting up of a Committee of Public Safety which, during the course of 1793, acquired a parallel Committee of General Security handling police functions. It had behind it a revolutionary momentum, and at the end of the following month National Guardsmen surrounded the Tuileries when the National Convention met there. Three exciting days followed from 30 May to 2 June when 29 Girondin members of the Convention, who had been increasingly under attack from the Paris *sans culottes*, were expelled, a move that provoked anti-Montagnard revolts in parts of the provinces. Some of the expelled escaped from Paris: others, including Brissot, were guillotined. Any citizen advocating a 'spirit of moderation' was suspect. The food problem was not solved, however, and a death penalty for hoarding was decreed on 26 July.

One day later Robespierre joined the Committee of Public Safety, which Danton, hitherto its dominating personality, had left on the 10th. (The members of the Committee were subject to monthly re-election.) A new democratic constitution for the nation, based on a unicameral legislature with annual elections and male universal suffrage, was promulgated on 10 August, and four days later a tough and efficient expert in what would now be called war logistics, Lazare Carnot, was made a member of the Committee of Public Safety: he was soon to be hailed as 'organizer of victory'. By the end of August a *levée en masse* of all single men from 18 to 25 years old had been decreed: 'until the enemies of France shall have been chased off the territory of the Republic, every French person must stand ready to serve and support our armed forces'.

Because of revolutionary upheaval the democratic constitution never came into effect. In September 1793, another cruel month, continuing popular disturbances led the National Convention (under pressure from the Paris Commune) to carry a *Maximum Général* Law which controlled the price not only of food but of other goods and services. In the same month a comprehensive Law of Suspects was passed which empowered watch committees, set up earlier in the year, to arrest citizens who 'either by their conduct, their contacts, their words or their writings, showed themselves to be supporters of tyranny, of federalism or to be enemies of liberty'.

The *levée en masse*, with a target of a million men, did come into force, backed by the enthusiasm of Paris *sans culottes* organized in sections (there were 48 of them, each sending two representatives to the Paris Commune) and by the militancy of provincial *armées revolutionnaires* which have been described by Richard Cobb, a historian who knew how to bring the past back to life, as 'the most original and characteristic of the many spontaneous institutional creations of the Terror'. Among their tasks was the policing of food supplies, among their delights blasphemous attacks on priests and the pillaging of church silver. From October 1793 onwards, therefore, the Convention was as much at the mercy of forces beyond its control as the King had been. It remained in existence for its allotted three-year span, but 120 of its members were under arrest for various periods of time and another 74 were executed.

The scale of 'the Terror', which reached its peak under Robespierre, may have been exaggerated, but in 1793 and 1794 there were 14,000 executions by guillotine, a revolutionary instrument which, like the steam engine in Britain, had its own rhetoric. Indeed, while the Terror lasted the guillotine, invented by Dr Guillotin in 1789 as a humanitarian instrument of death, painless and efficient – heads would 'fly off in the twinkling of an eye' – took the place of the cap of liberty as an image of revolution. 'Traitors look at this and tremble', ran one inscription attached to a picture of it. 'It will still be active while all of you have lost your lives.'

Most of those who lost their lives, the majority of them outside Paris, were not well-known figures, and the agents who sent them to death, often assisted by informers, were often little known too. It was not merely the guillotine which was employed. Ninety priests were disposed of in 1793 by sinking them in the River Loire, tied like animals, in a dilapidated barge with holes. As for the leaders of the Revolution during this period of the Terror, there have been profound disagreements between specialized historians concerning their personalities and their alignments, with Danton and Robespierre subject to almost perpetual review.

To the outstanding French radical historian of the Third Republic, Alphonse Aulard, writing a great four-volume political history of the Revolution at the beginning of the twentieth century, Danton was the hero, a man of intelligence, courage and realism, struggling for a 'democratic republic', and his guillotining in March 1794 was the great tragedy of revolution. (On going to his death he is reported to have said 'Show my head to the people, they do not see the like every day'.) To some later historians, however, Danton seemed to be paying the penalty for opportunism, even for venality.

Robespierre has been even more criticized from both right and left. He had served in the Assembly before he became a member of the Convention and the Committee of Public Safety, and originally opposed the war. A French nineteenth-century historian/politician, Adolphe Thiers, described him as 'one of the most odious beings that could have borne absolute rule over men' and the first English historian of the French Revolution, Thomas Carlyle, who began his study of it by studying a folio of portraits of the revolutionaries, called him more poetically, but equally damningly, 'acrid, implacable, impotent, dull-drawling, barren as the Harmattan wind'.

There is no doubt, however, that Robespierre dominated the scene, if he could not always control events, between October 1793 and July 1794. Eloquence was his main weapon. 'Democracy', he maintained, 'is the only form of state in which all the individuals composing it can call [their state] their own country.' 'The French', he went on, 'are the first people in the world to establish a true democracy [he also called it a 'republic of virtue'] by calling all men to enjoy equality and the fullness of civic rights.' To achieve and to maintain a 'republic of virtue', 'false' revolutionaries were the ones who had to be destroyed, with the guillotine serving as 'the scythe of equality'.

The 'moderates' went first – Brissot and the Girondins, defiantly singing the *Marseillaise* as they made their way to the guillotine. The 'ultras' on the left went next, including J. R. Hébert, the most outspoken Parisian journalist, and the 'indulgents', those who, like Danton, wanted to relax the procedures of 'the Terror', went last – last, that is, except for Robespierre himself and the young St Just, 'the angel of the Terror', who were guillotined in July 1794 (10 Thermidor, Year II), a month which claimed 1,400 victims. The peak of 3,500 had been reached in January 1794. St Just had suggested that moneys confiscated from 'suspects' should be distributed among poor citizens.

The forces which ultimately destroyed Robespierre constituted a curious and temporary domestic coalition, less tightly bound together, indeed, than the First Coalition that had been formed by Europe's great powers to fight the French revolutionary armies. The centralization of authority in France was one source of anger, active dechristianization another: Robespierre wished to nationalize the cult of the Supreme Being. Economic grievances were paramount. The further depreciation of the *assignat* added to hunger in Paris not only because prices rose (despite the *Maximum*) but because peasants held back food. There were personal quarrels too, like that between St Just and Carnot on the conduct of the military campaign in the Netherlands.

The Terror phase ended in 1794 in a kind of stalemate: after the fall and guillotining of Robespierre there was yet another group who contemplated restoring the monarchy with a boy of nine, Louis XVII. (He died in prison on 8 June 1795.) Within a few weeks it was clear that the 'revolutionary storm' had spent itself, and the Convention went on to reduce the powers of the Committee of Public Safety, abolish the Revolutionary Tribunal and the Law of Suspects, close the Jacobin Club, the main stronghold of Robespierre, reinstate the surviving Girondins, free many political prisoners, restore freedom of worship and abandon the system of controlled prices and state intervention in the working of the economy.

There were protests from the left, particularly about the last of these moves, and in May 1795 (Prairial, Year III) 'ultras' invaded the meetings of the Convention. In the past, such invasions might have been decisive. Now they were put down by force, and many of the surviving Jacobin activists were sent to jail or guillotined. Force was used also to put down the 'White

Terror' and an *emigré* invasion in the south. The Convention went on to draft a new and far from democratic constitution, known as the Constitution of the Year III. An Executive Directory was to be established, a five-man Board, to be elected indirectly by the Legislature which would consist of two chambers – the Five Hundred and 'the Senators' or 'Ancients'. The constitution set out 'duties' of citizens as well as rights. It also stated firmly that 'it is upon the maintenance of property . . . that the social order rests'.

There were protests against such an approach, including a conservative protest in October 1795, backed by royalists, which was dispersed with a whiff of General Napoleon Bonaparte's grapeshot before the Convention came to an end in the same month. A year later with the Directory in power, a premeditated left-wing plot of a contrasting kind, led by 'Gracchus' Babeuf – who called himself a 'communist', was put down also. Babeuf – who during his career had both collected and catalogued archives and destroyed them (he burnt seigneurial archives in an effort to protect the peasants of Picardy) – was responsible for an eloquent *Manifesto des Egaux* ('Manifesto of the Equals'). This was to be as famous after his death as it was when he was plotting to put its ideas into practice. The plot was handled gently. When it was crushed only Babeuf himself and one of his fellow conspirators were sentenced to death.

'Royalism' was not crushed, however, and at further elections in 1797 only 11 members of the old Convention were elected and many royalists were returned. The Directory was losing its grip, and there was ample evidence of corruption and profiteering. Not surprisingly, therefore, there was a *coup d'état* in September 1797 in which three of the Directors combined with General Bonaparte to get rid of the other two, along with two hundred members of the legislative chambers. This was a republican *coup*, and it was followed two years later in October 1799 with a further coup (Brumaire, Year VIII) which brought Bonaparte to power as one of three Consuls. He was believed to be a steadfast defender of the Revolution. Sieyès, who devised the new constitution, was another.

From war to Napoleon and through Napoleon to peace

The Directory had flirted with the generals as the revolutionary war continued, although it was never clear about how to deal with them once power was moving in their direction. Napoleon, the most remarkable of them, knew how to deal with himself. Born in 1759 in Corsica, a small Mediterranean island only just acquired by France, he joined the *Ecole Militaire* in Paris in 1784. Ten years later, after directing the artillery in the destruction of Toulon after it had been captured by the British, he became

General in command of the artillery in Italy, where he established his military reputation with a series of 'miraculous' victories, achieved not by initiating any new principles of warfare but by applying with verve the advanced military thinking of the old order in France.

Napoleon was the rare kind of man whose career raises every kind of question concerning the role of the individual – and, in particular, 'the great man' or 'hero' – in history. The Russian novelist Leo Tolstoy in his novel *War and Peace* suggested that ultimately Napoleon may have been a 'puppet': 'the more powerful a man appears to be the more he is a slave of history'. That was a late view. Further back in time, as early as 1784, the year when Napoleon entered his military school, the German philosopher Immanuel Kant had forecast that a legislator of outstanding genius might arise who would do for human society what great scientific thinkers had done for the study of the physical universe in the past. 'Nature [had] brought forth a Kepler, who reduced the eccentric orbits of the planets to an orderly formula in unexpected fashion, and a Newton who clarified the universal principles governing the natural order.' Might not Napoleon be this man, a new kind of genius?

When a later German philosopher, Hegel, saw Napoleon ride through Jena in 1806 after one of his great victories he considered him Reason personified. The remark throws more light on Hegel than on Napoleon, for 'history' could be approached in a quite different way from his. The nineteenth-century French politician/historian François Guizot may have simplified it in his own way, however, when he stated that if the Revolution had been a violent way of breaking out of the old regime, Napoleon offered a violent way of breaking out of the Revolution.

Napoleon had studied the *philosophes*, but he believed in his own destiny rather than other people's theories. He had no great plan in mind. 'I am a fragment of rock launched into space', he once said in one of the memorable phrases that he produced in great quantities. Revolutionary war helped to prepare the way for him to fulfil his own destinies, and it was because of the Revolution that he was able to prove his remarkable capacity to win the devotion of his troops. 'Every step of the Great Nation is marked by blessings!', one of his Italian broadsheets ran. 'Happy is the citizen who is part of it. Happy is he who can say about our great men: these are my friends, my brothers!' It was because of the Revolution too that despite the fact that his troops lived off the land that they conquered Napoleon could win the support of influential sections of the local population. He was more than a conqueror.

Within a year Napoleon brought Piedmont/Sardinia to heel and drove the Austrians out of their province of Lombardy, and within weeks of the *coup d'état* of September 1797 he was able to secure a peace treaty with Austria at Campo-Formio which established the 'revolutionary Cisalpine republic' in northern Italy, the first of his 'satellite states', and ratified the acquisition of the left bank of the Rhine by France. Yet by the same treaty

Plate 1.5 *Napoleon crossing the Alps* **by Jacques-Louis David (1748–1825).**
Already famous before the Revolution, and a relative of the famous
eighteenth-century artist Boucher, David threw himself into the Revolution with
gusto. Instrumental in the abolition of the old artistic establishment and influenced
by Renaissance art, David believed art should not be prostituted to depict pretty
landscapes or royal mistresses in the nude. His own art was serious, deceptively
simple and often austere. He developed a special relationship with Napoleon who
conferred upon him the title, *'premier de l'Empire'*.

the Austrians acquired the republic of Venice and the Illyrian coast, so that the French, who at that stage had alienated large numbers of Italians by their behaviour as occupiers, seemed to be taking away other people's freedom while offering it to the world.

It was the world, not Europe, that inspired Napoleon's next military moves – in his youth he had once described Europe disparagingly as a 'molehill' – for he turned across the Mediterranean to Egypt, and even though his Egyptian expedition was in effect an adventurous substitute for a direct campaign against island Britain it had a romance of its own. Having enjoyed what he later called 'the most beautiful time of my life because it was the most ideal', Napoleon returned to France in October 1799 a hero – and that despite the fact that the annihilation of the French fleet off Egypt in the Battle of Aboukir on the Nile in July 1798 had made his grand designs of finding lasting fame in the east impossible to follow through.

The demonstration of superior British naval power was to be repeated more than once during the long wars which were to be interrupted only once before 1815 at the Peace of Amiens in 1802; and the British admiral responsible for Britain's naval victory, Horatio Nelson, was himself to become a British popular hero in the future: London's main square, Trafalgar Square, named after Nelson's final victory, was to house his column on which was placed his statue. Napoleon, who continued to dream of distant conquests, even of India, rested his fortunes on war on land (outside as well as inside Europe) – and war was never to be the same again after his time. It was through war too that Napoleon would eventually lose all that he had won.

All this was in the glass in 1798. Nevertheless, Napoleon's elevation to the First Consulship for France, a new title with a Roman resonance, was less the result of any plotting on his own part than of the plotting of others. He went on to form a government of his own choosing which took the form of a Council of State in which no single minister had any authority independent of his own will. It was, however, broad-based in composition, including Lucien Bonaparte, his brother, as Minister of the Interior; Talleyrand, a highly talented and highly flexible aristocrat who had already been both revolutionary and *emigré*, as Minister of Foreign Affairs; Josèphe Fouché, a veteran of 'the Terror', as Minister of Police; and Martin Gaudin, an able accountant, as Minister of Finance. The chemistry of the mix was curious but potent. The generals were now brought under control to leave the way clear for Napoleon to make his own moves. He was now ensconced in the Tuileries, and Burke's prophecy had been fulfilled that 'the officers of the army will remain mutinous for some time and full of faction until some general who understands the art of conciliating the soldiery . . . shall draw the eyes of all men upon himself'. A very different Englishman, Jeremy Bentham, who had been made an honorary French citizen, cast his vote for Napoleon in 1799.

Before there could be any European peace, the necessity for which Napoleon himself saw – indeed, he now promised it to France – further victories had to be won, for within 14 months of Campo-Formio Austria had abrogated the treaty and a new Second Coalition, which included both Russia and Britain, pushed the French backwards towards their 'natural' frontiers. It was in a position to bring twice as many men into the field as France. The Russian General Suvorov's victories in Italy destroyed all Napoleon's work there, and Russian troops even entered Switzerland, which in April 1798 the French had converted into a Helvetic Republic. (At the same time the city state of Geneva had been annexed.)

Fortunately for Napoleon, Tsar Paul, who had succeeded Catherine the Great, was dissatisfied with the conduct of his allies, particularly Austria, and, leaving the Second Coalition, which lacked any unified strategy, recalled his troops by the end of 1799. In the new situation Napoleon went on to defeat the Austrians (by a slender margin) at Marengo in June 1800 and later in December at Hohenlinden. A new peace treaty at Lunéville in February 1801 did more than confirm Campo-Formio. The Austrians now recognized the Batavian, Helvetic, Cisalpine and Ligurian Republics and French annexation of the left bank of the Rhine. In the following month, by the Treaty of Aranjuez, a new kingdom of Etruria and a new Republic of Lucca were established in Italy, and Naples ceded the island of Elba to France. Not surprisingly – with Prussia neutralized and with Russia now friendly – Napoleon went on to settle minor disputes with smaller European countries during the early months of 1801. He also made a concordat with the new Pope, Pius VII, in April, and secured Louisiana from Spain.

Only Britain now remained hostile, and once again Napoleon had luck on his side when William Pitt, who had come to power controversially as a King's man, resigned the office of Prime Minister which he had held since 1784 in February 1801. Pitt remained a royal servant to the end, refusing to thwart George III's wishes on Ireland, where the French had launched an unsuccessful invasion in 1798, even though he had come to the conclusion that the King's refusal to allow the civil and political emancipation of Roman Catholics was wrong. Pitt's successor – Addington – lacked both his experience and his ability. He benefited from the fact, however, as Pitt had done, that by the beginning of the nineteenth century former friends of the Revolution, including Wordsworth, had become disillusioned with it, and few of them (William Hazlitt was an exception) had much sympathy with Napoleon.

Whatever the currents of opinion and whoever was Prime Minister, official British attitudes towards France and towards Napoleon were basically simple and consistent. France was an ancient rival, in the beginnings of the rivalry far stronger than England; and, going back no further than the reign of Louis XIV, Britain had had to struggle to prevent French domination of Europe. Yet fighting on land was desirable only when it was deemed necessary, as it had been when the French declared the navigation of the Scheldt open in 1792. Thereafter, fighting by sea to check French power in Europe and to guarantee British power overseas was essential. For Pitt, such an analysis, which he was to set out clearly in 1804, meant far more than any counter-revolutionary ideology. Burke was a political opponent of Pitt, not a supporter, when he had written his *Reflections on the French Revolution* in 1791. It was French policy in the Low Countries that led to Pitt's involvement in the First Coalition. And it was there at Waterloo near Brussels that the last battle against Napoleon was to be fought and won.

There was a brief spell of Napoleonic peace after Britain signed the Peace of Amiens in March 1802. It tacitly conceded French supremacy in Europe, while recognizing all British gains outside Europe. (The British negotiator, Cornwallis, had been Viceroy in Ireland, Governor-General in India and commander of the British troops at Yorktown in the American War of Independence.) What was missing from the settlement was a treaty of commerce, and without this – its British critics complained from the beginning – Article I, promising peace and friendship between Britain and France, was a piece of hypocrisy. Yet there was a desire for peace in both countries, and Napoleon, for the moment, was satisfied. 'At Amiens', he explained later, 'I had achieved the moral conquest of Europe.'

The word 'moral' begs all the questions, as, indeed, do Napoleon's policies inside France. 'We have finished with the romance of the revolution', he remarked in another of his many dangerously memorable aphorisms, 'we must now begin its history.' As First Consul and, after August 1802, Consul for life, he consolidated much of the work of the French Revolution. This was the necessary foundation of the power of his state. A new civil code of law was promulgated by his Council of State in 1804: experts had set to work on it in 1800 and it was completed under the Empire after he himself had taken the chair at 36 of its 84 sessions. The 1801 concordat with the Pope recognized Catholicism as the predominant religion in France, but the system of treating the clergy as paid servants of the state was retained. A comprehensive reform of local government involved the appointment of 'prefects' to each *département*: they obeyed central orders, and were committed to administrative reform.

Napoleon did not believe in universal free instruction, but the new kind of high schools he sponsored – the *lycées*, first created in 1802 – survived his regime as did the prefects. So, too, did the *Polytechnique*, an older educational institution for an elite, renamed in 1795. Napoleon's educational policy, directed by a 'University of France' which served as a Ministry of Instruction, was more concerned with ladders than with floors or ceilings. (The real educational reformer of the period, Pestalozzi, was working neither in France nor Britain but in Switzerland.) The same approach was reflected too in Napoleon's creation of the new Order of the *Légion d'Honneur* in 1802. In the light of this Napoleon's decision to become Emperor, announced in December 1804, surprised neither his friends, who

Map 1.1 Europe at the height of Napoleon's power

were already vying with each other to acquire titles and to attend his court, nor his enemies, revolutionary or royalist, although it caused the great German musician Ludwig van Beethoven, one year younger than Napoleon – they had never met – to strike out his dedication of the 'Eroica' symphony to him.

Napoleon himself believed always in his own stagecraft, and having induced the Pope to attend his coronation service in Paris in December 1804 he took care at the most solemn moment in a ceremony that was drenched in history to place his new crown on his head with no outside assistance. He had already played with the insignia and sword of Charlemagne and had even held court at Charlemagne's capital, Aachen. The 'Enlightenment' did not count at all in this web of ambition and fantasy. Yet both before and after he became Emperor Napoleon was in a sense carrying the policy of 'enlightened absolutism' to its logical conclusion, seeking to unify French administrative procedures and to give the country an efficient new order. This was a process that was bound to be marked both by successes and failures. Before lifting Charlemagne's sword he had always worn a revolutionary mask, and he had won far more support from below – from peasantry and *bourgeoisie* – than an 'enlightened despot' like the Habsburg Emperor Josef II had ever been able to secure as a hereditary ruler.

There was, nonetheless, a sacrifice of freedom in France before as well as after 1804. As early as January 1800 as many as 60 Parisian newspapers were suppressed, and seven years later all but eight of the 33 theatres in Paris were closed. An English biographer of Napoleon, Herbert Butterfield, who paid eloquent tribute to Napoleon's reforms, pointed out also that he depended upon 'an engine more dreadful than any of the absolute monarchs had at their command for the repression of the individual'. He inaugurated a 'type of polity more formidable as an organ of power than ancient feudalisms and ill-jointed dynastic systems could ever have hoped to achieve'.

Napoleon knew this, but he was always conscious of his lack of 'legitimacy'. As a German historian, Fritz Hartung, has written, 'the empire of the Bonapartes lacked inner security: it had always to be prepared for a renewed upheaval'. There was certainly an 'ill-jointed' dynastic element in Napoleon's own policies. He placed on satellite thrones members of his own family, thought of by members of old royal families as upstarts, and in 1810 he divorced his wife, the childless Josephine, to marry Marie Louise, the daughter of the Habsburg Emperor. He himself had already humiliated the Habsburgs more than once, but he was never secure enough to ignore them. Moreover, he was aware of ominous continuities. Like many Holy Roman Emperors before him, he was thinking as much of Italy as of Germany. When Marie Louise produced him the much-wanted child, the child was called 'King of Rome': even in his cradle the child was called 'the King' by his devoted father.

Napoleon's passage from Consul for life to hereditary Emperor was never a difficult one, although on the way it involved the mock trial by a staged military court of the young Bourbon prince, the Duc d'Enghien, heir to the throne, who was accused of conspiracy. The death sentence pronounced on him meant that Napoleon, like the revolutionaries before him, had now spilt royal blood. It was in such a manner that he moved to his throne. Yet there was a real throne to ascend, and an Irish visitor to his court could claim that it was much greater in splendour than the old court of France. More of those attending it came from outside the ranks of the nobility than those who attended the court of Louis XVI.

Napoleon appreciated royal as well as revolutionary continuities. Thus, when he went to the Cathedral of Notre Dame to celebrate the Concordat with the Pope before he became Emperor, he wore the Regent Diamond which Louis XVI had worn at the opening of the Estates-General in 1789. Some of his Chamberlains had attended on Louis XVI. The artist Isabey, who had painted miniatures of Marie Antoinette's ladies, now produced drawings for the Emperor and designed efficient costumes. There was to be forward continuity too. Napoleon's official architect, Pierre Fontaine, was to serve Louis XVIII, Charles X – and Louis Philippe.

Outside the court Napoleon looked to the future in other ways. He believed in natural science and encouraged it: an official report of 1808 on the progress of the mathematical and physical sciences since 1789 acknowledged what had been achieved and what might still be done. He found it easier to talk to engineers than to artists, and greatly improved the roads and bridges of France and the Empire. He was particularly proud of the mountain roads across the Alpine passes which linked France to Italy. He also reconstructed the *corniche* road along the southern Mediterranean coast, linking Nice with Genoa. It was that road which he had followed in 1796 when he first invaded Italy at the invitation of the Directory.

Napoleon's limitations as an 'enlightened' ruler were displayed most strikingly in his commercial and economic policy. A Bank of France was founded in 1800, which three years later was given the monopoly of issuing banknotes, and the system of collecting taxes was, at last, tightened up, but there was no French income tax, however, while Pitt had introduced one. Napoleon believed in solvency, but it was only because he could extract funds from occupied countries that he did not need to raise taxes inside France until 1813. He never accepted any of the arguments in favour of free trade, and when the British proposed to return to the low tariffs of 1786 after signing the Peace of Amiens, which lasted for scarcely more than a year – continued British retention of the island of Malta was the pretext for the rupture – he refused. Yet he allowed corn to be exported to Britain to make up for deficiencies in domestic supplies even when the two countries were at war and he was preparing an invasion of England. His 'continental system', introduced in 1807, was an attempt to close the whole of Europe to the British, but British ships used a variety of devices, including sailing under foreign flags, smuggling, and straight bribery in order to break the system. Their own attempts through Orders in Council to check international traffic and to search neutral ships on the seas provided a pretext for the United States to declare war on Britain in 1812, but the war was as inconclusive as the Treaty of Ghent which brought it to an end. It had none of the excitement for France of the War of American Independence.

Napoleon clearly recognized the importance of industry, particularly when it had a technological base, and succeeded, therefore, in encouraging the production of substitute materials for materials that he could not import: thus, he welcomed a new chemical process for making soda from salt. He was aware also of developments in the textiles industry, and in 1806 the state acquired the patent of the new Jacquard loom which perpetuated French superiority in silk manufacturing. As a result there was enough French industrial expansion to worry British manufacturers, many of whom objected strongly to the Orders in Council. Yet French industrial development, which lacked adequate momentum from below, fell far short of an 'industrial revolution', and did not effect iron production. Nor did it help Napoleon that there were signs of serious strain in the British economy in 1811 and 1812, stimulating radical ideas both among employers and workers. The British combination of industrial and maritime strength proved vastly superior to anything the French could offer.

The 'continental system', which broke down in 1813, was not a new idea of Napoleon. Nor were many of the particular schemes which formed part of the Napoleonic Empire. Indeed, there was no grand Napoleonic design in foreign affairs. Issues were taken up one by one, and there was an underlying restlessness, culminating in overextension. Having failed to invade England in 1804 he turned back to Italy. Having become Emperor, he could scarcely keep the title 'President of the Cisalpine Republic', but when he chose the new title 'King of Italy' (he was crowned at Milan in May 1805) the choice not unnaturally provoked the reactionary King of Naples as well as the Emperor of Austria, who saw the title as an undermining of the Treaty of Lunéville. In August 1805 Britain, Austria, and Russia formed the Third Coalition, and the armies which Napoleon had hoped would invade Britain were now rushed across Europe to defeat the Austrians at Ulm and the Austrians and Russians at Austerlitz. These were great victories, but 1805 was also the year of the Battle of Trafalgar. Nelson was killed in it but only one-third of the ships of France and its ally Spain ever regained their harbours.

Trafalgar was fought on 21 October, Austerlitz on 2 December. The Treaty of Presburg, which followed, was humiliating to the Austrians, for they were not only forced to recognize Napoleon's titles but to cede to him Venice and the Dalmatian coast. Territories were soon being disposed of thoughtlessly – often under threats or to keep promises – and after the

Tyrol had been handed over by Austria to Max Josef, King of Bavaria, at Presburg, the Duchy of Berg and Cleves was handed to Napoleon's brother-in-law, Joachim Murat. In 1806 the kingdom of Naples was assigned to his brother Josèphe and a new principality, Neuchatel in Switzerland, was created for General Berthier. Meanwhile, the Dutch were forced under threat of annexation to accept as King another brother of Napoleon, Louis.

Those parts of the Presburg settlement that related to Germany, particularly the end of the Holy Roman Empire and the creation of a Confederation of the Rhine, succeeded in irritating the Prussians who had previously been neutral, and their irritation was not appeased by the handing over to them of Hanover, a territory ruled by the British royal family, which since 1714 had called itself 'Hanoverian'. Prussia went to war, therefore, in 1806, only to be routed by Napoleon himself at Jena and by one of his generals at Auerstadt. Two weeks after Jena (14 October) there were French soldiers, led by Napoleon, in Berlin, sharpening their swords, it was said, on the statue of Friedrich II. Russia proved more difficult. The costly battle of Eylau was indecisive, but victory at Friedland on 14 June 1807 forced the Russians to ask for an armistice, and they were treated on 7 July to one of the most fascinating events of the whole Napoleonic period – a private meeting between Napoleon and Tsar Alexander I on a raft in the middle of the river Niemen at Tilsit.

The two men seemed for a moment to be settling there the fate of the whole of Europe. They reached compromises on Prussia, allowing the King to retain his throne, and on Turkey, casting aside without scruple an old Turkish-French alliance and sharing Turkish spoils. A grand duchy of Warsaw was created, and Napoleon's brother Jerome became King of Westphalia. As far as Britain was concerned, however, they could do nothing except prepare the way for an anti-British alliance which was signed in secret later in the year. The two rulers hoped to bring into the struggle all the small maritime countries, including Portugal, Denmark and Sweden, in a kind of crusade in reverse, to create a system of 'federated states', in Napoleon's phrase 'a true French empire'. But their hopes were dashed when a British force took the initiative and in September 1807 bombarded Copenhagen: an earlier British force had bombarded it in April 1801, and now within two months of Tilsit all that remained of the Danish fleet, the biggest of Europe's 'minor fleets', was in British hands. A familiar pattern was now repeating itself – command of the land by the French; command of the seas by the British.

The Tilsit agreements between France and Russia were no more likely to last than the Treaty of Presburg with Austria. Yet Napoleon began to consider himself above all moral law and ultimately invincible. Thus, when the Portuguese refused to close their ports to British ships – and Portugal was England's oldest ally – he made a secret pact with Spain to dismember Portugal which he invaded in October 1807. Lisbon was duly occupied by

General Junot's troops, but by showing an ignorant insensitivity both to Portuguese and to Spanish interests and susceptibilities Napoleon soon faced popular revolt in the Iberian peninsula. Disposing of the Bourbons and offering the Spanish throne to his brother Josèphe in the summer of 1808 – Murat was called upon to take his place in Naples – had not been a solution and he himself was to comment later that it was 'the Spanish ulcer' that 'destroyed me'.

It was in the Iberian peninsula, not in the Low Countries, that British land power – not this time, sea power – drained Napoleon's strength. The British General Arthur Wellesley – an Irishman who through war was to become Duke of Wellington – followed a highly effective strategy. In was in the Iberian peninsula, too, that the persistence and scale of popular resistance in Europe proved that not everyone without power was willing to respond to Napoleon's propaganda of revolution. Elsewhere in Europe, as far east as Poland, where his policies were bound in the long run to provoke Alexander I, Napoleon's armies carried a message which could attract both *bourgeois* and peasant backing, but the most support that he could get in Spain came from limited sections of the *bourgeoisie*. Meanwhile, as a direct result of Napoleon's switch of his *grande armée* to Spain, there was a rallying of the great powers that still remained hostile to him. Austria declared war on France in April 1809, three months after Madrid had capitulated to Napoleon.

It was not a decisive decision, for Napoleon won the Battle of Wagram in July 1809, and after occupying Vienna the Habsburgs were forced to cede territories. There was yet another redrawing of the map of Italy and Germany. There was one new element, however, in the Napoleonic victory. It ended with wedding bells. The Emperor Napoleon married Marie Louise, the daughter of the man who had been Holy Roman Emperor, Franz I. Napoleon's court now moved on to Dresden, the capital of the kingdom of Saxony, where acting as host, the warrior Emperor was attended both by Franz I and by the King of Prussia. His armies were now moving towards the Russian border. Napoleon said later that Destiny led him eastwards, but this was his greatest mistake and the cause of his final undoing. His armies were huge and included thousands of soldiers from many parts of Napoleonic Europe as well as France: there were Austrians and Prussians among them, and Franz I would have liked to join them.

Dresden, one of the most beautiful cities in Europe, provided a good vantage point. The boundaries of direct French rule now stretched from south of the Pyrenees to the Baltic Sea and from the North Sea to the Dalmatian coast, and within this huge, if sprawling, area there were other great cities as large, as important and as different as Amsterdam, Barcelona, Hamburg, Florence and Rome. Yet this was not enough for Napoleon, and all was to melt away as his soldiers struggled in Russia in 1812 and 1813, actually entering Moscow in September 1812 only to see it burning – on the orders of the Russian commander.

Plate 1.6 *Napoleon watches the burning of Moscow from the Kremlin Palace*, **by George Cruikshank.** When Napoleon entered Moscow on 14 September 1812 he found it almost deserted. The next day the fire laid almost two-thirds of the newly-occupied city in smouldering ruins and within five days the French had quit the capital. Weighed down by loot seized from the city, they were soon to lose their race against the Russian winter.

The winter retreat from Moscow was terrifying. During this period, Metternich, the Austrian Chancellor, who had served as Ambassador in Paris, offered Napoleon prospects of a peace settlement that would have guaranteed France's 'natural frontiers' – the Rhine, the Alps and the Pyrenees. Indeed, as far as France was concerned, the map of Europe would have returned to what it had been in the first year of the Directory, with France still controlling Belgium, the left bank of the Rhine and Nice-Savoy. Napoleon refused. The Empire meant more to him than France, and hegemony meant more than tranquillity.

His end was as dramatic as his beginning. In October 1813 a new Fourth Coalition, which included Austria, Russia, Prussia and Britain, defeated Napoleon near Leipzig – still far away from the natural boundaries of France – in a battle which acquired the name of the Battle of the Nations. No fewer than 50,000 French lives were lost. Napoleon won further victories against Prussia, but Paris surrendered to the Allies at the end of March 1814, and Napoleon abdicated two weeks later. He was exiled to the tiny island of Elba in his native Mediterranean – an island far smaller than

Corsica, where he had begun – and this, but for Napoleon, might have been the end of the story. Instead, he broke free, landed on the south coast of France and set out to rally Frenchmen to his cause again. The Allies had restored a Bourbon, Louis XVIII, a brother of Louis XVI, to the French throne, but he was no more capable of countering Napoleon's magic than the surviving democratic revolutionaries had been in 1799. In 1815 Napoleon had to emphasize his own commitment to the Revolution as he had done in 1799: 'I am not a military despot but the peasants' emperor. I represent the people of France.'

It was not France which counted in 1815, however, but Europe; and at Waterloo on 17 June British, Prussian, Austrian, Dutch and Belgian forces were together on the winning side. Napoleon now abdicated again, surrendering this time – and it seemed part of a predestined fate – to the commander of a British warship. He was exiled to St Helena, a small island in the South Atlantic, and died there in 1821, still only 51 years of age. His captors refused to give him books or letters addressed to the Emperor Napoleon: they settled for General Bonaparte instead. Napoleon spent much of his time weaving myths about what he had done, what he had wanted to do, and what he might have done. There was one lingering regret. 'I asked for twenty years and destiny gave me only thirteen.'

Social accounting: gains and losses

Historians have written about the Revolution and Napoleon – and the industrial revolution – from vantage points very different from that of Dresden, the centre of which was to be destroyed by a different allied coalition in 1945, or of Waterloo, just outside Brussels, where a European Commission was to issue orders for Europe in the late-twentieth century. Revolutionary change affects different people and different groups, whatever their country, in different ways: to some it means death, to others power. To some it means deprivation, to others liberation, to still more confusion.

If you were an aristocrat in France after 1790 – and survived the guillotine – you would be conscious, above all else, of the loss of privilege. Life would never be the same again even if you returned home. If you were a French lawyer in 1789, you would sense new opportunities, as Robespierre did. Merit could take you far ahead in 'a career open to the talents'. If you were a French peasant, you would most likely, but not necessarily, have gained economically from revolutionary decrees, and some peasants did extremely well. If you were a French soldier – and survived the wars – you would have seen more of Europe than most Frenchmen before or since. Yet large numbers of soldiers and sailors on both sides were wounded or killed. If you were a *sans culottes*, one of the very poor, you would be in some doubt in 1800 after ten years of revolution, much of it violent, whether you were better-off or not, although 15 years later you might feel that you *were* when you lived in the Paris of Napoleon, complete with its court.

There had been brief times during the Revolution when the revolutionary decrees had favoured the *sans culottes* and there had been revolutionaries like the young and fiery St Just, who had claimed that 'the unfortunate' (*les malheureux*) were 'the power of the world' (*la puissance de la terre*). Napoleon never felt that. There were, however, *sans culottes* counterparts in all European countries, just as there were aristocrats and lawyers, and lawyers did well in Britain too.

The French Revolution and the British industrial revolution can be compared in similar fashion – in terms of their effects on different groups of people (rich and poor: aristocrats, peasants and *bourgeoisie*) and on different parts of the country. In Britain you could either glory as a manufacturer in the new power of steam, comparing it with horse power – and profit from it – or, if you were an industrial worker in a new cotton mill, feel a sharp loss of personal independence even when you were materially better off. Could you be better-off and still unfree? America led the way in raising such questions and in opening up new possibilities before Europe did.

The effects of industrialization were always as debatable as the effects of the French Revolution, even though no-one could doubt the unparalleled increase in output. The English poet and biographer Robert Southey, originally fascinated by the 'outbreak' of the French Revolution but repelled from the start by the advance of the industrial revolution, was one writer who wrote feelingly about both, including a popular biography of Nelson. What he said provoked debate on both during the nineteenth and twentieth centuries. In particular, it roused the great nineteenth-century Whig historian Thomas Babington Macaulay who approved of the results of the French Revolution while deploring its violence. Southey, he complained, had not 'stooped to study in detail' the history of industrial development, comparing 'district with district, or generation with generation'. His preference for 'rose-bushes and poor rates' over 'steam engines and independence' was sentimental. Yet there were many people, not all of them poor, who were on Southey's side.

As far as the French Revolution was concerned, there was nothing sentimental in a positive verdict of 1814 – delivered before Waterloo – that 'the Revolution substituted a system more conformable with justice and better suited to our times. It substituted law in the place of arbitrary will, equality in place of privilege; delivered men from the distinction of classes, the land from the barriers of provinces, trade from the shackle of corporations . . . agriculture from feudal subjection and the aggression of tithes, property from the impediment of entails, and brought everything to the condition of one state, one system of law, one people.'

This was measured language – if the last sentence raised fundamental

FRENCH LIBERTY

BRITISH SLAVERY

questions about the role of the state which was far stronger in France than in Britain. And much of the language relating to industrial change was measured too in a way that Southey's judgements were not. Statistics provided one mode of measurement, as Napoleon himself recognized. More frequently, however, political revolutionaries dealt in words more enthusiastically than in figures, and most of the language of the French Revolution was as highly coloured as the events themselves. One problem with statistics concerned their selectivity: crucial figures might be missing. Another problem was how to interpret them. There was to be a vigorous twentieth-century debate on the standard of living during the first decades of industrialization. Some sections of the labour force, notably handloom weavers, were worse off, catastrophically so. Most skilled workers – and there was a demand for new skills – were better-off. The situation varied from region to region, and within one region, like industrial Lancashire, from place to place. Distribution facilities were limited and local prices varied. Other evidence, qualitative and not quantitative in character, must be taken into account in any assessment of standards of life. And the qualitative evidence relates too to the effects of industrialization on the community and on the environment.

In Britain no account of the industrial revolution is complete either that does not consider its impact on women and children's work and on the structure of the family. The shift from domestic work to factory work, associated with the rise of steam power, turned both women and children into wage earners who were paid less than men and were employed for that reason. Yet there were more domestic servants than cotton workers, and Lancashire (and later parts of the West Riding of Yorkshire) were special cases.

In France women figured prominently in the heroic mythology of the Revolution, playing the major role in the march to Versailles on 5 October 1789, and, as Charles Dickens observed in his novel *A Tale of Two Cities*, knitting and plotting while husbands and lovers killed. (Charlotte Corday passed into history by murdering the militant revolutionary J. P. Marat in his bath.) Yet women's clubs in Paris were dissolved in 1793, and from 1795 onwards women were not admitted unaccompanied into the spectators' gallery at National Assemblies. While the Revolution had promised political participation for all, it excluded females from public life on biological, not on political, grounds – their physical constitution. War, of course, revolutionary or counter-revolutionary, strengthened the supportive role of women. While their husbands and children were away

---

Plate 1.7 French 'Liberty' contrasted with British 'Slavery', James Gillray 1792.
This cartoon reflects British suspicion both of the achievements of revolution and the French way of life. (Notice the large pot of snails beneath the window.) The fat John Bull by contrast, has his own problems. The important symbol of British power for some (which symbolized slavery for others) is the pound sterling.

they had to cope. They were frequently left to run businesses also. In the Catholic provinces they were frequently the main defenders of the old faith. In Bordeaux, for example, when a brave female member of the Fumel family, owners of the great vineyard at Haut Brion, who had been imprisoned on religious charges, went to the guillotine before her father she immediately became a martyr figure. So, too, did Marie Antoinette.

More historical research is needed on the history of gender in years of revolution, and so, until recently, it was equally necessary in relation to the social consequences of the two revolutions, political and economic, on 'the poor', urban and rural. They escaped direct taxation in both countries, but were never free from deprivation, and in 'bad years' when harvests failed or employment ceased (the two were interconnected) they experienced complete destitution. Their 'annals' were recorded at the time, mainly by others, in the proceedings of the law courts, the logs of hospitals and mortuaries, the reports of the local clergy and of managers of charities and occasionally in official enquiries. They were not a homogeneous group either in France or in Britain.[5] Some were perpetually poor, some, particularly the young, were highly mobile in their search for food and employment. Some became beggars. In Russia and other parts of eastern Europe many were unemancipated serfs. They were tied to a system that in the nineteenth century came to seem anachronistic.

In Britain, where the system changed before the French Revolution, Sir Frederick Eden produced an invaluable book *The State of the Poor* in 1794, noting how the country poor were often victims of land enclosure carried through Parliament which changed their lives as much as it changed the landscape. And it was Arthur Young who, for all his trust in agricultural improvement, recorded how commoners bemoaned that 'all I know is, I had a cow and an Act of Parliament has taken it from me'. Some of them fought hard – and continued to fight hard – for their customary rights, but they succumbed to the power of property. Meanwhile, through revolution the French peasantry, 80 per cent of the population, had secured new rights, but they were an even less homogeneous group than the titled nobility to whom before 1789 they were expected to defer without question. One in five of them was already a labourer before the Revolution. In England there were few independent producers: 'yeomen' owned no more than 10 per cent of the land in the last decade of the century. There were, however, substantial tenant farmers, some of them keenly interested in new farming techniques, as were many of the 'squires' who owned the land, and indeed, some of the members of the aristocracy. King George III himself did not dislike being called 'Farmer George'.

The English did not use the term 'nobility', a term which was carefully defined in most European countries in legal charters, particularly in the east and which applied to a particularly large section of the population in Spain. The Prussians had a powerful entrenched nobility, the *Junkers*, on whose service to the state the kings of Prussia depended. In Britain the term 'aristocracy' was preferred, and some aristocrats profited substantially from industrial interests. Others married into trade, if not on the scale that some contemporaries suggested. They all recognized that even as far as land ownership was concerned they were not the only men of influence. The 'squires', small country gentlemen, some of them of very independent views, shared their local social and political power. They were magistrates and sometimes owned Church 'livings', and it was they rather than the aristocrats who were most suspicious in England of the new men of wealth who emerged in the City of London and in the new industrial districts, many of them wishing for nothing more than to become squires themselves. It was the squires too who took greatest pride in the defeat of Napoleon who represented everything that they most disliked.

References

Reader should note that place of publication is London unless otherwise stated.

1. D. Boorstin, *The Genius of American Politics* (Chicago, 1953) p. 68.
2. P. Mantoux, *The Industrial Revolution in the Eighteenth Century* (1928) p. 21.
3. Its chief populariser was A. Toynbee, *Lectures on the Industrial Revolution in England* (1884).
4. This image was used as a book title by D. S. Landes, *The Unbound Prometheus: Technological Change and Industrial Development in Western Europe from 1750 to the Present* (Cambridge, 1969).
5. O. H. Hufton, *The Poor of Eighteenth Century France, 1750–1789* (1974) p. 2.

Chapter 2

Order and Movement, 1815–1848

Restoration: idea or reality?

After the huge upheavals throughout Europe between 1789 and 1815 nothing could be quite the same again. The experience of revolution and war had gone so deep and had been shared by so many people, if unequally, that it could not be forgotten easily. Not everyone wanted to forget, however. Indeed, even before his death in 1821, Napoleon became a legend that still had the power to move men. In his *Memorial* which he wrote on St Helena, he blamed everyone else for his defeat, as he already had done in the Hundred Days, and claimed that had he been victorious Europe would have been a 'federation of free peoples' grouped in eternal peace around an enlightened France. 'There seems to have been something in the air of St Helena', an English politician wrote later in the century, 'that blighted exact truth.' And when Napoleon, who had seldom been concerned with 'exact truth', chose in his last years to depict himself both as a revolutionary and a liberal, those aspects of his career which did not fit into the picture were conveniently neglected.

Revolutionaries and liberals were to be found in most countries in post-Napoleonic Europe, both groups believing that the work begun in 1789 should continue. The former were often professional in their outlook and uninhibited in their methods. The latter sought to retain the positive gains in human freedom achieved as a result of 1789 while at the same time avoiding 'revolutionary excesses': they put their trust not in conspiracy but in 'constitutionalism'.

An Italian, Filippo Buonarroti, emerged as *the* professional revolutionary of this period, living in a world of spies and *agents provocateurs*. Born a nobleman in Tuscany in 1761, he had been an admirer first of Robespierre and then of Babeuf, and he attracted disciples and followers in countries from Poland to Italy, Belgium to Spain. Another professional, Auguste Blanqui, born much later in 1805, was in love with revolution. He divided his fellow conspirators into Years, Seasons, Months, Weeks and Days, sticking in that respect at least to the pre-Revolutionary calendar. The name of his leader was Sunday.

There was nothing 'liberal' about such activity, yet the word 'liberal', including Liberal with a capital L, was passing into daily politics in several European countries. An early example of its use comes from Spain: Southey in 1816 referred to the *liberales*, and four years later in Paris *Libérals* were being contrasted with Ultras. In 1822 a periodical appeared in London with the title *The Liberal*; and later in the decade 'liberal' minded members of Lord Liverpool's Conservative government, which had first taken office in 1812, were being singled out from the rest.

Political parties were still in an embryonic stage, but it was through their later development that 'liberalism' in a variety of versions, backed by a newspaper and periodical press, became a major political force. For some liberals, those, for example, who lived in Europe's great ports, economic liberty seemed a more urgent cause than political freedom – or rather the two were thought inextricable. Metropolitan liberals focused on assemblies and freedom of speech.

In the interim, before political parties emerged that could function freely and continuously, the politics of protest depended on riots in countries without liberal constitutions and on platform agitations and pressure groups in countries which possessed them. In Britain, as in France, urban protests were most likely in years when bad harvests and unemployment coincided. In the words of William Cobbett, an English radical who was in no sense a liberal but who had spent a formative period of his life in America, it was difficult to agitate on a full stomach. The advice had universal applicability. At the same time, there were many liberals who were as afraid of pressure from below – either from towns or countryside – as they were of authority from above.

Rural discontent usually took unsophisticated forms, including arson, even in England; and in continental Europe, where peasants accepted toil and poverty as facts of life, they were more difficult to draw into public protest than townsfolk were. Moreover, when they were so drawn, they usually sought for redress at the local level. Their religion, a popular religion, whether Catholic, Protestant or Orthodox, was a source of consolation to them. Nonetheless, peasant *mafiosi* in Sicily entered the streets of Palermo in 1820 to fight for home rule, and village labourers frightened Earl Grey's reforming Whig government before and after the Reform Act of 1832.

The years that followed the end of the Napoleonic Wars were particularly bleak throughout most parts of Europe, as the late 1820s were to be, serving to prove that peace was as hard as war. In France in 1816 the harvest was so poor that large quantities of grain had to be shipped from England, and there were fears of bad harvests in both countries in 1818 that pushed up the price of bread. There was heavy urban unemployment too.

In 1817, when huge radical meetings were being organized in Britain's new industrial cities, the authorities of the ancient industrial city of Lyons, as subject to fluctuations of the trade cycle as any British city, were also reporting 'meetings, plots and movements'. Only half the silk looms in the city were in operation. Two years later, when a large crowd gathered in Manchester in August 1819 to petition for parliamentary reform, the yeomanry charged the crowds, killing 11 people and injuring 400. Waterloo had been followed by Peterloo. One of the members of Lord Liverpool's government that responded by passing Six Acts seeking to suppress freedom of the press and free assembly was Lord Castlereagh, a key figure in the devising of the post-Napoleonic settlement.

For the time being, Europe in 1815 after Napoleon's fall was in the hands of men who wanted to restore rather than to change. Looking back, Revolution and Empire seemed for them like adventures that had at last been brought – very properly but at real cost – to a close. Respect for legitimately constituted authority and for the social hierarchy that sustained it now had to be restored, they believed, along with the rulers who returned to their kingdoms, some of them small rulers to small kingdoms. It was a critic of Rousseau, Ludwig von Haller, a Swiss writer not a Frenchman, who wrote in 1816 that 'the legitimate monarchs have been restored to their thrones, and we are likewise going to restore to its throne legitimate science, the science which serves the sovereign master, and whose truth is confirmed by the whole universe'.

This was the logic of the situation as it appeared to those participants and observers who used pre-revolutionary language. Yet anti-revolutionism, like revolution or Bonapartism (the *ism* of the legend) or nationalism (a new phenomenon), was often expressed in highly romantic language, tinged with sentiment. The philosophers of 'restoration' included a number who looked back nostalgically to times before both the French Revolution and the industrial revolution, before the Enlightenment, even before the Reformation. They placed their emphasis on the need to recover an organic social order, based on duties, not on rights; on unity of thought and of morals, not on variety of opinions or behaviour; on religious faith, not on 'the march of intellect'. René de Chateaubriand, who had served briefly as a diplomat under Napoleon, had already written in his *Génie du Christianisme* (1802) of the 'sublime Christian mysteries' as 'the archetypes of the system of man and the world'. For him Napoleon had 'bewitched' French youth by 'the miracles wrought through his arms' and had taught Frenchmen to 'worship brute force'.

The task of restoration

While the five leading statesmen who set about 'restoring Europe' in 1815 were of different temperaments and persuasions, they shared distaste for revolution and the sense that it had to be suppressed. None of them, moreover, needed nostalgia to prop them up. With the exception of Castlereagh, who had been British Foreign Secretary since 1812, most of them had had direct contact with Napoleon and had been prepared, not only at times of defeat, to make deals with him. At Tilsit, Tsar Alexander I had tried to settle the fate of Europe with him on a covered barge on the River Niemen decorated with two sets of imperial eagles. Metternich, while appreciating the fact that Napoleon 'marched right to his goal without lingering for matters which he treated as secondary', had not been taken in by appearances. He had found the Emperor 'short, squat' and 'careless' in 'the way he held himself while he attempted to appear imposing'.

Essentially Metternich was a man of the eighteenth century who appreciated Voltaire: 'I reason about everything and on every occasion', he once said. Well connected, he had been born not in Austria but in the Rhineland, and he thought in European terms. He was happier speaking French than German. He had no illusions concerning the permanence of the restoration, of which he was sometimes described as 'the rock', but he was determined to preserve it for as long as was humanly possible. 'Fate', he said, 'has laid upon me the duty of restraining as far as my powers will allow, a generation whose destiny seems to be that of losing itself upon the slope which will surely lead to its ruin.'

Revolutions were never 'the work of great masses of the people', Metternich told Alexander in 1820: they were stirred up by 'the agitated classes', small groups of ambitious men, among them 'paid state officials, men of letters, lawyers, and individuals charged with public education'. The lawyers were, in his view, the most dangerous. In 1819 he used the murder of the anti-liberal writer August von Kotzebue by a mentally unbalanced theology student as the occasion for drafting the repressive Carlsbad Decrees which outlawed demonstrations, imposed a stringent press censorship, and rigidly controlled appointments to universities and what was taught in them.

Castlereagh, the British Foreign Secretary, four years older than Metternich, would not have questioned either Metternich's diagnosis or his remedies. He too was 'bound by history and by tradition', and was well to the right in British politics (left/right terms were beginning to be used). As acting Chief Secretary for Ireland he had been responsible for the suppression of the French-aided rebellion of 1798 and for the Act of Union between Britain and Ireland in 1800. Like Metternich, he was suspicious of 'abstract and speculative' ideas and wanted more than all else a European period of 'repose'.

By contrast, Alexander I had many large and mystical ideas of his own, which became larger and more mystical the older he grew. In 1804 he had been in correspondence with William Pitt, Castlereagh's mentor, proposing to him a vague but high-sounding scheme for universal peace, based on a grouping of states, in effect a European government, that would be committed to the end of feudalism and to the introduction of constitutional rule. Pitt's reply ignored this vision and proposed instead a postwar settlement with guarantees that would be based on the principles of the balance of power. A decade later, in 1814 and 1815, Alexander retained a vision of Europe, still wishing to establish himself as its arbiter but arguing now that what was necessary was a new system of authority. He still preferred the idea of 'reconstructing' Europe to 'restoring' the status quo, and he was trusted neither by Metternich nor by Castlereagh. He had a number of advisers, however, from different backgrounds, who played a part in postwar negotiations, among them Count Nesselrode (of German descent) and Pozzo di Borgo (born, like Napoleon, in Corsica).

Friedrich Wilhelm III of Prussia had been interested in 'reforms' while Napoleon controlled the future of Germany, and his ministers Karl Stein and K. A. Hardenberg had set out 'to do from above what the French have done from below'. In appealing to his fellow countrymen to re-enter the battle against Napoleon in 1813, however, he had summoned up from the Prussian past for present inspiration the names of 'the Great Elector' and 'the great Frederick', recalling previous bloody battles for 'freedom of conscience, honour, independence, commerce, industry and science'. He was fighting, Friedrich claimed, 'for a secure and glorious peace and the return of better times'. When peace came he promised an extension of 'representative government', but he now did nothing to move even modestly in that direction, listening instead both to Metternich and to Alexander. His chief minister, Hardenberg, who remained close to him until his death in 1822, also showed little sign of his earlier radicalism at this stage in his career, though he had once been excited by 'the endless forces not developed and not utilized that slumber in the bosom of a nation'. In 1819 the King and his minister gave support to the Carlsbad Decrees, and it was in Prussia's capital city, Berlin, that the great founder of its university, Wilhelm von Humboldt, whose idealistic approach to higher education was to sway generations beyond his own, now resigned in disgust.

The settlement

Before Metternich took over the role of supervising post-Napoleonic Europe Castlereagh played a major part in trying to bind together in a Quadruple Alliance the four main wartime allies who had been involved in the four wartime coalitions, and before the final defeat of Napoleon they had signed a 20-year treaty at Chaumont in March 1814 in which they all agreed to work closely together. There was a further proviso looking beyond the territorial settlement itself. The great powers would hold a series of peacetime meetings to consult upon matters of common interest. This would have been enough for Castlereagh and Metternich; Alexander, however, wanted something more high-sounding, a compact that would rest not on *raison d'état* but a declaration of principle based on those 'sublime truths' that were enshrined in Christianity ('justice', 'Christian charity' and 'peace'). It would constitute a 'Holy Alliance' of monarchs, whom he described as 'fathers of families', to guarantee a Christian order 'in the name of the Most Sacred and Indivisible Trinity'.

'The course *formerly* adopted by the Powers in their mutual relations had to be *fundamentally* changed', Alexander urged in the first draft of his alliance. 'It was *urgent* to replace it with an order of things based on the exalted truths of the eternal religion of our Saviour.' After the Emperor of Austria read his draft he is said to have remarked that he did not know whether to discuss the proposals in his Council of Ministers or in the confessional, and Castlereagh described Alexander's final document as a 'piece of sublime mysticism and nonsense'. Not surprisingly, the Sultan of the Ottoman Empire was the only ruler of a European realm who was not asked to sign; and while Britain's Regent, the future George IV, expressed sympathy he did not sign.

The first difficult task of the peacemakers was practical, not ideological – to restore thrones, states and boundaries. The thrones came first because the legitimacy of hereditary rulership had been challenged both by the revolutionary regicides in France and by the clan kingmaking of Napoleon. Restoration of the states came second, because these were the territorial units within which rulers exercised authority. The peacemakers unanimously rejected what they held to be dangerous ideas concerning the sovereignty of the people. Restoration of the boundaries came third, although it was recognized that they could not be restored just as they had been. The map of Europe had changed so many times between 1792 and 1815 – often with the active connivance of surviving rulers from the 'old regime' – that it was necessary to look closely at what seemed to be basic geographical facts.

These were soon to change substantially with the coming of railways and the creation of a new communications system. Metternich, however, began with the geographical situation of the great powers as it was. 'France [which he significantly put first] and Russia have but a single frontier and this hardly vulnerable. The Rhine with its triple line of fortresses assures the repose of France; a frightful climate makes the Niemen a no less safe frontier for Russia. Austria and Prussia find themselves exposed on all sides to attack by their neighbouring powers. Continuously menaced by the preponderance of these two powers, Austria and Prussia can find tranquillity only in a wise and measured policy, in relations of goodwill and among each other and with their neighbours.'

The great powers had reached preliminary agreement earlier in the first Treaty of Paris (May 1814) after Napoleon had been dispatched to Elba. By then they had also settled a number of basic issues relating to the peace arrangements, including: the restoration of France to its 'ancient frontiers',

Plate 2.1 *The Congress of Vienna 1815,* **after a painting by Isabey.** From left to right: Duke of Wellington (Britain); Count Lobo da Silveyra (Portugal); Duke of Saldanha de Gama (Portugal); Count of Lowenheim (Sweden); (seated in foreground) The Prince of Hardenberg (Prussia): Count Alexis de Noailles (France); Prince Metternich (Austria); Count de Latour du Pin (France); Count Nesselrode (Russia); (seated) de Sousa-Holstein, Count of Palmella (Portugal); (seated) Viscount Castlereagh (Britain); (at round table) Duke of Dalberg (France); Baron von Wessenberg (Austria); (standing) Prince Rasoumoffsky (Russia); (standing) General Lord Stewart (Britain); Don Pierre-Gomez Labrador (Spain); Lord Calancarty (Britain); M. Wacken; M. Gentz; Baron Wilhelm von Humboldt (Prussia); General Lord Cathcart (Britain); (seated in foreground) Prince de Talleyrand-Perigord (France); (seated in foreground) Count Stackelberg (Russia).

the 1792 boundaries; the enlargement of Holland to include Belgium (the Austrian Netherlands before 1792) and Luxembourg; the independence of Switzerland; the division of Italy into independent states; the restoration of Spain, like France, to Bourbon rule; and the establishment of a confederated Germany. Saxony, which had remained an ally of Napoleon to the last, and partitioned Poland, where Napoleon had figured not as an aggressor but as a restorer, were deliberately not mentioned in this first Treaty.

Within this broad framework there was, indeed, scope for considerable disagreement, even among the Big Four, whose representatives met privately in Metternich's apartments almost every day during the Congress of Vienna which gathered together on 1 November 1814. It was a large and glittering congress, attended not only by representatives from every state but from many organizations that now would be considered 'nongovernmental'. Secret diplomacy went on behind the scenes on difficult topics, among them relations with defeated France which was represented at Vienna with great diplomatic and social skill by the 60-year-old Talleyrand, the man everyone knew. He could do nothing, however, to prevent (even had he wished to do so) British colonial gains during the revolutionary and Napoleonic wars from being taken into account as they had been in eighteenth-century treaties, like the Treaty of Paris in 1763 which ended the Seven Years War and which left Bourbon France seeking revenge. As far as Britain was concerned, the emphasis in 1815, as during the wars themselves, was not on acquisition of territory but on command of the oceans and the bases which would make this possible.

The Vienna settlement, discussion of which was interrupted by Napoleon's flight from Elba and the Hundred Days, was finally signed in June 1815. It was the most far-reaching agreement that had been reached in Europe since the Treaty of Westphalia in 1648. The very loose German confederation of 39 states (the *Deutscher Bund*) was to be presided over by Austria, and although it was never to develop a corporate sense of its own it was a creation of long-term importance for the future of Germany. At the same time, Austria was given direct control of lands in Italy that were to be of critical importance to the future of Italy. Lombardy and Venice were annexed and Austrian princes were handed key Italian duchies, Modena and Parma. There were now eight separate states in Italy.

Metternich thus ensured through the terms of the German and Italian peace 'settlements' that he and the multinational Empire which was controlled from Vienna would be at the heart of the new European order so long as he lasted. Yet only one element in that order was long to outlast him: Switzerland was not only granted independence but neutrality. The 'old regime' in Switzerland was not restored in its entirety. Formerly subject districts, like Geneva and the Valais, now became confederate cantons. The settlement allowed for the expansion of trade and industry, but it too was to change in 1846 through Swiss crisis and war two years before Metternich's own fall.[1]

Prussia, which was as anxious to protect the new status quo as Metternich was, received (after critical secret sessions) 40 per cent of Saxony and was also granted strategic lands on the Rhine and the Napoleonic Duchy of Westphalia as a defensive bulwark against France, eventually enabling it to emerge as a champion of Germany against France. This was long after both Friedrich Wilhelm III and Metternich had disappeared from the scene. The immediate effect was a doubling of Prussia's population. Berlin, however, was in the east, not all that far from Russia. The other German states had a different geographic orientation as well as a range of very different rulers.

Between disunited Germany and comparatively united France the old principality of Liège was arbitrarily merged with the former Austrian Netherlands and 'given' to Holland as compensation for its loss to Britain of Dutch colonies in South Africa. This was a settlement that could not last. In the east Russia was allowed to reconstitute part of the old Polish kingdom as a new but dependent Kingdom of Poland (a move which required Prussia to hand back the Warsaw region). It was not until after another protracted twentieth-century war that an independent Poland appeared on the map.

There were all kinds of compensation arrangements in 1815 of which this was one. Thus, when Austria secured the Italian duchies it lost its Belgian territories, and in the north Sweden 'gave' Finland to Russia and in return, as already agreed, 'received' Norway from Denmark. In Italy, where, as in Germany, the Habsburgs made substantial but in the long run dangerous gains, Vittore Emmanuele I, King of Piedmont-Sardinia, sporting an *ancien regime* peruke and pigtail, returned to Turin. Greeting his 'good and faithful subjects', he assured them that they would 'find themselves once more under the dominion of those beloved Princes, who have brought them happiness and glory for so many centuries', and offered them all the benefits of absolute government, although conscription was abolished and taxation reduced. As one item in the deal he received part of Savoy and Genoa which for centuries before French occupation had been an independent republic and which had been liberated by a British officer, William Cavendish Bentinck. In other parts of Italy the Grand Duke of Tuscany returned to Florence; the Pope, Pius VII (Pope from 1800 to 1823) returned to Rome (and the Papal States that straddled Italy); and Fernando IV, King of Naples – now renamed Fernando I, King of the Two Sicilies – was restored to his old throne of Naples: this, however, was only after he had signed a permanent defensive alliance with Austria.

Britain, so heavily and continuously committed to wartime coalitions, secured what it chose to seek. Command of the oceans was strengthened by scattered gains – Cape Colony in South Africa (a key position until the building of the Suez Canal, but a future cause of political conflict in both the nineteenth and the twentieth centuries), Ceylon, Mauritius, French islands in the West Indies, and – nearer home – Heligoland (off the German coast) and Malta, a Mediterranean shuttlecock during the Napoleonic Wars. Britain also secured agreements for the opening of certain rivers to navigation and a general condemnation of the slave trade, which was an insistent demand by influential British pressure groups that were represented at Vienna. Abolished by the French revolutionaries in 1792, slavery had been restored under Napoleon.

Unlike the other great powers present at Vienna, Britain was a country where pressures could register through Parliament and where policies of all kinds, however liberal, were open to debate. Castlereagh knew that all his actions would be subject to popular scrutiny and even to scurrilous attack at home. Cartoonists would be at work as well as journalists – and poets, among them Shelley, who in a famous poem, which had nothing to do with Vienna, described meeting 'murder on the way', wearing 'a mask like Castlereagh'. Although Castlereagh did not approve of the Holy Alliance, his political enemies in Britain drew no distinctions between the four-power treaty and the 'ideological' pact.

One participant in the Congress, Friedrich von Gentz, translator of Edmund Burke as well as secretary to Metternich, left a highly critical account of its work. Placed as he had been at the heart of the intriguing, he claimed that nothing had been achieved at Vienna except 'restorations which had already been effected by arms, agreements between the great powers which were of little value for the preservation of Europe, quite arbitrary alterations in the possessions of the smaller states, but no act of a higher nature, no great measure for public order or the general good which might compensate humanity for its long suffering or pacify it for the future'.

This verdict has been reviewed many times in the light of subsequent experience, particularly the experience of the two world wars in the twentieth century, the first of which was followed by a controversial 'settlement' that was to last for only 20 years, and the second, a settlement in instalments, out of which emerged the United Nations Organization along with a 'cold war' beginning almost immediately after the 'hot' war had ended. Judgements have varied. Woodrow Wilson as American President at the end of the First World War set out to devise a contrasting settlement on opposing lines which Harold Nicolson as a young diplomat present there criticized as strongly as Gentz criticized Vienna. Henry Kissinger, a later American Secretary of State during the Cold War years, who as a young historian had made a detailed and sympathetic historical study of the personalities at Vienna, praised the men who made the settlement for ushering in the longest period of peace in Europe that it had ever known. Moreover, it relied less on power to maintain itself than any other settlement would have done.

Undoubtedly the 1815 settlement secured a general balance of forces in Europe that survived local crises in particular places, including Italy and Spain, and one important change in the map of Europe, the creation of a new and independent Kingdom of Belgium in 1830. Within the overall balance there was to be an important place for defeated, though now royalist, Bourbon France, a very different place from that to be set aside for defeated Germany either in 1919 or in 1945. France had been forced to cease to be gigantic, it was observed, in order that it might be great. Depriving France of her revolutionary and Napoleonic conquests did not mean destroying the country, and it was by its own choice that it changed its regime in 1830.

Even after Napoleon had escaped from Elba and the settlement had to be reconsidered, it did not become vindictive. Slices of Savoy and Flanders, which France had retained under the first settlement, were now to be handed over to its neighbours along with lands in Germany and a fortress in Alsace; in addition, France was held responsible for limited indemnity and Allied occupation costs. The new settlement, signed in November 1815 in a second Treaty of Paris, brought an even greater element of justice in that countless art objects looted by the French during the Napoleonic Wars now had to be returned to their rightful owners.

The weaknesses of the settlement, which included such novel features as an international Commission for the River Rhine, were that it left a number of future trouble spots on the map and that it created new ones. Moreover, while 'Germany' and 'Italy' were kept in place – divided – until 1848, thereafter they were to upset the balance. The settlement also ignored one area that had been of diplomatic and military importance immediately before the revolutionary wars began and which was to bring many future troubles in the nineteenth century: the east of Europe and the Ottoman Empire. There was no Commission for the River Danube.

The 'Congress System'

Many problems became apparent soon after the initial period of peacemaking was over, and were not resolved during 1818 when the Quadruple Alliance became a Quintuple Alliance with the inclusion of France. This was a logical step which Talleyrand, always present at the right time, encouraged the other great powers to take. Yet, as he knew, France had interests and policies of its own within a 'Congress System', and these could now be expressed at the various congresses which met to monitor the postwar European order.

The five great powers who were now monitoring peace were the same great five who had dominated the European scene before 1789, but their interrelationships had changed after Britain had emerged from the revolutionary and Napoleonic wars with greater wealth at home and with access to far greater wealth in the world outside Europe than any other great power. At the same time Habsburg resources in relation to Habsburg commitments were inadequate to give Metternich the financial security he required in order to play the role in Europe that he felt necessary.

How wise he was to play it in the way that he did remains a matter of debate. The Habsburg Empire sprawled over many regions, and to suppress both liberalism and nationalism everywhere within it was a daunting task. Soldiers in his own armies, inadequately funded and difficult to reform, spoke many languages, including Magyar, Serb and Italian. To draw too much attention to this fact, however, violated military 'honour', a supreme virtue in Vienna. Politics from below could not always be suppressed, and Lord Palmerston told the Austrian Ambassador in London long after 'the system' had broken down that Metternich's approach to European questions was 'repressing and suffocating'. Immobility was not conservatism, and it would 'lead to an explosion just as certainly as would a boiler that was hermetically sealed and deprived of an outlet for steam'.

While the 'Congress System' was new and untried, the four European congresses held between 1815 and 1822 already made it clear, first, that the wartime Allies (with Britain on the periphery and Austria at the centre) had different standpoints in peacetime and, second, that it was misleading to claim without qualifications that an old world had been 'restored'. There were far too many signs of a new world in the making. From the start Castlereagh, while unsympathetic to that world, saw the difficulties of policing any European order, Christian or not, while Metternich rejected attempts by the Tsar to create an international army to guarantee the boundaries and existing governments of Europe. Yet when risings broke out in Naples and Spain against reactionary monarchist regimes, Metternich was deeply shocked by what he thought of in non-historical terms as 'earthquakes', 'volcanic eruptions', 'plague' or 'cancer'. He is said to have used eight such metaphors to describe society.

In the case of Naples, where, as in other parts of Italy, Metternich always encouraged ministerial attempts to improve domestic administration, he felt bound to act without resorting to metaphor. A secret treaty between Austria and Naples (one of several such treaties) provided for Vienna to receive a full supply of intelligence, and it was with the reluctant concurrence of Britain and the enthusiastic backing of Russia (which wished to join in the intervention) that an Austrian army entered Naples in 1821 and crushed a Neapolitan revolt as quickly as it had begun. There was, in fact, little local support for the Army leaders who had led the revolt and who had resisted the idea of a separate new constitution for Sicily. In consequence Fernando I returned to his throne. The financial cost to Austria was high: it necessitated a large loan and, in order to get it, a speedy part repayment of an earlier British loan, and it led to a substantial budget deficit.

Even before Austrian interventions in Naples and in the Kingdom of Piedmont-Sardinia, where rebels had plotted to depose Vittore Emmanuele I and introduce a new constitution, the 'Congress System' was in difficulties. At the very first conference at Aachen in 1818 Castlereagh had been told by his government to avoid 'continental entanglements' except that of keeping France in check; and in November 1820 at the time of the Congress of Troppau, at which he was not present, he objected strongly – and publicly – to a protocol drawn up to meet Alexander's wishes. It stated that states which had undergone a change of government, due to revolution, and which as a result threatened other states would cease to be 'members of the European Alliance', adding that 'if, owing to such alterations immediate danger threatened other states, the powers bind themselves, by peaceful means, or if need be by arms, to bring back the guilty state into the bosom of the Great Alliance'.

At the subsequent Congress of Laibach (January 1821) it was clear that there would be no compromise between Britain's position on the one hand and Austria's and Prussia's on the other, although one Austrian diplomat

1. United Netherlands
2. Neuchâtel (to Prussia)
3. Helvetic Confederation
4. Piedmont/Genoa (to Sardinia)
5. Parma
6. Modena
7. Lucca
8. Tuscany
9. Papal States
10. Naples (to Sicily)
11. Tarnopol (to Austria)
12. Montenegro
13. Catalonia
14. Valais (to Helvetic Confederation)
15. Piombino (to Tuscany)

Map 2.1 Europe after the Congress of Vienna

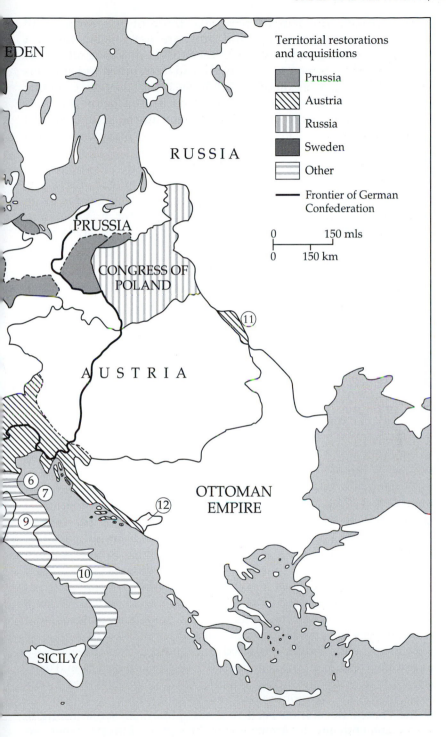

described Castlereagh's reactions as being like those of 'a great lover of music at church who wishes to applaud but dare not'. Before the next Congress, which was ,held at Verona in October 1822, at which all five of the great powers were present, Castlereagh had committed suicide (his reasons were private), and his more forthright successor, George Canning, reiterated in stronger language than had ever been used before Britain's complete refusal to take part in Allied intervention in the second area of disturbance, Spain, where rebels were asking for the acceptance of an abortive constitution drafted in 1812.

When French troops moved into Spain in 1823, with the support of Austria and Russia, the 'Congress System' was clearly at an end. There was a plaintive note, therefore, to Castlereagh's remarks to King George IV in his last interview with him four days before his suicide. 'Sir, it is necessary to say goodbye to Europe; you and I alone know it and have saved it: no one after me understands the affairs of the Continent.'

Signs of change

Between 1822 and 1830 it became abundantly clear that there were different interpretations of what 'Europe' meant. These were years when the word 'movement' was passing, like the word 'liberal', into the nineteenth-century political vocabulary as naturally as the term 'revolution' had passed into it during the late-eighteenth century, and it acquired a force of its own. Used vaguely in relation not only to the diffusion of liberal ideas and opinions but to the advance of nationalism, it was employed less vaguely in relation to new organizations and new political groupings, and strictly literally in relation to 'the movement of peoples'. In industrializing Britain the words 'labour movement' were used as early as 1828. By then, forming part of it, there were trade unions, cooperative societies and socialist organizations.

Belonging to a movement by choice carried with it new commitments and new loyalties. It might be either a secret movement based, like freemasonry, on oaths, or a public movement based on propaganda, including pamphlets and posters, and it might be national or international in its scope. The most famous of the post-1815 secret movements, engaged in plots rather than in campaigns, was that of the *Carbonari* (rural charcoal burners), founded in Naples in 1810. 'Apprentices' in its French counterpart, the *Charbonnerie*, were initiated in a mock trial of Jesus, and dedicated themselves to Faith, Hope and Charity.

Another group, with lodges scattered everywhere, was Buonarroti's League of Sublime and Perfect Masters, with their headquarters in Turin. There was a Greek society also, the *Hetairia Philike*, which linked Greek sympathizers in various cities of the Balkans. Some counter-revolutionaries attributed the French Revolution itself to a conspiracy, Masonic in origin; and anti-Semitism, endemic in various forms throughout Europe, generated deeply disturbing theories of conspiracy across the centuries. In Russia there was a distinctive twist to revolutionary conspiracy. On the death of Alexander I in December 1825 there was a misunderstanding about who should succeed him, and as the throne remained vacant for three weeks sections of the Army rebelled at St Petersburg, demanding the summoning of a national assembly. When Nicholas I, Alexander's younger son, succeeded to the throne as his father had intended, the so-called Decembrist Revolt was crushed with great severity, but the new Tsar was haunted for the rest of his life by the spectre of revolution.

France itself remained a centre of political conflict. Yet the Bourbon kings – Louis XVIII, twice restored, and his reactionary brother Charles X (the former Comte d'Artois, who succeeded Louis in 1824) – had to take account less of movements than of an ambiguous but to them inhibiting Constitutional Charter which had been drawn up in 1814 by a committee of former ministers, senators and deputies of the Empire: it guaranteed the land settlement of the Revolution, retained Napoleon's administrative and educational system, and provided for parliamentary government. Only the preamble, which stated that the Charter was the monarch's 'gift to France', belonged unequivocally to the *ancien régime*. Although the parliamentary franchise was severely restricted in 1822 – there were only 100,000 voters out of a population of 29 million – Charles X himself made the first moves that led to his downfall by trying to evade all the Charter's provisions. French opposition, whether in small clandestine groups meeting in secret or expressed openly in newspapers and in a Society of the Friends of the Freedom of the Press, could never be quelled, let alone crushed.

Nor could it in Spain, where the Bourbon Fernando VII followed in the footsteps of his uncle, Fernando I, King of the Two Sicilies, and tried ruthlessly to stamp out 'liberalism' through royal or 'white' Terror. One of Fernando I's chief ministers once said that 'the first servant of the Crown should be the executioner'. Yet he did not have at his command enough executioners to maintain uncontested order, and civil war was to follow his death in 1833. An all-out victory against 'liberalism' was also out of the question in Portugal, where a reactionary Regent took over in 1826 and civil war followed at once. The young Queen Maria II eventually won the struggle with the support of the liberals.

During the 1820s the issue of freedom was at stake not only in Spain and Portugal but in the east of Europe, where it was often to be threatened in the future. And once again rifts were revealed between Britain and the other four great powers. There were also new diplomatic complexities, including a temporary isolation of Austria. After 1815 two revolts began against the very loosely exercised imperial control of the Ottoman Turks. The first was in Serbia in 1827 when Milos Obrenović took control: it attracted relatively little attention outside the Balkans. The second was in Greece and, by contrast, this revolt attracted as much attention in Europe as the Spanish Civil War was to do during the 1930s.

In 1821 Greek rebels wrested the ancient Pelopponese from the Turks with deceptive ease and speed, and the Turks retaliated at once with savage reprisals against Greeks both in Turkey and in the Mediterranean islands. The Greek Patriarch and three archbishops were hanged in their ecclesiastical vestments in Constantinople, the centre of the Greek Orthodox Church, and as many as 30,000 people were killed or enslaved on the predominantly Greek island of Chios not far from the Turkish mainland. This was the beginning of a protracted struggle that continued for most of the 1820s. The Greeks, who had the American constitution in mind when they assembled in Epidaurus in 1822 to draft their own, secured immense public backing in all countries from 'Phil-hellenes' – writers, poets, politicians and rulers, like Ludwig of Bavaria, who sent an army brigade. Even Charles X had Phil-hellene sympathies.

The leaders of the romantic movement found a hero in Byron, England's 'brightest genius' and 'Greece's noblest friend', and leapt enthusiastically to the defence of what they took to be the greatest of causes. (One British supporter, Colonel, later Earl, Stanhope was described by Byron as 'the typographical colonel' because he equipped Greeks not only with arms but with a printing press.) Despite such backing, the Greeks seemed to be in danger of total collapse in 1827. With Athens besieged, they then elected as President for seven years Capo d'Istria, who had been one of Alexander's advisers at the Congress of Vienna.

Even if Metternich had not been in power, Austria and Russia would have been bound to disagree on the Greek question. Indeed, differences of interest and outlook on all east European questions were to remain, if often 'put on ice', into the twentieth century. In the 1820s Russians, committed neither to the classical world nor to Greek liberalism but to the Orthodox Church, had begun giving help to the Greek rebels even while they were urging joint European action against all rebels everywhere, but Metternich, considering the Greek rebels to be no different from rebels in Naples or Spain, was determined at least to prevent any inter-state action on their behalf.

The blow to him came in April 1826, when Nicholas I, who had succeeded Alexander as Tsar in 1825, entered into an agreement with Britain to impose mediation upon the belligerents in order to secure an autonomous Greece under the nominal suzerainty of the Ottoman Empire. In July 1827 France associated itself with the new agreement, bringing about an interesting – although temporary – alignment of the great powers who were to be in alliance again in 1914 when the First World War broke out. The climax of this phase came when a British admiral annihilated the Turkish fleet at Navarino in October 1827, the greatest Turkish disaster at sea since Lepanto.

Nonetheless, it did not seem to be in British interests then, or later in the nineteenth century, for the Ottoman Empire to be carved up and destroyed (although Charles X of France dreamed of doing so); and the Duke of

Plate 2.2 *Lord Byron,* **resplendent in orange and gold Albanian dress.** Hailed at his Greek funeral in 1824 as a martyr to the cause, he was described as having come 'to share our sufferings and our hardships; assisting us not only with his wealth, which was profuse; not only with his judgement of which he has given us so many salutary examples – but with his sword which he was prepared to unleash against our barbarous and tyrannical oppressors'.

Wellington, who after Canning's death succeeded him as Prime Minister in 1828, actually apologized to the Sultan as 'an old ally'. British fears seemed justified when the Russians advanced against the Turks on land and in August 1829 reached Adrianople, the nearest they had ever been to Constantinople. Nicholas halted, however – he had no desire to destroy the Ottoman Empire, preferring to keep it weak – and by the Treaty of Adrianople obtained a financial indemnity from the Turks (who pledged that they would not impair Christian rights, which were to be under Russia's protection) and, in more concrete terms, the Danube delta on the Black Sea. By a later London agreement, signed by Britain and France, Greece secured not only autonomy but independence. It was to become a kingdom rather than a republic, but it was not until February 1833 – after protracted negotiations involving different possible names – that Otto I, the son of the Phil-hellene King of Bavaria, ascended the Greek throne.

The significance of the Greek revolt did not lie primarily in the field of diplomacy. Metternich had been isolated, if only for the time being, and Britain and France (for different reasons and not for the last time) had revealed their own special interest in what was happening in Constantinople. Far more important, however, the Greek revolt had mobilized the kind of popular support, including support from the peasantry, that Metternich most feared. It had ended too with the recognition of a new country that took its place on the map not just as a state but as a nation state. The fact that the new nation acquired a dynastic monarch in 1833 did not minimize the extent of the change as far as Europe was concerned, although it was to complicate future Greek politics both in the nineteenth and twentieth centuries. Europe would move ahead, not stand still or, as some hoped, return to the past.

The statesman who best understood this was Canning. Like his predecessor Castlereagh, he was a conservative, although he favoured Catholic emancipation and knew that Europe – and the world – must change. 'Canning soars', Metternich complained, 'I walk. He rises into a region uninhabited by men. I keep on the level of human things.' (Canning called Metternich 'the greatest rogue and liar on the Continent, perhaps in the civilized world'.) Metternich was wrong in feeling that Canning was out of touch with reality. As Member of Parliament for Liverpool, his British opposite number was very much in touch with the hard issues of British trade and with the industry which increasingly sustained it. He was unwilling to subordinate British interest to the fears of a conservative concert of powers. 'Every country for itself and God for us all' was one of his mottoes. And, unlike Castlereagh, he had to deal with places outside Europe as well as on the continent.

The Spanish colonial territories in South America were in revolt against Madrid during the revolutionary and Napoleonic wars, and civil wars raged there in waves from 1812 to 1820. Byron sympathized with the liberationist cause there before he turned to Greece. There were dramatic events in the struggle too, like the crossing of the high Andes by 'the Liberator', Simon Bolivar, to create a republic of Venezuela in 1819, the year of Peterloo. It was of importance, therefore, that in 1825 and 1826 Canning did not hesitate to give his full support to the rebels, calling 'the New World into existence', as he put it in one of his famous phrases, 'to redress the balance of the old'.

This was 1776 in reverse, and Canning won great popularity in Latin America for his stand, which was shared by many Englishmen. Bolivar's dreams of a union of peoples were shattered, however, by the year of his death in 1830, and he died unpopular and reviled. After falling from power he was to declare that 'he who sows a revolution ploughs the sea'.

The revolutions of 1830: challenging the status quo

No such memorable aphorisms were pronounced in 1830 when Europe was swept by a revolutionary wave, although the French poet Victor Hugo, whose political views had evolved during the previous decade, chose appropriate and for him unusually concise words when he described the French Revolution of 1830 as 'a revolution stopped half-way'. There would have been no revolution at all in France in 1830, however, had it not been for Charles X's desire to make his regime even more authoritarian than it had been. Supported by extreme right-wing politicians, he invited trouble when he asked one of their number, the Comte de Polignac, who had been serving as French Ambassador in London, to become Prime Minister in August 1829. Polignac had been one of two members of the Chamber who had refused to take the Oath to the Charter of 1814, and the result of the royal *coup d'état* was direct confrontation. 'On the one side is the Court', one Paris newspaper put it, 'on the other the nation.' This newspaper, the *Globe*, was a new one. It belonged to Thiers, a young liberal politician (and later both historian and suppressor of revolution), who was supported – or patronized – by Talleyrand.

Charles X was subsequently disposed of with very little bloodshed in a July Revolution in Paris that was engineered mainly by the disgruntled *bourgeoisie* under the tricolour flag, supported by crowds of workmen willing, if necessary, to go to the barricades. The outcome, however, was not a new revolutionary republic but a constitutional monarchy, with Louis Philippe, the new monarch, designated 'King of the French' not 'King of France'. At the same time the 1814 Charter was revised and identified explicitly as a contract between King and People.

Louis Philippe was the son of 'Equality Philip' (*Philippe Egalité*) who had conspired against Louis XVI but had subsequently been guillotined. He had fought as a young man at Valmy, the crucial defensive battle of the Revolution in 1792, and at a critical moment in the July Revolution he now appeared on the same platform as Lafayette, whom some revolutionaries had wished to see appointed as President. There were historical echoes in all this, though they were echoes that stirred controversies as much as they brought back memories. The celebration of Bastille Day was revived. So, too, was the tricolour flag. But liberty caps were taboo, and after liberty trees had been planted in 1830 and 1831 the planting stopped under Louis Philippe's first conservative prime minister.

The immediate consequences of the Revolution were more striking outside France than inside, and they might have been sweeping had Louis Philippe been willing to place himself at the head of revolutionary forces in Europe. He was not. As a result events everywhere took their own course. Austria and Prussia remained quiet – for financial reasons Austria could take no action to intervene in events in France – but there was a violent uprising in Brunswick where the ducal palace went up in flames. (There were historical echoes for France too in the name Brunswick.) 'For fifteen years it seemed as if the eternal generative power of the world's history [had been] paralysed', a German liberal wrote years later. 'And then three days sufficed to overturn one throne, and make all the others tremble.'

The first throne to tremble was that of Holland. A successful revolt in Brussels in August 1830 fittingly followed a demonstration after an opera which had an anti-authoritarian plot. (Opera frequently served political purposes in the nineteenth century.) A provisional Belgian government demanded independence, and the Dutch King, William I, who had insisted on making the Dutch language the official language of the whole of his kingdom, was unable to re-establish his authority. The Holy Alliance seemed to have tumbled. 'Bold ardent hopes' sprang up 'like trees with golden fruit', according to the young German romantic poet, Heinrich Heine, a Jew who moved to exile in Paris in 1831. He had been disappointed when he visited 'materialistic' England a few years earlier as an admirer of Canning. 'Don't send a poet to England', he advised. For Heine it was Paris that was 'the new Jerusalem' and the River Rhine was the River Jordan 'which divides the land of freedom from the land of the Philistines'.

Nonetheless, Heine's fruits had also begun to appear even in Germany before he left it, for liberal constitutions were adopted in several German states, including Saxony, Hanover and Hesse-Cassel, and in May 1832 over 20,000 people from all parts of Germany held a festival at Hambach in the Palatinate at which the tricolour flag was hoisted. Toasts were drunk too to the sovereignty of the people and the brotherhood of nations. In the previous year the tricolour had even flown in Birmingham when Britain was in the throes of a protracted political and constitutional crisis centred on the passing of a parliamentary reform bill, which extended the franchise to a large section of the middle classes. The Whig Prime Minister, Earl Grey, who succeeded Wellington in 1830, believed rightly that political adaptability at the top was required to canalize popular pressure from below. By increasing the electorate by almost a half, the Act would hitch the 'middle ranks of society' to the constitution.

There were further fierce, if less successful, struggles for political and constitutional change elsewhere, with more evidence of repression than of reform. Before further German demonstrations were crushed in 1832 and 1833 – Metternich succeeded in getting the German Diet to carry Six Articles banning political associations and popular meetings. There had also been a terrifying revolutionary *débacle* in Poland. The Poles had risen against the Russians in November 1830, but the Polish nobility had made no attempt to win the support of the peasants, and there were fierce divisions among them between 'whites' and 'reds'. When in September 1831 the Russians were able to re-enter Warsaw their revenge was swift. An ordnance of 1833 declared Poland in a 'state of war': it authorized the death or imprisonment of thousands of patriotic Poles, the seizure of Polish lands, the closing of universities, and the military policing of Warsaw. Nearly 10,000 *emigrés* left Poland, most of them travelling to France. Some were to make their way to America, a route followed by thousands later in the century.

The fact that Belgium could secure its independence while Poland was crushed, and that the British could carry a Reform Act through Parliament while German Estates were being warned to accept decisions of the Diet without question, were signs of increasingly sharp and now obvious divisions between the east and west of Europe. The Belgian conflict did not end with the Treaty of London in December 1830, which guaranteed Belgium independence and, a month later, its neutrality. (Talleyrand was the French signatory, and Lord Palmerston, the ex-Canningite Foreign Secretary, the British.) In subsequent divisions, however – about who should be King and where the frontiers should be set – Britain and France drew closer together, standing out as 'liberal' powers arrayed against 'conservative' powers Austria, Prussia and Russia, the so-called 'Northern Courts'.

In Holy Alliance terminology Louis Philippe was no better than a 'king of the barricades'. Yet this was not the judgement of Palmerston, who (with breaks) was to serve as Foreign Secretary for more years than any other. He welcomed the fact that Louis Philippe preferred *entente* with Britain to the all-out support for other European revolutions which some of his own supporters were demanding. The King of the French even put on one side the idea of a French ruler of Belgium and accepted the nomination of Leopold of Saxe-Coburg, uncle of the British Queen, Victoria, who was to come to the throne in 1837. When the King of Holland refused to accept the new arrangements in Belgium, a French army and a British fleet moved together to force him to do so. The new Belgian constitution – with Leopold as 'King of the Belgians' – now constituted a new liberal model, more up-to-date than the American. It was to be widely studied.

The French and British also worked closely together in Portugal and in Spain in 1834, signing a Quadruple Alliance which Metternich, who tried to split them, was anxious should not take on any ideological significance.

And in Egypt too in 1833 they supported reconciliation between the Sultan and Mehemet Ali, an intelligent and ambitious rebel, Albanian by origin, who was *de facto* ruler of Egypt. Once again their interest was not ideological: it lay not in the strenuous efforts of Mehemet Ali to reform Egyptian politics and administration but in the diplomatic and military implications of his enlightened activities on Constantinople. The main problem there was the role of Russia, and in their combination they were no more successful in protecting the Sultan against the Tsar than they were in safeguarding the independence of Poland. By the Treaty of Unkiar Skelessi in 1833 Russia secured Turkey's agreement to close the strategic Dardanelles to all foreign ships. It was in the same year that Nicholas I described Metternich as his 'chief' and that Metternich 'acquitted' Russia of any aggressive views with regard to the Ottoman Empire. When a second crisis centred on Mehemet Ali's move into Syria in 1839 Britain and France took up different positions, and Palmerston himself worked in cooperation with Metternich to secure the Straits Treaty of 1841 which reversed Unkiar Skelessi (and isolated France).

Meanwhile, Russia had joined with Austria and Turkey in policies of repression in eastern Europe, in Germany and in Italy. After the *Deutscher Bund* had passed its Six Articles, joint commissions were established to monitor all subversive activity and to adjudicate in disputes about constitutions. Nicholas I, along with the rulers of Austria and Prussia, signed the Convention of Münchengratz (October 1833), which recognized the right of any sovereign threatened by revolt (as in the Holy Alliance of 1815) to summon Austria, Prussia and Russia to his aid. 'So long as the union of the three monarchs lasts', said Metternich, 'there will be a chance of safety in the world.' Thereafter until the 1840s Metternich's unflinching determination to maintain 'safety' proved stronger than any desire on the part of the British or French governments to support liberal regimes. The main interest of Palmerston, indeed, was not to change the European balance but to maintain as effective an 'equilibrium' as possible.

In Italy, after Austrian-backed rulers were driven out of Modena and Parma in largely uncoordinated moves in 1831 and a provisional liberal government had been set up in Bologna and the Papal States in the same year the Austrians had no difficulty in restoring order. Louis Philippe sent 'an army of observation' to Ancona, where it remained until 1838, but it played no part in the subsequent unfolding of events.

Nation and class

A more interesting development had taken place in 1831, when Giuseppe Mazzini, born in 1805, the year of Austerlitz and Trafalgar, founded Young Italy on French soil at Marseilles. Mazzini, a dedicated advocate of nationalism as a liberal and a liberating force throughout Europe, was influenced by other writers, but he always struck his own notes, and he enrolled more than 60,000 Italian supporters, all under 40 years of age, before he embarked on a bigger but related project to create a Young Europe.

Time was to prove that Mazzini was neither an effective nor a realistic politician: he allowed neither for the strength of alternative ideologies nor for localism and apathy, very strong in Italy both in 1830 and later; and he sacrificed more friends than he converted enemies. Yet he made his presence felt with small publicized raids, even when they turned into fiascos, like a crossing from Switzerland into Savoy in 1834; and his ideology of liberal nationalism deserves to be given pride of place at the opposite end of the political spectrum from 'safety in the world'. It has to be sharply distinguished also from nationalist philosophies that involved the exploitation of chauvinist aggression and the unleashing of the will to dominate. Different nationalisms were complementary, not competitive.

There were problems, however, in Mazzini's conception of 'national mission'. He did not believe in Irish nationalism and he was unimpressed by all versions of nationalism different from his own. After reading the writings of the exiled Polish poet Adam Mickiewicz, who lived in Paris, he thought that Poland, the 'Christ among the nations', might have as its mission the demonstration of national redemption through suffering, but he gave 'primacy' to Italy in relation to the remaking of Europe: 'the destiny of Italy is that of the world', 'God's word among the nations'. Not all French nationalists agreed. Whatever Louis Philippe and his ministers might say about the limits of French foreign policy, there were many Frenchmen – not all of them Bonapartists – who believed that it was France that had a special duty to act as 'the pilot of the ship of humanity'. No one believed this more strongly than Victor Hugo.

In Germany 'nationalism' took a different form. It was identified with trust in the *Volk*, a word very different in derivation and orientation from the French words (with Italian and Spanish equivalents) *peuple* and *nation*, which were now bracketed together by definition: they were associated also with two new French words coined after 1789 – *nationalisme* (still rarely used before 1815) and *nationalités*. J. G. Herder, the first German philosopher of nationalism, who died in 1803, thought in terms not of national power but of national cultures based on a shared language. Nationalism, he believed, would appeal to young people seeking 'unity of spirit'. As it subsequently developed, German nationalism appealed to the unsophisticated young more than to the meditative old and to the heart as much as to the mind. Throughout its development the word 'reason' was suspect. The young, it was appreciated, might live long enough to see Germany actually converted from a geographical expression (as Metternich thought of it) or a cluster of historical associations and loyalties (as Friedrich Wilhelm III thought of it) into a nation state appearing on the European map.

Where its borders would be drawn was not clear. Friedrich Ludwig Jahn, who encouraged the postwar youth movement to adopt a black, gold and red flag for a new Germany, thought that the state should be a big state – including Switzerland, the Netherlands and Denmark – and have its own capital, Teutonia. Nor was he alone in this. Others were prepared to include all the Habsburg lands. Prophecy could evade the issue. Heinrich Laube, who prophesied the end of nationalities and the coming of a new European republic in the first part of his *Das Junge Europe* (1833), had changed his mind when he wrote the second part in 1838. The German nation now came first.

Nationalism was a movement which emerged in the immediate postwar years when distinctions between different kinds of 'movements' were not being closely drawn. Later, however, they were, particularly after the word 'class' came to be used more widely, replacing, though not at once and not universally, the old language of ranks, orders and degrees. In Prussia, indeed, and even earlier in some of the smaller German states, representation through local Estates was restored after 1815 and in most parts of Germany power remained with the nobility, entrenched in an upper Estate, as it had been in France before 1789. There was a gulf between them and the merchant 'middle classes', strong in the Rhineland. Both in Germany and in Italy as well as in France the words *bourgeois* and *bourgeoisie* had a long history, leading back to the medieval city. It was to prove awkward, however, that in the German language *burgerlich* meant both *bourgeois* and 'civil': there was no distinction, therefore, between *bourgeois* society and civil society. And this could lead to confusion – then and in the late-twentieth century when the term 'civil society' was revived in political debate.

Such terms were used far less often in Britain, where pragmatism prevailed in the pursuit both of domestic and of foreign policy, but it was in Britain that a new entrepreneurial employer class emerged, proud of its energy and its will to innovate, and looking for profits, not for fees or rents. It was of this class that Marx and Engels, sons of well-to-do families of converted Jews living in the Rhineland, were thinking most when in exile in Britain they looked to a revolutionary future. They were to set out their forecasts in unforgettable language in a *Communist Manifesto*, written in six weeks and published in 1848, and were to go on to claim later (and far more systematically) that past, present and future could be approached 'scientifically' – as could revolution itself. Out of facts and ideas derived from the German philosophical dialectic of Hegel, from French histories of the 'class struggle', and from British political economy, particularly the labour theory of value of the English political economist David Ricardo, they forged a new synthesis.

Classes developed through movement, through economic change more than through political change, and their identities, often blurred at the edges, were established neither by law nor by custom. They were

Plate 2.3 Title page of the Communist Manifesto, 1848. Published by Karl Marx and Friederich Engels in London, the book was written by Marx although Engels contributed both money and ideas already articulated in his famous *Condition of the Working Classes in England* (1844). One of the key intellectual documents of the nineteenth century, the page bears the legend which was to become famous: 'Workers of the World Unite'.

articulated through common experiences, including 'combination', and through conflict. It is more dangerous, however, to generalize about 'classes', as Marx and Engels often did, even 'ruling classes', some of whom were very suspicious of all forms of movement, than it is to generalize about bureaucracy, whoever the rulers were. A close look at both the working class in the making and the *bourgeoisie* during these years directs attention as much to occupational and regional group variation within each class as to incipient or imminent class solidarity. In continental Europe the small-town *bourgeoisie*, entrenched and often traditionalist, could be comfortable, even deferential, in its own local communities, which were sharply distinguished from new industrial cities; its members were by no means attached in any obvious way to the cause of political movement.

Nor at a different level were shopkeepers (some serving the aristocracy), merchants (some very wealthy), industrialists (still a small group numerically, but some of them rich), and bankers, the greatest of whom constituted an ambitious *haute bourgeoisie* which might, like the Rothschilds, operate through a network of international links. As Metternich well knew, they were less attached to general causes than lawyers or 'intellectuals', another term little used in Britain.

British students, unlike their European counterparts, for the most part stayed out of political movements. In continental Europe they were vocal representatives of a new generation. So too were poets, who in France and Germany might be stronger advocates of 'movement' than railway promoters. Alphonse Marie Louis de Lamartine, who was to play a key role in the French Revolution of 1848, wrote to a friend 11 years earlier that 'the only road to power' lay 'in identifying oneself with the very spirit of a victorious movement at a time when no one can gainsay you'. Deciding on the right movement was, as the young Marx appreciated, perhaps the biggest of all the decisions that revolutionaries had to take.

Only in Britain, Belgium and parts of Germany and Austria was there an industrial labour force employed in mines, workshops, mills and factories that was big enough to count politically, and even there the 'force' was largely localized in industrial regions. Handicraft rather than machine production remained the dominant form of manufacturing employment in most countries, and during the 1840s there were always handicraft workers in France, Germany and Austria who behaved like Luddites in Britain a generation before, destroying machines that seemed to be taking away their employment. Everywhere more workers laboured on the land than in the towns and cities, and even in Britain it was not until the year 1851 that the urban population exceeded the rural.

Nonetheless, it did not require industrialization – and most of it was still small-scale even in Britain – for the *bourgeoisie* to assert its claims against the aristocracy or for socialist ideas to emerge in towns and cities. It was because of the sense of continuing revolution, hated though it was by substantial sections of the *bourgeoisie*, that socialist manifestos were drafted. 'Labour had arrived before capital was ready for it.' In France itself, where industrial progress was relatively slow after 1815, there was a profusion of socialist ideas, many of them propounded by intellectuals who knew the inside of libraries better than the insides of factories. Indeed, the word 'socialism' in its modern sense was invented in France.

The views of the socialists, most of whom Marx dismissed as 'utopian', diverged. Christian socialists looked back to Jesus as the first of the *sans culottes*. Louis Blanc, who published his *L'Organisation du Travail* (The Organisation of Labour) in 1839, believed in using the power of the state to control the market. Charles Fourrier and his disciples canvassed the creation of socialist communities, *phalanges*, as did the British cooperator Robert Owen, who used very different, and less bizarre, language. Proudhon distrusted all dogmas, claiming that social reforms could only be achieved by an 'economic combine' that would 'restore to society the wealth that another economic combine had taken from it'. St Simon and his followers, who in the 1820s used the word 'masses' as well as the word 'classes', thereby pointing to a further new scenario, believed in the necessity of industrialization. Past society had been a military society in which warriors had been supported by priests. Future society would depend on enterprise, not on force or reverence. St Simon's opinions evolved, and as they evolved they strongly influenced thinkers outside as well as inside France. So, too, did the writings of Marx who conceived of his task explicitly not as that of 'trying to bring some kind of utopian system into being', but 'of consciously participating in an historical process by which society is being transformed before our very eyes'.

Facts and dreams

It was not only nationalists, therefore, who dreamed dreams between 1815 and 1830. Robert Owen, who had been present at the Congress of Vienna to try to win support for his view on cooperation, thought in apocalyptic fashion of an imminent 'crisis' – the title of a British working-class journal of the early 1830s – that would lead to the world being born again. Abbé Lamennais, a French liberal Catholic, put Church before State and dreamed in 1832 of converting the Pope to liberal Catholicism. His journal was called *L'Avenir* ('The Future'), and his pamphlets, which stressed the need for unselfishness and justice, were very widely read. Richard Cobden, founder of the British Anti-Corn Law League in 1839, an efficient organization, pledged to secure by extra-parliamentary pressure the repeal of the protective British corn law, made the most of a new (1840) penny post in his campaigns, along with all kinds of meetings, including bazaars. Cobden dreamed of a new international order resting on universal free trade. For men like these and for their dedicated followers, states (with their aristocracies) and, as they developed, nations (with their armies) mattered less than principles. 'Let governments have as little to do with one another as possible', Cobden once wrote, 'and let peoples have as much to do with one another as possible.'

Influencing all political development then and into the 1840s were far-reaching structural changes – urban growth; industrialization; and, above all, new communications patterns. A 'railway age' had been ushered in when a line between Manchester and Liverpool was opened in 1830 (Wellington was present at the opening), and by 1838, the year when Russia built its first railway, there were almost 500 miles in operation in Britain. From the start, railways were symbols of movement (and speed), stimulating the imagination even more than the steam power that moved the locomotives. But they were far more than symbols. They reduced transport costs, opened up markets and created an unprecedented demand for coal and iron. Both freight and ideas were carried by railway and soon after its introduction by telegraph, a new invention with which they were quickly associated. Small countries could benefit from railways as well as countries with great spaces. In the middle of the 1830s Belgium was ahead of Britain in having evolved a 'railway policy', and the line from Brussels to Malines carried more passengers in its first year than all the railways in Britain.

It was to facilitate and increase the volume of movement of freight that Prussia, not Austria, took the lead in 1819 in creating a *Zollverein* ('Customs Union') which was soon to be a matter of concern to Metternich who saw it as a 'state within a state' but who knew that Austrian industries were then not sufficiently advanced to participate in it. The *Zollverein* was subsequently expanded in size and scope until in 1834 it included 18 states in central and southern Germany with a population of 23 million and a total area of 112,000 square miles. Its political advantages to Prussia were small: its economic advantages to Prussians substantial. By eliminating internal customs barriers it widened German markets and by sheltering its members behind the Prussian tariff of 1818 it restricted imports of manufactured goods from other parts of Europe: the duty on them was 10 per cent *ad valorem*. Fear of German economic competition from the *Zollverein* was expressed in the British Parliament in the late 1830s, and while the first administrator of the *Zollverein* was a Prussian admirer of Adam Smith, in Prussia a strong protectionist strand prevailed in Georg Friedrich List's *The National System of Political Economy* (1844). List had been an exile in America, where British free trade views never commanded universal assent.

America figured in European history in a variety of different ways between 1815 and 1848, but mainly because it too was both a symbol of open movement and a real place to which real people moved. It was people, however, not governments, who determined the pattern of overseas emigration, sometimes under the pressure of fear of their own governments; and every year in order to find new hope in a new land large numbers of people crossed the oceans, an increasing proportion by steam ship, often suffering great hardship on the way. Emigration from Britain alone rose from about 57,000 in 1830 to 90,000 in 1840 and 280,000 in 1850. The emigrants were drawn by more than dreams. The hard facts of daily life in Europe during the 1830s and 1840s drove some of the most enterprising people to seek to better their condition, and such betterment

Plate 2.4 The Irish Famine, c.1846. Pictures such as this illustration of Irish destitution elicited a great deal of sympathy in Britain, much of it of a practical kind. But there was also a feeling of revulsion, if not contempt, for the destitute Irish who were often depicted eating rotting or, all important, seed potatoes. Later, far more than at the time, the famine had a revolutionary impact on Irish politics.

was certainly more than a dream. 'Now father', one British emigrant wrote home in 1848 after reaching Australia, 'I think this is the Promised Land.'

Many moved from the countryside, some from the great cities. By 1848, 47 towns in Europe had a population greater than 100,000 – 28 of them in industrializing Britain – and all were centres of problems even while they were also centres of local pride, often expressed in rivalry with other cities. Industrial Manchester became the shock city of the age, and every social observer or critic who wanted to see how society was developing thought it necessary either to learn about it or preferably to visit it. Everywhere conditions in industrial centres and bulging capital cities received far more attention from social commentators than villages and country estates, although social conditions were often bad there also.

The hardest of all the European facts, perhaps, were those of the Great Famine which affected Ireland and large parts of eastern Europe too in the mid-1840s. The failure of the potato crop in 1845 and the years following led to widespread starvation, and over 20,000 people died in Ireland alone. A far larger number, however, emigrated to the United States. Some 1.5 million had left before the Great Famine began, a grim Malthusian phenomenon that the London government did not know how to handle, and by its end the Irish population had decreased by a third. Soon there were to be more Irish in American cities than in any city in Ireland itself. This had long-term consequences, extending from fact into myth.

Not all facts were as potent as the facts of city growth, migration and famine. Yet the years from 1830 to 1848 were years when there was as much talk about facts – hard facts – as about dreams. The urge to collect statistics, which had been described in the *Encyclopaedia Britannica* in 1797 as a word 'recently introduced' from Germany, was apparent everywhere, particularly, perhaps, in Britain and France – both official statistics in documents like the great British 'blue books' (the reports of committees of enquiry) or unofficial statistics collected by social investigators or voluntary societies. They were statistics not only about population – still rising in Europe despite emigration and reaching over 260 million by 1848, 75 million more than in 1800 – but also about industrial production, imports and exports, public health, literacy and, not least, crime. One common use of the word 'classes' related not to economics but to morals. The perception that there were 'dangerous classes', particularly in the great cities, was shared across the frontiers. So too – and the concept was refined later – was the sense of the existence of a distinct 'criminal class'.

The health statistics were particularly important, for it was through the analysis of differential mortality figures (different death rates in different regions of a country or even in different parts of the same city) that statisticians with a social purpose came to the crucial conclusion that it would be possible to eliminate some local and regional differences if proper social policies were pursued. Faced not only with endemic diseases, like typhus, which were related to poverty, but epidemic diseases, particularly cholera, which struck people from all classes (including one of Louis Philippe's prime ministers), they talked boldly of challenging Fate by deliberately altering people's chances of life and death through the public provision of better water supply and sewage systems.

This was not a dream, as it might have been in the eighteenth century, but an intention that could now be fulfilled (with the help of engineers even more than of doctors). Supplying clean water – and there were large parts of Europe where this was not assured – preceded the large-scale manufacture and distribution of cheap soap. Meanwhile, the supply of statistics increased annually. 'The pursuit of statistical enquiries', the tenth Report of the Statistical Society of London claimed in 1844, 'has already made such progress . . . as henceforth to be a necessity of the age, and one of its most honourable characteristics.'

Not all commentators on social change put their trust in statistics. The quest to collect them was sometimes satirized, sometimes described as a fad, sometimes treated as a less effective way of approaching the problems of society than 'the imaginative factor', better expressed in novels than in tables and in articles and reviews in newspapers and journals that were beginning to be thought of as a 'Fourth Estate'. Fortunately some statisticians could push forward imaginatively into difficult issues of social analysis. For example, the Belgian statistician Adolphe Quetelet, who loved to explore 'laws of large numbers', examined probabilities as well as aggregates and rates of change and introduced the notion of 'the average man'.

In France, social investigators like Eugène Buret and Louis Villermé related health to housing and housing to crime. It was to take many more decades to achieve by public policy an improvement in housing conditions that conservatives, believing in the family and the home, favoured even more than radicals. It was less easy to deal with housing issues – jerry building, overcrowding, and lack of necessary domestic amenities – than it was to deal with collective measures to improve public health. Sewers came before bathrooms. In 1829 Villermé was one of the founders of the *Annales d'hygiène publique et du médicine légale*, the first regular journal in the world to concentrate on problems of public health.

Few of the social investigators of the 1830s or 1840s were socialists. Edwin Chadwick, indeed, Bentham's last secretary, was associated in the public mind not only with public health reform (the first British Public Health Act was passed in 1848) but with the introduction of a controversial new Poor Law in 1834 which was also based on Benthamite postulates. Debates on how to deal with the poor were paralleled in other countries and were often bitter. They had been common in the late-eighteenth century. The 1834 Act, therefore, was a European landmark. By abolishing all outdoor relief for the poor and forcing them into 'workhouses', not a new institution but one which was to be introduced everywhere, money was saved and the care of the poor, previously associated with charity, was systematized. Conditions for the inmates of the workhouses were to be made deliberately worse than those in the worst forms of alternative employment. Not surprisingly, the poor compared the workhouses with Bastilles and their own conditions with those of black slaves.

Opposition to the Poor Law of 1834 in Britain played a key part in triggering off the great protest movement of Chartism, the first specifically large-scale working-class movement in Europe, as Marx and Engels recognized. Another element in the snowballing protest was the demand for factory reform, especially the limitation of working hours for women and children, still a major element in the factory labour force, particularly in the textile industry (the hare among the tortoises in the industrial race). A substantial instalment of factory reform was achieved in 1847, one year after the repeal of the corn laws, with some of the corn law repealers opposing the reform on the grounds that by extending the scope of factory inspectors it constituted governmental interference with industry. This was a relatively new political alignment. So, too, was rural aristocratic interest in the conditions of the urban poor as expressed, for example, by England's seventh Earl of Shaftesbury, an Evangelical reformer who was also a tory.

In Prussia there were strong paternalistic strains, and in 1839 a factory law was introduced (if not fully enforced) prohibiting the employment of children under nine years old and restricting the working day of children aged between nine and 16.

Politics centring on city improvement, on social intervention in factories and on measures to deal with pauperism – a serious problem in all countries, industrial or not – were 'social politics', and for many people without the right to vote at elections, and for some who had this right, this was now the only kind of politics that really mattered. It was complex, not simple, politics. The British Chartists, who drafted their key document, the Charter, in 1838, started with facts – the facts of a limited franchise and a grim 'condition of England' – but they had their dreams also, dreams of converting the British Parliament into a People's Parliament based on an electoral system with manhood suffrage, annual elections, and no property qualifications for members. When their Six Points had been achieved they could even offer roast beef on every man's table.

When the Chartists began to agitate during a severe business depression, the most serious depression since the industrial revolution, the first important measure of parliamentary reform had already been carried in Britain. This, indeed, afforded the Chartists with one of their main arguments – that they were only asking Parliament to grant the working classes what had already been granted to the middle classes by the Whigs in the Reform Act of 1832. Yet neither the Whigs nor Sir Robert Peel, a sensible and sensitive 'conservative', the son of a rich cotton manufacturer, who accepted the Act and who won a general election under the new franchise in 1841, had any sympathy with Chartist demands. The Chartists were left, therefore, with little opportunity except to organize and to demonstrate.

They were able to prove the strength of the new working-class presence in British life – for some a source of fear – but they seldom, if ever, threatened revolution. Many of them believed in the motto 'peaceably if we may, forcefully if we must', but there was little well-organized physical force in Chartist politics. Nor – until it was too late, in 1848 – was there a real junction between Chartists and disgruntled Irishmen, chafing against the 1800 Act of Union with Britain. The fact that the most popular Chartist leader, Feargus O'Connor, was himself Irish did not make for a Chartist-Irish alliance, since O'Connor was distrusted by (and himself distrusted) Daniel O'Connell, the Irish leader in Parliament.

Meanwhile, from 1841 to 1846 Peel carried out a programme of major reforms – including tax reforms, strengthening of the banking system and in 1846 the repeal of the corn laws – that laid the foundations for the security and prosperity of mid-nineteenth-century Britain. He did so, however, at the expense of dividing his own Conservative Party, one of the first parliamentary parties to have an organized base in the constituencies. Now a large section of it, including the squirearchy, turned against him,

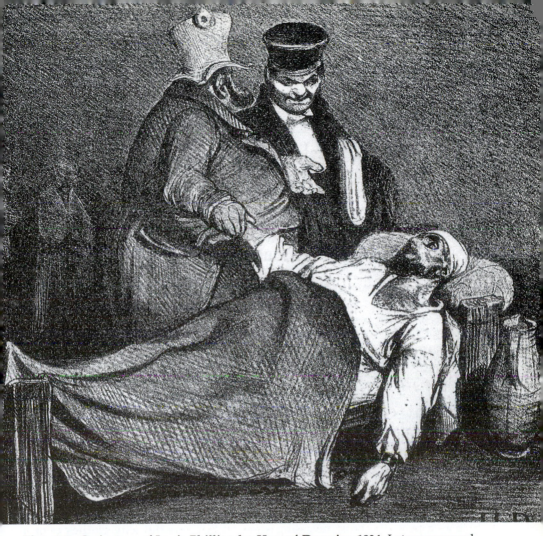

Plate 2.5 Caricature of Louis Phillipe by Honoré Daumier, 1834. Later renowned as a great romantic painter, Daumier was famed during his lifetime as a biting political cartoonist. Here the pear-shaped Louis Phillipe tests the pulse of a dying revolutionary and announces: 'It's safe to release this one!'.

rallied by the brilliant rhetoric of Benjamin Disraeli, a young politician in the making, for whom being a Jew (if a Christian Jew) was only a minor hardship. More important, therefore, than any social alliance in the British politics of the 1840s was a political rupture.

What happened in 1846 had long-term political consequences of great importance. The Whigs, a predominantly aristocratic party with a 'tail' of Protestant dissenters (or nonconformists), political radicals, Irishmen, ex-Canningites like Palmerston, and, after Peel's death in 1850, 'Peelites', dominated British politics for more than a quarter-century. Yet theirs was by no means a total Whig victory, for during this mid-Victorian period there was to be a gradual transformation of British party politics that started at the grass-roots level and culminated in the emergence of a new kind of liberal party. This was to be led by an ex-Peelite, Disraeli's chief opponent, William Ewart Gladstone.

The facts of British politics, which permitted such important adaptations, contrasted sharply with the facts of French politics in the reign of Louis Philippe, 'the July monarchy'. The 'Citizen' King admired Britain, as did one of his most able ministers, the Protestant François Guizot, who believed in economic progress and parliamentary government. Yet there was still no industrial revolution in France. Committed republicans continued to look back to the Constituent Assembly, to the Convention or to Napoleon, about whom songs were sung and whose body was brought back to Paris in 1840 and interred in imposing surroundings in the Invalides.

The red flag flew in the streets of Paris at the funeral of the radical General Lamarque (a cholera victim) in 1832, and there was a serious working-class insurrection in industrial Lyons in November 1831 when the local garrison was driven out of the city.[2] Five years later black flags were carried through the streets by marching silk weavers. This was the year when the first popular French daily newspaper *La Presse* was launched. Seven years later the radical newspaper *Le Réforme* was founded. Nonetheless, plots, assassinations and insurrections did not greatly disturb parliamentary politics between 1830 and 1848. Reform bills were introduced, but defeated, and the opposition was always divided. There were no fewer than 17 different governments holding office between 1830 and 1840.

Louis Philippe, ambitious and determined to rule as well as to reign, had few Napoleonic qualities and was the inevitable target of satirists and cartoonists. The most famous cartoon of him, often reproduced, showed him as a pear: the most revealing showed him wearing city clothes over a suit of armour. He loved restoring palaces, but he accepted a civil list of Fr. 12 million instead of Charles X's Fr. 32 million. The Chamber was subject to satire. Only one out of every 200,000 Frenchmen could vote, as against one out of 30 in Britain after the Reform Act of 1832.

It was generally recognized, moreover, that many French deputies – perhaps most – put their own private interests before those of the nation. So, too, did ministers: two of them were involved, for example, in an attempt to rig the salt market. While the British carried free trade, the French continued to pursue the protectionist measures of the Restoration; and while the British not only enjoyed a railway boom but actually built railways, the French mainly talked about them and speculated in them. There were only 1,200 miles of railway track in France in 1848, less than a quarter of the British mileage. (And, an equally pertinent comparison, there were by then far more railways in Germany than in France.)

In exile after 1848, Guizot, who had not hesitated to use the police to 'muzzle the country' in his last spell in office, wrote a flattering biography of Peel: his own accomplishments were less lasting. Nor was the motto with which the Louis Philippe regime was associated, *Enrichissez Vous* ('get rich'), which is said to have been devised by Guizot himself, calculated to make for acceptable leadership in a period of social tension. In 1840 a republican publicist claimed that seven million out of eight million of the 'active population', the *menu peuple*, were potential revolutionaries because of the poverty of their lives. The great French novelist, Honoré de Balzac, much admired by Marx, caught the distinctive atmosphere of the period. Some of his descriptions had a photographic character about them appropriate to a country that had displayed photography for the first time in 1839.

In Paris, growing rapidly in population, the financial and social scene was often hectic. It was the centre of finance, trade, administration and communication, and there was no comparable centre either of activity or of authority. The provinces, rural and urban, each with its own geography and history, were more set in their ways. Speculation was frowned upon, and there was more fear of disaster than display of entrepreneurial drive, more grumbling about usury than effort to widen the provision of necessary credit. 'We are staunch conservatives', Guizot wrote to the French Ambassador in Rome in 1846. 'It is the first and natural responsibility of governments. We are all the more staunch conservatives because our country has been through a series of revolutions.' It was only in retrospect that it could be claimed that while Britain had avoided revolution, France was moving towards one.

Nonetheless, one of Louis Philippe's most unwise remarks was a comment he made in January 1848 to General von Radowitz, the plenipotentiary of the King of Prussia, 'Tell your master that there are two things that cannot happen again in France – one is revolution, the other is war', for in the same month de Tocqueville made a prophetic speech in the French Chamber, in which he warned that there was trouble ahead. (He used the word 'storm' not 'revolution'.) 'It is true that there is no visible sign of disorder, but that is because the disorder is deep down in people's hearts. The ultimate reason for a man's losing authority is because he is not fit to hold it.' The speech was greeted with laughter.

The timing of the collapse of the French monarchy has been directly related to a serious worsening of the economic situation in 1847 following the same bad harvest (of corn and potatoes) that provided the occasion for the Irish famine and for Britain's repeal of the corn laws. Grain prices rose to new heights in May 1847. Political factors were more directly relevant, however, than economic facts. What was felt in many political circles to be 'the real character of the regime' headed by Louis Philippe was exposed in a series of scandals involving prominent figures in the news. In 1847 and 1848, therefore, there were two kinds of relevant social politics, the social politics of the deprived poor and of the grumbling *bourgeoisie* and the social politics of High Society. 'There is great disquiet in Paris', the *Gazette de la*

France reported on 16 January 1848. 'The funds are falling every day. In politics people have stopped being reasonable.'

There had also been a royal excursion into dynastic diplomacy in France that had brought friction with Britain. The King wanted Queen Isabella of Spain to marry one of his sons, and in 1847 and 1848 he seemed to be pressing this plan to a successful conclusion. Palmerston, back in power as British Foreign Secretary after the collapse of Peel's government, now used the occasion to rouse British opinion against the French regime. Under Peel, the *entente cordiale* of the early 1830s had been extended, Queen Victoria had visited France twice, and Louis Philippe had been received at Windsor, much to the annoyance of the rulers of Austria, Russia and Prussia. But Palmerston, who had broken the *entente* once before (on Mehemet Ali and the Turkish question in 1840) before Peel returned to power, did not scruple to break it again: he even communicated to some of Guizot's political opponents (Thiers, who had held government posts in 1836, 1840 and 1848, was prominent among them) political documents calculated to compromise the French government.

The end was not premeditated. A series of well attended 'reform banquets', *bourgeois* demonstrations in favour of an extension of the franchise, spread from Paris to the provinces in 1847 and 1848; and when it became clear that neither the King nor Guizot had any intention of yielding to pressure (as Grey was said by his opponents to have done) protest stiffened. While the socialist Louis Blanc declaimed that the 'phantom of revolution' was present at every feast, Lamartine chose more appropriate language to describe the situation when he spoke of a 'revolution of contempt'. The press played a key role, particularly *La Réforme* and *Le National*.

At the banquets toasts to the 'King of the French People' were proposed before the speeches, but there were also toasts to 'the improvement in the conditions of the working class'. From the outset 'real' revolutionaries were in a minority, but on 22 February 1848, after the banning of a banquet, rioting broke out in Paris, with students joining forces with artisans at newly erected barricades. On the following day after sections of the National Guard had joined the rioters, the King dismissed Guizot and tried to replace him first by Comte Molé and then by Thiers before losing confidence in himself, abdicating and fleeing in disguise to Britain on 24 February. A majority in the French Chamber probably would have accepted his nine-year-old grandson as his successor, but the Paris crowds, invading the Assembly, ensured that with the help of the radical press this would not be the solution. Simultaneously, a republic was proclaimed in the Paris Town Hall. Lamartine extolled the spirit of freedom rising from the ruins of a 'retrograde regime', and in language as dated as that of the Holy Alliance in 1815 asserted the 'sublime mystery of universal sovereignty'.

Plate 2.6 The National Workshop of Tailors housed in the Prison of Clichy, Paris, July 1848. The French Provisional Government hoped that National Workshops would help to maintain public order. In this former debtor's prison up to eight tailors were set to work in cells designed to house a single prisoner. The Tailor's Workshop was distinctive in being comparatively well organized. One of the tailors would read the newspapers of the day aloud to his fellow-workers.

The springtime of liberty: the dawn of the revolutions of 1848

The February Revolution in France and the consequent inauguration of the French Second Republic heralded a whole series of further revolutions that swept the capital cities of Europe, including Vienna and Berlin, during the exceptionally beautiful spring of 1848. There was even a massive Chartist demonstration in London on 10 April 1848 when the Chartists were joined for the first time by supporters of Young Ireland, an Irish nationalist group that had sprung into prominence after O'Connell's death. The accent there and elsewhere was on youth.

The new provisional government of the French Second Republic, heterogeneous in make-up, included a former opposition politician, Alexandre Ledru-Rollin, at the key Ministry of the Interior, Lamartine at the Ministry of Foreign Affairs, and Blanc, who insisted that the revolution should proclaim the right to work as well as the right to vote. In addition to fixing elections by universal suffrage for early April – this meant an increase in the electorate from 25,000 to nine million – 'national workshops' were now set up in Paris to provide labour for the unemployed. On paper the 'right to work' was guaranteed, while the length of the working day was reduced by one hour. Meanwhile, great caution was shown regarding dealings with revolutionaries abroad, who looked to Paris for leadership, but in phrases, at least, the provisional government saluted 'the great European republic', a federation of free peoples.

Such phrases were not needed to stir citizens of other countries into action. Before the February Revolution began, the civil war in Switzerland had ended in the victory of the liberal over the Roman Catholic cantons – with Metternich having been unable to intervene – and Switzerland now emerged as a federal state. There had also been a January revolt at Palermo in Sicily, the poorest part of Italy, against Fernando II of Naples, who was forced to offer a liberal constitution for the whole of his kingdom based on the French constitution of 1830 in the hope, unrealized, that this would stop the Sicilians from pressing for independence. There was a victory for 'constitutionalism' in Germany too, in Baden, where the liberal leader demanded the immediate summoning of a German national Parliament.

There had been several signs before 1848 both in Italy and in Germany that liberalism was at last in the ascendant. Indeed, a liberal-sounding Pope, Pius IX, had been elected in 1846 against expectations, and his papal reign began with an amnesty, a loosening of controls on the press and the creation of a state council of lawyers to advise him on foreign affairs. Decisions were taken too to build railway lines in the Papal States and to create a telegraph system. Pius's liberalism was not to prove durable, but at that time he seemed to echo the hopes of Vincenzo Gioberti, an eloquent Italian advocate of an Italian confederation of princes under the presidency of the Pope; and when in 1847 Metternich ordered Austrian troops to occupy the papal city of Ferrara Pius circularized the great powers in protest, and Carlo Alberto, King of Piedmont-Sardinia, offered to assist the Pope with troops. Metternich withdrew from Ferrara in December 1847. Piedmont-Sardinia would obviously have a crucial part to play in any moves towards Italian unification, and on 8 February 1848 Carlo Alberto I announced a draft new constitution which incorporated a bicameral parliament, elected on a limited franchise, and a citizens' militia.

For liberalism and nationalism to triumph either in Italy or in Germany it was just as essential that there should be a revolution in the multinational Austrian Empire and that Metternich should be removed from the European stage as it was that there should be a revolution in France. It was in Budapest rather than in Vienna, however, that the chain of events began that was to lead to Metternich's fall. On 3 March in aristocratic Hungary, Lajos Kossuth, who was to emerge as one of the heroes of 1848 (and then as one of the victims), delivered an impassioned speech to the Hungarian Diet – consisting only of the nobility, a huge group in Hungary, one in 20 of the population – demanding an end to absolutism and to centralized bureaucracy. 'Unnatural political systems', Kossuth told his fellow members, 'sometimes have a long life, for it takes a long time to exhaust people's patience. But some of these political systems do not grow stronger as they grow older, and there comes a moment when it would be dangerous to extend their life.'

These were well chosen words, and on 6 March petitions were circulating in Vienna also demanding free institutions and a free press. The fall of Metternich (through resignation) was accomplished in Vienna on a bright spring day a week later, when – after skirmishes in the streets and arguments behind closed doors in which Metternich urged resistance – he was dismissed by the Emperor and left the country to join Guizot in London. They were soon to meet on the steps of the British Museum.

A strictly pertinent question to ask is 'Did the revolutions of 1848 cause the fall of Metternich or did the fall of Metternich cause the revolutions?'[3] The feeble-minded Emperor Ferdinand, who himself was to abdicate later in the year (his abdication had been discussed in 1847), was willing to step down to protect the dynasty, although he was unaware of the full ramifications of Metternich's fall. Equally unaware were those sections of the nobility who pressed for Metternich to go, believing that he had surrounded himself with a 'forest of bayonets'. There were, indeed, some people, including the poet Franz Grillparzer, who considered that Metternich should have retired long before, after the death of the Emperor Franz I in 1835. Yet no-one had acted to get rid of him then or later. Now the Emperor in his capacity as King of Hungary accepted the Hungarian 'March Laws', and that too was to have ramifications of which few were aware.

Once in exile, Metternich, turning to autobiography, like other exiles, was publicly to blame the nobility, Hungarian, Italian, Austrian, as he had previously blamed them in private. 'To the list of symptoms of a sick, degenerate age', he wrote in 1850, 'belongs the completely false position which the nobility all too often adopts. It was they nearly everywhere who lent a hand to the confusion that was being prepared.' He had less to say of a financial crisis in Vienna, near bankruptcy, which had led him to appeal to the Rothschilds for urgent help in 1847. 'If the devil fetches me', he told Solomon Rothschild, 'he will fetch you too.'

Students – and their professors, hitherto quiet – were among the most active in the street-fighting in Vienna which preceded Metternich's fall, as were craft and factory workers who, like French and British workers, were feeling the strains of the economic depression: large numbers were unemployed. And when it came to the crunch Metternich had a surprisingly small police force at his disposal in the streets – only a thousand, far fewer than Louis Philippe – with a municipal guard of 14,000 men, and it was a newly formed civil guard and a student legion that now assumed control. Significantly there were no demands for a republic, but a new government, led by Count Kolowrat, who had worked (sometimes disloyally) with Metternich, promised freedom of the press and the convocation of delegates from the provincial Estates to frame a new constitution.

There were many different and contradictory elements in the subsequent disturbances (liberal, nationalist, peasant and, not least, anti-Semitic), inside the sprawling Habsburg Empire; and soon the great cities of Prague, Budapest, Milan and Venice were all in the grip of revolutionary fever. By the end of March, Hungary had acquired a set of new 'March laws' that transformed the country – on paper, at least – from a feudal into a modern state. They proclaimed equality before the law, abolished censorship of the press and took away from the nobility (this was the one sacrifice they made) their exemption from taxation. In Milan, with a population of 200,000, successful street-rioting (18–23 March), passing down to history as 'the Five Days of Milan', forced the veteran Austrian general Count Josef Radetzky, who had fought against Napoleon, to leave the city with his 13,000 troops. 'The whole country', he told Vienna, was in revolt. In Venice (there was no direct connection between events in the two cities) Daniele Manin, who had been imprisoned in January for urging moderate constitutional reforms, proclaimed a restored republic after a city crowd had raided a medieval armoury and the Opera House in search of weapons.

In Piedmont-Sardinia reformers turned for help to Carlo Alberto, untrusted in his own country and outside, but who now concluded on the advice of his chief minister Count Camillo de Cavour that 'the supreme hour of the Piedmontese monarchy had struck' – 'the state would be lost if we did not fight' – and troops under his command arrived in Milan on 26 March after Radetzky had already withdrawn, proclaiming that 'the destinies of Italy are maturing and a happier future is opening up for those who bravely stand up for their rights against the oppressor'.

In Germany, where there was also an upsurge of enthusiasm, there were demands everywhere in February and March for the freedom of the press and for constitutional government; and the Diet of the *Deutscher Bund*, meeting in Frankfurt, with a changed composition, cheerfully adopted the black, gold and red flag of Germany. The idea of a national parliament which would include representatives of each German state was successfully canvassed, and on 31 March a 'Pre-Parliament' (*Vorparlament*), the first relatively representative national assembly in Germany, met, also in Frankfurt, to work out the arrangements.

Excitement was high when on 18 May the members of the new Parliament walked in solemn procession to the Paulskirche (with church bells ringing and cannon roaring). They included some of the outstanding lawyers, judges, writers, professors, and artists in the various German states, some of whom had made their reputations as patriots during the War of Liberation in 1813–14. They included Jahn, the poet Arndt, the Roman Catholic leader Bishop Ketteler, and the historian Friedrich

Christoph Dahlmann, who had been dismissed from his chair at Göttingen University when the reactionary British Duke of Cumberland arrived in Hanover as King in 1837. Dahlmann's *Political Dictionary* and his later study *Politics* had focused on the need for a strong state. To him the state was as natural an institution as the family.

None of this German development would have been possible had not times changed in Vienna as well as in Paris. For the time being Vienna was in no position to intervene, and many members of the Austrian delegation to the Frankfurt Parliament arrived late. Yet there were even bigger changes in the Prussian capital, Berlin, than there were in Vienna. Friedrich Wilhelm IV, who had come to the throne in 1840, had vacillated before 1848 between liberalism and authoritarianism, and now he continued to vacillate in 1848 itself. Willing to reform the *Deutscher Bund*, as advised by his personal friend, General Radowitz, grandson of a Roman Catholic Croatian officer, he had been prepared early in 1848 to summon a congress of German princes in Dresden. Because of the fall of Metternich, who appeared in Dresden on the appointed day on his way to exile, this congress never met.

Berliners discussed the rapidly changing situation in beer gardens, while the citizens of Frankfurt discussed it, like Parisians, in cafes and clubs. There had been 'hunger riots' in 1847. Now there were none, but tension rose in Berlin on 16 March when news of Metternich's fall arrived, and two days later the King issued a proclamation lifting censorship and promising constitutional reforms in Prussia and in the *Bund*. He was cheered by his subjects, but by the end of the day the cheers had turned into groans and the laughter into tears. As crowds of people poured into the squares round his royal palace, the presence of visibly intimidating royal troops created alarm, and after two shots were unintentionally fired by his soldiers, there was fierce fighting in which workers from Berlin's craft guilds were prominent. Some of his subjects took to the barricades, some were taken prisoner or killed.

Now it was the turn of his officers to groan, for on the following morning a sad King, romantic at heart but tantalizingly vacillating in behaviour, issued a new proclamation declaring that while his subjects had been misled he offered them forgiveness and a withdrawal of all troops. As a result he was now compelled to pay his respects to the corpses of some of his subjects killed in the fighting and to appoint a new government headed by a liberal merchant from the Rhineland, Ludolf Camphausen. He was also driven to declare (however vaguely) that 'from now on Prussia will merge into Germany'. At such moments the King was as 'defenceless', wrote the American minister, as 'the poorest malefactor of the prisons'.

Later in the spring of 1848, on 22 May, four days after the opening of the Frankfurt Parliament, in which there was only one peasant and not a single industrial worker, the new Prussian National Assembly with a more varied social composition, including peasants, met in Berlin, a still deeply disturbed city over which civil guards could not exercise adequate control. The King spent most of the summer at Potsdam, surrounded by aristocratic conservative friends ('the *Kamarilla*') and well disciplined royal troops. It was unlikely, therefore, that the first gains of an exhilarating 'springtime of liberty' would now be consolidated.

There were to be surprises for many people in many countries in the sequences of events that followed and which are discussed in the next chapter. What already stood out, however, was that the Europe that had been opened up in 1848 after decades of 'order' was unlikely to last. The 1848 revolutions had been urban rather than rural and had been led by 'intellectuals' with little political experience, whose objectives diverged, and the workers who took part in them were for the most part not industrial workers but journeymen, artisans and small masters, a very different labour force from the industrial proletariat to which Marx and Engels appealed in the *Communist Manifesto*.

In Britain, where there were more factory-based workers than in any other European country, the strength of the middle classes had already been demonstrated in the spring of 1848. It did not need elaborate military precautions organized by Wellington or a host of special constables (among them the future Napoleon III) to save London from revolution on the day of Kennington Common. Most of the Chartists did not want one. When Lady Palmerston, wife of Britain's Foreign Secretary, wrote to a friend giving her what she called 'private' details of 'our revolution' she concluded cheerfully, 'I am sure that it is fortunate that the whole thing has occurred, as it has shown the good spirit of our middle classes'.

After April 1848, it still remained to be seen whether social peace in continental Europe would hold. Rulers had shown themselves reluctant to use force to suppress disturbances in the spring of 1848, and some of them, like Friedrich Wilhelm, had yielded even more readily than Louis Philippe. Would government, changed in composition and direction by revolution, act in the same way? Most of the new governments feared social disorder, rural and urban, as much as they hoped for change. So far, at the end of spring there were refugees, but no political prisoners. Would this always be so? Two of the refugees, the German radicals Friedrich Hecker and Gustav von Struve, had attempted a republican coup in Baden while the Pre-Parliament was discussing elections. It was totally ineffective, and both men made away across the Atlantic to the United States.

It was particularly ominous for revolutionaries that throughout the spring of 1848 Russia, where there were many rural but no urban disturbances, was waiting in the wings. Nicholas I had immediately mobilized a large army to support any possible victims of French aggression in February 1848. And although the European situation changed completely after the fall of Metternich and the revolution in Berlin, the great Russian Army – as liberals and nationalists everywhere knew – was still on the alert.

References

1. C. Hughes (ed.) *Switzerland and Europe: Essays and Reflections by J.R. Salis* (1971) pp. 32–4.
2. For its significance see A. Briggs, 'Social Structure and Politics in Birmingham and Lyons, 1825–1848', in *Collected Essays*, vol. I (1985) pp. 231–3.
3. A. Sked, *The Decline and Fall of the Habsburg Empire, 1815–1918* (1989) p. 41.

Chapter **3**

Nation Building, 1848–1878

The lessons of 1848

The mere fact of revolution carried with it great excitement in 1848 as it had done in 1789. An entrenched social and political order had collapsed. To everyone who had chafed under that order 'the March days' were days of unparalleled freedom and seemed to offer a future dispensation full of promise. Nonetheless, in every country, too, there were people who thought that Europe was suffering from March madness. There was general agreement on only one point – that the adjective *vormärzlich* ('before March'), like the adjective 'pre-war' in the years after 1918 or 1945, referred to days which were beyond recall.

One former German radical, David Friedrich Strauss, had complained as early as April 1848 that he had lived more happily in pre-revolutionary times, able to devote himself to 'true theory' without bothering himself about how to apply it. That was one individual's response. Another, not dissimilar, was the novelist Adalbert Stifter's in Vienna. The revolution had shown that 'people who are possessed by powerful desires and urges' were not to be trusted. People who promised 'to overwhelm you with immeasurable freedom' were 'mostly men corrupted by the power of their emotions'. These were very different responses from that contained in a Paris placard of March 1848 which read 'When only counter-revolution has had the right to speak for half a century, is it too much to give perhaps a year to liberty?' A contrasting response on the part of large numbers of people during and after the springtime of liberty, not usually put into words, had nothing to do with 'theory' or with past experience. They preferred to put their trust in individual self-help and their own material betterment rather than in communal revolutionary fervour.

Each revolutionary situation had its own history with tangled strands, confusing alignments and contrasting personalities, but there were elements that were common to them all, including ultimate disillusionment. For the twentieth-century American historian Bernardotte Schmitt 1848 was a 'terminus', while for the British historian G. M. Trevelyan, disappointed rather than disillusioned, it was 'the turning point at which modern history failed to turn'.[1] The liberal forces in which Trevelyan, descendant of Macaulay, believed had failed to take charge of events. In June 1848 France, which had led the way to revolution, had provided the first evidence of the despair that could accompany 'reaction', and by the end of 1848 revolutionary causes were in danger everywhere. It was not until 1849, however, that the revolutionary fires were finally put out in Germany and in central Europe. The Russians then played the role of firemen in a way that they had not been allowed to play the part of policemen after 1815. Authority had triumphed.

Both sides learned lessons from 1848 and 1849. 'Authority' learnt what it meant to have to prevaricate and to yield: for a time, as the King of Prussia put it, it had been forced to crawl on its stomach. 'Never allow that to happen again' was his lesson. The revolutionaries, who before 1848 had learnt most of what they knew from books – it was books, indeed, which had done the talking – learnt less, perhaps, from experience; and, divided as they always had been, they now gave way to others. But for new revolutionaries it was not simply that new chapters had been added to old books: the whole text required substantial revision. A major theme for the future was to be the national unification of Germany and Italy, not achieved in 1848. How could that be accomplished?

There were three main sets of lessons to be learnt from 1848 and the year that followed, although not everyone drew the same lessons and there were divisions inside the revolutionary or counter-revolutionary camps as well as between them. The first concerned the dynamics of social class; and in that connection what had happened in France was the main, though not the sole, source of instruction. The second related to the interplay of nationalisms, far more intricate than either nationalists or anti-nationalists had realized before 1848; and the third was the role of force in politics and in nation building, a subject which nationalists had increasingly begun to talk about in 1848 and 1849 while their opponents acted, driven by fear more than hope. There were two other themes that concerned all three sets of lessons – the relationship between monarchy and 'parliamentarianism' (which in future was to involve far more than the granting or withdrawal of constitutions) and the development of the apparatus, including the military apparatus, of the state.

The dynamics of class

Events between March 1848 and June 1849 revealed more about the dynamics of class within different social and political frames than the *Communist Manifesto* had done – first in France, then in Germany, and

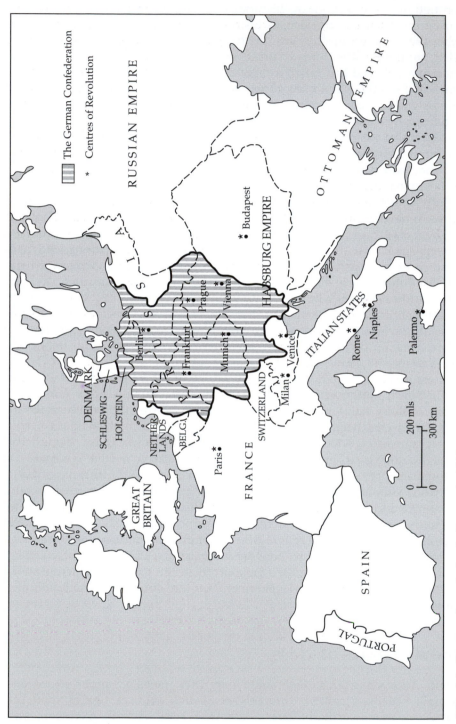

Map 3.1 Centres of revolution in Europe in 1848

throughout the whole period in Britain, where there was no revolution but where the Chartists continued to argue fiercely about class conflict and cooperation, political leadership and education even after the European revolutions had been put down. Everywhere there were disputes about property and its relationship to freedom. 'Where is the madman – or the charlatan – who claims that the liberty of the proletariat can be assured without the reorganization of property?' asked the French radical newspaper *Le Peuple Souverain* in March 1848.

In France, which was always the subject of special study for Marx and for Engels, antagonism between Parisian workers, most of them untouched by the industrial revolution, and *bourgeoisie* (likewise untouched) was apparent almost from the start; and 'socialization' claims, which sounded as revolutionary in liberal London as they did in aristocratic Vienna, rang alarm bells in Paris itself. 'The population of our kings in overalls grows larger day by day', wrote one of the alarmed several days before *Le Peuple Souverain* identified the issue. The republicans had promised elections in France as soon as they came to power, and when these took place – with universal male suffrage – in April 1848 before the spring was over, the outcome showed that there were real limits both to revolutionary zeal and to social commitment. Of the new deputies in the French Chamber 165 had sat in the previous Chamber under Louis Philippe. Monarchists far outnumbered radicals, and there were only 30 'workingmen'. Even in Paris itself only 12 socialists were elected. In total, out of 876 seats, radicals and socialists won only 100 in a poll of 84 per cent. When Frenchmen went to the ballot box 'ownership' constituted 'a sort of fraternity'.

Paris demonstrators, fearing the outcome, had tried to have the elections postponed, and true to the traditions of 1789, they were not prepared to abide by a national electoral verdict. As a result the revolution from below went on, and there were disturbances in the streets in May when a new revolutionary government, backed by Blanqui, was proclaimed in the Hotel de Ville. The National Guard came into action against the revolutionaries when they burst into the Chamber and made many arrests. The showdown came in the following month. The existence of the national workshops, providing labour for the poor, had sharply divided opinion on class lines, and one of the people arrested in May had been Louis Blanc. To their critics the workshops were 'temptations to idleness' (and disorder); to their defenders they were the only guarantee of the 'first vow of the Republic to provide bread every day for all its children by proclaiming the universal right to work'. The threat by the government to close them – or to run them down – triggered insurrection. Trees were chopped down and barricades built on 22 and 23 June.

The mood was very different from that of the March days, when trees of liberty were being planted everywhere; and when a soldier fresh from Algeria, General Cavaignac, acting on behalf of the government, ruthlessly put down all disturbances, he was helped in his task by the predominantly *bourgeois* National Guard. A siege was declared on 24 June, and in a civil war in the Paris streets on that day and the next more people were killed than in the whole of the revolutionary sequence that began in 1789. The outcome of the 'dreadful blood letting' was never, however, in any doubt. Cavaignac, with the help of French recruits from the provinces, broke all workers' resistance, with the Faubourg St Antoine being the last place to fall.

In November 1848 a new republican constitution was drafted which made no mention of the right to work and which entrusted executive power to a president to be directly elected by the people. He was not to be Cavaignac, however, the hero of the *bourgeoisie* in the 'June days' and now the 'order' candidate, but Prince Louis Napoleon, nephew of the hero of heroes during what in retrospect most Frenchmen were considering the most heroic age of French history. Cavaignac came in second in the elections, held in December, receiving only 1,442,302 votes as against Louis Napoleon's 5,534,520. (The left-wing radical candidate polled only 36,920, and Lamartine, the romantic hero of February, received only 17,910.)

Louis Napoleon was new to French politics (two earlier attempts at intrusion by conspiracy had failed), and his opponents, large numbers of whom were members of the second popular assembly to be elected in the year, judged him to be shallow and 'trivial'. Obviously, however, he had received large-scale support from many different quarters. Peasants, who had made such great gains in the first French Revolution, turned to him not only because they were totally opposed in 1848 to the idea of continuing social revolution but because liberal republicanism meant little to them. Working-class votes were even easier to explain. Why should any Parisian worker have voted for Cavaignac? It was as a conciliator, with a legendary name, standing above class and party, that Louis Napoleon made his first appeal to France. What had moved him personally from within was different – burning belief in his family inheritance and in destiny. 'I am sure', he had exclaimed in 1842, 'that the shade of the Emperor protects and blesses me.'

What happened in France by the end of 1848 was very different, therefore, from what revolutionaries and non-revolutionaries alike had expected to happen at the beginning of the revolutionary sequence. Nonetheless, there had never been any chance that disgruntled workers concentrated in Paris and large cities would win lasting gains (least of all, the right to work) in the economic, social and political circumstances of 1848. They would have to learn to organize – and to fight – in a different way – through trade unions and political parties – and even then the results of their struggles were to be limited. Republicans – and they came in different varieties – had had little real chance either. The events of the year had shown that under the prevailing circumstances the introduction of universal suffrage would not necessarily be followed by the coming to power of a democratic republican government. This was a political lesson which was to be repeated many times in the future. Napoleon III, indeed, was quick to see that national plebiscites could reinforce his personal authority. For Proudhon universal suffrage was counter-revolution.

Napoleon's success was bound to create uneasiness in other parts of Europe where older forms of authority were restored. Yet some of the same lessons could be drawn out from the revolutionary sequence in Austria which had interesting features of its own. In Austria, unlike France, revolution was a novelty. In Austria also, again unlike France, there was not one nation but many. The first achievements of an all Austrian Parliament (*Reichstag*), which met in July 1848, chosen not by universal suffrage but by indirect election – it included many members of the lower *bourgeoisie* and peasantry (some of them illiterate) – were impressive, recalling those of the French Revolution of 1789. In a time of continuing economic difficulty, it had carried through by early September, with the endorsement of the Emperor, emancipation of the peasants on grounds of principle – their human rights, thereby completing the work of Josef II in the eighteenth century.

Thereby, too, of course, it satisfied large sections of the peasantry in the same way as the French peasantry had been satisfied in 1789, while granting landlords compensation for losses of historic rights. As a consequence the militant revolutionary movement in Vienna, a precocious city movement led by professors, students and artisans, with little support in the countryside or in the *Reichstag*, was left to struggle on its own after the summer of 1848. The demand for public works to eliminate unemployment provoked the same responses and problems in Vienna as in Paris, following earlier disturbances in Prague and Budapest, aggravated when the wages of those engaged in public works were cut. There was street-fighting, the so-called 'Battle of the Prater', on 23 August.

October was the critical month in the Austrian capital. The Habsburg court, which had fled to Innsbruck in May and returned briefly in August, now had to flee from the city for a second time, leaving it in the hands of committed revolutionaries who strongly opposed the decision of the Austrian government to declare open war on Kossuth's Hungarian revolution. On 6 October, when an Austrian battalion was due to move into Hungary, rails were unbolted at the Northern Station and telegraph wires cut. On the same day the Minister of War was murdered and the arsenal attacked. Yet authority triumphed in Vienna as it had done in Paris – this time also, brutal military authority under the direction of Prince Windischgrätz. Martial law was proclaimed at the end of October 1848, political clubs were suppressed, the freedom of the press was abolished, and the students' organizations and the National Guard (in Vienna still a revolutionary force) were dissolved.

Three weeks after 'the fall of Vienna', Austria had both a new emperor who was to reign for 68 years, and a new prime minister, the brother-in-law of Windischgrätz, Prince von Schwarzenberg. Member of a powerful old family, he had been elected to the *Reichstag* and was intelligent enough to appraise the strengths and limitations of the revolutionary movement. It was he who persuaded Emperor Ferdinand to abdicate in favour of the 18-year-old Franz Josef. The Schwarzenberg ministry included some liberals, and the *Reichstag*, which was engaged in drafting a constitution, continued to sit and debate, not in Vienna, however, but in the small Moravian town of Kremsier.

The task would have been challenging in any circumstances. As things were, it was impossible. Yet the *Reichstag* was bold enough to introduce into the first draft of its constitution a clause, which it soon had to drop, stating that 'all sovereignty proceeds from the people'. It also decreed that the Emperor's ministers were to be responsible to Parliament. Other paragraphs in the constitution included the abolition of titles of nobility, the introduction of civil marriage, and, of key importance in the imperial situation, a statement that all peoples of the Empire (Hungary and Lombardy-Venetia were excluded for constitutional reasons) were equal in rights. 'Each people has an inviolable right to present its nationality in general and its language in particular. The equality of rights in the school, administration and public life of every language in local usage is guaranteed by the state.'

There were divisions in the *Reichstag* on some of these proposals which were far too radical to be acceptable to the Emperor or his ministers, and in March 1849 Schwarzenberg's Minister of the Interior informed the Kremsier deputies that the *Reichstag* had been dissolved. Although he also told them at the same time that the Emperor had approved a new constitution 'by God's grace', this constitution too was never to be implemented. Karl Kübeck, head of the Treasury under Metternich and a representative of Austria in the Frankfurt Parliament, advised the Emperor to return to the pre-March status quo, and on the last day of 1851 yet a third constitution was swept aside. Instead, Kübeck was to head a commission to examine all the laws passed since March 1848 to ensure that everything of a liberal kind would be eliminated. Schwarzenberg, who would have been prepared to work within a parliamentary system but did not object to personal rule by the Emperor, died on 5 April 1852. The only main substantial reform that was to last after 1852 was the emancipation of the peasantry.

In Berlin the failure of the Vienna revolution stirred the King of Prussia to action. He had already been roused when the newly appointed Prussian National Assembly, meeting in Berlin, had voted in favour of the abolition of aristocratic titles and of dropping the words 'by the grace of God' from his own royal title. On 2 November he appointed a new prime minister, a cavalry officer, Count Brandenburg, and a week later (in face of protests from the Assembly which called for a tax strike) he moved the meeting place of the Assembly from Berlin to the provincial town of Brandenburg. Two days later, a state of siege was declared throughout Prussia. Finally,

Plate 3.1 The National Assembly at Frankfurt, 1848. This lithograph depicts the impressive scene in the chamber. Beneath the *Reichsadler* (the Imperial eagle) hanging in the centre sits the President of the Assembly flanked by two vice-presidents and two secretaries. In front of them is the speaker's podium and the small tables on which the stenographers and secretaries work, although these trappings of power were not enough to guarantee the Assembly's power. By March 1849 it was already in decline.

the Assembly was dissolved on 5 December and a new constitution was imposed emphasizing the divine right of the monarch, leaving the control of the executive in the hands of the King, treating the Army as a separate establishment in the state, and creating a two-chamber parliament which favoured big landowners. The lower house was to be elected by universal suffrage, but since voters were divided into three groups according to the amount of taxes that they paid the constitution consolidated property interests. At the same time the Civil Guard was disbanded and the political clubs were closed. The freedom of the press too was restricted.

Then and later Friedrich Wilhelm was totally opposed to the view which had been expressed by a leading speaker in the Frankfurt Parliament that 'we derive our authority for [framing a constitution] from the sovereignty of the nation'. And when the Frankfurt Parliament, now placed in an awkward position because of the restoration of monarchical authority both in Berlin and Vienna, decided in March 1849 (by a majority, with almost as many abstentions as votes) to offer Friedrich Wilhelm the crown of a new Germany he refused it. He was 'deeply moved' by the offer, he told a deputation from Frankfurt – and it had made him turn his eye towards 'the King of Kings' – but in a considered statement made later he turned not to the King of Kings but to his fellow German kings, pointing out that he had earlier made 'explicit and solemn promises' that he would 'gain the voluntary assent of the crowned heads, princes and free states of Germany' in any move towards 'German unity'. More vividly, he stated in private that an imperial crown presented him by the Frankfurt Parliament would be a 'dog collar' that would make him 'a serf of the revolution of 1848'.

It was of critical importance in German history that Friedrich Wilhelm made no attempt after this to take advantage of the fact that no fewer than 28 of the existing German governments, beginning with Baden, declared their willingness to approve of the election of the King of Prussia as German Emperor within a German constitution decided upon by the Frankfurt Parliament. He would not accept such a constitution from a divided Parliament, the very existence of which he now disapproved. By April 1849 any hope of German unification under Prussian leadership (with liberal support) had disappeared. Instead, Prussian troops helped to suppress revolutionary disturbances in April and May in Baden, Bavaria and Saxony.

The fate of the Frankfurt Parliament was now sealed. From beginning to end it had no executive responsibilities, and to the very end it failed to develop organized formal groupings along the lines of political parties which might have given a focus to its decisions. The largest moderate liberal grouping favoured a limited suffrage, but most of the moderates abandoned the Parliament during the disturbed months of April and May 1849. The delegates from the Habsburg Empire withdrew *en bloc*, and the King of Prussia ordered that all the Prussian deputies should follow them. The rump of the Parliament (136), described by Friedrich Wilhelm as being 'in league with the terrorists' who took part in the scattered Spring uprisings, now moved on to Stuttgart where they were eventually to be forcibly dispersed by soldiers from Württemberg in June 1849. By then there were some liberals in Germany as well as conservatives who had concluded, as Friedrich Wilhelm had done, that the Parliament had urged the unity of Germany as a pretence. The rump of its members had really been fighting 'the battle of godlessness, perjury and theft'.

The interplay of nationalisms

The liberalism or radicalism of the Frankfurt Parliament in face of authoritarian power, particularly when it was left as a rump, stood out less at the time and stands out less in retrospect than its nationalism. It became almost immediately apparent after the Parliament met that one of the major problems confronting it was deciding which Germans it should exclude from the orbit of geographical unification and which non-Germans it should incorporate. Of the Habsburg Empire's 36 million subjects, fewer than six million were German-speaking, most of them Roman Catholic, while of Prussia's 16 million, most of them Protestant, there were 14 million. A 'big Germany' (*Gross Deutschland*), which would include the German-speaking areas of Austria, would involve the disruption of the Habsburg Empire: a 'little Germany' (*Klein Deutschland*) would involve not only giving a preponderant share of power to Prussia within a new Germany, but leaving large numbers of German-speakers outside the German borders.

Some Germans always believed that it was an advantage to their cause that the Habsburgs as Germans ruled non-Germans, and there were few people in Austrian politics and government who believed that the Habsburgs should surrender their non-German areas. At the same time, there were some Germans who believed that Germany was not a territorial but a metaphysical concept: anyone of German stock and language owed allegiance first and foremost to the German Fatherland, and that Fatherland had its roots deep in the past. Germans were different from Italians or Slavs.

Practical as well as metaphysical or historical problems dogged the Frankfurt Parliament just as they dogged the Habsburg court. What was to happen, for example, to Poles living in Prussia? If Poles were still prepared to remain subjects of the King of Prussia – and many Prussians in 1848 were far more willing to acknowledge Polish linguistic and cultural claims than the Russians were – they were not prepared to be submerged in a German nation state. The members of the Frankfurt Parliament held a wide variety of views concerning the 'Polish question', ranging from those who wished to undo the injustice of the three Polish partitions of the eighteenth century to those who wished to prevent the establishment of an independent Polish state. Initially the pro-Poles were in the majority, but opinion shifted later. And when at last open fighting broke out between Germans and Poles in Posen, the Prussian-controlled districts of Poland, German national solidarity triumphed over support for Polish nationalism and over a cosmopolitan belief in the complementarity of different national causes.

There were awkward issues also in relation to Denmark. Many chauvinistic speeches were made in the Frankfurt Parliament about

Germans and Danes (as, indeed, there were about Germans and Czechs). There was even contemptuous general talk of 'puny nationalities' (*Nationalitätchen*) attempting 'to found their own lives in our midst and live like parasites to destroy ours'. The Czech politician and historian Frantisek Palacky had made it clear from the outset that Czechs did not wish to be represented in the Frankfurt Parliament: in words that became famous, 'If the Austrian state did not exist', he told the Parliament, 'we should have to create it in the interests of Europe.' Just 500 years before the revolutions of 1848 the University of Prague had been founded as a German university. Now Bohemia looked in the future to a multinational Habsburg Empire, to be reorganized on a federal basis, an outcome never to be realized then or later.

Within the Habsburg Empire there had long been a persistent tendency on the part of the authorities to play off one nationality against another, and in 1848 there was considerable confusion as to who or what could be called 'revolutionary' or 'counter-revolutionary'. This was largely because the Hungarian revolution, successful in its first phase because the Emperor as King of Hungary accepted its demands, seemed to carry with it not a social threat but a threat to the 'submerged nationalities' of the Habsburg Empire, among them Croats, Czechs, Slovaks and Ruthenians: all of these were represented in Hungary itself. Kossuth himself supported Magyar hegemony in Hungary, and when a new national assembly met in July 1848 the Croats revolted against it. The Hungarian Diet had decided that all candidates for election should speak Magyar (Latin had hitherto been the official language) and that the older Diets of Croatia and Transylvania should disappear.

Already by then events in Prague had followed a pattern of revolution and reaction. A Congress of Slavs convoked by the Czechs in Prague on 2 June 1848 and presided over by Palacky was thought of by him as a deliberate counterpoise both to the Hungarian and to the Frankfurt Parliaments. Yet this Congress too revealed a remarkable number of nationalist inter-Slav tensions – between Czechs and Slovaks, for example, and between Czechs and Poles – with the Poles being well disposed to the Magyars and far less well disposed to the Czechs. The Congress carried a resolution that a 'general Congress of European Nations' should be summoned 'for the discussion of all international questions'. There was never any question of this. Instead, an uprising in Prague, which began on the day that the Congress ended, and which was led by the same kind of combination of workers and students as was active in Vienna, was put down in five days by Austrian troops.

The suppression of the Hungarian revolution followed, although it took far longer than five days and went through many different phases. In September 1848 the Emperor, who now wished to see the March Laws revoked, declared war on the revolutionary Hungarian regime, provoking the further autumn disturbances in Vienna, and Windischgrätz entered

Plate 3.2   Hungarian emigrants on the march to Shamula, December 1849.
Across Europe the failed revolutions caused considerable numbers to emigrate to
the west. However, while the westward movement of emigrants brought much that
was good, it also brought cholera. The epidemic had begun in China in 1844,
spread through Russia and reached Eastern Europe by 1848. The movement of
refugees after the collapsed revolutions brought it to western Europe by the end of
the year.

Budapest on 5 January 1849. In February 1849 the Austrian Army defeated
the Hungarians at Kapolna, and when the Austrian *Reichstag* was dissolved
in the next week the new unitary constitution that was promulgated took
no account of Hungarian or Czech demands for a federal system in the
Habsburg territories.

As a result, Hungary, abandoning the Habsburgs for the first time,
declared its independence in April 1849, making Kossuth Supreme
Governor, only to fall – after initial victories, valiant resistance, complex
manoeuvres and Russian intervention – in August 1849. (One castle held
out until November.) For several years the Magyars remained under
martial law, administered by German officials sent from Vienna. Kossuth,
who had buried the Hungarian crown near the frontier, fled to Turkey, and
later visited London, where he was given a hero's welcome, but he was not
received by Britain's Foreign Secretary, Palmerston. He also visited the
United States which by the end of the nineteenth century was to house
millions of immigrants from different ethnic groups in central Europe and

the Balkans. There were to be more of them in some cases than there were in their own capital cities.

To sum up, the second lesson of 1848 and 1849 was that nationalism had revealed itself as a force making for conflict and even for confusion as much as for liberation. Leaving Germany on one side, it was apparent in the light of Magyar and Slav experience alone that a new *international* order based on coexisting nations would involve just as many conflicts of interest as the older dynastic order seeking after a 'balance of power'. The same lesson had been taught further east, too, in the Ottoman Empire, where risings had broken out in Bucharest, capital of Wallachia, where an independent government was set up in June 1848 proclaiming the unity of Wallachians, Moldavians and Transylvanians as free Romanians. There were deep divisions, linguistic and cultural, between Magyars on the one side and on the other Wallachians and Moldavians, speaking a Latin language, as there also were with German minorities living in these lands. And when Nicholas I gave aid to the Sultan to suppress the Romanian revolt it was the fraternity of the great dynasties not of the revolutionaries that was demonstrated to the world.

'The year 1848', wrote Sir Lewis Namier, the distinguished British historian of Polish extraction, marked 'for good or evil the opening of an era of linguistic nationalism, shaping mass personalities and producing their inevitable conflicts'. And while the term 'mass personalities' begs questions, 'linguistic nationalism' was to become an increasingly strong force after 1848–49 with the 'language chart' serving as 'the revolutionaries' Magna Carta'. There was as much prejudice as idealism in the way that national differences were often asserted (not unlike the religious differences that could sustain nationalism). Nonetheless, prejudice was more dangerous to the future of Europe than the language in which it was expressed, and it could be revealed even when the languages were the same. In May 1848, for example, a French Army officer reported that French navvies working on the Dunkirk railway line had 'attacked Belgian workers, who after collecting their pay, returned home'.

In Italy, where lovers of the language were cultivated, often learned people, and where, whatever the dialects, it was largely one language that was being read, local and regional differences (as well as imperfect communications) kept apart people who spoke varieties of Italian but many of whom still did not consider themselves to be 'Italians'. There were massive problems, national and non-national, in fighting for principle. When the King of Piedmont-Sardinia, Carlo Alberto, neither a liberal nor a romantic, announced in March 1848 (with the hope of avoiding French intervention) that Italy would fend for itself (*Italia fara da se*), he was too optimistic. And before his armies were defeated by the Austrians at Custozza in July 1848 he had already discovered that the Lombards of Milan were unhappy about being incorporated in a Piedmontese-Sardinian state governed from Turin.

The defeat at Custozza had general counter-revolutionary implications, for it left the Austrians free to fight the Hungarians. Nonetheless, it did not mark the end of the Italian struggle. In March 1849 Carlo Alberto took to the field again, only to be beaten this time at Novara. He was forced, in consequence, to recognize Austrian authority in Lombardy and Venice and to pay a large indemnity to Vienna. He also abdicated, little lamented, to spend the rest of his life in Portugal, which was to become a home for many later royal refugees. He was succeeded by his son, Vittore Emmanuele.

In the meantime, a short-lived Republic of Rome had come and gone, and Pope Pius IX, who was to become one of the most implacable enemies of all versions of liberalism, outside as well as inside Italy, had been restored to power by Louis Napoleon. There seemed to be little principle here on the French side, at least, for it was to Napoleon that many Italian nationalists had looked for support. French troops sent to Rome met with brave resistance from guerrillas led by Giuseppe Garibaldi, one of the greatest guerrilla fighters in history, but the resistance failed and the French were to stay in Rome, continuing to protect the Pope until the Franco-German War of 1870 and Napoleon's fall. For a brief moment Mazzini, who earlier in his life had solemnly maintained that 'the worship of principle' had begun, had been a 'Triumvir' in the Republic of Rome which had been proclaimed on 9 February 1849 by a Constituent Assembly elected by universal suffrage. After 1849 he was never to hold any kind of power again.

The role of force

The third lesson of 1848 and 1849 was that force had triumphed over principle in battle as well as at the barricades. *Einheit, Freiheit und Macht* (Unity, Freedom and Power) had been a German slogan in 1848: now the emphasis was to shift to *Macht*. It was in Germany too that the term *Realpolitik*, the politics of power, was invented, and that the greatest military theorist of the nineteenth century, the Prussian Karl von Clausewitz, was to exert major influence, inspiring long after his death Helmuth von Moltke, Chief of the Prussian General Staff in a new phase of German history. Moltke placed Clausewitz on a par with Homer and with the Bible. Clausewitz had joined the Prussian Army in 1792 and within a year had been pitched into battle against the French. His military experience, however, was not entirely Prussian. He learned from the French how important it was to involve the whole nation in war, and he learned too from a spell with the Russian Army. He had fought at Borodino (he had watched Moscow burn) before taking part in the Battle of Waterloo.

It was experience as well as 'science' that led Clausewitz to conclude that 'true military spirit is to be found only in an army that maintains its cohesion under the most murderous fire, that cannot be shaken by imaginary fears and resists well-founded ones with all its might; that proud of its victories, will not lose the strength to obey orders and its respect and trust for its officers even in defeat; [and] whose physical power, like the muscles of an athlete, has been steeled by training in privation and effort'. The Prussian Army sought to achieve this resolution of spirit, but it was in German economic matters, however, not military ones that Prussia rather than Austria had taken the lead before 1848 through the activities of the *Zollverein*, which in the words of a British observer in 1840, 'brought the sentiment of German nationality out of the regions of hope and fancy into those of positive and material interests'.

In politics and diplomacy Austria retained primacy in 1849 once the vacuum created by Metternich's dismissal had been filled by Schwarzenberg, and one man who hoped that Prussia could have taken the lead, General Josef von Radowitz, a friend of Friedrich Wilhelm, failed in his plans to control a newly founded federation of German states, the Erfurt Union. Schwarzenberg shrewdly bided his time, and agreed on what was called an 'Interim', during which both Prussia and Austria would jointly supervise the affairs of Germany. Once the 'Interim' expired, however, on 1 May 1850, with order re-established in the Habsburg Empire, he succeeded in restoring the old Diet of the *Deutscher Bund* as it had been before 1848. There had been tense moments when Austria and Prussia were on opposite sides in relation to troop movements in the duchies of Schleswig-Holstein and Hesse, but it was Prussia that backed down.

Radowitz lost his power and was dispatched to London as Prussian Ambassador, and in November 1850 the Prussians reached an agreement with Austria at Olmütz by which they dropped their independent policies and virtually accepted Austrian leadership in German affairs. Finally in May 1851 a three-year treaty was signed between the two countries that was manifestly one-sided in character. Prussia guaranteed Austrian power in Italy, but there was no corresponding guarantee of Prussian power in the Rhineland. Only in economic matters was Prussian primacy still assured. The *Zollverein* held firm against Austrian attempts to dilute it, and in 1853 it was renewed for another 12 years. In the longer term Austria, weaker economically, was not able to sustain its primacy in German political affairs which had been reinstated in 1849 and 1850, but it required war, not diplomacy, for Prussia to secure it – a short, sharp war which, according to the rules of Clausewitz, was 'the continuation of policy'.

The language of power had been heard in 1848 and 1849 outside both Austria and Prussia in the Frankfurt Parliament itself – and from the left, not from the conservatives. 'If I knew that the unity and future greatness of Germany had to be attained through a temporary renunciation of all the freedoms', a liberal deputy had declared in February 1849, 'I should be the first to submit to such a dictatorship.' (The declaration complemented the famous phrase of Ludwig Ühland, one of Germany's most popular poets, a month earlier: 'No head will shine forth over Germany that is not anointed by a full drop of democratic oil.') When the Prussians were forced by Austrian (and significantly, Russian) pressure to withdraw from southern Denmark, where they had intervened in 1848 and 1849 to support 'Germans' living in Schleswig-Holstein, it was the left in the Frankfurt Parliament that protested most strongly about the affront to German 'national spirit' and 'military honour'.

The man who found the successful way to German unification was Otto von Bismarck, the son of a *Junker* landowner in Prussia, although he was not to become President of the Prussian Ministry until 1862. Born in 1815, the year of Waterloo, he first came to prominence as a conservative politician at the time of the 1848 revolutions. After hearing that Friedrich Wilhelm IV could not sleep because of worrying about the revolution, Bismarck commented simply that 'a king must be able to sleep'. He urged the King to resist as well as to sleep. Yet Bismarck himself was the most sensitive and the most volatile of conservatives, a man of nerves as well as of iron; and although he stands out in retrospect as the main architect of German unification, he followed subtle and devious policies before and after achieving it. Indeed, it has been claimed by A. J. P. Taylor that in 1870 he unified Germany to defeat France rather than defeated France to unify Germany.

Certainly the kind of unification that Bismarck achieved did not imply centralization except in diplomatic and military matters. Germany then (as now) retained within it a high degree of regional and local initiative. Bismarck's greatest skill was displayed in using individuals and groups for his own ends, selecting and discarding them when they had ceased to fit his purposes. Serving Prussian kings, as he did, he had no illusions about their personal limitations, particularly their dependence on their relatives. He was well aware of the limitations of dynastic diplomacy in a Europe networked by royal marriages, although he knew how to exploit it.

Even so far as serving Germany was concerned, Bismarck always put the interest of Prussia first. 'What the devil do I care about the petty [German] states?' he once asked 'My only concern is to safeguard and increase the power of Prussia.' 'The only healthy basis of a large state which differentiates it essentially from a petty state, is state egoism and not romanticism, and it is unworthy of a great state to fight for that which is not connected with its own interest.'[2] This was a classic expression of *Realpolitik*. It had nothing in common with the liberal German nationalism of the Frankfurt Parliament, even when that nationalism demanded the use of force. 'Germany', Bismarck consistently maintained, 'does not look to Prussia's liberalism, she looks to her power ... Since the treaties of Vienna our frontiers have been ill-designed for a body politic. The great questions of our time will be decided not by speeches and resolutions of majorities, but by blood and iron.'

Bismarck achieved power in 1862 after roughly attacking 'the chatterers' who were incapable, he said, of ruling Prussia. In foreign politics, in particular, they were 'children'. Foreign politics always interested him profoundly, not least when he was Prussian representative on the revived *Deutscher Bund* from 1851 to 1858. He had gone on to serve as Ambassador to Russia from 1858 to 1862 and for a few months in 1862 Ambassador to Paris. He learned from these useful experiences how to deal with Russia and how to assess Napoleon III in a decade of change. Both countries played a key part in his thinking about the international scene, while Britain came a low third.

His relations with Austria were even more central to his planning, however, for there could be no German unification unless Prussia replaced Austria as the main influence inside Germany. Frustrated by what he described in 1852 as the 'measureless ambition' of the Austrians, he had been aggravated too by Schwarzenberg's confident anti-Prussian moves at Dresden. Yet before and after what he thought of as a 'necessary' war between Prussia and Austria in 1866, Bismarck wanted a strong Austria, not a weak one. He attached supreme importance to maintaining long-term Austro-German ties. Ties with France, so important to German politicians after 1945, played no part in his vision. He wished to balance forces in Europe, not to integrate Europe, whether the old Europe of the rulers and the aristocracies, a group to which he himself belonged, or the new Europe of manufacturers and merchants. He believed also, however, that since France encouraged, even represented, forces of movement in Europe, Prussia could benefit from this disposition during the transitional period. France was only 'one piece – although an essential one – in the chess game of European politics'.

Diplomacy and war

There were, in fact, many signs of international change during the 1850s, a decade of economic growth when Bismarck from different post-1848 vantage points (and London was not one of them) was surveying the scene. At the beginning of the decade Schwarzenberg's policy of tightening Austria's hold on the smaller south German states and isolating Prussia politically and diplomatically by retaining the goodwill of Russia seemed to be highly successful. The middle German states were suspicious of Prussian ambitions, and Russia, the saviour of Habsburg interests in 1849, continued its vigilance. 'No one needs a strong and powerful Austria more than I do', Tsar Nicholas I had told the mother of Franz Josef, the young Austrian Emperor, in December 1848.

It was Russia, however, increasingly isolated during the early 1850s, that was to be at the forefront of European diplomacy after 1851, and having avoided revolution in 1848 was to be drawn into war. The danger points in the European balance were at the geographical edges of the continent – in the north Schleswig-Holstein, historic key to the Baltic, and in the south the Ottoman Empire, thought of by Nicholas I (and others) as 'the sick man of Europe'. And after the complex question of Schleswig-Holstein was apparently settled (if uneasily) in May 1852 by the Treaty of London, which determined the succession to the Danish throne and recognized Danish authority in the two duchies (while allowing Holstein to continue to be represented in the *Deutscher Bund*), attention moved eastwards. The first important shifts of alignment since 1815 came not from moves towards German or Italian unification but from the Crimean War of 1854 to 1856, the first war involving Britain since 1815 – this time in alliance with France against Russia – and a war in which neither Austria nor Prussia took part.

Napoleon III rightly believed that a strong policy in eastern Europe and an alliance with Britain would give his regime the security and prestige it required, while British opinion (even more than British governments) believed that there were vital British interests at stake. There was to be British official and unofficial support too in 1859 and 1860 for Italian unification, although it was now coupled with suspicion of France and of French intentions not only in Italy but elsewhere. It was only at the end of the decade that Italy came into the centre of the picture. The war then between Austria and France (in which Prussia, though seized with Francophobia, did not take part) not only changed alignments but altered Europe's map. Ending as it did in Austrian defeat and in partial Italian unification, it gave a fillip to German nationalism.

Internal politics had changed too by then, not least in Austria and in France. In Austria the *Reichstag* was enlarged in 1860 to make it more representative, and Franz Josef in defeat agreed to exercise his power to legislate only with its 'cooperation' and with that of the provincial diets. A Viennese liberal, Anton von Schmerling, became the leading Habsburg minister. In France, where Napoleon III had ruled in authoritarian (if arbitrary) fashion since a new imperial constitution had been promulgated in 1852, parallel concessions were made to the Liberals in 1860. The Legislature, elected by universal suffrage, was now allowed to debate government policy and the press was permitted to report debates. As the mid-nineteenth century boom years continued there was no return in either country to the state of affairs in 1849 or 1850.

Yet all this was around the corner when the Crimean War broke out in 1854. Its immediate causes, some of them lying outside Europe, were more complex than its consequences. Control of the so-called 'holy places', religious sites in and near Jerusalem, became a matter of dispute between France and Russia, and when in 1852 the Ottoman government allowed Roman Catholics equal rights with Greek Orthodox Christians (and full control of the Church of the Nativity in Bethlehem) Russia put strong pressure on the Sultan, moving troops to the borders of Moldavia and Wallachia, sending a commission to Constantinople to demand Russian

Plate 3.3 Roger Fenton in the Crimea, 1855. A former solicitor who achieved fame with his photographs of the Crimean War, Fenton travelled fully equipped to develop his pictures near the battlefield but never showed battles. In his mobile darkroom shown here, he was able to process photographic negatives within ten minutes of their exposure.

rights to protect Orthodox Christians everywhere, and proposing to the British Ambassador there a scheme to partition Turkish territories. When the commission, headed by Prince Menshikov, failed, Moldavia and Wallachia were occupied, provoking popular as well as governmental protests in both Britain and France. After Austrian attempts to avert war failed, Turkey declared war on Russia in October 1853, and in March 1854 Britain and France declared war on Russia: for the first time in centuries they were on the same side.

War lasted long enough in the Crimea to reveal military and administrative ineptitude on both sides. The losses in men were substantial, more than in any other war between 1815 and 1914 (300,000

Russians, 100,000 French and 60,000 British), with more deaths from sickness, particularly typhus, than from battle, and with cholera, which had added to the problems of Europe during the aftermath of revolution, once again proving impossible to control. Florence Nightingale, 'the lady of the lamp', who organized the nursing of the British sick, the wounded and the dying, became a national heroine. Russia, which had neither heroines nor heroes, took the initiative in seeking to end the war not through a change of government (there was one such change in Britain) but through a change of tsar. In March 1855 Nicholas died and was succeeded by Alexander II who, faced with threats that Austria might enter the war, made peace overtures before the full strength – or weakness – of either side had been fully tested.

Paradoxically, the Peace of Paris, which followed in 1856, prepared the way for a future understanding between France and Russia – as Bismarck, watching from the sidelines, recognized. 'You wish to change in part the Treaty of Paris', Napoleon could write to Alexander II in 1858, writing also that he too 'would change in part the treaties of 1815.' The two treaties were, indeed, closely related. By the terms of the 1856 peace, which neutralized the Black Sea and checked Russia's freedom to intimidate Constantinople, the free navigation of the Danube was achieved. At the same time the Ottoman Empire was admitted to 'the Public Law and System of Europe', the 'concert', from which the Sultan had been excluded in 1815. The idea of such a 'concert' had survived the failure of the regular Congress System devised in 1815, and a 'Declaration respecting Maritime Law' was agreed upon by the great powers represented at Paris.

Napoleon emerged from the Crimean War with his prestige greatly increased, while Britain, shaken in victory, became aware of the problems that had to be faced by a 'liberal state at war' (with militant anti-Russian radical groups pressing for a more comprehensive victory). Piedmont-Sardinia, which had joined Britain and France in an alliance which strengthened its claims to be considered a power on the European stage, gained, if not territorially, from being present at the Congress of Paris. Russia lost in territory as well as in prestige, being forced to cede parts of Bessarabia to the Turkish province of Moldavia, the core of the future Romania. The Ottoman Empire was propped up but not strengthened. Indeed, the Sultan agreed to grant a substantial degree of delegated authority not only to Moldavia and Wallachia but to Serbia which was to secure its full independence in 1878. (Turkish garrisons in Belgrade were withdrawn in 1867.) There was ample scope, therefore, for intensified Balkan rivalries between Austria and Russia after 1856, and at many times these were to prove stronger than counter-revolutionary community of interest.

In time Bismarck was able to put the memories of the Crimean War to good account. And he was able to put economics to good account also. Austria suffered economically as a result of the Crimean War, and throughout the 1850s it was losing ground every year to Prussia and to the

Zollverein. In the very year that Bismarck came to power, 1862, a trade treaty between Prussia and France destroyed any continuing hope of Austria ever being able to join the Prussian-led economic grouping. Politically some of the smaller German states might wish to look to Vienna: economically they were already looking towards Berlin even though the iron in Bismarck's 'blood and iron' was not yet fully forged. As late as 1860 France was still producing more pig iron than Germany. Significantly the most striking portent of Prussian economic power was military – the rise of Krupps and the German armaments industry. At the Great Exhibition of 1851 in London, where the gospel of peace was sung, Alfred Krupps had displayed a huge gun – and the biggest ever block of steel.

In retrospect there seems to have been an unfolding logic behind Bismarck's sophisticated diplomacy, backed by growing military power, between 1862 and 1871, the year when Wilhelm I, who succeeded Friedrich Wilhelm IV in 1861 as King of Prussia, was crowned German Emperor. He had served as Regent since 1857 after the Emperor became incapacitated; and although deeply conservative he believed strongly in Prussia's mission to unify Germany. Nonetheless, as in the case of the 'revolutionary logic' of the 1790s or of the years 1848 and 1849, what happened thereafter was not premeditated or worked out according to plan. Bismarck thought primarily in terms of the present, making use of its fluidity in all his calculations. 'When I have been asked whether I was pro-Russian or pro-Western powers', he wrote in a letter of 1857, 'I have always answered I am Prussian, and my ideal in foreign politics is . . . independence of decision reached without pressure or aversion from attraction to other states and their rulers . . . I would see our troops fire on French, English or Austrians with equal satisfaction.'

Before Bismarck acquired the power in 1862 to exploit or to fashion events, the position of Austria and France had completely changed. This was a result of the unification of Italy, and it was this change of position that made his policies during the 1860s possible. The chronology was important. As late as 1860 the Prussian Prince Regent told Napoleon III that he did not expect to live to see German unification, and when he was crowned King of Prussia at Königsberg neither he nor Bismarck could have foreseen that he would be crowned Emperor of Germany nine years later not in Germany but at Versailles. Nor was that to be the end of the story. There was to be a French revenge for Versailles after the First World War in 1918 when the Hohenzollerns lost their throne, and following the Second World War when Königsberg was to be turned into a Russian city.

Italian unification

The key figure in the Italian context was the Prime Minister of Piedmont-Sardinia, Camillo di Cavour, five years older than Bismarck, who entered parliamentary politics in Turin in June 1848, and who became Prime Minister in 1852, ten years before Bismarck. Like Bismarck he made full use of the increased fluidity of European diplomacy, seeking to achieve the possible. He was prepared, therefore, to use treaties, battles and back-stairs intrigues to achieve his purposes. Although he edited *Il Risorgimento*, he despised 'frenetic, ferocious and absurd' revolutionaries, and once said that he would willingly use them as manure for his sugar beet.

Cavour was the younger son of a nobleman, and his mother, French by origin, had lived in Switzerland. He himself wrote French more easily than Italian, and with his European perspectives was well aware of all the problems of what he once called 'our poor peninsula'. He even described Italian unification as 'nonsense'. For him, indeed, it was essentially a by-product of the struggle for independence and of a series of exceptional and unforeseen events inside Italy from which he could profit. He knew that there were other personalities involved in the process of unification besides himself and that for some of them unification was the goal. In some respects he had more in common in his general outlook with Peel and with Guizot, both of whom he admired, than with Bismarck. Moreover, many of his policies were necessarily concerned with issues derived from an earlier age than that of Bismarck. Thus, he dissolved half the monasteries in Piedmont-Sardinia as an enlightened despot might have done, and supported the abolition of ecclesiastical courts which had survived in their original form in Italy but nowhere else in Europe.

With a very different agenda in mind, he also shared Peel's ideas on free trade, the need for economic progress (including agricultural improve-ment), and the importance of forestalling 'general political and social upheaval'. He had visited Britain in 1835, when he was greatly impressed by industrial Birmingham and commercial Liverpool, where he saw a workhouse and caught a train for Manchester. Railways, he recognized, were symbols of prosperity. As late as 1859 half the railways in Italy were in Piedmont-Sardinia.

The British minister in Turin, who greatly admired Cavour's work and helped him to achieve his objectives, called him 'a financier who has Adam Smith at his fingers' ends, not a conqueror who aims at debt and empire'. But this was to underestimate Cavour's diplomatic subtlety and the range of his preoccupations. They were never exclusively economic; and if he was uninterested in empire himself, he could not ignore the existence of the Habsburg Empire. Independence meant primarily independence from Austria, which had a different role to play in Italy – with a quite different history behind it – from the role that it played in Germany. Cavour could talk naturally of 'the barbarians' from outside, 'encamped' as they were in Lombardy, who oppressed Italy. Even had he wished to do so, Bismarck could never have employed the same kind of language about the Austrians in Germany. He had to be content with taking off his jacket when he talked to their envoys and ostentatiously smoking cigars in their presence.

The movement of Italian politics and the achievement of Italian unification in two stages – 1861 and 1870 – depended on many people in many places, outside Italy as well as inside it. Cavour had no sympathy with those Italian revolutionaries like Mazzini, who renamed his followers 'the Party of Action' in 1853; and when in that year Mazzini and his followers tried to organize a republican revolution in Milan, Cavour attacked them openly and for doing so was thanked by the Austrians. Nonetheless, after 1856 he courted the National Society, the main agency of the Italian *Risorgimento*, even though it was led by and included radical Italians whose views about social politics and Italian unification were different from his own, and it was a triumph for him when the Society began to refer to Vittore Emmanuele as King of Italy. Cavour described Daniele Manin, one of its leaders, as 'always a little Utopian', but he realized shrewdly that even such utopianism might on 'a practical occasion' be 'useful'.

He then proceeded by a different route to show that he was just as anxious to get rid of the Austrians as Mazzini was. Looking around for allies, he recognized realistically from the outset that Italy would have to win French support above all else, and when in 1855 he deliberately chose to embroil Italy in Crimean War politics, he did so fearing that Austria might join the war first. At the end of the war he had useful discussions with Napoleon III at the Congress of Paris, which were followed up at Plombières in the summer of 1858.

By the so-called pact of Plombières (details of which were not disclosed by Cavour to his cabinet) Napoleon accepted 'the principle of nationality' and declared that he would join in a war to drive Austria out of Lombardy and Venice. This would be a repeat performance, of course, of the achievement of Napoleon I, and there was another Napoleonic repeat in that Napoleon III and Cavour agreed that a marriage would be arranged between a middle-aged cousin of Napoleon, Jerome, and Vittore Emmanuele's 15-year-old daughter. The most cynical aspect of the deal – a demonstration of the bargaining aspect of Cavour's *Realpolitik* – was that Piedmont-Sardinia would cede Savoy and Nice to France. The informal agreement at Plombières was turned into a formal treaty in January 1859. A Franco-Russian understanding followed. Russia would accept change in Italy, and France would support Russia in overturning the still recent decisions of the Congress of Paris to close the Black Sea.

It was left to Cavour to find an occasion for war. At first this seemed difficult, since there was pressure even from friendly countries, like Britain, for a European settlement of 'the Italian question' without recourse to war. (Palmerston had always recognized the need for a secure Austria, not least in the excitements of 1848 and 1849.) But in the course of a 'war scare', something that was to become a familiar event in the years before 1914, the Austrians conveniently played into Cavour's hands, as they (and in 1870 the French) were later to play into Bismarck's hands. When Cavour mobilized the relatively small army of Piedmont-Sardinia in March 1859, the Austrians retaliated in April by mobilizing their own far bigger one; and when they went even further and in April 1859 sent an ultimatum to Piedmont-Sardinia demanding Italian 'disarmament' within three days, Cavour rejected the ultimatum and Napoleon III, as promised, marched into Italy.

The war did not go entirely according to plan, for Napoleon was no Bismarck. Yet it lasted only for six weeks, and the two bloody and costly Franco-Italian victories at Magenta and Solferino were decisive. Railways were brought into use in the warfare, and it was out of the carnage of Solferino that the Red Cross was born: a Swiss observer on the battlefield, Jean-Henri Dunant, had been appalled by the treatment of the wounded on both sides. The peace did not go according to plan either, for Napoleon in a sudden switch of tactics made overtures to the Austrians before Cavour wished, and, unknown to him, agreed in talks with Franz Josef to leave Venice and the central Italian duchies in Austrian hands. Only Lombardy was to be given up. He also proposed an Italian confederation with the Pope as President and with Austria as a member. A deeply shocked Cavour resigned after as stormy a scene with his king as any that Bismarck ever had with his.

But the wheel of fortune had not stopped turning, and within a year of the peace, Piedmont-Sardinia had doubled its size, incorporating not only Lombardy but the three central Italian duchies and part of the papal territories. Moreover, within that same year the British government had made it clear that it would not allow these moves to be resisted. Palmerston, the British Prime Minister from 1859 to 1865, and his Foreign Secretary, Lord John Russell, were so passionately pro-Italian at this crucial moment in Italian history that they were nicknamed 'the two old Italian masters'. Gladstone, the future leader of British liberalism, who had served under Peel but had joined Palmerston's government as Chancellor of the Exchequer, was equally pro-Italian. Italy contributed directly to his political development as a popular politician.

The expansion of Piedmont-Sardinia took place in separate phases. After Villafranca constituent assemblies in Parma, Modena, Tuscany and the Romagna formed an alliance with a common army and turned to Piedmont-Sardinia for leadership. Cavour returned to power, confident of British support, and when Napoleon also (in another *volte face*) accepted this total modification of the terms of Villafranca, Cavour declared himself willing to allow Nice and Savoy to pass to the French. And this they duly did after French troops had moved in not to wage a campaign but to arrange a plebiscite.

Cavour was still not the only character on the stage, however, and at first he was deeply alarmed, not enthused, by what was happening further south in Italy. Two months after Napoleon had secured Nice and Savoy, Garibaldi and a thousand Redshirts – soon to become even more famous

throughout Europe than his heroic defenders of Rome in 1849 – landed in distant Sicily, where there had been a popular uprising against the King of Naples, Francisco II. The 'thousand' (there were actually 1,088 men and one woman, the largest single group among them from Lombardy) soon captured the city of Palermo, and within three months crossed the strategic Straits of Messina and moved on to the Italian mainland. On 7 September they entered the city of Naples and paused before marching on Rome.

Such spectacular success was far more dazzling than anything that had happened in northern Italy, and it was happily achieved, moreover, without deviousness. Garibaldi had little use for diplomacy; indeed, before landing in Sicily he had contemplated as an alternative a landing in Nice, his birthplace, to thwart the French. His actions – in the name of 'Vittore Emmanuele and Italy' – were certainly too spectacular and too direct for Cavour, who at this critical moment in time needed every resource of *Realpolitik* to decide what to do. He had been strongly opposed to Garibaldi's expedition, but he had been able neither to prevent it nor publicly to criticize its outcome: 'the ministry could not have lasted', he wrote later, 'if it had tried to stop Garibaldi'. Writing privately six days after the Sicilian landing he noted that 'if the Sicilian insurrection is crushed we shall say nothing: if it succeeds we shall intervene in the name of humanity and order'.

Afraid of Garibaldi's impulsive spontaneity, of his natural radicalism, and of his immense prestige, Cavour made a number of moves to check Garibaldi before finding the one that worked. Knowing that there would be serious international implications if Garibaldi's troops entered Rome – for Napoleon III, as self-appointed defender of the Pope, might intervene and might on this occasion be backed by Austria – Cavour concluded that what was necessary was a still more spectacular triumph than Garibaldi's. He had to make news. And he succeeded. On the day that Garibaldi entered Naples, Cavour sent an ultimatum of his own to the French-protected Papal States. Claiming that the Pope was incapable of controlling revolutionary movements in his territories, Cavour sent in his own troops, and on 18 September, at Castelfidaro, the Piedmontese defeated a Papal army that was commanded by a royalist French general who was a bitter opponent of Napoleon. Bypassing Rome, they moved towards Naples and there they converged with Garibaldi's troops who had defeated a Bourbon army of 30,000 at Volturno. Vittore Emmanuele and Garibaldi rode together into the city of Naples.

The great powers had not been able to intervene directly in this story, although Britain, in particular, approved of its outcome, and Cavour had

---

Plate 3.4 Napoleon III at Solferino, 1859. A contemporary depiction of the carnage at Solferino – the battle that led to the creation of the Red Cross. Note the amputated, mangled human limbs beneath the horses' hooves on the right of the picture; to the left, the massed ranks of reinforcements march over fallen comrades.

coordinated beforehand (very cynically) this boldest of moves with Napoleon, whose troops stood in the way of Rome. The whole of Italy except Venice and the area immediately round Rome was now under the physical control of Piedmont-Sardinia.

Garibaldi's 'irregulars' were soon disbanded without fuss, and the great hero went away to live quietly, Cavour hoped, in an island off Sardinia. Plebiscites which were held on the basis of universal adult male suffrage in Naples, Sicily, and the captured Papal territories, confirmed the wishes of the inhabitants to become subjects of Vittore Emmanuele (they were not given the choice of voting to belong to independent kingdoms), and the 1848 Constitution of Piedmont-Sardinia, which Carlo Alberto had granted to his subjects, was now extended to the new kingdom of Italy. Vittore Emmanuele II, who had made many moves of his own during this extraordinary sequence, was proclaimed King and Cavour became the first prime minister. The first national Parliament met at Turin in March 1861. Only around 2 per cent of the population, however, had the vote. This was not a plebiscitary assembly, and from the start it faced serious problems in seeking to determine the extent of administrative decentralization.

The word 'national' begged many questions, just as did the inevitable choice of Turin, the capital of Piedmont-Sardinia, as the national capital. There were enormous regional differences – economic, social and cultural – between north and south, and in many of the cities also, old and new, there were differences between 'clericals' and 'anti-clericals' and 'respectable' politicians and radical revolutionaries. Vittore Emmanuele refused to call himself Vittore Emmanuele I, while one surviving federalist deputy asked, in the first national parliamentary debate, why Milan, Florence and Naples should be ruled from Turin. There were troubles in Naples almost immediately after the union. Pro-Bourbon riots were one manifestation of discontent. Another was the so-called 'brigands' war' in which large numbers of civilian lives were lost through peasant disturbances. And there was another moment of drama further north when in 1862 Garibaldi failed to seize Rome (*O Roma, o Morte*: 'Rome or death') with an army of volunteers who were checked at Aspromonte not by the French but by Italian troops. By then Cavour was dead, a victim of 'fever' (probably malaria) at the age of 51. He had already stated publicly in March 1861 that Rome, the key to Italy, should become Italy's capital. Now he suddenly disappeared from the stage when he was at the very centre of it.

There were to be more tensions in the new but still impoverished kingdom of Italy than there were in the prosperous new German Empire, as ministers who claimed to be as dedicated to Cavour's memory as the Peelites were to Peel's memory in Britain tried to hold the country together. Yet the prime minister who succeeded him came not from Piedmont-Sardinia but from Tuscany, and Turin was temporarily to give way as a capital to Florence. The man who now moved into the centre of the European stage was Bismarck, who achieved power in 1862 by

Map 3.2 The Unification of Italy

ensuring that it was possible for his king to govern through himself without depending on Parliament. Taxes were raised to support a substantial military budget – and collected – without Parliament approving of them. Bismarck, contemptuous of liberalism (though prepared to use even that) had the right personal qualities to counter the liberal watchword of 'a people's army behind Parliament' with the King's watchword 'a disciplined army that is also the people in arms, behind the King, the warlord'. The Austro-Hungarian envoy to Britain, Count Karolyi, fully approved. 'If democracy is suppressed inside Prussia, its damaging influence on the rest of Germany will also be crippled.'

German unification

In making it possible to employ the Prussian Army effectively as an instrument of policy, Bismarck, who wished any wars in which it was engaged to be short, had to avoid the creation of foreign alliances or coalitions that would stand in his way. The first critical year for him was 1863, when a Polish revolt began after Russia had tried to draft urban Poles into the army. Following the revolt, Russia suppressed all remaining Polish liberties and even the old name 'Kingdom of Poland' disappeared. Bismarck won Russian good will by dismissing all the protests of Prussian liberals in favour of Poland, and was equally brusque with the Prussian Crown Prince when he protested too. In the same year Bismarck began a series of moves on his northern borders which were to place him in a position whereby he could successfully go to war against Austria in 1866.

When King Frederick of Denmark died in November 1863, the question was raised again of who should rule the southern Danish/German duchies of Schleswig and Holstein, and a German pretender appeared, Friedrich of Augustenberg, who proclaimed himself Duke of Schleswig-Holstein. Bismarck avoided European intervention in the dispute – partly by skill, partly by accident – and after successful military intervention, authorized by the German *Bundestag*, he reached a settlement, the Treaty of Vienna, by which, ignoring Friedrich, the King of Denmark renounced all his rights in the Duchies of Schleswig and Holstein to the King of Prussia and the Emperor of Austria. In 1865 by the Convention of Gastein it was agreed, and this was clearly transitional, that Austria would occupy one duchy – Holstein – and Prussia the other – Schleswig. The presence of Austria in distant Holstein, a predominantly German duchy, would give future grounds for Prussian manoeuvre.

No European congress was called despite the fact that both Prussia and Austria had defied the recently signed Treaty of London, and this seemed to have proved Bismarck's powers of calculation. In London itself Palmerston, who had made promises to the Danes and who claimed that he was one of the few people who understood the issue, won no support for any British intervention from his cabinet or from the Queen. Meanwhile France and Italy were won over by Bismarck: two months after Gastein he visited Napoleon and had friendly talks with him at Biarritz. Throughout, Russia, already won over, gave no support to the Danes. In 1860 *The Times* in London had derided Prussia for 'always leaning on someone, always getting someone to help her, never willing to help herself; always ready to deliberate, never to decide; present in congresses, but absent in battles'. Now the tables had been turned, and there was no 'concert'.

Already there was Prussian revenge for Olmütz. When the Austrian Emperor travelled to Frankfurt to present to the German princes a plan for a five-man German directorate under his own leadership and a new German Diet composed of representatives from the German state diets, Bismarck persuaded the King of Prussia not to attend. The Emperor was welcomed by *Gross Deutschland* politicians and was received with cheering crowds, but his plan had no chance of success. Instead, Bismarck put forward a far more popular alternative plan in July 1866, proposing the abolition of the Diet and the summoning of a German Assembly to draft a new constitution. It would then create a new German parliament to be elected by universal suffrage.

Bismarck's object, of course, was to outbid Austria, not to give the German people a share in their government, but it was difficult, once his plan had been published, for liberals to oppose it. Ex-members of the Frankfurt Parliament, in particular, could scarcely find reasons for protest. Bismarck had already won the support of the nationalists of 1848 when he invaded Schleswig-Holstein: they had protested sharply, after all, in 1848, when Prussian troops had been withdrawn.

Secret diplomacy counted for more than public appeals, important though the latter were in Bismarckian tactics. Behind the scenes he quietly won the support both of Piedmont-Sardinia (which, after all, had been at war with Austria in 1859) and of France (Piedmont's ally in that struggle) in the eventuality of Prussian military action against Austria. 'Prussia and France', he flatteringly told Napoleon at Biarritz in 1865, 'are the two nations of Europe whose interests are most nearly identical.' In securing promises of French neutrality in a war between Prussia and Austria the possibilities of an understanding between France and Austria – with so many eighteenth-century echoes – were effectively discounted. And in Schleswig-Holstein, as he had hoped, he found ample material with which to provoke Austria, even though the Austrians had successfully set out to be moderate and conciliatory.

It was not Prussia but Austria (backed by the smaller German states – Bavaria, Saxony, Hanover and Baden) that declared war in 1866, with the Austrian minister responsible for the declaration hoping optimistically that it would 'make amends for Magenta and Solferino'. 'Without a war', he added, 'there is only the prospect of insecure peace or revolution.' This was total miscalculation. The Prussian Army, well drilled and well armed,

121

made the most effective use possible of superior weapons and, not least, of railways and telegraphs as instruments of mobilization and deployment. The war lasted only seven weeks and culminated in a decisive Prussian victory at Königgratz on 3 July.

Had the war gone badly, Bismarck would not have scrupled to call on Italian, Magyar, Polish, Czech and Croat resistance groups in a struggle against Austria; and it was significant, perhaps, that the final treaty was signed in Prague. Yet he did not seek a vindictive peace, and he told his Minister of the Interior to work hard so that Berlin newspapers did not demand one. He believed that he would need Austrian 'strength' in the future – a somewhat dangerous belief, given ample evidence of increasing Austrian weakness – and he had to argue with his own king to get his way, as he had earlier been forced to argue with him about Schleswig-Holstein. Whatever the newspapers might have said, the peace would have been far more severe had Wilhelm I determined it.

The Peace of Prague in effect excluded Austria from both Germany and Italy, and in the following year the Magyars gained full control of their own internal affairs. A Dual Monarchy was set up by which Franz Josef, dividing his territories at the River Leithe, a small tributary of the Danube, became simultaneously Emperor of Austria and King of Hungary. Liberals in Vienna supported the change which brought with it parliamentary government and guarantees of civil liberties. Yet this partition, as significant as any unification, could not quell the claims of other 'nationalities' in the Empire, and when these were vigorously put forward directly or indirectly they made it difficult for ministers to govern firmly. Bargains had to be made in the interests not only of conciliation but of executive action. In the process Europe lost.

Matters were different in the new North German Confederation of which the King of Prussia became President and Commander-in-Chief. It was in effect a greater Prussia, although it did not and could not centralize all aspects of government and life. Much that mattered could be determined far away from Berlin. Those north German states that had opposed Prussia during the war were annexed, except Saxony, but other German states with a different set of traditions remained in existence within their old boundaries. And in Prussia itself Bismarck won a political victory when after years of obstruction moderate liberals in the *Landtag* now voted for an Indemnity Bill which indemnified the government from responsibility for the previous four years of unauthorized public expenditure. Bismarck was victorious in the new Germany too when he refused to make himself legally responsible to the *Reichstag*. In a new *Bundesrat*, where representatives still voted under mandate, as in the old Federal Diet, the fact that a two-thirds majority was required ensured Prussian power, and in a new *Reichstag*, elected by universal suffrage, popular power was restricted: there was to be no annual budget for it to discuss and ratify.

The age of Metternich had been left far behind. Inside Europe, thanks to Bismarck's diplomatic skills, as great as those of Metternich, and Prussian economic and military power, which was to grow throughout the decade, the work of the counter-revolution of 1848–50 and the Vienna settlement that preceded it had now been undone. The age of Palmerston (who died in 1865) had been left far behind also. Britain, indeed, did no more during the Austro-Prussian War than it had done during the Schleswig-Holstein crisis. It was preoccupied with its own affairs.

Bismarck's next war, that against France in 1870, had its immediate origins, as had so many previous European crises, in the issue of the Spanish succession. The Spanish Queen, Isabella, whose marriage had been a diplomatic issue just before the fall of Louis Philippe, was driven into exile in 1868 following a successful revolution; and a constituent Spanish assembly offered the vacant throne to a reluctant member of the Prussian royal family, Leopold of Hohenzollern. Bismarck encouraged Leopold's candidature and in 1869 was secretly spending money in Spain to ensure Spanish backing. The French government, backed by an excited press, became increasingly uneasy about Leopold's candidature. The Prussian press too fanned the flames in 1870 as the British press had fanned the flames before during and after the Crimean War.

Bismarck's active role in stirring intrigue and excitement was very cleverly thought through, for he knew that in France there was never any shortage of combustible material. Napoleon was always interested in possible deals, and when with Bismarck's encouragement he showed himself willing to contemplate French territorial gains in Belgium and Luxembourg he was falling into Bismarck's trap. There were many people in Europe in 1870 – not least in London – who saw Napoleon, not Bismarck, as the main threat to peace. Bismarck was even attempting behind the scenes to win the support of Mazzini for this interpretation.

Faced with French protests about the Hohenzollern candidature, Wilhelm I was prepared to back down, and Leopold subsequently withdrew his name (for the second time). The crisis, however, was not solved. The French government foolishly went on to ask for further guarantees. When Wilhelm refused – Bismarck was manoeuvring very cleverly behind the scenes, as became known years later, manipulating the wording of a royal telegram – it was France, described in its press as 'insulted', that declared war on 19 July 1870. Once again Bismarck had so organized affairs that it was not he but his opponents who were made to take the initiative: he was able to tell the German Parliament 17 years later – with no one to contradict him – that Napoleon had 'launched into the war' because he had 'believed that it would strengthen his rule at home'. Once again the Prussian victory, achieved at Sedan on 2 September, was swift, if not immediately decisive, and this seemed to justify all the tactics employed. Napoleon's empire had collapsed within two months. Prussia was now the strongest nation in the world in military terms.

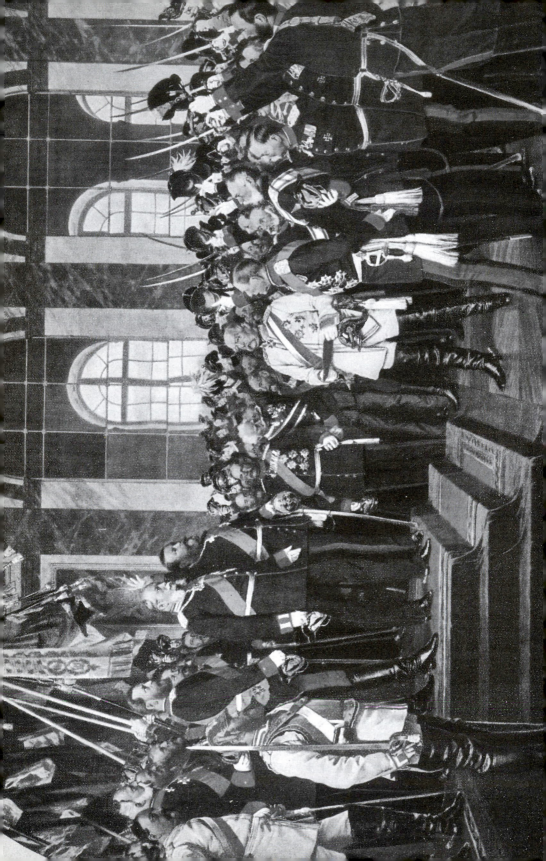

Britain and Russia both stayed on the side-lines, as did Franz Josef, with whom Napoleon had had abortive treaty discussions following Königgratz. The French defeat at Sedan resulted, however, in continuing domestic divisions in France itself. After Napoleon capitulated a republic was proclaimed in Paris – now in a state of siege – and a staunch republican politician with a future, Léon Gambetta, escaped in a balloon to organize provincial resistance. It was not until 18 January 1871 that an armistice was signed with Bismarck. And even then the divisions continued. Paris held out in appalling circumstances (and with many deaths) until the end of May under a revolutionary Commune which was crushed not by Germans but by Frenchmen, led by Adolphe Thiers. The Commune included socialists and anarchists, but fierce republicans besides, and, hailed as it was by Marx, it created an even greater set of myths than the Italian *Risorgimento*. Violence and myth went together. In the twentieth century Lenin's dead body was to be shrouded in a Communard flag, and a ribbon from that flag was to be carried into space by Soviet cosmonauts in 1964.

Whatever the future power of myth, the capitulation of France in 1871 demonstrated that, imperial or republican, France no longer possessed the great advantages in Europe that it had less than a hundred years before. Its population in 1870 was five million less than the 39 million in the united Germany that Bismarck created, and it was Germany that experienced large-scale industrialization after 1870, not France. The new Germany was a triumph both of blood and of iron.[3] Money played its part, too, however, for it proved necessary to persuade the King of Bavaria to join the new German Empire by bribing him with money acquired from the King of Hanover after its annexation in 1866.

After victory Bismarck demanded from defeated France a large financial indemnity as well as the cession of the provinces of Alsace and Lorraine, the latter rich in minerals. This cession, urged on Bismarck by his king, by generals and by popular pressure inside Germany, was a mistake. Even in 1848, when the Frankfurt Parliament was rallying Germans everywhere, no-one had suggested that there should be delegates from Alsace-Lorraine, and after 1870 the issue was to bedevil future Franco-German relations down to the First World War of the twentieth century. After 1870 Bismarck professed that Germany was 'satiated' and that his only interest was peace. Here, however, was oversatiation and a 'cause of war'.

There were also flaws in the new imperial structure, in this case most of them quite deliberately put there by Bismarck himself to stem 'democracy'. No elected representatives of the German people were present at Versailles when Wilhelm I was crowned (there was to be no hint of the gutter this

---

Plate 3.5   King Wilhelm I of Prussia is proclaimed *Kaiser* **(Emperor), 18 January 1871.** The ceremony took place in the Hall of Mirrors at the Palace of Versailles. Standing on the raised dais, the new Emperor, accompanied by his son Crown Prince Frederick Wilhelm (to his left), receives the congratulations of Bismarck (dressed in white) and other German nobles and officers.

time), and although the new German constitution, like that of 1867, was based on universal suffrage, it was clear from the start that the relationship between Chancellor (Bismarck) and the new Emperor would continue to be more significant than the relationship between Chancellor and *Reichstag*. The relationship began less triumphantly than appeared on the surface, for Wilhelm had to be persuaded tactfully by Ludwig of Bavaria to accept the new Crown, and it required Bismarck's insistence to force the King to call himself 'German Emperor' and not 'Emperor of Germany', a controversial title given the existing German states. In the words of the Crown Prince of Prussia there were 'sobs and tears' before the coronation.

Bismarck's insistence demonstrated, if it needed to be demonstrated, that he held the same views on the constitution after 1871 as he had held before 1870. Given the importance of the Army, there was to be no *annual* debate on the military estimates which accounted for 90 per cent of government expenditure. The government could be outvoted in the *Reichstag*, made up of political parties, but the Chancellor of the *Reichstag*, who was President of the *Bundestag*, had to be a Prussian, and all ministers were responsible only to the Emperor. After 1870 the Prussian system of administration was introduced throughout the imperial institutions of the new confederal Germany, ensuring that while there was to be no democracy there would always be a bureaucracy. It was difficult within the new constitution, therefore, to envisage how any movement towards a 'constitutional government' resting on a greater degree of individual freedom and responsibility would be possible; and the system, which at the same time allowed for initiative and devolution in the internal affairs of the states, was to survive his own fall from power in 1890. Thereafter, as the German economy boomed, it was to create *impasses* in German domestic politics that were to have disastrous consequences.

The biggest difficulty in 1871 – in national terms – was a different one. So many Germans were left outside the new Empire (a *Klein Deutschland*) that the Austrian poet Franz Grillparzer could say, 'you think you have created an empire, when all you have really done is destroyed a nation'. Likewise, many non-Germans were left within the new boundaries: nearly three million Poles, for example, lived in West Prussia and Posen. Those Germans who were left outside the new frontiers could become dangerously radical – a threat to the peace that Bismarck, having unified Germany, now wished to maintain. In 1873, like Metternich before him, he encouraged the Emperors of Austria and Germany and the Tsar of Russia to sign a Three Kings' Pact to work in concert and resist revolutionary ideas. It was a more formidable task than Metternich had faced. Ethnic relations within the Habsburg Empire were often to reach boiling point, and it was equally ominous that German intellectuals inside the German Empire – even intellectuals who were suspicious of Bismarck – could rally to the defence of Germans living outside. Pan-Germanism was to increase its appeal after Bismarck disappeared from the scene.

Because of the way in which the Empire was made, there were immediate difficulties in getting the new imperial symbols right. At first, for example, there was not even a new German national flag or a national anthem. (By contrast Britain's 'God Save the King' – or Queen – had been written in 1745.) It was not until 1892 that an imperial tricolour was devised of black, white and red (the black and white colours of Prussia were dominant); and even then, this flag, like many of the other emblems, was never popular in Bavaria. *Deutschland über Alles* (its music had originally been composed by Haydn for the Habsburg Emperor) was sung frequently as a kind of national anthem during the 1890s. So, too, was *Die Wacht am Rhein*, a nationalist song that reiterated and emphasized all the old enmities between Germany and France.

In 1871 Bismarck believed that a 'satiated' Germany had nothing to gain from a new war, yet nationalism, often inflamed by the press, still pointed towards new wars rather than towards new harmonies. Moreover, strident nationalism could also exploit, as it often did, anti-Semitism, anti-Catholicism and anti-socialism inside the country. The writing on the wall was beginning to be plain before Bismarck completed his work. 'Nationality', wrote the British historian Lord Acton in 1862, 'does not aim either at liberty or prosperity, both of which it sacrifices to the imperative necessity of making the nation the mould and measure of the state.' Four years later Emile de Laveleye, who knew as much about French nationalism as German, commented despairingly that 'nationalism . . . mocks at treaties, tramples on historic rights, puts diplomacy in disarray . . . and tomorrow perhaps will unleash a cursed war'.

Acton was writing as a liberal Roman Catholic, and the Roman Catholic Church was itself directly affected by the political changes that took place in Europe in 1870. The destruction of the temporal power of the Papacy was made possible by the grace of Bismarck, for Italy was able to profit from the Franco-German War of 1870 and Napoleon III's withdrawal of French troops from Rome enabled Italians by themselves to seize the city and turn it, as Cavour himself had wished, into Italy's capital. It had been by Bismarck's grace too that Italy had secured Venice by the Treaty of Prague in 1866 after Italian forces had been defeated by the Austrians at Custozza. The two unified states owed much to each other.

1870 and beyond

By a coincidence, when the political and military crisis of 1870 was at its height, the Pope had summoned to Rome a Vatican Council from 'the whole of Christendom' which proclaimed the dogma of papal infallibility in *ex cathedra* spiritual pronouncements, a dogma which the historian Acton, like many German theologians, found difficult to justify. Already in 1864 Pius IX had attacked liberalism of every kind (and with it socialism and confident belief in 'modern civilization') in a *Syllabus of Errors*. After 1870, bereft of temporal power, the Church was to become involved in disputes in many European countries, not least Germany and Italy. It was not until a new Pope, Leo XIII, was elected in 1879 that the Papacy regained any capacity to manoeuvre and to adapt, and by then there was no possibility that it would regain its temporal power. Until 1888 the Pope declared himself a prisoner in the Vatican and would not even leave it to go to the great cathedral of St Peter's across the square.

This was because of Italian rather than European politics. Right-wing in their policies, Cavour's successors were far less agile than he had been in attracting the support of other centre and centre-left groups. While drawing on the myths of the *Risorgimento* they did not want nationalism to be converted into continuing revolution, and they were unwilling to change the status quo. It was only after Mazzini was dead, in 1872, that a statue was erected in his memory. Some of his last thoughts on the new regime were that having sought to evoke the soul of Italy, all that he now saw before him was its corpse. Few Germans would have been so depressed or so frank. Garibaldi fared better: the personal relics of his campaigns had become museum relics of the *Risorgimento* in his lifetime.

There was a change in mood but not of system after a new parliamentary left, *la Sinistra*, acquired power in 1876, with the liberal Agostino Depretis, a Piedmontese with a Mazzinian past, as Prime Minister. Under the new regime there was as much patronage and bribery as there had been either under foreign rule or under Cavour, with Depretis offering to accept 'the help of all honest and loyal men'. The result was a system of *trasformismo*, taking your political opponents into your orbit rather than competing with them, a system associated in retrospect with Cavour himself; and it did not change in 1887 when Depretis died and gave way to his rival Francesco Crispi who venerated Bismarck and pushed Italy into colonial ventures in Africa.

When it proved impossible to take over all opponents, the remaining splinter groups looked around for new, often opportunist, coalitions. Gladstone, who had sharply criticized the old Bourbon regime in Naples when it was not fashionable to do so, had once described the unification of Italy as 'among the greatest marvels of our time'. Yet there were few signs that it was such a marvel during the 1870s and 1880s. In the twentieth century it was to be claimed by the highly intelligent Italian Marxist, Antonio Gramsci, that the most important aspect of the *Risorgimento* had been the 'missing revolution' (*rivoluzione mancata*).

In Germany, less bedevilled by regional poverty and by parliamentary squabbling, there were quite different political problems, and the Bismarckian era, which lasted until 1890, was a distinctive era of unchallenged power, with a strong belief in the nation's future. There were problems, however, in the rate and scale of industrialization and its political implications not least for the court and old *Junker* establishment. It was very different from industrialization in very different circumstances in late-eighteenth century Britain. Yet like industrialization then and later it was an uneven process. Bismarckian Germany after 1870 did not enter a period of exceptional prosperity. Economic crisis in 1873 brought to an end a 'promoters' boom' and the economy limped through the 1870s.

The most important difference between Germany and Britain in their century-separated industrial revolutions was structural – the role of the state. In Germany it intervened, often directly. And there was a tradition to fall back upon. Long before the German industrial revolution began German historians and political economists had identified economic with political nationalism. Political economy was given a historical dimension, and British classical political economy, culminating in a theory of universal free trade, was dismissed as at best abstract and theoretical and at worst an ideological justification of British economic interests. During the 1860s Prussia made good use of free trade policies in its rivalry with Austria, but when in 1879 Bismarck introduced a tariff in the 'national interest', in order to raise national revenue which would be outside the control of the constituent German states, he met with only limited opposition. Such independent revenue made it possible to implement imperial policies.

Throughout the Bismarckian era, German bankers, backed by the state, positively encouraged German industrialization, and German railways (there had been no railways during the early stages of the British industrial revolution) passed directly into the hands of the state and were managed in a highly disciplined fashion with impressively uniformed railway workers: mileage almost doubled between 1870 and 1880. The acquisition of the rich iron deposits of Lorraine, one of the results of the German victory against France, made possible a huge expansion of iron and steel production, ironically made easier to exploit through the application of a new steelmaking process devised in Britain.

In engineering the invention in 1867 of the dynamo by Werner von Siemens prepared the way for an 'age of electricity' in which Germany was to take the lead. The *Allgemeine Elektrizitäts-Gesellschaft*, founded in 1883, was an outstanding example of the power of German industry to combine in large organizations, contrasting sharply with the small-scale organizations which had emerged during the early years of British industrialization. Competition in industry was restricted, and industrial cartels were formed both to fix prices and to control production.[4]

Many branches of business, including the flourishing chemical industry, were scientifically based, and science was taught in institutions strongly supported by local, regional and national government, including the great Charlottenberg Technische Hochschöle, set up in 1879. It was recognized that German capacity to compete depended both on research and on education, and that competition meant a widening of markets. The Potash Syndicate, founded in 1881, aimed deliberately at the exploitation of new foreign outlets, and in 1910 the state insisted on its further continuation.

In trade too the *Deutsche Bank*, founded in 1870, was encouraged by the state to extend German 'spheres of influence' abroad. As Germany climbed higher in what was already thought of as an international league table, Germany and Britain inevitably became economic rivals. Although each was a good customer of the other, the rivalry was a new factor in international relations which received more and more public attention both in Germany and in Britain just before and just after the fall of Bismarck. There was particular publicity for the fact that Germany's commercial fleet, one of the smallest in Europe in 1879, came second only to that of Britain by the end of the century.

Protection was the key to Bismarck's domestic politics during the last decade of his power. On coming to power in 1862, he had been strongly opposed by liberals, but from the mid-1860s down to 1879 he relied on the parliamentary support of the majority of 'National Liberals' among them. After Königgratz they not only gave him an indemnity for measures which he had taken without the support of Parliament before 1866, but strongly supported his active foreign policy. Many of them came to attach more importance to the rule of law than to constitutional freedom. As one of them put it, 'the time for ideals is past, and the duty of politicians is to ask not for what is desirable, but for what is attainable'.

More positively, they supported his attack on Roman Catholic privileges (and 'clericalism') in the so called *Kulturkampf* (struggle of cultures) of the early 1870s, when a new Centre Party emerged in 1871 to defend the Church. Some of the National Liberals would even have been prepared to support his open move towards protection in 1879: in a climate of economic uncertainty a majority of them failed to oppose a new tariff designed to protect both German grain and iron, and to appease both the agrarian interest, fearful of its future, and the then 'depressed' industrialists. Refusing to make even verbal compromises to satisfy dissident liberals, Bismarck now turned instead to the Centre Party and the newly formed Conservative Party, which won 79 seats at the general election of 1897, when the National Liberals lost 24. Bismarck had always despised the concern of the National Liberals for parliamentary debate, and disapproved of their unwillingness to subordinate themselves completely to his purposes.

After 1879, therefore, his descriptions of the National Liberals began to be as cruel as his descriptions of the members of the Frankfurt Parliament 30 years before. They were, he once said, 'the gentlemen whom our sun does not warm and whom our rain does not moisten'. By making them appear disloyal not only to their Emperor but to their country, Bismarck ensured that they suffered heavy defeats at the election of 1881 from which they never recovered. The liberals were in decline in Austria at the same time, and Franz Josef used his influence against them at the elections of 1879. Never again in the nineteenth century did they achieve a majority in Parliament.

Splits in German liberalism made it difficult for German politics to take full account of the social and economic changes which followed in the wake of Germany's economic transformation, speeded up after Bismarck left office. The National Liberal Party that survived after 1881 propped up government rather than served as an independent political agency, willing to argue about political issues and to enhance political awareness. It was in character, therefore, that in 1887, a year when for reasons of foreign policy Bismarck needed *Reichstag* support, the National Liberal Party reached an agreement with the Conservative Party, called at the time a *Kartel* deal, whereby neither party would put up candidates to oppose the other's at the election in constituencies that were safe for them.

Bismarck's dependence on conservative groups during the 1880s accelerated the growth inside Germany of social democracy, a new force distrusted by liberals just as much as – if not more than – by conservatives. Bismarck tried to buy himself out of danger on this front by introducing sickness insurance in 1883, accident insurance in 1884 and old age pensions in 1889, the first statesman in Europe to follow this social policy. He could claim, as some German conservatives and professors of political economy claimed, that 'protection of the rights of labour' was one of the necessary forms of protection, fully in line with the traditions of German history going back to the Middle Ages. He could also claim that, like agricultural protection, it was in the national interest.

Bismarck's own instincts were paternalistic, and like Disraeli in Britain he was willing to make sizeable bids for working-class support. Thus, as early as the 1860s, he had held secret talks with one of the first independent German socialist leaders, Ferdinand Lassalle. Bismarck could not prevent the rise of German social democracy, which adopted Marxist or near-Marxist programmes, but he made it as difficult as he could for the socialists to rely on German mass support. They nonetheless created at Eisenach in 1869 what later became the most powerful Social Democratic party in Europe. They were divided in their attitudes towards the Franco-Prussian War of 1870, with the followers of Ferdinand Lassalle supporting it, and August Bebel, a Prussian, and Wilhelm Liebknecht, a follower of Marx, opposing it, but they united again in 1875 – with a new political platform, the 'Gotha Programme'. In 1871 Bebel had been the only Social Democrat in the *Reichstag*: in 1877, however, the party won 12 seats and attracted 9 per cent of the total German vote.

It was in these circumstances that in 1878 Bismarck carried an anti-socialist law providing for the dissolution of all social democratic, socialist and communist associations. It also included clauses threatening printers, booksellers and innkeepers with loss of licences if they collided with the law. As a result many Social Democratic institutions, including newspaper and publishing firms, went out of business and the powerful German trade unions, although not affiliated to the party, were affected too. Between 1878 and 1890, when the law was repealed after Bismarck's fall, 900 persons were expelled from their homes and about 1,500 imprisoned. Nonetheless, whatever Bismarck did either by way of repression or 'social insurance' he could not stop the advance of social democracy. The Social Democratic vote fell by a quarter in 1881, but was larger in 1884 than in 1878 and more than tripled in 1890.

Within the new German nation a largely insulated Social Democrat subculture took shape, always under the scrutiny of the Police. The Erfurt Programme (1891) was explicitly Marxist (there were fierce disputes about Marxist theory and tactics), and because the party was kept out of power it retained a belief in revolution without being prepared to make one.[5]

Unlike his opposite numbers in most other European countries, Bismarck was never a party leader, drawing his supporters out and encouraging them to participate in power. He made no effort to educate his country-men, and when he had to make constitutional statements fell back on unqualified support for the monarchy. This was to prove his own political undoing when a new German emperor, Wilhelm II, took over in 1890. Young, ambitious and more in tune with the restless mood of the new and richer Germany which had taken shape between 1871 and 1890, Wilhelm II was determined to make his own policies. The Chancellor had to go, and Germany entered a new phase, dangerous and wayward, in its history.

What remained was the national ideology which Germans had fostered in place of liberalism. Bismarck spoke the language of duty, but many German exponents of national power expressed their ideology in language that could veer between sentimentality and totalitarianism. For the National Liberal Professor Heinrich von Treitschke, the worst sin of the state was feebleness and its highest moral duty was to increase its power. Only great and powerful states deserved to exist. It was the great sociologist Max Weber, however, who emphasized most strongly that unification in 1871 was a beginning for Germans and not an end. In his inaugural lecture delivered at Freiburg University in 1895 he demanded that Germany should become a world power. Unless unification became the 'starting point for a German *Weltmachtpolitik*', 1871 would seem like 'a youthful folly, which the nation committed in its declining days and would have been better dispensed with because of its expense'.

Nations and empires

No account of nation building in the nineteenth century would be complete if it dealt only with Germany and Italy or even with those two countries and the multinational Habsburg Empire. Nationalism was a force in all parts of Europe, associated in many instances (as in Austria-Hungary) with partition as much as with unification. It was also associated, however, with dreams of huge national territories on a new map of Europe, including a revived Poland that would cross the existing frontiers of dynastic empire.

The idea of 'nation', emotive and rhetorical, was different from the idea of 'region' and drew on a different (if related) set of symbols. In both cases history, including distant history, was evoked, history that could, if necessary, be invented. In both cases there were strong correlations with religious differences, and religious revivalism could spur on 'national awakening'. At the same time the religion of the nation (or state) was sometimes the religion of those who had no other.

In the west of Europe was Ireland, an agrarian and largely Roman Catholic appendancy of a Protestant and increasingly industrial Britain (with Irish industrialization concentrated in the Protestant north). There were people of Irish origin scattered throughout the British Empire and Irishmen serving in the British forces, but Ireland's representatives in the Westminster Parliament remained hostile to the Act of Union, the existence of which was reaffirmed in 1886 when the Liberal Party split on the issue. A 'Home Rule' Irish Party had been founded in 1870 which in 1878 chose Charles Stewart Parnell as its leader. He remained in that position until 1889 when his political career was ruined in a much publicized divorce case. In a different part of Europe's west, Flemish nationalism was asserted inside Belgium, with demands being made as early as the 1890s for the use of the Flemish language in the Army, in courts, in schools, and in the University of Ghent.

In the north of Europe was Norway, an independent-minded community of farmers and fishermen, largely Protestant and still tied to Sweden by the settlement of 1815 in which it had been treated as a pawn. The Norwegians adopted and fostered their own national language, *Landsmaal*, had their own Parliament (*Storting*) and after constitutional disputes secured their own control over ministers (but not over foreign policy) in 1884. In Finland, following Tsar Alexander I's granting of a measure of self-government to his new subjects in 1819, a four-Estate Parliament (*Landtag*) met regularly after 1863, and in the same year Alexander II issued an edict obliging officials and courts to accept documents and pleas in the Finnish language. A small Finnish Army was created (the men were selected by lottery) between 1877 and 1878.

The Russians, for all their repressive policies inside their own borders – in the Baltic areas as well as in Poland and the south – often advocated action outside. The support they had given to the Greek cause during the Greek struggle for independence was extended now to Slavs both in the Ottoman and the Austro-Hungarian Empires. It was not a coincidence that in 1867, the year of the Dual Monarchy's foundation, the second Pan-Slav Conference was held in Moscow. Yet Pan-Slavism in its later phases was an imperialist rather than a nationalist movement and could be identified with reactionary philosophy and policymaking. Danilevski's *Russia and Europe* (1869), which went through five editions before the end of the century, not only unabashedly proclaimed Slav superiority but extolled Russia's 'special mission'.

Relations between different Slav communities were as complex as their relations with the empires of which they formed a part, as had been demonstrated before 1867 at the Slav Congress in Prague in 1848. Slavs lived in large numbers inside the boundaries of the Ottoman Empire, but there were other submerged nationalities, including often sizeable 'pockets' of German-speakers who had migrated across the centuries. The different minorities within the Ottoman Empire, some of whom had been converted to Islam, enjoyed varying and fluctuating degrees of autonomy and cultural expression. 'Massacres' made news, but there was usually a high degree of tolerance, not least to Jews – and Gypsies – both to be tragic victims of twentieth-century racist nationalism grounded not in empire but in ideology. Turkey too had its nationalist movement. Confronting an autocratic Sultan, Abdul Hamid II, 'Abdul the Damned', who ruled from 1876 to 1908, the 'Young Turks' secured from him the setting up of a parliamentary system in 1907 before deposing him and replacing him with his younger brother Mohammed V.

Russian nationalism was itself a powerful, if latent, force within an expanding Russian Empire. Alexander II's emancipation of the peasants in 1861, however, without a revolution, did not turn them into a politically conscious force at the base of society. They were no longer forced to provide dues in cash, kind or labour to owners, but they had to pay redemption money, often borrowing it from the state. They held their land not as private property but as a share in the collective property of the village community (the *mir*). They were not free to move to the towns. The sense of Russia being distinctive in Europe in its institutional frame was strong, although land problems were common to most parts of eastern Europe, particularly as population grew.

In most, but not all, of Europe, great power rivalry influenced patterns of allegiance and of aspiration. The Irish had something in common with the Poles, but they were not subject to influences from three directions – Austria, Russia and Prussia – as were the Poles. Nor, for all the religious differences, were there any places outside the Balkans where local populations included both Christians (of various sorts) and Muslims. It was not until after the First World War – and then not completely – that the map of Europe began to show most of its boundaries as national boundaries, and even then it was to reflect imperfectly, as any map must, the distribution of 'nationalities', some of whom thought in terms of bigger affiliations, 'Pan-Slav', Pan-German or 'Pan-Scandinavist'.

The nineteenth-century developments within the Habsburg Empire (itself appealing to history) were always revealing, for within its extensive frontiers nationalism, including German nationalism, could express itself at the same time in pure and in perverted form. When Hungary secured equal rights in 1867 and the Empire became a Dual Monarchy (Franz Josef was crowned with the crown of St Stephen in Budapest), there were some Hungarians, as there had always been some Austrian Germans, who hoped that moderate policies would be followed towards the other national minorities. Yet most Hungarian nationalists cared little for such considerations. Their intensely proud nationalism reached its nineteenth-century climax in 1896 with the celebration of the 'millennium' of Magyar power on the Danube.

The position of the Czechs was often equivocal. After the founding of the Dual Monarchy they were unable to secure similar arrangements in Bohemia, and they went into total opposition to centralizing 'liberal' administrations in Vienna from 1867 to 1879. ('Liberalism' in the Austrian Empire at this time had no concern for anything other than German nationalism.) They returned to the Vienna Parliament only under Count Taaffe's Conservative regime, which came into power in 1879. Thereafter, a Czech university was established in Prague in 1882, and local officials were obliged after 1886 to use Czech as well as German. There was also a Czech majority in the Bohemian Diet.

Disturbing 'ups and downs' – to be so prominent in twentieth-century Czech history – continued, however, for as Czech demands increased in strength Prague was put under martial law in 1893. For two years there was the most severe repression, including the end of press freedom and trial by jury. A lull followed, during which Professor Masaryk and a new generation of Czech nationalists were able to develop their philosophy of 'realistic' nationalism, which included the necessity of joint action between Czechs and Slovaks.

Masaryk was friendly to Russian-orientated Pan-Slavism, recognizing that it was always something more or less than an instrument of Russian foreign policy; but Pan-Slavism met with little support among the Poles, or immediately after 1878 from the Croats and Serbs. This was because in 1878, after the most serious and the most significant of the nineteenth-century Near Eastern crises, the Russians threw all their weight behind the creation of a new big Bulgaria, carved out of the disintegrating Ottoman Empire. The politically active Slav-speaking Bulgars had pushed demands for increased use of their language since the 1860s, and in 1870 the Sultan, pressed by Russia, had recognized the ecclesiastical authority of the Patriach of Bulgaria as head of a Bulgar Church which no longer accepted the authority of the Patriarch in Constantinople.

In 1875 mountain revolts in the Ottoman provinces of Bosnia and Herzegovina adjacent to the Austro-Hungarian border triggered off this crisis. They were occasioned by a bad harvest in 1874 which drove peasants to flee from Turkish tax collectors, and as revolt spread it drew in volunteers from Serbia, Croatia, Slavonia, Slovenia and even Russia. There were also Garibaldists from Italy. Many peasants were killed, and the roads were crowded with large numbers of refugees; more than 100,000 left Bosnia in conditions of great hardship.

A subsequent uprising which followed in 1876 in the Bulgarian provinces of the Ottoman Empire, was put down savagely, and as news

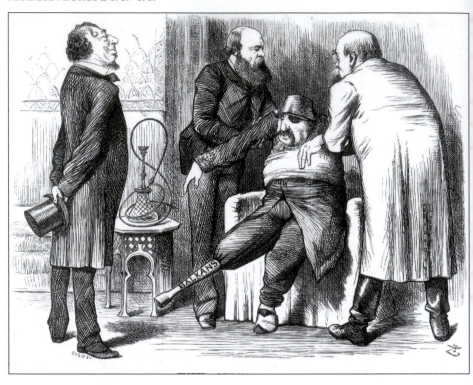

Plate 3.6 *The New Leg.* This cartoon from the periodical *Punch* was accompanied by the caption: 'Dr Benjamin Disraeli. "Cheer up, Sir, Cheer Up! You'll find it so much better than the old one!"' However, the patched-up Sultan of the Ottoman Empire recognizes that British repairs to his failing 'body politic' are not enough to enable the empire to stand alone.

spread the principalities of Serbia and Montenegro declared war on the Ottoman Empire, having agreed beforehand that Serbia would annex Bosnia and Montenegro Herzegovina. Serbia was quickly defeated, but Montenegro held its own, and the crisis reached its climax when on 24 April 1877 Russia declared war on the Ottoman Empire, backed by Pan-Slavs who were as much opposed to the Austrian Empire as they were to the Ottoman Empire. The campaign was not well handled, but it ended in disaster for Turkey. The Russians entered Sofia in January 1878, and as they swept forward to Constantinople, the Turks sued for peace.

In March 1878 the Treaty of San Stefano, in effect dictated by Russia, was signed between them. Romania, Serbia and Montenegro were recognized as completely independent national states, and an enormous new principality of Bulgaria was created, reaching from the Black Sea to the mountains of Albania. It even included a stretch of the Aegean coast. This was a Pan-Slav peace, although it divided the Slavs against each other and left Bosnia and Herzegovina under Turkish suzerainty.

This was a crisis that could not be 'localized'. It stirred and divided foreign public opinion at the same time as it provoked conflicting foreign policies in Europe's major capitals, with the main divisions of opinion about what was happening and how to respond to it appearing in the country farthest away from the action, Britain. There the liberal Gladstone – a very different kind of liberal from Cavour or from the German National Liberals – emerged from retirement to support the Bulgarians. Thundering against Turkish atrocities, he drew on – or rather was guided by – popular liberal enthusiasm expressed at huge public meetings and demonstrations. He knew little of the Bulgarians, but then he knew even less of the Afghans when in 1879 he urged a large and enthusiastic popular audience in Scotland to 'remember that the sanctity of life in the hill villages of Afghanistan, among the winter snows, is as inviolable in the eye of Almighty God as can be your own'. Moral and political principle 'passes over the whole surface of the earth and embraces the meanest along with the greatest in its unmeasured scope'.

The Conservative Prime Minister, Disraeli, highly suspicious of Russian designs in the Balkans and further afield – and afraid of Russia gaining access to the Mediterranean through the Black Sea – tried to eschew all moralizing. Britain's interests mattered just as much to him as German interests did to Bismarck. There had been divisions in Austria too before San Stefano. Should it become involved with Russia in the partition of the Ottoman Empire? Should it resist a further growth of Russian power on its borders? Should it take independent action? Even before decisions had to be taken, it was apparent that earlier agreement reached between Austria, Russia and Germany (the Three Emperors' League) to resist revolution and to maintain the status quo was a broken reed.

As a bilateral peace San Stefano went too far to be acceptable to the other great powers. Indeed, in February 1878, before it was signed, Disraeli had ordered a British fleet to sail through the Dardanelles and anchor off Constantinople. He was determined to demonstrate Britain's interest in the survival of the Ottoman Empire. And after the signing of the treaty in March 1878, Austria proposed, with British support, that it be referred to a congress of the great powers. The Russians had to give way, and the Congress was held at Berlin during June and July 1878, with Bismarck willingly offering to play the part of honest broker. Unharassed by any expressions of free public opinion inside his own country, he was unwilling to give Russia a free hand against Austria; and in 1879, when the crisis was over, his support of Austria was to be enshrined in a dual alliance of the utmost long-term significance. Yet in 1877 he had taken no steps to restrain Russia from attacking the Ottoman Empire, and in a famous speech, contrasting in content and style with Gladstone's great speeches on this issue, he argued that 'the Eastern question' involved 'no German interest which would be worth the bones of a single Pomeranian grenadier'.

Plate 3.7 The Congress of Berlin, June 1878. The Congress consisted of what were know as the 'Great Powers' of Europe. They were Germany, Russia, Austria-Hungary, Turkey, France, Britain and Italy. Chancellor Bismarck, centre stage in this picture presides over proceedings.

Attended by the chief ministers of the great powers, including Disraeli from London and Julius Andrassy from Vienna, the Congress of Berlin was the last glittering gathering associated with what came to be thought of after the First World War of the twentieth century as the 'old' European diplomacy, the diplomacy in which Bismarck excelled. Essentially, the Congress was a 'carve-up'. The Ottoman Empire was 'saved' and its integrity guaranteed, but it lost most of its European territories to the new national states. Following San Stefano, Romania, Serbia and Montenegro were recognized as independent, but the big Bulgaria was split into three. One part became an autonomous principality; the second became an Ottoman province under a Christian Governor; and the third, Macedonia, was handed back to the Sultan. (In 1885 the first and second portions were to become united under a Battenberg – and not a Slav – King of Bulgaria.) Bosnia and Herzegovina were handed to Austria for occupation and administration, and Britain received Cyprus.

The Austrians expected to be welcomed, and sent the news of the decision of the Congress to Sarajevo by telegram ten days before it was printed in the newspapers of Europe's capital cities. They were not. Religion came into the reckoning when a green Islamic flag was flown outside the Sarajevo mosque, and it was only after victory in battle at

Klokoti near Vitez and an assault, house by house, on Sarajevo that they won control. The troops had been commanded by a Croat nobleman. There were some Austrians who had opposed the occupation, fearing that it would be dangerous to add millions of Slavs to their large ethnic minority, and the new provinces were neither added to Hungary nor kept by the Austrian government in Vienna. They became Crown lands, administered through the Minister of Finance.

There was little to enthuse about in Vienna. In London, however, there seemed to be. British jingoism in 1878 ('we don't want to fight, but by jingo if we do') showed that Britain was not immune to nationalist fever, although the jingoists were subject to fierce internal criticism. Disraeli exploited the jingoism when he talked of bringing back from Berlin 'peace with honour'. The Italians could never make that claim. They secured no territorial gains, and when the Italian delegate boasted on his return to Rome that he had kept 'clean hands' he was mobbed by his compatriots and thrown out of office.

The new Balkan nations, each of which moved quickly to develop all the familiar apparatus of nationalism – anthems, flags, schools and barracks – were not satisfied nations. Romania, which lost Bessarabia to Russia (only a part of the Russian share of the final carve-up), actually had fewer Romanians within its new borders than within its old, and Romanian eyes were turning longingly towards possible territorial gains in Hungarian Transylvania. Serbia, which aspired to become the Piedmont-Sardinia of the Balkans, was now confronted with increased Austrian dominion over fellow Serbs living within the boundaries of occupied Bosnia and Herzegovina. Bulgarians, who had been dazzled with the prospect of a big Bulgaria, saw their territories dismembered in the very year when they had been put together. Not surprisingly, therefore, the Balkans began to be thought of as 'the cockpit of Europe'. They were also, however (to use another contemporary metaphor), a 'cauldron', and out of the cauldron little but further trouble for Europe was to come.

Not all the problems were ethnic or religious, although Croatia was devotedly Roman Catholic and Serbia Orthodox. Ownership of land remained contentious. In 1876 the Turks had allowed serfs to free themselves by paying an indemnity, and many did so, but Austrian attempts to improve agriculture (without introducing a major land reform) were little appreciated. Serbia, dependent on Austria-Hungary for trade, resented Austrian economic and political power, and many of its citizens dreamed of a greater Serbia.

For the American historian and analyst of nationalism, Carlton J. H. Hayes, all that Berlin had done was to substitute for one sick man (the Ottoman Empire) half-a-dozen maniacs: 'For the Congress of Berlin drove the Balkan peoples mad.'[6] It is an inadequate and incomplete final verdict, but it points to another important conclusion. Insofar as there was madness in changing Europe, it would require more than *Realpolitik* to control it.

References

1. G. M. Trevelyan, *Manin and the Venetian Revolution of 1848* (1923) pp. vii–viii. A. J. P. Taylor took up and sharpened the phrase (A. J. P. Taylor, *A Personal History* (1983) p. 190).
2. Quoted in D. Hargreaves (ed.), *Bismarck and German Unification* (1991) pp. 23, 32.
3. A Roman Catholic critic of Bismarck, Edmund Jörg, feared after the victory of 1871 that the 'humanity and civilization of the nineteenth century will give way in its final third to a new iron age'. H. Böhme, *Die Reichsgründung* (Munich, 1967) p. 26.
4. See A. D. Chandler, *Scale and Scope, the Dynamic of Industrial Capitalism* (Cambridge, Mass., 1990) ch. 12.
5. The story is told briefly in G. Lichtheim, *Marxism* (1961) pp. 259ff.
6. See C. J. H. Hayes, *Essays on Nationalism* (New York, 1928) ch. 5, 'Nationalism and International War', for Hayes's views on the relationship.

Chapter 4

Rivalry and Interdependence, 1871–1914

'The causes of war'

As was fully revealed during the 1870s, there were many contradictory forces inside and outside Europe during the 44 years of European hegemony that separated the founding of the German Empire in 1871 from the outbreak of the First World War in 1914, a European war that became a world war. It was fashionable, indeed, during and after that war to look back and identify these contradictory forces, domestic and international, as 'causes' of the war, distributing blame. More recently the word 'origins' has replaced 'causes', with one American historian, L. Lafore, describing its 'long fuse'.[1] Before the period began Disraeli predicted what the future might be like when he told Parliament in 1871 that the war between France and Germany was 'no common war like the Crimean War, the Italian War or the Austro-Prussian War. It represented a greater political event than the French Revolution last century', adding percipiently that he did not say 'a greater, or as great, social event'. 'You have a new world, new influences at work, and unknown objects and dangers with which to cope.'

One identifiable force in the 'new world' around the turn of the century, militarism, was not new. It had never been confined to one country or group of countries, and in some places it had the force of a religion. Now it was intensified, and Disraeli's great opponent, Gladstone, saw it as the biggest danger in an unpredictable future. Brightly uniformed men on horseback were proud of their rank and of their code of honour, but they were proud too of their weaponry. There was a 300 per cent increase in the level of armaments, military and naval, in Europe between 1870 and 1914, made possible not only by decisions taken by political leaders but by the increasing wealth and advancing technology associated with industrialization.

Another force was autocracy, which was prominent on each side during the First World War when the Russian Empire was pitted against the

Habsburg Empire. In Vienna liberalism and populism had checked it. In Russia Tsarist authority went unchecked before 1905 except by assassination. Three attempts were made to assassinate Alexander II before he was killed by an anarchist's bomb in 1881. When the first Russian socialist party came into existence in 1883 it was organized not in Russia but in Switzerland, and when revolution came in 1905 in circumstances which the exiled revolutionaries did not plan or foresee, they arrived too late to influence events. Seventy thousand people were arrested and 15,000 people killed before the revolution was put down. As a consequence the Tsar summoned a national assembly (the *Duma*) which met in April 1906, but dissolved it after two months. Three more met before 1914, but they achieved little.

Autocracy was prominent in Germany too, where, if anachronistically, industrialization was accompanied by a 'neo-absolutist culture of the court' to which 'military brass' had special access. The annual cost of the court was more than the cost of the Reich Chancellor and his Chancellery, the Reich Justice Department, the Foreign Office (including the whole diplomatic corps) and the Colonial Office put together. The office of the Senior Marshal of the Court had an establishment of nearly 500 persons.[2]

A third force was imperialism, which usually referred to empires outside Europe rather than within it and to the fierce rivalry to gain profit as well as power. For 'realistic' politicians, particularly in Germany, imperial policies seemed capable of diverting attention from internal social conflicts. Fürst Bernhard von Bülow, who took over the Foreign Ministry in an important ministerial reshuffle in 1897 and was soon to become Chancellor, wrote in retirement in 1914, in a widely read book, that *Weltpolitik* (a world policy) was 'the true antidote against social democracy'.

A fourth force, more contentious and more difficult to pin down, was moral disintegration, whether expressed in demagogic leadership or in mass hysteria. 'The popular imagination is by no means a thing to be left out of account when calculating political probabilities', a writer in a popular journal, *Science Siftings*, stated in 1897. The word 'masses' came into increasing use during that decade and the next in Germany, France, Austria and Britain, where there was more talk of *Masspsychosen*, the psychology of the masses, than of 'popular imagination'. One of its manifestations was anti-Semitism. Jews became scapegoats in Berlin, Vienna, Moscow and Paris. And attacks on them contributed to the unleashing of forces that it was difficult to keep under control. In a much publicized study, *The Crowd*, the French sociologist Gustave le Bon shifted attention from individuals to what he called 'a collective mind'. One of his key phrases was 'social contagion'.

Militarism, imperialism, autocracy and social contagion were all related to each other in the work of the English liberal writer, J. A. Hobson, who influenced Lenin, born Vladimir Ulyanov, and who came to believe that successful revolution would come through war, as it eventually did in

Russia in 1917. In searching for the 'causes' of war, however, most people looked no further than what a German under-secretary of state (in August 1914, the month when European war broke out), called 'this d...d system of alliances, the curse of modern times'. In October 1916 the American President, Woodrow Wilson, whose country was outside the system, blamed the war upon 'a concatenation of alliances and treaties, a complicated network of intrigue and espionage which unerringly caught the entire family in its meshes'. The fact that the network had been developed to a considerable degree in secrecy was for Wilson an additional factor responsible. 'Leaks' of secret information, some of them deliberate, had served as a weapon of diplomacy. So, too, had espionage, code-breaking and other forms of military and naval intelligence.

The origins of the European treaty system lay far back in time, although it was under Bismarck – who worked in terms of options, preferences for deals with particular countries or groups of countries according to the circumstances of the case – that the system was perfected; in his view, as an instrument of peace. Already, before the founding of the German Empire he had proved himself a master of treaty-making, using resourcefully both open and secret treaties as best suited his purpose. And after 1870, when he proclaimed the German Empire a 'satisfied' power, he was determined to use treaties, as Metternich had tried to do, in order to keep other powers in order. His skill was unmistakable. So, too, was the military power that lay behind its deployment and which he had demonstrated before 1870 that he was prepared to use. In addition to knowing exactly what he wanted, he had a keen sense of exactly how far he dared go in order to get it.

Nonetheless, the Bismarckian peace was a peace in which rivalries and conflicts were exploited rather than eliminated, and Bismarck himself had no commanding sense of European interest. Sometimes the exploitation involved a degree of subtlety and subterfuge that generated new misunderstandings, not least in his own country. He himself remained prone to nightmares. If inside Europe there was often fear on the part of rulers, officials and large sections of the public, particularly fear of social revolution, there was always fear inside Bismarck himself.

It could be argued – after Bismarck was dead, of course – that the subsequent hardening of the European alliance system into rigid blocs after 1890 was caused by the fact that Bismarck was succeeded by lesser men than himself. He had, after all, maintained peace in a period of considerable economic, social and cultural change, where Germany was changing later and faster than many other countries. Yet the lesser men who succeeded him thought in terms of options also, including war as a legitimate continuation of policy. Another favourite word in their vocabulary was 'sphere of interest'. The term was used in relation both to Europe and, just as frequently, to the world. Britain was already a world power in 1871. Indeed, it had been one since the eighteenth century, and over a long period of time it had identified its own 'spheres of influence', extending the notion in the late-nineteenth century to include what Lord Rosebery, a Liberal imperialist, called 'precautionary' zones that other powers might claim. Germany, which was not a world power in 1871, developed a conscious thrust to become one only after the fall of Bismarck in 1890.

There was intellectual as well as economic backing for Wilhelm II's professed desire to wield a world trident. The economist and economic historian Gustave Schmoller predicted in 1890 that the great world empires of the twentieth century would be Germany, Russia, Britain, the United States and possibly China. Europe, it was claimed, was too small and crowded. Expansion was necessary. Moreover in Europe itself Germany was 'encircled'. After 1897 its leaders wished to break through – and out. And this inevitably implied confronting Britain.

The Bismarckian alliance system

While Bismarck was in office the power equations were worked out rationally. His favourite preference was for mutual understanding among three great powers – Austria, Russia and Germany – with a fourth, Italy, added when necessary. This combination left defeated France and neutral Britain in isolation, and it was important for Bismarck that they should never work closely together over a significant period of time. This Bismarckian preference – always subject to review in the light of changing circumstances – was expressed in the League of the Three Emperors in 1873 (Figure 1).

Fig. 1

Britain   Germany —— Russia —— Austria + + + + + + Italy

France

Key (for figures 1–8)

———   alliance
+ + + + + +   entente
- - - - - -   commitment to remain neutral if one of allied parties finds itself at war
· · · · · ·   commitment to cooperation over imperial issues
···············   naval agreement
←———   alliance/entente directed against

With their divergent interests, particularly in the Balkans, Austria and Russia were drawn into a common 'conservative' understanding with Germany similar to that when Metternich ruled in Vienna, to resist revolutionary forces, including one new force which had not been present in Metternich's time – the Workers' International which Marx and Engels monitored.

Even before the Near Eastern crisis of 1875 to 1878 exposed the problems inherent in this alliance, Bismarck had engineered or exploited a Franco-German 'war scare' that drove both Russia, inside his alliance system, and Britain, outside it, into common protests. 'Is war in sight?' a German newspaper headline asked after the French had passed a law in 1875 adding a fourth battalion to each regiment of the Army. The idea of a 'preventive' war by Germany so soon after 1870 was anathema both to London and St Petersburg.

It was not so much a combination of Britain and Russia that Bismarck most feared, but a combination of Tsarist Russia and Republican France. After the Congress of Berlin in 1878, which brought the eastern crisis to an end, his nightmares grew more frequent, for he realized that Russia was now an aggrieved as well as an 'unsatisfied' power: it could gain something from change, as France had done under the now deposed Napoleon III, although what Russians most wanted – access to the Mediterranean through the Black Sea – could scarcely be secured peacefully. The League of the Three Emperors had become a dead letter even before the Congress of Berlin, the work of which the Tsar was disposed to look upon as that of 'a European coalition against Russia under the leadership of Prince Bismarck'.

Bismarck's nightmares included what in his own lifetime was an unlikely Prussian isolation, and it was in the aftermath of the Congress of Berlin that he decided – in spite of bitter opposition from Emperor Wilhelm I, an uncle of the Tsar – to seek a Dual Alliance with Austria (Figure 2).

Fig. 2 (for key; see Fig. 1, p. 144)

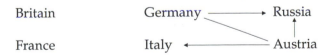

The result was a comprehensive treaty which Count Gyulov Andrassy, the Austrian negotiator, well judging Bismarck's fears, insisted should contain very specific clauses. The first clause stated that if either one of the two contracting parties, 'contrary to their hope' and against 'their loyal desire', should be attacked by Russia, the other party would go to its assistance with its 'whole strength'. The second clause, covering attack by any other power, pledged 'benevolent neutrality' at the least, unless Russia supported the other power 'either by active participation or by military measures which constitute a menace to the party attacked'.

The Dual Alliance between Germany and Austria, defensive though it was, proved to be far more lasting than any other nineteenth-century treaty. Concluded originally for a period of five years (Bismarck watched the dates of the expiry of treaties as keenly as Americans watched dates of presidential elections), the Alliance was renewed in 1883 and in 1902, and it lasted until the collapse of the Austrian Empire in 1918. It was, indeed, the prop of the pre-war alliance system which developed into a confrontation of alliances; and by drawing Germany into Austrian politics in the Balkans – Germany had other interests of its own there, particularly economic – it contributed directly to the war of 1914–18. Bismarck, however, certainly did not see future dangers in this way. Nor did the Marquess of Salisbury, then British Foreign Secretary, who hailed news of the Alliance from the Austrian government as 'good tidings of great joy'. For Bismarck, it would be necessary to supplement the Alliance with further treaties – if possible, with the Tsar, to whom, at the Emperor's insistence, details of the treaty were sent secretly.

Before further agreement with Russia, a revived Three Emperors' League was recreated in 1881. Differences between Britain and Russia in the Near East and Asia had predisposed Russia to sign it. The treaty was to be brought into operation in the first instance for three years. This time Bismarck had to win over the Austrians. Germany and Austria agreed that they would not assist Britain against Russia (the names of the countries were not spelled out), and Russia agreed to remain neutral in a war between France and Germany or between Italy and Austria. Attached clauses stipulated in some detail the policies that Austria and Russia would follow. The new League, far more formal and specific in its arrangements than the old League, was kept a secret from the other powers. It was renewed in 1884, and when it came to an end in 1887 (in the same year as other Bismarckian treaties) the implications were serious.

The arrangement reached in 1881 represented the best that Bismarck could obtain. And he soon had a supplementary agreement, at first sight of a remarkable kind. One year after the signing of the Three Emperors' League, a secret Triple Alliance was signed between Italy, Germany and Austria, with five years' duration (Figure 3).

Fig. 3 (for key; see Fig. 1, p. 144)

The Italians, so recently within the orbit of Vienna, naturally would have preferred an alliance with Germany alone, but Bismarck insisted on

Austrian participation. This time particular countries were named in what was a purely defensive treaty. 'In case Italy without direct provocation on her part should be attacked by France for any reason whatsoever, the two other contracting parties shall be bound to lend help and assistance with all their forces to the party attacked.' Austria did not insist on Italian help against a Russian attack. The Italian negotiator had already refused to promise military assistance to Germany against an attack from France.

Bismarck had no illusions about Italian military power, but the value of the Triple Alliance to him was obvious. Just as the League of the Three Emperors kept Russia apart from France, so the Italian Alliance kept Italy aloof from France and lessened the chances of what to Bismarck would have been an unnecessary conflict between Italy and Austria. Meanwhile, the two smaller powers, Serbia and Romania, both at this stage anxious to keep aloof from Russia, secretly moved into the German-Austrian orbit in 1881 and 1883 – the former through a ten-year alliance with Austria in 1881 and the latter through a five-year alliance with both Austria and Germany in 1883.

In 1884 Bismarck showed the range and resilience of his diplomacy when he cooperated closely with France, forced Britain into isolation, and secured the first colonial gains for Germany in Africa (Figure 4).

Fig. 4 (for key; see Fig. 1, p. 144)

British isolation was always possible in the nineteenth century, and sometimes the British themselves thought of it as 'splendid'. There was nothing splendid for Britain, however, about 1884. In several respects it was a year of mounting domestic tension and national humiliation, an *annus horribilis* in Gladstone's political career when far away in the Sudan General Gordon, whom he had dispatched there, met his lonely death. It was also a peak year in Bismarck's life.

The alignments of 1884 were short-lived, however, and by 1887 Bismarck was preferring a quite different option as far as Britain and France were concerned. A 'Mediterranean agreement' reached between Britain, Austria and Italy was designed to preserve the status quo in the Mediterranean, Adriatic, Aegean and Black Seas and to provide a barrier both against Russia and France (Figure 5).

Fig. 5 (for key; see Fig. 1, p. 144)

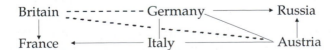

There was a bonus. The signing of the agreement persuaded the Italians to renew the Triple Alliance (albeit in changed form). There were two main reasons why Bismarck was anxious to secure its renewal even though in its new form it allowed for changes in the status quo for the benefit of two of the three partners. In France a new nationalist Minister of War, General Boulanger, Bonapartist in his sympathies and an 'apostle of revenge', seemed to be threatening the peace, and in Russia there was a clamorous agitation against the renewal of the Three Emperors' League on the grounds that it limited Russian freedom to manoeuvre in the Balkans. Earlier there had been tension in Austria and in Hungary, and Bismarck had to tell the Austrians that if they attacked or provoked Russia they would be doing so at their own risk and that Germany would not come to their aid under the 1879 treaty.

The year 1887 was as dangerous for Bismarck as the year 1884 had been propitious, although he secured from a newly elected *Reichstag* an increase in the size of the German Army which had been denied him a year earlier. He now felt it essential to secure an agreement with Russia, which he did in June – in a secret Reinsurance Treaty, signed in the month that the Three Emperors' League expired and one month after France (very fortunately for him) dropped Boulanger from office. By this treaty, which few knew about or suspected, Germany was assured of Russian neutrality if attacked by France, and Russia was assured of German neutrality if attacked by Austria or Great Britain (Figure 6).

Fig. 6 (for key; see Fig. 1, p. 144)

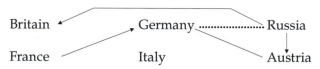

The Reinsurance Treaty was not incompatible with the Dual Alliance of 1879, but it required great nerve to maintain both it and the Dual Alliance at the same time. This was not Bismarck's favourite preference, for it pledged Germany to recognize Russia's historic rights in the Balkans and its 'preponderant and decisive influence' in Bulgaria. It was the most acceptable treaty in the circumstances, however, and it seemed effective enough to continue to ward off the dangers of a Franco-Russian alliance.

With great difficulty the treaty stood up to the strains of a year when Russia, still deeply embroiled in the politics of the Bulgarian dynasty, rearmed along the German and Austrian frontiers. Bismarck had to resort to other diplomatic and economic moves, such as restricting Russian credit in Germany and publishing the text of the 1879 Dual Alliance to show how deeply committed Germany was to the support of Austria. 'We Germans fear God and nothing else in the world' was his message to Europe. He was right to direct attention to the brute fact that in the last resort German diplomacy rested on superior power.

Bismarck's own position as juggler-in-chief, however, was limited in one crucial way. Unless he were backed by the Emperor, he would be nobody. This was the key relationship within the constitution of the German Empire, and Bismarck himself had so fashioned it. Before the Reinsurance Treaty came up for renewal in 1890 not only had Franco-Russian economic and military relations drawn a little closer (German withdrawal of credits was followed by Russian borrowing and purchase of military equipment in France), but the 91-year-old Emperor, Wilhelm I, with whom Bismarck had often quarrelled, but who had always yielded on major matters to Bismarck, however reluctantly, was dead. His first successor in 1888, married to Queen Victoria's daughter, reigned for only three months; his second successor, Wilhelm II, was barely 31 (Bismarck was nearing 75), and he was to reign until his deposition in 1918 after Germany's defeat in the First World War.

A new *Reichstag*, elected in 1890, reduced Bismarck's parliamentary support – the National Liberals lost 57 seats, and the Conservatives lost 24. By itself, however, this would not have mattered. Bismarck had bold plans for calling new elections and, if need be, for introducing martial law and amending the constitution. What did matter was that Wilhelm II, who had begun by admiring Bismarck, did not like this approach. He feared not only that Bismarck would lead the country into civil war but that he would establish his own dictatorship for ever. 'It was a question whether the Hohenzollern dynasty or the Bismarck dynasty should rule.' After weeks of growing disagreement following the elections, Wilhelm demanded Bismarck's resignation on 17 March, and nine days later they had their last meeting. 'I am as miserable as if I had again lost my grandfather', Wilhelm wrote to a relative. But he ended with the words 'Full steam ahead'.

It was of crucial importance at this point that the chief official in the German Foreign Office, Friedrich von Holstein, had long opposed the Reinsurance Treaty, which was due for renewal, on the grounds that it was incompatible with the Dual Alliance. The Emperor was willing to renew the treaty, but Holstein was able to persuade Bismarck's successor, General von Caprivi, a soldier with no previous diplomatic experience, that the Bismarckian system was too complicated. To him it seemed irrelevant that the Russians with a pro-German Foreign Minister wished to renew the treaty. A more open foreign policy would be desirable, one that would involve not only a loyal understanding with Austria but increasing friendship with Britain.

The Reinsurance Treaty was not renewed, therefore, and while Wilhelm II expressed continued desire for Russian friendship, a bilateral Anglo-German agreement was signed in July, involving an exchange of the island of Heligoland (which the British had held since 1795) for colonial territory held by the Germans in Africa (Zanzibar and Uganda). In May

1891 the Triple Alliance with Austria and Italy was renewed for 12 years. And when British ships paid a ceremonial visit to Venice and Fiume in June 1891 – in the same year Wilhelm visited London – there was much talk that the Triple Alliance would turn into a Quadruple Alliance with Britain as the fourth party (Figure 7).

Fig. 7 (for key; see Fig. 1, p. 144)

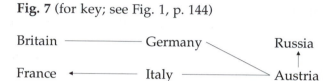

It did not need a Bismarck or a diagram to deduce what would happen next given the fears of isolation and the trust in the power of alliances that characterized this period of European history. Yet there were strong reasons why Russia and France should *not* join together. There were Frenchmen, committed to the cause of revolution, who feared any association with the most 'reactionary power' in Europe, and even more there were Russians who thought that France was still not only revolutionary 'at heart' but notoriously undependable.

The first moves were more dramatic than consequential. Thus, the Tsar listened bareheaded to the playing of the *Marseillaise* when French warships visited Kronstadt in July 1891. Eventually, however, in December 1893 (after the Germans had carried a new Army Bill and the French had been embroiled with the British in the colonial politics of the Far East) a secret Franco-Russian convention was signed. 'If France is attacked by Germany', the first clause read, 'or by Italy supported by Germany, Russia shall employ all her available forces to fight Germany.' The second clause dealt with the Triple Alliance: if the Triple Alliance powers mobilized, Russia and France would mobilize too, and the Treaty would remain in force for as long as the Triple Alliance lasted.

In the first instance the signing of this new treaty – which was to become the second cornerstone of the early twentieth-century alliance system – did not harden the European power blocs. They still remained side by side, not face to face. This was largely because Britain never joined any alliance with Germany, Austria, and Italy – either in the early or the late-1890s – but partly also because in 1897 Franz Josef, on a visit to St Petersburg, agreed with the Tsar to cooperate to maintain the status quo in the Balkans and the Straits. It was as important a feature of this agreement that Austria and Russia checked their own 'satellites', the new nation states, as that they themselves were in agreement.

As far as Britain's role was concerned, it was often easy during the 1890s to align all the European powers together – Triple Alliance, France and Russia – against Britain on colonial and other issues; and there was more cooperation between Germany, Russia and France than there was between

Germany and Britain, Russia and Britain, or France and Britain. Thus, Germany supported France in 1894 in blocking an African land deal between Britain and the Congo Free State, an enterprise in central Africa under the personal control of King Leopold of the Belgians; and a year later, to Britain's irritation, Germany, Russia and France intervened to check Japan after it had defeated China and went on to acquire bases for themselves on the Chinese mainland.

Almost every year there was some such episode. In 1896 Wilhelm II sent a congratulatory telegram to President Kruger, the head of the Boer Republic of the Transvaal, after the failure of the Jameson Raid (a freebooter raid by white settlers of British descent in South Africa that was arrived at with the connivance of Joseph Chamberlain, Britain's energetic and ambitious Colonial Secretary). When Britain went to war with the Boers in 1899 and soon became involved in a messy and surprisingly protracted conflict – a big power against a small one – most European countries expressed sympathy for the Boers. It proved possible, however, for Britain to survive any such international disapproval since it was secure in command of the seas. This was as vital an underpinning of Britain's 'isolation' as Germany's land power was of the alliance system to which it belonged. Neither now thought in terms of 'concert'.

The politics of empire

Before considering by what stages the European alliance system hardened after 1900 – and sea rivalry was to play an important part in drawing Britain into the system – it is necessary to consider in more detail the politics of late-nineteenth-century empire. They were even more complex than the politics of Europe and cannot be summed up in diagrams. Decisions were made not only in European foreign offices but on the spot, miles away, and many people were involved in making them. Pressures came from missionaries preaching the gospel and adventurers dealing in gold and guns. Communications were improving, but were still slow. Orders could arrive too late.

Until the end of the 1860s the word 'imperialism' – one of many *isms* of the late-nineteenth century – had been used mainly with reference to the France of Napoleon III. It was not until 1869 that a British writer drew attention in a magazine to what he called 'imperialism in its best sense', by which he meant 'the consciousness that it is sometimes a binding duty to perform highly irksome or offensive tasks such as the defence of Canada or the government of Ireland'.

Profit was not mentioned in this statement, although there was clearly money to be made out of foreign investment whether in territories controlled directly by European countries or in other countries open to 'informal empire', the empire of development and trade. The statement

Plate 4.1 *La leçon de Gymnastique de John Bull*. Drawn at the time of the Boer War, this French cartoon shows an outwitted, out-manoeuvred John Bull attempting to trap an unconventionally small, but typically troublesome, Boer soldier. The final frame shows an exhausted John Bull sending a telegram home to announce that 'the enemy has disappeared'. Meanwhile the Boer perches happily unobserved on his hat.

concentrated also on white settlement, whereas most of the 'colonial gains' between 1869 and 1900 were in the Tropics.

The gains in territory were striking in quantitative terms. The British Empire increased its territory by a half and its population by a third during the last three decades of the nineteenth century, although anti-imperialist governments were sometimes in power in London. (Gladstone never approved of imperial expansion.) Likewise, France, where the imperialists never had their own way, added 3.5 million square miles of territory during the last two decades of the nineteenth century. Germany too added 1 million square miles. Bismarck had once stated that his map of Europe was in Africa, and he loved to dissipate or to divert dangerous rivalries inside Europe by encouraging distant competition. Yet it was he who began the German colonial expansion.

Others, more committed than Bismarck, and with all the rhetoric of empire at their disposal, could follow expansion through to the point where it excited fear in Britain. Meanwhile, the old empires of Spain and Holland continued to exist on the map – the latter growing in wealth, if not in size – and the old empire of Portugal grew in both. Italy took part with little success in imperial competition (it failed in 1896 to establish power in Abyssinia), and Belgians, nominally without any empire, managed Leopold's Congo State until it was left to them in his will in 1889. Even the United States, with its long anti-colonial record, acquired colonies during the 1890s.

Statistics tell only a part of this story, which was usually told at the time in non-statistical terms – in maps, in adventure stories, in travel books, in popular songs, and in rousing speeches on flag-draped platforms.

Imperialism shared some of the same folklore as nationalism, for it always had its heroes and its myths. And like nationalism, it could claim that the world was being partitioned not so much between competing but between complementary imperialisms, each with its own 'mission'. Sometimes, indeed, the different imperialisms could come together, united in the cause of 'civilization' and 'progress'.

British spokesmen usually drew a sharp distinction between themselves and their 'kith and kin', and the 'natives' or 'aborigines' they conquered or controlled. In the first case – Canada and Australia were obvious examples – settlers, among them waves of new immigrants, acquired substantial independence during the last half of the nineteenth century. The federal government of Australia dates back to 1900. In the second case there was talk of 'burden', but there could also be exhilaration. There was also a will to 'get things straight'. 'We find by practical experience', wrote Sir Francis Younghusband, explorer of Central Asia (where British and Russian interests clashed in what was sometimes called 'the great game'), 'that the affairs of the world will not work while there is disorder about.'

So many people were involved in 'imperialist' adventures, at so many levels and in so many places, that it is difficult to generalize. In Africa, a scene of rivalry, there was a general sense of a 'dark continent' being explored and exploited, whereas in Asia, 'strange and mysterious', there were old religions and old cultures that could never be ignored. Before 1875 not 10 per cent of Africa had been appropriated by European nations, but India was on the eve of having Queen Victoria proclaimed Empress, a move initiated by Disraeli. It was easier to partition Africa than Poland, but it would always have been difficult to 'stabilize' central Asia or 'the Far East'.

By the last decade of the nineteenth century the question of 'the Far East', a term which reflects European dominance in the world, was brought to the fore not so much by direct European expansion as by the rise of an Asian power, Japan, which had already taken over much of the apparatus of European nationalism. (In 1880 the German bandmaster of British troops at Yokohama had been invited to set the words of a ninth-century hymn to music to provide a national anthem.) Japan was also in the first stages of an industrial revolution that was supported by the power of the state and which was to transform the whole basis of its power in the twentieth century. In 1894–95, war between island Japan and mainland China – the British noted the parallels – demonstrated both Japanese strength and Chinese weakness.

Was the Chinese Empire the Ottoman Empire of the Far East? France, Russia and Germany were able to put pressure on Japan to modify the Treaty of Shimonoseki (April 1895) and make gains for themselves. Yet before the century ended the anti-foreign Boxer Rebellion in China alarmed European countries and the United States more than anything that had happened in Japan. By 1908 China was to have a draft constitution – something that the Sultans had never been prepared to do much about in Constantinople – and in 1912 it was to become a republic.

Plate 4.2 *The Closed Door*, **11 July 1900**. As a fiercely determined *Europa* batters at the closed door of China, it triggers a bloody response (trickling under the door) with the Boxer Rebellion.

Looking at the 'imperializing' world as a whole – Africa, Asia, and the Pacific – the people involved in the intricate processes of expansion included explorers (Leopold, a latter-day *conquistador*, launched his African project at an international geographical congress in Brussels in 1876); missionaries of all denominations, spreading the gospel or rival gospels and much else besides, including education; emigrants, acquiring new homes, far from their places of birth, along with new lifestyles; businessmen, big and small, seeking new materials (as different as rubber, minerals, and vegetable oils) or new outlets for manufactured goods; contractors, the builders of cities, harbours and railways; soldiers, for the record of imperial achievement was never short on blood spilt in what were called, often misleadingly, 'small wars'; and administrators, also big and small, with some big enough to be called – and to think of themselves in Napoleonic terms as – 'pro-consuls'. Such were the big three of the late-nineteenth and early-twentieth-century British Empire: Evelyn Baring, first Earl of Cromer in Egypt, a country that linked Africa and the Ottoman Empire (as Napoleon, the First consul, had known); the first Marquess Curzon in Persia and India; and Alfred, first Viscount Milner, a new recruit, in South Africa.

The place of profit in this story is not easy to assess, although it was given a central place in theories of 'imperialism' that were developed on a Marxist basis by Lenin in the twentieth century. It was an English liberal writer on empire and one of its sharpest critics, J. A. Hobson, who had suggested that the mainspring of imperialism was to be found not in trade but in investment. Colonies offered new outlets for capital, and capital invested overseas could bring higher returns than capital invested at home; it could also provide employment and raise domestic standards of living. Hobson's *Imperialism: A Study* appeared in 1902, and Lenin took over the main elements of the thesis, fitting them into an extended Marxist chronological framework, according to which the age of imperialism followed naturally and inexorably from the age of European capitalism.

The explanation he offered was no more comprehensive than Marx's explanation of capitalism which was now being 'revised', particularly by Marxists in Germany and by Fabian socialists in Britain, many of whom had not read Marx. There are many examples of colonial expansion that can be explained only in non-economic terms: Russian expansion by land into Central Asia and towards the Far East in the nineteenth century was one variant of such expansion. Nor was it the case that investment followed the flag. Little British capital in the late nineteenth century went to the new territories painted red on the map, except South Africa. Far more went to Latin America and the United States. Norway, with an oceanborne commerce exceeded only by that of Britain and Germany, had no empire: it was not even yet a nation state.

The place of government in the story is almost equally difficult to assess in general terms, for imperial processes usually went on without break as governments changed; and any government could always be faced with *faits accomplis*, miles away, which it could not foresee or control. There were also many different and sometimes conflicting motives among 'imperialists' in European political parties and cabinets. Some thought of colonial territories providing outlets for surplus population. This, indeed, was a favourite conservative argument, advanced by people who had no connections with trade or investment. Others thought of power or prestige. Again this was conservative thinking, natural to men like Disraeli or Bismarck, although they were both clever enough to exploit it rather than to share it. Jules Ferry in the defeated France of the 1870s made much of *esprit* and *élan*: he also argued, whenever he was talking of places as far apart as Tunis and Tonkin, that if France did not create a new empire, it would 'descend from the first rank to the third or fourth'. Later in the century, Joseph Chamberlain, whose radical background in Birmingham civic politics made him think in terms of action, treated empire as 'underdeveloped estate'.

Even after Chamberlain had broken with Gladstone and the Liberal Party on the Irish issue in 1886, the surviving Liberal Party remained divided between Liberal Imperialists ('Limps') and men like Hobson, who were critical not only of the economics of empire but of the jingoism that imperialism encouraged in 'the masses'. These contradictions – and the dreams – are all present in Cecil Rhodes, who arrived in South Africa just when diamonds were discovered in Kimberley in 1870. He was interested in everything imperial – money, power, development, welfare, education – yet he admired Irish nationalism and gave money to Parnell.

The effect of non-European rivalries on European politics varied from year to year. So, too, did the particular rivalries that hit the headlines. By any standards, however, the years 1884 and 1885 stood out. These were years when the great powers met at Berlin to consider Africa, the first and last time that they did so. (The United States was one of them.) It was an impressive conference which coined the term 'sphere of influence' and which agreed, with little concern for African sensibilities, that the powers could, in effect, acquire African territories by possession, provided that they respected the claims of other countries and notified them of what they were doing. These were the years when Leopold's Congo State was recognized (suppression of slavery was made a condition) and when Bismarck made his 'bid for colonies'. Hitherto he had condemned 'our colonial jingos'. Now he found no difficulty in choosing the right language: 'colonies would mean the winning of new markets for German industries, the expansion of trade and a new field for German activity, civilization and capital' (in that order). New Guinea was involved as well as Africa, and after its non-Dutch territories had been partitioned between Germany and Britain, the Germans went on to acquire Samoa (not without argument) and gave Bismarck's name to an archipelago in the Pacific.

And all this did not exhaust the themes of 1884 and 1885. There was trouble for the British in India to the north-west and to the north-east. There was great alarm in Calcutta and London in 1884, when the Russians occupied Merv, a Turcoman centre that was only 200 miles from what was believed to be one of the key points on the road to India, Herat. To the east, when the King of Burma gave railways and other economic concessions to the French in 1885, the British sent him an ultimatum, captured him, and annexed Burma to India on 1 January 1886.

Other years of incident were 1896, 1897 and 1898. The first was the year not only of the Jameson Raid, but of the British conquest of the kingdom of the Ashanti on what was called the Gold Coast; of the French subjugation of Madagascar; and of the rout of the Italians by the Abyssinians at Adowa (a rare example of the defeat of a would-be colonial power at the hands of a non-European opponent). It was the year, too, when a French Army officer, Jean Marchand, was given orders to march into the Sudan, where the British General Horatio Kitchener had just defeated a native Sudanese army at Omdurman. (One of the young British officers present there was Winston Churchill.) Marchand declined to obey Kitchener's request to retire, and the impasse was reported back to Europe.

What happened next was felt later to have been of great significance, of more significance than it was. The French, represented by a new foreign minister, Théophile Delcassé, agreed to retire from the Sudan, and a more general agreement, reducing friction, was subsequently signed by the French and British in 1899. This was seen later as the beginning of a Franco-British *rapprochement*, which was to move through an *entente cordiale* in 1904 to a full Franco-British alliance during the First World War, although as late as 1900 a Franco-Russian military convention was still envisaging war with Britain.

Characteristically, the *entente*, signed by Delcassé, merely liquidated overseas rivalries: no mention of Europe was made in it. Characteristically, too, Britain's first move out of isolationism (just when the Boer War was coming to an end) had already been made – an alliance not with a European power, but with Japan – in January 1902. This might have been an alliance between Germany, Britain and Japan, for the Germans were interested in such an agreement at the time. As it was, however, Britain was to become further estranged from Germany in drawing closer to France between 1904 and 1914. Wilhelm II was fascinated by a *Weltpolitik* backed by sea power, as was recommended to him by some of his advisers, notably Admiral Alfred von Tirpitz, and Delcassé believed quite simply that Germany was France's 'hereditary enemy'.

World interdependence

Talk of friends and enemies among nations was becoming just as commonplace in the late-nineteenth century as talk of the need for competition between them, and the language of competition itself was influenced as much by biology as by economics. Darwin's theories of the 'survival of the fittest' were vulgarized in various forms (some, to use a later pejorative adjective, were blatantly 'racist') to cover the survival of the fittest among nations and to justify the triumph of the strong over the weak. Von Bülow, who became German Chancellor in 1900 – only the third Chancellor after Bismarck – was convinced that there was no such thing as permanent peace, nor should there be: 'War is an essential element of God's scheme of the world.'

Yet at the very time that such language was most fashionable – it was often nasty, and it was never profound – the facts of economics, if not all its theories, were pointing to an unprecedented degree of world inter-dependence. Never before had the economic ties binding different countries together been so close or so essential to the daily well-being of millions of people as they were in the quarter of a century before 1914. However much talk there might be once the First World War started of the need to move away in the future from 'the international anarchy' of the pre-war period, there was always contrasting talk when economics was mentioned of getting back to pre-war 'normalcy'. Only Marxists and a number of non-Marxist socialists saw the origins of the war in straight economic terms.

The interdependence rested, however, on European dominance and on a system of economic specialization developed to meet European interests. The first countries to industrialize in the Western world were now the richest – Britain, Belgium, Germany, France – but their industrialization had depended on imports from overseas. Cotton led the way and linked the interests of the still economically-backward plantations of the American south, with their slave workers, to the mills of one of the most economically-advanced regions of the world, industrial Lancashire with its confident factory owners and operatives and its busy commercial exchanges. Other textiles followed. By 1914 half the world's supplies of wool were coming from Australia and New Zealand, new lands of white settlement that were almost exclusively British (English, Scots, Welsh and Irish) in composition and background.

The great change during the last years of the century was the increasing dependence of Europe on non-European parts of the world for food as well as for raw materials for industry. The mid-West plains provided wheat (the value of United States exports of wheat increased more than 20 times between 1850 and 1914, although France and Germany did their best to maintain their own production); Argentina provided meat (refrigerated ships, first introduced in the 1870s, made this trade possible); the West Indies provided sugar (although European countries produced larger quantities of sugar from beet); New Zealand provided dairy products; West Africa provided cocoa and vegetable oils; India (and to a lesser extent China) provided tea; and Brazil provided coffee (64 per cent of Germany's coffee imports in 1914 came from Brazil).

These are only representative statistics, partial in their range of reference, and, like the statistics of empire, they tell only a part of the story. Alongside the maps painted in imperial colours in the new school atlases must always be set the maps of trade and communications. And alongside the chronologies of treaties and battles should be set the chronologies of the trade cycles – some short-term, with peaks and troughs in output, employment, prices, and incomes; and some long-term, covering movements of rising and falling prices (and innovation trends) over a whole generation. It is important to note that the general price level, which had been rising through the middle decades of the century, was falling between the mid-1870s and the mid-1890s, and that there was ample complaint of 'depression'. Some of it was misplaced. Low interest rates favoured particular forms of investment, and while profit margins narrowed, the real income of employed wage earners increased. In bad years, however, like 1902, many industrial workers in all countries – and service workers like dockers, the most 'casual' of all labourers – were thrown out of employment.

There was an interdependence of disaster as well as benefit. Many European farmers were ruined by imports of cheap American wheat in the 1880s. Protection helped them to only a limited extent – with France, most successful of the European countries in the pursuit of this policy, raising its tariffs on wheat regularly between 1881 and 1897; and with Germany protecting itself against both American and Russian wheat. France raised industrial tariffs too in 1892 – they amounted to more than a third on British manufactured goods – following in the wake of the United States. Britain, however, stood by free trade, although the area of cultivated land dropped by nearly 10 per cent between 1897 and 1912 and old industries with increasingly obsolete equipment were being hit hard by American and German competition.

The role of Britain was crucial to the working of the international system, even more crucial than the role of Bismarck's Germany was to the working of the post-1870 alliance system. In 1914 Britain was the only European country that was selling more goods outside Europe than inside it. It was also the world's greatest importer, banker and provider of business services (such as insurance). The Bank of England was a private institution. Behind the pound sterling was gold, and it was Britain's role as a free-trading country with a dominating interest in the world's commodity markets and a highly flexible money market that allowed the gold standard to operate as automatically as possible, free from intervention by govern-ments. The apparent automatism of this system, which relied on tacit understandings, contrasted with the contrivance of the political system and, even more, of the diplomatic system. Meanwhile, Britain exported capital as well as manufactures to the rest of the world: 43 per cent of the world's foreign investment in 1914 was British when the share of Germany was only 13 per cent and that of the United States only 8 per cent.[3]

The extent of interdependence was apparent in Europe itself. Half the total recorded trade of the world was made up of the exports and imports of seven European countries. Germany was Britain's main industrial rival inside Europe (the theme of a fascinating book, *Made in Germany* by Edward Williams, published in 1896), but Britain was Germany's best customer, and Germany came second only to India as a customer for British goods. British coal was being burned in Berlin when war broke out, and German sheet steel was being used to make ships for the British Navy. In France the building of blast furnaces was going ahead in 1914 with the help of German capital, and Germans were making chemicals in Russia – a hitherto backward country with a high growth rate in the immediate pre-war years and an unprecedented momentum in a few industrial regions. There were a few powerful international trusts and cartels, also, that cut across national boundaries, 'carving up' national shares by formulae that they devised for themselves.

It is important not to idealize economic interdependence. The international division of the world into 'green' (agricultural) and 'black' (industrial) regions was accompanied by a division of population inside countries between 'rich' and 'poor', and it was easy to think of both divisions as works of nature rather than as human dispensations. In Europe itself there were marked differences in the standard of living from Palermo to Milan and from Milan to Luxembourg and from Luxembourg to Lübeck. Nor did intervention by the state, whatever the reasoning behind it (welfare or power) necessarily make things better. Bureaucracy frustrated and intimidated. Social compensations, while necessary, were uneasy. Thus, German landowners benefited from agricultural protection, but German workers suffered. Finally, international horizons were changing. Europe dominated international trade, but the United States was forging ahead in production, benefiting from enormous reserves of materials, a huge home market, and an advanced labour-saving technology. In new industries – such as the automobile industry, as much a key industry in the twentieth century as railways had been in the nineteenth – the United States very quickly established a lead that was never lost.

The Japanese industrial revolution proved also that industrialization was in no sense a monopoly of white peoples. Japan was closest in political relations to Britain after the signing of the Anglo-Japanese Treaty, but it was Germany rather than Britain that provided models of economic development, and it was competition from Japan that was to break the world power of British textiles manufacturing, the original pioneering industry of Britain's industrial revolution. This was still around the corner, however, for in 1914 no less than 80 per cent of the huge output of the British cotton textiles industry was being exported. (India, whose own pre-industrial revolution textiles industry had been finally destroyed by British competition, was taking no less than 40 to 45 per cent of the whole.)

No account of interdependence would be complete without bringing in communications. Without railways and steamships (supplanting sail in the 1870s and 1880s) the unprecedented expansion in output and trade could never have taken place. Nor could the growth of the coal, iron and steel industries. Brazil got its first railway in 1854, Argentina in 1857, Australia in 1854, and South Africa in 1860; but by 1840 North America operated half the world's total mileage. Long before the coming of the automobile, therefore, it was the United States and Canada, following Britain's technological lead, that made the maximum use of the first stages of a communications revolution – the transportation phase – a necessary stage in economic integration.

Out of transportation other forms of communication developed (as the Canadian historian, Harold Innis, teacher of Marshall McLuhan, twentieth-century prophet of communications, realized). The British, with their scattered Empire, were carriers of the telegraph during the 1850s and 1860s, and it was in London that in 1851 Baron Reuter, born in Hesse Cassel, created his huge news agency based on telegraphy not carrier pigeons. The telephone, however, invented in Canada in 1876 by a Scottish immigrant, Alexander Graham Bell, was exploited far more effectively in Canada and in the United States than in Europe. Wireless, an invention of the 1890s, following in the wake of X-rays, was thought of at first as a substitute for communication by wire – Morse Code, not words, was its language – just as the automobile (a luxury product invented not in Britain but in France and Germany) was at first thought of as a horseless carriage. The aeroplane was still a dream, although it was a dream that enthusiasts believed would come true.

It was not until the second half of the twentieth century that people were to talk of a 'communications revolution', of 'media of communication', and of electronic 'global networks'. However, by the middle of the nineteenth century, the laying of the great transcontinental cables was already heralded as a way of uniting the world through science, and by the 1890s there was an increasing emphasis on the possibilities of further enhancing human interchange through 'wonderful new inventions'. It was not only to be business or government that was to benefit. Everyone, it was forecast, would gain, for the home would be penetrated as well as the factory or the office, now equipped with typewriters as well as telephones. Meanwhile, the daily newspaper, which made its way into the home along with the products that were advertised in it, would not have been able to provide the news that it did from all corners of the world had it not been for the telegraph, which in the words of Britain's last Victorian prime minister, Salisbury, 'combined together almost at one moment . . . the opinions of the whole intelligent world with respect to everything that is passing at that time upon the face of the world'.

Once again, it is important not to idealize. The telegraph could be used to twist diplomacy, as Bismarck used the Ems telegram from the Emperor

Plate 4.3 Woman worker operating a telephone exchange. It was the introduction of the telephone exchange system, accompanied by the growth of a network of telephone lines, which turned Graham Bell's 'toy' into an economic and social instrument of immense influence. The new system, like typesetting, also offered a welcome source of employment for single girls wishing to escape the drudgery of domestic service. Typists were first known as 'typewriters'.

on the eve of the Franco-German War of 1870, and the newspaper could be used to exploit prejudice as much as to spread facts. Even when the press was not controlled by government it could heighten tension behind the scenes, as it did at the time of Fashoda. Mass circulation was the object. The year 1896 saw the founding of Alfred Harmsworth's cheap *Daily Mail* in London. This was also the year when the young Guglielmo Marconi arrived in London from Bologna with his wireless devices and when Paris and London held their first cinema shows. By 1900 the *Daily Mail*, which trumpeted every new invention, had a circulation of over a million.

Le Petit Parisien was by then selling 800,000 copies, and *Berliner Morgenpost* was read by over half a million people. All these newspapers had far more to say of 'crises' and of 'rivalries' than of interdependence. And Marconi displayed his wireless not only to the Post Office but the British and Italian navies and armies. By the end of the century his newly founded company, which made no profits in the first 12 years of its life, had a German rival, the Telefunken Company which had the backing of Siemens and of the German government and court.

From crises to war

In retrospect, it is easy to overemphasize those aspects of European diplomacy between 1904 and 1914 that pointed towards the First World War, as many German official (and unofficial) papers do. There were, in fact, parallel efforts to regulate international rivalries and disputes, including an international conference on telegraphy in Berlin in 1904 called by Germany. A Nobel Peace Prize was on offer along with the other prizes for Science and Literature and was won in 1905 by the Austrian novelist Baroness Bertha von Suttner who had persuaded Nobel to endow it: her book *Die Waffen Nieder* ('Lay Down your Arms') went through 37 editions between 1889 and 1905.

More questions of contention were settled by arbitration during the last 20 years of the nineteenth century than during the previous 80 years, and there were over a hundred such arbitrations between 1904 and 1914. The article on arbitration in the eleventh edition of the *Encyclopaedia Britannica* (1910) stated optimistically that 'with the help of world-wide Press, public opinion can always be brought to bear on any state that seeks to evade its moral duty'. Unfortunately there was no consensus on what 'moral duty' meant. It was a concept too large for the lawyers, more so, indeed, than *raison d'état* had been a century before. Nor did it even carry the weight more recently attached to the term 'concert of Europe'.

Towards the end of the nineteenth century, in 1898, Tsar Nicholas II circulated to diplomats in St Petersburg an imperial rescript stating that 'the preservation of peace has become an objective of national policy', and a Peace Conference opened at the Hague, capital of Holland, on his

A VIEW OF THE STERN

ANCHORING OFF SPITHEAD

birthday in 1899. Salisbury said that it should not be taken 'too seriously', Wilhelm II in Berlin described it as 'utopian'. In fact, it adopted a number of 'rules of war' and strengthened the position of the Red Cross, as did a second Hague Convention in 1907, but it did nothing to reduce armaments, as Nicholas had hoped (if only for economic reasons).

Many of the people who attended the convention were powerful advocates in their own countries of increased expenditure on armaments – among them the British Admiral, Sir John Fisher, and the German military expert, Colonel Schwarzhoff, who told the convention bluntly that he did not see why Germany should be expected to restrict its military power because other countries could not afford to compete. The United States had among its representatives Captain Alfred Mahan, author of a classic study of naval power (published in 1890) which explained how essential power was to national prosperity. In 1900 the German geographer Friedrich Ratzel had urged Germany to 'be strong on the seas to fulfil her mission in the world'.

The naval armaments race between Britain and Germany, seeking always to catch up, was to speed up. One year before Nicholas produced his imperial rescript, Germany passed a new Navy Law announcing its intention to build a battle fleet. Without it, maintained Admiral Alfred Tirpitz, the initiator of the new policy, Germany would be 'a mollusc without a shell'. Navy Laws passed in 1898 and 1900 equipped Germany to take limited action in the North Sea, but not to challenge Britain on the oceans of the world. Thereafter, as questions of relative naval strength hit the headlines, there was no issue more calculated to disturb British policymakers and British public opinion.

In military strength Germany was far ahead. As early as 1894 Count Alfred von Schlieffen produced the first version of his battle plans to prevent the two new allies France and Russia from meeting on German soil. It was based on a lightning attack on France through Luxembourg and Holland. A further version was agreed upon in 1905, but this was amended in 1911. Instead of invading Holland German forces would move through Liège and across Belgium. By then the German military leaders were deeply concerned about the growing military strength of Russia, and the *Reichstag* agreed to the biggest increase ever in the German Army (to be financed from a wealth tax).

The Russians themselves had not demonstrated strength, either naval or military in the first of the great twentieth-century 'crises' which was of

---

Plate 4.4 HMS *Dreadnought*. The launch of the *Dreadnought* in 1906 enormously enhanced the fighting power of the British Navy. The first big-gun ship – it had ten of them, 12 inches wide – she made obsolete all existing battleships, including the British. Anglo-German naval rivalry became as familiar a topic to newspaper readers as it was to admirals, among them Britain's First Sea Lord, Admiral Sir John Fisher.

particular interest to Britain. In 1904 Russia was drawn into war with Japan in what seemed to be the inevitable culmination of a Russian policy of expansion in the Far East, an alternative expansionist policy to expansion in the Balkans (which had been checked following a visit by Franz Josef to St Petersburg in 1897). The Japanese, checked themselves by the European reaction to the Treaty of Shimonoseki which followed their success in their war with China, wished to turn the Russians out of Manchuria; the Russians, interested in Korea, wished to have it neutralized at the thirty-ninth parallel. (The Anglo-Japanese Treaty of 1902 had recognized that Japan was 'interested in peculiar degree' in Korea.) On 6 February 1904 Russian troops crossed the Yalu River, and two days later the Japanese occupied Seoul and attacked the Russian fleet at Port Arthur. All this was before either side had declared war. Japan did so on 10 February. In the war Port Arthur fell after a five-month siege, and in May 1905 a Russian fleet brought round the world from the Baltic was defeated in the Tsushima Straits.

France, Germany and Britain watched the war with varying degrees of concern, but it was the President of the United States who lent his assistance when a peace was signed in the United States at Portsmouth, New Hampshire, in August 1905 – itself a marked departure from nineteenth-century patterns of diplomacy. The peace recognized Japan's permanent interest in Korea, not dissimilar to Britain's interest in Egypt. A Japanese Governor was appointed in Seoul, and in 1910 the whole of Korea was annexed by Japan. The following year there was an uprising in China and 260 years of Manchu imperial rule came to an end.

Russian imperial rule had looked more shaky in 1905 than ever before as revolution threatened the country that for decades had been immune to it and that helped other countries to put it down. It began in January 1905 when a large and powerful crowd, led by an Orthodox priest, Father Gapon, was shot down on the Tsar's orders after demanding the summoning of an assembly based on universal suffrage, land reform and an eight-hour day. Defeat in the Russo-Japanese War added to what had long been endemic discontents and forced it out from the underground into the open.

Taken by surprise, the exiled socialist leaders, Lenin and Trotsky, returned to Russia, but not before there had been a wave of strikes and a mutiny on the battleship *Potemkin* which has passed into myth as well as into history. When they arrived in late November they created a Soviet in St Petersburg which was brutally crushed after 50 days of life, as were other peasant and workers' uprisings. The failure of the revolutionaries seemed decisive, but little imagination was shown in its aftermath. The nature of the peace blocked any thought of further Russian expansion in the East and thereby pushed Russia back again into Balkan politics.

This took some time, however, and meanwhile there had been a second crisis, which stood out as 'a turning point in the diplomatic history of

Plate 4.5 Barricade in Odessa, 1905. The events of Bloody Sunday, as the Tsar's attack on Father Gapon and his supporters became known, caused a wave of revulsion and violence to sweep the country. Events in Odessa were among the most bloody. In mid-June, striking workers were joined by the mutinous crew of the *Potemkin*. Despite barricades hastily constructed from trams, carts and iron railings, like this one on Niejinskaia street, it was said over 2,000 protesters died with another 3,000 gravely injured in clashes with the Tsar's forces.

modern Europe'. It began not with a revolt but with an agreement. An *entente cordiale* between Britain and France was reached in 1904 – an *entente*, not an alliance – which settled longstanding colonial differences and included an understanding that in two of the north African territories in the Ottoman Empire, France would take no further steps to hinder British activity in Egypt and Britain would take no further steps to hinder any French activity in Morocco. The German government had never believed that an *entente* of this kind between Britain and France was possible (it still seemed possible to some Germans that Britain could be drawn into an alliance with Germany), and it now determined to test it by a counterstroke. Wilhelm II, who was *en route* for a Mediterranean cruise, was induced to disembark at Tangier in Morocco and pay his respects to the Sultan in March 1905, thereby providing an opportunity both for a naval demonstration and for a declaration of German interest in the affairs of Morocco 'not only on economic grounds, but far more to maintain her prestige'.

This was a dangerous form of counterstroke that was likely from the start to be counterproductive, and when the idea was first proposed by

Bülow and Holstein, Wilhelm himself did not like it and the visit was postponed until March. He was right to have had doubts, for the effect of his speech, which hit the headlines, was to strengthen the *entente*. First, however, there was a pyrrhic victory. When Germany demanded that France should agree to submit the Moroccan question to an international conference, the French government, fearing war, accepted the demand, and Delcassé resigned in protest. Not surprisingly, he became a national hero. Also not surprisingly, when the international conference was held at Algeçiras in Spain in 1906, all countries except Austria supported the French case. Italy, which by a treaty with France in 1900 had recognized French interest in Morocco in return for French support of Italian interest in Tripoli, stood by this arrangement, although still a member of the Triple Alliance. Another supporter of France was the United States. Britain and France were drawn closer together. The least of all the surprises was that Holstein resigned.

The following year, the full implications of the counterstroke became apparent when Britain, after long negotiations, reached an agreement with Russia designed to reduce frictions. Like the *entente cordiale* it dealt directly only with issues outside Europe, but it had obvious European implications, given the existence of the Franco-Russian Alliance, and the French naturally gave it their full support. The agreement partitioned Persia into 'spheres of influence' and recognized Britain's interests in the Persian Gulf, Afghanistan's neutrality was to be respected, and Tibet was to be treated as a buffer state. Nothing was said about the old issue of contention between Britain and Russia – the 'Eastern Question' – except that the territorial integrity of the Ottoman Empire was guaranteed and that the British would show goodwill if at a later date there were to be international discussions about the Black Sea and the Straits. The opening of Constantinople to Russian warships was a Russian objective that had always been opposed by Britain from the days of William Pitt.

Wilhelm II had every reason to be disturbed by this arrangement. He had, in fact, signed a short-lived alliance with the Tsar at Björko in 1905, which failed – on the surface at least – because it was pushed too far and too fast. Before the Russian-British agreement was reached, Holstein had talked (not for the first time) of German 'encirclement' (*Einkreisungspolitik*). Now Wilhelm became conscious of his own imminent isolation: 'A nice outlook. We must bargain the future of the Franco-Russian Alliance, the Anglo-French *entente*, and an Anglo-Russian *entente*, with Spain, Italy and Portugal as secondary satellites.' Isolation was the wrong word, however. There remained the defensive 1879 Alliance with Austria which had never been designed to be exclusive. Between 1907 and 1914, however, it was to drag Europe into the worst war in its history (Figure 8).

The significance of the alliance was soon tested in what came to be called the 'Bosnian ordeal' of 1908–9 which had its origins in 1903 when the Obrenovic dynasty was overthrown in Belgrade and a new Serb dynasty favourable to Russia, the Karageorgenics, brutally seized power.

Fig. 8 (for key, see Fig. 1, p. 144)

The balance had changed, and in 1906 Austria-Hungary, fearful that Serbia was following in the path of national resistance that Italy had followed earlier in the nineteenth century, imposed import duties on Serbia's main export, pigs, beginning what became known as the 'Pig War'. When two years later the Young Turks disposed of the Sultan, an opportunity was provided for taking other measures and the Habsburg Foreign Minister, Baron Aloys von Aehrenthal, announced the full annexation of Bosnia-Herzegovina on 5 April 1908. By the terms of the Treaty of Berlin in 1878, Austria had been empowered to 'occupy and administer' the Turkish provinces of Bosnia and Herzegovina, and one of the confidential stipulations in the Three Emperors' League agreement of 1881 was that Austria-Hungary reserved 'the right to annex the provinces at whatever moment she shall deem opportune'. Nonetheless, the news of the annexation without preliminary warning in October 1908 shocked not only Serbia, as Aehrenthal had intended it to do, but Russia, which he had not intended to do. Russia now offered support to Serbia which wished to take over the provinces itself.

Tension mounted, but peace was preserved after the Russian Foreign Minister, Alexander Izvolsky, who had been engaged in earlier talks with Aehrenthal, advised Serbia to 'remain quiet... and ... do nothing which could provoke Austria and provide an opportunity for annihilating Serbia'. As a result the Austro-Hungarian and Turkish governments signed an agreement in February 1909 under the terms of which Austria-Hungary acquired full rights over Bosnia, withdrew from the Sanjak of Novi-Bazar, guaranteed full freedom of religion for Bosnian Muslims, and paid an indemnity to Turkey. But even then the crisis continued for several months.

The fact that there was no European war in 1909 offered no guarantee that war on such an issue could be avoided in the future since the only reason why Russia ultimately did not press the issue was that Germany backed Austria without qualification. Wilhelm had disliked the annexation, which he heard of as a *fait accompli* and which seemed to undo 20 years of increasingly close German cooperation with the Ottoman Empire, part of a *Drang Nach Osten*, which included the German-backed building of a railway from Berlin to Baghdad. Yet as the crisis continued Germany gave Austria a *carte blanche* and sent to Russia what was in effect an ultimatum stating that, like Serbia, it should accept the annexation without question. Izvolsky concluded that he had no alternative but to give in. Any possibility of a revival of the Three Emperors' League, which Aehrenthal had thought possible, was now lost for ever.

This time there was not even a pyrrhic victory for Germany. Wilhelm had stood by his ally 'in shining armour', as he put it, but it was his ally who had chosen the issue and who had led Germany along. Austria, unbacked by Britain, almost immediately signed a secret treaty with Bulgaria, a further threat to Balkan stability; Russia quickly recovered from any diplomatic humiliation and increased its armaments programme (ironically drawing on the German armaments industry); and Serbia, which had to sign a humiliating declaration that it would 'modify the direction of her present policy towards Austria-Hungary, and live in future on good neighbourly terms', waited for revenge. France became increasingly suspicious of German policy, and Britain augmented its programme of naval construction.

Before two Balkan wars further disturbed the relations between empires and nations in 1912 there was a second Moroccan crisis, again directly focused on Germany and France. A Berber rebellion in Morocco in 1911 provided the excuse for France to send an expedition to occupy Fez, the Moroccan capital, and this in turn provided the excuse for Germany to send a battleship, the *Panther*, to the Moroccan port of Agadir to protect German nationals. (There were none in Agadir, although a year earlier the French had arrested three German deserters from the French Foreign Legion at Casablanca.) The ensuing crisis lasted for several months as the Germans put pressure on the French to offer the French Congo as 'compensation' for recognition of their claims in Morocco. The French government then in power was keen to reach a bilateral understanding with Germany but the British on this occasion were more anti-German than the French.

It was a Liberal leader and future prime minister during the First World War, David Lloyd George, who caught the mood. He had hitherto been known as an advocate of friendship with Germany and, as Chancellor of the Exchequer, as an opponent of heavy British naval expenditure on giant Dreadnoughts. Now in a widely reported speech he declared that 'peace at any price would be a humiliation intolerable for a great country like ours to endure'. When all that the Germans could secure from the French in an agreement of November 1911 was the handing over of small sections of the French Congo in return for recognition of the French protectorate over Morocco, it was their turn to feel humiliated. And as they blamed Britain more than France, Tirpitz used the crisis to try to gain support for an enlarged naval programme.

It was during this crisis that details of military and naval cooperation between France and Britain in case of war were settled. Moreover, since the French government had seemed too willing to reach a political accommodation with Germany, it was replaced by a 'patriotic' government headed by Raymond Poincaré. Finally there was an Italian epilogue to this crisis that led almost immediately to a broader war. Seeing the weakness of the Ottoman Empire in Africa, Italy declared war on Turkey in September

1911 and landed troops in Tripoli. The Turks soon ran into difficulties, and the war spread from Africa to the Dodecanese Islands. When the beleaguered Turks closed the Straits, Russia protested, triggering off a new Balkan crisis that was to lead directly to war. Once again Serbia, watching with envy Italian advances in Tripolitania, Cyrenaica and the Mediterranean, was a key player in the scenario. In March 1912 it joined in alliance with Bulgaria and later Greece, setting out to share the spoils in a partition of the Turkish Balkans. Serbia was to gain lands on the Adriatic, part of a greater Serbia; Bulgaria was to acquire Macedonia; and Greece was to take Salonika. It was a fourth country, mountainous Montenegro, adjacent to Serbia, that declared war on Turkey on 8 October 1912, with the immediate consequence of forcing the Turks to make peace with Italy. Its further consequence was to alarm both Austria-Hungary, fearful of Serbian aggrandizement, and Russia, fearful that Bulgaria would take possession of Constantinople.

It was not the League of Balkan Powers, however, but the great powers that worked out a settlement in London in May 1913. They even drew closer together in the process. And they did not intervene when a second Balkan war started almost at once over the division of the spoils; a bigger Bulgaria attacked both Serbia and Greece, Romania attacked Bulgaria, and the Ottoman Empire recovered Adrianople. Nor did they intervene in the Peace of Bucharest, arrived at by the Balkan states themselves, which forced Bulgaria to disgorge almost all its gains of the first war.

Gains made by Serbia, which seemed yet again to be playing the part of the Piedmont of the Balkans, angered Austria-Hungary, and when the Serbs contemplated a further move into Albania, Austria-Hungary secured German backing. In October 1913 Wilhelm II promised Field-Marshal Conrad von Hötzendorf, who had been Austrian Chief of Staff since 1906, that if Austria marched against Serbia (Hötzendorf had been pressing for this since January) he would go with him, 'ready to draw the sabre if ever your action makes it necessary'. Nor would he be the only one. In March 1913, Germany had introduced its new Army Bill designed to put it ahead of Russia in the following year. The Russians responded by increasing their own forces, with a target of an extra 40 per cent by 1917, thus clashing not only with Austria-Hungary but with Germany, which now sent a military mission to Constantinople.

'Russo-Prussian relations are dead once and for all', Wilhelm recorded in an excited minute that would have shocked Bismarck. 'We have become enemies.' The knowledge that Russia was growing stronger each year gave weight to the military judgement that if Germany did not go to war in 1914 it would not be able to stand up to a conflict that was now inevitable. Early in that year the Austrians decided to start military manoeuvres in Bosnia, knowing that they would provoke the Serbs.

The final crisis began on 28 June 1914 when the heir to the Habsburg thrones, Archduke Franz Ferdinand, and his wife were murdered by a

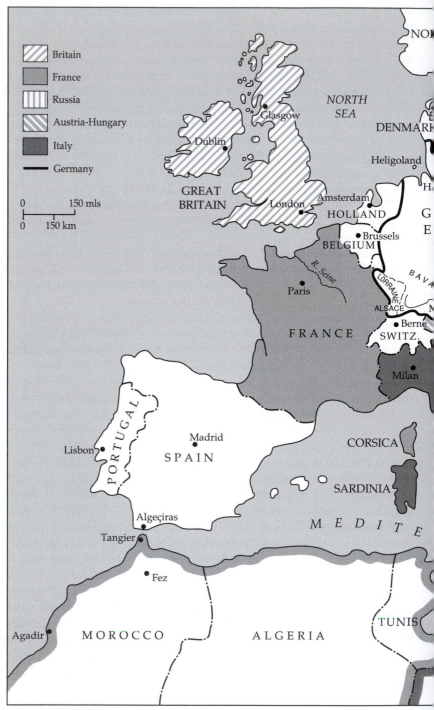

Map 4.1 Europe on the eve of the Great War 1914

Bosnian Serb at Sarajevo. Von Hötzendorf did not want to wait for a judicial enquiry. Berchtold and the Austrian and Hungarian Prime Ministers did. Wilhelm II asked no questions. He wanted to act. 'Now or never.' The treaty of 1879 stood. For von Hötzendorf it was a matter of principle or rather of principles, two of which were in sharp conflict: 'the maintenance of Austria as a conglomerate of various nationalities ... and the rise of independent national states claiming their ethnic territories from Austria-Hungary'. Serb activities had brought this conflict to a head.

The German Chancellor, Theobald von Bethmann-Hollweg, aware of the implications of his actions, promised full support to Vienna on 5 July, but the government in Budapest needed persuasion, and it was not until 19 July that a ten-point ultimatum to Serbia was agreed upon and presented to Belgrade on 23 July with the demand for a reply within 48 hours. This was nearly four weeks after the assassination, another of the reasons for the delay being a planned three-day visit of the French President, Poincaré, to Russia starting on 20 July. When the Serbs asked for more time to reply they were abruptly reminded that they were living in 'the age of railways, telegraphs and telephone'; and when they failed to accept all ten points the Habsburg Empire declared war on 28 July. For Germany, well armed and ready with imposing war plans in the west and in the east, this was the moment to strike. Once Russia mobilized, which it began to do slowly before the Serbian reply was received, the Germans wanted to start what they believed would be a short war as quickly as possible.

Thereafter the treaty system moved into gear in the summer of 1914 – Triple Alliance versus Triple Entente – although there was a final exchange of dynastic telegrams between Wilhelm II and Nicholas II, cousins soon to be at war, and abortive efforts by Sir Edward Grey, Britain's Foreign Secretary, to call for a conference. On 1 August Germany declared war on Russia, and France mobilized. On 2 August the Germans presented an ultimatum to Belgium, which was immediately rejected, and two days later crossed the Belgian frontier. On that same day, 4 August, Britain declared war on Germany. That there was little regret among the peoples, and in most countries even great enthusiasm, requires a different kind of explanation from that given in books of diplomatic history or in the memoirs of foreign ministers and generals.[4]

References

1. L. Lafore, *The Long Fuse: An Interpretation of the Origins of World War I* (1965). Compare Lafore's *An Interpretation of the Origins of World War II* (1970).
2. J. C. Röhl, *The Kaiser and His Court* (1995), ch. 5.
3. See B. W. E. Alford, *Britain in the World Economy since 1880* (1996), chs 2 and 3.
4. For a vivid popular account of the sequence see B. W. Tuchman, *August 1914* (1962).

Chapter 5

Classicism, Romanticism, Victorianism, Modernity

Cultural change

The great Italian liberal historian, Benedetto Croce, who lived through stirring years of twentieth-century history and survived the Second World War, argued forcibly that after the year 1870, the period covered in the last chapter, there had been a profound change in 'the public spirit of Europe', directly associated, he thought, with the unification of Germany and Italy. And other historians have extended his argument by identifying a profound change also in human consciousness and perception, tracing back to this period, which links nineteenth and twentieth centuries, the origins of 'a modern movement' expressed alike in literature, painting and music.

It was not an unprecedented change. In the mid-eighteenth century there had been an equally strong sense of change, although when the word 'modern' was used then there had always been reference back to the 'ancient world' both for comparison and for example. Change was thought of then as more than intellectual. It was d'Alembert, joint editor of the *Encyclopédie*, who wrote in 1759 that 'if one looks at all closely at the middle of our century, the events that occupy us, our customs, our achievements and even our topics of conversation, it is difficult not to see that a very remarkable change in our ideas is taking place, one of such rapidity that it seems to promise a greater change to come'.

By the time of the French Revolution, which was not quite 'the greater change to come' that d'Alembert and most of his fellow writers of 'the Enlightenment' expected, there had been further significant changes in tastes as well as in ideas, including reactions to 'Nature' and assessments of 'human nature'. What was artificial (or trivial) became suspect. The 'picturesque' and the 'sublime' were viewed in new ways – mountains, moors, tombs and ruins. The 'sentimental man' was held up for approval. So, too, was Rousseau's 'noble savage'. Bernardin de St Pierre's *Paul et*

Virginie (1788), an exotic island idyll, suggests, as Rousseau did, that tragedy follows from contact with European 'civilization'. More than 20 years earlier James Macpherson's *Poems of Ossian* (1762) had recalled a mythic Celtic twilight. 'We call back', Macpherson wrote in his preface, 'the years that have rolled away.'

Recall went with novelty, and for all the dwelling on the past in Ossian's poems, the poems themselves were inventions. Public reaction to them, like reaction to 'novels' (the very name 'novel' is linked with the sense of the new), is of interest to cultural historians who seek to uncover feelings as well as to trace ideas. There have always been what have been thought to be 'significant' novels like Rousseau's *La Nouvelle Héloise* (1761) and Goethe's *Werther* (1774), to be set alongside autobiographies like Rousseau's *Confessions* (1781). To appreciate the range, the historian Edward Gibbon's *Autobiography*, published in 1796 in edited form two years after his death, should also be considered.

The novelists themselves were interested in evidence, and it is of more than symbolic interest that the British novelist Henry Mackenzie, author of *The Man of Feeling* (1771), used the device of an incomplete bundle of papers discovered after the event to introduce one of his plots. Sir Walter Scott, too, uncovered all kinds of historical evidence in his Waverley novels. Later in the nineteenth century there were to be other *genres* that would directly bring history back to life, particularly biographies, often focusing on 'great men', some of them 'heroes'; and these usually rested on the evidence of letters, diaries and autobiographies. It is of interest, however, that when Thomas Carlyle, who created his own literary style, began his massive work on the French Revolution, it was to prints and portraits of the revolutionary leaders that he first turned.

It is extremely difficult to periodize cultural change, for there are always overlaps, time-lags and throw-backs. At times 'fashion' seems to dictate the process, as it did in the late-eighteenth century in 'the Gothic revival' or enthusiasm for *chinoiserie* (Chinese style paintings and objects). Yet in every generation there were to be writers like the young French poet Arthur Rimbaud, born in 1854, who hailed what was new for reasons which had nothing to do with fashion: 'let us ask the poet for the *new* in ideas and forms', he wrote: it was he who would 'arrive at the unknown'.

Rimbaud, who published his first volume of poems while he was still at school and composed little of importance after the age of 19, claimed that a poet makes himself a *seer* 'by a long and rational *disordering of the senses*. He consumes all the poisons in him and keeps only their quintessences. This is an unspeakable torture during which he needs all his faith and superhuman strength, and during which he becomes the great patient, the great criminal, the great accursed – and the great learned one among men'. Samuel Taylor Coleridge, poet and philosopher, had put it differently when in relating excitement in the discovery of the new to the years of youth he had written of discovering 'the charm of novelty' in the 'things of every day', 'a feeling analogous to the supernatural, by awakening the mind's attention from the lethargy of custom'.

The shock of the new was to be a source of thrill in the early-twentieth century, for example in 1911 when Igor Stravinsky's shattering musical composition – noisy, rhythmic, 'primitive' – *Sacré du Printemps* ('The Rite of Spring') was performed in Paris. Of the previous year, 1910, the English novelist Virginia Woolf was to make the startling statement in 1924 (after the shocks of the First World War) that 'on or about December 1910 human character changed'. It was then that a controversial Post-Impressionist Exhibition had been shown in London where most British viewers saw for the first time paintings by Vincent Van Gogh, Paul Gauguin, Henri Matisse, Pablo Picasso and, the one who most stood out for her, Paul Cézanne.

Virginia Woolf's attempt to place this 'transformation' in perspective brings out the importance of distinctions that have often been drawn between the 'modern' and the 'contemporary', although the words were often used as alternatives. Much that was merely 'contemporary' – most indeed – was ignored or despised by self-consciously 'modern' writers and artists, some of whom had come to the conclusion long before Virginia Woolf – long, indeed, before 1910 – that 'human character' had changed. For them the essence of 'the modern' was that it was 'problematic'. The past had provided answers: the present posed questions. The 'primitive' offered one way out of it. 'I wanted only to try to live in obedience to the promptings which came from my true self', says one of the characters in a German novel by Herman Hesse. 'Why was that so difficult?' In his quest the writer or the artist was prepared to scorn any sense of 'responsibility' to a 'public', a concept which had its origins in the late-eighteenth century.

Social imperatives set the context for individual 'promptings'. There were five significant structural changes in the late-eighteenth and nineteenth centuries, not always immediately understood, which provided a new and changing context within which writers and artists worked: the shift, never total, from literary and artistic patronage, largely provided by royal or aristocratic patrons, to individual or institutional purchase; the emergence of new 'publics' for books, paintings, sculptures, pieces of music and the performing arts (theatre, dance, opera, ballet, concerts); the emergence of *avant gardes*, minorities prepared to defy convention and tradition; the development of new technologies, as different as, for example, electroplating and photography, which enabled relatively low-priced copies to be made and distributed through extended markets; and the creation and evolution of cultural institutions, some 'voluntary' in their organization, some dependent on subsidy. These operated either alongside educational institutions – schools, universities, academies, conservatories – or within them.

If only because of the second, third and fourth of these shifts, it became possible in the nineteenth century to speak of cultural policies and of

cultural politics. It also became common for the public (or publics) to put their trust in cultural prophets like John Ruskin, who lived through to 1900, or in cultural tastemakers like Viollet-le-Duc, who restored cathedrals and castles in France.[1] Both treated 'the Gothic' as the highest form of 'organic architecture'. The influence both of tastemakers and of critics was bound to increase when there was no longer any general acceptance of 'rules of taste' common to all periods and to all peoples as there had been in the early-eighteenth century. Gothic – or what passed for it – never completely won the day.

There was no distinctive new nineteenth-century style either, and if only for this reason the eclecticism of the mid-nineteenth century encouraged a quest on the part of clients – or disciples – for guidance and at a deeper level education. There were reactions against mid-century cultural prophets, however, before the century ended, with advertisers taking over from tastemakers to an increasing extent as mass production and mass distribution developed.[2] At the same time, *avant gardes* emerged in all the arts, minorities that appealed to minorities, as Virginia Woolf's Bloomsbury was to do. The twentieth century, which was ushered in with a parallel but contrasting movement towards 'specialization' and 'professionalization', was to be very different from the nineteenth, and this was obvious by the end of its first decade.

In retrospect, the nineteenth century was no single person's century. Nor was it a century of consensus. Argument prevailed. The currents of change could often direct people into whirlpools or over waterfalls. Pursuing what to them was a favourite metaphor, there were watersheds too and sometimes 'meetings of the waters'. The currents were seldom simply national or class-based. Ideas (or styles) might be born in Germany or France or Britain and make their way everywhere, sometimes strangely transformed in the process. This was a century of travel on a far bigger scale and far more commercially organized than the aristocratic 'grand tours' of the eighteenth century. Thomas Cook, pioneer of the guided tour, founded his travel agency in 1841. The German Karl Baedecker had pioneered guidebooks in the two decades before his death in 1859. Italy, Switzerland and the French Riviera were on a new tourist map long before the century ended.

Through cultural history we approach political, social and economic history in a way that enables us to understand more clearly the processes of change. In approaching the past through 'political culture' political

---

Plate 5.1 The Gothic revival. Restoration, as well as creation, was a theme in the Gothic revival. Depicted here is the citadel restored during the nineteenth century at Caracassone in Languedoc, by Viollet-le-Duc, the Great French exponent of the Gothic style. His British contemporary, A. W. Pugin, believed that medieval Gothic was the peak of European artistic expression. The nineteenth century revival was particularly fed by nationalism.

historians have gained new insights into the structures and dynamics of politics. So also have economic historians when in relation to recent economic history they have re-examined the nature of 'political economy' and through studies of *entrepreneurs* have explored the evolution of the notion of 'corporate culture' in business.[3] Statistics are never enough. Cultural historians have drawn also on a far wider range of historical evidence than the written (or spoken) word. The music of Beethoven (and for a later date Wagner) is an obvious example, as is the art of David (or at a later date Eugène Delacroix). Such forms of cultural expression may be set alongside the evidence of buildings, many of which survive. Medals are revealing, too, and in the case of economic history such items as 'tokens', paid to workers in lieu of coins, banknotes which could take the place of coins, and share certificates, some of them worthless from the start. Ephemera (labels, tickets, forms), objects that were thrown away, have been collected and examined also. Waste has become part of history.

Classicism and neo-classicism

In the eighteenth century there was a different sense both of time and place and above all a different sense of proportion. When d'Alembert, consciously cosmopolitan, was summing up both the whole of human knowledge and the whole sense of his own age, there were 'correct' or 'true' styles that were considered universally applicable, styles to which men and women of a later age, who had reacted against them, attached the labels 'classical' or 'neo-classical'. 'Rules', derived ultimately from antiquity, covered all the arts from drama to architecture, and they were universal in their application. Having been set out in Italy from the fifteenth century onwards, they were easier to apply (although they needed little enforcement) in pre-revolutionary France, with its court and its Academy, than they were in Britain, where there were always non-conformists, religious or secular, or in the separate states of Germany. There the rules were not always known, and Gotthold Ephraim Lessing, playwright of the Enlightenment, who certainly knew them, could contrive to make them seem absurd. So long as the rules held – and in France, while stretched, they survived the Revolution – they not only set standards but provided a common framework of reference.

The dominant styles both of Revolutionary and of Napoleonic France were neo-classical, and there was no real break in art or architecture in 1789 or 1800. Jacques Louis David, born in 1748, had painted for Louis XVI before he made his way through the Revolution and revelled in his new responsibilities as 'painter to the Government' of Napoleon. Two of his best known paintings are *The Death of Socrates*, a classical topic, and *Marat Assassinated*, the most topical of subjects, and he sketched Marie-Antoinette on her way to the guillotine. David dealt not only in canvasses but in the presentation, direction and management of such solemn occasions as the Feast of the Supreme Being, held on 8 June 1794, a feast of neo-classicism as well as of revolution, for a huge statue of Hercules dominated the Paris scene. The poet André Marie de Chénier, romantic, not classical in his sensibilities, wrote a poem on Hercules also: his *Hymn to Liberty* had begun with the 'hell of the Bastille' and its collapse into debris.

Throughout the Revolution the word *sacré* (sacred), once applied to kings, now related to 'the people' or 'the nation', and this had important cultural ramifications. While Marx was correct when he stated that the Revolution was played in Roman clothes, the *sans culottes* did not wear togas. And while Maximilien de Robespierre in some of his stirring speeches referred back to the ancient world, blending Cicero with Rousseau, members of his audience drew most of their ideas from the ephemera of the Revolution which included flags, music, 'street theatre', exhibitions and above all, 'festivals' (*fêtes*). The destruction of old monuments was as significant as the erection of new ones. Bits and pieces of the destroyed Bastille were being sold as mementoes in 1789, just as bits and pieces of the Berlin Wall were to be sold 200 years later. That the new buildings were in neo-classical styles was a sign that Revolutionary leaders were determined that the revolution should last and that it should display its own order.

It was an order, however, that could not obliterate Christian memories. When the great Paris cathedral of Notre Dame (to be 'restored' in the nineteenth century by Viollet-le-Duc) was rededicated to the Goddess of Reason in the presence of the enthusiastic Robespierre, the ceremony drew on Christian rituals as well as on classical allusions. The great procession stopped at five points. At one there was a huge pile of discarded feudal charters and coats of arms, huger than a David painting. At another there was a mountain, the symbol of the revolutionary Jacobins. Such ceremonies were not exclusive to Paris. In Nevers, for example, the opportunist Josèphe Fouché, who must have been sceptical about the Supreme Being and who in later life was to be Minister of Police under both Napoleon and the restored Bourbons, had unveiled a bust of Brutus in the local parish church. More to the point, perhaps, he gave orders to all priests to marry.

In architecture, at least, neo-classicism had reached its peak before the Empire – although it was to survive Napoleon's fall – while in the design of furniture and interiors there were stiff and ostentatious elements in 'Empire style', particularly when the neo-classical was embellished with Egyptian or self-consciously imperial decorations. There was a contrast at this stage with the simplicities of much of earlier neo-classical art and architecture, but in Britain, long before Napoleon claimed that it was right to expect the nation 'to give birth to masterpieces', the Scottish architect and designer Robert Adam, who died in 1792, expressed the hope that the reign of George III might 'fix an Aera no less remarkable than that of Pericles, Augustus or the Medici'. Adam was a friend of C. B. Piranesi, an

Italian source of inspiration throughout Europe. Later British neo-classicists stimulated a Greek revival which reached its peak after the fall of Napoleon. Robert Smirke's British Museum (1823–47) housed among its great collections the Parthenon sculptures that Lord Elgin had brought back to London from Greece, still controlled by the Turks, between 1806 and 1812.

The fact that Adam's designs were identified as 'Adam style' long before the word 'neo-classicism' was invented shows how impossible it is in practice to separate the ancient and the modern, the private and the public, the inherited and the original. Tendencies that were later to be identified with 'romanticism' were plainly there by the mid-eighteenth century. Thus, Adam's sceptical compatriot, the philosopher David Hume, was one of a number of Enlightenment figures who were prepared to question rules of form that would restrict 'the sallies of the imagination'; while in France, Diderot, d'Alembert's partner, left a place in his world for 'genius' that would break rules. His novel, *Rameau's Nephew*, known in manuscript to Goethe and Hegel, focuses on a nihilistic character who would have had no place in a classical world, old or new. Napoleon himself had little taste for classical allegory. When David incorporated a hovering Victory in the sky in his painting 'Distribution of the Eagles' Napoleon asked him to remove it.

Allegory went with heroism, and even in industrial settings, like Coalbrookdale or Boulton and Watt's Soho, it could find a place. 'Enthusiasm' was more difficult to fit in. Indeed, it was a word that always created difficulties within the eighteenth-century classical framework of reference. To accept its influence, as Voltaire did, only if it was 'reasonable', that is to say held in check, was not to deny its force but to fear it, as Samuel Johnson did in England. It was in England that the evangelical Anglican John Wesley was condemned for mobilizing religious enthusiasm in the open air, but it was in Revolutionary France that Robespierre himself demanded passion more than reason in a notorious impromptu speech presented to the National Convention on 25 December 1793, a date which for him had no religious significance. His object was to denigrate revolutionaries who in a period of Terror were appealing to the law to protect them from the guillotine. 'By its nature patriotism is ardent. Who can love his homeland with a cool love? Patriotism belongs particularly to simple people, who have had little training in determining the political consequences of an act of state.'

Romanticism

Robespierre's affirmation of the need for passion and his direct appeal to the simple reflected what were commonly held even at the time to be 'romantic', not classical, qualities. Yet to place 'romantic' and 'classical' in sharp opposition was a later development in a rapidly changing culture. Greek classicism itself incorporated 'Apollonian' and 'Dionysian' elements, the latter uninhibited, even frenzied. Many of the greatest poets and writers defy the easy application of labels like 'classical' and 'romantic'. Goethe, for example, who created the suffering young romantic 'hero' Werther – Napoleon took a copy of *Werther* with him on his Egyptian campaign – admired classical forms and was critical of many aspects of romanticism which he did not hesitate to condemn. 'The most impetuous painter', he wrote as early as 1781, 'has no right to daub any more than the fiercest musician should strike wrong notes.' In 1805 he complained at an art exhibition in his city of Weimar that 'feeling' was being exalted 'over mind and spirit'.

One painter who is difficult to fit into any *schema* is the Spaniard Francisco José de Goya, born in 1746, three years before Goethe, and, like him, living deep into the nineteenth century. His early work was *rococo*, the style which neo-classical artists considered trivial. His dark and mysterious etchings, *Disasters of War*, suggested by the Napoleonic invasion of Spain – so different in style from his earlier paintings, including his satirical works – are among the outstanding artistic triumphs of a period in which superimposed official order was often no more than a facade. When Goya returned to his villa at the age of 70 he chose to decorate it with paintings that had subjects like 'Saturn devouring his children' and 'the Witches' Sabbath'. These were the kind of subjects that appealed most to some of the German romantics.

The word 'romantic' itself was of seventeenth-century origin. It derived from the older word 'romance' that had been used in the Middle Ages, and already before the French Revolution it had come to be applied widely not only to novels (*romans*) and poems but to scenes and paintings and to manners and dress. In a very general sense 'the same impulse – in different guises' lay behind both 'the mounting spirit of Revolution' and the 'romantic current' that swept Europe in the late-eighteenth and early-nineteenth centuries. Indeed, as early as 1803 the German novelist Jean Paul Richter observed that 'the revolution', 'more intellectual, more vast than that of Paris', which was 'surging up in the minds of men, was not so much an effect of the French Revolution as the result of forces before it broke out'.

Chasing the changing use of the word 'romantic' back in time is an even more difficult quest than chasing the political and constitutional ideas that were 'in the air' in 1789 back into the eighteenth century. It is clear, however, that the view that there were 'classical' and 'romantic' elements in the literature of the past – with Shakespeare standing out as a towering romantic genius – preceded the view that there was a 'romantic movement' in current thought, taste, writing and art. It is clear, too, that the most interesting early expressions of eighteenth-century 'romanticism' were to be found outside France. The romantic poets of Britain and Germany are still read more widely than any of their French contemporaries, just as

Plate 5.2 *Saturn devouring one of his children* **by Francisco Jose de Goya y Lucientes (1746–1828) Prado, Madrid/Bridgeman Art Library, London.** The fourteen 'black paintings' which decorated the two main rooms of Goya's country retreat, Quinta del Sordo, encompass an array of nightmare visions. The monstrous and inhuman painting of Saturn is the centre-piece of the series. Art historians remain undecided as to whether the painting represents the triumph of ignorance and darkness, or melancholy and old age – it could represent both – yet it remains a profoundly disturbing work.

German composers of this period are still listened to in almost every twentieth-century concert.

The terminology of 'romanticism' was German and British too. In 1797 Friedrich Schlegel in 125 pages drew a distinction between 'classical' and 'romantic'; and in the same year Wordsworth wrote his preface to the

Lyrical Ballads which rightly came to be regarded as a manifesto of romantic poetry, although it did not employ the word 'romantic' at any point. For Schlegel there was a sharp division between the north of Europe – the literature and art of which was medieval and Christian in origin and ultimately romantic – and the south of Europe, pagan and classical in pedigree and mediated through the Renaissance. Schlegel did not bring Spain into his picture; nor did the influential book *De L'Allemagne* ('Of Germany'), written by the erudite and witty Madame de Stael (Necker's daughter), completed in 1810 but for political reasons published first in England, not France, in 1813. She emphasized in particular the distinctiveness of German literature within this north-south pattern.

By then the first generation of German 'romantics' – centred at first on the university town of Jena, the home of the Schlegels and near the site of one of Napoleon's great victories – a generation which had an unusually strong *esprit de corps*, was already dead. Wilhelm Heinrich Wackenroder had died in 1798, and Novalis (pseudonym of Friedrich von Hardenberg) in 1801. Herder, who had moved to Weimar through the influence of Goethe, died in 1803, and Friedrich von Schiller, who had also moved to Weimar in 1787, two years later. Johannes Christian Friedrich Hölderlin, Dionysian prophet, was mad, and Heinrich von Kleist, despairing of knowledge, had committed suicide. It was Schiller, however, who had written the *Ode to Joy* (1785) which was to be used by Beethoven for the finale of his *Ninth Symphony*.

The next generation of German romantics (the so-called 'high romantics' such as Uhland, Count Karl von Arnim and Ernst Theodor Hoffmann), who were fascinated by the past, became interpreters of *volk* and *kultur*, often drawing on old tales, as did Jacob Grimm, one of the founders of comparative philology, who compiled with his brother Wilhelm the famous collection of *Fairy Tales* which appeared between 1812 and 1815. On the side-lines Heinrich Heine, Jewish, ironical and outcast, understood all that his fellow German romantics were saying and writing, but could not participate in their ventures. In this he was the most romantic of them all.

Although, partly because, conscious 'romanticism' came to France late, after 1815, the idea of a 'romantic movement' was stronger there than it had been in Britain and, indeed, Germany; and it was in France that the poet Victor Hugo produced far more rhetorical manifestos of romantic literature than that of Wordsworth in 1797. The prolix prefaces that he wrote for his plays *Cromwell* (1827) and *Hernani* (1830) frontally attacked 'classicism' and 'neo-classicism', dismissing all rules, including the dramatic 'unities' of time and place, as 'petty' and 'conventional'. Hugo extolled genius ('mediocrity has no existence as far as art is concerned: art supplies wings, not crutches'), and found a place (as did some of the German romantics) for 'the grotesque' as well as for 'the natural'. The fact that Hugo's plays were banned or hissed when they were presented on the Paris stage added to the power of his attack.

When Hugo was forced to be concise, he oversimplified, for example in calling romanticism 'liberalism in literature'. There were 'romantics' in France as well as in Germany who were not liberals, and the first outstanding English romantics – Wordsworth, Coleridge and Southey – moved far away from their earlier enthusiasm for revolution. Sir Walter Scott, a great storyteller whose novels had immense appeal in Europe, was made a baronet in 1820 when Castlereagh was Foreign Secretary. Although his novels strongly influenced European composers of opera – and fashionable costumes – he is not easy to fit into a romantic schema. Nor is Byron, whose poetry was so different from Wordsworth's (and Keats's and Shelley's) that despite his European popularity as a romantic genius British literary critics never found it easy to relate it to the romantic 'mainstream'. What is certain is that Scotland, through its images, played as important a part in the whole romantic movement as it did through its ideas in the eighteenth-century Enlightenment.

For Stendhal, 'romanticism' (and he used the *ism*) could be defined as simply (if inadequately) as Hugo defined it. It was 'at any time the art of the day', while 'classicism was the art of the day before'. After attending the first night of *Hernani* Stendhal wrote briskly 'champagne and *Hernani* did not suit me at all'. Few critics, however, have found romanticism so easy to define as Stendhal or Hugo, although so many definitions (many of them blatantly contradictory) have been attempted that the difficulty in approaching romanticism 'is less that of finding *a* definition than of finding one's way through the mass of definitions that have already been put forward'.[4]

At the heart of the romantic attitude was compelling concern for the inner self, for the authentic individual experience, spontaneous and unique, that accompanied the realization or frustration of that concern, and for the imaginative ('original' and 'creative') expression of that experience. In the course of the romantic quest, pursued through light and shadow, there were moments both of desire and guilt, accomplishment and regret, ecstasy and agony, melancholy (*ennui*) and elation. Above all, there was always a sense of the unattainable. *Sehnsucht* (longing), a key word in the romantic vocabulary, belonged to the night as well as to the day.

Unresolved tension was a necessary part of the individual and social psyche, and Hugo's declamatory rhetoric could not conceal it. However inner-directed, solitary and isolated, 'romantics' might be, they were also concerned inevitably both with the 'wonders' and with the pressures of an outer world which they might grasp intuitively but which they could never control.[5] To them it was an 'organic', not a mechanistic, world, and there was always an ultimate romantic disenchantment with it (*Weltschmerz*) just as there was always a *mal du siècle*, a time disease. The facts of the nineteenth century – and its underlying structures – and, above all, the strength of the *bourgeoisie* – who stood for all that the romantics claimed most to dislike – were always, in their view (if mistakenly), against them.

They could feel 'alienated', therefore, a term with a spiritual content that was appropriated by Marx.

A. W. Schlegel, who believed that history is the 'self-consciousness of a nation', sharpened the sense not only of a romantic style – and of a romantic geography – but of a romantic century. The eighteenth century, an old hag, was not, he wrote for a pageant performed on 1 January 1801, the parent of the nineteenth. Its true parents were Genius and Liberty. And in his pageant the withered old hag was carried off to Hell by the Devil, a familiar romantic character. Insofar as 'romanticism' was to influence the whole pattern of the nineteenth century, more preoccupied than any previous century with establishing its own distinctive identity, Schlegel was right. History was no longer fixed within a universally accepted framework. Nor were historical characters and events judged in terms of timeless criteria. In the new history, a subject developed at all levels far more many-sidedly than in any previous century, characters and events were to speak for themselves, as were 'peoples' and 'nations'. One of the greatest romantic historians was a Frenchman, Jules Michelet, who concerned himself with the French Revolution within the history of France. In his own word he 'resurrected' it.

Michelet had no obvious foreign counterpart, but there was more than one romantic version of the history of the century while it took shape. Long vistas were explored too as some romantics compared their own century unfavourably with the Middle Ages, particularly the thirteenth century. Distaste for the nineteenth century was vividly expressed by Ruskin and the Scot Thomas Carlyle, who criticized the dehumanizing division of labour: for Adam Smith and for later political economists, that had been the main cause of the increase in industrial production that reflected and influenced so much else. Carlyle was equally critical of the power of the machine that St Simon extolled. 'Not the external and physical alone is now managed by machinery, but the internal and spiritual also ... Mechanism has now struck its roots down into man's most intimate primary sources of conviction.'

Later in the century William Morris, in a direct line of descent from the earlier romantics, looked back to Ruskin and Carlyle and, after he became a socialist, sideways to Marx. Scornful of machine-dominated and steam-driven industry he dismissed contemptuously the pride of modern civilization:

> Was it all to end in a counting-house on the top of a cinder heap, with
> Podsnap's drawing room in the offing, and a Whig committee doling out
> champagne to the rich and margarine to the poor in such convenient
> proportions as would make all men contented together, though the pleasure of
> the eye was gone from the world and the place of Homer was taken by
> Huxley?

Huxley was the main spokesman of nineteenth-century science. Podsnap was a character created by Charles Dickens, England's 'special correspondent for posterity', in his brilliant novel *Our Mutual Friend* (1865) which focused on the rubbish heaps of nineteenth-century civilization. His Podsnap was a stock English type, self-assured, complacent and incapable of speaking except in platitudes. 'You shall have the poor always with you.' Podsnap had a remarkable ability to evade or to dismiss all 'disagreeables' or unpleasant realities: 'it is not for me . . . to impugn the workings of Providence'. Morris demanded action, not satire. If all were not to end in 'a counting house at the top of a cinder heap', there would have to be collective action, and for there to be collective action there would have to be collective 'hope'.

In romantic music and painting, as in poetry, individual hope had been associated with *Sehnsucht* and *Weltschmerz*. Yet romantic musicians could soar as well as console (not least their fellow romantic writers), and romantic painters could inspire. Ernst Hoffmann, composer, romantic painter and music critic as well as writer, whose tales were to be set to music by Jacques Offenbach, wrote of closing his eyes 'to all the strife and war in the world' and retreating 'into the land of music as the land of faith, in which all our doubts and sorrows sink into a sea of sounds'. Yet the one undoubted musical genius, Ludwig van Beethoven, who never doubted his own claim to the title, composed music that for Hoffmann, as for thousands of others, did far more than close eyes to strife and war. It 'set in motion the lever of fear, of awe, of horror, of suffering and awakens that infinite longing which is the essence of romanticism'.

There were many tangled strains in romantic music from Karl Maria von Weber, who introduced ample horror into his opera *Freischütz* (1821), through to Franz Schubert and Robert Schumann, both of whom, to complete the circle, greatly admired Hoffmann. And there were many different modes of musical expression, as different as lyrics and epics or novels and poems in literature, with musicians often attempting them all. The *Lieder*, the supreme expression of German romanticism, could 'tear the heart strings'. Yet there was a thrill in listening to symphonies and great operatic arias and choruses, Russian as well as German, Italian as well as French, with Britain providing great concert audiences if not great composers. From Italy, Giuseppe Verdi could steal romantic – and nationalist – hearts, opera and politics often going together. Heart strings could be torn also, however, by the melancholy movements of string quartets.

There seemed to be no limits in music; and in painting also two very different romantic painters carried painting far beyond any limits set by neo-classicism. J. W. M. Turner, described by the late-nineteenth French musician Claude Debussy as 'the first creator of mystery', looked at nature, at life and at light in a totally different way from any painter before him. 'All is without form and void', his critics complained, but he won the enthusiastic approval of Ruskin, who loved light. In France the great romantic painter Eugène Delacroix, reputed to be an illegitimate son of Talleyrand, was admired by a romantic musician of a very different

Plate 5.3 *The train at Gare Saint-Lazare*, **Claude Monet.** Shimmering, luminous colours characterize the paintings of Claude Monet. Although more obviously representational than his landscapes, this painting puzzled his public. Contemporaries argued that while the impressionist technique of painting might be suitable for painting water or foliage, it was difficult to accept buildings and people painted this way. Where was the technique? What was the audience supposed to admire? What did the paintings mean? Railway locomotives and stations had always interested nineteenth-century painters. The impressionists responded that in painting a railway station they could paint what they liked. Although unpopular at first, the move away from representation arguably gave painters a new lease of life, rescuing as their art from competition with the camera.

generation from Debussy, the great Polish pianist Frédéric Chopin. The huge Delacroix canvasses included many that dealt with revolutionary upthrust, among them 'Liberty Guiding the People', painted in 1831 and frequently reproduced in the age of photography that was soon to begin.

Photography had imposed its own order when the Impressionist painters held their first great Impressionist Exhibition in Paris in 1874, only four years after the collapse of the Empire of Napoleon III. It took place in a photographer's studio. One of the paintings, Claude Monet's *Impression* provoked a derisory critic to coin the word 'impressionism' in a hostile review. It was a label that stuck. The Impressionists had been painting new kinds of paintings since 1863, experimenting both with colour and with light, and looking at people, nature (and cathedrals and railway stations) in a new way, but it was only after 1874 that tastes began to change. Nonetheless, as a group whose paintings were handled by one dealer, the Impressionists shocked viewers who were disturbed by the sight on canvas of a 'world perceived momentarily by the senses'. One of the characters in an Emile Zola novel said of their art that it 'contradicted all the regular habits of the eye', and one hostile critic called their second exhibition a disaster, second only in magnitude to a recent fire at Charles Garnier's Paris Opera House, work on which had started in 1861. It was one of the most famous buildings of the century.

The Impressionists were to hold six more exhibitions before 1886 – and to triumph over opposition until they in their turn were pushed aside by painters of a new generation, grouped together vaguely (by an English observer at the 1910 Exhibition) as 'post-impressionists', among them Cézanne, Van Gogh, Gauguin and Henri Matisse. Both Impressionists and Post-Impressionists were represented at the great World Exhibition held in Paris in 1900 which attracted more than 40 million visitors (more than the total population of France) and left behind as part of its heritage the Grand Palais and the Petit Palais, where many future exhibitions were to be held, and the ornate Alexander III bridge, named after the Russian Tsar.

Science

Exhibitions were even more concerned with the display of scientific advance than with the work of painters or architects. Some of the inventions on display, including the most ingenious, had no future. Some, however, pointed to a new age. Electricity, which had figured prominently at a Paris Exhibition of 1889, was dominant at the Exhibition of 1900. All the great exhibitions were photographed: all were seen too through tinted spectacles. 'Optical science', most highly developed in Germany, was a subject of scholarly study in a continuing 'Age of Spectacle' which produced far more pairs of spectacles, thought of increasingly as 'common things', than any previous age in history. (How did people manage without them before?) They were not thought of as 'common things' in early periods, however: 'a pair of spectacles', Carlyle's father wrote, 'is a thing I have often looked at and thought of, but could never call any of them my own before'.

Photography was a nineteenth-century invention with a long pre-history, conceived of both as science and art. The first fixed photographs, 'heliographs' or 'sun drawings', had been taken in France during the 1820s. It was not until 1839, however, that Louis Daguerre, like so many men of his century a born impresario, demonstrated his photographic processes in Paris, and later in the same year in London, Henry Fox Talbot displayed his first 'photogenic drawings', 'calotypes', for 'lovers of science and nature' at the Royal Society. Daguerre had presented his first 'daguerreotype' to the Curator of the Louvre gallery in Paris.

During the decades that followed, photography was employed in many different settings from photographers' studios (portrait photography became an industry) to houses and gardens, theatres, hospitals and prisons and even during the Crimean War to military tents. It was a photographer born in Germany but a naturalized Frenchman, Edouard Baldus, who took pictures of places on the route of Victoria and Albert's visit to Napoleon III in 1855 and of the railway from Paris to Marseilles opened by the Emperor in the same year. And by the end of the century the camera too was coming to be thought of as a 'common thing'. The box camera, with a branded name, Kodak ('branding' of products was now becoming more general), was introduced from the United States in 1888. The first moving pictures had been taken in 1872, and in 1896 the Lumière brothers exhibited moving pictures in Paris and in London. It was not until the twentieth century, however, that the cinema captured a regular mass audience, directly influencing the relationship between Europe and the United States.

It was not entirely easy to fit photography into the story of nineteenth-century science, and in a collection of essays, *The Progress of the Century*, published in 1901, it was possible for the writer on physics to describe 'the development and the art of photography' as 'not of the first importance', while admitting that it had 'contributed much to the pleasure of life'. 'Serious science' was best represented by chemistry, the science which had most directly affected daily life. The work of the great German chemist Justus von Liebig had been influential in improving public health as it had been in transforming agriculture and food processing. The French chemist Louis Pasteur influenced the preparation both of milk and wine as steps in the development of bacteriology, a science that changed the basis of the understanding of disease. Theoretical chemistry made advances, too, both through classification and through experiment. There was a place in the atomic table, first set out in 1872, for chemical elements which had not yet been discovered. At the end of the century it seemed 'obvious', Professor William Ramsay wrote in 1901, 'that the nation which possesses the most competent chemists, theoretical and practical, is destined to succeed in the competition with other nations for commercial supremacy and all its concomitant advantages'.

By comparison, physics, a new word, often seemed less exciting, although there were great nineteenth-century physicists like Michael Faraday, James Clerk Maxwell, Herman von Helmholz and William Thomson (later Lord Kelvin), to place alongside Liebig and Pasteur. The laws of thermodynamics were enunciated *after* the invention of the steam engine, which depended on them, but impressive theorizing about electricity and magnetism preceded its application, as did the experiments of Heinrich Hertz and others with radio waves. There was little intimation that physics – theoretical, experimental and applied – would become the major science of the first half of the twentieth century, culminating in the harnessing of the split atom during the Second World War. 'Concerning the nature of matter', one prominent physicist wrote in 1901, 'the ablest physicists of the century have thought and written much, and doubtless our present knowledge of the subject is much more nearly the truth than that of a hundred years ago.' In the light of what was soon to come he was right not to linger on the point. Instead, he concluded his account with a salute to 'the great and rapidly increasing number of well-organized and splendidly equipped laboratories in which original research is systematically planned and carried out'.[6]

The advance of science in the nineteenth century, he claimed, had hitherto been 'more or less a guerrilla war against ignorance'. Now in an age when warfare itself seemed to be becoming more 'scientific' the research war in science was to be organized through campaigns in which teams would be involved as well as individuals. The participants were to be professionals, too, for while discovery in geology and 'natural history' earlier in the century had often been the work of 'amateurs', some of them 'gentlemen', some self-taught, laboratory science, passing far beyond observation and classification, required a professional base. This was first provided in Germany, although it had been in Britain that the Cambridge philosopher William Whewell, inventor in 1840 of the word 'scientist' (and the word 'physicist'), foresaw the shape of things to come when he described 'the tendency of the sciences . . . to an increasing proclivity of separation and dismemberment. The mathematician turns away from the chemist; the chemist from the naturalist; the mathematician, left to himself, divides himself into a pure mathematician and a mixed mathematician, who soon part company.'

Nonetheless, in Britain, both in the provinces and in London, great emphasis was placed on publicizing science through lectures and demonstrations and through the opening of museums, and there was stimulating argument about the place of science and classical studies in the curriculum. There was also a noisy debate about evolution after the publication of Charles Darwin's book _The Origin of Species_ in 1859. Darwinian biology was even more controversial than geology which had already dramatically lengthened the span of the Earth's history and disturbed beliefs in the _Book of Genesis._ The _Origin of Species_ was one of the 'great books' not only of the nineteenth century but of all time, although it was an essentially nineteenth-century work and could have been written in no other century. It had a nineteenth-century centrality too. Marx, nine years younger than Darwin, emerging from a completely different background and with a sharply contrasting personality, wished to dedicate his huge treatise on political economy, _Das Kapital_, the first volume of which appeared in 1867, to the English scientist. 'Darwin has interested us in the history of Nature's technology', Marx wrote. 'Does not the history of the productive organs of man, of organs that are the material basis of all social organization, deserve equal attention?'

When Darwin died in 1882 he was buried, although a religious agnostic, in Westminster Abbey, proof of the authority of a new 'scientific priesthood' as one scientist called it. For the liberal John Morley 'the Darwinian creed' (itself a religious term) 'runs through all the best thought [he did not add the worst thought] of our time. It tinges our unformed public notions; it reappears in a hundred disguises in works on law and history; in political speeches and religious discourses . . . If we try to think ourselves away from it we must think ourselves entirely away from our age.'

Yet not all nineteenth-century evolutionist writing was a by-product of *The Origin of Species*. Much of it developed independently. Indeed, the idea of evolution had a long pedigree, and the literature of the period, including the poetry – Alfred Tennyson's *In Memoriam* was an example – was full of references to it. Ideas interconnect. So do pedigrees. If there had not been a transformation in the study of geology, there could have been no Darwinian achievement in biology leading ultimately to a new appreciation of Man's place in the long process of evolution. Darwin, like Marx, was looking for 'laws', but he saw 'grandeur' also in a view of life that started with 'the war of nature' and ended with 'the most exalted object which we are capable of conceiving, the production of higher animals' – including man. That Man was not set apart from the animal kingdom – and this was the theme of Darwin's *Descent of Man* (1871) – seemed to Darwin's admirers to be 'the grand and special discovery of natural science in our generation'. It was not, however, to be the end of the story.

Positivism and liberalism

The advance of science must be related to its economic and social setting, even though individual scientists seemed often to be oblivious to it. Religion must always be brought into the picture also – along with philosophy. 'Our species from the time of its creation', Whewell wrote in 1837, 'has been travelling onward in pursuit of truth, and now . . . we have reached a lofty and commanding position with the broad light of day around us.' The idea of 'progress', including scientific progress, often coupled with the idea of evolution, remained central to the nineteenth century and to its strong sense of history.[7] It was propounded, however, before both the French Revolution and the industrial revolution in one of the first novels set in the future – *L'An 2440* by Sébastien Mercier, published in Amsterdam. The novel was banned in the France of the *ancien régime*, but was soon translated into both English and German.

Not surprisingly, Mercier forecast that there would be no such banning in 2440, but there would still be censorship. People defending dangerous principles would be forced to wear a black mask. There was little that was 'liberal' in this. Mercier also forecast, however, that slavery would have disappeared, that there would be few domestic servants and no monks, and that all marriages would be determined by personal inclinations. He also referred to the sciences. 'Where can the perfectibility of man stop, armed with geometry and the mechanical arts and chemistry?' Yet he did not foresee either the upthrust of technology or the emergence of a French Republic. One agreeable change would be that France and Britain were to be bound in an indestructible alliance in 2440.

The term 'perfectibility of man' is associated most with another French writer, 'the last of the *philosophes*', the Marquis de Condorcet, who renounced his title in 1789 and whose *Esquisse d'un tableau historique du progrès de l'esprit humain* ('Sketch of a Historical Picture of the Progress of the Human Spirit') was posthumously published in 1795, after the French Revolution had gone through its early phases. Condorcet, who put his trust in equality among individuals and peoples, offered his readers 'a vision of the human race, emancipated from its shackles, released from the empire of fate and from that of the enemies of its progress, advancing with a firm and sure step along the path of truth, virtue and happiness'. But he did not tread that path himself. He was gaoled by the Jacobins during the Terror, and after writing his book died in prison, probably by suicide, before he could be sent to the guillotine.

It was not so much Condorcet's own fate in the Paris of the French Revolution that made his vision seem unduly optimistic, but the critique of it written by the English clergyman and political economist Thomas Malthus, whose *Essay on the Principle of Population* was first published anonymously in 1798: it was to go through many later editions in expanded form, beginning with a two-volume edition of 1803 under his own name. The first essay began as a refutation of Condorcet and of the English social philosopher William Godwin. In 1793 Godwin had published a ponderous *Enquiry Concerning Political Justice*, highly sympathetic to the French Revolution, which influenced Wordsworth, Coleridge, Southey, Shelley and Hazlitt. Malthus's view that population always rises faster (geometrically) than the means of subsistence (arithmetically) had a continuing influence far outside anti-revolutionary circles, not least on Darwin. His ratio seemed by itself to block any dreams of human perfectibility from being realized. Fate meant famine and war.

Until 1750 Europe's population had grown slowly as it had done during the previous century. From 1750 onwards, however, when there were 120 to 140 million Europeans, the rate of growth began to accelerate, and by the time that Malthus wrote there were between 180 and 190 million. Growth was to continue in even more spectacular fashion – but not evenly – throughout the nineteenth century, with the population of France – and no one foresaw this – growing less than that of any other European country.

By the end of the nineteenth century Malthus's bogeys seemed to have been more fanciful even than Condorcet and Godwin's dreams. Indeed, while he did not foresee ways in which his grim ratio might not always apply, both Condorcet and Godwin had themselves foreseen that at some stage – very far away (Godwin talked of 'myriads of centuries') – the number of people in the world might press on food supplies. And during the nineteenth century, when the quantities and range of available foods, including foods carried over great distances, multiplied in unprecedented fashion, both Godwin and Condorcet continued to influence believers in progress. Robert Owen learned from Godwin and wrote his own *View of Society*: St Simon was in direct line with Condorcet who had promised 'a science to foresee the progression of the human species'. In seeking to discover 'laws' of progress as binding as the laws of science, St Simon prepared the way for one of his secretaries, Auguste Comte, founder of 'positivism', which along with 'liberalism' was one of the most widely diffused *isms* of the nineteenth century. Comte believed fervently that 'the determination of the future must be regarded as the direct aim of political science, as in the case of the other positive sciences'.

St Simon, who as a French aristocrat had fought with the Americans in the War of Independence, contrasted the eighteenth and nineteenth centuries: the philosophy of the former was 'critical and revolutionary', the philosophy of the latter was to be 'inventive and organizational'. He also maintained, in presenting a project for a new *Encyclopédie*, that it was absurd to set golden ages in the past. Through industrial change machines would 'replace human arms' in a society managed by industrialists, scientists [men of knowledge] and artists. There would be no need in this golden age of the future either for politicians or for soldiers.

St Simon's views influenced thinkers in many countries, including the liberal John Stuart Mill in England – he, too, contrasted the two centuries – and helped to form and to promote both thinkers and engineers in France. Yet the nineteenth century was not to be either St Simon's century or Mill's. Politicians were to gain in influence through the extension of the suffrage, the forging of political parties and the evolution of parliamentary government. Soldiers (and sailors) were to gain in importance also during the last decades of the century when 'militarism' was added to the many nineteenth-century *isms*. Scientists were to be less prominent than scholars in other disciplines, and social scientists (some of whom, among them the French sociologist Emile Durkheim, looked back to St Simon) were to be less numerous than historians. Artists and writers were to develop the concept of 'art for art's sake' rather than to adjust in functional fashion to the possibilities of a new society.

The idea of progress was challenged throughout the century by a range of both 'romantic' and 'realist' writers and artists, and was to lose much of its appeal (though not yet its popular hold) in the last *fin de siècle* decade of the century and in the first decades of the twentieth century, when the laws of thermodynamics could be cited to draw the gloomy conclusion that the earth was running down. There was to be talk then and later of 'degeneration' and 'decline'. And although the development of medicine, particularly surgery, was taken to be one of the great triumphs of the nineteenth century, making possible longer life and the relief of pain through the discovery of anaesthetics and antiseptics, there were fears of the physical 'deterioration' of large numbers of human beings and ominous pleas for 'genetic control'. 'Genetics' became as much a topic of discussion as anthropology, where one seminal work appeared, James Frazer's *The Golden Bough*, the first two volumes of which were published in 1890.

One of the great liberal works of the century, Mill's *Essay on Liberty*, had appeared in the same year as *The Origin of Species*. The thought and experience that lay behind it derived from a different kind of eighteenth-century thinker from Condorcet, Jeremy Bentham. Mill's father James had been one of Bentham's close confidants, and young Mill was given a carefully programmed utilitarian education from which he emerged after a personal crisis to write outstanding books on political economy and political philosophy. While acknowledging and praising human progress, he warned of dangers making for social and cultural conformity in his own society.

Liberalism and positivism had many features in common, although in Britain and France, in particular, there were obvious strains of 'romanticism' in the pursuit of liberal causes. There could have been nothing more romantic, for example, than the language used by Gladstone when he expressed his personal feelings in 1860 at the height of the struggle for Italian unification. 'I feel within me the rebellious unspoken word. I will not be old. The horizon enlarges, the sky shifts around me. It is an age of shocks; a discipline so strong, so manifold, and so whirling that only when it is at an end, if then, can I comprehend it.'

It would be misleading, however, to make too much of this element in assessing Gladstone, although it figured prominently in his voluminous diaries which chart, sometimes it seems relentlessly, his own history. Like some other liberals, Gladstone turned also to the classical world, speculating about Homer and translating Horace, while Mill described the Battle of Marathon as being 'more important', 'even in English history', than the Battle of Hastings. Macaulay too published his poems *Lays of Ancient Rome* before he produced his *History of England*. At a different level too there were elements in British liberalism that were neither romantic nor classical – middle-class self-interest and pride; provincial prejudice; nonconformist conscience; temperance (some liberals advocated total abstention from all alcohol); individual thrift; governmental parsimony. Which element predominated varied at different times and in different places. Temperance, for example, had dedicated spokesmen in Norway, the country which produced Henrik Ibsen, critic of most of these values.

There were other elements in continental liberalism, where there was often a strong tradition of anti-clericalism, particularly in Belgium and in

France. It was possible under the Third Republic to advocate freedom of enquiry and speech while urging repressive measures against Church orders and Church education. The words 'liberty' and 'liberalism' were for some writers and politicians synonymous with organized state anti-clericalism. There was an additional element in German and Austrian liberalism, emphasis on *Bildung*, a long-term process of character formation. Action was not a simple response to outside events: it was 'inner directed'.

The idea of individuals being formed through education as well as through experience greatly appealed in England to Matthew Arnold, who stressed how narrowly based the English middle-class character could be, and to Mill, who denounced the 'pinched and hidebound type of character' to be found in provincial places that he himself seldom ever frequented. The Prussian Von Humboldt, romantic in his sensibilities, had urged the need for 'human development in its richest diversity', and this included an openness to new experience and an appreciation of the aesthetic. Economic success in itself, 'getting on', was not enough.

One link between most liberals everywhere was the cause of free trade, as fervently pursued in Hamburg as it was in Manchester, and it is significant that before Gladstone became an advocate of the widening of the suffrage he had made his name as an active free trader. The cause of free trade could be proclaimed in the positivist language of economics, in formidable statistical comparisons, in moralizing sermons, in highly romantic platform rhetoric, or even in images, like those of a big and small loaf. It could also be linked to nationalism. For Cavour, writing 12 years before the major moves towards Italian unification, 'in working to lower the barriers that divide us, we are working for the intellectual and moral progress of Italy as well as for its national prosperity'.

Along with the gospel of free trade went other liberal economic gospels which were deemed to have universal applicability. More widely publicized even than free trade was the gospel of work, a gospel which in Britain had Puritan roots but which could be preached equally from Catholic pulpits in Vienna or Milan. Its missionaries condemned both aristocratic and working-class idleness, but they praised work positively also, claiming that it was only through hard work that people could develop their individual talents and that society as a whole could progress. 'Not what I have but what I do is my kingdom.' Max Weber was a careful student of the 'work ethic', examining in detail the relationships, as he saw them, between vocation, work, Protestantism and capitalism. In parallel he was studying bureaucracy and bureaucratic organization.[8]

One of the most active missionaries of the 'gospel of work' was the Scot Samuel Smiles. Trained to be a doctor, he became a railway administrator and an editor. His works were translated into many languages, beginning with *Self Help*, loved both by Garibaldi and the Queen of Italy. It appeared in 1859, the same year as the *Origin of Species* and the *Essay on Liberty*, to be followed by *Character* (1871), *Thrift* (1875), *Duty* (1887) and *The Lives of the Engineers* (1877). It is not difficult to see how Smilesian philosophy was related to that of Gladstone, who urged his hearers to 'be inspired with the belief that life is a great and noble calling; not a mean and grovelling thing that we are to shuffle through as we can, but an elevated and lofty destiny'.

The positivists would have agreed with Gladstone on this, although when foreign issues were being discussed they went further than Gladstone and other liberals did, turning to organized workers as allies. According to Comte, who invented the word 'altruism', a word that appealed alike to liberals and to traditionalists, it was 'among the working classes that the new [positivist] philosophers will find their most energetic allies. They are the two extremes in the social structure . . . and it is only through their combined action that social regeneration can become a practical possibility'.

The concept of 'social regeneration' did not appeal to most liberals, although some of them (on both sides of the Channel) were as prepared as the positivists were to try to encourage working-class aspirations. For them it was 'reform', a word that came to be substituted for 'improvement', that was most required. Institutions had to be 'improved'. They attached great importance, too, to free speech, even though there were limits to what was discussed, limits set by class, by convention and by reason.

The term 'positivism', like other nineteenth-century *isms*, particularly 'liberalism', could be used inclusively or exclusively; and in its exclusive form, as expounded by Comte, it diverged increasingly from 'liberalism', to such an extent, indeed, that Mill, deeply interested in all the points that the positivists raised, could describe it as 'the most complete system of spiritual and temporal despotism that ever issued from the brain of any human being – except perhaps Ignatius Loyola [founder of the Jesuits]'. The reason was not simply that Mill was nervous of 'complete systems', Comtist or Marxist, but that Comte's belief in the need for 'order' as well as for 'progress' seemed to him contradictory. Not least, it overvalued the 'organic' Middle Ages, just as many 'romantics' did.

This was a basic difference. The Comtists took religion seriously – creed and ritual. Aware that respect for old ecclesiastical authorities was breaking down – and with it respect for the authority of religion as a whole – Comte offered the world a new 'religion of humanity'. It had widespread appeal, but it was so interpreted by some of his disciples that they came to constitute a sect, with their own 'temple' in the heart of Paris, with their own chronicles of the great men who had made history, and with their own annual calendar of festival days for celebration.[9] It was in the knowledge of all this that Huxley called positivism of the Comtian variety 'Catholicism without Christianity'.

In its non-exclusive form positivism did not necessarily provoke liberal protest. Natural science, including Darwinian biology, rested on laws which Darwin's spokesman T. H. Huxley was happy to propound; and

Herbert Spencer, whose three-volume work *The Principles of Society* was published between 1876 and 1897, had far more influence on both sides of the Atlantic than Comte's faithful English disciple, Frederic Harrison. Spencer, a utilitarian and an evolutionist, came from a provincial nonconformist background and was infuriated when he was sometimes described as a disciple of Comte. Indeed, in best Victorian fashion he declared that the only debt he owed Comte was 'an antagonism which cleared and developed my own views'. His intention, however, was the same – to trace and to explain the laws of progress, the central law being evolution from the simple to the complex.

Like 'the other laws of the universe', the laws of society were for Spencer 'sure, inflexible and ever active, and they admitted of no exceptions'. Nor did they depend on coercion. Spencer, unlike Mill and Smiles, believed in social as well as economic *laissez faire*. Ironically he was to be buried at Highgate Cemetery in London in 1903, very near to Karl Marx who had propounded a theory of revolution which magnified (in the short run) the power of the state. Yet Marx too believed that 'social movement is a process ... governed by laws not only independent of human will, consciousness and intelligence, but rather, on the contrary, determining that will, consciousness and intelligence'.

Spencer had published his *Social Statistics* in 1851, the year of the 'Great' international Exhibition in the Crystal Palace when progress was made visible (three years after the revolutions of 1848); and in 1857 Henry Thomas Buckle, after 18 years of solitary study published the first volume of his *History of Civilization in England* which propounded – or promised – historical laws as firm as any proposed by Spencer or Comte. 'Just as astronomers had found the principles governing the motions of the stars, so ultimately will historians discover the laws which govern mankind.' 'Nothing is anomalous, nothing is unnatural, nothing is strange. All is order, symmetry and law.'

Buckle had originally hoped to write a 'scientific' history of civilization everywhere and not just in Britain, a task that in an age of increasing specialization was already impossible. He looked forward to the time when 'the history of man' would be taken out of the hands of 'babblers of vain things ... biographers, genealogists, collectors of anecdotes, chroniclers of counts, of princes and of nobles' and would be written only by those 'whose habits fit them for the task'. Neither Burke nor Michelet would have fitted the bill. Hippolyte Taine, who set out in France to make literary criticism a positive science, might well have done. He wrote a history of English literature which appeared in 1863. He explained psychology through physiology.

It was Spencer, not Buckle, Darwin or Taine, who invented the unforgettable phrase 'the survival of the fittest' (Darwin used the term 'natural selection') which was to be used later in the century by politicians and militarists of whom he would have disapproved. 'Social Darwinists' employed some of Darwin's concepts, including 'the war of nature', to relate to political rather than to natural processes. Their argument was that there was a human struggle similar to the natural struggle in which the fittest, that is the strongest and most capable, not only *would* win but *should* win. Spencer, extremely influential in the United States, was opposed to all 'sentimental' interventionism on the part of Church or State. Other writers – British, French and German – who used Darwinian language drew very different conclusions. It was just before the First World War that a British writer, in the periodical the *Nineteenth Century*, insisted that 'amidst the chaos of domestic politics and the wave-like surge of contending social desires the biological law of competition still rules the destinies of nations as of individual men. And as the ethical essence of competition is sacrifice, as each generation of plants or animals perishes in the one case, or toils or dares in the other, that its offspring may survive, so with nations the future of the next generation is determined by the self-sacrifice of that which precedes it.'

Not all social evolutionist argument was crude. There were sophisticated evolutionary anthropologists – and their inspiration was not necessarily Darwinian – who believed, like historians, that there had been an evolution from 'primitive' to 'advanced' societies, with Western culture as the highest form. Men of primitive culture were – to revert to the language of geology – 'moral fossils'. The process of 'advance', too, could be thought of in terms of law. As an early anthropologist put it in 1876, 'the history of human society is that of a development following very closely one general law, and ... the variety of forms of life ... is ascribable mainly to the unequal development of the different sections of mankind'.

The sense of the primitive that was to appeal in the twentieth century provoked very different reactions by the middle years of the nineteenth century when in an age of discussion a liberal-conservative writer like Walter Bagehot, editor of *The Economist*, studying the English constitution, was disturbed by the fact that 'the polity' was required 'to deal with a community in which primitive barbarism lay as a recognized basis to acquired civilization'. Similar perceptions were shared by continental liberals. In Vienna, for example, controlled by Liberals from the 1860s to the 1890s and given a new face, there was an awareness of the contrasts between a highly civilized city and some of the remote rural regions of the Habsburg Empire. The Liberals attached even more importance to aesthetic culture, including music and art, than they did to the improvement of public services.

The new face of Vienna was the *Ringstrasse*, built to 'contain' the old inner city and adorned with monumental public buildings (schools, theatres, museums and Parliament House) and impressive and much sought after private blocks of apartments. They were perhaps less conscious of the contrasts within their own city, and were not prepared for the upsurge of anti-liberal forces from below, mobilized by men like Georg

Plate 5.4 The Ringstrasse, c.1889. On the left of the picture modern apartment
blocks, on the right, the baroque facade of the *Hofoper* (Opera house of the Imperial
court or *Hof*), and centre-stage the Ringstrasse. The scale and grandeur of the
street's arterial design reflected Viennese society's pre-occupation with the modern,
but the street was also designed with military considerations in mind: to enable the
rapid movement of men and materièl to defend any part of the city centre.

Von Schönerer, son of a railway engineer, who employed rancour to ruffle
polite politics and who stirred up virulent anti-Semitism in the crowds.
Karl Lueger, two years younger, manipulated this and other illiberal forces
as he shifted from liberalism to populist control of the city. This was the
Vienna to which the young Adolf Hitler moved and which strongly
influenced his feeling and thinking. Theodor Herzl, a generation older, the
prophet of Zionism, had moved to Vienna too, just as fascinated as Hitler
was with the dynamics of mass psychology.[10]

Victorianism

The Habsburg Empirè did not rest on an industrial base. By 1851 Britain did. The facts of material progress were most obvious there in the first home of industrialism, although London itself was never an industrial city. It was the provinces that possessed an industrial face in Britain, or rather, perhaps, in Ruskin's phrase, wore an 'Iron Mask'. By the end of the century the iron had given way to steel. Yet the country was still ruled over by Queen Victoria, born in the same year as Ruskin. It was during the middle years of the nineteenth century, when what came to be thought of as 'Victorian values' were at their most firm that the term 'Victorian' came to be commonly used: 'Victorianism' came later.

British historians have rightly emphasized the dangers of dealing with Victorian experience as if it were one large, single block: there were at least three Victorian Englands – conveniently classifiable as early, middle, and late – covering a period when in France there were three markedly contrasting regimes. They have also warned, rightly, of the dangers of 'selective Victorianism', choosing particular facets of thought or behaviour and assuming that they were general.

Just because there were so many changes of regime in France, no French historians would be tempted to make easy generalizations about the 1840s, when Louis Philippe's 'citizen monarchy' was undermined by scandal and torn apart by social discontents; or about the 1880s, when a new republic was also concerned with scandals and seeking, never without strain, to find a place for itself in Bismarckian Europe. Likewise, no German historians – however strong their sense of the identity of the nineteenth century – would confuse the moods of 1848, of the 1850s and 1860s, of the 1870s and 1880s, and those of 'Wilhelmine Germany' where there was also something of a break after a court scandal involving Philipp Eulenburg, 'the Kaiser's best friend', in 1908. Wilhelm II, as prominent in the press, including the British press, as his uncle Edward VII, spoke a different language and fostered completely different images from any of his Prussian ancestors, though he shared most of their prejudices.

Victoria was the only occupant of a modern throne to give her name not only to an adjective (as Wilhelm II did), but a noun. By reigning alone for 40 years after her German husband, Prince Albert, died in 1861, she offered a sense of continuity which most other countries lacked; although Franz Josef in Vienna, just as conscientious but less imaginative, obviously represented continuity from his accession in 1848 to his death in 1918. Unlike her, however, he had less interest in and hope for the future. A. J. P. Taylor wrote 'the Habsburg Empire brought on its own mortal crisis to prove that it was still alive'.

To complicate matters, *Biedermeier*, an Austrian term often treated as equivalent to 'Victorian', preceded Franz Josef and there were many signs of Victorianism before Victoria came to the throne, notably a tightening up of moral codes and a proliferation of styles. By the 1870s, a watershed decade in Britain, Victorianism was ruffled and by the 1890s *Biedermeier* was obviously out-of-date. Both had implied a certain ultimate confidence in standards and in human destiny, however rapid the currents of change might be and however strong the sense of transition from past to future, and both carried with them a sense of moral obligation. By the late-1890s, when Victoria was celebrating her Diamond Jubilee and Franz Josef his Golden Jubilee, to their reverent and irreverent subjects alike they had become something of idols.

The term *'Biedermeier'* was invented by the Austrian writer Ludwig Eichvodt. Little knowing how widespread its use would be, he created a character called Biedermaier based on a worthy provincial versifier who extolled homely qualities. With the *a* changed to *e*, it was applied at first (mockingly) to styles of furniture and only later (more mockingly) to styles of living. There were many parallels between the cult of the private and the stress on family values in London and Vienna – as there were, indeed, in other countries inside and outside Europe – and some critics, considering them to contain compromises both in tastes and in conventions, have dwelt on the element of cant and hypocrisy which they have held to be inherent in them. They have ignored the fact, however, that the Victorians, though not the devotees of *Biedermeier*, were their own best critics.

Much that is associated with 'Victorianism' – including both values and artifacts, and much of the criticism of both – was as prominent on the other side of *La Manche* and in the south and east of Europe as it was in Britain itself. French liberals were just as prone as British liberals to attribute working-class poverty to indolence, apathy and improvidence and middle-class success more to character than to ability. Germany invented the Christmas card and the Christmas tree for the greatest of all the annual Dickensian festivals of the home. Not even the Albert Memorial in London is a more 'Victorian' building than the monument of Vittore Emmanuele in Rome, completed in 1884. And what could be more Victorian than the following passage from the great Russian novel *Dead Souls* (1842) by N. V. Gogol?

> She had been brought up in one of the most exclusive establishments where three objects are regarded as of the highest importance. First comes French, then the piano, that she shall be able to amuse and soothe her husband, and lastly a thorough acquaintance with the principles of household economy in its highest and most aesthetic sense, including the art of knitting purses.[11]

The literature of the so-called 'Latin countries' was far more accessible to the rest of the world than the literature of Russia, both in western and in eastern Europe, although the special characteristics of Russian literature – and music – came to be appreciated in the last decade of the century.

In this and some other contexts France, by then allied with Russia, comes into the picture more prominently than Britain or Germany. In

Poland, Hungary, and Russia, it was said, rich readers used to fashion their house *à la Balzac*, and in Venice merchants used to assume the names and manners of Honoré de Balzac's characters. (He was a novelist much approved of also by Marx.) The novels of Emile Zola, deliberately realistic, attempting to leave out nothing, provoked equally sharp reactions 20 years later. In exploring the ramifications of 'Victorianism' or *Biedermeier*, therefore, it is essential to focus on the sharp national contrast during the middle years of the century – the sharpest of all the national cultural contrasts in Europe – between the British and the French.

When Gustave Flaubert's *Madame Bovary* appeared in 1857 it was so different from English novels of the same period that the *Saturday Review*, a brilliantly written London weekly with an edge to it, could remark generally that 'French novels differ from ours in so many respects that it is hard to believe that they belong to the same period of civilization'. British critics felt that the French lacked all the strengthening qualities of a Puritan heritage: there were touches of 'decadence' to be found there before 'decadence' became a cry of the day in the late-nineteenth century, and there were no politicians who followed Gladstone in relating everyday political decisions to profound moral choices. Even Matthew Arnold, who admired French culture and education and attacked cultural 'philistines' in his own country, condemned the French for 'taking the wishes of the flesh and of current thoughts for a man's rights' and for believing that if such wishes were to be obeyed 'human happiness and the perfection of society' would be realized. He attributed the defeat of France by Germany in 1870 to a 'want of a serious conception of righteousness and the need of it'.

For their part, the French complained of 'chaste or modest England', with the first of the two adjectives being the one that rankled most. Illuminating evidence comes from the pages of Hippolyte Taine's record of his travels in Britain. Taine liked much of what he saw as a writer and critic of art and literature, but he was distressed by the plight of the working classes in the big industrial cities, and he was amazed by the extent of 'spiritual touting' in such unfavourable circumstances – the diffusion of religious tracts, for example, and the display of religious slogans. One of his comments on a Victorian Sunday in London was particularly evocative: 'A rainy Sunday in London; shops closed and streets nearly empty. The rare passers-by under their umbrellas in a desert of squares and streets look like ghosts: it is horrible.'

In France itself Flaubert, who once described himself disarmingly as 'a bourgeois living a retired life in the country, occupying myself with literature and demanding nothing of other people', and the poet Charles Baudelaire were prosecuted in 1856–57 for offending public morals through their writings. They could scarcely have been surprised, particularly Baudelaire, whose book of poems *Les Fleurs du Mal* ('The Flowers of Evil') appeared at the same time as *Madame Bovary*. He was a poet for whom the mention of the word 'progress' was rather like mention of holy water to the Devil. 'Poetry will die', Baudelaire maintained, 'if it assimilates itself to science and morality', and he associated himself with every poet who protested against the marketplace, the government office, and the pulpit. The Paris of the Second Empire, glistening in its gaslight, Baudelaire's Babylon, seemed to the English critics, particularly those who lived in England's flourishing provincial cities, to sum up all that was wrong with France, even if it did not stop large numbers of them from travelling there. 'Everywhere in the Latin nations', Arnold wrote in 1874, 'you see the old indigenous type of city disappearing, and the type of modern Paris, the city of *l'homme sensuel moyen* [average sensual man] replacing it.'

It was in Germany and German-speaking Switzerland that *bourgeois* ways of life were established most firmly during the middle years of the century. And there, where the quest for comfort was most apparent also, it was also criticized most strongly. After the revolutions of 1848 there was a consolidation of 'respectable' *bourgeois* tastes, and middle-class Germans established a reputation for regular habits, sentimentality, and *Gemütlichkeit* (a comforting word that has been translated into twentieth-century English as 'sedative benevolence'). *Gemütlichkeit* was completely compatible with Bismarckian reliance on blood and iron. Indeed, as German liberalism diverged increasingly from the kind of universalist liberalism advocated by Gladstone in Britain, the operational moralities of the two countries – based on character, duty, work and thrift – increasingly converged.

The great German-speaking Swiss historian, Jakob Burckhardt, who coined the phrase 'age of revolutions', realized far-sightedly that the prevalence of such moralities would not necessarily save the world from militarism and war. He feared, moreover, that 'large sections of society' would readily give up all their national literatures 'for the sake of through sleeping-cars' which carried travellers across frontiers, often by night, on the great international railway expresses. Burckhardt believed that nineteenth-century people, jejune, perfunctory, many-minded, were quite incapable of fully appreciating 'greatness': 'Our starting point might be ourselves ... Greatness is all that we are *not*.' There were similar judgements in other quarters. Thus, the Russian exile in London, Alexander Herzen, thought that it was the people, not the railway carriages, which were the real sleepers. How, he asked, could they be awakened? 'In the name of what shall the flabby personality, magnetized by trifles, be inspired, be made discontented with its present life of railways, telegraphs, newspapers and cheap goods?'

The speeding-up of communications by rail and by sea was one of the most noted phenomena of the nineteenth century, and in Europe – with all its economic, political, social and cultural differences – there was a strong sense of interdependence. The operas of Giuseppe Verdi could be heard in every opera house, some like *La Traviata* (1853), raising moral as well as musical issues. (It is interesting to note that in her youth Queen Victoria was an ardent opera-goer, and she also surprised Paris by her enthusiasm

for dancing on her visit in 1855.) The French musician, Hector Berlioz, sublimely romantic, always received a warm welcome in Britain, which produced audiences if not composers. The music of Richard Wagner, who began to create his great new opera house in Bayreuth, Bavaria, in 1871, was controversial everywhere, claiming 'disciples' and arousing critics.[12]

Russian writers, like Ivan Turgenev, author of *Fathers and Sons* (1862), and Leo Tolstoy, whose *War and Peace* (1865–69) is thought by many critics to be the greatest novel ever written, were regular travellers, and Russian composers heard their works performed in different capital cities. Many of the latter drew on literature for their themes. Pushkin made his name known to many European audiences through Tchaikovsky's *Eugene Onegin*. Fyodor Dostoevsky, whose *Crime and Punishment* appeared in the same year as *Fathers and Sons*, asked fundamental questions – without ever claiming to answer them simply or unambivalently – about the extent of the power of humans to make of the world and of themselves what they desired. These were central questions in a century when the world was being remade – in the opinion of many of its most creative writers – completely unsatisfactorily.

In Britain the mid-century years were a 'high-noon period'. In the decade which began with the Great Exhibition, machines, like industrial cities, came to be taken for granted, and the fact that the country – in defiance of its industrial structure (or was it because of it?) – had escaped the revolution in 1848 that Carlyle thought would come, increased confidence. So, more profoundly, did great economic prosperity which lasted until the mid-1870s. Real wages rose at the same time as profits, rents, and prices, so that there was a balance of interests, agricultural and industrial, aristocratic, middle-class, and working-class. Not surprisingly there were few demands for 'organic' economic or political reform during these years, when the unwritten British constitution, which antedated both industrialism and the rise of democracy, was extolled. So too was the fact that Britain as 'a home of freedom' allowed exiles from foreign despotisms to settle in it and remain relatively undisturbed – often to the chagrin of their own governments. Police decentralization and the absence of armed police appealed far outside Britain's shores as they were to appeal to Croce in the twentieth century.

This was the golden age of the English novel, when readers, who might have been tempted to be smug, could read not only Dickens, one of the most successful writers in reaching a wide audience, but George Eliot, an outstanding woman writer of remarkable sensitivity and moral judgement,

---

Plate 5.5 Original set for Wagner's opera *Parsifal*, c.1887. This set was designed by the Brükner brothers and their partner P. Joukovsky for its first performance at Bayreuth in 1882. Music for Wagner was not an enclosed language, but rather one to be exploited and adapted to convey moods. In *The Ring* cycle and his other mature masterpieces, he employed all the resources of the theatre and orchestra to create what he called a *Gesamtkunstwerk* (a total art work) in his purpose-built temple of opera at Bayreuth in Bavaria.

and Anthony Trollope, who could also engage his readers in self-examination. The word 'realism' has been loosely applied to some of this writing. Poetry, much of it late-romantic in style, was more often thought of as a means of escape, although Tennyson and Browning shared a deliberate concern for 'the modern'. Writers knew, of course, that there were large numbers of people in their society who could neither read nor write, even though literacy rates were improving before the advent in 1870 of publicly-provided elementary education, soon to become free and compulsory.

Prussia had led the way on this road early in the century, and it was not until 1870 that Britain passed its first national Education Act. In 1882 primary education in France, made free the year before, became compulsory and secularized. Jules Ferry, the initiator of this policy, made the schoolmaster the agent of the Republic, at the expense of conflict both in Parliament and, above all, in French provincial towns and villages where the clergy were bitterly opposed to 'secularization'. In all countries compulsory education for the young, even if it was of the most elementary variety, inevitably changed the terms of daily life, secular and religious.

During the last decades of the century, when the state was increasing its power in all countries and while Britain's economic lead was lost in several branches of industry, there was a loss in British cultural power also – despite the advance in education and in literacy. It is interesting within the British context to compare two poems of Tennyson, *Locksley Hall* (1842) and *Locksley Hall Revisited* (1882). In the first poem Tennyson, like Victor Hugo in France, put his faith in science: 'Science moves but slowly, creeping on from point to point.' And while he was more clearly aware than some of his contemporaries of the needs and demands of a 'hungry people', he had – again, like Hugo – great confidence in the future:

> For I doubt not through the ages one increasing purpose runs,
> And the thoughts of men are widened with the process of the suns.

By the 1880s Tennyson was less sure about science and more afraid of 'the power of Demos' than disturbed by the needs and demands of a 'hungry people'. And he was pessimistic rather than optimistic about the future:

> Gone the cry of 'Forward, Forward,' lost within a growing gloom;
> Lost or only heard in silence from the silence of the tomb.

This was more than the gloominess of old age. There was doubt also about direction. It was during the 1870s, when agnosticism and relativism were winning new adherents, that Morley talked of the air in Britain being full of missiles. 'Those who dwell in the tower of ancient faiths look about them in constant apprehension, misgiving and wonder ... All is doubt, hesitation and shivering expectancy.'

Tennyson and Morley were interested in *isms*. Those people who were not were less affected by such doubts, for despite intellectual ferment, life could retain (even enhance) its comfort. There was a thrill too in the adventure and glory of empire. The main social fear was the rise of independent working-class power, with new pressures apparent on the part of the unskilled workers and, more ominously still, the unemployed. Now the tables were turned; and for rebel voices like those of Oscar Wilde and George Bernard Shaw, both claiming that it was not the 'respectable poor' who were most worthy of care, it was axiomatic that 'the virtues of the poor are readily admitted and are much to be regretted. The best among the poor are never grateful. They are ungrateful, discontented, disobedient, and rebellious. They are quite right to be so.' Both Wilde and Shaw used the stage as a place for argument as well as for entertainment.

There were many different kinds of rebels, with two types standing out: aesthetes, like Wilde, savouring every aspect of experience, particularly the forbidden and the bizarre; and 'primitives', seeking a simpler and less 'artificial' life. Most of the latter read the poems of the American Walt Whitman and enjoyed the paintings of Paul Gauguin with their South Sea themes. Many, like Edward Carpentier, were willing to reject all accepted conventions. Women rebels were prominent, too, asserting rights that had been unclaimed a few decades before. The idea of the 'new woman' was as influential during the *fin de siècle* years as the idea of 'new art'. Indeed, the adjective 'new' became increasingly popular as the century grew old.

Even in the middle years of the century behind the great new boulevards of Paris, which Napoleon III ordered and which Baron Haussman had constructed (they were impossible to barricade), there lay the courtyards and garrets of *Bohemia*, a place not on the map that was known in every language. '*La Bohème*, the ideal, free, pleasurable life of Paris', Arnold went on, 'is a kind of Paradise of Ishmaels.' And in most European capital cities there was also a Bohemia, a clustering of artists and writers, many of them seeking to escape both from the conventions and from the commerce of nineteenth-century society and culture. Arnold paid little attention to it in his critical writings, though when he discussed 'intellectual and spiritual purposes' he treated Europe as 'one great confederation, bound to a joint action and working to a common result'. Nonetheless, much that was to be thought of as 'modern European' was born in Europe's Bohemias. And some of the people who contributed most to the making of what has been called 'the modern European mind' had lived there before 1870 when the great break in European consciousness was said to have occurred.

Modernity

The concept of 'modernity' can confuse as much as the concept of romanticism when it is used to describe as wide a range of cultural expressions as the stagecraft of Henrik Ibsen and the symbolism of the French poet Stéphane Mallarmé. Yet Mallarmé's poem *L'Après-midi d'un*

Faune, published in 1887, was not only set to music by Debussy but became a famous stage ballet presented by Sergei Diaghilev who founded the *Ballet Russe* in Paris in 1909.

'Modernity' worked through a series of connections between arts and between countries; and if Paris was a centre, so too, in the years before 1914 was Vienna, home not only of Sigmund Freud but of the musicians Richard Strauss, Gustav Mahler, Arnold Schoenberg, Alban Berg and Anton von Webern; of the poet and librettist Hugo von Hofmannstal; of the novelists Karl Kraus and Robert Musil; of the painters Gustav Klimt and Oskar Kokoschka; and of the philosopher Ludwig Wittgenstein; all key names in every dictionary of modernist biography, spanning nineteenth and twentieth centuries. Berlin and Munich were other centres too, the former 'making up in "modernity" for what it lacked in antiquity', the latter the cradle of German 'expressionism'. It was there in 1908 that Wilhelm Worringer, a proponent of 'abstraction', followed in the wake of Madame de Stael early in the century by seeking to explain the differences between 'Northern' and 'classical' (and 'Oriental') art. It was there too that Wassily Kandinski, a Russian pioneer of abstract painting, moved in 1897.

Much of the 'modern movement' has been described – and was, indeed, so described at the time – in terms of *isms*, however misleading they can be. Symbolism was the first, with the symbolist manifesto, *La Symbolisme*, published in 1886. There was no similar cubist manifesto, although the poet Guillaume Apollinaire, who introduced Picasso to Georges Braque in 1907, did much to diffuse knowledge of it (and of African art). 'Futurism' was proclaimed in 1909 in one of the most famous of manifestos, the first of several, written by the Italian poet Filippo Marinetti. One of its objects was to make a 'clean sweep' of 'all stale and threadbare subject-matter in order to express the vortex of modern life – a life of steel, fever, pride and headlong speed'.

Between and across the *isms*, connections can be traced back before and after 'symbolism' through *art nouveau* (called, in Klimt's Vienna *Sezession*), through *fin de siècle* 'decadence' – comprehensively condemned in one of the most discussed books of the 1890s, Max Nordau's *Degeneration* (1892) – through opera (from Strauss's *Salome* to Berg's *Wozzek*), through literature (from Ibsen to James Joyce) and through philosophy (from Nietzsche to Wittgenstein), and they can be traced geographically too. *Art nouveau* was developed in Scotland (Charles Rennie Mackintosh), Belgium (Henry van der Velde and Victor Horta), France (René Lalique), Finland and other countries; and when Strauss turned Wilde's play *Salomé* into an opera in 1905 (the play had been performed in Berlin two years earlier) this was 'a bridge' which joined the England of Wilde and Aubrey Beardsley, who illustrated *Salomé*, with the Austria–Hungary of Klimt.

There was symbolism in Ibsen too as his last plays – *The Master Builder* and *John Gabriel Borkman* – bring out, and within France itself in Zola's 'realist' novels. And in the background both to symbolism and realism were changing attitudes towards both time and place. They had been changing throughout the nineteenth century, but before time was unmoored in the twentieth, it was regulated. 'Standard time' was settled in 1884 when representatives of 25 countries met in Washington and established Greenwich as the zero meridian and divided the world into time zones. The system was slowly accepted between 1884 and 1900, with surviving exceptions like St Petersburg that retained their own time.

Individuals had their own times too, and 'modern literature' made much of them. The American philosopher William James invented the term 'stream of consciousness' in 1890. Marcel Proust played with time in his great modern novel *À la Recherche du Temps Perdu* ('Remembrance of Things Past'), the first volume of which appeared in 1913, to be followed by James Joyce, the Irish novelist in exile in France, whose *Ulysses*, considered to be one of the most important of modern novels, appeared in 1922. It was banned in Britain. Preoccupation with time and space was apparent in the work of painters – and sculptors – too. Thus, the French painter Marcel Duchamp described his *Nude Descending the Stairs* (1913) as 'an organization of kinetic elements, and expression of time and space through the abstract presentation of motion'.

This sounded completely new, yet 'modernity', self-conscious as it became, was not a new concept during the late-nineteenth century nor even during the 1860s and 1870s. It has been chased back to the Renaissance, Stendhal's favourite period, and even to the fall of ancient Rome, the period Oxford and Cambridge Universities deemed 'modern Europe' to have begun. It was during the last years of the nineteenth century, however, and the first decade of the twentieth, that old senses of perspective and purpose were most under attack. Ibsen probed all the accepted values that had dominated mid-nineteenth-century society. Nietzsche, intuitive and anti-intellectual, was at war not only with the purposive nineteenth century but with all the Christian centuries that had preceded it, dwelling on 'the feeling of power in man, the will to power, power itself', insisting that the positive passions which had to be released included pride, joy, health, sex, enmity and war. Nietzsche did not care that he had many enemies, including all systematizers: 'I mistrust all systematizers and I avoid them. The will to system is a lack of integrity.' Freud, different in background, temperament and talent, explored the unconscious, revealing 'the night side of nature and the soul'. His *Interpretation of Dreams* was one of the last books of the century. 'These wishes in our unconscious', he wrote, 'ever on the alert . . . remind one of the legendary Titans.' 'In the unconscious nothing can be brought to an end, nothing is past or forgotten.'

Other writers or composers, born earlier, notably Marx and Wagner, were admitted into the select group of 'modern' thinkers; Marx because his ideas were active in the shaping of twentieth-century history; Wagner (with Nietzsche's blessing) because in the three great operas, composed at different times, that made up *The Ring* – and in other operas, notably *Parsifal*, first performed in 1882 – he delved deep into the psychology of love, trust, hate, power and redemption and in the process created a realm of myth that was to retain, even to increase, its power in the twentieth century. There was a place also for the German philosopher of 'pessimism' Arthur Schopenhauer, who died in 1860, and for the French poet Baudelaire, who was read more after his death in 1867 than before.

As a key figure, the Norwegian prophet of modernity, Ibsen, saluted along with Wagner by George Bernard Shaw, was renowned throughout Europe during the last decades of the nineteenth century for his treatment of drama as social criticism, seeking to expose the errors both of convention and superstition. In particular, the morality of 'respectability' (a key word of the nineteenth century) offended him: the view expressed by Podsnap that there should be nothing in any book unfit for the reading of any 'young person', nothing that should bring a blush to that person's cheek. Sex had to be kept a secret in the mid-century middle-class home, and outside the home much was made in Scandinavia as in Britain of the need for 'purity' in thought and deed.

There was a great flowering of Scandinavian culture at this time, related in part to nationalism. Julian Christian Sibelius, born in Finland in 1865, composer of seven symphonies, composed his symphonic poem *Finlandia* in 1900. There were also cross-linkages between the arts. Thus, the musician Edvard Grieg composed the music for Ibsen's *Peer Gynt* as an opera. One of the greatest expressionist painters was the Norwegian Edvard Munch, who frightened himself as much as the people who looked at his pictures. There was a link here with Ibsen; as one critic has said, 'expressionism makes painting a vehicle for pure emotion, for inner drama, often in the raw state'. A later Swedish playwright and novelist, August Strindberg, bitter and at times obsessive, employed experimental expressionist techniques that influenced twentieth-century theatre, but his derogatory attitudes towards women scarcely qualified him to be a prophet of a new century which was to end with a feminist upsurge.

One of the people who influenced Ibsen most, the Danish critic Georg Brandes, gave a lecture in 1871 that Ibsen hailed precisely because it placed 'a yawning gap between yesterday and today', adding that anything was better than the existing state of affairs. There were other 'yawning gaps' in what had once seemed the safe structure of social life. Ibsen, who dwelt on the influence of the personal past on the lives of his characters, was aware also of the significance in mid-century morality of a 'double standard' in prescribing the behaviour of men and women. The 'manly man' was expected to behave in ways quite inappropriate to the chaste 'womanly woman', and the much cherished 'sanctity of the home', based on a family ideal in most European countries, was maintained in practice by the coexistence of widespread prostitution, regulated in most countries through licensed brothels. In Britain, where it was not, prostitution was

Plate 5.6 The 'new woman' enters a railway compartment, (anon.). Those who feared demands that women be granted legal and political equality with men sometimes argued, as here, that if granted equality, women would take on masculine characteristics. Yet many nineteenth-century feminists based their claim to the vote on women's differences from men. Millicent Garrett Fawcett, a future leader of campaign for women's suffrage in Britain, argued that women should be granted the vote '. . . because I want to see womanly and domestic side of things weigh more and count for more in all public concerns.'

described as 'the Great Social Evil': 'the prevalence of this vice tends, in a variety of ways, to the deterioration of national character – and to the consequent exposure of the nations among whom it abounds to weakness, decline and fall'.

It is always difficult to generalize about attitudes towards sex or about sexual behaviour, not only because there is that much that is hidden away from outside scrutiny but because there are both individual and class differences. There is no doubt, however, about the existence in nineteenth-century Europe of many forms of repression, and of the complex reactions of 'modernists' to what were their current values. Some were homosexuals, others libertines, some solitaries. The fact that 'the working classes' seemed to have kept free from some of the shibboleths of *bourgeois* morality encouraged some of the modern rebels to seek an alliance with them, curiously similar, though for different reasons, to that which the positivists had sought.

There had obviously been both cultural and social contradictions. Thus, romantic love, idealized in prose and poetry, particularly in the middle years of the century, was as much in sharp contrast with the competitive drive which sustained the private enterprise economy in its progress towards increasing industrialization as it was to dynastic and aristocratic approaches to family strategy. In mid-century middle-class circles the home, presided over by *pater familias*, was conceived of, therefore, as a place of release from the business pressures of daily life, above all a place of peace. 'The family', it was claimed in Britain in 1874, 'is the unit upon which a constitutional government has been raised which is the admiration and envy of mankind . . . The husband and wife, however poor, returning home from whatever occupations or harassing engagements, have found there *their* dominion, *their* repose, *their* compensation for many a care . . . There has been a sanctity about this.'

The problem, of course, was, as all 'realist' commentators were forced to note – and this was a link between 'realism' and 'modernism' – that all homes were not like this. Ibsen, in particular, dwelt on the tendency for husbands to treat wives and even children as property, at best dolls in dolls' houses; and in most countries, north or south, east or west, women were slow to secure their own property rights or (if they could divorce at all) to free themselves from their husbands on grounds of cruelty or desertion. Despite increasing pressure for women's rights, the husband remained 'the lord of creation' until the end of the nineteenth century, presiding over what were usually large nineteenth-century families. Children were present in such large numbers that the one Victorian maxim about them which is still remembered is 'little children should be seen and not heard'. Child mortality was high, and the death of young children was a common experience.

'Modern' writers, like Samuel Butler in Britain, were fascinated by the implications (sometimes 'unconscious') of authoritarian family relationships. So too, of course, was Freud. Preoccupation with the 'unconscious' was growing throughout the period, as Stuart Hughes demonstrated in his study *Consciousness and Society*, and there was no interest more calculated to erode the basic liberal and positivist philosophies of the mid-nineteenth century. Significantly, Freud himself, emerging from a *bourgeois* background in the Vienna of the late Habsburg Empire, retained a liberal belief in toleration and a positivist faith in science.

The 'well-ordered home' whether in Vienna or London required an ample supply of regimented domestic servants, and, despite occasional press publicity to the contrary, they remained in ample supply (if at rising cost) until the First World War. In all countries families were divided in status according to whether or not they employed domestic servants and if they did, how many. Working-class homes with no servants could be 'respectable' – even if by then this was bleak praise – but they could be no more. The mid-nineteenth-century middle-class household had to be full of *things* too, and there was change here – as there was in the size of families – before 1914.

It was another sign of 'modernity' when fullness began to be called clutter during the 1880s and 1890s, and it was an even greater sign of change when the design of the houses themselves began to change during the 1900s, particularly in Germany. During the early-nineteenth century, eighteenth-century objects had been relegated to attics or to cellars: they were too simple and balanced in design, and in house building there was a sharp reaction against 'monotonous' Georgian canons of taste. Now, in the late-nineteenth century, when many 'new things' made their way into the home, there was a further reaction against the mid-century predilection for solid, preferably highly decorated, furniture designed to last. There was ample scope, however, for luxury. The quest for wealth and for material progress did not cease as the doubts and anxieties of the philosophers and artists multiplied. Nor did the advance of socialism which accompanied the great burst of European economic development. The first decade of the twentieth century saw far more willingness to spend ostentatiously (at the table or the shoot, in the country or in the town) than there had been during the middle years of the nineteenth century. Plutocracy mingled with aristocracy. There was also an even more strident 'philistinism', not least in Britain, which went alongside demands both for greater wealth and for greater power. Edwardian Britain tried hard not to be Victorian in spirit. It did not help the apostles of 'modernity', nor did the economic and social configuration of Wilhelmine Germany.

If enjoyment was what the spenders wanted (even when they were in debt), permanence was what 'modernists' most despised. Fascinated by speed, the group of futurist painters and writers in Italy who prepared a *Manifesto of Futurism* (1909) demanded dynamic, individual action sustained by human energy and the new technical power of the machine.

There was political ambivalence in this, for some modernists of this kind turned more and more to the revolutionary left and some to the radical right. One French critic of reason, Georges Sorel, who owed much to Marx, managed – and he was not alone in this – to look both ways. In rejecting the liberalism of the ballot box and demanding direct action through the general strike, Sorel was searching for 'myths of action'.

It is partly because of such dualities that the twentieth century took on a quite different shape from the nineteenth. There was even to be a place for Victorian revivals after generations of revolt. There was often to be a disturbing preoccupation with violence, domestic and international. On the very eve of the 'Great War' of 1914–18, which so transformed history, a young British philosopher, Bertrand Russell, who was keenly interested in mathematics and the new sciences, was writing of the 'barbaric stratum of human nature, unsatisfied in action' finding 'an outlet in imagination'. Russell did not have long to wait for the action; and he did not like it when it came.

References

1. For Ruskin, see J. D. Rosenberg, *The Darkening Glass* (1963).
2. See A. Briggs, *Victorian Things* (1988), ch. 1.
3. W. Olins, *Corporate Identity* (1990); and J. M. Peddings (ed.), *Organisational Strategy and Change* (San Francisco, 1985).
4. For changes in the use of the term, see L. R. Furst, *Romanticism* (1969).
5. For romanticism in action, see J. R. Talmon, *Romanticism and Revolt* (1967).
6. See E. N. Hiebert, 'The Transformation of Physics', in M. Teich and R. Porter (eds), *Fin de Siècle and its Legacy* (1990), ch. 12.
7. For the classic study, now dated, see J. B. Bury, *The Idea of Progress* (1913).
8. See A. Briggs, *Victorian People* (1965 edn), ch. 5.
9. For the development of Comte's thought, see F. E. and F. P. Manuel, *Utopian Thought in the Western World* (Oxford, 1979), ch. 30, which also relates Comte to St Simon and Marx.
10. See C. E. Schorske, *Fin de Siècle Vienna, Politics and Culture* (1980).
11. Quoted in G. M. Young, *Victorian Essays* (1962) pp. 158–62, where Young points out that 'much that we call Victorian [in Britain] is a picture at second-hand, a satirical picture drawn by the Victorians themselves'.
12. For the place of Wagner and controversy about 'the music of the future', see C. Dahlhaus, *Nineteenth-Century Music* (English trans by F. Bradford Robinson, Berkeley, 1989), ch. 6, 'Modernism as a Period in Music History'.

Chapter **6**

A European Civil War, 1914–1918

'Germany has declared war on Russia – [went] swimming in the afternoon.'[1] So it was that the author Franz Kafka recorded the outbreak of the First World War in the hot first week of August 1914. His phlegmatic diary entry was in marked contrast to the jingoistic reactions to the declaration of war in most European capitals. Crowds gathered in Berlin, St Petersburg, Vienna, London and Paris during the final days of the Sarajevo crisis, cheering the escalation of international tension and the likely imminence of war. Berlin newspaper vans carrying the *Tägliche Rundschau* were stormed by crowds anxious for news of the Serbian response to Austria-Hungary's ultimatum, and Serbia's rejection of the Austrian demands was greeted with jubilant cries in Berliner dialect: '*Et jeht los!*' (It's on). During the weekend crisis of 1–2 August 1914 almost 2,000 emergency marriages were performed in Berlin, and when the Rector of Kiel University made an impassioned address on the declaration of war, almost the entire male student body enlisted.

Whether motivated by the desire to preserve a glorious present (Britain? Austria-Hungary?), to restore tarnished honour (France? Turkey? Russia?) or to create a glorious future (Germany? Serbia? Italy?), citizens, subjects and governments alike appeared eager to wage war. Cross-frontier ties were wrenched apart and the International Socialist brotherhood was broken. The enthusiasm for war can be explained in part – but only in part – by the widespread conviction that the war would be over in a matter of months. Most war strategists in 1914 foresaw a quick resolution to the conflict, despite ample evidence from the Crimean War, the American Civil War and the Boer War, which indicated that a major conflagration would involve long, drawn out and bitter fighting. This miscalculation was to change Europe forever. Fifty-one months and nine million deaths later the war was over, in time for Christmas 1918, not Christmas 1914 as had been widely predicted.

Plate 6.1   Masses at war. Gathered in London's Trafalgar Square to hear the news that Britain was at war with Germany, members of the cheering crowd salute the Union Jack. Similar scenes were enacted in other European capitals.

The dawn of 'total war'

By 5 August 1914 Britain, in proclaimed defence of Belgian neutrality and, more significantly in fear of German hegemony in Europe, had joined France, Russia, Germany, Serbia and Austria-Hungary at war. The war thus became the first major conflict since the Napoleonic wars which involved all the major European countries. They had been split into opposing camps of Central and Entente or Allied powers during more than a decade of diplomacy. During the course of the war, however, while Germany's erstwhile ally, Turkey, and Bulgaria fought alongside the armies of the Central alliance, Japan and the United States joined the side of the Entente, alongside Italy (after the 1915 Treaty of London), to be followed by a number of independent states in Latin America, by China and by Siam. Some of these powers, like Italy, entered the war because participation in the conflict seemed less dangerous than neutrality. The entry of the non-European nations, like Japan and the United States, had an important long-term effect for Europe. In particular, the entry of the United States was to shift the balance of power away from the European nations in the twentieth-century world.

Soldiers from distant imperial lands were heavily involved in the war also, but for the most part it was a European civil war, waged between countries which were either industrialized or on the way to being so. Paradoxically, it was because of the nature of European industrialization that military planners were led to believe that there would be a quick end to the war, typified by Prussia's ninteenth-century victories over Austria and France. The military believed that railways would move men quickly to the front, machine-guns would create a powerful offensive force, and mighty ships and artillery would overwhelm the enemy. Speed of attack was the key to the German Schlieffen plan (or rather plans as there were several versions) on which the beginning of the war hinged. With its stress on a quick strike to be followed by a decisive victory on the Western Front, and a turning east to confront the large and cumbersome Russian force, the plan promised dramatic action. For von Schlieffen:

> the whole of Germany must throw itself upon *one* enemy, the strongest, most powerful, most dangerous enemy and that can only be France.

Instead, the nature of the industry behind the war ensured that it would become a bloody and protracted conflict in which success along the Western Front was to be measured in inches rather than in miles.

Europe's economic growth, which had fashioned the most prosperous and privileged continent in the world, also created both the wealth and organizational potential to raise large armies that could be supplied on an impressive scale with industrial products. Meanwhile, individuals could contribute more in taxes towards the cost of waging war and endure greater reductions in living standards long before being reduced to subsistence level. Industrial and social progress in itself determined that the war would be a protracted conflict lasting over four years. No country had the freedom to wage war as it had claimed.

It was the large-scale development of Europe's metal, engineering, chemical and power industries, especially after 1870, that had helped to secure European economic dominance, which could now be applied in warfare. Given that the quantity of military hardware in Europe increased by 300 per cent from 1870 to 1914, Europe's powers could now kill one another far more efficiently. There were also many more Europeans to do the killing. In 1800 the five main belligerents (Britain, Germany, 'Austria-Hungary', France and Russia) had a combined population of around 98.8 million; by 1910 this had risen to 355.5 million. In 1914 the universal infantry weapon was the rapid fire rifle with a magazine of six to eight rounds. Refined machine-guns, too, had enhanced killing power. Innovation in the chemical industry had finally replaced the black gunpowder used for centuries with high explosives containing nitro-glycerine, developed by the chemist Alfred Nobel (1866) after whom future Peace Prizes were to be named.

Already by September 1914 Britain and France were buying liquid

Plate 6.2 German cavalry crossing a pontoon bridge in Russia. Throughout the war hundreds of thousands of men in cavalry divisions waited in vain for the decisive encounter which had characterized European warfare in the Napoleonic era. In the twentieth century experience of war, however, cavalry, for the most part, was consigned to the less glamorous role of intelligence gathering, and horses to transport and supply.

chlorine to produce poisonous gas, and the technology of chemical warfare developed quickly from chlorine to phosgene and mustard gases. The Germans were the first to use gas extensively and methodically. Flame-throwers and trench mortars were other German innovations in the field of battle. Denounced by 'the Tommies' (British forces) for their 'barbarism', the 'Boches' were also quicker than the British and the French to exploit sophisticated new devices like tanks and submarines.

Nonetheless, it would be a mistake to see the war as an entirely modern conflict. Seasoned methods of warfare continued, co-existing uneasily with the new. 'Old-fashioned' forms of transport – donkeys, mules, horses – were still essential, and military pride often stubbornly resisted change, even in the uniforms of war. To protect their troops in combat the British had already changed their uniforms to khaki and the Germans had moved from Prussian blue to field grey, but in 1914 the French army still wore the same blue coats, red kepis and red trousers which they had worn in 1830. Making the French soldier less conspicuous on the field of battle would undoubtedly have saved lives, but as the *Écho de Paris* reported, to banish the red trousers was 'contrary to French taste and military function'. The final verdict came from France's Minister for War: 'Eliminate the red trousers? . . . Never! *Le pantalon rouge, c'est la France!'*

During the first months of the conflict, Germany, well prepared, appeared to take the initiative in its choice of methods, tactics and instruments of war. But as the war continued and the resources of an entire nation had to be mobilized in what came to be called an age of 'total war', a phrase popularized by the German General Erich von Ludendorff in the 1920s, this lead was lost. It was the underlying economic strength, social cohesion and political stability of the nation, alongside the support or opposition of the United States, that were crucial in determining the 'winners' and the 'losers'.

The Schlieffen plan failed when French and British troops halted the initial German advance from Belgium to Paris, and by November 1914 the mobile war had shuddered to a halt with troops of the Allied and Central powers dug in behind trenches stretching across northern France. Technological developments had already determined that the war, contrary to expectation, would be largely a defensive one, although until 1917 most politicians and strategists did not abandon the hope that one successful offensive could turn the conflict in their favour. Meanwhile, European governments were slow to develop strategies to fight a long war as they were to do during the Second World War. They extended their control over their human resources, men (for the army), women (for factory and field), only in a haphazard and short-term fashion, if at all. Austria-Hungary, the Ottoman Empire and Russia paid the ultimate price – not simply defeat but political revolution.

The evolution of British policy towards the war provides a typical example of how the conflict 'surpassed' the expectations of politicians, military personnel and ordinary people alike. When the British government decided to fight in the summer of 1914, its immediate objectives were to restore Belgian neutrality and to prevent France and Russia from succumbing to the domination of the Central powers. Yet separated from continental Europe by 'the English Channel', the British were as suspicious from the start of the long-term ambitions of their fellow allies as they were of their enemies. Nineteenth-century experience had taught British governments to be wary of Russian expansionism in the east (the Crimean War, imperial rivalry in Asia) and of French colonialism in the south and east. The British government wanted any future peace settlement, therefore, to secure not only a Germany that would be tamed but a Russia and France that would not become so strong as to threaten the British Empire.

The question was posed inevitably, as it had been during wars against Napoleon, as to whether Britain could offer greater assistance to its allies by limiting the size of its own army and supplying money and equipment *or* by raising a large conscript army which would demonstrate that Britain had not abandoned its allies. The island of Britain, with its large empire to

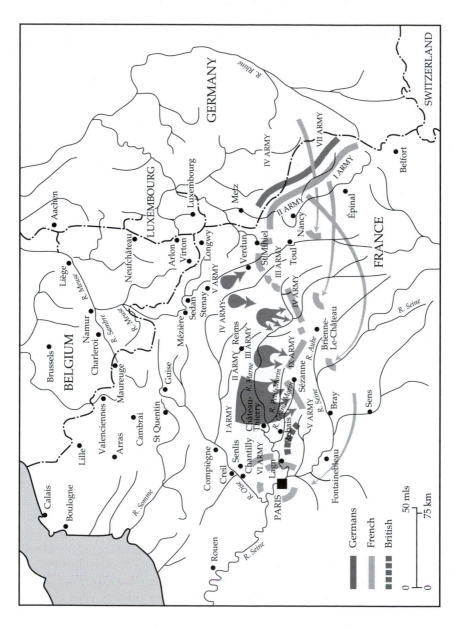

Map 6.1 Battle lines on the eve of the Marne

back it, seemed to have a greater range of strategic options than other Entente powers, another choice being whether to concentrate its military effort on initiatives on the Western or the Eastern Front?

Like the Central powers, the countries of the Entente alliance worked together at a number of levels – military, political, naval, economic – and among them Britain assumed that the main burden of the land war would fall on France and Russia, with troops from the BEF (British Expeditionary Force) making a limited contribution, while Britain's role in the war effort would be to impose a naval blockade on the Central powers and to provide financial support. In the late summer of 1914 a favourite slogan was 'business as usual'. The country appeared set to become the economic powerhouse of the Entente, by providing war materials and making a profit on loans granted to its allies. 'Maximum victory' was to be achieved at 'minimum cost'. By December 1914, however, it was clear that such a strategy was wildly unrealistic. France and Russia were unable to fight without large-scale military assistance, and the Russians already joked caustically that 'the British are prepared to fight to the last Russian'. So it was that by December 1914 British and later imperial troops (including Canadians, Australians, New Zealanders and Indians) became bogged down on the Western Front. The first months of the war were enough to shatter any illusions that the conflict would find a speedy resolution.

The course of the war

Losses in the first phases of the war set the pattern, for already by the end of 1914 France and Germany had sustained around 600,000 wounded or missing soldiers with over 300,000 dead in the 'battle of the frontiers', and nearly every family in both countries had suffered some bereavement. There were logistical problems also – ammunition and shell shortages – and grave concern about long-term food provision for the civilian population. Added to these difficulties came growing awareness of the terrible reality of trench warfare. Endless rain – the heaviest December rainfall since 1876 – turned the field of battle into an impassable, muddy swamp. Water pumps, hose pipes, shovels and pick-axes became as important as guns and ammunition in the struggle for survival.

The horrors of trench warfare continued until the end and left abiding memories. The first Battle of the Marne (September 1914), the Battle of Ypres (April–May 1915), the struggle for Verdun (February–November 1916), the Battle of the Somme (June–November 1916) and the recapture of the fortifications of Verdun by the French in December 1916, all took place within a remarkably small band of territory. The Battle of the Somme and the third battle of the Ypres campaign, Passchendaele (1917), stand out equally for their 'bloodiness' and for their 'futility'. Gains were small and the cost in life was very high. Death came by bullet, shrapnel, gas, high explosive shell and, at Passchendaele, by drowning in mud: the very name seemed to convey the image.

Away from the Western Front, Russian defeats at Tannenberg (in August 1914, where the Germans took over 100,000 Russian prisoners), in the region of the Masurian Lakes (November–December 1914), and in the winter campaign in the Carpathian mountains were the prelude to what was to follow. It was on the Eastern Front that German Generals, Paul von Hindenburg and Erich von Ludendorff, important actors in the future history of the Weimar Republic, established their military reputations. Then the Ottoman Empire entered the war. On 28 October 1914 the Turkish Caliph proclaimed a Holy War against the infidel and Turkish forces bombarded the Russian port of Odessa.

In the long run, the Turkish decision to join the Central powers was disastrous for the Ottoman Empire which, by 1918, faced dissolution; and the collapse of imperial rule created new territorial boundaries for the Middle East in the twentieth century – Palestine, Syria, Iraq, Saudi Arabia, Yemen. Yet in the short term, Turkish intervention added greatly to the problems of the Allied powers. The Russians, always chronically short of war supplies, were placed in immediate and long-term difficulties when Turkey closed the Black Sea Straits, thereby preventing Allied provisions from reaching Russian lines and factories. For Britain Turkish involvement also threatened the oil-fields of the Middle East, and Muslim insurrections in Mesopotamia, Persia and Afghanistan posed a grave potential threat to the British Empire.

With Anglo-French efforts on the Western Front trapped in a bloody stalemate, the British controversially decided to launch a naval assault on the Dardanelles, and in April 1915 an imperial army landed on the Gallipoli peninsula. The failure of the first assault prompted a second landing at Suvla Bay in August, but all to no avail. After weeks of indecision and at a high cost in ships and life – particularly among Australian and New Zealand forces – the Allied troops were driven into the sea and forced to withdraw. By the beginning of 1915, therefore, the Allies, in the words of Lord Kitchener, Secretary of State for War, had recognized that 'unfortunately we had to make war as we must, not as we should like to'. Britain, like France and Russia, now raised a large conscript army, and after military setbacks at Neuve Chappelle, Festubert, Arras and Loos on the Western Front, the Entente powers finally recognized the need for a common plan. Notwithstanding, the year 1916 proved as bleak for the Allies as 1915 had been. They held firm against a concentrated and determined assault by the Germans, now led by General Falkenhayn at Verdun, but in the battles both sides sustained losses of around 800,000 men.

The war in eastern Europe remained far more mobile than the war in the west, if only because the thin railway network reduced the ability of the belligerents to bring up reserves quickly to resist attack. In October 1914, for example, it took the Russians one month to transport 18 divisions from east of Cracow to south of Warsaw. Comparable troop movements on the Western Front took a matter of days. Strategically, however, the east did not differ greatly from the west since troops on the offensive invariably ran ahead of their communications, supplies and reserves, and defenders could easily assemble their reserves to counter-attack.

The offensive staged at Lake Narotch in March 1916 was typical of the inept efforts of the old Russian Army (as distinct from the 'new' Army led by 'sensible technicians' which emerged in the summer of 1916). Launched in the spring (18 March 1916), soldiers faced alternating heavy frost and thaw which turned road and field from ice to morass. This made the movement of heavy equipment impossible, shooting difficult and camouflage awkward: XX Corps was sited in marshy ground, easily visible to German artillery. The Germans also had good intelligence of the offensive two weeks before it began. The Russians lost over 100,000 men, as well as 12,000 men who died of frostbite. The Germans lost 20,000.

This typically horrendous defeat condemned the Russian Army to passivity. Russian generals argued that if the effort and resources of this campaign could not bring success, then only a mammoth increase in their supply of shells could. Even the brilliance of General Aleksei Brusilov could not rescue the Russian war effort, and when, for once, during the Brusilov offensive, launched on 4 June 1916, the bravery of the Russian soldier was matched by sufficient support in equipment, food, coordinated leadership and communications to offer the possibility of conquest, the advance faltered in the next month. Thereafter, the Central powers recaptured Galicia and Bukovina, and in September 1916 the Germans took Riga.

By 1916 more nations had joined the war: Italy, Bulgaria, Greece and Romania. Japan also entered the war in 1916, not to influence events in Europe but to eliminate the German naval threat; to extend its influence into China (especially Manchuria); and to spend more money on armaments which pleased those who had ambitions for Japan's role as a world power. Hopes receded of the 'one great offensive' which would create a turning point in the conflict, and instead, the war became one of attrition, 'the last resort of a paralysed strategy'.[2] Resources were severely strained, and the Allies, like the Central powers, under increasing pressure from within, were saved by the entry of the United States in April 1917. The United States, with its seemingly boundless supply of commodities, manufactures, loans and ultimately men, was the only country which could break the stalemate in the European war.

Men in trenches

For the men battling in the trenches, the war brought horrors far beyond the imaginations of politicians in the hot summer of 1914. What lingered in the mind as the 'Great War' helped fix the standard imagery of mass

Plate 6.3 Trench warfare. Some of the dense networks of interconnecting trenches, like this one, were carefully constructed. Others were not. Where the poet Rupert Graves fought, ate and slept, for example, '. . . the trenches have made themselves rather than been made, and run in and out; it is most confusing. The parapet of a trench which we don't occupy is built up with ammunition boxes and corpses. Everything here is wet and smelly. The Germans are very close.'

warfare until the deployment of atomic weapons some 30 years later: networks of interconnected trenches, uncut barbed wire and grenades, 'deafening artillery barrages', long lines of attacking men 'going over the top', moving as if in slow motion to be confronted by machine-gun fire. Men on the attack were left almost entirely defenceless. For a British soldier, Germans appeared to 'fall like shooting gallery targets'; a German machine-gunner depicted an Entente attack:

> The officers went in front . . . I noticed one of them walking calmly, carrying a walking stick. When we started firing we just had to load and reload. They went down in their hundreds. You didn't have to aim, we just fired into them.[3]

There were other horrors. On taking over one waterlogged trench, a Frenchman quipped, 'It'll be all right so long as the U-boats don't torpedo us'. Terrible mutilations of comrades in arms were common. So were decomposing corpses. Soldiers attempted to cover rotting bodies with dirt, but sometimes bits of corpses would find their way into sandbags – arms and hands were known to pop out unexpectedly from burst bags. Decaying bodies also attracted lice, and rats the size of cats. Poison gas attacks were the only way of killing the vermin, although, of course, this had the unfortunate side-effect of killing men too. For men on the front dirt and filth were constant companions. A spell of trench duty normally consisted of three to four days and nights in the front line and three to four days in the support trenches. This was followed by a similar length of time in the reserve, and only here could they wash, change and rest before returning to the front. For those troops behind the front line the principal feature of the war was boredom. Not surprisingly, there was a loosening of public morality. In 1914 soldiers were warned off wine, women and song, but by 1915 brothels were a standard component of base camps.

The gulf between officers and other ranks did not diminish to any substantial degree on either side during the course of the war. Europe's pre-war armies, with an officer class recruited from the traditional elites, and the regular rank and file often drawn from the lowest members of society, were not especially representative of society as a whole, and no European army witnessed a dramatic revision of its 'class-orientated' structures in the aftermath of the war. This was even true, in part, of the Russian Imperial Army when it became the Red Army under Lev (Léon) Trotsky's leadership in 1918. The status and privilege of officers were marked in many different ways: better food, cleaner dugouts, segregated eating places and cinemas, separate brothels, and longer periods of leave. There had been some changes in the West, however, among the regular rank and file when the patriotic rush to enlist was followed by conscription. Workers in commercial or distributive trades and many other occupations were now put in uniform, remaining at war for longer than most people employed in key occupations – industrial workers, transport workers and farm labourers.

With all the hardship and inequalities of trench life, the terrible sacrifice demanded of millions of men across Europe and the obvious confusion over what each nation was fighting for, why did the soldiers continue to fight? Unlike the ideologically-driven Second World War (the fight for liberal democracy and freedom on the part of the Allies: the fulfilment of national destiny on the part of the Axis powers) and the Cold War ('communism' versus 'freedom'), the First World War lacked any substantial ideological thrust. This difficult question becomes even more puzzling given that by the end of the war these were not professional but mass armies of relatively poorly trained conscripts and volunteers, many of the latter even unused to wearing uniforms. Moreover, military discipline was not intolerably harsh, although desertion remained punishable by death and the label 'conscientious objection' carried with it considerable social stigma.

Among the German and British troops, aside from a relatively minor incident at the British base camp at Étaples, soldiers remained remarkably loyal until the end. In the French lines, by contrast, there were widespread mutinies in 1917 after a series of disastrous and futile offensives. As in Russia, which in political turmoil experienced the most dramatic breakdown in military discipline, soldiers' protests centred on basic grievances – the quality of food, the cost of tobacco and the regularity of leave. Objections rested, therefore, on the poor administration of the war, not on the war itself. Perhaps, as was often suggested, the reality of life in the trenches helped to dull the senses and to suppress seemingly futile questions, while menial work – digging latrines, cleaning equipment, preparing rations – meant that there was little time for contemplation.

It would be wrong to conclude that soldiers were 'bludgeoned' into passive submission. Once the passion of patriotism had cooled, there still remained a sense of 'duty', *'devoir'*, *'pflicht'*, along with a gritty determination to see the conflict through, thereby making sense of the sacrifices that had already been made. But it is a small wonder that, given the appalling conditions which soldiers on all sides endured, men emerged from the war brutalized and alienated, although there were some soldiers who were inspired to depict the 'pity of it all' or to recreate in prose after the war ended the appalling conditions soldiers had suffered. A later generation of writers argued that the road to the Holocaust began in the dehumanized slaughter of the First World War.

War at sea

Before the outbreak of the war, Britain's position as the pre-eminent world power and the attempts of Germany to achieve a similar *Weltmacht* status had resulted in a spectacular naval rivalry between the two nations, and popular interest in naval rivalry did not end in 1914. The British public awaited a second Trafalgar when the upstart German Navy would be rapidly defeated by a Royal Navy superior in numbers and imbued with a fighting spirit honed by generations of naval supremacy.[4] But public opinion was to be disappointed. Although the Royal Navy had superiority in numbers – in August 1914 it had 24 Dreadnoughts with 11 building while Germany had only 15 with six building – it failed to win a decisive victory against the German High Seas Fleet, and the war at sea settled into a similar pattern of attrition and stalemate as the war on mainland Europe.

At Jutland in the North Sea (31 May–1 June 1916), the only significant sea battle in the war where firing was over a range of 16,000 yards – at Trafalgar it had been at 200 yards – the Royal Navy was not unequivocally victorious, for Britain lost more men and ships than the Germans. Set in a different perspective, however, Jutland was a victory for the Allies. Thereafter, the High Seas Fleet remained in harbour where its morale collapsed and its sailors eventually mutinied. The German Fleet was finally scuppered at Scapa Flow, Scotland, in November 1918.

In the war of attrition at sea, which entailed blockading supplies to the Central powers and providing convoy support for Allied merchant shipping, the Royal Navy was undoubtedly successful, but Germany was innovative and bold in its employment of submarines or U-boats – a form of operations largely unforeseen by the British – until Admiral Jellicoe's opposition to the convoy system was finally overcome in 1917. The change came just in time, for between 1914 and 1916 over one million tonnes of shipping had been lost, and with the final onslaught of unrestricted German submarine warfare in 1917 Britain's situation became critical. One in four ships coming to Britain was being sunk and only nine weeks' supplies of grain were left in the country. Even after the war British industry continued to suffer the effects of the U-boat campaign: in some British waters it became impossible to trawl for fish because of the large number of wrecks on the ocean floor.

Why continue to fight?

Given the apparent deadlock in military operations until 1917 and the terrible sacrifice of life and resources, it was perhaps surprising that governments in Europe did not make a more concerted effort for a negotiated settlement to bring an end to the war, as American statesmen, like Colonel E. M. House, wished. The first step to any negotiated peace, or even to initiate 'talks about talks', would have been for each belligerent to identify clearly what it was fighting for: its war aims, *buts de guerre*, *Kriegsziele*. But these aims were inherently difficult to define and, as the war continued, their range was widened.[5] This can clearly be seen in the evolution of German war aims from 1914 to 1916, a period when the Central powers generally held the initiative in the land war. In 1914 German war aims had been formulated on the basis of establishing the security of the German Reich. This was a difficult enough concept to specify, but by 1915, with German territorial expansion into eastern Europe (especially Poland), there was talk of a Central European Customs Union or *Mitteleuropa*.

The more territory Germany and Austria-Hungary occupied, the grander their war aims became. By 1915 in Germany, as elsewhere, there developed an imposing, unofficial movement strongly opposed to a compromise peace and firmly in favour of sweeping annexations. This lobby included German princes, and Conservative, Free Conservative and National Liberal politicians. In the same year a 'Petition of the Intellectuals' calling for 'the most ruthless humiliation of England' was signed by, among others, 352 university professors. A competing, anti-annexationist petition boasted only 141 names. Thereafter, there was little hope of the Entente powers or of the United States facilitating a negotiated peace.

The war aims of the Entente powers were no easier to define. Britain, France, Russia, Italy and Japan had been rivals in the past and were likely to be so in the future. Within the alliance, therefore, each ally hoped to profit from the war to 'stake out' its own position. There were also differences within countries as well as between them. There were people in Britain who shared Wilson's approach to a peace that would be liberal in 'tone' and national in its approach to communities and boundaries. Lord Lansdowne, Minister without Portfolio in Britain, for instance, called for a 'realistic balance sheet approach to war aims' in which war aims would be 'balanced' against the tremendous human cost of the war, but he was quickly denounced by cabinet colleagues who asserted that 'only cranks, cowards and philosophers' would consider peace before the enemy had been crushed. In Russia, too, the Tsarina was well-known to be entirely opposed to a compromise peace.

The same view also dominated the French cabinets of René Viviani (1914–15) and Aristide Briand (1915–17), although political tensions in France erupted in 1917 when Socialists in the short-lived cabinet of Alexandre Ribot demanded that the French government negotiate with fellow socialists across Europe for peace. It was a demand strongly and successfully denounced by the French right. It was only in 1917 that Britain and France were finally able to spell out their broader war aims, then to embark on a further reassessment when Russia collapsed in revolution and the United States entered the war.

As the bloody fighting continued, it also became clear that war aims were moving further apart. Indeed, like the alliances which increasingly had divided Europe irrevocably before the war, war aims could become barriers to peace and not the means by which peace could be negotiated. Equally destructive to hopes of bringing the war to an end was the inclination of governments to behave like addicted gamblers with an 'in for a penny in for a pound' mentality. Once the war was under way, they became entangled in a web of 'incremental commitment': they had to decide whether to launch the next offensive in the hope that this would create a decisive breakthrough and secure victory, or whether to cut their losses and negotiate peace.[6] War acted to deaden governmental sensibilities, and it was easier to sacrifice the *next* 50,000 lives after the first had been lost. It was only when the carnage ceased and wartime passions cooled that the cost of war appeared out of all proportion to the benefits of victory.

Plate 6.4 Tanks at the Battle of the St Quentin Canal, September 1918. The cribs attached to the front of these Mark V British tanks enabled them to break through the Hindenburg line, the most formidable entrenched system on the Western Front. It was protected by immensely deep fields of wire, many on reversed slopes, but the tanks crossed them with comparative ease.

The Church and war

In August 1917 the Vatican also attempted in vain to bring an end to the war with the publication of a peace note from Pope Benedict XV. Aside from the obvious humanitarian concern behind this gesture, the Roman Catholic Church wanted to terminate a war which had set Catholic against Catholic and undermined the Vatican's authority over its congregations. In Italy, in particular, the Catholic Church became an indispensable prop to a weak state fighting an unpopular war.

Organized religion across Europe had been seriously damaged by the unprecedented enthusiasm with which many ministers greeted the war, often urging their parishioners to further slaughter. As Pastor Phillips, a German Lutheran clergyman exhorted, 'Put more steel into your blood! German women and the mothers of fallen heroes must also not tolerate a sentimental attitude towards the war'.

In the longer run, while death and suffering in family circumstances might encourage spiritual concern, the association of organized religion with other traditional forms of authority – the military, the imperial monarchy – significantly undermined it in a conflict which appeared to banish God's benevolence from Europe. For the English painter, Paul Nash 'no glimmer of God's hand is seen anywhere'. The Churches of Europe had already been under threat before 1914, both from intellectual and social changes – the increasing urbanization of society; the movement of population; the growing tolerance within Europe of non-Christian ideas; new approaches to both sciences and the scriptures. Now there were new challenges, particularly to local parish priests. Some of them responded by serving at the battle front – with open air mass becoming a regular feature of army life. Others took the lead in organizing relief work – exchanges of sick or wounded prisoners, the repatriation of displaced civilians – and in local initiatives on the Home Front. In Italy, for instance, Catholic Action founded rural banks, Catholic newspapers and promoted peasant cooperatives. Some of the war's many casualties flocked to Portugal in the hope of solace and recovery after a vision of Fatima in 1917.

Two further challenges to the Church – communism and extreme nationalism – were also significantly strengthened in the course of the First World War. Communists who were to seize power in 1917 saw religion as the 'opiate' of the masses, the means by which the poor and destitute remained passive under the oppression of society's middle and upper classes. Extreme nationalists, like Houston Stewart Chamberlain, for instance, strongly rejected Christian teaching that all men and women are equally children of God by asserting that some peoples (for Chamberlain it was the German people) were clearly superior. Each of these creeds was to pose organized religion with important challenges in the decades which followed the war, creating new justifications for the persecution of Christians.

The United States enters the war

The entry of the United States on the side of the Allies won their war. In 1914 the American people, who included large numbers of first-generation immigrants, had treated the war in Europe as an outbreak of madness, and even as late as 1916 American involvement on the side of the Entente powers was far from a foregone conclusion. Some American statesmen, like Secretary of State William Jennings Bryan, believed that the United States had a distinct world role, based on its unique history, which meant that it should remain aloof from European conflict in order to pursue an impartial, mediating role between the warring parties.

Yet between 1914 and 1917 there was a gradual accretion of American support for the Entente powers, generated, in part, by the cultural sympathy between the United States, Britain and France. They were all democracies, and they had many interests in common. France was an old ally, Britons spoke the same language. Before the war, Britain and France had been important trading partners for the United States, and after 1915 they became important debtors. There were barriers, however, to going beyond sympathy. The Royal Navy had violated American 'freedom of the seas', as it had during the wars against Napoleon; both Britain and France had empires; British policy in Ireland, especially in the aftermath of the Easter Rising (Dublin, 1916), alienated the American Irish; and, leaving Britain and France on one side, Russia was an autocracy. It was American outrage at German submarine activity – the sinking of the *Lusitania* (7 May 1915), with 124 American deaths, and the *Sussex* (24 March 1916) – that turned public opinion against Germany, as did German attempts to incite Mexican support against the United States.

In January 1917 the newly appointed German Foreign Minister, Arthur Zimmermann, authorized Germany's diplomatic representative in Mexico to propose a Mexican alliance with Germany should the United States declare war on the Central powers, offering such incentives as the return of Mexican territory lost to Texas in 1848. British Naval intelligence intercepted Zimmermann's telegram, and this German intervention in the American continent, followed by the Central powers' resumption of unrestricted submarine warfare (1 February 1917), and the abdication of Nicholas II of Russia, certainly increased the likelihood of American involvement.

In the end, it was a desire to play an effective, if not pivotal, role in the formulation of the peace settlement which caused the Democrat President Woodrow Wilson to abandon his pacifist principles in the spring of 1917 and to enter the war on the side of the Entente powers (6 April 1917).

Governments at war

As well as irrevocably altering the lives of the veterans of the battlefields or the ocean ways, the war also had a profound effect upon those who remained 'at home'. Some of the effects might seem trivial. Some were irreversible. In Belgium, northern and eastern France, not only were families divided but property was destroyed or requisitioned by the occupying Germans. Belgium, occupied for over 50 months, was starved by a British blockade, and families struggled to find sufficient food to survive. The calorific shortfall of the average civilian was over 56 per cent, whereas in Britain it was 3.5 per cent. When in France the industrial town of Lille was finally liberated most homes were said to be without a mattress.

It remains hard to quantify how much social and political change was attributable to the war or how far the war merely accelerated trends which were apparent before 1914. Some change was unplanned: other change followed from the marshalling of national resources on an unprecedented scale. Every man, woman and sometimes child, it was now felt, had to be put to good use. Politicians, in consequence, found themselves taking on new administrative and social responsibilities far beyond their peacetime activities: they organized manpower, industrial production and distribution, rationed food, made agreements with organized labour, attempted to control public access to information, distributed propaganda, borrowed money and in the process imposed taxes on society at unprecedentedly high levels.

The most immediate challenge to government in the winter of 1914 was to muster sufficient numbers of men to fill the ranks of rapidly expanding armies, and then to organize enough manpower (women; the redistribution of workers from non-essential to essential industries) to maintain vital wartime industrial production. Within a matter of months, a large pool of unemployed labour had been absorbed and governments across Europe were faced with acute labour shortages. European society was dramatically changed by this search for labour. Those in work became more prosperous, as did those who owned factories – the industrial dynasties of Thyssen, Krupp and Vickers, for example – while the fortunes of Europe's landed classes were under threat. Businessmen were also recruited into government both in Britain and Germany, although the transformation from politicians into managers of a sometimes effective war machine was never complete. Nor did it happen overnight.

One such businessman who was successfully recruited to serve his government was Walther Rathenau, heir to one of the biggest concerns in Europe, the *Allgemeine Elektrizitäts Gesellschaft* (AEG), with ambitions as a writer, philosopher and social thinker. Appointed as head of the *Kreigsrohstoffabteilung* (war materials administration) to tackle Germany's desperate shortage of raw materials – by October 1914 Germany's food and fuel reserves were almost entirely exhausted – Rathenau created hundreds of 'war companies' to manage all the materials essential to the war effort. Tough measures for civilians followed and the German people began to suffer deprivations which did not affect Britain for another two years. By March 1915 Rathenau had returned to his business interests, although he played an important, if short-lived, role in the Weimar Republic founded after the war.

While Rathenau's wartime accomplishment was important, his writings, notably in *Von kommenden Dinge*, also foreshadowed the development of European governments in the later-twentieth century. Rathenau exhorted that the economic and social life of society ought to be ordered to 'equalize' property and income. To some observers, Rathenau's ideas were akin to revolutionary communism, but others recognized the positive role that he assigned to industry in opening up access to education and culture. His system, which sought to moderate the manifest evils of capitalism, presaged aspects of state corporatism which emerged in Europe after 1945.

In democracies like France and Britain, party political rivalries often surfaced when the war went particularly badly or was judged to be going badly, while authoritarian governments, like Germany, Austria-Hungary and Russia, found themselves riven by constitutional and ethnic rivalries, as well as by party politics, when it was sensed that defeat was at hand. In a three-step evolution during the course of the war, governments often passed through a first 'honeymoon' period of 'business as usual' into a period when problems were encountered that the state had never envisaged in 1914, and from then into a third stage when, threatened by subversion or revolution, it was necessary to promise postwar 'reconstruction'.[7]

Society at war

In a 'war of attrition' which came to be a 'war of exhaustion' each government was forced to borrow money and to tax its subjects more than ever before. France borrowed heavily from Britain ($3,000 billion) and the United States ($4,000 billion), and Britain borrowed from the United States ($4,700 billion), while allies like Canada, New Zealand and Russia borrowed from Britain and France ($11,600 billion). Germany and Austria-Hungary relied less on international credit and had little choice but to extend the tax burden, particularly to war profits: in 1917 profit tax was fixed at 60 per cent. Moreover, all nations issued government bonds (by 1918 the German imperial debt was 156.1 billion marks; it had been 5.4 billion in 1914) and printed money with insufficient reserves in order to pay for the war effort.

Financing the war had important implications for the long-term health of Europe's economy, but even during the war most countries experienced considerable inflation causing serious hardship: in France the wholesale price index rose from 100 in 1913 to 340 in 1918 (over the same period the German price index rose to 415, Britain's to 227 and Italy's to 409), and in Russia prices rose by around 500 per cent, wages by 100 per cent from 1914 to 1918.

The magnitude of social upheaval varied across Europe, and on the whole the challenge was managed more effectively in Britain and France than in Germany, Austria-Hungary and Russia. On 8 August 1914, for example, the French government introduced a rent freeze and acted to help families deprived of their principal breadwinner by granting a family allowance of Fr. 1.25 a day. In Vienna, by contrast, where there was no attempt to develop a social policy. Poor families had to forage from dumps and collect firewood from the Wienerwald where, by the end of the war, there was precious little 'picking wood' left on the ground of the forest.

Government intervention had its paradoxes. For example, at a time when millions of lives were lost in senseless battle, the working classes in Britain and France found their standard of living enhanced and their health improved. This was largely because they were able to earn more. In Germany, Austria-Hungary and Russia, by contrast, food shortages

Plate 6.5 A ration queue in Berlin, 1918. It was women, young and old, who took responsibility for feeding their families. Rations were often insufficient, particularly in Germany. The food situation became a critical index of the success or failure of the German war effort. It was commonly said that 'When old Bill's [the Kaiser's] lady wife queues for spuds, then the war'll be over.'

amongst the urban population were a considerable problem throughout the war. Germany in its encircled and blockaded position introduced *ersatz* bread made of potato and later turnip in October 1914, and ration cards for bread, fats, milk and meat were compulsory by early 1915. Meanwhile, German agriculture went into a steady decline, with vital manpower carted off to the front, and the farmers who remained behind had their best horses requisitioned by the Army, were forced to slaughter their pigs and were allocated insufficient fodder for their surviving animals. When the 1916 harvest fell below official expectations by over a million tons, it was clear that Germany's arable land was also suffering the effects of extensive overcultivation. Even requisitions from newly conquered territories (areas of Poland, Rumania and the Ukraine, for example), and imports from Austria and neutrals such as Holland and Denmark could not make good this shortfall.

In Austria-Hungary food was also in short supply. Fighting in the eastern half of the empire, Czech and Croat nationalist resistance, and the decision by the Magyar owners of large estates in Hungary to keep large quantities of grain to feed their animals all worked substantially to reduce grain supplies. In Italy, too, farmers' incomes decreased and levels of production declined: over two-and-a-half million peasants and labourers had been taken into the Army, leaving only older men, women and adolescents to till the fields. French farmers, by contrast, began to enjoy an increase in their profits, despite a fall in the overall levels of production, from the increased prices their goods could command, and some of them even took the opportunity to improve their equipment or animal stock.

In Europe's towns and cities the dislocation caused by the war was felt more directly. Food and accommodation rose considerably in price, but working-class labour was in unprecedented demand, enhancing both working-class ability to consume and political power. This was reflected in the changing size, character and strength of bargaining power of many trade unions, some of which, however, like the Genoese and Viennese munitions workers' unions, were ill-equipped to cope. There was a serious shortage of union officials, as the unions found themselves flooded by new workers and they were no longer dominated by skilled artisans. In cities like Petrograd, Milan, Turin and Berlin, radicalized workers in the munitions industries sometimes seized control of their factories, against explicit union directives, to make their grievances known. Through the 'Hindenburg plan' (*Hilfdienstgesetz*), passed in 1916, German trade unions had already markedly increased their authority to hire and discipline German labour under the watchful eye of the German military.

For large sections of Europe's middle classes the impact of the war was disastrous. Families living on unearned incomes, members of the liberal professions, the dwindling numbers of craftsmen and even civil servants, were badly affected by the consequences of the war. When 'heads' of families were called up for military service, they often left their families badly provided for, and their social status and pride often prevented them from claiming allowances which were available. The perception that the working class was doing considerably better out of the war than the middle class was particularly strong in Germany.

Despite the equalizing power of death on the battlefield, the perceived gains made by Germany's working class encouraged the birth of the *Dolchstoss* ('stab in the back') theory. As early as 1915 in a highly prophetic essay, the German sociologist Max Weber, warned that while

> the prolongation of the war is entirely the result . . . of a fear of peace . . . to a
> far greater extent still . . . people are afraid of the domestic political
> consequences of the disillusionment that will inevitably set, given the foolish
> expectations that have now run riot.

These 'foolish expectations' were to haunt post-war German politics.

In France, too, there was potential for future trouble. Members of the middle classes frequently served far longer spells of duty than their working-class counterparts and, with their higher standards of education, they were often subalterns of the reserve with an increased chance of becoming casualties. For the middle-class family the loss of the father often made it very difficult to regain social status once the war was over.

For all men returning home from the front, wherever they had been serving, readjusting to peace and family life magnified many of the subtle changes society had undergone in their absence. When the 'storm of steel' finally stilled, disabled men struggled to survive on meagre disability pensions, and some of the marriage vows hastily made in the heat of war were abrogated in peace. Fathers who felt their authority within the family damaged by their absence often battled, sometimes brutally, to reassert it over their children and wives. One man described his father thus:

> Of course he was sick from the war. He had had malaria, he had bouts of fever for the rest of his life, you know, and shivering fits. Actually he was pitiful, a pathetic figure. But the worse he felt, the more he played master and we were all the more afraid of him.

With the end of the war, an unprecedented number of veterans returned home leaving a dramatic impact upon the public's perception of war. Europeans were no longer confident in the 'Idea of Progress' which had dominated the nineteenth century. Instead, Europe had been plunged into an 'abyss of blood and darkness'.

Women at war

The First World War appeared to revolutionize the place of women in European society. Women, who were often 'invisible' in the political and economic history of Europe at peace, made tangible political, economic and social advances during, and especially after, the war. Much of this progress was more apparent than real. It is clear that for some middle and upper-class women the war offered an excellent opportunity to escape the stuffy vacuum of knitting, good works and polite conversation in which they had been swaddled for much of the nineteenth century. As the inspirational nurse Florence Nightingale reflected earlier, (prosperous) women often suffered from 'the accumulation of nervous energy which has had nothing to do all day ... [making] women feel every night as if they are going mad'. The contribution of some 'gentlewomen' to the war effort was more effective than others. The bravery of nurse Edith Cavell, shot by the Germans for aiding British as well as German war-wounded, stood in marked contrast to the activities of Lady Fanny Byron who sent a consignment of footballs (bearing the inscription 'simple mirth kept high courage alive') to the Western Front, being convinced that this 'manly' sport was the main foundation of the British character.

Nursing the dying and wounded was the most immediate contribution made by women across Europe to the war. In Britain the Queen Alexandra's Imperial Nursing Service, for example, grew from a force of 463 trained nurses in August 1914 to a force of 7,710 trained and 5,407 partially or untrained volunteers at the end of the war. In the brutal conditions of the battlefield it was a profession which demanded considerable courage. Before the invention of antiseptic paste the dressings on bad headwounds had to be changed several times a day, yet even the high-speed butchery of the operating theatres did not extinguish the compassion and care of these, often poorly trained, nurses for their patients.

The war served to enhance the standard of living and health of working-class women who discovered that they could secure employment and command wages at levels undreamt of before the war. Women were employed in munitions production (they were called munitionettes in Britain) – in France they provided a quarter of all personnel in war factories. In Germany the proportion was even higher: the German Krupp arms factories, which had employed 2,000 to 3,000 women before the war, employed 28,000 women by 1918. Other women became bus conductors or worked on the land in a variety of jobs where they had never been employed before. Yet very few occupations were feminized as a result. During and especially after the war, women continued to be employed predominantly in nursing, secretarial work and school teaching. In 1921 there were only 17 female solicitors in England and Wales, 49 architects and 41 civil engineers; in postwar Germany large numbers of working women were concentrated in unskilled industrial, agricultural and domestic jobs which were demanding in effort and carried with them lower status and income than ever before. These characteristics of women's employment remained unchanged for the next 30 years. Women's wages remained lower than those of their male counterparts. They were not encouraged to acquire new skills, and when men returned from battle the women were expected to return home to the hearth.

War propaganda portrayed women to their husbands or lovers as browbeating them to join the forces, saying goodbye, and bearing dead heroes' babies. Public 'concern' was also voiced that women earning money would upset the traditional 'male-centred' lines of authority within the family – the father as breadwinner with mother acting to reinforce his authority – but while families were often split up, family life continued much as before as eldest sons, uncles and grandfathers stepped in to replace the absent father. Daughters also became more important: their duties now included waiting in queues for hours on end for potatoes, margarine and horsemeat. Many women did not expect recognition for their contribution to the war effort from their fellow man. In 'Red' Clydeside, beneath a Kitchener poster ('YOUR KING AND COUNTRY NEED YOU'), was scribbled:

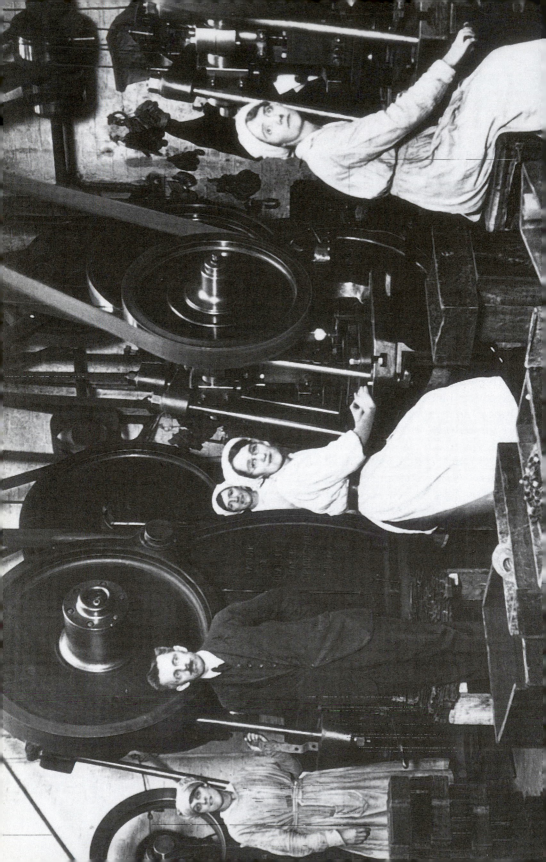

Your King and Country Need You,
Ye hardy 'sons' of toil,
But will your King and Country need you
When they're sharing out the spoil?

The most obvious spoil which came to women in the aftermath of the war was the vote, but even here it is difficult to quantify whether the women's war effort had contributed to this decision (taken by male politicians). In Britain and Germany, for example, the battles had already been won before the war. By 1914 specious arguments that women were illogical; lacked talent, productivity and common sense; and were unstable in opinion and allegiance largely had been refuted. By 1912 H. H. Asquith, then Britain's Liberal Prime Minister, although opposed to giving women the vote, had prepared his line of retreat into democratized women suffrage. In pre-war Germany women had become increasingly organized – the *Allgemeiner Deutscher Frauenverein* had over 12,000 members – and they were already an indispensable factor in industrial production (between 1882 and 1907 the female proportion of the manual labour force increased from 13.3 to 18.2 per cent, while in Britain women made up around 30 per cent of the manual labour force). In 1908 German women were granted the right to participate in political meetings and associations and by 1913 the German writer Gertrud Bäumer was confident that 'the state has come nearer to women, has become more alive and responsible to them'.

However, it is also clear that women's war effort helped to fortify changes in attitudes to female suffrage and the diminution of party divisions on the issue. This was most evident in France, where the academic lawyer and conservative politician Joseph Barthélemy was in no doubt by 1918 that the war had 'accomplished rapid and extraordinary progress for the cause of sex equality'. When the bill on women's suffrage came before the French Chamber of Deputies in January 1918, deputies both on the left and right of the political spectrum spoke in favour of enfranchising women on the same terms as men. (The bill was finally thrown out in 1922 when radical and socialist politicians got cold feet, fearing that women's votes would lead to clerical rule and the subversion of republican institutions. French women were finally granted the vote in 1945.) During the war, men spoke freely and frequently of their admiration for the courage of nurses and the efforts of women in factory and field, although often their political judgement was still disparaged. A (male) English author described a political protest of Berlin women in July 1915 thus:

Plate 6.6 Women war workers in a Manchester munitions factory, 1918.
Governments across Europe made much of the contribution of women munitions' workers to the war effort. They were usually paid less then men, however, and employers often went to great lengths to avoid replacing a skilled man with a woman worker (a strategy warmly supported by the trade unions).

These women were rather vague in their demands. They called Von Bülow an old fathead for his failure in Italy, and complained that the whipped cream was not so good as before the war.[8]

Women certainly appeared more emancipated during the war, most obviously in the way they dressed. Many women wore trousers or uniform – they delighted in the their new-found freedom of movement and pockets – but women were by no means emancipated from their central responsibility for raising the family. In France, for example, continuing concern over the declining birth rate led to propaganda efforts to encourage couples to have children. By December 1915 even the feminist newspaper *Le Féminisme Intégral* had reversed its stance on such matters for fear of being branded unpatriotic and now urged its readers to provide 'children, lots of children to fill the gaps'.

Historians have not been able to agree whether the war altered how women understood themselves and their position in society. Early wartime propaganda certainly encouraged women to think of the war as a conflict between men; women were told to stay at home. Many women, of course, did no such thing, and labour shortages and the need to enlist more men soon prompted European governments to enlist the manpower of women on the Home Front and to launch propaganda urging women to urge men to wage war. But while they began to enjoy their new found economic freedoms – buying dinner for themselves in restaurants, for example – the war continued to emphasize an essential difference between men and women: women were not combatants. Men were expected to kill and women were not. Moreover, as the social historian Susan Pedersen has demonstrated, the state's determination to 'relieve the minds' of its fighting men by providing separation allowance reinforced a notion of the man as 'head of the household' while the wife and children became 'dependants' for whom the husband – or in his absence the state – had to provide. This development prompted the Leicester branch of the Women's Labour League to protest: 'for the hardworking wife to be called a "dependant" is offensive and even insulting'. The advancement of such welfare provisions, coupled with the continued cultural emphasis on the family and the need for women to have children left many women, especially in Germany, Russia and France, without an obvious role in society as the war had killed or maimed a large number of their would-be husbands. The sight of women partnering women at tea-dances in postwar Europe was a poignant reminder of this lost generation.

Political change

Some features of social, organizational and political change during the war were common to all countries. Others, however, were specific. There were obvious differences, for instance, between France and Britain. At the outbreak of war the French President, Raymond Poincaré, spoke in Paris of a *union sacrée* (sacred union) which bound the nation, needlessly provoked by German aggression, together in a common cause. This unity, which embraced statesmen across a broad political spectrum and most of French society, was also evident in Germany, Austria-Hungary and Russia. In Britain, however, there was less unity amongst British politicians than elsewhere in 1914, doubtless, in part, because the war did not automatically challenge British national security. Within the Liberal government, the Foreign Secretary, Lord Grey, urged caution, fearing that 'if we shall suffer more . . . than if we stand aside'. But the violation of Belgian neutrality and, more importantly, a German-dominated Europe, helped to create a pro-war majority and anti-war minority. The latter largely consisted of socialists who, unlike many socialists in both France and Germany, were not prepared to support war credits.

The long-term impact of the war on British politics was great. The Liberal Party, which had held office since 1906, never regained power after the war. Divided over conscription and over the qualities required for wartime liberal leadership, it acquired a new leader in 1916, David Lloyd George, who under political pressure and with press support replaced Asquith as Prime Minister of a coalition government which now included Conservative and Labour members. Lloyd George hastily established a small cabinet and set up new departments of shipping, food production, national service and labour. All this was designed to encourage 'efficiency'. Nonetheless, so long as military success continued to elude the Entente powers, the domestic situation was never stable, and in 1917 workers' unrest, already evident in 1916 (notably amongst the militant, but atypical, workers of 'Red' Clydeside), broke out once more among engineering workers in Coventry, Sheffield and Liverpool. All in all discontent on the Home Front was ominous but not serious, and in a 'Coupon election' (so-called because the Unionists agreed not to contest 150 Liberal seats, a ration akin to the coupons in the nation's ration books) Lloyd George's governing coalition won a massive victory.

Political life in France remained relatively stable until 1917 under the government of the *union sacrée*. By 1915 French life was restored to some semblance of normality, and Parisians, who had fled from their city in fear of the advancing Germans, returned. Theatres reopened, undaunted by Zeppelin raids, one of the new hazards of war. It was only when the war reached a critical phase in 1917 with the failure of the Nivelle offensive at Chemin des Dames, followed by mutinies in the French Army, massive industrial unrest at home and the collapse of Russia, that cooperation within the *union sacrée* became strained. In secret sessions of Parliament, the ruling cabinet was severely criticized from both the left and right. On the left, many socialists were now arguing that the war should be brought to an end by peaceful negotiation, while the right denounced the Interior Minister, Louis-Jean Malvy, as a German agent and pressed for a more energetic prosecution of the struggle.

In November 1917 the 76-year-old Georges ('The Tiger') Clemenceau, who had been an unremitting and sometimes unrealistic critic of French failure to score a decisive victory against the Germans, took office as Prime Minister. Given the name *Père-la-Victorie* he immediately took a hard line against all his political opponents. Pacifists, declared guilty for seeking an end to the bloodshed, found themselves clapped in jail; while the socialists were bitterly denounced, particularly after a massive wave of strikes swept France in the spring of 1918. Clemenceau retained the loyalty of the Army. Yet he was keen to limit the growing power of the military in French civilian life, and he set the tone of postwar politics in France.

In Germany, unlike France, the outcome of widespread industrial unrest in 1918 led to the collapse of the established political order, the abdication of Kaiser Wilhelm II, and the creation of a democracy. Nonetheless, while the socialists played an important role in the political history of the new Weimar Republic, they were never able to shake claims that the strikes they had launched at home had brought about their country's defeat. Germany's conservative leaders, like the military commanders were able to assert, therefore, that Germany had been defeated by the Reds, rather than by the British and French. Industrial interests, too, increasingly came out on top before and after 1918, while national minorities also began to make substantial gains in return for agreeing to cooperate with the German war effort. As one Polish deputy boasted: 'the Foreign Office is as soft as prunes these days. It is willing to make concessions for us'.

It was not merely strikes which had contributed to a mood of defeat in Germany. The standard of living for ordinary Germans had deteriorated sharply – as it had in Italy – and young civilians were said to be dying from malnutrition before they had time to get to the front: it has been calculated that there were about 300,000 'excess deaths' among those aged between 15 and 19 from 1916 until the end of the war. Clearly, while imperial military forces were holding their own on the Eastern and Western Fronts, imperial bureaucracy was losing the war at home. In 1917, after the failure of the so-called Hindenburg plan, designed to limit shortages of food and labour, grievances burst out into the open. The Kaiser had already begun to negotiate with leaders of Germany's burgeoning trade union movement when widespread strikes and food riots erupted in major cities. In a momentous 'Easter Message' of April 1917 he opened the way for greater postwar democracy, but the Russian Revolution and the International Socialists' Conference held in Stockholm in June 1917 – a short-lived attempt of Europe's Socialist International to forge a path to peace – precipitated further German unrest. While floundering cabinet ministers were sacked and replaced, society disintegrated into chaos. Germany's administrative structures had proved incapable of coping with the demands of total warfare, and by 1918 no scheme – economic, political, or military – was effective enough to save the German Empire from defeat and dissolution.

During the first two years of war the Austro-Hungarian Emperor, Franz Josef, had succeeded in bringing together the Empire's different political parties, churches and people, but in 1916 there was a striking change in public sentiment. Following the lead of the Social Democrats, other opposition groups began to express doubts about the military leadership, and in July of that year a new Independence Party came into existence – led by Count Mihály Károly, the future President of the Hungarian Republic – which demanded internal political reforms and a peace without annexations.

Ironically, German propaganda did little to help its Central power ally when it portrayed the war as a 'decisive struggle between Germandom and Slavdom'. This poisoned the Slavic population's relationship with the military authorities. There was opposition in Hungary also, where industrial strife reached new heights in 1917, and in January 1918 a munition workers' strike in Vienna spilled over into Hungary, encouraging greater unrest, and infecting other national minorities. In the wake of defeat in 1918, all that remained for the government of Emperor Charles, who had succeeded Franz Josef in 1916, was to dissolve the existing state, and two separate republics of Hungary and Austria were proclaimed on 11–12 November 1918.

Russia in revolution

In February 1917, the Russian Empire was the first imperial casualty of the war. After repeated military defeats and internal chaos, Tsar Nicholas II was forced to abdicate and for the next nine months the ensuing leadership vacuum was filled by the dual regime of a Provisional Government – created from the former *Duma*, first under Prince L'vov and then under Alexander Kerensky (from July 1917) – and the Petrograd Soviet, a self-styled workers' council dominated by socialists. By October 1917 the Provisional Government, too, had failed to provide the Russian people with a military victory or with relief from massive food shortages, industrial disruption and calls for a redistribution of Russian land, and Russia succumbed to a Bolshevik revolution followed by civil war.

The war alone was not responsible for the ruin of the Russian Empire. In July 1914, on the eve of war, following a strike at the Putilov armaments works, industrial unrest had swept the Russian capital and within days over 110,000 Petrograd workers were on strike. Visiting French Premier Raymond Poincaré was greeted with the sight of Cossacks and police struggling to control demonstrators who were waving red flags, singing revolutionary songs, and seeking to smash their way to the centre of the capital. It took the suffering, deprivations and defeats of the war, however, to fuse the discontents of the Russian peasants, workers and middle classes, and it was because Nicholas lost the support of his armed forces that the Romanov dynasty perished. He had mustered an army of one million, ill-equipped men in 1914, but there were huge losses: between 7.2 and 8.5 million Russians were killed, missing or wounded. As Mikhail Rodzianko, Chairman of the Duma (an elected, but powerless chamber established by Nicholas II), wrote of the February 1917 street protests:

> 'Unexpectedly for all, there erupted a soldier mutiny such as I have never seen. These, of course were not soldiers but *muzhiki* [peasants] taken directly from the plough. . . . In the crowd, all one could hear was 'Land and Freedom', 'Down with the Dynasty', 'Down with the Romanovs'.[9]

When Nicholas abdicated in February 1917, his German-born wife disappeared from the scene with him. With the disreputable monk and mystic Grigorii Rasputin at her side, she had been left in charge of the Home Front while Tsar Nicholas led his troops in battle. But Tsarina Alexandra Fedorovna was unable to appease mounting popular discontent with the imperial government. In the month before the Tsar's abdication there were over 1,330 industrial strikes involving around 680,000 workers.

Writing in April 1917, Weber described what happened in Russia as the 'elimination' of an incapable monarch, not a revolution, and certainly for some members of the Provisional Government the events of February merely marked a political transformation that did not challenge the existing social or economic order. The Kadet (liberal party) leader, Paul Milyukov, typified this view with his fervent belief that the Tsar had lost the throne through his inept conduct of the war. But such a view was not confined to the Russian liberals. The Socialist Revolutionary Party (SRs), the Menshevik Party and even some Bolsheviks, like the future leader of the party, Jusip Stalin, at first supported the Provisional Government in its efforts to continue the Russian war effort. The SRs awaited a promised general election, while the Mensheviks cooperated with the Provisional Government because they were orthodox Marxists who postulated that Russia had to develop a larger working class before the time was ripe for a Marxist revolution.

Marx had argued that a communist revolution in which an exploited, industrial working class would unite and revolt against its capitalist employers, thereby abolishing private property and creating a 'classless society', was most likely to take place in countries which had a large working class, like Germany, Britain, Belgium and Holland. Indeed, for many Marxists the peasantry were a reactionary force. Hence the determination of the Russian Mensheviks to await the emergence of a Russian industrial proletariat with a revolutionary consciousness. By March 1917, however, V. I. Lenin, leader of the Russian Bolshevik Party, believed he had resolved the Marxist dilemma posed by Russia's small industrial working class. Eager for power (although, as always, cloaking his political ambition in Marxist theory), Lenin determined that the new Bolshevik formula should be 'a revolutionary dictatorship of the proletariat and the poorest peasant'.

Plate 6.7 Troops loyal to the Provisional Government fire on Bolshevik demonstrators on the streets of Petrograd, July 1917. One of the few pictorial records of violence in the Russian Revolution, this photograph shows Provisional Government forces firing on Bolshevik demonstrators on 4 July 1917. Despite later claims that the demonstrations were 'peaceful' and 'spontaneous', the demonstrators' actions were orchestrated by the Bolsheviks planning a coup d'état. At the last minute, Lenin lost his nerve and though Petrograd was there for the taking, the Provisional Government temporarily regained the initiative.

Only the Bolsheviks, revitalized and reorganized on Lenin's return from exile in April 1917, began to sing a different revolutionary tune to that of other political parties. Since his elder brother's execution for the attempted assassination of Tsar Alexander III in 1887 at the age of 19, Lenin had called himself a 'professional revolutionary'; and for 30 years this St Petersburg-trained lawyer and his similarly intellectual comrade leaders – men who later helped create the Soviet Union, like Nikolai Bukharin, Grigori Zinoviev, Karl Radek – had withstood imprisonment and exile in Siberia, London and Switzerland. Under Lenin's leadership the Bolsheviks developed a distinct programme of their own, promising 'Peace, Bread and Land' to Russia's workers and peasants. Driven by the profound conviction that 'history will not forgive us [the Bolsheviks] if we do not assume power', Lenin cleverly exploited the frustrations of the Russian peasantry, as well as those of the working class, in his quest for political control. But it was not all plain sailing. Despite the continued slaughter of Russian troops on the battlefield and the failure of the much publicized June offensive against the Germans, the Bolsheviks themselves were discredited when starving workers took once more to the streets of Petrograd in the 'July Days'. Bolshevik fortunes plummeted as party members fled into hiding or were arrested by forces loyal to the Provisional Government.

There was an economic crisis too. Growing anarchy in the countryside had profound implications for life in Russia's towns and cities, and by July 1917 food supplies to the capital had become erratic – Voronezh, some 300 miles east of Moscow, for example, produced only 30 per cent of the grain it had harvested in 1916 – and prices were spiralling upwards. Starving workers now fled the towns for the countryside and, as a consequence, industry continued to collapse.

Reflecting on his short-lived career as Russian Premier, the Socialist Revolutionary Alexander Kerensky claimed that he had been undone by two plots of a very different kind. The first had been hatched by Lenin and by Ludendorff, the latter providing the sealed train used to transport Lenin from exile to foment unrest at home, unrest on a scale undreamed of by the Germans. The second plot took place in August 1917, when Russia's Commander-in-Chief, Lavr Kornilov, marched on Petrograd in a counter-revolutionary attempt to impose martial law. Kornilov's rash act had dramatic consequences: Kerensky's authority collapsed, Russia's traditional conservative elites – judges, civil servants, priests and military officers – were discredited, the Army was in disarray and the Bolsheviks were able to come out of hiding and pose as defenders of the February Revolution. Florence Farmborough, a field nurse from Britain, noted how uncertainty fostered despair amongst the soldiers: 'if only they had someone in whom they could put their trust . . . Whom were they to believe?'

The Bolsheviks certainly made a big effort to capture the trust of the Russian soldiers, issuing their own army newspapers – *Soldiers' Pravda* and *Trench Pravda* – which urged disgruntled troops to fraternize with the enemy along the Russian Front. Authority and discipline began to collapse as servicemen formed their own soldiers' committees (soviets) and desertions from the front rose to unprecedented proportions. By then, the Petrograd Soviet – which in its Order Number One acquired control over Russian weapons and created soviets in all regiments, battalions, batteries and squadrons – was dominated by Bolsheviks and reinforced by its own Red Guard which numbered between 70,000 and 100,000. The Provisional Government was slow in calling a general election – Russia's Constituent Assembly met for the first and last time in November 1917 – and did little to satisfy the peasants' hunger for greater landownership or the workers' hunger for more food and better working conditions. It was by promising to fulfil the aspirations of these groups that Lenin ensured that the

Bolshevik coup in the Marrinsky Palace (on the night of 24–25 October) secured the support of a wider audience. Far from being a bloody, jacobin revolution, the Bolshevik revolution was a quiet affair. A deputy of the now defunct Provisional Government recorded his bewilderment when told an armed insurrection was under way: 'I laughed since the streets were absolutely quiet and there was no sign of any uprising.'

Once in control of the Russian capital, Lenin and his party needed to secure the support of the peasantry, numbering more than 100 million and by far the majority of the population, in order to provide a popular mass base to help them retain power. Their apparent determination to address the concerns of the Russian peasant broadened their appeal enormously. The peasants were embittered by years of redemption payments (payments to the government for land granted during their emancipation in 1861), as well as hunger and slaughter in the Russian Army. They were also frustrated by a pattern of landholding which determined that the gentry still owned 47 per cent of the land, with the ever increasing numbers of Russian peasants squashed within the remainder.

When the honeymoon of the February Revolution passed, peasants began to demand action on the distribution of land and food, and only the Bolsheviks appeared to promise immediate answers. Peasant soviets were created on an *ad hoc* basis across the former Russian Empire and peasants began to seize land for themselves. In Petrograd, those that remained increasingly supported the Bolsheviks, in search of a democratic republic, a just peace and a decent standing of living.

Peace and civil war

Having taken Petrograd in October 1917, Lenin declared a republic based on soviets, urban and rural, and set about arranging a peace with the Central powers. In the elections for the Constituent Assembly held in November 1917, however, the Bolsheviks polled less than a quarter of the vote. The election result clearly pointed to the strength of Bolshevik support in large urban areas and its weakness in the countryside. Despite this, the Bolsheviks kept a determined hold on power and in January 1918, though defeated in elections by the Socialist Revolutionaries (SRs) and the Mensheviks, they dissolved the Constituent Assembly.

After tense negotiations the Peace of Brest-Litovsk was signed on 3 March 1918. Some Bolsheviks, like Nikolai Bukharin and his 'Holy Group', had wanted to extend Russia's war effort into a Marxist revolutionary war across Europe, The terms of Brest-Litovsk were harsh and made it all the more difficult for Lenin to peddle the treaty to comrades reluctant to lay down arms: Russia lost 27 per cent of its cultivated land (particularly damaging was the agreement that surplus food supplies from the fertile Ukraine be given to the Central powers), 26 per cent of its population (some 55 million people), and 75 per cent of its iron and coal. Nonetheless, with peace to the west, Lenin could now concentrate on securing the Bolshevik revolution at home.

By July 1918 the Bolsheviks faced serious opposition from disgruntled SRs and Mensheviks unable to translate their electoral votes into political power, from traditional conservative and liberal elites and from the Allied troops now landing at Archangel and Siberia. British, French, American and Japanese troops became embroiled in the Russian Civil War, albeit in limited numbers and to limited effect, for a number of reasons. For Britain, France and the United States, Ludendorff's punishing offensives in the west and the signs of an alliance of sorts between the Bolsheviks and the Germans threatened to halt their progress towards victory, especially as Germany's penetration of Russia undermined the Allied blockade. There was hostility towards a Bolshevik victory, especially in the United States, France and Japan – the latter also determined to use its invervention to establish a permanent base in Siberia.

In Russia severe food shortages continued throughout that year, and on 30 August there was an attempt on Lenin's life. The first months of the Bolshevik government, far from putting out the flames of social unrest, fanned an even greater conflagration. The economic policy of 'state capitalism' gave way to 'war communism', based on grain seizures and complete nationalization, as the Bolshevik Party embarked on a civil war which outstripped fighting on the Eastern Front in its savagery and brutality.

The 'creation' of Poland

By returning Lenin to Russia, Germany had played an important role in the creation of the new Union of Soviet Republics. Likewise, when Germany transported Józef Pilsudski, the 'Prophet of Polish Independence' to Warsaw in November 1918, the collapsing *Kaiserreich* was also instrumental in forging the character of the new Polish Republic. When Europe was engulfed by war in 1914, Poland did not exist in any practical sense. Some 20 to 30 million people called themselves Poles, but they were imperial subjects of Germany, Austria-Hungary and Russia. The great Polish cities were similarly dispersed: Warsaw lay in Russia, Danzig (Gdańsk) in Prussia and Kraków in the Austro-Hungarian Empire. It was because the belligerent powers needed to win and to retain Polish support for their war efforts that they revived the issue of an independent Poland. What role it would play was as contentious and unresolved as it had been in the nineteenth century.

As early as August 1914 the opening gambit to the Polish people had been offered by the Russians. The Poles were promised 'a reborn Poland . . . free in her own faith, language and self-rule' under the sceptre of the Tsar. From then until November 1918 similar bids were made by

Austria-Hungary, Germany and, perhaps most notably, by American President Woodrow Wilson in the thirteenth of his Fourteen Points (January 1918) which called for a 'united, independent and autonomous Poland'. Meanwhile, the bitter and bloody fighting on Polish lands helped create both a sense of solidarity and political structures which Polish nationalists were able to exploit.

Poles, who had numbered 30.9 million in 1914, fought in the armies of Russia, Germany and Austria-Hungary, often against each other, and sustained over a million military casualties and a population decrease of 4.5 million people. But now Polish military and political organizations burgeoned on all sides, including the Polish National Committee under Roman Dmowski, based first in Lausanne and then Paris, calling for Polish autonomy under Russia; the Polish Information Committee, based in London; and the Polish Relief Committee with strong links to Polish-American groups in the United States of America. These groups, led by Dmowski, were the 'passivists' who hoped to achieve an independent Poland through diplomacy and cooperation with the Allied powers. They stood in marked contrast to the 'activist' grouping led by General Pilsudski – who worked to make his Polish troops indispensable to the Austro-Hungarian military – which sought an independent Poland through the Central powers.

From August 1915 until November 1918 it was the German military authorities who ruled Warsaw and it was this – plus the rudimentary Polish administration created by the region's Governor-General, General Hans von Beseler, and the return of Pilsudski to Poland by the Germans – which forestalled the implementation of the victorious Allies' plans for the rebirth of Poland. On 14 November 1918 Pilsudski was declared Chief of State of a nation without a frontier, government or constitution. Many Poles believed they had fought in the war for an independent Poland, and although this was erroneous, the sacrifice and courage of Polish soldiers and their families were instrumental in the years which followed, not only in the series of local wars (1918–21) which defined the boundaries of Poland far more than the Paris Peace Conference, but in the struggle to maintain an independent Poland in the face of future German and Russian territorial ambitions.

Important, too, was the notion of a distinct and respected Polish culture in the establishment of the Polish state in the twentieth century, exemplified by the work of Nobel 'laureate' Stefan Żeromski. In the famous verse of Edward Słoński, written on the eve of war, the sacrifice of blood and the notion of an immutable, common identity amongst all Poles found popular expression:

> Now I see the vision clearly,
> Caring not that we both will be dead;
> For that which has not perished
> Shall rise from the blood we shed.

Writers and the war

The glory of warfare was a common theme amongst writers on the eve of war. At first, many of Europe's artists and writers welcomed the outbreak of war as a revolt against the selfishness and greed of the pre-war world. In England Rupert Brooke wrote of soldiers as 'swimmers into cleanliness leaping'; in Germany Thomas Mann greeted the war as a 'purification and release . . . and a mighty hope'. Other writers and poets as diverse as England's Thomas Hardy, Italy's Gabriele D'Annunzio and France's Charles Maurras (later leader of *Action Française*), welcomed the war as an opportunity to reassert their national or imperial identity and the chance for adventure and heroism. As the German author Ernest Jünger recorded in his war diary, 'having grown up in an age of security we were all of us filled with longing for the unusual, for great risk . . . the war would give us that mighty, powerful, awesome experience'. Without experiencing the horrors of war, Brooke could write:

> Now, God be thanked Who has matched us with His hour,
> And caught our youth, and wakened us from sleeping.[10]

Even Sigmund Freud was not immune to the atmosphere which surrounded him in the summer of 1914: for the first time in 30 years, he felt himself to be Austrian – 'All my libido is given to Austria'. But for Freud and writers like the German Rainer Marie Rilke, this early enthusiasm was soon extinguished by a moral repugnance for the reality of the war. It was a rejection which found echoes amongst writers on the left in Britain and France – H. G. Wells, George Bernard Shaw and Romain Rolland. And in France and Britain, at least, writing which had glorified war soon lost its appeal and value in the eyes of younger generations.

The most searing stories and critiques of the war were published after, not during, the First World War. Erich Marie Remarque's *Im Westen Nichts Neues* (All Quiet on the Western Front), Robert Grave's *Goodbye to All That*, and Ernest Hemingway's *A Farewell to Arms* all appeared in 1929. The freedom of authors and poets during the war depended greatly on the level of government censorship and propaganda. In Vienna the satirist Karl Kraus's publication, *Die Fackel*, sought to highlight the incongruities and, whenever possible, the horrors of war against the welter of official propaganda. In 1916, for example, Kraus reported of children's essay titles at the Kaiser Karl Realschule: class Vb were given the choice of 'A walk during the holidays' or 'The latest methods of warfare' and class VIa were offered the choice of 'The main characters in Goethe's *Egmont*' or 'The intensification of U-boat warfare'. For the families at home, their perception of the war was coloured far more by propaganda and their distance from the war fronts, although in real terms the mileage was not great – an officer on leave from the Western Front could breakfast in the trenches and dine in his London club.

The poems and writings of men like Siegfried Sassoon and Erich Maria Remarque reflect both the horror and camaraderie of the war. But historians now argue that perhaps too much has been made of the 'spiritual bond' forged between men of different social classes in war. While Sassoon and Remarque helped reflect the bitter disillusionment of men who had gone to war for romantic ideals, the plethora of ex-servicemen's institutions – the British Legion, the 'Association of Italian Volunteers', *Vaterländische Kampfverbände* (cartel of German activists) – indicated that ex-servicemen were more concerned with the conditions of resettlement into civilian life than they were with sharing any common experience of military service.

The experience of women writers during the war was as varied as that of the men. Some, like St Clair Stobart, saw war and militarism 'as maleness run riot', while for others, like the volunteer nurses who cared for the wounded on the front (such as the 18-year-old Scots nurse Mairi Chrisholm and her English colleague Baroness T'Serclaes, known as 'The Heroines of Pervyse'), the war was an opportunity for adventure. But men and women did not share precisely the same stressful experiences during the war, and this is reflected in their writings. Women had no experience of trench life, and while they risked death in munitions factories or as auxiliaries behind the lines, they did not have to endure hours of endless bombardment or the sight of friends blown apart before their eyes. As one German carpenter wrote to his wife in 1914:

> You know more about the war theatre than we, except that everything is painted in bright colours for you. Would that some of those propagandists and superpatriots could be in a position now to see the corpses . . . piled high.

Such letters home were comparatively rare. Few soldiers wanted to cause futile unease at home, and if they tried to tell the truth, it was excised by company officers who censored all outgoing mail.

For the unprecedented numbers of war veterans returning home the sense of isolation and brutalization precipitated by their wartime experiences was oppressive. As Remarque's returning war veteran reflects in *All Quiet on the Western Front*: 'A terrible feeling of foreignness suddenly rises up in me. I cannot find my way back.' For some veterans it was easier to continue fighting – in communist insurrections in eastern Europe, in patriotic societies in Germany and Italy – than it was to face the realities of peace in 1918.

References

1. M. Brod (ed.), *The Diaries of Franz Kafka, 1910–1923* (Harmondsworth, 1964) p. 301.
2. C. Sorley, in a letter to his mother, 10 July 1915, quoted in Modris Eksteins, *Rites of Spring* (1990) p. 200.

3. J. Ellis, *Eye-Deep in Hell* (1977) p. 94.
4. B. Ranft, 'The Royal Navy and the war at sea', in J. Turner (ed.), *Britain and the First World War* (1988) p. 54.
5. B. Hunt and A. Preston (eds), *War Aims and Strategic Policy in the Great War* (1977) p. 16.
6. D. Stevenson, *The First World War and International Politics* (Oxford, 1988) p. 87.
7. The three stages are delineated by Arthur Marwick in *War and Social Change in the Twentieth Century: a Comparative Study of Britain, France, Russia and the United States* (1974) p. 24.
8. J. W. Gerard, *My Four Years in Germany* (1917) p. 301.
9. G. S. Gill, *Peasants and Government in the Russian Revolution* (1979).
10. For this and other examples of Brooke's enthusiasm for war, see G. Keynes, *Letters of Rupert Brooke* (New York, 1968).

Chapter 7

A New Order? 1919–1929

For Woodrow Wilson, as for Lenin, the end of the First World War in Europe marked the beginning of a new age. In Russia, Lenin and his party cohorts had seized power in November 1917 and set about consolidating the Bolshevik Party's slender control by dismissing Russia's new Constituent Assembly on 5 January 1918 and fostering the growth of local councils, or 'soviets' loyal to Bolshevik ambitions. Everywhere else in Europe, Wilson's vision inspired hopes for the future – from Poland in the east to Ireland in the west. In his Fourteen Points unveiled to Congress on 8 January 1918, Wilson had defined principles which he believed would bring peace, prosperity and greater democracy to Europe as a whole. Yet while 1919 brought much that was new to Europe – new nations, a new diplomatic order, a striking extension of democracy – many of the old social, economic and diplomatic structures survived to interact unhappily with the new. Within three years democracy was banished from Italy, and the political and social fabric in nations as diverse as Germany, Spain, Poland, Britain and Hungary became increasingly strained.

The 'price' of war

Managing the peace was the most immediate problem which faced a war-weary Europe in 1919. The situation was different from that after the Second World War, for in 1918 few plans for postwar Europe had been drafted by the Allies – or by the Central powers – during the First World War. The damage wrought by the war, however, was substantial, with intense though concentrated fighting in the West and sweeping military campaigns in the East. The war had affected every aspect of European society, and the loss of life and monies were amongst the most easily quantifiable of its costs. The number of deaths and casualties was unprecedented. Over eight million men were killed in active service, with another seven million severely disabled. Germany lost 1,800,000 men, Russia 1,700,000, France 1,385,000, Austria-Hungary 1,200,000 and Britain 947,000. Only American casualties were substantially less, with 48,000 killed in action.

Nonetheless, Europe's population was to recover. In the west it rose from 170.2 million in 1920 to 189.9 million in 1940, although there was only slight growth in France and Austria, and a static population level in Ireland. In the east and south the statistics were more impressive. In the former it rose between 1920 and 1940 by 84.4 million to 102.4 million in 1940, and in the latter from 68.6 million to 84.9 million. The impetus for the rise came from the continued popularity of marriage at an early age and continued improvements in health-care. (Celibacy, partly because of the decline of organized religion, has not proved popular in the twentieth century.)

The character of population migration had also begun to change. Scots, Germans and Russians, for instance, no longer migrated in large numbers to the United States as the open door of New York gradually edged shut. Europe's population also became increasingly urbanized. In the more industrialized nations, people no longer moved from a rural to urban environment in search of work, but rather from city to city. In Britain, for example, men and women moved from Manchester, Newcastle and Belfast to the new, light industrial areas located in the south-east of England around towns like Slough.

It proved more difficult for many European governments to recover from the financial cost of the war than from the loss of life. The physical damage wrought by the war was concentrated in northern France, Belgium and western Russia. In all, some 15,000 square kilometres of France were laid waste, and damage to French municipal, private and industrial buildings amounted to $17,000 million, a high proportion out of a world loss of $29,960 million. Indeed, it was France that appeared to have sacrificed the most in pursuit of victory amongst the victorious nations. All the European belligerents had lost loans and bonds invested overseas when war broke out, and large debts to the United States had been accumulated during the course of the war, in particular, by Britain and France, to fund their victory in Europe. The latter, in turn, had lent some of their own resources to subsidiary allies, like Australia and Canada.

Before the First World War Britain had been the world's banker, the primary source of overseas investment capital, and British banking and monetary pre-eminence, alongside the promotion of free trade, had helped to foster stability and growth in the international economy. After the First World War, the United States replaced Britain as the world's greatest creditor nation, with an important role (though different from Britain's) in supporting the world economy. This financial supremacy of the American economy was soon confirmed by the pressure of American technology, products and methods of industrial organization which generated both attraction and resistance. The term 'Americanization' became synonymous with 'scientific' management and production through simplification, standardization, and time and motion studies. The name of the American entrepreneur Henry Ford, an initiator of these practices, was equally well-known on both sides of the Atlantic. So were his automobiles. Dubbed 'Ford the Conqueror' by the British press, the American tycoon had big plans for Europe's postwar production and consumption of cars, many of which remained unfulfilled, in part, because of Europe's slow recovery from the war.

In 1919 few statesmen or businessmen appreciated the scale or, indeed, the nature of the economic consequences of the war. There were dreams of a return to 'normalcy'. From the spring of 1919 until the summer of 1920 Europe experienced a short and misleading economic boom – in Britain, France and the United States it was one of the shortest, sharpest booms ever recorded – fostered by consumer demand between 1919 and 1921 which sent out the wrong signals. The boom depended both on pent-up demand for products which had been unavailable during the course of the war, and spending on government orders to replace war-damaged goods like ships and railways. Once the mist of this spending spurt had cleared, however, the problems of the British economy, in particular, loomed large. Some of the old industries had already begun to decline before the war, and after 1921 the demise, notably of heavy industries, was to continue for much of the remainder of the twentieth century. For the shipyards of Glasgow and Belfast, and the cotton finishers of Lancashire, the days of prosperity and expansion were over. It was the United States which enjoyed a spectacular boom during the mid-1920s · that optimistic Americans felt would last forever.

The Paris Peace Conference

By then the government of the United States had passed from the Democrats to the Republicans, and Wilson's 'new age' in Europe had faded. His Fourteen Points aspired to a 'healing' and flexible European peace settlement based upon the principles of self-determination (points five to thirteen), open diplomacy (point one), an open world economy (point three) and a coherent international community which would abandon the sterile and dangerous practice of bilateral alliances and secret treaties (points two, four and fourteen). The language was lofty, but the American President descended from his Olympian heights on the other side of the Atlantic to chair the proceedings at the Paris Peace Conference. His rapturous welcome from the European public belied the hard bargaining that was to take place between the victorious powers, especially amongst the 'Big Four': British Prime Minister Lloyd George, French and Italian Premiers Clemenceau and Vittorio Orlando and, of course, Wilson himself.

Plate 7.1 Delegates representing the Allied powers watch the signing of the Treaty of Versailles, 28 June 1919. Delegates both inside and outside the Hall of Mirrors had to strain to see proceedings, for although the 'German representatives sat on a slightly raised dais in the middle of the room, unless one was in the front row it was very difficult to see what was going on. The Germans were marched in with very little ceremony or dignity', and when 'the signing was finished, the session was closed and the Germans were escorted out again like prisoners who had received their sentence.'

To many it seemed that Clemenceau, with 'the face and figure of a Chinese Mandarin' (according to the American Secretary of State, Robert Lansing), dominated the Paris proceedings.

The Peace Conference proved a miserable affair for all concerned. The unwieldy, haphazard structure of Conference deliberations did little to soothe the discomfort of the delegates, many of whom suffered from the 'Paris Cold', a worldwide influenza epidemic which killed more people than the war.

Germany and the Treaty of Versailles

For John Maynard Keynes, the British economist who was at the Peace Conference, the treaty was 'a Peace which, if . . . carried into effect must impair yet further . . . the delicate, complicated organisation already shaken and broken by war'. In a devastating and highly influential critique, *The Economic Consequences of the Peace* (1919), written after he had resigned from the British delegation, Keynes argued that the 'honest and intelligible' French policy to irreparably weaken Germany, which had gone uncurbed at Versailles, posed a tremendous future danger for the 'perpetual prize-fight' of European politics.

Keynes had a point. The spectacle of the Peace Conference had underlined Germany's status as a defeated power. The German government was not consulted during the negotiations, and only when the final draft of the settlement was completed were the Germans allowed to see the Treaty of Versailles. They were given fifteen days to put their complaints in writing to the Allies before minor emendations were scratched in red ink onto the completed treaty. Before signing, the German delegates to the conference, Hermann Müller and Johannes Bell, were humbled in front of an audience of 2,000 in the Hall of Mirrors of Louis XIV's magnificent palace (where Bismarck had humbled the French in 1871). The date was 28 June 1919, the fifth anniversary of the Sarajevo assassinations. In their defence, supporters of the Versailles Treaty argued that the treatment of the German delegates was no different from that which Prussia had inflicted upon France in 1871 or which Germany itself had imposed on Russia in 1918.

Nonetheless, despite this humiliating treatment (and, according to Harold Nicolson, a member of the British delegation at Paris who wrote a vivid account of what happened, the 'forlorn and deathly pale' demeanour of the German delegates), Germany had not been resoundingly defeated in 1918.[1] Rather, the German people had accepted Wilson's Fourteen Points as the basis for armistice negotiations and the new German democratic government, known to history as the Weimar Republic, watched proceedings in Paris with mounting dismay. It was clear to all Germans that their country had not been treated as an equal. It was not surprising then that the peace came to be thought of as a *'diktat'* (dictated peace) or *'Schandvertrag'* (treaty of shame). Instead of bringing peace to Europe, it provided a source of social, political and economic discontent for years to come.

Anti-German sentiment ran high in Britain and France in 1919, although there were differences on the two sides of the Channel. (The poet Robert Graves professed himself too weary for war unless it was against the French when he would be 'off like a shot'.) In both countries, sections of public opinion, stirred by the press, wanted to extract their pound of flesh from the German people. Lloyd George, Clemenceau and even Wilson eventually appeared to respond to calls to 'Hang the Kaiser', but were saved the embarrassment of a public trial of the former German Emperor when the Dutch refused to hand over their unwanted guest. There were no such fortunate solutions to other issues in Paris. Even when French and British national interests coincided, they did not always match those of the

United States. Moreover, if and when the Allies reached an agreement in the *ad hoc* muddle of committee meetings in Paris, their findings rarely, if at all, matched German aspirations for a just and honourable peace.

Arguably the hardest development for the German people to accept in 1919 was defeat in a conflict which, until the summer of 1918, they had believed they were winning. The terms of the peace were tough. Germany lost over 27,000 square miles of territory, containing about seven million people – about 10 per cent of Germany's pre-war resources – and its brief flirtation with empire was cut short with the loss of imperial territories in Tanganyika and South West Africa. Closer to home, German territorial losses greatly modified the map of Europe. They included the return of Alsace-Lorraine to France and the creation in western Prussia of a Polish corridor to provide the new independent nation of Poland with access to the sea. The former German Hansa trading city of Danzig, at the end of the corridor, was given the status of Free City since Lloyd George, echoing many of the prejudices of the older, powerful European nations, baulked at the notion of granting outright to the Poles the prosperous, cultured city with its 90 per cent German population. To have handed Danzig over to the 'primitive' Poles, he felt, would have been like putting a 'watch in the paws of a monkey'.[2]

These and other new territorial arrangements were bitterly resented by the German people, appearing to them as a gross violation of Wilson's Fourteen Points and of Allied promises that a democratic Germany would be treated fairly. The German peoples of Austria were not allowed to unite with Germany and over three-and-a-half million Sudeten Germans became part of the new Czechoslovakia. The French government would have gone further, however. It demanded an independent German Rhineland, for example, and it was only through Lloyd George's last minute pleading that plebiscites were held in the east Prussian districts of Allenstein and Marienwerder; and as a result these territories were allowed to remain in Germany.

Allied demands for a reduction in German arms, though greeted with resentment by conservative elements in German society, met with little dissent amongst the German population as a whole. The Rhineland was demilitarized, the Army was reduced to 100,000 volunteers, and Germany was deprived of a High Seas Fleet. These military injunctions, plus economically-motivated extractions, like the lease of the coal-rich Saarland to France for 15 years, did not provoke popular outrage in Germany to the same degree as the cuts to its 'national flesh' in extractions of territory, and a hastily drafted 'war guilt' clause which placed responsibility for the origins of the war firmly on the shoulders of Germany and its Allies. The 'war guilt' clause has remained controversial ever since, providing employment for a legion of historians, not least those first engaged by the German Foreign Ministry in 1919 in a strenuous effort to refute this Allied claim. Reparations were equally controversial and the issues involved remained intricate long after 1919.

Reparations and war debts

When Britain and France outlined their conditions for peace in 1918, they made no mention of an indemnity – a payment to be made by Germany for damages caused to the Allies during the war. During their war-dominated election campaigns, however, both Clemenceau and Lloyd George promised to 'make Germany pay'. Significantly, their election as Prime Ministers was to cabinets described by the colour of military uniforms – in France (November 1919) the *Horizon Bleu*, in Britain (December 1918) the Khaki government.

Of all the powers assembled at Versailles, the United States stood alone in refusing to demand 'tribute' payments from Germany, but the Americans were powerless to prevent their former allies from demanding reparations. In the years which followed, however, this moral stance rang increasingly hollow when the United States itself continued to demand war debt payments on loans granted to their allies during the course of the war. Its refusal to recognize any link between Germany's ability to pay reparations and the capacity of Britain and France to make war debt payments bedevilled their diplomatic as well as their economic relations.

In 1919 France took a 'realistic' and flexible bargaining position on reparations. A careful assessment was made of Germany's capacity to pay, and its government expressed willingness to reduce its demand significantly if the United States agreed to guarantee French security. And this was the nub of the longer-term problem. It was on the vexed questions of American involvement in Europe and France's preoccupation with national security that the Versailles settlement floundered. In the committee rooms of the Paris Peace Conference and on the floors of the Congress and Senate of the United States, it soon became clear that most of the people involved in the bargaining were not so much invigorated by Wilson's ideas for the future as burdened with the experiences of the past.

France's determination to secure reparations was born as much from a desire to rebuild its own economic base as from any impulse to ensure that Germany remained economically toothless. It did not. Indeed, some Britons and Americans argued that the requirement on the Germans to deliver both gold and goods to the victorious Allies as reparations would strengthen rather than weaken the German economy. The sticky problem in the Paris deliberations, once the principle of reparations had been accepted by the Big Four, was determining Germany's capacity to pay. For Britain and France the figure had to be fat enough to satisfy public opinion; for the United States the agreed sum had not to be so high as to starve an already emaciated Germany. After much foot dragging, a veneer of compromise was finally achieved with the creation of an inter-Allied reparation commission to fix the final sum after an initial German payment of £1,000 million in gold.

Neither Britain, France nor the United States profited from the reparations saga. The European victors collected nothing like the specified reparation payments, while the United States took up what, from the point of view of Britain and France, was a rather baffling position. It refused to demand reparations from Germany, yet insisted that France and Britain pay war debts to the United States. Eventually the United States did forgo much of this debt: by 1930 it had waived 35 per cent of Britain's debt, 82 per cent of Italy's and 65 per cent of French and Belgian debts. By then, however, the economic situation had changed radically. At least such issues had proved open to modification and negotiation. A far greater test for Allied cohesion and aspirations for a healing, flexible peace in 1919 came quickly with increased signs that the American Senate harboured profound misgivings about any American commitment to French security or to the League of Nations which lay at the centre of Wilson's vision.

The League of Nations

The American President dreamed in 1919 of an organization which would safeguard international peace and serve as a forum for a more orderly management of the world's political, economic, financial and cultural affairs, but while he worked hard to foster European support for his idea, enthusiasm in the United States for such an international commitment soon began to wane. Increasingly fearful of repeated involvement in European squabbles and suspicious that the League would cripple America's cherished freedom to take independent action whenever and however it pleased, the American Senate, in November 1919, refused to ratify the Covenant of the League of Nations. In so doing, it also rejected the Peace of Versailles. For all his pains to secure agreement in Paris and at home, Wilson, the idealist, had failed through the resistance of his fellow countrymen. He suffered a severe stroke and passed out of history.

The damage to European confidence in the United States was profound. The original Covenant of the League of Nations aspired to 'elasticity and security' in international relations. Now America withdrew from Europe – to mounting German and British frustration. There was a knee-jerk reaction too from France. During the 1920s France resolutely maintained that the

---

Plate 7.2   French Prime Minister Edouard Herriot addresses the League of Nations, September 1924. While public opinion across Europe looked to the new League of Nations to effect disarmament, the negotiations in Geneva increasingly turned on the question of rearmament. Herriot, mindful that French pride was still smarting from defeat over the Ruhr and increasingly subject to British and American pressure to accede to German demands for treaty revision, here justifies the rearmament of France: 'My country has a dagger pointed at her breast, a centimetre from the heart . . . I cannot renounce the security of France.'

Paris deliberations had determined the status quo in Europe. For security reasons it could not and should not be changed. Ironically, when by the 1930s France adopted a more conciliatory approach to German demands, Germany was under a new regime, that of Adolf Hitler whose dreams encompassed far more than a change in the status quo.

The difficulties for European peacemakers were stark after the effective withdrawal of American support for the peace settlement. The European Allies lacked the power, military or diplomatic, to enforce the Versailles peace terms. Moreover, when France did not win the much prized guarantee for its security from the Americans, this provided an opportunity for Britain to take a longed for step out of Europe. Although the British government remained committed to the security of France's borders with Germany, it grew profoundly wary of becoming embroiled in French foreign policy and the Republic's network of Little Entente alliances with Poland (1921 and 1925) Czechoslovakia (1925), Romania (1926) and Yugoslavia (1927). France had courted these alliances in an attempt, which proved forlorn, to contain any potential German ambitions of aggrandizement: the Little Entente was designed to recreate the sense of security and counter-balance provided before 1914 by France's former alliance with Imperial Russia. Instead, the French government's decision to establish mutual guarantees of security with these struggling new powers, which had their own differences, only served to emphasize the potential mismatch in conflict between a French nation of 40 million people and a Germany of 65 million.

The dearth of military or diplomatic authority to support the peace became more dramatically apparent in the 1930s, but even as early as 1919–20 the League of Nations lacked the clout to provide sufficient economic aid to the emerging nations of central and eastern Europe, and it was the Americans who stepped in, despite the abandonment of Wilson's vision. Flexing its new economic muscles, the American government created the American Relief Administration which supplied food to the value of $1,145 million, spearheaded by Herbert Hoover, future Republican President of the United States. As 'Food Regulator of the world', Hoover was enthusiastic in his duties, but he was never above giving a political twist to American aid. Thus, he offered the carrot of food to capitalist Austria, while granting none to a Hungary which stood under threat of communist domination by Béla Kun. His Relief Administration also arranged exchange deals which cut across wartime divisions: Austrian machines for Polish eggs and ham, Yugoslav wheat for Polish gasoline, and German coal for Polish potatoes.

Even after the immediate postwar period of rehabilitation had ended, agricultural problems persisted. Europe's diverse agricultural community, which ranged from small tenant farmers in Spain and Italy to British and German landowners (*Junkers*) who tilled larger estates, was in trouble during the 1920s. All farmers were affected by the sharp drop in agricultural prices which had several causes. Among the most important was the opening of huge new grain fields in America, Canada and Russia; more intensive use of farmland with the spread of mechanized farm equipment, like tractors; and the mounting popularity of chemical fertilizers. Europe's population also grew more slowly, and its diet had changed too, in favour of dairy over cereal produce. These challenges spelt trouble for Europe's farmers and for countries highly dependent on income from agriculture, most notably the new nations of eastern Europe.

The settlement in central and eastern Europe

The Paris Peace Conference marked the beginning of a wider concept of Europe as the empires of east and central Europe – Ottoman, Habsburg, Romanov and Hohenzollern – gave way to new nations and new democracies. If there was a moment when the nineteenth-century 'principle of nationality' triumphed it was at the Paris Peace Conference. In creating new nations from old empires, Wilson's fifth point, that of self-determination – the right of 'nations', largely defined by language, to choose their own form of government – was crucial, and Wilson could claim that in respect of the last he had fulfilled his vision.

For the victorious nationalists themselves – leaders like Thomas Masaryk, the highly respected Slovak President of the new Czechoslovak Republic – the creation of a jigsaw of new states in eastern Europe was a victory against the 'Caesarism' of Europe's former empires. His hope, as idealistic as Wilson's, was that 'these political changes will stimulate endeavours to bring a renascence and regeneration in ethics and culture'. The new states were broadly defined both as nation states and as parliamentary democracies. For Masaryk this, too, offered an exciting opportunity for democracy. Indeed, he argued nobly that the nation of Czechoslovakia could only be preserved 'through freedom increasingly perfected'. Not all 'nationalists' shared this vision in 1919, and the link between nation state and democracy in eastern Europe, increasingly weathered by economic, social and political pressures in the years ahead, proved extremely short-lived.

At first Britain and France had been uncertain as to whether they wished to destroy the old Habsburg Empire or merely to 'reform' it, but the swift disintegration of Austro-Hungarian rule, the threat of communist insurrection – during 1918 troops were used over 50 times to restore civil order in Austria alone – and Wilson's determination to uphold the principle of national self-determination wherever possible, forced the Allies' hand. A radical revision of national borders in the Balkans followed; many of the boundaries 'fixed' at Versailles were decided by the more junior members of the Allied delegation.

In Wilson's eyes, national identity could largely be determined by the language spoken and the choice of the individual: men and women could chose to be Polish or German or Serb or Bulgarian. But in eastern Europe, where the rich intermingling of language, history and religion were important determinants, such an approach was, at best, problematic. Unlike émigrés to the United States who had 'chosen' to become American, individuals in eastern Europe could not 'choose' to be Polish or Lithuanian or Serb or Bulgarian; they either were or were not. Ironically, the application of 'self-determination' alongside strategic and economic considerations made an already complex task impossible. So, too, did the creation of states based on more than one 'nation'. The Serbs, Croats and Slovenes who made up most of the new Yugoslavia had very little else in common: the Serbs looked eastward for cultural and political models, the Croats looked westward. Serbo-Croat was one language with two distinct alphabets.

There were certainly clear 'winners' and 'losers' in the radical revision of national boundaries in central Europe and the Balkans. The Treaties of Saint-Germain-en-Laye with Austria (signed 10 September 1919), Neuilly with Bulgaria (27 November 1919), Trianon with Hungary (4 June 1920), and Sèvres with Turkey (10 August 1920) marked out who they were. Germany and Russia lost territory too, and it was land taken from Russia which helped to create or redefine the national borders of Finland, Estonia, Latvia, Lithuania, Bessarabia and Poland. Germany contributed territory to the new Poland, while Austro-Hungarian land was incorporated into Romania, Czechoslovakia and Yugoslavia. Bulgaria, a late entrant into the war on the side of the Central powers, conceded territory to the new Yugoslavia, and although its territorial and population losses were small, they were felt acutely as a penalty because of the territorial expansion of neighbouring Yugoslavia and Romania.

Hungary, for centuries amongst the most stable and well defined powers in the region, was arguably, the most aggrieved. Its defeat in war cost it dear at the Paris Peace Conference. So, too, did its ethnic diversity. The punitive Treaty of Trianon left it with only 32.7 per cent of its pre-war territory and 41.6 per cent of its pre-war population. Nor was that all. To the Magyar people of Hungary the peace treaty appeared to endorse the dubious assumption that all non-Magyar people ought to be freed from the Magyar yoke. (The idea that the Slovaks, for example, might not want 'liberation' from Hungary was never taken seriously.) Yet for all these losses, the Treaty of Trianon did not promote national homogeneity within the 'new' Hungary. Over 15 per cent of its peoples remained of non-Magyar descent. After Trianon Hungarians harboured a profound sense of injustice, and their governments were vigorously to follow revisionist policies which spelt trouble for the future.

It was not only the 'losers', however, who were appalled by the application of the peace settlement. The British diplomat Harold Nicolson reflected disquiet in the former Allies' camp. For all Wilson's principles,

Map 7.1 Europe in 1914

'provinces and peoples were, in fact, treated like pawns and chattels in a game. The territorial settlements ... were based on mere adjustments and compromises between the rival claims of States.' He did not note, however, that the idea of forcibly moving peoples was rejected. Instead there were tensions and anomalies. Even the most apparent 'winners', the newly created states of Yugo(meaning south)-Slavia and Czechoslovakia faced problems. Their boundaries were so arbitrary that quarrels were bound to

Map 7.2 Europe after the Paris Peace Conference, 1919

follow, especially as these new nation states contained the largest proportion of ethnic minorities in eastern Europe. Indeed, while the Wilsonian peace settlement had strongly espoused the 'right' to self-determination, neither the nations of eastern Europe nor the former Allies were willing or able to protect the rights of these minorities and it was estimated that in 1930 around 52 per cent of Czechoslovakian and 57 per cent of Yugoslavian citizens were members of minority nationalities.

Natural frontiers – a river, the sea, a mountain range – did receive attention, and Wilson ensured, for example, that Yugoslavia incorporated the Dalmatian coast. But this decision itself created problems. It frustrated Italian ambitions by breaking promises made to Italy in the secret Treaty of London (1915) which had secured Italian intervention on the Allied side during the war. The Italian Prime Minister, Orlando, was so incensed that three years of fruitless battling against Austrian defences at a cost of 1,400,000 wounded and dead amounted to so little, he stormed out of the Conference and returned to Rome. Yet while Italy could not annex the Dalmatian coast because it was not 'Italian', it was given the German-speaking territory of the South Tyrol in the Dolomite Mountains for strategic reasons. Even in Poland where, as in Romania, the ethnic minorities were a smaller proportion of the total population (approximately 30 per cent for both nations in 1930), the advantages were more than outweighed by the fact that it shared a common frontier with Germany and Russia. Indeed, during the interwar period ethnic minorities in Poland were increasingly seen as the 'Trojan horses' of these revisionist powers, with Poland's large Jewish population sometimes also cast as potential communist agents.

The Paris peace treaties, which went some way towards creating a new geographic order for Europe and which reduced by half the number of people living in eastern and central Europe under alien government, fuelled the nationalism of the new nation states in eastern Europe, and not just among the dominant national groups – the Serbs in Yugoslavia, for instance. They did nothing, however, to provide Europe's minorities with national outlets for their 'nationalism' and offered them even fewer guarantees of their rights.

Meanwhile, the stress on self-determination enhanced the determination of the former Central powers – notably Germany, Hungary and Bulgaria – to 'return' their minorities, like the Sudetenland Germans in Czecho-slovakia, to the 'fatherland'. Given the unwillingness of national groups to live in countries where they did not form the dominant nationality – and there were over 30 million of them – nationalism was to become increasingly inseparable from political ambitions. As former Italian Prime Minister Francesco Nitti asserted in 1922, the 'keen contest of nationalism, land-grabbing and cornering of raw materials renders friendly relations between the thirty states of Europe extremely difficult'. Wilson, himself rooted in history, later professed his surprise at the virulence and variety of eastern European nationalisms. On his return to Washington, he told the Senate unhappily: 'When I gave utterance to those words [that all nations had the right to self-determination], I said them without the knowledge that nationalities existed, which are coming to us day after day. . . . You do not know and cannot appreciate the anxieties that I have experienced as the result of many people having their hopes raised by what I have said.'

National – and regional – tensions were to be subdued during the

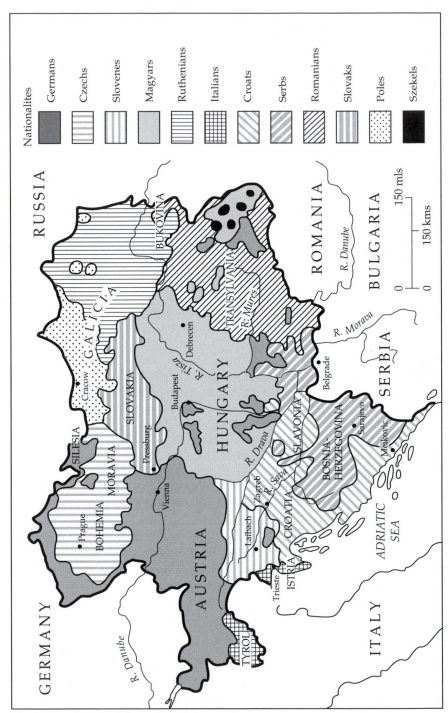

Map 7.3 The main ethnic groups of the Austro-Hungarian Empire

post-Second World War period with the extension of Soviet political authority into central and eastern Europe and the Balkans, but after the collapse of the Soviet Union, ethnic tensions were all to revive. Old dramas were to be replayed.

It was in the immediate aftermath of the treaties, however, that problems were to flare further east. The Allies saw the crumbling Ottoman Empire, which over the centuries had left its mark – religious as well as political – on the European map, as the ideal territory with which to pacify resentful Greek and Italian delegates who believed they had been shabbily treated by their former allies. In May 1919 the decimated Ottoman Empire, which comprised only 77 per cent of its pre-war population and 80 per cent of its former territory, was invaded by a nominally inter-Allied (but in fact overwhelmingly Greek) force at Smyrna (modern day Izmir) on Turkey's eastern coast. The Smyrna occupation only served to fuel anti-Greek and anti-Allied hostility (although the Italians and later the Americans opposed it), and helped precipitate a 'modern', nationalist revolt in Turkey itself which was led by Mustapha Kemal. The Sèvres peace settlement of 1920 dealing with the former Ottoman Empire had already proved unworkable, and it was replaced by the Treaty of Lausanne in July 1923. By then, the formidable task of trying to create an effective peace for Europe had taken longer than the prosecution of a seemingly endless war.

Russian civil war and peace, 1918–21

The boundaries of eastern Europe were not determined solely by weary peacemakers in Versailles. The bloody civil war in Russia, which erupted in the summer of 1918, also helped define the borders of the Soviet Union and Poland. It was a war between the Bolshevik Red Guard and a White Guard composed of disparate political opponents, including former imperial troops, who received military assistance from European, American and Japanese allies.

After the conclusion of the Brest-Litovsk Treaty in March 1918 the Bolsheviks confronted three principal problems: quietening domestic political opposition, which by July 1918 had taken up arms against the Bolsheviks; extending the Bolshevik revolution beyond Russia's urban centres, like Petrograd and Moscow; and determining the territorial boundaries of the new Soviet Republic and its policies towards non-Russian nationalities. The Bolsheviks faced a formidable challenge. The Soviet Republic was in economic disarray and the Red Guard, unlike its domestic enemy, had to be built almost from scratch. It lacked resources, and few of its commanders had a military background. It was soon transformed, however, by its Commander-in-Chief, Léon Trotsky, from a relatively informal force of volunteers to a highly disciplined and effective army recruited by rigorous conscription. The control of Red officers over their men was harsh: for Trotsky, discipline could not 'possibly be maintained without revolvers'.

The Bolshevik Party, which had already consolidated its hold on the main organs of political power in the Russian heartland, provided its Red Guard with a clear war aim: a Soviet Republic. Control of the railways, to maintain lines of communication, supply, and propaganda further benefited the Bolshevik side. As the Railwaymen's Union was told: 'the future historian will most likely say "the railwaymen saved the revolution" or "the railwaymen ruined the revolution" '. By contrast, the White Guard, dispersed across Russia and fighting under a variety of commanders – General Anton Denikin, Admiral Aleksandr Kolchak, General P. Wrangel, General N. Yudenich – was disunited. It had diverse, and sometimes conflicting, strategies and goals. Its administrative hold on the surrounding countryside was weak. It was plagued, too, by a third force, the so-called 'Green Armies' – peasant and Cossack troops who gave allegiance to neither side but were most active in the areas where the Whites were based.

The Civil War, the mood of which was so evocatively captured in Boris Pasternak's novel *Doctor Zhivago*, was hard and bloody for soldiers and civilians alike. Both sides resorted to terror to silence opponents and requisition food, with important consequences for the victorious Soviet regime, which created the Cheka (a brutal commission dedicated to the struggle against counter-revolution). According to Bolshevik figures for European Russia, it shot around 9,000 persons without trial and arrested another 90,000 between January 1918 and July 1919 alone. By November 1920 the final Red offensive had successfully defeated Wrangel in the Crimea and a Red victory was assured. The British author, Arthur Ransome, who travelled in Russia during the Civil War, described vividly the hasty evacuation of Wrangel's troops from the Crimea, leaving in their wake – to the mercy of the Red Army – 'portmanteaux, rifles, machine guns . . . undamaged tanks, undamaged aeroplanes' and Cossack troops.

The intervention of Czechoslovakia, Britain, the United States, Canada and even Japan on the side of the White Guard in the Civil War was insufficient to provide practical aid and helped to unite Russians against them. It merely helped to prolong the Civil War. The commander of the White Army, General Denikin, reflected, 'never had the Entente Powers been offered such a golden opportunity. . . . [But] time went on . . . and help was not forthcoming'. Entente troops in Russia's Civil War meant that foreigners trapped behind Red Army lines had an uncomfortable time. When Englishman Gerard Shelley, under house arrest in Moscow, demanded food from the Soviet authorities, he was told: 'If you don't like starving to death, dance! In any case, there will be one English dog less!' Foreign intervention also left a bitter legacy for international relations. The young Soviet Union continued to fear the intervention of the West in its domestic affairs.

Plate 7.3 Comrade Lenin sweeps the world clean, c.1919. This propaganda poster underlines the party's commitment, later abandoned, to promoting world revolution. The poster's message, reinforced by the establishment of the Comintern in the same year, alarmed employers and property-owners across Europe.

Nearly every facet of Bolshevik Party life was changed by the tribulations of the Civil War. The ruthless suppression of opposition outside the party and the increasingly undemocratic character of Lenin's party itself – elective party committees within the armed forces were abolished lock, stock and barrel, for example – were the price paid for a Bolshevik victory. The Bolshevik leaders had underestimated the dangers of authoritarianism and centralism in their struggle for victory, and by failing to build institutional bulwarks against authoritarianism – such as freely elected national and local government organizations – the Bolshevik revolution was betraying the workers and peasants it was supposed to protect. In 1921, however, the brutal economic policy of War Communism was abandoned and succeeded by the so-called New Economic Policy (NEP). This was a more liberal economic regime, but it was not to last.

Peace was sealed when Soviet Russia signed the Treaty of Riga with Poland on 18 March 1921. World war and civil war had cost Russia dear in life, material and territory. To its north-west, Finland and the Baltic states of Estonia, Latvia and Lithuania had all achieved independence from Russia by 1919 and had staged democratic elections by 1920. Elsewhere in the Soviet Union, the 'nationalities issue' presented the Bolsheviks with a dilemma. The former Russian Empire had ruled over a host of different ethnic groups, including Ukrainians, Turks, Azheris, Siberian Yakuts and Buryats. Lenin had cautiously endorsed the principle of self-determination as set out in a 'Declaration of the Rights of the Peoples of Russia' (15 November 1917), drafted by Comrade Stalin, People's Commissar for Nationalities Affairs. In the declaration the party set out what it considered to be a constructive approach to the nationalities question under the slogan 'National in Form, Socialist in Content' which provided an encouragement to minority self-consciousness yet denied any ambitions to political nationalism or claims to autonomy.

For Marxists considerations of 'class' were always more important than national considerations, but the dangers inherent in working-class nationalism had become clear to the Bolsheviks in 1920 when the Red Army marched into Poland in 1920 and Polish workers resisted the invasion.

Among the remaining ethnic groups within the former Russian Empire, the Ukraine with its own form of recently created Soviet (March 1917) – the *Rada* – appeared to present the greatest separatist threat to the Bolsheviks, but it remained within Lenin's Soviet republic largely because over half its population was Russian and because its peasants, as elsewhere, were more interested in acquiring land than regional autonomy; intellectuals often complained of their indifference to the nationalist message. In 1920 Mikhail Hrushevsky, the 'father' of Ukrainian nationalism and President of the *Rada*, was allowed to return from exile to lead the movement for Ukrainian cultural progress.

To the outside world, the most conclusive proof of the Bolshevik tolerance of national minorities came with the formation of the Union of Socialist Soviet Republics (USSR) in December 1922 – which appeared to allocate equal status to the Soviet republics of Russia, Transcaucasia, the Ukraine, and White Russia (Uzbek and Turkmenian joined in 1924, Tajikistan in 1929) – and the new Soviet constitution in July 1923 which established a Soviet of Nationalities. According to the historian Richard Pipes, however, the Bolsheviks' apparent commitment to minority rights quickly became mere 'window dressing' as the revolution and the imposition of Bolshevik control destroyed many religious and cultural institutions, and independent parties.

As the 1920s progressed, many minorities found themselves worse off than they had been under Tsarist rule. Even the favoured ethnic groups of Byelorussia and the Ukraine, closest to the Russian borders, were repressed when the Bolsheviks realized that the nationalism they had encouraged could backfire against them; and after 1928 the demands of Stalin's economic programme, in sharp contrast to the relatively liberal regime of the NEP, put paid to the few remaining freedoms enjoyed by the USSR's minorities. Stalin's Five Year Plans demanded the collectivization (or industrialization) of Soviet agriculture and the massive build-up of heavy industry – collective farms would feed industrial workers, heavy industry would provide machinery for agricultural workers to farm more efficiently. Karl Marx had given no guidance to communists on how to plan an economy of the type that Stalin desired, so he implemented his own policies to make the USSR an industrial workers' state. Indeed, Marxist analysis would have suggested that the first revolution during or just after the First World War would have taken place not in Russia but in Germany.

Revolutions in Germany and Hungary, 1918–19

There was a German 'revolution' in early November 1918, when the monarchy was replaced by a democratic constituent assembly after popular mass protest across the length and breadth of Germany; and there were German communists, like Karl Liebknecht, who believed that it could lead to a total social revolution of the kind Marx had envisaged. Instead, although there were dramatic events, the outcome was quite different. Capitalism was to become more concentrated, and new, large-scale production and trading units emerged. Out of a 'rationalization mania' came the great German mergers of Vereinigte Stahlwerke in 1926 (United Steel Works) and I. G. Farben (1925), a conglomeration of chemical producers.

In the chaos of defeat and abdication in the early winter of 1918, it came as a great relief to Frederich Ebert, the highly responsible leader of the German Socialists, when he was assured that the Army would support the new German Republic. The once illegal and persecuted German Social Democratic Party (*Sozialdemokratische Partei Deutschlands*, SPD), with its Marxist roots, was set to become the main party of government in 1919. Yet fear of 'class war' led politicians like Gustav Stresemann, founder of the conservative *Deutsche Volkspartei* (the German Peoples' Party), to accept a German Socialist regime led by Ebert. Opposition to him and to other moderate leaders of the SPD came, in the first instance, from independent socialists, communist Spartakists fired by the Russian Bolshevik Revolution, which they believed would become worldwide, and from hungry workers, some of them organized in self-appointed revolutionary factory councils inspired by the soviets in Russia. There were street protests also in industrial centres outside Berlin in Leipzig, Nuremberg, Thuringia and Saxony.

The effect of the street violence was different from that which had been anticipated. The badly organized Spartakist revolt in Berlin – championed by Liebknecht and his rather more reluctant conspirator, Rosa Luxemburg – met a bloody end. On 11 January 1919, five days after it had begun, the murdered corpses of the two leaders were dumped in a canal in Berlin. A similar revolution fizzled out in Bavaria, where a short-lived ultra-democratic state founded by Kurt Eisner ended its fraught life with Eisner's assassination. The upsurge of street protest on the left prompted a response from the German right which, in the long run, was to seem more significant. In March 1920 came a 'putsch', the first major right-wing attempt to overthrow the new German constitutional order by force; and when the *Reichswehr* ignored government orders to fire on Walter Kapp and his armed volunteer *Freikorps* supporters (men newly returned from the battle fronts), there was evidence of the tacit support that the right-wing 'boot-boys' appeared to enjoy amongst 'respectable' people and the authorities. Indeed, bungled revolutionary attempts from the right were treated more leniently than attempts from the left. Kapp's co-conspirator, General Walther von Lüttwitz, was merely retired on a military pension; the then unknown Adolf Hitler (an ex-corporal, not a general) was also treated indulgently after his abortive Beer Hall putsch in Munich in 1923. Further north, in Germany's industrial heartland, the Ruhr, force had been ruthlessly employed to scupper a left-wing army of 50,000 volunteers in May and June 1920. The size of the army indicated the frustration and radicalization prevalent amongst sections of the German working class.

In the winter of 1918–19 left-wing revolutions had also erupted in Austria and Hungary. They were inspired by the example of the Bolshevik putsch in Petrograd and by the education in Marxism of former imperial soldiers who had been captured and interned in Russian prisoner of war camps on the Eastern Front. In February 1919, amid considerable economic and military confusion, power in Hungary passed to one such Bolshevik-educated prisoner of war, Béla Kun, who had returned to Hungary armed with Bolshevik funds and promises of assistance. General Smuts, a South African representative at the Paris Peace Conference dispatched to Hungary, sensibly concluded that Hungarian Bolshevism 'was not a serious menace and cannot last'.[3] He was right. Kun had been promised Russian support which did not materialize, and advocated radical social reforms (including the nationalization rather than the redistribution of Hungary's agricultural land) which were hugely unpopular in a country where more than half the population was engaged in farming. An energetic anti-God campaign and Kun's resort to organized terror against his opponents – orchestrated by his bloodthirsty aide, Tibor Szamnelly – turned the tide against him, and by 1 August 1919 he and his associates had fled the country.

Further confusion followed. Kun was succeeded by a right-wing government under Admiral Horthy, and even the professedly homesick ex-Emperor Karl I attempted to exploit the situation and to recover his throne by returning to Hungary in April 1921. His action proved fruitless, although rumours of a monarchist coup continued to bedevil Hungarian politics. In fact, Kun's 133-day Soviet-style republic had a far greater impact on Hungarian politics. As in Germany, a threat from the left had aroused an energetic response from new radical right-wing political groups. As elsewhere in Europe, workers' protests, born of hunger, inflation and unemployment during the first winter of peace, revealed very little ideological commitment to an international Marxist revolution across Europe except in Italy and Spain (a conclusion Lenin himself reluctantly reached). Meanwhile, the spectre of a communist revolution which would eliminate God, private property and national pride continued to haunt the middle classes, sections of which had grown deeply hostile not only to the left but to the ideals of liberal democracy.

The magnitude of political violence in postwar Europe augured ill. There was a renewed upsurge in political assassinations in 1920–22, accompanied by an increase in overt anti-Semitism. (Many of the communist revolutionaries were also Jewish: Luxemburg, Liebknecht, Kun and Szamnelly amongst the most prominent.) In Germany, E. J. Gumbel, the author of *Zwei Jahre Mord* ('Two Years of Murder'), calculated that there had been 334 political murders from March 1919 until June 1921, 318 committed by the German right, 16 committed by the left. Prominent casualties included representatives of liberal democracy, the Catholic leader Matthias Erzberger and the Jewish economic organizer, Walther Rathenau, who had arranged the German war economy.

The surviving empires: Britain and France

While the map of Europe was being redrawn, Britain, France and Germany were also forced to reassess their imperial relations. Rivalry between the European empires, especially between those of Britain, France and Germany, had contributed to the mounting tension in Europe before 1914. After the war, Britain and France modified their imperial ties. The notion of a British Commonwealth, grouped around White Dominions like Australia and Canada, helped to release a weakened Britain from some of the burdens of empire. But Britain now also had to protect territories mandated by the League of Nations in the 'Middle East' and Africa, as the Paris Peace Conference had also taken decisions which modified the maps of both these areas, as well as that of China.

Closer to home, the declaration of independence by the self-constituted Irish parliament, *Dail Eireann* (21 January 1919), marked a new stage in, although by no means an end to, the long history of troubled Anglo-Irish relations. The newly proclaimed republic launched an appeal for recognition by the powers assembled at the Paris Peace Conference; and by the end of 1919 the two 'nations' were effectively at war, although the British government did not admit that it was a war. The Irish republican challenge – led by Michael Collins, Cathal Brugha, Eamon De Valera and Arthur Griffiths – was determined, if sometimes divided, and British forces in Ireland had to be increased in numbers. The Royal Irish Constabulary recruited amongst ex-soldiers in England – hereby establishing the notorious Black and Tans. Indeed, *The Times* suspected that government use of force in Ireland, would perhaps deliberately arouse a state of rebellion in which a settlement would be impossible.

Progress in the British Parliament on the Irish question was as troubled as the 'policing' activities of British forces within Ireland, but on 23 December 1920 the Government of Ireland Act became law. The North was partitioned-off as a Unionist stronghold, the Protestants there being enthusiastic in their loyalty to the United Kingdom. The war in the South continued until May 1922, when the republic government in Dublin wrung substantial concessions from a reluctant British government. The civil war was over, although for decades to come, masked gunmen continued to fight the war either in the name of Irish independence or of loyalty to the British Crown.

The First World War and, less significantly, the struggle for Irish independence, had taxed Britain's resources immeasurably, yet the British Empire was larger after the First World War than at any other period in its history. It extended over almost 14 million square miles of the globe and contained a population of over 454 million. The only nation which could possibly hope to compete with Britain on such terms was China, and its population was still 123 million less than that of the British Empire. There were few changes in the pattern of colonial empire, and the idea that there existed a 'sacred trust' between the civilized peoples and the 'backward' natives remained dominant: it was even incorporated into the Covenant of the League of Nations. The ideology of empire gradually changed, however, with an increasing emphasis on the notion of 'responsibility' over that of 'power'. This was also true of French colonial relations, as Albert Sarraut, French Minister for the colonies and an important colonial theorist, argued in 1923: 'Colonizing France does not work only for itself . . . its efforts must be beneficial to the colonies as to itself, for there France assures economic betterment and human development.'

At home Britain's 'established democracy' went on to extend the franchise to men in 1918, enfranchising all men over 21, and all soldiers regardless of age, and in 1921 women over the age of 30 were finally granted the right to vote. But as quickly as the working classes of Europe were given the vote, they uncovered their continued political impotence on issues which immediately concerned them: the price and availability of food, and unemployment.

Despite new legislation, like the Unemployment Insurance Act (1920) and the Pensions Act (1925), many working-class people in Britain grew increasingly frustrated with the failure of government to support the ailing domestic economy, which suffered from outmoded methods of production and a chronic loss of export markets. Even the short-lived, first (minority) Labour government of 1924 offered few new policies to tackle Britain's industrial difficulties. There had been large-scale industrial unrest every year since the end of the war, and on 3 May 1926 a miners' strike became a nine-day General Strike. The fact that it was short-lived, that it was never general, and that it was led by local union and party stalwarts (the General Council of the Trades Union Congress did not direct the strike) demonstrated that British socialism and indeed British politics as a whole were dominated by moderate politicians determined to preserve British democracy and some form of capitalist system. It was not apparent at the time, but the General Strike marked the end, not the beginning, of widespread social unrest. The same could not be said for parliamentary politics elsewhere in Europe, and soon the gap widened.

Italy: the first casualty, 1919–24

During the first years of peace, democracies in Germany, Hungary, Austria and Poland had charted routes which were to be travelled with increasing frequency in European politics in the years that followed: an increasingly pronounced division between reformist socialists, prepared to cooperate with the existing democratic order, and revolutionary communists striving for a worldwide working-class revolution; the power of nationalism as a political force; the tendency of malcontents to resort to street violence; and the decline of Europe's liberal parties, to be replaced by fragmented, interest-group parties.

In Italy the level of street violence and the mounting confrontation between forces of the left and right established a pattern which was to be repeated elsewhere. Before the war Italy's Premier, Giovanni Giolitti, an accomplished manipulator, had attempted to accommodate the left into the Liberal movement, but he failed to preserve the dominance of the Italian Liberal Party, just as the divided but powerful British Liberal Party soon lost out to the Labour Party after the war. Italian postwar electoral reforms, which introduced universal male suffrage and proportional representation (1919), were followed by a Liberal loss of votes to the radical left and to the increasingly troublesome *Partito Popolare Italiano* (PPI, Italian Popular Party). The latter was a curious blend of right, centre and left-wing Catholics, supported mainly by the small peasant proprietors and tenants of northern and central Italy.

In November 1919 and again in May 1921, two successive Liberal Premiers, Nitti and Giolitti, called general elections to try to staunch the flow from the ranks of Liberal supporters into the parties of the left and right. But the Liberal Party was unable to resolve the tension between history and modernity, so well portrayed in the paintings of artists like Giorgio de Chirico and Alberto Savinio. On a more practical level too, they faced a broad range of social and economic problems for which they had no satisfactory answers: urban unemployment, land hunger amongst peasants in the south, high rents for tenant farmers in the north, and an economic crisis in the now largely superfluous munitions industry. Times were so hard for the Perrone Bros. Munitions Company, for instance, that they funded right-wing groups in the hope that government would spend more on military equipment.

Italy's middle classes went on to desert the Liberal Party in droves, complaining bitterly that the tired old clichés of Liberal politics offered no new answers, and matters were made worse by Italy's soaring rate of inflation: the wholesale price index (1913=100) rose from 413 in 1918 to 591 in 1920, wiping out salaries, pensions and savings. As in Germany three years later, white-collar workers were especially badly hit and Italy's middle class as a whole grew increasingly uneasy at the mounting levels of street violence. Their fears of a communist revolution increased as their confidence in the existing political order diminished.

To add insult to already substantial injury, the shoddy treatment meted out to the Italian people by their Liberal coalition government was mirrored by the victors at Versailles. Prime Minister Orlando's inability to secure the territories promised to Italy in the Treaty of London rankled, especially amongst the 'tens of thousands of new, young officers, drunk with patriotism and greedy to command'. Italian nationalists trusted that the First World War would cement a disparate people and create a truly united Italy, but postwar economic hardships and disappointment in Paris brought regional tensions to the fore once again. As revealed by the march of the flamboyant poet Gabriele D'Annunzio to take Fiume (September 1919), there were plenty of eager, young Italian men ready to strut like peacocks and resolve their disagreements with the Italian government by force. The era of mass politics and potentially disloyal military forces had descended upon Italy.

The extension of the electoral franchise in Italy, as in Germany and Hungary, had heightened the challenge to the dominant liberal democratic order: there were violent food riots in central and northern Italy and factory seizures in Piedmont. But while the working class swarmed to support the socialists and the newly formed Italian Communist Party, and the peasants of the south turned to the PPI, Italy's ultimate political fate, like that of so many liberal democracies in interwar Europe, pivoted on the arbiters of political power in nineteenth-century Europe: the middle class. Industrialists and shop-owners along with tenant farmers, artisans, civil servants, business-men, members of the Italian government and the King himself, became increasingly frustrated with the government's inability to contain mounting insurrectionist violence: their factories and land were being seized, their shops being looted, and their salaries and profits were shrinking.

By the end of 1920, with rising support for the PPI and the socialists, they concluded that the political system was unable to cope and that Italy's liberal order had had its day. The answer they reached was an ominous one. Frustrated by the failure of the traditional liberal parties they turned to a journalist and former PSI (*Partito Socialista Italiano*) socialist, Benito Mussolini, who, after a highly successful career as the editor of the Socialist *Avanti!* newspaper, had impulsively broken with the PSI in 1914 in favour of an interventionist stance on the First World War. By the end of the war in Europe, Mussolini had adopted the aggressive nationalist garb of founder and leader of the *Fasci di Combattimento* (Fascists), offering land reform to the peasantry, and the abolition of the Senate and the summoning of a new Constituent Assembly. None of these policies was new. What *was* new was the large number of armed gangs who roamed both rural and urban Italy, under the new banner of Fascism, recruiting most successfully in regional capitals. Mussolini was able to make electoral and financial capital from Italy's rising revolutionary violence, aware that his own squads had been contributing to the problem.

By the end of 1921 Italian fascism had already taken on its chameleon form: it promised to please all except Italy's socialists, who played into fascist hands by creating a rival communist party with links to Red Moscow; this was a tremendous propaganda coup for the fascists. Pledged to break strikes, to discipline labour, to offer local political representation, and an end to widespread public disorder, Fascism also presented a new, national leader: *Il Duce*.

Trapped in a pattern of consensus, coalition politics, the Liberals did not offer imaginative proposals to staunch the fascist tide. Instead, the King invited Mussolini to join a coalition cabinet as Prime Minister in October 1922. By May 1924 Mussolini faced allegations, made by a socialist Deputy, Giacomo Matteotti, that recent Italian elections were fraudulent, distorted by violence and torture. Mussolini was furious at Matteotti's efforts to discredit his 'respectability' and allegedly told his thugs, 'if you were not cowards, nobody would have the courage to make a speech like that'. On 10 June 1924 Matteotti disappeared, and everyone rightly assumed that Mussolini's boot-boys had wanted to make good their earlier oversight by murdering him. Mussolini defused the crisis by sacking a number of his most unpopular henchmen and, with the opposition bitterly divided and public opinion apparently reluctant to blame Mussolini for Matteotti's murder, he maintained a clear majority in parliament. Rather than weaken *Il Duce*, the Matteotti crisis made Mussolini's position stronger. From now on he made promises the 'conservative' middle classes wanted to hear: the freedom of the press would be curbed, opposition parties would be disciplined and Italy would be governed by a strong, efficient leader.

The collapse of Italy's democracy came far sooner than that of Germany – or Spain – despite the fact that Italy had been a victor in war, but certain elements of the Italian story were to be repeated in the collapse of liberal

democracy in those two countries, and were also to threaten the more established democracies of France and Great Britain: the frustration and impoverishment of the middle class; unemployment amongst the urban working classes; land hunger amongst the peasantry; and a growing disillusionment with the much heralded extension of democracy. Securing the vote did not, after all, solve the problems of the less privileged in society. Moreover, those groups who had been favoured by nineteenth-century political structures – the upper and middle classes – grew fearful and resentful at the extension of the suffrage. Economic collapse in Europe at the end of the 1920s was to fan to life tensions in Europe which had already destroyed Italian democracy at the beginning of the decade.

Danger signs: western Europe, 1920–24

From January 1925 Italy embarked on a painful journey to a dubious goal: the fascist state, basing its authority on mass popular support. Mussolini brought the fascist squads under more rigorous control, the Fascist Party's highest body, the 'Grand Council', was constitutionalized, and he himself assumed responsibility for the Ministries of War, Air and Navy. Although most of the party's actions were the 'huff and puff' of theatrical propaganda rather than the product of hard, clearly defined policies, Italian spirits were lifted in the early years of fascism by higher levels of employment, while admiring foreigners – and there were many of them – were impressed by the fact that trains ran on time.

In 1923, in Spain, the dictatorship of Primo De Rivera, a man of 'immense optimism,' was the Spanish answer to rising inflation and agrarian unrest. As in the nineteenth century, Spanish politics continued to see-saw from reaction to reform as the keepers of political power struggled to come to terms with the changing nature of society. Farmers in Catalan Spain and southern Italy had grown to resent the traditional patterns of landholding which milked the labour of tenant farmers without enabling them to enjoy the rewards of owning their own land. Southern Spanish agriculture, by contrast, was dominated by large estates (*latifundia*) run on a factory-style system. This enabled employers to keep wages down to starvation level by means of huge reserves of unemployed labour. For Spanish peasants there were few alternatives to radical, anti-clerical political protest and 'civil wars' albeit on a localized scale, were not uncommon. With only two

Plate 7.4 Fascists in Rome celebrate the seventh anniversary of the March on Rome, 28 October, 1930. Assembled before the Palazzo Venezia, the massed ranks of Blackshirts and 'Representatives of National Strengths' commemorate the seventh anniversary of the March on Rome and Mussolini's accession to power. During the 1930s such 'oceanic assemblies' became increasing important to the public presentation of Italian fascism. Mussolini boasted that just by ringing a bell, he could produce an applauding crowd.

million workers employed in industry, urban migration was no real solution to Spain's heady rate of population growth at the turn of the twentieth century, and the country faced a grave political crisis.

De Rivera, too, came to power on the shoulders of King and Army, and sought to guide Spain with a strong hand. But his authoritarian approach was clumsy. By 1930 he had offended almost every section of Spanish society. He alienated his strongest supporters on the right with his attempts at army reform and on the left his repressive measures against the Catalans (he even banned the Catalan national dance, the *Sardana*) stirred up regional republican sentiment. Worse unrest was to come.

Portugal, too, was hit by wave after wave of strikes in the mid-1920s, while worker anti-clericalism also provoked a reaction from the Portuguese right. Unlike Spain, Portugal was not riven by ethnic conflict, but the failure of the First Republic which had been inaugurated in 1910 to regenerate the country politically, socially, and materially triggered widespread disenchantment with democratic politics. At first, the declaration of the Republic had appeared to place Portugal at the vanguard of European politics – the only other republics were France and Switzerland – but its democracy soon faltered, There were 45 administrations between 1910 and 1926, each lasting on average four months; the national budget ran a consistent deficit, and the army and navy officer corps became increasingly involved in national politics inspired, in part, by the example of Primo De Rivera in Spain.

In 1926 a national revolution replaced the democratic republic with a military dictatorship. Yet social unrest continued and in early 1927 demonstrations and riots swept the country once more. In Oporto 80 people were killed, a further 100 lost their lives in Lisbon, and over 600 alleged trouble-makers were exiled. The following year António de Oliveira Salazar, a Catholic Professor of Economics from Coimbra, joined the dictatorship as Finance Minister. Influenced by Charles Maurras and other French and Italian right-wing activists, Salazar was determined to bring Portugal's rampant budget deficit under control. He also wanted a corporate government that would act in the interests of all, not just the majority of individuals. To Salazar 'man in isolation is an abstraction, a fiction mainly created under the erroneous principles during the last century'.

Salazar's record as Portugal's financial *supremo* was impressive. During 1917–28 the budget deficit totalled 2,574,000 contos, yet in the next 11 years – which included the world's worst depression – he achieved a total surplus of 1,963,000 contos (then equivalent to around £20 million). In initiatives which extended far beyond his portfolio as Finance Minister, and while other ministers were appointed and dismissed, Salazar spent the budget surplus on public works, social assistance, rearmament, communications, ports, irrigation and hydro-electric schemes and education. A widely respected financial dictator, overseas as well as at home, he also came to be regarded by the younger generation of nationalists and army officers as the answer to Portugal's political problems. As a result in July 1932 Salazar became Prime Minister of Portugal (confusingly his official title was President of the Council of Ministers), a position he was to hold until his health failed in the autumn of 1968. Yet, although his *Estado Novo* (New State) bore many similarities to De Rivera and later to Franco's Spanish state, Iberian cooperation remained limited. During the Spanish Civil War Portugal was to act as a clearing centre for Nazi supplies to Franco and to surrender Republican refugees to the nationalists; but Portuguese canniness in its relations reflected the old proverb, 'Neither good winds, nor good marriages come from Spain'.

In Germany the new right, sometimes known as the 'extreme of the centre', received a powerful impetus for growth with the onset of an unprecedented hyper-inflationary crisis in 1923. Never before had the economy of an industrialized nation experienced such uncontrolled destruction of the value of money. The German mark was already in trouble in the summer of 1921, slipping to one-fiftieth of its 1914 value, and by the summer of 1923 the spiral of inflation reached its zenith. It was a good time for American tourists to visit Germany. In November 1923, one dollar could buy 4,200 billion marks. Inhabitants of both town and country began to abandon the *Reichsmark* in favour of direct bartering: swopping household items, like saucepans and furniture, for food.

Much of this inflation had been generated by domestic economic difficulties. The imperial German government had financed its war effort by selling war bonds in preference to taxing the German people. This large domestic debt, which had to be paid back with interest, was compounded by Entente reparation demands and paying for the costs of demobilization – care for the wounded and widowed, finding employment for the able. It was easier for German governments to tolerate and even generate inflation than to try to control it, as the dwindling value of money depreciated their debts and, in the short term, enabled them to pay their bills.

The rest of the world sat up and took notice when, after Germany had failed to meet repeated French demands for reparation payments, French troops marched into Germany's industrial heartland, the Ruhr, in January 1923. The French suspected that the Germans were deliberately trying to destroy their economy so that they would not have to pay reparations – there was some truth in this accusation – while the United States and Britain expressed outrage at France's deployment of black colonial troops on German soil. The German government won international sympathy, and a temporary victory over the French, by encouraging a policy of passive resistance in the Ruhr. Nonetheless, by the summer of 1923 the German government was forced to concede that 'we are sitting on a volcano and we are on the threshold of revolution unless we can ameliorate the situation'. Whereas a British cartoonist could flippantly refer to the 'ruhrnation of Germany', the German people could ill-afford to be so sanguine.[4]

Plate 7.5 German boys play with kites made of Reichsmarks, 1923. The novelty of wall-papering rooms or fashioning kites from worthless notes brought light relief from the acute hardship most families faced during hyperinflation. Arnold Bauer, a Berlin theatre critic, recalled '. . . there was awareness of great poverty on the streets . . . people bought enough for one or two days – that was as far ahead as they could buy. There was a lot of bartering too – big flea markets sprang up as people tried to make some money or they became exchange places for goods, clothes, anything which there was no money left over to pay for in the normal way.'

For most Germans, especially the middle classes, who saw their pensions, savings and salaries wiped out, the ordeal of hyper-inflation was not one they wished to repeat, and this conclusion was to have profound consequences for German politics during the Great Depression when Chancellor Brüning (1930–32) believed he could not resort to inflationary methods to combat the problem. More immediately, the crisis shocks of 1923 enabled government to reduce wages by 18 per cent, while confirming the deepest fears of Weimar's sceptics among the lower-middle artisan class. For traditional craftsmen – the carpenters and cabinetmakers of a former age – an industrialized, capitalist Germany prone to crisis appeared to offer no special place for them. Increasingly they, and groups like them, found refuge in nationalist, romantic movements, like the 'Militant League of Beggars', which harked back to a fictional age when the German race was 'pure' and the countryside unpolluted by greedy capitalists.

At first these right-wing movements, like their revolutionary communist counterparts, posed no immediate threat to the Weimar Republic. But Weimar's hyper-inflationary experience, followed by the introduction of a new currency, exacerbated social and economic divisions within Germany and led to a loss of support for liberal, democratic and centre parties. The division between ostentatious rich and deprived poor grew more pronounced within the context of a 'modern' culture at its most vibrant – and tense – in Berlin. 'We needed very little sleep and were never tired', the celebrated German dramatist Carl Zuckmayer wrote; 'Berlin tasted of the future and that is why we took all the crap and coldness'.

In 1923–24 Germany was saved by Gustav Stresemann and American dollars. Stresemann, the charismatic leader of the *Deutsche Volkspartei* (DVP), briefly became Chancellor in 1923–24, before becoming Foreign Minister, a post he occupied with considerable skill until his death in 1929. He put an end to passive resistance in the Ruhr and set about overseeing arrangements for a new currency – the *Rentenmark*. Though a nationalist, Stresemann was prepared to work with the Socialists – notably President Ebert – to restore stability to Germany. Indeed, in their efforts to resolve the Ruhr crisis, Ebert and Stresemann repeatedly resorted to Article 48 of the German constitution which enabled them to bypass the *Reichstag*, suggesting that even amongst the defenders of German democracy there was only a superficial commitment to the rigours of democratic politics.

Their efforts were also aided by Anglo-American hostility towards France after the Ruhr invasion, and most important of all, by a $200 million American loan granted in September 1924, under a new Dawes plan which enabled Weimar to begin again.

Danger signs: eastern Europe, 1920–28

The Dawes plan influenced the pattern of economic recovery in central and eastern Europe, where there had been many danger signs during the early 1920s. The chaos, destruction and dislocation in the states of eastern Europe, both old and new, far outstripped those experienced in the west, and while by 1921 Finland, the Baltic states, Poland, Czechoslovakia, Austria, Hungary, Yugoslavia, Bulgaria and Rumania had all held some form of relatively free democratic elections, there were formidable social divides between aristocrats and peasants, and business and trade was largely managed by minorities, notably Germans and Jews. Most of eastern Europe's immediate postwar leaders were of peasant stock. Masaryk was the son of an ex-serf; and the Bulgarian Agrarian Prime Minister, Alexander Stambolisky (1919–23), was the son of peasant, as was Engelbert Dollfuss, the Chancellor of Austria (1932–34).

These peasant prime ministers helped to give eastern European politics its populist character, moulded by romantic images of common folk and an intense nationalism. They were also viewed with incredulity, if not

Plate 7.6 Crowds massing in St Wenclas Square, Prague, October 1918. In the days before the announcement of an independent Czechoslovak state, huge crowds were drawn to the 'old town square'. On 14 October, when the new state was announced, the square became the venue for an impressive meeting to celebrate the birth of the new republic. Here Social Democrat MP, Antonin Němec, addresses the crowd gathered in front of Prague's Old Town Hall.

hostility, by the old nobility. A typical reaction was that of the Polish diplomat Count Potocki, who described Poland's Prime Minister in 1919, Ignaz Paderewski (a concert pianist who had delighted President Wilson with his performances of Chopin), as 'a remarkable man . . . Do you know that he was born in one of my villages? And yet when I speak to him, I have absolutely the impression of conversing with an equal.' The social legacies of the old empires contributed to the character of politics in eastern Europe which could be divided into three, broadly defined camps: first, the old nationalist movements, championed by men such as the Polish National Democrat Roman Dmowski, and characterized by bourgeois, conservative politics; second, the new nationalists – Pilsudski in Poland, Monsignor Fan Noli in Albania – and, later, the new 'radical right' which was less interested in democracy than in nationalism; and third, the numerous peasant parties whose spokesmen argued that society should be governed in the interests of the peasant majority.

These distinctions were enhanced by the large variety of language, religion, history and constitutions in the new nations. In Austria, Poland and the Baltic states, and to a lesser extent Czechoslovakia, the democratic constitution was modelled on the Third Republic of France with its dominant legislature and weak executive. Even in Romania, Yugoslavia, Greece and Bulgaria, where the Crown had retained important powers, the political power of a parliament elected by universal suffrage became increasingly important.

Such commitment to the ideals of democracy was laudable, but generated enormous problems in societies as ethnically divided, economically impoverished, and deprived of democratic experience or strong support from overseas powers as the nations of eastern Europe. Instead, violence and instability became the hallmarks of eastern European politics. Instability was exemplified by Poland, where civil war threatened and government changed hands 14 times from 1919 until Pilsudski launched a successful military coup in 1926; violence was exemplified in Bulgaria by the assassination of Stambolisky in 1923. By 1928, Yugoslavia, too, was riven by dissent over the constitution and the need for agricultural reform to provide improved living standards for the peasantry who made up 80 per cent of the population. In December 1928 King Alexander announced that 'the [democratic] machine no longer works' and introduced a royal dictatorship in Yugoslavia. Romania, too, fell under complete control of its monarch, King Carol, from 1930 until his abdication in 1940; while in Albania, after bitter rivalry between Fan Noli of the progressive Popular Party and Ahmed Zogu, a local clan chieftain, democratic government fell to Zogu. A year later he heralded a republic with himself as President. By 1928, having tired of this title, Zogu proclaimed himself 'Zog I, King of the Albanians'.

By the end of the 1920s France's political, diplomatic and economic role in eastern Europe was increasingly challenged by German economic penetration and diplomatic involvement. Far more menacing, however, was the rising popularity in the region of new German political models, notably National Socialism. Despite its emphasis on free choice, democratic government required the creation of majorities to work effectively. Eastern Europe was bedevilled by too many conflicting and minority groups which the government was unable to absorb. Only the Czechoslovakian state, with its relatively efficient economy, successful land reforms and strong executive, provided stable government during the 1920s, and even this rare success-story was profoundly challenged by the economic crisis which swept Europe in 1929.

A semblance of stability, 1925–28

Germany's continued interest in eastern Europe was signalled by the Rapallo Treaty (April 1922) – ostensibly a Russo-German 'economic agreement' – which, at the cost of French hostility, broke the diplomatic isolation of Germany and the USSR. The two outsiders of international politics established full diplomatic and consular ties between themselves, and agreed to renounce all their debt claims on one another. They not only secured important economic markets and diplomatic cooperation, but the two powers had thumbed up their noses at their Western creditors, notably France. By 1924, however, Britain, Italy and France had all granted *de jure* recognition to the USSR. (The USA recognized the Soviet government in 1933.)

In 1923 Franco-German relations, as we have seen, deteriorated further with the French invasion of the Ruhr, but many German politicians increasingly recognized that their country would grow stronger only through cooperation with the West. Stresemann was the leading exponent of improved relations, especially with France. The crowning achievement of his career was the Treaty of Locarno, signed in December 1925, which proved his determination to use economic diplomacy and conciliation (rather than the assertive revisionism which had characterized Rapallo and passive resistance in the Ruhr) to effect a peaceful revision of the Versailles Treaty.

Stresemann's efforts were undoubtedly aided by the coincidence of a 'Cabinet of the left' in France. The French Foreign Minister, Aristide Briand, shared Stresemann's view that European stability would be better served by incorporating Germany into the League of Nations and French security arrangements, than by treating the German people as outcasts. The Treaty of Locarno, signed by Germany and France and supported by Britain, was a landmark. It swept away the old distinction between 'Allied' and 'enemy' powers. French troops left the Ruhr, and the frontier between France and Germany was guaranteed, with British support. Thereafter, Britain became as suspicious of French ambitions to revise Versailles as of Germany's revisionist rhetoric, and by 1928 the RAF had drafted plans for an attack on France should it violate Locarno.

The Locarno Treaty contained echoes of a 'European rhetoric' which was to resurface in Briand's diplomacy in 1930 and, with greater consequence, after 1945. For Stresemann 'everyone' was a citizen of Europe, pledged to 'the great cultural idea that finds expression in our continent', and for the Belgian government, ever anxious to promote international cooperation and European unity to guarantee its national security, the pact was 'a decisive step towards the formation of the United States of Europe'.[5]

The optimistic signals of Locarno were confirmed in 1928 when Briand, now French Prime Minister, and the United States Secretary of State, Frank

Kellogg, signed the Kellogg-Briand Pact which outlawed war as an instrument of policy. To its critics, however, it amounted to little more than an 'international kiss', particularly when the United States, anxious to avoid any commitment to French security, invited all other independent powers to sign it; 65 powers eventually did so. The Soviet Union, however, remained excluded from this European reconciliation.

Improved international relations were also enhanced, if not fostered, by the apparent recovery of the European economy. Lenin's NEP (New Economic Policy), introduced in 1921 to counter some of the unproductive excesses of War Communism, had begun to produce encouraging results by 1924, and the USSR began to trade overseas after Lenin instructed that 'communists must learn to trade'. In the West, meanwhile, the Dawes plan was followed by a massive infusion of American capital into Germany. From 1924, over $4 billion of foreign money was lent to Germany – the latter paid only $1.8 billion on account for reparations – and this credit effectively locked the Americans into the rise or fall of Europe's economy (and tied Europe's fate to that of the United States). Meanwhile, Belgium, Italy, Czechoslovakia, France and Yugoslavia all signed new war debt schedules with the United States, and France, too, managed to bring runaway inflation under control in 1926. Many countries in Europe showed a determination to return to the gold standard, which they believed was designed to limit inflation, to make trade easier, and to remove uncertainty from the world's money markets.

Elsewhere in Europe the levels of trade had increased to their pre-1914 level, with industrial products notably in much greater demand than agricultural output. Trade within and beyond Europe also benefited from the loosening of government economic controls, although the plight of Europe's farmers soon encouraged tariff walls to rise again. Many of the wartime economic controls were abolished in the rush to return to the freedom of pre-war business transactions, despite the fact that government interest in planning remained, notably in the Soviet Union, Germany, Hungary and Czechoslovakia. In Britain there was considerable criticism of the government when the Chancellor of the Exchequer, Winston Churchill, returned the pound sterling to gold in 1925 at the same rate of exchange as it had been in 1914, with all his critics complaining that this made British exports uncompetitive.

However sharp such criticisms might have been, European nations, both old and new, appeared to have turned the corner. European prosperity remained patchy, but a tentative optimism began to emerge. Material progress was evident as modern technology brought electric cookers, toasters and frozen or tinned food into the home (a more comfortable place than it had been in 1914). The Weimar government helped build almost two million new houses and there was an extensive public housing policy in Britain too. With greater social security and more adequate educational provision, 'modern' life seemed more acceptable. There was more leisure, although much of it was used for escape. Hollywood, with its stars, influenced America-European relations as much as the Dawes plan. In Britain most people visited their local cinemas ('picture houses') at least once a week, and both Germany and France developed their own thriving film industries, each with its own style and appeal. Radio was organized on national lines, as were large circulation, popular newspapers which, it was claimed, contributed to the formation of a more democratic society.

A stability built on fragile foundations, 1929

The dislocation of the postwar decade liberated and promoted an unprecedented flourishing of artistic activity which reflected the uneasy coexistence of the modern and traditional. While the architect Walter Gropius (of the 'Bauhaus' movement), excited by the challenge of urban life, was determined to design buildings that would 'avert mankind's enslavement by machine', conservative writers wrote urgently of the importance of the family and of tradition, and young men and women joined movements, like the German *Wandervogel*, to explore the countryside and sing folksongs. Perhaps most resonant of the period was the writing of Thomas Mann and André Gide. It reflected a scepticism and despair which proved prophetic.

Europe's relative prosperity had masked substantial diplomatic, economic and political tensions – aside from some eastern European countries where democracy and prosperity had already proved a chimera. The peace of 1919 had satisfied no-one. Thirty million Europeans still lived under governments of which they were not the dominant ethnic minority and tension in European diplomacy remained. France continued to regard Germany with a wary eye and fresh anxieties surfaced after the death of Stresemann in October 1929. It was reported that Paris received the news of his death 'as though the greatest living Frenchman had died'. France was suspicious of Italian expansionist ambitions in central Europe, while British contacts with France were also prone to misunderstanding and illwill. The 1920s had shown that Europe was not ready for the kind of cooperative internationalism espoused by Wilson in Paris as each European nation continued to jostle with its neighbours to assert its own national interest. In the relative prosperity of the 1920s this rivalry posed no threat. But after the whirlwind of the 1929 stock market crash and the ensuing depression, the desire for economic and social regeneration within each European country provided an insuperable challenge to peace.

Not only did Europe's economy show signs of potential weakness – debt burdens, the decline of heavy industry, uncertainty about the gold standard – but a persistently large number of Europe's working class remained unemployed throughout the 1920s. In Britain unemployment never dropped below the level of one million and in Germany it averaged one-and-a-half million from 1926 to 1929. The alleged beneficiaries of the 'new order', the workers, increasingly perceived their new won freedoms as illusory. For working-class men and women little, in reality, seemed to have changed. Working conditions were still poor, with most employees working 10–12 hours a day. Housing provision, too, remained inadequate, and frustration with democracy was often translated into increased recruitment for the Communist Party.

This rising swell of support for the radical left was matched by the rise of the 'new' right. The disaffected elements in 'traditional' European society, the lower middle class, the artisans and the large landowners turned to extreme political parties on the right to give vent to their discontent. In the 'revisionist' states of Germany, Hungary and Austria, in particular, democratic politics had taken on a negative and destructive character, with politicians and elites well able to criticize and destroy democratic politics, but offering little constructive in its place. It left a vacuum that the radical right, among them Germany's National Socialists, was to fill with its own brand of 'revolution'. As the Earl of Birkenhead, a former Conservative minister and close friend of the future British Prime Minister, Winston Churchill, prophetically cautioned in 1930:

> Will Germany's rancour die down with the flux of time or will some unforeseen and untoward incident upset the balance of power? Then Germany might stretch out a hand to clutch at Poland and all Europe once again will be dragged in.[6]

References

1. H. Nicolson, *Peacemaking 1919* (1933) p. 368.
2. M. Howard, 'The Legacy of the First World War', in R. Boyce and E. M. Robertson (eds), *Paths to War: New Essays on the Origins of the Second World War* (1989) p. 46.
3. H. Nicolson, *op. cit.*, p. 302.
4. *The Star*, London, 5 January 1923.
5. G. Stresemann, *Reden und Schriften*, vol. 2 (Dresden, 1926) pp. 219–20.
6. Earl of Birkenhead, *Turning-Points in History* (1930).

Chapter 8

Guns and Butter, 1929–1939

The Great Depression, 1929–33, an unprecedented world slump, had a profound impact upon European history. Its effects lingered on throughout the 1930s until Europe was engulfed by tragedy of a different order – the Second World War. There had been only a superficial recovery, for by 1937 the European economy began to turn down once more and the peoples of Britain, France, Scandinavia and eastern Europe were saved from further unemployment and deprivation only by an increase in expenditure on rearmament. It was poor consolation for the workers of Sheffield and Lille to find jobs in factories when it became increasingly clear that more military orders signified the likelihood of a European war which promised to be even more terrifying than the last.

As politicians struggled and failed to find effective answers to mass unemployment, moderate politicians in Germany, France, Spain, Poland, Romania and Britain were challenged by populists. They came both from the left and from the right of the political spectrum. In Germany and Spain new nationalisms emerged victorious over the left, and even Britain chose a nationalist route in 1931, albeit a moderate and conservative-dominated one, with the collapse of the Labour government and the creation of a so-called National Government under the same Prime Minister, Ramsay MacDonald. France, with a political system which failed to throw up a coalition government, endured 11 different cabinets in four years (between 1932 and 1936). There were also numerous national budget crises.

'Bread and butter' issues came to dominate European political life. How could farmers secure a reasonable price for their produce in a world of falling prices? How could workers in Europe's cities find enough work to buy food? The depression also disrupted diplomatic relations as the severity of the world slump pushed countries to protect their national interest above all else through discrimination, tariffs and import quotas. The globe was divided into protected and warring trading blocs, and it was in an atmosphere of intense economic competition, sometimes between nations who shared common diplomatic and strategic interests – like Britain, France and the United States – that German National Socialism and Italian Fascism entered the international scene. For Germany, Italy and Japan, taking pride in their peoples' 'racial superiority', economic nationalism was a step on the road to the creation of empires.

Causes of the depression

The causes of the depression were complex. The European recession did not originate in the USA, but the shock of the Wall Street crash on 'Black Thursday', 24 October 1929, undoubtedly affected Europe adversely, just as American economic involvement had buoyed the European economy in the 1920s. At the most elementary level, the European economy had not entirely adjusted to changes wrought or accelerated by the First World War. There were long-term, 'structural' changes in the world economy which had already contributed to Europe's considerable unemployment problem in the 1920s.

The vulnerability to economic dislocation of even the largest European powers, like Britain, France and Germany, was already plain in the 1920s when Europe was rendered more sensitive to its economic shortcomings by the virulent economic competition it faced not only from the United States but from Japan. Competition was aggravated by the growing uncompetitiveness of German, and to a lesser extent, British labour. From 1925 until 1930 real wages in Germany grew considerably, at a rate of 4.6 per cent per annum. Productivity did not. Among Britain's 'old industries' textiles faced as many problems as iron and steel, coal and shipbuilding. The official *History of Munitions*, published in 1922, described British manufacturers as 'behind other countries in research, plant and method . . . with competition becoming impossible'.

By early 1929 most policymakers in Italy, France, Germany, Britain and the United States recognized that the upswing in the world economy had ended. Demand for machinery from Germany and Czechoslovakia, for manufactures and wines from France, and for new housebuilding in Britain and Scandinavia, were all falling. To the German-born economist Joseph Schumpeter, who was interested in the relationship between economics and politics, depression was cyclical, and other economists identified cycles of differing lengths, among them the Kondratieff long cycle covering decades, not years.

But the causes of the initial downturn in prices and production in 1928–29 were not the same as the causes which led to this recession becoming the most protracted and profound economic depression of the twentieth century. There were four distinct elements in the situation – the loss of American investment in Europe; the collapse of world primary prices and the subsequent rise in trade protectionism; the clinging to the gold standard – Britain was the first power to abandon it in 1931, while France stuck with it until 1936; and the failure of politicians to promote international, as distinct from national, initiatives for economic recovery. Even in 1929 many politicians failed to appreciate fully the degree to which their national prosperity had become dependent on that of their European neighbours and the United States. As the shadows of depression fell across Europe each nation was determined to secure its own interests.

American loans had helped to paper over some of the cracks in Europe's economy before 1929. They now became increasingly visible. The prosperity of Germany, of all the European powers, was the most dependent upon a stream of American Dawes plan credit which stimulated not only German economic growth, but that of the central and eastern European nations around it. Its supply to the German economy ominously began to dry up in 1928. The United States, whose intervention in the First World War was decisive, had an equally decisive, and this time totally destructive impact on Europe after 1929.

It was ironic that American credit to Europe evaporated not because of economic weakness but because of economic success in the United States. From 1924 to 1928 American investors had been drawn to European investment by high rates of return, but in 1928 it became clear that even more money could be made by investing in the American stock market. A river of gold now began to converge on Wall Street while credit became scarce in Europe. American overseas investment fell from $2,214 million in 1928 to $1,414 million in 1929 (in 1930 it was to fall to $363 million). In a vain attempt to retain foreign investment, Italy, Germany and Britain increased their discount (interest) rates, but this made it more expensive for the weaker economic powers (as well as their own businessmen) to borrow money in London, Berlin and Paris when their American credit dried up. A dangerous chain reaction had begun. The first signs that America was failing the international economy were already apparent. Yet during the 1920s the American people had come to believe that their new found prosperity was permanent and assured, and their boundless optimism was reflected in a stock market boom of unprecedented dimensions. On 1 January 1925 the total value of all shares on the New York Stock Exchange was around $27 million. Four years later, the value exceeded $67 million – an increase of over 250 per cent. When Herbert Hoover accepted the presidential nomination for the Republican Party in 1928, he spoke for millions of Americans as he declared: 'We shall soon with the help of God be in sight of the day when poverty will be banished from all the nation.'

Hoover would have done well to exercise greater caution. Within a year of this speech there were clear signs that all was not well in the American economy itself, and the Wall Street crash, which involved the stock market, shook American confidence to the core. On 'Black Thursday' almost 13 million shares changed hands at vastly reduced prices. The only diversion from this terrible news for the crowds amassed in front of the Stock

Exchange on Wall Street was the spectacle of a would-be suicide balanced on a nearby skyscraper.

The European slump, 1929–36

Different European countries hit economic rock bottom at different times over the next four years. The first misguided policy decision came in the United States: American bankers believed that Wall Street's 'melt-down' had been triggered by too much 'cheap' money sloshing around within the economy. Their conclusion prompted the Federal Reserve Bank of New York to increase base lending rates, making it more expensive to borrow money. This was an action which made the depression more severe as consumer demand and business investment now dried up altogether. The economist John Maynard Keynes, whose ideas were to shape the world after 1945, was in no doubt: 'the fall of investment . . . I find – and I find without doubt or reservation whatsoever – the whole explanation for the current state of affairs'. It was only as the depression progressed that the Americans and British gradually reduced their interest rates and introduced a policy of cheap money. This helped to revive industry and to stimulate demand.

Without American investment after 1929 Europe's banks became increasingly unstable. Representatives from eastern and central Europe – Germany, Poland, Austria, and Czechoslovakia – now went to London, instead of New York, in search of loans just at a time when Britain was least able to provide them. Matters came to a head in May 1931 when Austria's largest commercial bank, the *Creditanstalt*, collapsed. A banking crisis quickly followed in Germany.

European bankers were not the only businesses with problems and as banks appeared unsafe, frightened Germans and Austrians began to withdraw investments and savings to hoard and to hide them under beds and, it was said, in chamber-pots and tea-caddies. At the heart of Europe's difficulties lay the global collapse not in the prices of stocks and shares, but in primary prices (notably the price of wheat, meat, coal and steel). During the 1920s agricultural prices had already fallen between 20 per cent and 50 per cent. After October 1929 this trend continued and accelerated. With over 67 per cent of the world's active population still engaged in agriculture, falling prices spelt disaster and had several important consequences.

At the most obvious level European farmers became politically militant and began agitating anxiously for governments to address their plight. As a result, the governments of France, Germany and Spain, amongst others, began to modify and increase protectionist measures which were already in place in the 1920s. Countries now attempted to protect their disgruntled farmers behind protectionist walls of tariffs, import quotas, depreciated

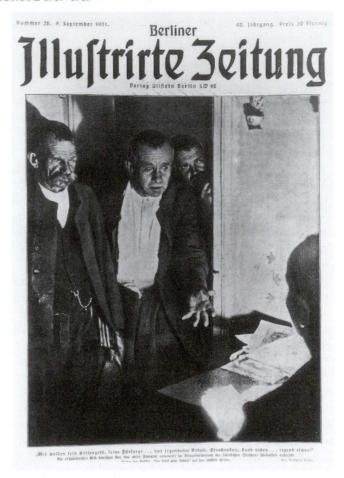

Plate 8.1 The *Berliner Illustrirte Zeitung* depicts German desperation as the depression deepens, October 1931. The photograph on the front of Germany's leading picture magazine underlines that this is a common-place scene: it was taken 'without being noticed in the mayor's office of the small Franconian village Wallenfells'. The caption which accompanies it reads, 'We don't want any compensation for the crisis, no handouts . . . only some work, road-building, work on the land . . . anything.'

currencies and (sometimes bogus) sanitary regulations – these policies became known as 'beggar-thy-neighbour' economics. In 1931 the Nazi publication *Der Deutsche Volkswirt* ('The German Economist') wrote, in typically florid prose, of the 'bondage of tariffs tearing into the body of international trade'. It was increasingly difficult to challenge this sentiment. German import duties soon increased by over 50 per cent, by 1932 French quotas covered more than 3,000 goods, and Romania had imposed quotas on 80 per cent of its imports.

The most dramatic transition to protectionism took place in Britain. After the withdrawal in October 1931 of many of the Liberals from a newly formed National Government, it decided to abandon its historic promotion of free trade and, following the depreciation of sterling in September 1931, passed a series of tariff acts. These included a General Tariff (April 1932) and a number of Imperial Protection Agreements signed in Ottawa (August 1932). Imperial preference did not mean that the British had plans to make the Empire self-sufficient: by 1932 the mercantilist concept of an industrialized mother country linked to primary producer countries had become grossly anachronistic. The Dominions, too, had begun to industrialize and would have resented such a paternal approach from Britain.

For frustrated national-imperialists in Germany and Italy, however, Britain's move towards the Empire appeared to emphasize the inequality created by the Versailles Treaty between the *have* and *have not* powers, and a sense of injustice was compounded when nationalists in Germany and Italy surveyed the remainder of the globe during the depression. France fostered its imperial connections in North Africa and the 'B' mandate territories of Eastern Togoland and the Eastern Cameroons, Japan had established a protectorate in Manchuria (1931), and the United States showed renewed commercial interest in Central and South America. Mussolini fantasized of a Second Roman Empire in the Mediterranean, while for Hitler, Germany's imperial destiny lay on its doorstep – the security of *Lebensraum* (living space) for the German people in eastern Europe.

The division of Europe into exclusive trading blocs was, from the start, accelerated by currency instability. This began in the summer of 1931 when pressure increased on the pound sterling, the Labour government fell and the National Government was formed. The confidence of investors who owned large amounts of sterling evaporated amid mounting political and economic uncertainty, and they began to convert their paper pounds into gold. Gold, in turn, began to drain from the Bank of England at an uncontrollable rate and, on 20 September 1931, the Bank's Governor, Montagu Norman, announced that the British government had decided to float the pound: sterling was no longer on the gold standard. Countries which had large reserves of sterling – Britain's Empire and Dominion partners, and Scandinavia – quickly floated their currencies too. Once Britain was off the gold standard, prices at home began to rise, but British exports became more competitive overseas.

While Britain declared it had been 'forced' off gold, President Roosevelt deliberately chose to float the United States dollar as part of his New Deal recovery measures in April 1933: by the end of that year the dollar had depreciated by around 40 per cent, American domestic prices had improved and jobless figures had begun to fall. This American recovery helped sponsor a rally in the world economy as a whole. United States citizens gradually regained their appetite for overseas imports, and it gradually became possible once more to borrow money for investment.

Abandoning the gold standard had not led, after all, to the economic disaster which many critics believed it would in the 1920s, for the gold standard had damaged Europe's economy before 1929 in two principal ways. First, as we have seen, some currencies (like the British) were fixed at the wrong exchange rate. Second, the maintenance of the standard required each participant in the system to follow an 'orthodox' economic policy, balancing its domestic budget (no government should spend more than it collected in revenue). The net effect of a gold standard 'ideology' in 1929 was to create government economic policies in Europe which acted to depress economic growth rather than encourage it in the aftermath of the Wall Street crash.

When it came to abandoning the gold standard after 1931, European nations fell into three broad categories. In the first group were countries like Britain and the United States, who had been forced off, or had opted to abandon gold. Second came gold bloc nations (France, Italy, Poland, the Netherlands, and Switzerland), dominated by the leadership of France and Italy who stuck to the gold standard. These countries believed that the gold standard had helped to generate prosperity in the 1920s and that to abandon gold would destroy their economies. Through the relative undervaluation of the French franc and the predominance of agriculture in France (unemployment was more easily concealed in the countryside), the depression came to France relatively late – largely after 1931 – but by 1934 it had taken hold with a vengeance. Yet it was only in 1936 that France finally devalued the franc, and then with bitter regret.

Italy, like France, proved a stalwart supporter of the gold bloc. For Mussolini a much vaunted 'Battle for the Lira' in 1927, two years before the Wall Street crash, had been more than a struggle to defeat moral disgrace and economic disaster.[1] According to him 'the fate of the regime is tied to the fate of the lira'; a stabilized currency was a reflection of Italy's determination to achieve great-power status in economic and diplomatic terms. But for these nations such an approach to status often carried a heavy economic price. The third category of European gold bloc powers, exemplified by Germany and Hungary remained on the gold standard because they were terrified of the potential social price of leaving it, the encouragement of inflation within their economies, but they severely restricted the way that the standard was allowed to operate in their countries.

The international and national responses, 1929–36

In the rush by politicians to preserve national economies, international efforts to revive the world economy were stillborn. Britain, France, Germany, Italy, Belgium, the Netherlands and Austria, amongst others, continued to express the need for international economic cooperation to tackle the rising levels of international protectionism and competitive currency depreciation. In practice, efforts at international cooperation were, all too frequently, stymied by domestic priorities.

After the failure of a 1927 World Economic Conference in Geneva to tackle the growth of protectionism in Europe, the next concerted effort at international cooperation came in the depths of the depression with the momentous Hoover Moratorium. In June 1931 President Hoover announced that Europe could postpone its debt payments to the United States for a year and this, in turn, enabled Britain and France to forgo German reparations for that year. The European economy failed to improve, however, and the Lausanne Conference (June 1932) finally abolished German reparations and the hated 'war guilt' clause which had accompanied reparations in the Treaty of Versailles.

From the Lausanne Conference grew the initiative for a second World Economic Conference. This was an unprecedented gathering. Sixty-five nations came to deliberate the condition of the world economy in London's newly opened Geological Museum in the summer of 1933. But for all the hot air generated by politicians debating the world's economic troubles, the balloon for international economic revival failed to go up. The World Economic Conference soured rather than improved the economic and diplomatic climate. Representatives were more anxious to preserve the protectionist measures they had already introduced than to secure any loosening of international restrictions. Britain, for example, was anxious to preserve its tariff levels and the depreciated status of the pound, while the United States wanted the freedom to depreciate the dollar further. As in any crisis, politicians chose to protect their own backyard before taking account of any broader, international considerations.

Many European delegates, particularly those from eastern Europe, returned embittered from London. These smaller powers were dependent solely on the good offices of their larger European neighbours, and they had been let down. The prognosis for these countries was poor. They were heavily dependent on agriculture, the most severely affected industry in the depression, and their productivity was far lower than that of west European farmers. In Bulgaria, for example, there were around 450,000 wooden ploughs to 250,000 iron ones in 1936, while Yugoslav and Romanian farmers spread 0.2 kilograms of fertilizer per hectare of land – their Dutch counterparts used 311 kilograms.

Nor did eastern Europe, inextricably drawn into the network of European financial relations, find help outside. Indeed, its powerful neighbours, Germany and the Soviet Union, not only failed to provide economic support or cooperation at the London conference, they soon came to threaten the very territorial integrity of Europe's newest nation states. In the wake of the depression, competition, not cooperation, became Europe's watchword. With the escalation of 'beggar-thy-neighbour' economics, European nations became engrossed in commercial rivalry and

Mr. MacDonald said that the Profits of the world were with them. They must co-operate.

M. Daladier of France favoured co-operation in so far as it gave other nations the opportunity to make sacrifices for France.

Mr. Chamberlain of Britain believed in co-operation if it gave Britain an advantage over other nations.

Signor Jung of Italy supported co-operation if Italy got the thick end of the deal.

An interval here took place during which Dr. Dollfuss was exhibited free of charge.

Baron Neurath of Germany would co-operate if everybody would give Germany something.

Litvinoff of Russia said that all the Capitalist System needed was a stick of dynamite. It was felt that he was trying to turn the occasion into an Economic Conference and he was voted no gentleman.

THE CONFERENCE THEN ADJOURNED, THE HALL BEING NEEDED FOR A CONFERENCE OF AMERICANS TO DECIDE WHO HAS THEIR POLICY, IF ANY.

CONFERENCE HALL

failed to find the common ground which would have enabled them to fight the depression more effectively, despite the fact that the symptoms of the slump were the same across Europe: industrial unemployment rising in Britain from an annual average of 12 per cent in the 1920s to 15.4 per cent from 1930 to 1938, and in Germany from 9.2 per cent to 21.8 per cent during the same period. Translated into human terms, this meant two to two-and-a-half million unemployed in Britain in the 1930s. In Germany the jobless total was even more startling, reaching a peak of almost six million in 1932.

European governments chose national and generally ineffective policies to defeat the depression. Politicians had not foreseen how serious the depression was to become, any more than they had foreseen the character of the First World War. Britain, France, Germany and Italy evolved and modified their economic policies as each new crisis unfolded, with only Sweden combining realism and imagination. It was not that politicians were reluctant to get their hands dirty in managing the economy. Indeed, in many European nations, government intervention had increased greatly already during the 1920s. Even in Hungary, which had one of the most liberal economic policies in the Balkans, there was strong pressure to extend government involvement. By 1931 the Hungarian state owned many large industrial enterprises such as the Diósgyör iron and steel works, and the Nitrokemia gunpowder factory.

For many European governments the slump revived notions of economic planning which had been hastily abandoned at the end of the First World War. In Germany, Italy, Hungary and Romania the metaphors of war found a new purpose in the planning of industrial and agrarian 'fronts', 'shock' workers and recovery 'campaigns'. But despite greater levels of political economic management, strict financial orthodoxy, associated with the gold standard, continued to be popular. Europe's major economic powers – Britain, Germany, France and Italy – remained determined to balance national and trade budgets and, as far as practicable, maintain their exchange rates. It was only once countries abandoned this orthodox strait-jacket that their economic fortunes revived.

The experience of the 1920s was another element which helped to condition the response of Europe's democracies to the depression. This trait was most easily recognizable in Germany where the dominant fear was that the hyper-inflation of 1923 would return to destroy the economy and

---

Plate 8.2 The Failure of International Co-operation. The *Evening Standard*, 22 June 1933. Low's cartoon illustrates the preoccupation of the leading European delegations to the World Economic Conference with national interests and the personal rivalries which plagued the American delegation. On the opening day of the conference, the Austrian Reichstag was attacked by National Socialists. The 'exhibition' of the Chancellor Dollfuss is a wry reference to the Austrian premier's reception by the conference. The delegates responded with warm applause but offered no practical aid to his defence of Austrian independence.

knowledge of what happened in Germany was fully appreciated elsewhere. Whatever Keynes in Britain might say – or senior civil servants like Wilhelm Lautenbach and Günter Gereke in Germany, and the American Raymond Moley – large-scale government expenditure to boost employment was largely unpopular with politicians between 1929 and 1932. It was only after 1933 that increases in government expenditure contributed to the reduction of unemployment in Germany and the United States.

Depression and democracy

The Great Depression was a global crisis which left few unscathed and it had a devastating effect on European governments. It is difficult to overestimate the impact of this economic collapse on European democracy. Everything that happened from then on seemed sinister and of evil omen.[2] For some democratic governments in Europe – Germany, Spain, Greece – the depression was the final blow. Even in Britain and France liberal democracy came perilously close to collapse, and the Soviet Union, while proclaiming loudly that the depression sounded the death-knell of capitalism, found that its economy was not entirely insulated from the slump's devastating effects.

In Britain in May 1929, shortly before the Wall Street bubble burst, Prime Minister Stanley Baldwin (Conservative) was replaced by Labour's Ramsay MacDonald, following an election which marked a milestone for the Labour Party: it was the largest party in the House for the first time ever. His government was a minority government, however, and his cabinet – complete with its first ever woman minister, Margaret Bondfield – was to stumble at the same hurdle as Hermann Müller's Social Democratic Grand Coalition in Germany. The problem Labour faced was how to resolve the spending demands of social welfare provision with existing methods of economic management during an unprecedented economic crisis. Once the depression hit, demands for government to spend more on unemployment insurance and on measures to combat unemployment naturally increased, at the same time as it became particularly important for government to reduce its expenditure as dictated by orthodox economic policy. Unfortunately for the minority Labour government, it had made life more difficult for itself by introducing an Unemployment Insurance Bill in November 1931 which increased the number of people eligible for unemployment benefit.

The British economy had been one of the most depressed in western Europe during the 1920s, and the Wall Street crash further discouraged British investment while primary prices and levels of trade continued to fall. But Labour's ministers, like their luckless socialist counterparts in Germany and France, had no new weapons to combat the economic slump. In Britain Jimmy Thomas was Minister for 'Unemployment'. He had plenty of ideas for national relief schemes, but British public works policy was severely limited by budgetary constraint. When it became clear that the minority Labour government was to adopt cautious and conservative strategies to defeat the depression, Thomas's deputy, Sir Oswald Mosley, resigned to pursue a more sensationalist career in British politics, becoming founder of the 'New Party' and later of the British Union of Fascists.

In the summer of 1931, while central European financial systems wobbled and sometimes crashed, Britain's political and economic problems reached fever pitch. Sir Clive Wigram, private secretary to George V, warned the King that 'We are sitting on top of a volcano'. The foreboding atmosphere was enhanced by the May Committee's financial report which pointed to serious problems in Britain's industry and finance, and estimated that by April 1932 the British government would be £120 million in the red. The Committee urged the Labour government to increase taxes and introduce economies, largely by cutting unemployment benefit. It was this latter call which split the Labour Party: those on the left, like Glasgow's James Maxton, believed any reduction of benefits was a betrayal of party principles; those on the right, like the Chancellor, Philip Snowden, asserted that reducing expenditure was the only way to preserve the viability of the British economy. An alternative was proposed by Lloyd George who, motivated by what he considered a deplorable waste of human resources, urged that government increase its spending to reduce unemployment and stimulate demand to produce benefits which would ripple across the entire economy. Such ideas, later given theoretical justification in J. M. Keynes's *The General Theory of Employment, Interest and Money* (1936), were pooh-poohed as, at best expensive, at worst 'crackpot', by senior Conservative and Labour politicians alike.

By August 1931 the Labour government was in crisis and after two visits to the King, MacDonald, to the stupefaction of his Labour cabinet colleagues, informed them that although they were no longer in office, he was. MacDonald had agreed to head a National Government composed of individuals rather than parties, as a temporary expedient to settle the financial crisis. Instead, events that summer heralded nine years of Conservative government beneath the National Government banner, with many of MacDonald's party colleagues branding their leader a traitor. As Schumpeter, writing in 1942, recognized, in the long run the Labour Party 'recovered and consolidated its position' in the years which followed the split. In the short term, however, the crisis was catastrophic.

To observers overseas and at home it appeared that dramatic changes were afoot as Britain followed the depreciation of the pound with its series of tariff acts designed to protect British trade. The closest Britain ever came to a dramatic political upheaval, however, was on 15 September 1931 when 12,000 sailors refused to work after they heard that their pay was to be cut (the wage cuts were uneven: a 3.7 per cent reduction for lieutenant commanders, with up to a 13.6 per cent cut for unmarried able-bodied seamen). Some fearful voices compared this incident at Invergordon to the military rebellions which had preceded the Russian Revolution, but the depression never seriously threatened the stability of British political life.

After the depreciation of sterling in 1931 the British economy began to show tentative signs of revival, a recovery which was made all the more dramatic by the economic collapse which continued to grip Germany, France and the United States. Political extremes, like the National Unemployed Workers' Movement on the left and Mosley's British Union of Fascists, were only successful in areas where unemployment remained high, and British politics did not take an anti-democratic or revolutionary path. The country had a strong parliamentary tradition, sound financial and banking institutions, and relatively moderate levels of unemployment (2.5 million at its peak). There was a widespread feeling that British democracy was 'superior'. As MacDonald's successor as Prime Minister, Stanley Baldwin, put it, it was 'the only country where parliamentary government has grown up, the only country . . . where it is flesh of our flesh and bone of our bone'. A believer in conciliation, Baldwin had replaced MacDonald after the latter's resignation in 1935. His Chancellor of the Exchequer, Neville Chamberlain, was to succeed him in 1937 after Baldwin had safely steered the country – and the Empire – through a royal abdication crisis.

The collapse of Weimar, 1930–33

It was in Germany that liberal democracy faced its greatest test. Here, too, the left was unequal to the challenge of the depression, but there were forces on the right whose strength and character were not paralleled in Britain. In the spring of 1930 a Great Coalition, dominated by the Social Democratic Party (SPD), and led by Hermann Müller, failed to weather the economic storm. The final SPD government of the Weimar period collapsed in the spring of 1930. Although the left continued to command substantial support in the *Reichstag* – the KPD (German Communist Party) and the SPD together held more seats than the NSDAP in November 1932 – the SPD and KPD did not join forces to defeat the right (the German communists had been forbidden to do so by their Stalinist directors in Moscow). But, as in Britain and France, Germany's socialists were also impeded by their economic principles. They were wedded to balancing the national budget, which inevitably entailed cutting unemployment benefit and the pay of public employees.

Germany's budgetary difficulties had been made more acute by the expansion of German social security legislation in 1927. Whereas social expenditure had amounted to 19.3 per cent of all public expenditures in 1913, in 1930 it was 40.3 per cent. Successive German chancellors were faced with the dilemma of paying ever rising unemployment benefits while their income from taxation was falling because of business failure and declining income tax yields. In March 1930 a new right-wing coalition under Heinrich Brüning took office. That spring, German unemployment stood at over three million and the Nazis collected 107 seats in the German *Reichstag* – a new high. Brüning quickly introduced draconian measures to rescue the German economy. He rigorously cut government expenditure, real wages were reduced and prices fell while levels of taxation were increased. On the face of it Brüning had few policy alternatives given the German electorate's deep fear of inflation and the dearth of foreign investment available to Germany.

Such harsh measures, of course, made Brüning few friends within the German electorate. Lower-middle-class businessmen saw profits slump, salaried public employees saw their wages cut – the income of a petty bureaucrat earning 260 marks per month in 1927 was slashed to 202 marks by 1932 – taxes increased, farmers were unable to sell their produce, some industrialists went bankrupt and the unemployment figures continued to rise. Every social class in Germany was affected. To distract hostility at home and hopefully provide an alternative remedy to Germany's economic downturn, Brüning began to pursue a vigorous foreign policy for the abolition of German reparation payments and modifications to the military restrictions imposed by the peace of Versailles.

In May 1931, however, matters grew worse when there was a run on German banks. Large amounts of foreign and German money fled Weimar and now there was even less money available for investment and loans to be employed in reviving the German economy. But, unlike in Britain or France in 1936, neither Brüning nor his successors – Franz von Papen, Kurt von Schleicher and Adolf Hitler – ever entertained the possibility of devaluing the *Reichsmark* for fear of the political repercussions. After the 1923 hyper-inflation it was firmly believed that currency devaluation, to make German goods cheaper on the international market and to create capital for investment and purchases, was not an option open to German politicians.

By early 1932 it was clear that Brüning's measures were having little effect. German unemployment had risen to six million: one in five Germans was without work. The year 1932 was a hungry and demoralizing one for many. Everthing helped to undermine German democracy as the early disappointment of Germany's political elites – the Army, the judiciary and landowners – with the Weimar Republic grew more profound. As in Britain, it was centre-liberal parties who lost out as the German political scene began to fragment with dire consequences.

The business classes, for example, became increasingly divided as the German government introduced legislation to protect the small shop-owner. In response to this and to harsher economic conditions, German big business began to strengthen cartels to keep up prices. This move, in turn, was resented by those who had to pay more for their goods, notably other members of the middle class and the working class. Big

Plate 8.3 Chancellor Hitler and President Hindenburg, August 1933. The eighty-six-year-old Reichspresident and the newly-installed German Chancellor pictured together at the commemoration of the battle of Tannenberg of 1914 in which Hindenburg, then a Colonel-General, had commanded German troops to victory. Long suspicious of the 'intolerance', 'noise' and 'indiscipline' which characterized Nazi party activity, Hindenburg had forlornly opposed Hitler's appointment as Chancellor. By the time this photograph was taken, Hindenburg was preoccupied with his succession. He, like many conservatives and some Nazi party members, wanted to see monarchy restored to Germany, but Hitler was determined that he and no one else should succeed to the Presidency.

business, despite its reputation for actively assisting Hitler to power, was in reality a passive contributor to his success. True, it had no allegiance to Weimar. The heads of large concerns blamed wage rises and the deteriorating economic situation on the new German state and they were prepared to tolerate and even support anti-democratic and anti-parliamentary rule. Nonetheless, businessmen did not automatically fly into the arms of the National Socialist Party.

German farmers also became divided in the harsh economic climate. The small peasant farmer grew indignant at the preferential treatment accorded to the *Junkers* (large Prussian landowners) and the trend towards small, specialized splinter parties – facilitated by Weimar's proportional representation system – accelerated during the first two years of the depression.

Parties like the Christian-National Peasants and Farmers' Party, the Green Party, the German Peasants' Party and even the 'Militant League of Beggars' began to collect votes. And while German workers took to the streets demanding jobs, conservative groups began to claim that Germany stood under threat of imminent 'Bolshevization'. The German electorate were becoming radicalized, drawn to the political extremes of the right and left for an answer to economic distress.

As Brüning found his political support wearing thin, he, like his predecessors, increasingly employed emergency decrees to avoid the need for a majority in the Reichstag. German democracy was undermined already before Chancellor Adolf Hitler came to power. In June 1932 Papen became Chancellor and few mourned Brüning's parting. Even the Americans condemned Brüning as 'ascetic, scholastic, fanatic and despotic',[3] yet neither Chancellor Papen nor his successor Schleicher, remained in office long. They could not muster sufficient support to withstand 'no-confidence' votes now that the National Socialists and the Communists commanded over 50 per cent of the Reichstag. On 30 January 1933 the Nazi Party came to power, at a time when its electoral support had actually been declining and its party funds running low.

Adolf Hitler proved to be the politician to square the circle of interest-group politics. The NSDAP, for instance, actively courted small peasant farmers, and within the first six months of holding office, the Nazis had introduced further protective measures favouring the peasant farmer over export industry – the latter was silenced with promises of German rearmament and threats of civil war if business failed to support the National Socialists. Germany was revived by lavish rhetoric, the subordination of labour to the state which enabled employers to push down wage costs (they fell by around 24 per cent over the next four years), increased taxation and, of course, Hitler's famous public works schemes. It is important to note, however, that Hitler did not abandon orthodox economics – the *Reichsmark* was not devalued and money supply was kept constrained. In its remarkable rise to power, the National Socialist Party had successfully harnessed what has been termed the 'coalition of no' with its promises of 'bread and work'. The disgruntled peasant farmers, the industrialists, members of the white-collar middle class and the artisans who had felt ignored and impoverished within a modern, industrialized Germany were all drawn to the energy of the NSDAP.

Like Mussolini, Hitler was also able to rally Germany's youth to his cause. Both leaders were young and dynamic (Mussolini was 39 when he became Prime Minister, Adolf Hitler was 44 years old when appointed Chancellor), and both conducted their juvenile propaganda drives in an atmosphere of passion and violence. The success of the German National Socialists gave credence to the widespread sentiment, held by opponents as well as promoters of fascism, that, in Mussolini's words, 'fascist ideas were the ideas of the age'. In some respects National Socialism was a very distinct form of fascism – it was the most virulently racist movement, determined to free the German people of the twin and interchangeable evils of Judaism and international socialism.

These familiar leitmotifs of Hitler's ideology were hardly original. Popular anti-semitism and crude Social Darwinism (which divided the world into 'races' competing for survival) had been circulating in Europe for several decades. Hitler bound these themes with more concrete political goals: a centralized, national community, 'equality of treatment in international affairs' and total autarky (a self-sufficient economy). As Nazi Party chief George Strasser proclaimed: 'a nation which is dependent on foreign countries is in the final analysis never in a position to solve its foreign policy problems'.

The case of Sweden

Germany's economic recovery under the Nazis had important implications for its trading partners, notably in eastern Europe and Scandinavia. Eastern Europe was penetrated increasingly by German political ideas and economic policies, while the economies of Scandinavia, notably that of Sweden, benefited from Germany's revived appetite for raw materials. Swedish iron ore exports grew from three million tonnes in 1933 to 12.5 million tonnes in 1939 – over 70 per cent of this ore was shipped to Germany.

Sweden, the most industrialized Scandinavian economy, also adopted less conventional, and more successful, policies for tackling the depression which attracted the interest of German and American economists at the time and historians ever since. Rejecting accepted othodoxy, the Swedish economists Bertil Ohlin and Gunner Myrdal advocated greater state intervention and expenditure to stimulate demand, and their ideas were adopted with gusto by the 1932 coalition government dominated by the Social Democratic Party. This government and its economic policies marked a sharp break with past thinking, even on the part of Swedish Social Democrats, as the new Finance Minister, Ernst Wigfors, implemented radical and innovative recovery strategies. Sweden's tax burden was redistributed and the government's budget deficit was balanced over a number of years (around three to four) rather than year by year, which increased the amount of revenue available to the government. This revenue was then ploughed back into the economy by public work projects and subsidized building schemes.

Even in Sweden, where these 'Keynesian' policies had found a receptive audience, the benefits of currency depreciation, low interest rates, price stability and the recovery of German and British export markets (especially as the drive for rearmament accelerated) was as important as deficit spending to its economic recovery. Sweden's depression was undoubtedly serious, as the suicide of well-known industrialist Ivar Kreugar (March 1932) and a bitter labour strike (from April 1933 until February 1934) testified, but a stable political environment, an innovative policy response, an outward-looking economy and international recovery also contributed towards the country's exemplary recovery from the depression.

France, 1932–38

The same could not be said for France. Developments in Germany may have offered temporary benefits to the Swedes, but were viewed with mounting anxiety by the French, many of whom began to fear not only a resurgent Germany, but for the stability of liberal democracy home. The French Republic was slower than Britain or Germany to feel the full impact of the great depression and its comparative good fortune earned it the nickname 'L'île heureuse' (the fortunate island), but by 1932 the French economy was in difficulties. As the depression began to bite, the political climate became increasingly unstable. Like Germany, France had introduced proportional representation after the First World War, and from 1932 onwards its government became fragmented between varying shades of radicals, radical-socialists, socialists, conservatives, nationalists and populists.

In June 1932 Edouard Herriot, a Radical, came to office. He lasted six months, defeated over the issue of cutting national expenditure to balance the national budget and France's failure to meet its war debt payment to the United States; his successor Edouard Daladier lasted nine months. This pattern was to become typical in a political system which was hijacked by narrow coalitions focused on individuals like Herriot, Daladier and Camille Chautemps, although French democracy did not fall prey to anything as extreme as National Socialism. By early 1934 the Radical and Socialist Parties were increasingly discredited by a series of well-publicized political scandals and by their failure to initiate any effective policy to spare France from the worst effects of the depression.

Fascist movements began to flourish in France too. Popular right-wing, anti-semitic and nationalistic politicians found a willing audience amongst lower-middle-class Frenchmen who feared Marxism and resented the Third Republic which had allowed this 'fifth column' to grow. In 1934, some 370,000 people – set against 35,000 communists – belonged to four separate French fascist movements (Action Française, the Légion, Jeunesses Patriotes and the Faisceau). The ideology of French fascism was influenced by foreign fascist movements, but it also boasted an older pedigree. Much of its anti-semitism dated back to the Dreyfus case, while its anti-parliamentarianism and support for the Army grew out of the conservative backlash to the liberalism and socialism prevalent in France in the late nineteenth century.

In February of the same year bloody fighting broke out on the streets of Paris as right-wing demonstrators marched in protest against the new Radical government led by Daladier. People threw marbles under the hooves of horses, slashed horses' bellies with razor blades and tore up iron-railings from the streets. Two years and several right-wing cabinets later, the French left (Radicals, Socialists and Communists) finally united to defend the Republic, and in May 1936 the Popular Front came to power. Drawing an important lesson from the fatal divisions amongst the German left, French communists and socialists had bound together to save France from increasingly subversive elements. The German remilitarization of the Rhineland and a physical assault on Socialist leader Léon Blum by the *Action Française* in the early months of 1936 had reinforced the apparent danger to the Third Republic.

Under the leadership of Blum, the Popular Front introduced economic and social measures which were popular largely with French workers. Such economic recovery as there was came almost by accident when the Popular Front was forced to devalue the French franc in September 1936 by around 25–33 per cent, even though without a vigorous recovery programme the devaluation had limited effect. The government represented a significant milestone in French political history, but this alone did not guarantee success. In May 1937, the French economy took a tail spin and the Popular Front collapsed in disarray over the issue of the 40-hour week. Blum was defeated by the conservative Senate's refusal to grant the extraordinary powers he required to enact his economic programme and by the collapse of support among his Radical coalition members. He complained, 'I've had enough. All I have tried to do has been sabotaged.'

In France's political turmoil, the role of the middle class, as in Germany, proved especially important. It was this group which was most anxious that orthodox economic policy be followed to preserve the value of their pensions, savings and salaries. But while the position of farmers and big business was crucial in undermining Weimar, in France and Britain this stratum of society remained essentially conservative and loyal to the existing political order. When the 371st regiment of the French heavy artillery hatched an insurrectionist plot with their local branch of *Action Française*, for instance, the local police were rightly confident that it would not succeed 'because of the sincerely Republican spirit of the local population'.

Civil war in Spain

France had come close to civil war, but for Spain the election of a Popular Front government in 1936 was the catalyst, not the antidote, to a bitter and bloody internal conflict. Neutrality during the First World War had brought a much needed era of prosperity to a Spain humiliated by defeat in the Spanish American War (1898), and impeded by relatively low levels of population growth and a predominantly agrarian economy. But the end of the war brought economic recession, as it had across Europe, and the conservative interests which had dominated Spain under a constitutional monarchy since 1875 found themselves increasingly bereft of support.

War and recession had encouraged the growth of powerful movements on the left. The Spanish Socialists, *Partido Socialista Obrero Español* (PSOE), and their influential trade union, the *Unión General de Trabajores* (UGT) alongside the Marxist *Partido Obrero de Unificación Marxista* (POUM) – of which George Orwell became a member – and the Anarchist union, the *Confederación Nacional de Trabajo* (CNT) had all emerged with strong, though conflicting, visions of Spain's future. As in France and Germany then, the Spanish left was split into revolutionary and reformist movements and these divisions were made yet more complex by anti-clerical and separatist tendencies, most notably the struggles for autonomy in the Catalan and Basque regions.

The industrial unrest and unauthorized land seizures by peasants in the south of Spain, which had characterized the early 1920s, were temporarily repressed by the relatively benign dictatorship of General Primo de Rivera from 1923 to 1930. But de Rivera soon alienated the Army with ill-conceived military reforms, and big business with his tendencies towards economic nationalism; and added to this heady mixture came economic depression after 1928. In 1931 the grip of the Spanish right on power finally loosened. 'We are', as King Alfonso XIII admitted, 'out of fashion.' He then hastily left Spain for exile.

Spain became a republic overnight, and after five more years of frequent cabinet changes and a brief revival of the right in 1933, the Popular Front – an alliance of Republicans, Socialists, Communists and Anarchists – narrowly won a hard fought election in 1936. These years had witnessed the mass politicization of Spanish life, perhaps even more so than in Germany and France. But while rivalries and differences amongst the Republic's governing Socialists grew more bitter, the left's election victory galvanized the Army to mount a military coup against the Republic. Of the three generals leading the coup, the youngest, Francisco Franco, came to dominate an alliance of the right which included defenders of the Catholic Church and Spanish unity, alongside conventional political parties: the *Confederación Española de Derechas Autónomas* (CEDA), the fascist *Falange* and the *Carlists* – the traditional Catholic and conservative party of Spain.

In the Civil War which followed, the Republic at first appeared to hold the stronger hand strategically and in the resources at its disposal. But acrimonious feuding within the Popular Front became more divisive as the war proceeded – the Communists and the CNT on one side, and POUM on the other, began shooting at one another on the streets of Barcelona in 1937 – and their organization was weak as the left proved ill-suited to the

Plate 8.4 General Franco at Burgos, 1936. The diminutive Franco is seen surrounded by victorious soldiers and supporters in the city of Burgos in Old Castile. Burgos was taken almost without a shot, for its politics had long been monarchist and agrarian. The crowd, containing women in *mantillas* wearing scapularies and men in blue *falange* shirts, sang *Salve Regina* in celebration of easy victory.

discipline of war. Of the Republic's potential allies, only the USSR came to its aid; France and Britain did not. The Soviet Union's intervention was not always positive. Its unfair condemnation of POUM as 'Trotskyist' and the activities of its secret police (the GPU) in Spain only fuelled divisions within the Popular Front. The International Brigade, perhaps the most widely publicized element in foreign assistance (evocatively portrayed in George Orwell's *Homage to Catalonia* and André Malraux's *Days of Hope*), never played a decisive role in the war although its losses were substantial: of the 20,000 volunteers, almost half were killed.

The right, on the other hand, suffered no such impediments. The Army coordinated discipline and the various political groups were firmly united in their desire to defeat communism, defend the Church and preserve the unity of the Spanish nation. They also had generous help from their 'friends' overseas. Italian aid to General Franco was far more plentiful than that from Germany and at one point almost 50,000 Italian soldiers were fighting in Spain. But Germany's contribution became the most infamous when the *Luftwaffe's* Condor Legion attacked the small Basque town of Guernica. In the slaughter, vividly commemorated in a painting by Pablo Picasso, the town was destroyed and civilians machine-gunned as they fled.

By 1936 the right was controlling a band of territory in the east stretching from Algeciras in the south to the Franco-Spanish border. Almost all of New Castile, Catalonia and the Basque territories were in the hands of the Republic. By the end of 1938, however, the right's advance on Catalonia had become a rout and by 1 April 1939 Franco's forces had engulfed New Castile and emerged victorious. Franco, the puny, bullied schoolboy dubbed *cerillito* (little matchstick) by his classmates, had become a ruthless political as well as military leader. He successfully managed to unite the disparate forces of the right by judicious use of the 'carrot and stick'.

In 1939 Franco's government appeared a rather old-fashioned, traditional dictatorship when set against the dynamic, new-style leaderships of Hitler and Mussolini. Yet he survived for nearly 40 years as ruler of Spain – one of the longest terms of one-man rule in modern European history. His monolithic power always rested on two foundations: the Army and the Catholic Church. Spain, still a predominantly rural country in 1939, thus took a separate and isolated path from the remainder of western Europe.

Eastern Europe, 1929–38

Like Spain, eastern Europe, too, was ravaged by the severe agricultural depression. In Poland, Romania and Bulgaria agricultural income collapsed by 50–60 per cent, and in Hungary it fell by 36 per cent. Industrial production also was reduced considerably (Czechoslovakian and Austrian industrial output fell by over 40 per cent during the depression). Land hunger, widespread indebtedness and low peasant incomes had threatened political stability in the 1920s, now politicians had to confront international depression.

Democracy was soon beaten, or on the retreat, across all of eastern Europe, with the notable exception of industrialized Czechoslovakia. Unlike in much of the west, here it was peasant parties which made a distinct contribution to political and economic life during this period. They promoted agricultural cooperatives in Bulgaria and Slovenia and attempted to encourage more modern methods of farming and finance in the countryside. (The Agrarian Premier of Bulgaria, Alexander Stambolisky, even made grandiose plans for 'electrified' peasant villages, connected by a network of railways, each with a 'hall of popular culture' and a silo store.)

But without western investment or markets, it was difficult for the economies of eastern Europe to recover, particularly given the pervasive and longstanding character of their political, economic and social problems. Autarkic economic policies were followed by a sequence of increasingly inward-looking nationalist governments which became ever more intolerant of their ethnic minorities, especially the Jewish community with its popular association with *Finanzkapital* (financial-capitalism) and 'internationalism'.

By the mid-1930s most of the Balkans had succumbed to authoritarian government, and in Poland, after Pilsudski's death in 1935, his successors, a small group of old military associates known as the 'Government of Colonels', perpetuated his policies and encouraged popular nationalism with a dream to create a 'Great Power Poland'. In contrast to the relative longevity of Pilsudski's reign in Poland, Hungary endured a succession of conservative, nationalist leaders – Count Gyula Károlyi, Gyula Gömbös, Kálmán Darányi and Béla Imrédy – each more nationalist than the last. When Imrédy took the helm in May 1938 he promptly introduced anti-semitic legislation into Hungary, supported German policy in Czechoslovakia and paved the way for Hungary to join the Anti-Comintern pact (January 1939).

Austria, too, was racked by nationalist tensions – in 1934–35 there was even a movement dedicated to a Habsburg restoration – with the conservative countryside increasingly at odds with the Socialists in 'Red' Vienna. On 25 July 1934, Engelbert Dollfuss – the Austrian Chancellor and head of the coalition of conservative parties, the Fatherland Front – was murdered by members of an Austrian Nazi unit. Their putsch was unsuccessful. Dollfuss was succeeded by Kurt von Schuschnigg who took the bold step of attempting to broaden the appeal of the Fatherland Front. He reduced the powers of the *Heimwehr* (the 'homeguard' of the Fatherland Front) and even attempted to include a token number of Social Democrats – members of a party which had been outlawed since 1934. But, despite Schuschnigg's determination that Austria 'remain independent', his country had neither the unity nor the strength to withstand the powerful alliance of Austrian and German Nazis. It was annexed (the *Anschluss*) to Germany on 11 March 1938 with the German Field Marshal, Hermann Göring, satisfied that 'the existence of Austria is past history'.

The Czechoslovakian President, Thomas Masaryck, unlike his Austrian counterpart, took repressive action against pan-German nationalism as early as 1931. But although Nazism was outlawed, it regrouped into the *Sudetendeutsche Partie* (Sudeten German Party) led by Konrad Henlein. In secret, Henlein continued to foster links while his party grew in electoral strength. In 1935 Czechoslovakia's non-German parties unanimously endorsed Masaryck's successor, Edvard Beneš, but such cross-party cooperation was rare. The government faced mounting ethnic opposition, not only from Germans, but also from its Polish, Hungarian, Ruthenian and, most important, Slovak population who now demanded an independent republic. As Czechoslovakian democracy became increasingly prone to intolerance towards its minorities, these ethnic tensions, described by the Germans as an 'authentic chemical process of disintegration' provided the German Nazi government with an invaluable pretext to intervene in Czechoslovakian affairs.

Hitler's appointment as Chancellor in 1933 had sent shock waves across central Europe. His government was determined to extend Germany's economic and strategic involvement in eastern Europe (for example, in 1929 Germany imported 20 per cent of all Hungary's exports, by 1938 this had risen to 41 per cent). Nor was this involvement necessarily unwelcome. In May 1934 King Alexander of Yugoslavia was reported to have complained that Yugoslavia was 'tired of being treated like a puppet by the French, and would gladly free themselves of the tutelage by a *rapprochement* with Germany'. The National Socialist movement was also an inspiration and model for fascist movements across the region, most significantly in Hungary (the Arrow Cross), Romania (the Iron Guard) and the Bulgarian Chain (*Zveno*) movement.

Communism and fascism, 1933–41

In the 1930s Europe became dominated by political leaders and groups with strong revolutionary aspirations. In the Soviet Union Stalin continued and accelerated an economic and social revolution, determined to create 'Socialism in one country'. Beyond an insatiable greed for personal power, Comrade Stalin aspired to fulfil Lenin's dream of a Soviet Republic peopled with dedicated and educated working-class citizens, but elsewhere the spectre of Marxist revolution, economic crisis and populist politics often helped to promote fascist movements dedicated to an alternative 'revolutionary' vision. Fascist movements sprang up across Europe. Germany, Italy, Spain, Hungary, Greece, Poland, Portugal, Bulgaria, Romania and others, all adopted strongly authoritarian, if not fascist governments.

But despite, or perhaps because of, the large array of fascist movements in the 1930s, historians have faced substantial problems in defining fascism. In 1920 the word 'fascism' was known to very few people. Even Mussolini placed the word in quotation marks when he used it to describe an 'organized, concentrated, authoritarian democracy on a national basis'. Mussolini's definition here would also encompass the government of Franco's Spain, Dollfuss's Austria and Szálasi in Hungary, yet though these groups were anti-communist and anti-intellectual, they made no real ideological contributions to fascism. Franco, for example, was more a military dictator in an old-fashioned sense than a fascist *Führer* in the Hitler mould.

Other movements, like Germany's National Socialism and the British Union of Fascists, actively sought to emulate Mussolini's movement. But, despite their differences, fascist organizations, which stretched from the Atlantic to the Baltic, did share a common set of characteristics summarized by the historian RAH Robinson as:

> a nationalist, anti-Marxist, mass-mobilising, political movement, normally headed by a charismatic leader, aiming at the complete conquest of power and seeking the fullest control over all aspects of life in a polity by means of a single party system.[4]

The *Action Française*, the NSDAP, the Italian Fascists, the Romanian Iron Guard and the Nordic Fascists shared some common features. Beyond an ideology which was strongly nationalist, anti-communist and anti-Marxist, fascist movements often attempted to appeal to all social groups while at the same time establishing elitist party structures. Party members, proudly attired in their black and brown shirts, joined a movement whose image was one of a tightly organized, semi-military machine.

These movements also cultivated imperial and racial myths – German *Lebensraum* in the east, a second Roman Empire in the Mediterranean – and appealed to Europe's youth by promoting a cult of violence and action in preference to ordinary political discussions. The emergence of fascism has been closely identified with Europe's middle classes, the lower-middle class in particular; but, of course, they were not the only social group to provide the fascists with a legitimate avenue to power. It was the Great Depression which offered fascism a mass audience. They were also successful among the working classes of eastern Europe, for example (the Iron Guard movement was the third strongest party in the Romanian elections of 1937). In Scandinavia, on the other hand, the ideas of the Nordic racists (espoused by men like Hans Günther), with their pretensions to scientific objectivity, had greater success amongst the educated bourgeoisie. The leaders of a fascist movement held a uniquely powerful position; a role which Mussolini and Hitler expounded on at length (the *Führerprinzip*). In particular, they cultivated a mystical, superhuman aura.

In Germany, the constitutional policy of the NSDAP evolved around the personal rule of Adolf Hitler. Unlike established political parties such as the British Labour Party and its European socialist counterparts, fascists stressed the 'organic' character of their movement. Thus, the leaders of the movement could rapidly alter political policy, unfettered by party constitutional 'niceties'. This flexibility enabled Mussolini to make political compromises – with the monarchy, Army, state bureaucracy, large landowners and the Catholic Church – and Hitler to abandon quietly the socialist elements of the National Socialist Party programme to help secure the support of traditional conservative elites in business, the Army and the judiciary.

Fascists, in contrast to the nineteenth century's liberal focus on the individual, stressed a collective national or racial goal. This led them to favour corporate structures for the state. It also led them, however, to seek for scapegoats. Then reason fled.

Nazism, 1933–41

For Hitler, the door to unfettered political power opened when he was appointed Chancellor on 30 January 1933; few people realized that once the National Socialists were in power it would take an earthquake to move them. Hitler was able to achieve legal access to the Chancellorship by forming a temporary alliance with the conservative elites and the DNVP under Alfred Hugenberg. The day after Hitler's accession to power, Hugenberg is supposed to have remarked: 'I've just committed the greatest stupidity of my life; I have allied myself with the greatest demagogue in world history.' Hugenberg was right.

While Hitler's opposition was divided in the wake of his appointment as Chancellor, the *Reichstag* fire (27 February 1933) and Hitler's boot-boys stoked the atmosphere of terror. This allowed the NSDAP to pass the Enabling Act (23 March 1933) and begin the process of *Gleichschaltung*: the 'coordination' of German society, bringing everything under National Socialist control down to its bowling clubs and bee-keeping associations. In the march towards total power, the NSDAP concentrated upon dissolving what remained of Weimar's constitution and creating a total 'leader' state in which the economy, society and culture were to be coordinated under the untrammelled rule of one party and a government subordinate to the party.

To this end the NSDAP had created party offices in the 1920s to be superimposed upon those of the state, like the NS Development Department which addressed issues of race, culture, agriculture and internal affairs. But, in reality, the Nazi state was far from monolithic. Different bureaucratic structures came to rival and conflict with one another and Germany did not become the totalitarian nation to which Hitler aspired. Some historians have even gone so far as to describe the National Socialist state as a 'chaos state'.

Hitler used the democratic process to achieve power. He then set about destroying it. As he had explained in 1930, 'the constitution only marks out the arena of battle, not the goal ... once we possess the constitutional power, we will mould the state into the shape we hold suitable', and the acquiesence of Germany's administration and institutions in these changes certainly simplified Hitler's task. The veneer of legality which accompanied Hitler's revolution was complete when Hitler appointed himself 'Supreme Judge' in June 1934. Henceforth all magistrates and civil servants were required to take an oath of allegiance to the *Führer*.

Hitler used violence, as well as the rule of law, to eliminate his opposition. At the end of January 1933, the National Socialists embarked upon a legal and physical attack, with the help of Röhm's SA (*Sturmabteilung*), against the German Communist Party. The SPD and the German trade union movement were soon drawn into this oppressive net and by 14 July the NSDAP remained the only legal party within Germany. For those associated with parties on the left and centre of German politics, January 1933 marked the dawn of years of imprisonment, exile or fear of discovery – the endless, 'panicky fear' which pervades events in Anna Seghers's moving novel *The Seventh Cross*.

In all areas of German life, a Weimar institution was replaced by a National Socialist one. Trade unions, for example, were smashed and workers now became members of the Labour Front (*Deutsches Arbeitsfront*: DAF); agricultural organizations 'chose' to dissolve themselves and were replaced by Walter Darré's agricultural marketing corporation, the National Food Estate (*Reichsnährstand*: RNS). The Army was the only conservative group, at this stage, to maintain its independence from overt Nazi infiltration as the combination of legally orchestrated state power, grass-roots terrorism and the acquiescence of Germany's conservatives had all combined to ensure Weimar's destruction.

Like Stalin, Hitler was also prepared to launch an attack on his own party faithful. In the Night of the Long Knives (June 1934) he challenged the considerable influence of the SA to eliminate the personal power of Ernst Röhm – one of his keenest supporters from the early days. Röhm had no stomach for Hitler's compromises with Germany's conservative elites, and said so. But Hitler scorned Röhm's talk of a second revolution. He was anxious to placate the German Army, court international opinion and consolidate the gains of the first year in power, so he murdered Röhm and purged the SA.

The Nazis shamelessly propagandized every advance of their 'revolution'. Joseph Goebbels persuaded Hitler to give him control, not only over the press, radio, films and theatres but over books, visual arts and music as well. Propaganda was a vital element of the social revolution which Hitler sought to engineer, a revolution whose muddled ideological vision sought to embrace all pure (*rassenrein*) Germans in a *Volksgemeinschaft* (a folk/people's community) based on racial superiority. Its ultimate ambition was to fulfil Germany's destiny as a rearmed, 'assertive' nation determined to establish a German Empire in eastern Europe.

Germany's youth came in for particular attention in the Nazi propaganda machine because, according to Hitler, their own parents were 'a lost generation', one which had acquired its values in a different, non-Nazi world. To this end new guidelines for schools were drafted to educate Germany's 'youth in the service of nationhood and state in the National Socialist Spirit'. University students were to serve compulsory labour service, while universal military service was introduced in March 1935. There were elites too, with most being expected of the SS (*Schutzstaffel*). This was the party's weapon of racial terror and its head, Heinrich Himmler, aimed to create new Nazi leaders. The SS was based on racial criteria, an explicitly anti-Christian ideology and unconditional obedience.

Plate 8.5 Hitler photographed with members of the Hitler Youth. The organization comprised distinct leagues for boys, girls, and students to promote their physical and mental education according to Nazi prescription. Membership rose quickly. Already by 1934 over 1.25 million young Germans had joined. As Margarete Fischer, wife of the German historian Fritz Fischer, recalled, the appeal of the *Bund der deutschen Mädchen* (League of German Girls) lay in activities like camping, hiking, and singing : 'These girls I brought together found it terrific something of this kind was happening in the village. It wasn't like today where every village has a discothèque or a swimming pool.'

Women, too, had a particular place in Hitler's vision. In the blunt words of one party activist, the goals were:

> Produce babies and educate them according to Nazi party doctrine . . . Support men's activities in whatever roles the leadership deems necessary . . . maintain family-orientated values.[5]

Like Mussolini, Hitler wanted women to produce future soldiers. But the Nazi vision for women was rife with contradictions. Hitler's attacks on the Catholic and Protestant Churches and Himmler's breeding schemes, which briefly appeared to sanction promiscuity for three million SS members in 1933, undermined Nazi statements on the sanctity of the German family.

The Nazis did not intend to banish women from the workforce. Rather, they wanted to rationalize the process of deciding which women should perform which functions: manufacturing goods or producing children. Even in peacetime German women's involvement in the labour force increased twice as sharply as men's, although the type of jobs open to women was predominantly low-skilled. During the Second World War the search for manpower (*sic*) led to a new policy to encourage young women into higher education previously barred by the Nazis. By 1943 women made up 48.8 per cent of the German workforce – in Britain the figure was 36.4 per cent – and propaganda posters proclaimed, 'Earlier I buttered bread for him, now I paint grenades and think, this is for him'. By expanding the contribution of women to the national economy the National Socialists went some way to modernizing the position of women in German society, but the Nazis' determination to control the role of women, whether at work or at home, made it clear that docility was the only trait in women that counted.

At the heart of Hitler's world view (*Weltanschauung*) lay his anti-Semitism. In 1933 the world received reports of Jews expelled from public service, of shops boycotted, of concentration camps, mass arrests and torture. During the following years Hitler's fanaticism and tireless anti-semitic propaganda acted as encouragement and sanction to the growing persecution of Jews, gypsies, beggars and homosexuals. At the Nuremberg Rally in 1935, with laws *inter alia* forbidding marriage or sexual relations outside marriage between Germans and Jews, Hitler satisfied impatient voices across the Nazi Party demanding greater discrimination against the Jews.

In September 1937 Hitler made his first big attack against the Jews: in 1936 and 1937 he had been relatively quiet. His tirade was followed by agitation by the party rank and file in the summer and autumn of 1938 and the expulsion of some 17,000 Polish Jews living in Germany. In the so-called Crystal Night (*Kristallnacht*) pogrom of 9–10 November, initiated by Goebbels in an attempt to curry Hitler's favour, the SA were given 'the freedom of the streets' in a wild night of terror. Two hundred synagogues were burned down, 91 Jews murdered and 7,500 Jewish shops and business were destroyed. Germany's streets stank of schnapps from the ransacked shops as the SS arrested a further 26,000 Jews.

It is unclear when the decision to murder Europe's Jews was taken by Hitler and his cabinet. War and the rapid conquest of Poland transformed the Jewish question as forced immigration schemes and plans to sell Jews for foreign currency were no longer an available option. To 'manage' the Jewish problem now, totaly separate ghettos were created – the first of which was erected at Lódź (Litzmannstadt) in December 1939 – and compulsory labour, with the inevitable death of thousands, was introduced for all Jews. These steps contributed to a momentum which culminated in the Final Solution. The mentally and physically handicapped suffered too, in a Nazi euthanasia programme which liquidated over 70,000 mental patients between 1939 and 1941 to 'free' beds for those who could be 'cured'. The killing process escalated during the war against the Soviet Union, and by the end of 1941, German policy towards the Jews had become one of full-scale annihilation. One of the many sinister aspects of the process was the perversion of science and medicine, and it was a topic of Nazi cinema even before 1939.[6]

Active resistance to Nazi terror amongst the German population remained sporadic, subdued by propaganda, the strength of state control and, after 1939, by the daily struggle to survive described by a German journalist, Berndt Engelmann, as the 'evil of banality'. Virtually all gave their assent to Nazi rule. But while employment prospects for most had improved, the basis of Nazi economic success came partly from reducing the living standards of the working class – wages fell from 64 per cent to 57 per cent of national income between 1932 and 1938 as the production of guns took priority over that of butter.

Hitler fulfilled his promise of providing 'bread and work' to the German people, although his interest in a vibrant German economy was founded upon his foreign policy ambitions. The Nazi government wanted economic recovery, greater autarky to avoid the danger of blockade and the recreation of a broad military capacity for Germany. The economy was Hitler's fourth 'arm' for war – alongside a rebuilt Navy, Army and Airforce. It was the importance of producing guns for Germany's racial struggle, rather than any genuine interest in the welfare of the German worker, which determined the increase in government investment and the creation of public work schemes in Germany before 1939. And war itself was an instrument of policy.

Stalinism, 1927–41

The ultimate target of Hitler's aggression was, of course, the Soviet Union, and in this country, too, citizens and the party had been terrorized by a dictator's unbridled ambition. Like the Night of the Long Knives, in which Hitler rounded upon some of his most loyal and longstanding party cohorts, 1934 saw Stalin turn the reign of terror he had so successfully introduced against the ordinary Russian people (the *Narod*) – peasants and workers – during the period of collectivization and industrialization, to attack the Bolshevik Party itself (the *Aktiv*). After the chaos of the First Five Year Plan (1929), heavy industry continued to expand at the expense of Soviet agriculture (guns over wheat). The year 1932 saw a return to more sober economic planning in Stalin's drive for industrialization. The Second Five Year plan, instigated that year, was less ambitious than its predecessor, although Stalin's targets for industrial output remained characteristically unrealistic.

Like Hitler's attempts to transform German society, in 1932 Stalin found that his self-styled industrial revolution for the Soviet Union sometimes threatened to run away from his control through the zeal of local party workers who were growing 'dizzy with success'. The desire to 'consolidate', as the Communist Party's new slogan demanded, was made more urgent by a famine which spread across the Soviet Union in 1933. Once again the conflict between towns and villages, land and industry, characteristic of Russian history this century, became overt as food became scarce and the need to feed Soviet workers took priority.

Comrade Stalin continued to propagandize his role as protector of the proletariat, although he had already terrorized their class and was about to turn on their professed 'representatives' within the Communist Party. His appetite for political power grew with the eating. During the 1920s dissenting voices had been quelled by the unquestioned dominance of the Bolshevik Party; during collectivization, a ruling oligarchy centred on Stalin emerged, only to be replaced from 1934 onward by the personal rule of one man. His power and penchant for violence had germinated, however, in a fertile environment. Precendents were available in nineteenth-century Imperial Russia, in the jacobin tradition of the Bolshevik Party, and in the bloody civil war, while Lenin's ban on factionalism (March 1921) appeared to provide legitimation for Stalin's brutal assault upon his own party cadres. Stalin was desperate to confirm his position as Lenin's natural and most loyal heir. The Five Year Plans had effectively waged war against the Soviet working class – Stalin himself conceded that the battle for industrialization had been Russia's true civil war, and it has been estimated that ten million people 'demographically disappeared' inside the Soviet Union between 1926 and 1939. (Many estimates now go higher as more details emerge from the archives of the former Soviet Union.)

By 1930 the pace of industrialization had created an acute labour shortage, and in order to prevent workers from abandoning their jobs and returning to the countryside, Stalin reintroduced wage differentials. More serious to the credibility of the Soviet Communist Party, however, was the corruption which lay at the heart of its pledge to end the exploitation of the working class and create a more humane society. The increasing involvement of the OGPU (the state's security services) and the Army to enforce collectivization and to manage the enormous expansion of labour camps clearly negated any pretence of a just and equal society. The contradiction between the party's declared aims and its methods became glaringly obvious. By 1934 the Bolshevik commitment to equality amongst its citizens had already been abandoned.

After 1934 life became more stable for the working and peasant classes: the provision of housing, education and employment for men and women all improved. The peasantry continued to struggle on, but for the privileged *Nomenclatura* the terror was just about to begin. During the 1920s Stalin had rewritten history to make Lenin sole architect of the revolution with Stalin at his right hand, thereby establishing a 'cult of personality': he had fed on idolatry of Lenin to enhance his own mystique. Now, while never describing his regime as 'Stalinist', he nonetheless engineered a bloody and unprecedented political 'revolution' against his own party members to secure his personal political power and to consolidate the economic revolution he had already forced upon Soviet society.

Plate 8.6 Courtroom scene of a Moscow show trial. The public presentation of the
trial was central to Stalin's determination to remake the Bolshevik Party. Mass
terror became an inherent technique of the regime. One of the most interesting
features was the willingness of the defendants to confess. In May 1937 the exiled
Trotsky published *The Revolution Betrayed* just as the trials of the old Bolsheviks
entered full swing and noted that, 'the bureaucracy superstitiously fears whatever
does not serve it directly, as well as whatever it does not understand'.

Stalin's suspicions became obsessional and, in his boundless lust for power, purges within the Communist Party swept away one million people between 1935 and 1939. For Eugenia Ginzburg, 'a model communist and teacher', the reality of Stalin's brutality began to unfold with the murder of Kirov, Secretary of the General Committee, in November 1934. For her, and loyal party cadres like her, allegations against fellow Bolsheviks accused by Stalin 'must be true' because they were printed in *Pravda*. But by 1937, convicted of trumped-up charges and imprisoned in solitary confinement, Eugenia had uncovered the true nature of Stalinism. Among her fellow prisoners were German and Italian communists who had fled Hitler and Mussolini only to fall prey to the leader who had claimed to be their ally. She described the solitary cell in which she was imprisoned for almost 24 hours a day:

> I remember the anxiety of my whole body, the despair of my muscles as I paced out my dwelling, five paces by three, five and a quarter if I took very short steps. One-two-three-four-five one way, turn on the toes not to waste an inch, one-two-three the other.[7]

In 1930 GULAG, the statute authorizing the 'Main Administration of the Labour Camps', was passed, and by the mid-1930s these camps, according to recently released estimates from the archives of the former Soviet Union, contained 1.5 to 2 million people.[8] By then, arbitrary arrest and execution without trial had become commonplace. The Great Terror acted as a political revolution to reinforce the economic and social transformation of the USSR which had begun with collectivization and industrialization. Many of Lenin's revolutionary Bolshevik Party – men like Aleksei Rykov, Nikolai Bukharin and later, and most famously, Trotsky – were murdered at their former comrade's behest. Even the Red Army, which, like the NKVD and the Soviet Navy, had greatly benefited from Stalin's policies during the First and Second Five Year Plans, found itself victim of Stalin's insatiable suspicion. In 1937 he executed the Red Army's leading commanders for treason as a prelude to a drastic purge of the entire High Command and the Russian Officer Corps – a purge which murdered three of the five Soviet Marshals, 13 out of 15 Army commanders, and eight out of nine Fleet admirals.

Of course, Stalin could not have been responsible for all the individual decisions of the purges, but he alone allowed the purges to assume such proportions – a charge supported by General Secretary Gorbachev in 1987. Indeed, Stalin often resorted to carefully calculated but equally brutal measures to ensure the loyalty of even his closest advisers. For instance, he arrested the wife of his personal secretary, A. N. Poskrebyshev, to ensure the latter's unswerving loyalty and allowed him to remain a trusted servant until 1953.

There was, however, a facade – and behind the facade there were social achievements. Most impressive, certainly to social commentators like the British Fabians Beatrice and Sidney Webb and the writer George Bernard Shaw, was 'Stalin's Constitution' for the Soviet Union, ratified by an extraordinary Soviet Congress in 1936. It spelt out equality between races and sexes, and guaranteed each Soviet citizen the right to work, to welfare benefits, to education, and to housing. As a consequence, and for the first time, priests and former members of the White opposition were able to vote, although other political parties remained outlawed. For young men and women from even the lowest social classes, industrialization, the growth of the party machine, a government-promoted drive to increase adult literacy, and open access to technical colleges and universities brought greater scope for advancement and a better life. The Kremlin also launched a major propaganda campaign to promote family life and sexual abstinence, after earlier legislation legalizing divorce and abortion resulted in almost one out of two marriages failing and three times as many abortions as live births in Moscow during 1934. Unlike other countries in the west, however, government support for 'family values' did not result in women being forced from the workplace.

These achievements, thought to be essentially twentieth century, contributed towards making the 1930s a remarkable decade – certainly its leaders were among the most infamous. Yet its contradictory and sometimes confusing features, like individual insecurity, governmental brutality, and forced population movements, were all present in the nineteenth century. Some governments, like those of Germany and the USSR, inflicted inestimable suffering under the pretext of acting for the 'collective good' of their 'chosen people', whether determined by race or class. Others, which claimed a broad, popular base – the Popular Front governments of Spain and France, for example – were unable to cling to power because they lacked a unity of vision and the desire, or means, to use coercion. In the struggle to overcome economic depression, many countries had waged a 'civil war' of sorts. The brutal, confrontational character of domestic politics, typified by Franco's wartime dictum 'distrust any bargain' and 'decide everything by arms' was increasingly reflected in international relations.

References

1. R. Sarti, 'The Battle of the Lira', *Past and Present*, no. 47, May 1970, p. 98.
2. E. Canetti, *The Play of the Eyes* (New York, 1986, 1987 edn) p. 89.
3. Financier Russell Leffingwell writing to 'Bunny' Carter, 16 June 1932, Private papers of Walter Leffingwell, Baker Library, Harvard University, box 3, file 63.
4. R. A. H. Robinson, *Fascism in Europe, 1919–1945* (1981, 1989 edn) p. 4.
5. C. Koonz, *Mothers in the Fatherland. Women, the Family and Nazi Politics* (1987).
6. M. Burleigh, *Death and Deliverance, 'Euthanasia' in Germany, 1900–1945* (Cambridge, 1994) ch. 6.
7. E. Ginzbourg, *Into the Whirlwind* (1967, 1989 edn) p. 149.
8. Chris Ward, *Stalin's Russia* (1933) pp. 135–7.

Chapter 9

From European to World War, 1933–1945

Europe's greatest economic crisis had created a frightening legacy. It fostered nationalism and the search for empire and it encouraged rearmament. Ultimately, indeed, the means which nations, like Nazi Germany and Imperial Japan, employed to stabilize their political and economic conditions led them to wage a war that spanned the globe. Economic and political issues also determined the response of Europe's remaining democracies to a new expansionist menace – six years of negotiation and then six months of mounting confrontation when war became 'unavoidable'. Politics and economics taken together explain why Britain and France, in particular, were ready to challenge the might of National Socialism in September 1939, largely on the pretext of defending Poland's national integrity. The year before they had been prepared to sacrifice, albeit reluctantly, Czechoslovakia to Hitler's ambitions.

The events of 1936 dramatically encapsulate the changing nature of diplomatic relations within Europe, and between Europe and the remainder of the world. In this critical year, Hitler took the bold but calculated move of cancelling the Locarno Treaties and remilitarizing the Rhineland. The step permitted industry in the Rhineland to be brought into a Four Year Plan implemented to remilitarize Germany. Hermann Göring, the powerful Prussian Minister for the Interior, was put in charge and announced in July that year, 'Carrying out the armaments programme according to the schedule and planned scale is the task of German politics.'[1] Returning Germany's industrial heartland to military production in March 1936 gave a clear signal to those who were in any doubt – and there were many – that Hitler's diplomatic intentions stretched beyond the policy of revising Versailles. Returning German troops to the Rhineland was a calculated risk. Before the gamble Germany was at its most vulnerable to foreign intervention. After remilitarization Germany now had the economic and military base to make it a formidable foe.

But no European power was prepared to challenge Germany in 1936.

The most vulnerable power, France, was in the throes of a political crisis, and diplomatic cooperation within the League of Nations stood in tatters following the debacle of attempted sanctions against Mussolini after the Italian invasion of Abyssinia (October 1935–May 1936). The disapprobation of the international community made little impact on a man who offered Italy the 'gospel . . . better to live for one day like a lion than a hundred years like a sheep'. Britain, while politically stable, nevertheless faced strong pacifist sentiment and attached priority to the need to defend its worldwide empire. The United States was preoccupied with domestic affairs, with pacifist and 'isolationist' sentiment running high in the 1936 presidential elections.

The Axis powers

The future direction of world diplomacy was now set along a loosely established axis in an anti-Comintern pact spanning first Germany and Italy, and then broadened to include Japan. Facing these nationalists were the 'democracies'. The pact created the spectre of full-scale cooperation amongst the world's most ambitious and militaristic powers, although, in reality, it was never more than a loose understanding: Germany's cooperation with Japan was limited, and inside Europe the fascist partnership of Mussolini and Hitler was fraught with conflicting objectives and interests. In 1934 Mussolini used his troops to defend Austria's territorial independence from Germany, but *Il Duce* grew to respect *Der Führer*, a man whom he had once considered neurotic and vulgar. By 1938 Mussolini was prepared to tolerate the invasion of Austria, and by shifting Italy's imperial ambitions southwards, he left eastern Europe to German influence.

The Abyssinian War was popular at home, reinvigorating Italian fascism and enhancing his personal reputation, but it also proved costly and took its toll on Italy's military and economic resources. Nonetheless, successful intervention in the Spanish Civil War and the invasion of Albania (1939) were one thing, involvement in a world war another. Even the Pact of Steel (May 1939) did not make the Nazi-Fascist alliance completely binding. Italy did not enter the Second World War until the German invasion of France was about to reach its successful climax in 1940. Until then, Britain and the United States continued to harbour hopes that the Italians would abandon their neutrality and join the side of the 'democracies' as they had, for a price, during the First World War.

The governments of Germany, Italy and Japan committed their peoples to war when their national interests – *Lebensraum* in eastern Europe, the aggrandizement of the Italian Empire in north Africa, the search for raw materials (especially oil) and markets in the Far East – determined that no other course was available. Aside from ambition and militarism, these three powers believed that they were the 'have not' powers, denied the empires and status achieved by Britain, the United States and France. To Hitler 'the Englishman had reason to be proud' and German men and women did not. This perception was heightened by the impact of the great depression which had worked greatly to increase international tension. The military incursions and conquests of Manchuria, Czechoslovakia and Abyssinia all illustrated Axis resentment. According to Axis rationale, economic collapse had come about by excessive dependence upon other nations and their raw materials. With the creation of empires, this dependence would cease.

The net result of growing nationalism and imperial ambition was a sharp increase in rearmament. There was no country in Europe which did not begin to rearm in the 1930s, although the major arms race was once again between Britain, France and Germany. All had begun new rearmament programmes in 1936 and Germany's was by far the most ambitious. By 1938–39 the burden of producing armaments was so heavy – for Britain the expenditure on rearmament threatened a crisis of confidence in the pound sterling, in Germany consumer goods and food became increasingly scarce – that some historians have argued that by the end of 1939 waging war was the only alternative to widespread social unrest.

Hitler's foreign policy tactics, as well as the ambitions which underpinned his foreign policy, have generated much heated debate amongst historians. They have largely rejected suggestions that Hitler's aggressive foreign policy was born simply of an 'unprincipled opportunism', despite the fact that changes to Hitler's diplomatic strategy sometimes surprised even his closest advisers. It is now clear that Hitler had four broad ambitions: the restoration of German military power; the expansion of German frontiers; the gathering together of Germany's *Volksdeutsche* (German people); and the creation of a German Empire to provide *Lebensraum* (living space) in eastern Europe which might possibly entail a racial war against the Soviet Union. It was possible for Hitler to hold 'principles', however repugnant these beliefs may seem, and at the same time be 'opportunistic' in their execution. Hitler doubtless seized the moment in timing the remilitarization of the Rhineland, but the need to rearm Germany for the racial conquest of eastern Europe was a long-term, 'principled' consideration.

What was striking in Germany's foreign policy ambitions was the way that Hitler was able to place the 'revision' of Versailles at the forefront of Europe's diplomatic agenda. All of Weimar's chancellors had, to some degree, sought to revise the Versailles Treaty, be it by abolishing reparations or covertly training German troops inside the Soviet Union, but only Hitler succeeded in hijacking events to ensure that the 'German Question' became the world's foremost diplomatic consideration, even determining, to a degree, the conduct of British, French and American foreign policy towards Italy and Japan.

Why was Germany, relatively weak and demilitarized in 1933, able to threaten not only European but global peace by 1937–38? On the positive side Germany had a number of legitimate diplomatic grievances which Europe needed to redress. Indeed, a process of redressing them had already begun with the revision of reparations in the 1920s. Far more important, however, were the 'negative' considerations which determined that Britain and France were unwilling and/or unable to resist Hitler after he seized the initiative until the magnitude of his ambitions became absolutely clear. In all these diplomatic discussions, as was so often the case, the smaller powers of Europe stood largely on the side-lines while Britain and France bargained for their national integrity and for future peace.

In the same way as Hitler had exploited Weimar's law and democracy to overturn it, so too he exploited the language of Wilsonian liberalism, using lofty phrases like 'restitution' and 'repudiation' to attack the Versailles Treaty. His attacks found a receptive audience, at home and abroad, amongst those who believed that Versailles had ensured the instability of Weimar or that French intransigence and rearmament had left Germany with little alternative but to rearm. In reality, the moral tenor of this argument was false: Versailles aspired to a fairer peace than that signed by Germany with Russia at Brest-Litovsk (1918) for example, while in the case of reparations, Prussia had demanded similar 'tributes' from France in 1870. Nor was Germany's sense of injustice unique: it was shared by others.

The policy of appeasement

Until 1938 Hitler consolidated the labours of Brüning and Papen, who had worked to wipe the reparations slate clean by attacking the territorial and security arrangements of Versailles, and he remilitarized the Rhineland, achieved *Anschluss* with Austria in 1938, and began to move in on Czechoslovakia, while Britain and France appeared to do nothing. Nor, according to Göring, should these developments have been of any real concern to them. In December 1937, he informed a British visitor:

> You know of course what we are going to do. First we shall overrun Czechoslovakia, and then Danzig and then we shall fight the Russians. What I can't understand is why you British should object to this.[2]

To the Nazis it seemed clear: Britain and France already had empires, and it was Germany's right to establish an empire in eastern Europe.

French, American and especially British attempts to reach a negotiated settlement with Hitler have been called 'appeasement', a policy that affected notions of diplomacy in the same way that the First World War affected notions of war. Debased by overuse, it is still often used by late-twentieth-century politicians to denote a policy of weakness and

Plate 9.1 Berlin café society on the eve of the war, 3 June 1939. In 1929 Berlin was blessed with over 16,000 different cafés. Ten years later they were still crowded, but the combined effects of the great depression, the mass exodus of the city's greatest artists after 1933 and persistent shortages had robbed café society in Berlin of its variety, creativity and excitement.

capitulation. The realities of diplomacy are, and were, more complex. Appeasement – the skills of arbitration, negotiation and tackling each new problem as it arose – were tactics long associated with British diplomacy. On the whole, French and British leaders were not naive but dealt with each new crisis as it happened, and it was this which gave the 'democracies' the appearance of weakness, especially when Anglo-French efforts at arbitration were set against Hitler's bold initiatives. Britain and now France were prepared to make readjustments to the postwar settlement provided these revisions did not damage their national interests – although this was almost impossible in the case of France. Many French politicians now wanted to reach a settlement with Germany.

That Hitler's ambitions extended far beyond the revision of Versailles was only fully clear when he tore up the Munich agreement (29 September

1938) – whereby three million Sudeten Germans, formerly citizens of the Czech Republic, were incorporated into the Third Reich (Slovakia and the Capartho-Ukraine were also granted autonomy) – and ordered German troops to invade the remaining rump of Czechoslovakia in March 1939. It was obvious then that appeasers, men like Chamberlain, Halifax and Bonnet – charged as 'the Guilty Men' by a trio of radical journalists including the future leader of the British Labour Party, Michael Foot – had failed. It was also then that appeasement became a term of abuse. Britain and France had hoped desperately that the Munich agreement would be Hitler's final demand, a view that Hitler encouraged. They were certainly not persuaded by Nazi logic, but had to take pressing domestic and international difficulties into account when responding to Hitler's sequence of demands.

The western powers, 1933–39

Cooperation between Britain and France on military and diplomatic matters had never been easy. European 'harmony' in the later 1920s had been built on fragile foundations. Important issues remained unresolved and returned to plague relations in the 1930s: France's quest for security; the contradiction in Britain's obligations to the Empire and Europe; the diplomatic isolation of the United States; and the relations and responsibilities of western Europe to a 'new look' eastern Europe.

Good Anglo-French bilateral relations became essential once it was apparent that the League of Nations was ineffective, if not a liability, as an instrument of international cooperation. When League directives were ignored by Japan (over Manchuria 1931), Germany (over disarmament in 1933), and Italy (over Abyssinia, 1935), cynics had good reason to accuse the League of hypocritical moralizing about the status quo. According to the journalist Robert Dell, the League was 'a fraudulent institution betraying the confidence of the public', and he dubbed it 'the Geneva racket'.[3] European statesmen ignored the League when it suited them, preferring to revert to the bilateral treaties so criticized by Wilson. The alliances between France and the Little Entente powers were typical of such revived bilateralism, though these were alliances of unequals and by the late 1930s France was in no condition to help the countries of eastern Europe. Conveniently for Hitler, France could barely help itself.

It was a sense of national 'weakness' accentuated by conflicting pressures on national policy, not the persuasiveness of Hitler's case, that determined Britain and France's response to his demands. France was weakened primarily by political strife as the late impact of the depression grew more severe, and nowhere were the consequences of unstable domestic politics on international policy denoted more obviously than in France's reaction to Mussolini's invasion of Abyssinia in 1935.

The British were hostile to an Italian presence in north Africa, but France, at first, wanted to pursue a more conciliatory policy against the Italians in order to prise *Il Duce* away from *Der Führer*. France's reaction was surprising given that the Italian invasion threatened imperial routes to Algeria and north Africa, and that Italian propaganda and bribery sought to undermine the French Empire. Pierre Laval, the unfortunate French statesman who negotiated with Mussolini over Abyssinia, quickly found himself isolated at home and abroad, a symbol of sullied patriotism and *facilité* – cheap appeasement. On the eve of the invasion, Mussolini boasted, 'I have reflected well; I have calculated all; I have weighed everything'. But the invasion was completed at no small cost to the Italians who had discounted the determination of the Abyssinians to resist European involvement in Africa. Nonetheless, Africa, once again, was trapped in the jaws of European rivalry, with Mussolini's greedy claim that 'if for others the Mediterranean is a route, for us Italians it is life'.

The failure of the League's sanctions and Anglo-French disagreement only served to bring Mussolini closer to Hitler. Division amongst French politicians in 1936 grew when Hitler remilitarized the Rhineland and Belgium renounced its security treaty with France. The public withdrawal of Belgian confidence was a hard blow to a France already struggling under a caretaker government with widespread labour unrest. The prospect of German rearmament and the recently agreed Anglo-German Naval Treaty (1935), which sanctioned the recreation of a German Navy at a ratio of 35 to 100 British ships, made the situation worse.

Nor did matters improve with the accession of the Popular Front government in France in 1936. Although domestic politics became more effective, France's foreign policy was still filled with contradiction. Léon Blum, leader of the cabinet and a lifelong pacifist, now argued that France's best hope of securing peace was by preparing for war: France could produce peace abroad by a position of military and political strength at home. But when the Popular Front collapsed under a wave of strikes and currency depreciation in 1937, France appeared weaker, not stronger, for its efforts. Premier Chautemps succeeded Blum and Blum then succeeded Chautemps. By March 1938 the time had come for a new man and new measures, but when a veteran of 15 cabinets, Daladier, became Prime Minister and French politics shifted dramatically to the right, France's relative diplomatic weakness continued.

Like many of the Socialists in Blum's Popular Front government, the Labour Party in Britain began to demand a more assertive, if not aggressive, policy towards European fascists and National Socialists in 1936. The decisive struggle was played out between the minority, pacifist wing of the party, represented by party leader George Lansbury, and those who saw Europe's fascists as murderers of working-class men and women and wreckers of free trade unions, represented by Ernest Bevin, the most powerful trade union leader of the day and a future Labour Foreign

Minister. At the 1935 Labour Party conference in Brighton, many agreed to abandon their longstanding hostility to the League of Nations as an agent of capitalist oppression and support sanctions against Europe's aggressors. Bevin's pragmatism had won the day. Lansbury resigned from the party leadership and was replaced by Clement Attlee, the future Prime Minister of the first postwar Labour government. Seen in retrospect, this transition marked a watershed in the development of the Labour Party.

'Peacenik' sentiment was evident, too, in the centre and right of politics and grew strength from grisly newsreel footage of the Spanish Civil War, particularly the bombing of Guernica, and later from news of Japan's invasion of China. In the 1930s, in sharp contrast to 1914, there were widespread horror stories of what a war against Germany would cost the British people, fuelled, in many instances, by the experience of the First World War. Civilians feared mass gas attacks and civil unrest culminating in communist revolution, and there was particular alarm about large-scale bombing of civilians. All of these fears made public opinion hostile to the prospect of war. Among the most persistent rumours was the tale that in the first week of a German air offensive, Britain would suffer over 150,000 casualties. In reality Britain suffered less than 147,000 casualties from all forms of bombing in the *whole* of the Second World War.

The Munich crisis, 1938

For France the best hope for peace appeared to be a strong Anglo-French *entente*. It was, however, an *entente* of unequals. France was dependent upon British military and material help, but could not provide such useful assistance to Britain. As a result, France had to tow the British line on Abyssinia, the *Anschluss* and, perhaps most significantly of all, sign the Munich agreement after repudiating its alliance with Czechoslovakia in July 1938 and informing the Czech Premier, Edvard Beneš, 'that France would not go to war for the Sudeten affair'. Constrained by coalition politics and the slow pace of rearmament at home, Daladier could do nothing to save Czechoslovakia – France's ally – from Hitler's demand that Czechoslovakia's three million Sudeten Germans join his greater Germany. In reality, Hitler was as anxious to lay hands on Czechoslovakia's raw materials (bauxite, oil and wheat) as to reunite the three million *Volksdeutsche* living on Czech soil. When at Munich Beneš was forced to accept the cession of the Sudetenland to Germany – with Chamberlain famously, and prematurely, branding it 'Peace in our time' – there were other political repercussions. Thus, Hitler's move to annex the remainder of Czechoslovakia prompted Poland, in a desperate scramble to reinforce its own fragile security, to annex Teschen.

In September 1938 France, embattled by political division and economic weakness, had had little choice but to abandon its ally. Meanwhile, Britain, too, had shown itself unwilling to become enmeshed in a 'quarrel in a far-away country between people of whom we know nothing'. Even before Munich, however, Daladier found himself increasingly at odds with Foreign Minister Georges Bonnet, who was willing to do deals with Hitler. By October, Daladier had reverted to a policy of *fermeté* (firmness) in French foreign policy and ordered a massive increase in rearmament spending, Fr. 93 billion against a 1937 level of Fr. 29 billion.

The alarm with which the peoples of western Europe regarded Hitler's foreign policy grew further when German troops invaded and occupied the remaining rump of what was once the Czechoslovakian Republic on 15 March 1939. It was now clear that Hitler's appetite for conquest extended further than revising Versailles, that his promises made in negotiation were worthless, and that Poland was the next target of German ambition: on 24 October 1938, only a few weeks after Munich, the Poles were informed by the Reich's Foreign Minister, the former 'champagne salesman' Joachim von Ribbentrop, that it was now time to settle outstanding issues in German-Polish relations. In October 1938 German demands included the return of Danzig – the seaport at the end of the Polish corridor which had been dominated by Nazis since May 1933 – and the right to establish transportation lines across the Polish corridor to East Prussia. The Poles, unpopular with both eastern and western Europe, bravely rejected these demands out of hand.

Poland was determined not to abandon Danzig (now Gdansk) to the Germans and support came from a surprising quarter: on 31 March 1939 Chamberlain announced to the House of Commons that should Germany clearly threaten Polish independence and were prompted to use force to resist, Britain and France would come to its aid. Britain had drawn a line in the sand in an attempt to make it clear to Hitler that he would no longer be able to expand into Europe on his own terms. In reality there was not much Britain could do to save Poland.

As in France, the aftermath of Munich also encouraged the British Treasury to initiate increased armament expenditure. The locust years of British military spending had been 1932–38. In 1919 Britain spent £604 million on its three armed services, by 1932 the figure had dropped to £101 million. Yet it was only in February 1939 that staff talks were initiated between Britain and France, and military planning began in April. By September 1939 British and French aircraft and tank turnout exceeded that of Germany, and by May 1940 France alone, contrary to contemporary belief, matched German output in aircraft production (with a new generation of combat aircraft: the Dewoitine, the Morane-Saulnier 406 and the Bloch 152). French tank output was higher also and of better quality than Germany's. Given the potential of the German economy, the singular purpose of Hitler's cabinet and his determination to achieve a totally mobilized war economy by 1941–42, it was unlikely that the balance of armaments would remain in Britain and France's favour for long.

The development of radar, too, influenced the timing of the war. In 1937 work had begun to build a chain of 51 radar (Radio Detection and Ranging) stations around the British coast. While Göring dismissed radar as 'simply a box with wires', this early warning system was revolutionary and of decisive importance. Although incomplete, the radar stations were brought into continuous operation in the spring of 1939. In consequence, that year increasingly appeared the most opportune year to challenge the now global nature of the Nazi threat.

The British Empire and Hitler, 1933–39

France welcomed a firmer British commitment to maintaining the territorial status quo in Europe in 1939, but British foreign policy had more than Europe to worry about. It retained an 'imperial dimension' that affected all diplomatic calculations. As we have seen, the British Empire was larger during the 1930s than it had been in 1914. This was not simply because Britain 'inherited' parts of Germany's rather meagre empire at the Paris Peace Conference, but because Mandate territories were acquired in the Middle East. While supplying an increasingly valuable energy source (oil), they were proving costly to defend. In particular, political tension and military involvement dogged Britain's presence in Palestine from 1929 onwards, and problems in Iraq proved a further diversion. (France faced similar pressures in Morocco, Indochina, Syria, Algeria and Tunisia.)

Britain was caught in a paradox. The apparent source of its world power status – the Empire – was becoming a liability. British military power was stretched around the globe in order to protect it; and sometimes it was stretched so thin that Britain had to tolerate aggressive expansionism – Japan's incursion into Manchuria (1931) and later full blown war against China (1937) – so long as its own trade links with its Empire, and especially India, remained secure. Even the imperial 'jewel', India, was in political upheaval and a drain on British resources, and the White Dominions (Australia, Canada, New Zealand and South Africa), were becoming more significant in the formulation of British diplomacy.

After the First World War Britain's imperial allies were most unwilling to become embroiled in another European war so far from their own shores, and Chamberlain had to cultivate carefully the support of Dominion cabinets for a potentially more interventionist European policy. His efforts received an important boost after the fall of Prague. From then on Australia and New Zealand were committed to British policy, although South Africa and Canada refused to be drawn into support of Britain until the eve of war. Until 1939, according to its Prime Minister, MacKenzie King, Canada 'was resolved to maintain neutrality in war at any price'.

Britain was all too aware of the need to 'educate' the Dominions as to the relevance and reality of the European situation. By careful propaganda and by fostering a relationship of trust with their Prime Ministers, Chamberlain's 'management' of the Dominions was a success. But perhaps of greatest help in Chamberlain's efforts to secure Dominion support (and that of the United States) in the event of war, was the increasingly *global* nature of the National Socialist threat. By March 1939 Germany dominated all of central Europe, while Hitler's allies, Italy and Japan, threatened the Mediterranean and the Far East.

The economics of appeasement

The British government was more conscious than ever before of the cost of empire because of the relative decline of the British economy since 1914. Persistent unemployment, a reduced share in the world's export market and the decay of heavy industrial capacity (problems made more acute by the great depression) all underlined Britain's fall from grace as number one world power. The British industrial engine no longer appeared able to sustain a large and expensive defence commitment. Finding the money to pay for rearmament was made more acute by the increased social expenditures pledged by British governments of every political hue after 1918, and by the abolition of conscription from March 1920.

The same was true of France, although French expenditure on armaments was proportionately higher than that of Britain in the 1920s. The late impact of the depression, however, meant that investment stalled at the same time as Germany began to rearm. By 1938 the German *Luftwaffe* was five times larger than the French airforce. Real progress on French rearmament only came after the Munich crisis.

Economic considerations in diplomacy and in the preparations for war played a more overt role on the road to the Second World War than they had before the 'Great War', a war which had brought home the cost of modern warfare. Budget preoccupations in Britain and France helped to determine the pace of rearmament and the timing of war. Rearmament had to be speedy and efficient in order to prevent a balance of payments crisis and the collapse of sterling and the French franc. Both British and French governments carefully targeted expenditure into the production of tanks and aircraft. Then there were the political factors that influenced rearmament. Good labour relations, especially with Britain's skilled workers, were needed in order to ensure that new weapons were delivered on time. The Conservative-dominated National Government was never entirely confident of the 'responsibility' of British labour which, as elsewhere in Europe, had become affected by the widespread pacifism.

Economic bargains and deals entered diplomacy in a more calculated fashion than ever before as Britain and the United States came to believe that some form of 'economic appeasement' – providing Germany with economic concessions and economic satellites of its own – might work to

SOMEONE IS TAKING SOMEONE FOR A WALK

Plate 9.2 Cartoon of the Nazi-Soviet pact, by Low, August 1939. The two dictators had more in common than their moustaches. But although the pact reflected shared interests in Eastern Europe and temporarily bound their fates together, Low, always an astute commentator, appreciated the depth of their mutual antipathy.

assuage Hitler's expansionism. It was a strategy particularly favoured by those banks and industrialists who invested and traded with the 'Axis' powers. But the approach appealed only to the 'moderates' in German politics, a group whose political star was on the wane. Hitler and his cohorts were pledged to political annexation, although any profitable trading concessions would not be passed up if they were offered.

By 1938 Germany was supplying an average of 29 per cent of annual imports into eastern and south-eastern Europe, largely thanks to Anglo-French concessions, and by 1939 German capital, as well as German goods, had largely replaced British and French investment and imports. Yet Hitler, Mussolini and the Japanese nationalists could not be bought off by economic concessions. Economic collapse had helped foster an aggressive nationalism across the globe, but economics by itself could not now solve the crisis.

The final crisis: Poland, 1939

Europe's diplomatic crisis intensified with continued agitation of Nazi storm troopers on the streets of Danzig and continued German pressure on Poland. There was an astonishing new development also when Ribbentrop and Molotov on 23 August 1939 signed the Nazi-Soviet pact. For Hitler the alliance was his 'trump card. Perhaps . . . the most decisive gamble of my life.'

The Nazi-Soviet pact surprised the West. It should not have done. Britain and France, even during August 1939, never pursued an alliance with the Soviets with any degree of enthusiasm, nor did such an alliance offer Stalin any great advantages. Stalin preferred to let the West carry the risk while concentrating on the Japanese menace on the Manchurian-Siberian border. Self-interest and the historic enmity between the capitalist powers and communist Russia helped, therefore, cement the unlikely alliance of two self-confessed enemies – fascism and communism.

Poland was now encircled by hostile powers and *Der Führer* expectantly waited for news that Britain and France would abandon Poland as they had abandoned Czechoslovakia. Poland, on the other hand, was defiant, confident of Western assistance, especially when the Franco-British guarantee became a formal alliance on 25 August – unknown to them, the day before Hitler had planned to attack Poland. The reaffirmation of Franco-British support for Poland delayed Hitler's attack for five days during which time there was frenetic diplomatic activity and meetings between Hitler, Ribbentrop and the British Ambassador to Berlin, Sir Nevile Henderson, which sometimes degenerated into shouting matches. But neither side had anything to offer, although, ironically, Britain showed renewed confidence that Hitler might back down at precisely the moment when Germany was mobilizing for war. At lunch on 31 August the British Foreign Secretary, Lord Halifax, remarked that he had the 'first sight of a beaten fox'. At the same time the Reich's Chancellery in Berlin was abuzz with the activity of Hitler's closest supporters. That evening Hitler signed the Directive Number One for the Conduct of War, and at 4.45 a.m. on the morning of 1 September 1939, 'Operation Fishing' against Danzig had begun.

But France and Britain did not immediately issue declarations of war against Germany. Stunned incredulity typified the West's response to Danzig's destruction for although many had recognized that war over Poland was likely, this did not mean that, in the words of the historian D. C. Watt, 'in their hearts they had expected it'.[4] There followed two more days of furious diplomatic activity, mainly between Britain and France, with both powers making it clear that new negotiations would only be possible after a complete German withdrawal from Poland. The American President, Roosevelt, Pope Pius XII, and the neutral 'Oslo group' of states (Belgium, Norway, Denmark, Sweden, Finland, the Netherlands and Luxembourg), also made vain attempts to secure peace in the final days before the outbreak of war. But the German government, with the possible exception of Hermann Göring, were not interested in peace. While the Polish Ambassadors in London and Paris became frantic at Western inaction in the face of reports of the terrible atrocities committed in their homeland, public and parliamentary pressure on the cabinets of Britain and France grew. The British cabinet met on the night of 2 September amid rumours that French resolve was weakening (there was some truth to this) and, while a terrible thunderstorm raged, they agreed to issue Germany an ultimatum the following day: Sunday 3 September. No-one at the meeting dissented from Chamberlain's conclusion that 'this means war'.

The British ultimatum expired at 11 a.m. that Sunday; the French ultimatum expired six hours later. The West was now at war with Germany, although there was little it could do to help the encircled and outmatched Poles. Hitler was flabbergasted by the news that Britain and France intended to stand by their guarantees to Poland. For the first time he had miscalculated the Anglo-French response, and this time, unlike 1914, Germany had no plans for a general war. Until August 1939 Hitler had been able to fulfil his ambitions by negotiation or unresisted force, with his ultimate sights set on a racial war with the Soviet Union two or three years later. To Britain and France, however, 1939 seemed as good a time as any to confront Hitler's greed. On both sides of the Channel, government was resolved. Indeed, Chamberlain's tactics of exploring every avenue of peace, which were so hastily discredited after 1939, had probably helped bring about national unity on the need to 'stand up' to Hitler – a potent memory in British politics after 1945. Public opinion in Britain was firmly behind the fight. For Chamberlain, however, the events of 1939 were a personal disaster. He did not remain in office for long and was quickly replaced by a man of a very different temperament who had long opposed appeasement: Winston Churchill. Britain and France now fought to preserve their power not only in Europe, but in the Mediterranean and Far East as well.

The course of the war, 1939–41

The cynical friendship treaty signed by Molotov and Ribbentrop in 1939 had promised to guarantee the Polish people 'a peaceful life in keeping with their national character'. These were empty promises, of course. The citizens of Danzig were the first to taste the horrors of the war. Every Pole whom the Germans found was hunted down and beaten to death. Their bodies were then dumped into a mass grave and above it a wooden placard proclaimed: 'Here lies the Polish minority'.

The Poles fought bravely against overwhelming odds and managed to withstand the German onslaught for 17 days – their target had been two weeks. 'Operation Case White' against Poland quickly mobilized the three million German soldiers already amassed on the Polish frontiers under the age-old pretext of 'manoeuvres and exercises'. Strength of numbers, military technology and the confusion amongst Britain, France and Poland meant that only one-third of Polish troops were mobilized when the German invasion began, and a rapid German victory followed. The Soviet Union was not so quick off the mark. The Red Army only moved to occupy eastern Poland on 17 September. By 1940, however, the possibility of Britain and France declaring war on the Soviet Union was no longer a threat – it had been one of the considerations which caused Stalin to delay before invading Poland – and Stalin greedily annexed Estonia, Lithuania, Latvia and Bessarabia to his empire. Finland proved a more difficult 'morsel' to swallow. When Russia began an offensive there in October 1940 they did not reckon on the Finnish Army's ability to use Finland's snowbound forests to its advantage. By the time victory came in March 1941 the USSR had been forced to commit over a million men to defeat only 175,00 skilful and courageous Finns.

The Polish people were forced into labour service for their Nazi occupiers and their land was given to German settlers. It was a pattern of conquest intended to harness the productive resources of western and central Europe to enable Hitler to launch a war against Germany's 'true' racial and political enemy: the Soviet Union.

After Poland, German attentions shifted northwards to Norway and Denmark. Despite Hitler's anxieties and the substantial losses sustained by the German Navy, the battle for Norway lasted little more than six weeks (it capitulated on 10 June 1940). The fall of Scandinavia (bar neutral Sweden) did nothing to boost Anglo-French morale. Indeed, the Allied campaign to defend Norway had been mismanaged – the RAF, for example, had used obsolete Gloucester Gladiators which lacked oxygen provision for their crews, and it lost all but one aeroplane. Thus far, Germany had enjoyed easy victories and still had to turn the might of its forces to confront the Allies in the west.

Britain, France, Belgium, the Netherlands and Luxembourg, unlike their eastern and northern European counterparts, had to wait for seven months until it was their turn on the German timetable for war. The period was nicknamed by the popular press the 'phoney war' because the civilian population waited for German bombs to fall, but nothing appeared to happen except a large number of futile air raid warnings which dragged them out of their beds for nothing. The bustling preparations undertaken on war's eve – the evacuation of children and mothers from urban areas, the introduction of rationing, the construction of large air raid shelters and the family-sized, Anderson shelter, the issuing of gas masks and the launch of vast barrage balloons into the air – signified that the British public, though alarmed at the prospect of war, believed they were prepared. In France the fear of war was no less, but preparations for it were not so well advanced. In both countries the mood was sombre and serious. There were too many terrible memories of 1914 for it to be otherwise.

Preparations for war continued after 3 September 1939. New taxes were levied; the blackout was enforced; censorship was introduced; entertainment was restricted; armament production, conscription and the organization of labour were stepped up; and the world's press corps waited to report the opening of the Western Front. Indeed, the public was so thirsty for news that wild rumours of German espionage were commonplace. Military preparations, too, continued to escalate, although without orders for action, there was little for the troops to do except undertake training exercises. Morale declined and people began to wonder what kind of war this was. Some hoped against hope that the war would soon come to an end, perhaps through an internal revolt against Hitler – a false hope which had been shared by Chamberlain in August 1939.

Few Allied military commanders shared this optimism, particularly as Germany's military success soon rallied the German people behind *Der Führer*. Franco-British military cooperation was established in the Supreme Inter-Allied War Council, and by January 1940 the British Expeditionary Force had taken up its positions on the Franco-Belgian frontier after Allied efforts to coax Belgium out of neutrality had come to naught. As in the First World War the blockade of Germany was an important plank of the Allied strategy, although it was undermined by the willingness of some of Germany's neutral neighbours, notably the Netherlands, to become warehouses for produce intended for forwarding to Germany. The blockade was also weakened because the Allies allowed Italy to make considerable purchases abroad, including coal and raw materials, in the hope that they might yet prise Mussolini away from Hitler.

Throughout the Polish campaign, Hitler had instructed the Army, the *Wehrmacht*, to exercise the greatest caution in the west, indeed to remain completely on the defensive. Until Germany was ready, Hitler ordered that 'any hostile initiative should come from Britain or France'. Thus, Germany could avoid, for as long as was practicable, the need to wage war on two fronts, and there was even the possibility that once Britain and France had

witnessed the might of Germany's forces they would back down. The approach of winter, too, played its part. By October 1939, however, Hitler had altered his priorities and was anxious to wage war in the west. But autumn had given way to winter. Eleven times he gave the order to attack and eleven times poor weather forced him to cancel the order.

War in the west, 1940

The 'phoney war' finally ended on 10 May 1940 with the launch of Hitler's 'Operation Case Yellow'. Countless discussions between Hitler and his generals – the latter fearing the strength of the Royal Navy, the RAF, and the resources of the British Empire and France would prove too great for Germany – had come to an end. The battle for western Europe had begun and Hitler was proved right: victory was Germany's. Although the German war economy was not fully mobilized until 1942, in 1940 France's forces were poorly trained, demoralized and badly led, its political leadership in disarray as Premier Paul Reynaud struggled to form and keep a majority. General Maurice Gamelin complained of France's 'inferiority of numbers, inferiority of equipment, inferiority of method' – only some of this was true – and added to these difficulties came strategic mistakes. The French general staff failed to see that Germany might concentrate its attack on France through the Ardennes, not just via Belgium and the Netherlands, and so France quickly capitulated to the German invaders. The 500,000 British troops dispatched to France under the command of Lord Gort were unable to help their ally.

By 24 May 1940, ten days after the German attack had begun, Gort received orders to retreat across the Channel. Thus began the undignified British scramble from the port of Dunkirk which somehow managed to turn a devastating defeat for the Allied forces into a famed victory. 'Operation Dynamo' shipped British and Frenchmen from Dunkirk in small boats and the operation became the stuff of legend. Certainly, the firepower of the *Luftwaffe*, which had been so efficiently married with military power in the battle for France, had limited effect on the beaches of Dunkirk. But France was now certain to be defeated (its army was outnumbered 2:1), and the British Army had lost the bulk of its equipment and almost 70,000 men. On 22 June 1940, Marshal Pétain concluded armistice negotiations with Germany in the same railway carriage as Germany's humiliating armistice of 1918. With this final piece of theatre,

---

Plate 9.3 A German soldier keeps guard beneath the Eiffel Tower, 2 July 1940. The photograph was one of the very first taken of the German occupation of Paris. It marked the beginning of a relentless German propaganda campaign: the Third Reich had spectacularly defeated one of the world's leading military powers and had occupied Paris, widely regarded as the capital of modern civilization.

Hitler's ambition to overturn the *'Schandvertrag'* ('treaty of shame') of Versailles had reached its destructive conclusion.

Hitler's ambitions did not end here. Germany's generals and its people (who had shown little enthusiasm for war in 1939) were elated with the triumphs of 1940, and this mood was reflected in popular propaganda films like *Front in Himmel* ('Front in the Heavens') and *Sieg im Westen* ('Victory in the West') which used authentic footage alongside the usual tricks of propaganda. Film propaganda during the war, ranging from the subtle message of Allied films like *Casablanca* to the overt propaganda of German 'news reels', was more sophisticated than that of the First World War. Civilians were not only able to offer their labour and their lives to wage 'total war' but they could now watch the results of their efforts on film. The world's 'dictatorships' and 'democracies' alike were quick to exploit the media, and especially film, to maintain morale and to 'educate' their audience as to the cause and course of the war.

From the Battle of Britain to the Battle of the Balkans, 1940–41

By July 1940 Britain stood alone, although with the potential resources of the British Empire ranged behind it – a fact which Hitler and his generals were aware of more often and more acutely than the British people. Preparations for the probable German invasion of the British Isles had begun early in the war. Windows were blacked out, signposts were removed from roads, and later a 'Home Guard' was mobilized. But Hitler and his High Command were united in their belief that the invasion of Britain was 'an act of desperation', not an inevitable step on the road to dominating all Europe. Germany's real ambitions lay in eastern Europe.

When Germany's half-hearted peace overtures to Britain came to naught, 'Operation Sea-Lion' (following Hitler's directive of 16 July 1940) was launched with Göring's *Luftwaffe* leading the assault. Göring boasted: 'by means of hard blows I plan to have this enemy, who has already suffered a crushing moral defeat, down on his knees in the nearest future'. But this was not to be. The carefully timed interception of incoming German aircraft, the ability of RAF pilots to learn 'on the wing' from their more experienced adversaries, good intelligence and the development of radar all contributed to Germany's defeat in the 'Battle of Britain'. So, too, did Germany's fateful decision, in August 1940, to send 100 aircraft on a bombing raid to London. This decision altered the whole course of the battle, for not only did the British order a retaliatory strike against Berlin (which infuriated Hitler) but, far more importantly, it diverted German attacks from Fighter Command's bases in the south of England. Britain's industrial heartlands – Coventry, Liverpool, Birmingham, Glasgow, Leeds,

Plate 9.4 Coventry during the Blitz, 16 November 1940. The German air raids on Coventry began on 14 November and marked a new phase in air warfare. The centre of the medieval city was set ablaze by incendiary devices – one of the losses was the cathedral whose spire can be seen in the background, Using the blaze as a target, the raiders then dropped hundreds of tons of bombs on the city. Around one-third to the city's houses were destroyed and half of its buses put out of action.

Manchester and Belfast – were more difficult targets for the *Luftwaffe* and attacks there were less damaging to the British war effort.

The RAF was victorious in the Battle of Britain and German hopes that the bombing would cause British morale to collapse were mistaken, as were British hopes that raids on Hamburg, Dresden and Berlin would prompt the capitulation of the German people. Britain was now determined to avenge the 23,000 lives taken in the Blitz. Churchill immortalized the 537 brave fighter pilots who had given their lives in the battle, when 'so much [was] owed by so many to so few', and the film *Britain Can Take It* glorified the nation's battle. But although this conflict was over in December 1940, battles at sea, in the Balkans and the Near East, continued to rage. As Hitler's prime objective was to prepare Germany for racial war against the Soviet Union, he drained the material and labour strength of his conquests. Germany did not simply plunder obvious war resources: *The Times* reported that over eight million kilograms of butter had been removed from the Netherlands in the first weeks of occupation.

In the summer of 1940 Hitler also attempted to limit severely Britain's access to the Mediterranean and to improve the Reich's relations with the Balkan powers. But matters did not go according to plan. Franco, the 'Jesuit Pig' so carefully cultivated by Hitler, finally decided to abandon Spain's imperialist aspirations to Gibraltar and French colonies in north Africa, and informed the German Chancellor that Spain – exhausted by its civil war – would not enter the European war. After his 1940 meeting with the Spanish dictator, Hitler confided that he would rather have all his teeth pulled without anaesthesia than undergo such an experience again. This, plus only limited cooperation from Vichy and Italian suspicion of German ambitions, put paid to Hitler's aim to close off the Mediterranean to British ships.

But Hitler's frustration did not end here. While the German government worked to draw Romania, Hungary and Bulgaria into alliance with Germany (they were successful April–June 1941), Mussolini launched an attack on Greece which threatened Hitler's entire strategy in the Balkans. Mussolini's late entry into the war in June 1940 helped to extend the conflict to Yugoslavia, Greece, Bulgaria, Romania, Hungary, the Mediterranean and north Africa in the coming months. For Churchill the political and strategic reasons for intervening to counter-attack the Italians were overwhelming, and 'Operation Lustre' saw British troops shipped to Greece. Hitler, in the meantime, was not idle. He needed to secure the 'support' of Yugoslavia to enable German troops to reach Greece to aid the Italians and in preparation for the imminent invasion of the Soviet Union. As in the 1930s, he first tried diplomatic means, and when these proved fruitless he invaded Yugoslavia, successfully manipulating the Croat people against the Serbs in 'Operation Punishment'.

German troops had begun to attack Yugoslavia and Greece even before the British had time to work out their strategy. By 27 April 1941, German troops had entered yet another European capital: this time Athens. It made for great newsreel footage back home and crestfallen faces in London and Washington, especially when some 18,000 Allied soldiers had to be hastily withdrawn from Crete in another emergency evacuation. Churchill's instruction to 'keep hurling all you can' was to no avail. Although Hitler had been drawn into war in Greece by Mussolini, with its fall, Germany and Italy controlled most of the Mediterranean, their dominance only partially neutralized by the British Navy. The German Army had also secured the 'crossroads of Europe', the Balkans, in preparation for its assault against the Soviet Union, and now controlled the important oil-fields of Romania for the German economy.

Eastern Europe's traditional vulnerability to Russian and German ambitions was never more clear than during the Second World War. Its minority groups, most obviously its large Jewish population, were especially vulnerable to the victimization and brutality which is always heaped upon minorities during war. Some minority groups were so numerically small that a single act of war was apocalyptic. In April 1941, for example, German bombing of Yugoslavia devastated Zemun, the Gypsy quarter of Belgrade, destroying in one day a substantial portion of the entire Yugoslav Gypsy population. Patriotic hysteria, chauvinism and suspicion were also fuelled by war. In the First World War, stories of Jews signalling to German troops and acting as Habsburg spies were commonplace. In the Second World War Jews were again the most persecuted minority in eastern Europe, suffering at the hands of natives and occupiers. But there were other internecine conflicts of which that between Serb and Croat was the most bitter, reaching its bloody climax in the 1940s when the fascist *Ustasha* movement declared a 'holy-war' of 'purification' against all non-Croats. Of the 2,300,000 military and civilian casualties in the Mediterranean area during the Second World War, around 1,800,000 were lost in Yugoslavia in this terrible war between Croats and Serbs. In both world wars, the same minority groups suffered disproportionate losses – Jews, Gypsies, Serbs, Poles, Ukrainians and Byelorussians.

The 'Desert War', 1940–41

The outlook for the Allied forces was similarly bleak in Africa in 1941. The 'Desert War' in Africa, like Axis involvement in Greece, was triggered by Mussolini's ambition to establish a Mediterranean Empire 'to the east and to the south, in Asia and Africa'. In August 1940, again without Hitler's prior approval, from his base in Ethiopia, *Il Duce* launched a successful attack against British Somaliland. Italian troops outnumbered the British six to one and they made easy progress heading east towards Egypt. But Britain was determined to protect its strategic interests in the Mediterranean and its access to the Suez Canal and the precious oil resources of the Persian Gulf. On 8 December 1940, the British, led by General Sir Archibald Wavell, opened a surprise offensive and began to push the Italians back across the desert.

The Desert War highlighted the fact that the Second World War, unlike the First, was a war of movement, not of trenches. The extension of the conflict into Africa and the composition of the Axis and Allied forces emphasized the global character of the conflict – Italian troops were reinforced by indigenous forces from Ethiopia, Eritrea and Somaliland; the British Army was supported by, amongst others, men from Somaliland, Sudan, Egypt, Kenya and later from India and South Africa.

The desert battles soon began to turn to Britain's advantage, and in less than three months the British took 113,000 Italian prisoners and 1,300 guns at the expense of 438 British dead. Mussolini's rhetoric about the creation of a new Roman Empire now looked like empty boasting. But at the same time as Churchill withdrew some of Wavell's men to help to defend Greece, Mussolini once again prevailed upon Hitler to bail him out. Hitler obliged. In February 1941 the Afrika Korps was hastily assembled. Under the command of Lieutenant-General Erwin Rommel, a man who had made his name commanding the 7th Panzer division in France, the Afrika Korps soon demonstrated its mastery of mobile operations against the Allied opponents. Nicknamed the 'Desert Fox', Rommel succeeded in pushing Allied troops back across the frontiers of Egypt and became Germany's first genuine war hero. An Australian garrison at Tobruk was cut off which, according to Churchill, had 'undermined and overthrown all the projects on which we had embarked'.[5] As a result Wavell joined the ever lengthening list of military commanders sacked by Churchill. He was replaced by Field Marshal Claude Auchinleck.

Rommel's success opened up the tantalizing possibility of a German advance to Suez, Iraq and the Persian Gulf, but such prizes had to wait. It was now the turn of Hitler to divert resources to the Balkan campaign. In the heat and expanse of Africa supplies and reinforcements were even more critical in determining military success or failure than in Europe. By December 1941 Rommel was forced to withdraw to Tripolitania and the seige of Tobruk was temporarily lifted.

Despite spectacular victories against an ill-equipped and ill-prepared Italian Army, and victory over the German *Luftwaffe* in the Battle of Britain, the British Empire was in desperate straits in 1941. In the Far East developments were equally grim. Already in July 1941, with the connivance of the Vichy French government in Saigon, Japan had absorbed Indochina.

Peace for some, 1939–41

From September 1939 until the summer of 1941, however, there were a number of nations intimately concerned with the outcome of war in the west, who at first chose to be isolated from it. The USSR, the United States and Japan were important protagonists still waiting in the wings.

Isolation was nothing new to the Soviet Union. It was only after Munich that the Axis and Western powers sought Stalin's friendship. To many people communism appeared as great an evil as fascism (for some the distinction lay in the moustaches of the dictators), and, typically, Stalin trusted neither Axis nor the West. His prime concern was to keep the USSR out of a major war to consolidate the gains of the Five Year Plans and, perhaps more important, to allow the Red Army to recover from the vicious bloodletting of the purges. Stalin certainly had good reason to distrust Hitler, the man who had expressed the ambition 'to cut a road for expansion to the East by fire and sword . . . and enslave the Soviet peoples'. Yet Stalin also had good reason to distrust Britain, France and the United States. The countries which had attempted to intervene on behalf of the White forces during the Russian Civil War had been reluctant to recognize the legitimacy of the Bolshevik government, and had appeared to fear the menace of communism as much as, if not more than, the menace of fascism. This had been typified by their failure to construct an international front to defend the Popular Front in Spain. The occupation of the eastern territories of Poland, Romania, Lithuania, Latvia and Estonia was Stalin's prize for isolation in 1939. Finland, too, had proved to be an irresistible temptation.

The United States and Japan observed from the side-lines. The former, under the dynamic leadership of Franklin D. Roosevelt, chose a nationalist path to economic recovery. At the depths of America's depression over 25 million Americans were unemployed and the collapse of the domestic economy made Roosevelt cautious in foreign affairs. His caution was more than matched by that of the majority of American citizens who had grown 'gun-shy' of Europe: a widespread revulsion against foreign wars which had intensified in the wake of the First World War and criticism of America's failure to ratify Versailles by an 'ungrateful' Europe. During the 1930s the desire to isolate America grew. Neutrality legislation was passed in 1935, 1936 and 1937, with many Americans fearful that the United States would be infected by the social and political diseases which had swept Europe: a successful pro-Nazi party rally at Madison Square Garden in 1934 struck an icy chill in many hearts; subsequently, an American Legion commander in California demanded 'Down with all Isms!'

Yet if the icy waters of the Atlantic appeared to protect America from the German menace, the USA faced a new threat to the west: Japan. The rising power in the Far East, with an enhanced economic and military capacity, Japan now also hungered for an empire. Its recently acquired and fragile liberal political tradition (established under the Meiji restoration, 1868) collapsed under the strain of economic crisis, and the military gained increasing influence in government. In 1931 Japan sent troops to protect its economic interests in Manchuria, and by 1937 the Japanese people were engaged in war against China. It was a development which threatened Britain and, in particular, the USA.

By 1940 Japanese military operations had extended into Indochina in the search for oil and other raw materials essential to military expansion, and on 7 December 1941, in a pre-emptive strike against the United States, Japan attacked the Phillipines and Pearl Harbor in Hawaii. Within four months of this sensational attack the Japanese were complete masters of the whole of south-east Asia and much of the Pacific. The sinking of British as well as American ships gave Japan a naval supremacy which the Washington treaties of 1921 had never anticipated, and in air power also it was Japanese supremacy which made inevitable the fall of Hong Kong,

Malaya, Singapore and the Philippines by February 1942. Even India was now under threat. These Japanese victories, particularly the speedy capitulation of Singapore, triggered a lengthy debate on the future of British colonial rule, now that the Japanese had dealt a series of devastating blows to European authority. But the Japanese had also brought the Americans into the war.

The attack on Pearl Harbor ended American isolationism. The United States declared war on Japan, and the global spread of the conflict was complete when Hitler declared war on the United States. In many ways, American neutrality had already become a pretence by 1941. Munition supplies to Britain ('cash and carry' followed by 'lend-lease' schemes) and propaganda offensives through the media of film, radio and print, all served to illustrate the President's sympathies for Britain, sympathies cemented by the friendship of Roosevelt and Churchill. With American entry into the war, Britain no longer had to fight alone and Churchill was at last able to sleep 'the sleep of the saved and thankful'.

From 1939 until September 1941 the course of the world's second war had appeared to follow that of its predecessor: apart from the Sino-Japanese war, the conflict was concentrated inside Europe. But with the bombing of Pearl Harbor in December 1941, the theatres of war in western Europe, north Africa, the Balkans, the Soviet Union, at sea and in the air, linked to Japan's struggle for dominance in the Far East, forming a continuous chain of conflict and destruction around the globe. This time, unlike 1914–18, the war was highly mobile. Characteristic of the ever accelerating pace of technological change in the twentieth century, the development and improvement of aircraft, tanks and armed vehicles enabled well equipped and organized forces to sweep forward and engulf their opponent. As long as their supplies lasted, their communications remained cohesive and their organization strong and effective.

The turning point, 1941–42

Two events in 1941 turned the tide in favour of the democracies. The first was Hitler's decision, contrary to the advice of his Army leaders, to launch 'Operation Barbarossa' against the Soviet Union. The second came with Japan's assault against the United States. Germany, as in 1914, now faced the prospect of a war on two fronts, while the United States entered the Second World War with the commitment to 'Europe First', despite the misgivings of men like General Douglas MacArthur who wanted to concentrate America's offensive against the Japanese in the Pacific.

The first phase of the world war had brought some searing defeats for Britain. Europe had been overrun by the National Socialists. Singapore, the linchpin of the British Empire's defences in the Far East, had fallen in February 1942, and on 21 June 1942 Tobruk finally succumbed to Rommel after a renewed offensive by the Afrika Korps. According to Churchill, it was 'one of the heaviest blows I can recall during the war'.[6] At sea, too, the British Navy suffered some terrible losses: more than 3 million tons of shipping from June 1940 to March 1941 (as in the First World War, the convoy system; and recently invented radar and code-breaking skills eventually reduced these losses). Until the circle of conflict was completed by Germany's invasion of the Soviet Union and Japan's surprise assault on the United States, Britain, fighting alone, had few answers as to how to defeat its enemy.

Without sufficient troops to invade continental Europe, Britain's main hope lay with strategic bombing. But Bomber Command lacked both the equipment and expertise to carry out a strategic offensive. Early airborne offensives also appeared to undermine the bombers' case: in 1941 it was estimated that over 50 per cent of British bombs were landing in open fields. The entry of the United States into the war held out a lifeline to Britain and opened up new strategic options to win the war.

The Germans had made elaborate plans for the invasion of the USSR. Army generals who argued that an effective campaign against the Soviet Union would enable Germany to harness 75 per cent of the Soviet armaments industry found favour with the *Führer*. Those who counselled caution did not. Detailed plans were also drafted on the treatment of the Soviet population in the coming 'ideological war': Jews and Soviet Commissars were to be shot. On 22 June 1941 Germany attacked the Soviet Union without a declaration of war, echoing Napoleon's invasion of Russia almost to the day. Despite warnings from Britain, the United States and his own secret agents, Stalin was shattered by news of the invasion – he did not appear in public until 3 July. Churchill, meanwhile, was quick to silence those who did not wish Britain to ally with the communists:

> Can you doubt what our policy will be? We have but one aim and one single, irrevocable purpose. We are resolved to destroy Hitler. . . . It follows, therefore, that we shall give whatever help we can to the Russians and the Russian people.

In reality, Anglo-American support for the Soviet Union amounted to very little until 1944. Stalin's repeated calls for the creation of a second front in Europe were impossible for Britain to meet, even with American help. Troops needed to be amassed, trained and supplied. But Churchill's sometimes disingenuous remarks to Stalin on the timing of the Western Front stored up trouble for the future. Britain did try to assist the USSR, but set against the terrible losses the Soviets endured, almost any quantity of British and American aid appeared paltry.

In the meantime, like the first stages of Japan's campaign in the Far East, the Germans had a number of spectacular victories inside the Soviet Union. By 16 July 1941 they had taken Smolensk and by 19 September 1941 Kiev. The agricultural and industrial resources of the Ukraine thus fell into German hands; in the fall of Kiev alone, the Soviets lost 655,000 men, 884 tanks and 3,718 guns. From October to December the Germans were engaged in a bitter battle for Moscow and here the first signs of their fallibility appeared: their soldiers were exhausted and lacked sufficient materiel and communications to sustain them. But while the infamous Russian winter worked against the Germans in 1941–42, Stalin often worked for them. He repeatedly undermined his generals' strategies and, like Hitler's 'Nero order' in 1945, called for 'fanatical resistance' from his troops in the face of overwhelming odds. For those on the Home Front, however, Stalin appeared to be the author of the Soviet Union's victory in this 'Great Patriotic War'. Like many others, a young Jew who had escaped the clutches of the occupying Germans in Poland, found inspiration in Stalin's speech to the people on 3 July 1941:

> He [Stalin] found some apt expressions to show how this time was not a matter of an ordinary war between two countries and two armies, but a trial of strength between two visions of the world, and how therefore the Red Army fought not only to defend its own soil, but the freedom of all peoples who 'groaned under the yoke of German fascism'.[7]

By September 1942, the Germans had successfully countered the Soviet winter offensive, no thanks to directives pouring forth from the office of the *Führer*, and by 10 September Hoth's 4th Panzer Army was fighting on the streets of Stalingrad – the furthest point of German penetration. The Soviets put up a spirited and successful resistance in a bloody battle fought from house to house. But it was the Soviet Republic's victory at Kursk, to the north east, which provided the USSR with more than a psychological victory over the Germans. Hitler's elite forces – the SS division, *Totenkopf, Adolf Hitler, Das Reich* – all sustained heavy losses in one of the bloodiest battles of the war. The battle for Kursk cost Hitler half a million men, and now all possibility of avoiding total defeat had gone. The German Army was in retreat and Russian military production now outstripped that of Germany. Stalin had conducted the engagement with meticulous efficiency. He had improved relations with his generals, and the USSR now outnumbered and outgunned its German enemy. The tide had turned in Stalin's favour and his troops now pushed up towards Poland.

Beyond Europe the situation also began to improve for the Allies. Japan's expansion in the Far East was checked in 1942, this time within reach of Australia. The Battle of the Coral Seas in May 1942 was followed in June by that of Midway Island; while in the west, air attacks on Ceylon were repelled and Madagascar, still under Vichy control, was occupied by the British. Meanwhile, after the fall of Tobruk, General Bernard Montgomery took command of Allied troops in north Africa, breathing new confidence into an army sunk in despair after defeat. For Churchill the defeat was a particularly 'bitter moment' for defeat was 'one thing; disgrace another'.

The Desert War had seen exceptional commanders – Rommel for the Axis, Wavell, Auchinleck and Montgomery for the Allies – play out a finely balanced encounter. After the humiliation of Tobruk, Churchill was determined on a victory in the field. That year saw the final defeat of the German-Italian Panzer Army in the desert and the Battle of El Alamein was the centre-piece (November 1942). Rommel was defeated by superior Allied numbers, resources and military intelligence, and by his own dwindling resources – German and Italian tanks and jeeps were under the constant threat of an empty fuel tank. Britain lost a large number of forces at El Alamein but Montgomery had succeeded in halting the German advance. With the landing of American troops in the region in 'Operation Torch' that same month, the Allies were now in a position to tighten the net around the Axis forces in Europe.

The tide had turned in favour of the Allies, but the war was by no means won. Divisions between Britain and the United States as to how to defeat Germany still needed to be ironed out: Britain favoured an attack from the Mediterranean, through Italy and the Balkans, to deliver the final blow to Germany. The United States, on the other hand, disagreed with what they condemned as Britain's 'periphery pecking' approach and remained determined to launch a full-scale invasion of France. Whereas this issue brought endless friction to Anglo-American relations, Churchill arrived in Moscow in the summer of 1942 to inform Stalin that there would be no second front in Europe that year. At the end of 1942, then, no immediate end to the war was in sight, although the Allied victories had dealt an important blow to Axis morale. As a secret report of the German *Sicherheitsdienst* (security service) put it: 'A certain gloominess and anxiety exists among many people because they "cannot quite cope" with events any more and fear an unknown danger they cannot grasp.'

The Home Front

Hitler, Stalin, Roosevelt, Mussolini and Churchill, the principal wartime leaders, were amongst the most influential political leaders in the history of their nations in the twentieth century. They all gave strong and often uncompromising direction to their countries, although the policy decisions taken by Adolf Hitler ('Operation Barbarossa' and the Final Solution, for example), perhaps more than those of any other leader, determined the outcome of the war. For governments in the Second World War, as in the First, the principal task was to mobilize manpower and resources, balancing the needs of industry against those of the armed forces. In Britain and the Soviet Union, this problem was especially acute in the early stages of the war.

In the Second World War, as in the First, failures in the war effort had an important impact on domestic political life, although the degree of public criticism permitted depended upon the character of the ruling regime. In Germany, Hitler's leadership went unchallenged. Italian political

Plate 9.5 A couple transporting a dead body during the siege of Stalingrad, 1942.
Although the Germans had captured much of the city and controlled most of the
Volga river by September 1942, the citizens of Stalingrad and the Sixty-second
Russian army put up brave resistance. The centre of the city was the battleground,
and its principal buildings, some of which changed hands as often as five or six
times a day, were the tactical objectives. When the siege finally was ended in
February 1943, burning stumps of buildings and corpses piled high greeted the
Russian liberators.

356

life, by contrast, was more complex. By 1942 the Italian Fascist Party had begun to disintegrate from within. The factions and in-fighting which had long characterized Mussolini's party grew increasingly bitter, particularly when the 'Petacci clan', the friends and family of Mussolini's mistress, Claretta Petacci, joined in the squabbling groups attempting to revive Italy's collapsing war effort. Four major anti-Fascist parties also began to revive in 1942 – the Actionists, the Communists, the Socialists and the Catholics. Although these parties had yet to develop party organizations and manifestos, politicians who were to play an important role in Italy's postwar history, like the former Popular Party leader and future Christian Democrat, Alcide De Gasperi, set about helping to destroy Fascism and establish a democratic political system for Italy.

The year 1942 brought the most serious political challenge to Churchill. The military failures of 1940–41, notably in Norway, Dunkirk, Greece and north Africa, were compounded in 1942 by news of the fall of Singapore and Tobruk. It was not Churchill's skill as a military commander, however, which was in doubt. In particular, the government was criticized for its management of the war economy and for its failure to help the Soviet Union. That summer Stafford Cripps – Britain's former Ambassador to the USSR and a popular, young Labour politician – challenged Churchill for the leadership of the British war effort. Neither his personal appeal – he was described as an *éminence beige* – nor the breadth of his political support was a match for Churchill. By November 1942 a Mass Observation report concluded that the public was 'completely disillusioned' with Cripps. Churchill's position was secure.

One of Britain's main difficulties was the short supply of munitions. Until December 1941, Britain was heavily dependent upon supplies from an unreliable source: a United States President busy bending the rules of American isolationism. Businessmen were once again central in the struggle to marshal Britain's resources for total war. Learning the lessons of the First World War, the British this time quickly established that for every soldier there should be one worker in the defence industries, and two more workers in the civilian economy producing food, clothing and other necessities for the war-worker and soldier. These figures alone give some indication of the importance of the Home Front to the war effort.

Miscalculating the proportion of workers to soldiers could be costly. In the Soviet Union, the excessive mobilization of troops in the front line in 1941–42, by drafting industrial workers and skilled defence workers into the Army, seriously undermined the Soviet war economy at a time when German forces were marching across the Soviet Union's industrial heartland. As Hitler had stressed throughout the 1930s, managing the economy effectively was the key to winning the war. Yet despite Germany's extensive preparations in peace, the German economy was amongst the least efficient in war. This was partly due to the fact that Hitler had been planning for a large-scale war in 1941–42; war in 1939 prompted some hasty improvizations. Moreover, whereas the British war effort was comparatively well directed by a coordinated bureaucracy, Germany's war economy lacked such coordination. Regional administration under the *Gaus* resisted the centralized priorities of the war. There were also intense rivalries for resources and power amongst men like Göring (responsible for the Aircraft Ministry) and Funk (in charge of the civilian economy).

Göring claimed that 'no problem is so great that it could not be solved by a German'. Yet even the efforts of Albert Speer, a former architect with a flair for administration, appointed in February 1942 to coordinate Germany's war production, achieved only mixed results. Speer, like Rathenau, believed in centralized, capitalist control and despite ministerial rivalries, crippling shortages and Allied bombs, he succeeded in more than doubling German war production in early 1943. By the summer it had more than trebled, although many of the weapons produced were of inferior quality to those of the Allies.

As during the 'Great War', government extended its control over economy and people to new heights and, once again, the war provided an important stimulus to the development of the American economy. From 1940 to 1944 American manufacturing output increased by 300 per cent. Ingenious American businessmen used every opportunity afforded by the war to increase sales – Coca-Cola persuaded the American Army that buying their drink was essential for morale – so that even consumer industries prospered from the war. Most Americans enjoyed an exceptional level of prosperity during the Second World War and thus rejected the need for greater social provision for their less privileged citizens. The experience of the Second World War, in contrast to the experience of the 1930s, confirmed that capitalism could bring untold riches to the United States.

Europeans, by contrast, were offered the hope of postwar social security. In Britain in June 1941, Sir William Beveridge presided over an inter-departmental committee of civil servants to survey 'social insurance and allied services', and his long report, published in November 1942, a largely technical document, attracted immense popular interest: a surprised Beveridge described its reception, which was greatly publicized abroad, 'like riding on an elephant through a cheering mob'. Behind the back of an unimpressed Churchill, who was preoccupied with winning the war, the foundations were being laid through this and later White Papers for a comprehensive social security system 'from the cradle to the grave'. The war fostered a feeling that all members of the community should be involved in postwar social spheres just as they were involved together in the war itself. It also spotlighted the importance of 'fair shares for all'. The Labour Party was to benefit from this in 1945 at the next general election, the first in 10 years.

While class barriers continued to remain rigid, there was a growing determination to create a society where each individual could play his or her part for a common, worthwhile cause. A similar drive for 'social justice' was also evident amongst European resistance movements in their plans for the postwar order.

Women at war

The notion of 'Fair Shares' for all was in part in response to the contribution of women to the Second World War effort. On the outbreak of war women across Europe were again warmly welcomed into the workforce. Drawing on the experience of the First World War, most countries recognized the importance of mobilizing women as soon as war began, although in the Soviet Union women had already become a very important part of the workforce in the drive for collectivization and industrialization in the 1930s. Moreover, it was only in the Soviet Union that the war prompted the state to announce that 'there are no longer so-called "male" professions'. Soviet women had shown that 'there is no profession that is beyond them'. In the rest of Europe women at war were employed in what were traditionally considered 'male' occupations – support services for the Army, Navy and Airforce, farming, manufacturing, civil defence, driving buses, steering barges and even flying aeroplanes – but this, as during the First World War, did not mean that women remained in these occupations once war was over.

There was a tremendous variety in women's experiences of the war. Many went to work on the land: in Britain the Land Army was one of the more popular auxiliary services for women to join. They were also employed as farm labourers in France, Germany and much of eastern Europe, although many more 'farmed' unofficially to scavenge extra food and fuel for their families. Women made an important contribution to manufacturing, too. The proportion of women employed in industry varied greatly across Europe. By 1943 in Britain over seven million women were employed in the armed forces, civil defence and industry – responsible for almost two-thirds of manufacturing output. As we have seen, the Nazi government, too, attempted to bring more women into the labour force, but the role of German women as child-bearers, as in Vichy France, continued strongly to be emphasized by the state. (The Vichy '300 Law' declared abortion to be a crime against society, the state and the race. It was an act of treason punishable by death.)

In Nazi Germany there was another, uglier side to this pro-natalism: the state's conviction that racially and eugenically 'inferior' women must not be allowed to bear children. At the outbreak of war Polish and Russian women from the occupied territories who were conscripted into forced labour were no longer permitted to return home when pregnant. Instead, they were encouraged or compelled to have abortions or to be sterilized,

and those children who were born often fell prey to their employers: Himmler's race experts or Nazi doctors. This was but a taste of plans for the occupied territories designed to reduce the number of children born. Worse was to come. Jewish and Gypsy women rounded up in concentration camps were subjected to sterilization experiments which were intended to establish efficient methods to sterilize hundreds of thousands of 'inferior' women in the future. Women were also involved in the killing – as nurses in the killing centres, as social workers, as doctors, as researchers and as camp guards.

The horrors of the Second World War – civilian bombing, mobile front lines, occupation, resistance and, in some cases, combat – determined that the gulf of experience between men and women in this war was considerably less than it had been in the First World War. Nonetheless, in most countries as many women remained at home as came into the workplace. In part, this was because the state remained poor at recognizing that women required encouragement, by way of childcare, decent wage rates, and shopping facilities near their places of work. For women with young children the average working week of 12 hours a day for six days a week on top of looking after children, home and (sometimes) husband was too great a burden. It was also because some women did not want to work (or their husbands disapproved).

But war-work brought additional, much welcomed, housekeeping money and, for young single women, a more active social life. (A British commentator was horrified to note that 40 per cent of single women now socialized in pubs.) Sometimes there was even enough to provide women with a little freedom to spend money on themselves, although the work was not without its risks. An 18-year-old volunteer recalled:

> It was putting the caps on the detonators of bullets. It was dangerous . . . the cordite used to fly about, fly up into your face. It caused a rash, impetigo, and it would come up in big lumps. Your eyes swelled up. We used to work seven [days or nights] a week. It was good money. I was earning £10 a week.

As in 1918, at war's end few professions were feminized as a result of the war. In western Europe women all but completely disappeared from the armed services, transportation (particularly women-drivers) and certain types of manufacturing. Only in the divided Germany and the USSR did the loss of men in the war ensured a strong demand for working women. The indications of change for women reflected changes in attitudes, particularly among women themselves. In 1945 many more married

---

Plate 9.6 Women at war. Advertising campaigns to recruit women workers were conducted thoughout Europe during the war. Yet of the principal belligerents, only Britain and the Soviet Union drafted womanpower; Italy and Germany did not. Women in the military, who almost without exception were unmarried and childless, provided support services for the male armed forces or worked on the land.

women were determined to remain in employment (traditionally most female employees were single), and most had an increased sense of self-worth as a consequence of their war-time experiences. But although across Europe politicians loudly praised the contribution of women to the war effort, they took considerably longer to legislate for change which recognized the economic value of women. Typical was the response of Ernest Bevin when women demanded equal pay to men (women worked for 50 to 70 per cent of men's wages) in the House of Commons:

> *Dr (Edith) Summerskill:* Even he admits my figures are right.
> *Mr Bevin:* I think your figure's perfect.

The fall and rise of 'great powers'

Britain's war experience was clearly set apart from that of the rest of Europe. Its land was not fought over, as in the Soviet Union, nor was it as extensively bombed as Germany, and apart from the Channel Islands, there was no occupation or resistance. The war did, however, emphasize the decline of Britain as a world power. That the Empire was in crisis was clearly signalled by unrest in India and by Britain's dependence on the United States for financial aid. But while Britain's star was on the wane, the Soviet Union arose in the east as the world's latest great power.

The first year of the 'Great Patriotic War', which claimed over 20 million lives, brought terrible suffering to the USSR. Retreating in the face of the advancing German forces, the Soviets lost territories containing 63 per cent of all coal production, 68 per cent of pig-iron, 84 per cent of sugar, 38 per cent of grain and 60 per cent of pigs. Food shortages appeared within days of the outbreak of war – milk, sugar and fats were all very hard to come by and even cabbage disappeared from the market-place. Workers often walked four or five miles to and from work on an empty stomach, and housing conditions were often grim, usually without any heating. The USSR's most remarkable achievement during the war was to evacuate entire factories from the west to the Urals, Siberia, Kazakhstan and central Asia. Moving these special defence industries was an essential foundation to the mobilization of the Soviet economy as a whole.

Winning the war after 1942 brought little relief for the Soviet peoples as the Germans carried out a policy of systematic destruction as they retreated, although the war went some way towards healing some of the divisions in Stalinist society prompted by the purges of the 1930s. But whereas these purges had effectively discriminated against particular social classes in the Soviet Union, under the impact of the war, belonging to a certain ethnic group now began to distinguish loyal workers from traitors. Volga Germans, Karachi, Kalmyks, Chechens, Ingushis, Jews, Crimean Tartars and others were shipped off to Siberia in a wave of Russian chauvinism which sought scapegoats and 'enemies within' to explain the early success of the Germans.

Other former enemies of the Soviet state fared better under the conditions of war. The Church and some artists discovered a new freedom as Stalin worked to sustain the morale of his people. Propaganda concentrated on liberation: thus, in a poster, a crab, complete with Hitler moustache, was shown crushed beneath the tracks of a Soviet tank. There was a challenge which needed to be met purposefully at all levels.

The German people did not experience starvation to the same degree as the Soviet Union's, although their standard of living was nevertheless substantially lower than that of Britain from 1939 to 1947. Life in the cities was especially tough with food in short supply and, by the end of the war, many families were driven by Allied bombs to living in cellars. As in Britain, the National Socialists attempted to provide their *Volk* (people) with an inspiring social vision, but plans drafted by Robert Ley, leader of the German Labour Front, came to naught under the demands of war. Instead, the Nazi vision became one of death and destruction. By 1941, the promised 'racial renewal' began to take place through genocide and subjugation. Hitler waged the war to provide *Lebensraum* for the German people, yet few understood what this concept meant. Scant numbers of Germans settled for long in occupied eastern Europe and those who did – leading party members, large corporations – began to abandon their assets and plans for expansion in 1944 when it became clear that the dream of victory had become the nightmare of defeat. To his supporters, Hitler's claim that 'in this war, not luck, but justice will finally triumph' appeared increasingly hollow.

Resistance in the Axis countries

It was impossible to measure the degree of support or hostility Hitler's regime engendered during the war but active resistance amongst the German population was low. As Speer noted, 'apathy ... despite all the great triumphs' appeared to be the prevalent sentiment. Most were far too preoccupied with the task of daily survival. Under the ever watchful eye of the Gestapo, large-scale resistance was, at best, difficult. The experience of the 'White Rose' group, founded by brother and sister Hans and Sophie Scholl, illustrated the obstacles faced by organized resistance in the Reich. The group courageously printed leaflets which were distributed in Munich, Stuttgart, Frankfurt, Freiburg, Vienna and Hamburg. But their activities were short-lived. In 1943 all members of the group were arrested, tried and executed. Sophie was 22 years old when she died.

Carl Goerdeler, the former Lord Mayor of Leipzig, was representative of more elevated opposition to Hitler. He organized the 1944 'Officers' Plot' to assassinate Hitler. Such high-level protest was directed more against the dishonour Hitler was heaping upon Germany during the war than at murder in the concentration camps. In Italy, resistance to the mass murder of Jews in German-dominated Europe came at a more senior level. Encouraged by the character of semi-official Italian life, diplomats, civil servants and administrators conspired against their orders to deliver Jews to the gas chambers. But their efforts, however valiant, did little to diminish the incomprehensible horror of the Holocaust: six million European Jews were slaughtered or murdered in the gas chambers of Auschwitz, Chelmno, Belzec, Sobibor and Treblinka. While most Germans had heard rumours of the concentration camps, the full horror came as a shock to many. A 17-year-old German prisoner of war recalled:

> Barely a week went by that the Americans did not show pictures of . . . the concentration camps. Many of my fellow prisoners cried. Others, however, left the cinema after the film and laughed in the faces of American soldiers, because they believed the films were *Greuelmärchen* [horror stories], similar to the sophisticated propaganda they had been subjected to by Goebbels.[8]

Participation and resistance in occupied Europe

Just as the First World War had shaken Europe from its belief in human 'progress', so the crimes of the Second World War worked to erode European claims to moral superiority over the rest of the world. In Nazi-occupied Europe, the choice between participation or resistance was a painful one. The Polish poet Czeslaw Milosz went so far as to describe his country as a 'Gangster Gau' (the German-occupied Vistula basin bore the name Government-General, or GG for short), in which the entire Polish nation turned to criminal activities to survive the occupation.

Germany's occupation policy for Europe was by no means consistent. The Nazi occupiers wanted to exploit the economic and strategic resources of the Reich's new territories while imposing a new racial order. But different 'regions' were exploited in different ways, depending on how the territory was defeated, the strength of local Nazis and the form of the existing political structure. France, Belgium, Greece and Serbia were strategically important and so remained under military control. Holland and Norway, by contrast, had fledgling fascist parties which were allowed to establish powerless consultative cabinets (the most infamous was Vidkun Quisling's cabinet in Norway), while real power rested with a German *ReichsKommisar*. 'Native' fascists – like Quisling, Anton Mussert in Holland and Léon Degrelle in Belgium – were caught in a vicious spiral of concession to their Nazi occupiers; men who were usually more extreme and ruthless than themselves. The local fascists provided the henchmen to do the Nazis' dirty work. They carried out raids and reprisals, rounded up and transported their compatriots to concentration camps, and even recruited volunteers to fight for Germany. Twenty-thousand supporters of

Mussert served in the German Army, and the Grand Mufti of Jerusalem recruited a Moslem Legion which paraded in Berlin alongside Bosnian or Soviet prisoners of war from Azerbaidzhan and Turkestan.

Denmark, at first, was treated rather differently from other countries in occupied Europe. King Christian X refused to go into exile and instead formed a national government to negotiate directly with the Nazis. The Danes were thus spared the degradation and horror of a Nazi occupation until 1943 when it became clear that here, as in Norway, there was little chance of home-grown Nazis mustering sufficient public support to take office. Occupied western Europe as a whole, however, received better treatment than its eastern counterpart, although there, too, the Nazis had their 'quislings'. In Hungary it was the Regent Horthy, in Croatia it was Anté Pavelič and his fascist *Ustasha* party: they instituted a reign of terror against Serbs, Jews, Gypsies and communists living in Croatia, and provided troops to help the Italians in their war against Tito's communist partisans. Even in the USSR the *Wehrmacht* sometimes received a warm welcome, especially from Estonians, Ukrainians, Armenians, Tartars, Caucasians and Moslems, who, if they did not join the German Army, were taken prisoner by it in abnormally high numbers. Nonetheless, French, Danish and Norwegian men and women stood higher on the Nazi racial scale and so merited larger food rations and better conditions in their labour camps.

What of France – a country whose land mass, if not the size of its population, was equivalent to that of Germany? At first, only the northern half of France was placed under military occupation, while the south-west region remained unoccupied to form Vichy France under the government of Pétain. It was on the other side of the English Channel that a former junior minister, Charles de Gaulle, took up the Free France cry. But not all Frenchmen and women shared de Gaulle's hostility to the Vichy government. Some inside France argued that Vichy was an opportunity to right the wrongs of earlier, weak French governments. Whatever their noble claims, the reality of Vichy France was an ugly one. Unlike the Netherlands and Belgium, where brave efforts were made to hinder the mass murder of their Jewish citizens, Vichy France had an appalling record of anti-semitism. After 1942 all of France was occupied by the Germans and the French *Service d'Ordre Légionnaire* cooperated energetically with France's occupiers. Just as some French people argued that collaboration with the Nazi occupiers was essential to national survival, the memory of resistance to the Germans was vital to national morale in the immediate postwar years.

There was resistance to the Nazi occupation throughout Europe, but it was never unified or coordinated. The resistance fighters had much in common: a hatred of German and of foreign or local fascism, and an unflinching patriotism. They also shared poverty – lacking weapons, money and trained personnel – and their sentiments and actions brought them into direct conflict with their compatriots, the collaborators, so that resistance often became civil war. Most listened regularly to the British Broadcasting Corporation (BBC) which sustained morale.

The early resistance to Axis occupation was passive – demonstrations in Wencelas Square in Prague or at the Arc de Triomphe in Paris. Then came underground newspapers and leaflets, and direct action – sabotage and attacks on important figures, sometimes with the collusion of the Allies. But there was also enormous variety in European resistance, conditional on the character of the Nazi occupation, the local geography and history. In Norway military resistance was organized into a single group under the command of the Norwegian Army's General Ruge. This, plus mountainous terrain, created an effective, unified, guerilla unit, in sharp contrast to the resistance movements of Denmark and Holland, countries unsuitable for this type of warfare. Here resistance was restricted to acts of sabotage, rescuing Jews and collecting intelligence for the Allies. Resistance movements in Belgium and France, by contrast, did plan and execute military operations, although Belgium's 35 intelligence networks – employing over 10,000 people – were a much more vital part of the Allied war effort. Resistance in Belgium, unlike France, was unified under the control of the 'Secret Army'.

In France, organized resistance movements like the *ITLAIC Combat Libération, Franc-Tireur, Front National* and *Organisation Civile et Militaire* played a vital role in defeating the Germans and opening a Western Front. French resistance increasingly formed competing splinter groups after June 1941 when the French Communist Party joined the movement. Eventually, these groups were united under the command of General de Gaulle in 1942, but while they could fight together to defeat the Germans, peacetime political cooperation proved impossible.

In eastern Europe the rivalry between communist and non-communist resistance movements was fiercer than in the west because of the proximity of Soviet forces. Czechoslovak resistance from 1939, for example, was first led by the exiled President from France, but the defeat of France was a second 'Munich' for Beneš and the Czech resistance was increasingly guided by Soviet directives. In Yugoslavia and Greece, rugged terrain again made guerrilla-style resistance more practicable, but here, too, there was strong competition between non-communist and communist groups. Yugoslavia's forces had capitulated quickly to the *Wehrmacht* in April 1941 (only 151 of the German invaders were killed). Draza Mihailović was the only Serbian commander who escaped the demoralized collapse of Yugoslavia's forces and he took to the hills with his remaining troops, calling them *Chetniks* in memory of the struggle against the Turks. Within months these Serbian freedom fighters, who were loyal to the Crown, were in fierce competition with the communist partisan forces led by Marshal Jusip Tito. The pan-Serbianism and monarchism of the *Chetniks* had little in common with the Croatian, communism of Tito, bent on the creation of a federal South Slav state, and cooperation between the two groups proved impossible. The *Chetniks* came off second best, and Tito's political agenda and his struggle against the *Chetniks* and Croatian fascist *Ustasha* meant that Yugoslavian resistance, as in Greece and Romania, provoked civil war and revolution as well.

Intellectual and spiritual resistance

In eastern Europe, Soviet-style communism provided the intellectual backbone for many of the resistance movements. Elsewhere in Europe, and sometimes from exile, writers, artists and churchmen attempted to provide intellectual and spiritual support for those engaged in active and passive resistance. There was even an intellectual 'resistance' movement of sorts in Britain.

The need for security and unity in the face of the enemy imposed limits on the freedom of expression of leading British intellectuals. Although, as George Orwell noted, 'the British government started the war with the more or less openly declared intention of keeping the literary intelligentsia out of it', by 1943 almost every writer, 'however undesirable his opinions', was sucked into 'the BBC or some other essentially literary job'. The contribution of writers like Orwell and J. B. Priestley to the British propaganda effort was important, but their official work sometimes rested uneasily with their left-wing convictions. Orwell, for example, had a deep distrust of authority and the collectivist tendencies of the state at war. In his public broadcasts he, like Priestley, stressed that the war was being waged to defend a 'unique island people' and expounded on the 'great' qualities of the British. He did not always tow the government line, however, as he attempted to convey his concern that the extension of the powers of the state in war and, subsequently, in peace (via the Beveridge plan) would destroy the inherent 'gentleness of English civilization'.

Above all, like many left-wing luminaries who were among the most popular BBC performers, he wanted British working-class people to think positively of the future and the need to eliminate 'inefficiency, class privilege and the rule of the old'. The need for social justice was an especially popular message – so much so that in 1942 a leading conservative complained that too many left-wingers had been elevated to 'positions of eminence'.

The need to convey a positive vision of the future was also a powerful image in French intellectual resistance. In 1941 the French writer Jean-Paul Sartre – released from a German prison camp and inspired by his view that 'each writer is implicated in each era', each author 'measured his responsibility' to society – took a leading role in French intellectual resistance to the German occupation. His main aim was to convey to the French people that 'French sins' had not brought about a German victory and that, rather than dwell for ever on the mistakes of the past, they should turn their attention 'to the future that they were still free to shape'. This was the theme of his play, based on a Greek myth, *Les Mouches* ('The Flies').

Censorship in occupied France was strict, but not so strict as to prevent the publication of plays and books on classical and historical themes. Indeed, this tactic was also adopted in Germany to circumvent far harsher controls on censorship. As the editor of *Deutsche Rundschau*, one of the few Weimar publications which continued to be printed under the Nazi regime, explained: 'One criticized despots and crimes committed in all periods of history, illustrated with the figures of such tyrants of antiquity, Roman Caesars of the late Empire, Genghis Khan . . . and left the reader to draw the proper conclusions.'

In France and Italy there was also an underground press, with *Combat*, *L'Humanité* and *Les Lettres Françaises* clandestinely published in Paris. The editorial board of *Les Lettres Françaises* included such authors as Sartre, Edith Thomas, Jean Paulhan and Albert Camus. In 1943 its circulation was over 12,000 and its readership many times higher as the paper was secretly passed from hand to hand. In common with anti-fascist writers across Europe, and those in exile, the paper sought to formulate a set of moral ideals opposed to fascism. Many politically radical intellectuals rallied to the defence of traditional freedoms: freedom of expression, freedom of conscience and the defence of human dignity. The paper also denounced writers, such as Françoise Mauriac, editor of the prestigious *Nouvelle Revue Française*, who wrote in praise of their German occupiers.

There were other French authors who counselled not active physical and intellectual resistance but stoic self-respect expressed in stubborn silence. The French call for passive resistance – typified by Vercors's (Jean Bruller) novel, *La Silence de la Mer* ('The Silence of the Sea') – found echoes in the resistance writing of critics of Nazism who had remained in Germany after 1933. German poets and writers emphasized the notion that the German nation was a prisoner awaiting freedom that could only be earned through suffering. As Werner Bergenruen wrote:

> He who endures to the end
> is crowned most truly,
> No breadth of constancy is lost.[9]

For the most part, opportunities for intellectual resistance in Germany were extremely limited. Hundreds of prominent German writers, poets, scientists, artists and musicians had fled Germany for Switzerland, Britain, America or the USSR after 1933 and they played an important role in 'educating' opinion outside Germany. Thomas Mann broadcast to the German people from Geneva; his son, Klaus, published his memoirs and stories in the United States, as did their fellow artist and friend, the Austrian, Stefan Zweig. Life in exile was by no means easy. As Klaus Mann put it, 'in this world of nation states and nationalisms a man without a nation, a stateless person, has a difficult time'. Of those that remained, many employed their skills in the service of the Reich. Typical was the vision of party functionary and author Werner Beumelburg, who explained his mission to 'purify and shape the German destiny'. Nazi writers were also encouraged to write about military and heroic themes to stimulate wartime morale.

Nonetheless, in Italy, where Fascist censorship was never as strong as in Nazi Germany, the war marked an important turning point in intellectual resistance to fascism. The Second World War was unpopular in Italy from the outset. The number and output of resistance publications, such as the Milan-based *L'Unità*, increased after 1940, and paintings like Renato Guttuso's *Crucifixion* depicted the suffering and futility of war. A number of leading writers, notably Elio Vittorini, broke with their Fascist past to criticize both the management of the war effort and the moral character of the government.

The efforts of Italy's writers and artists did not receive much support from the Church of Rome until 1943. Until his Christmas message of 1942, which denounced 'state worship' and 'racialism', Pope Pius XII was comparatively silent on the impact of Fascist and Nazi policies in Europe. In 1940 the Pope allowed himself to be used as a secret channel of communication between German conspirators against Hitler and the British government in the hope that this would save lives. For the most part, all Christians believed that resistance to an immoral government must be passive. The Church of Rome was also mindful of temporal considerations – the threat of the Bolshevization of Europe and the risk of, first, Italian Fascists and, later, German soldiers, overrunning the Vatican. In 1944 Hitler threatened, 'I'm going to the Vatican right now. Do you think the Vatican bothers me? We'll grab it at once.'

Many local nuns, monks and churchmen, however, actively resisted their fascist governments and occupiers. Hitler hated Roman Catholics and despised Protestant pastors. He was determined to eliminate the influence of the Church once the war against Russia had been won because, as head of the Party Chancellery Martin Bormann argued, 'all influences that could impair, or even damage, the Führer's and the Party's rule must be eliminated'.

Bormann's warning to the 'Churches and their agents, the pastors' came after a number of vocal protests by Protestant and Catholic pastors against the party's euthanasia programme. Most famously, Bishop Clemens August von Galen, the Bishop of Münster, publicly denounced the euthanasia campaign as a 'violation of the fifth commandment', and filed a declaration to this effect with the police chief and the public prosecutor's office. This, amongst other complaints, helped to curtail the programme severely. There was no comparable protest about the murder of Jews.

Dietrich Bonhoeffer, a leading anti-Nazi Lutheran pastor, who chose to return to Germany from the United States of America in 1939, went further than many. He attempted to provide an intellectual and spiritual legitimation for active resistance in his writings, notably *Ethiks* ('Ethics', 1943). He was arrested in 1943 and executed in Buchenwald in 1945, but his example, perhaps more than any other, was important for postwar Germany as an instance of heroic resistance. The most significant contribution of many writers and artists came not during the war but after, in the powerful vision they presented of how society should be in the postwar era. It took more than ideas to defeat the armies of the Axis powers.

Allies on the offensive, 1943–45

Montgomery's victory at El Alamein effectively marked the beginning of Allied efforts to liberate western Europe. 'Operation Torch' was the largest amphibious landing so far, and between November and May 1943 the Germans and Italians were evicted completely from north Africa. The reconquest of Sicily and Italy followed. It took 58 days to prepare the Sicilian landings and 38 days to achieve success. It was another 17 days before the Italian mainland was attacked, but this difficult fighting produced important political results. In July 1943 the first Fascist Grand Council to convene since 1939 deposed Mussolini, and, in September 1943, the Italians made a separate peace. The Allied reconquest of Italy was by no means easy. Few Italian troops were like Private Angelo, hero of Eric Linklater's novel of the same name, who reflected, 'it has taken us a long time to lose the war, but thank heaven we have lost at last'. By December 1943 Allied troops were outside Cassino and it was only in December 1944 that they reached the Dolomite mountains.

Hitler retained a warm enough regard for his Italian ally to send German parachutists to release Mussolini from his mountain prison (13 October 1943) and reinstate him in the north in Gargano, but the psychological effect of Italy's withdrawal from the war was immense nevertheless. Unable to provide his people with an adequate explanation of why Italy was in the war, a shortcoming compounded by serious food, fuel and clothing shortages, Mussolini forfeited their support. The Allies squabbled over whether an Italian government should be led by Marshal Pietro Badoglio or dissident intellectual Carlo Sforza, and toyed with the notion of supporting the *Chetniks* in Yugoslavia, but in the end they decided to support Tito's partisans because they were killing more Germans. In Albania, too, the Communist resistance movement led by Colonel Enver Hoxha was triumphant over the Republican resistance, with important consequences for the character of that country's postwar government.

With Greece threatening to disintegrate into civil war at the beginning of 1944, it was clear that Germany would not be easily defeated via this route. American determination to launch an invasion through France remained

Plate 9.7 Dresden after the bombing. Bombed for 40 successive hours, little of the historic centre of one of Europe's most prized cities remained. Around 100,000 people are estimated to have died, although exact figures are hard to calculate since by that time the city was full of refugees fleeing from the Russians in the east.

undiminished. They angrily dismissed British fears of a second Passchendaele or Dunkirk, and pointed to the advancing Soviet armies in the east to illustrate the mobility of the war and the need for a Western Front in France. By the end of August 1943 the Red Army was pushing through Bulgaria, by December 1944 it had reached Yugoslavia and was advancing through Czechoslovakia, and by April 1945 the Eastern Front was in Königsberg and Pillau. Here the Soviet forces ran amok in an orgy of looting, rape and murder, and horror stories about the barbarous Red Army quickly spread.

Throughout the war Hitler and Stalin trumpeted that this great struggle was the supreme test of their respective political visions. In reality, however, the war tested the resilience of their economies, the skill of their military leaders (when they were allowed to do their job without the damaging interference of the dictators), and the willingness of every family to sacrifice its menfolk in battle, labour in war production, and to submit their homes and lives to enemy bombs.

The final stages of the war were accompanied by ever more numerous and terrifying bombing raids. To counter the failures of British bombing raids against Germany in 1940 and to prove the value of Bomber Command, Air Marshal ('Bomber') Arthur Harris began to advocate saturation bombing: filling the skies with over 1,000 aeroplanes at a time. Yet despite lavish claims, massive Allied bombing assaults failed to prevent increases in German industrial production during 1943–44. Nor did the terrible fire-bombing raids on Hamburg and Dresden (the latter described by Harris as 'more like firewood than human habitation') on the night of 13–14 February 1945 have much effect on German morale, although some historians now argue that Bomber Command's campaign against the German transport system in late 1944 did contribute significantly to the collapse of the German war economy and war effort. The populations of 'Allied Europe' endured their own share of bombing terror in the closing stages of the war from Hitler's 'secret weapons': the V1 and V2 rockets. These weapons came too late to have a significant impact in the war, although the 9,300 terrifying 'doodlebugs' which fell on England made a great impression on public morale.

American strategic attacks on the German aircraft industry, however, had a greater impact on their enemy and, like German rocketry, anticipated future military technology. Bombing cities only succeeded in taking life: 25,000 were reported dead, 35,000 missing after the Dresden attacks. Behind such statistics lay appalling human tragedy. A young German woman recorded in her diary the tragedy of an Allied raid on Berlin: a girl of 16

> was standing atop of a pile of rubble, picking up the bricks one by one, dusting them carefully and throwing them away again. Apparently her entire family was dead, buried underneath, and she had gone mad.

The dead citizens of Rotterdam, Hamburg, London, Coventry, Dresden, Warsaw and Berlin are prominent among those still remembered victims of enemy assaults. But other places, like Hull or Le Havres, suffered calamitously. Outside towns and cities mistargeted bombs fell at random while women farming in the field made good target practice for passing fighter aircraft.

The 'second front', which Stalin had demanded for so long, was launched at last on 6 June 1944 when the Allied forces, under the command of the American, General Eisenhower, landed at Normandy. Not all went according to plan. Allied landings on the Cotentin peninsula, for example, were a shambles, although this served to bemuse the Germans who were now entirely confused as to the Americans' true intent. Had the Germans reacted more effectively, the operation might have been disastrous for the Allies. As it was, however, Paris was liberated in less than three months (German General Dietrich von Choltitz disregarding Hitler's instructions to reduce the capital to 'a heap of rubble'). On 19 March Hitler issued his 'Nero order' instructing his troops to destroy everything in the path of the invader. The order was ignored and sabotaged by leading Nazis, including Speer. Nothing could now save Germany from inevitable defeat. In April 1945 the German troops in the Ruhr surrendered and, with Allied troops slowed down by the fanatical resistance of the SS in the Harz mountains, the Red Army reached Berlin first on 22 April 1945. Hitler and Eva Braun, whom the *Führer* married in the final days of the Reich, took their lives in their Berlin bunker on 30 April; and on 9 May 1945 Germany signed an unconditional surrender.

The world war continued long enough in the Far East for the 'conventional' weapons, as they came to be called, to be abandoned in the search for peace. These weapons paled in their horror when set against the work of project 'Manhattan' in the United States. The National Socialists had abandoned their work on a nuclear weapons in 1942, believing that it would not bring dividends in time to help to them win the war. American and British scientists, aided by émigrés from occupied Europe, pursued the quest and covertly developed their own 'secret weapon'. On 6 August 1945 the 'Enola Gay' dropped a 14 kiloton Uranium bomb on Hiroshima. The world had changed forever. Nuclear technology, first employed not in Europe but in Japan, now could destroy more than towns, cities and thousands of the population. Ultimately it could destroy the earth.

Allied relations 1943–45

With Germany defeated, tensions amongst the Allies, or the 'United Nations' as they had come to call themselves, burst out into the open. There had been some disagreement in Anglo-American relations over the conduct of the war, and especially over Britain's relations with its Empire, but these were nothing when set against the mounting frustrations in their relations with the Soviet Union. The mutual suspicion of the 1930s, greatly compounded by delay over the 'Second Front', the extent and character of the Soviet advance, and planning for the peace – particularly the vexed questions of what to do with Poland and Germany – was to replace the hot war which had ravaged Europe for 6 years with a Cold War which was to dominate political relationships for the next 45 years.

The Allies' wartime conferences at Casablanca (January 1943) and Teheran (November 1943) were genial affairs, and the Yalta Conference in February 1945, ominous in retrospect, at the time appeared little different. Yet compromises arrived at there were dearly bought. It was clear that Stalin would not contemplate any return to the 1939 Polish frontiers or any

future Polish government which was not dominated by communists. There were also divisions over the shape of the future United Nations Organization, the new peacemaking agency which, it was hoped, would prevent any future war from breaking out. Frustration with the outcome of the Yalta Conference soon set in as it became apparent that the world's balance of power had shifted drastically in favour of the Soviet Union. It was now beyond doubt the greatest power in Europe.

Tension amongst the 'United Nations' were not eased when Japan unconditionally surrendered on 14 August 1945 after the Soviet Union had declared war on Japan on 8 August. Atomic bombs on Hiroshima and Nagasaki had sealed the fate of the Japanese Empire, and as one senior American recorded: 'the relief to everyone concerned when the bomb was finished and dropped was enormous'. But such relief as there was was short-lived. The last of the great wartime United Nations Conferences took place at Potsdam (July–August 1945), a short distance away from the ruined shell of Berlin. It was a very different conference from Teheran or Yalta, however. Of the great wartime leaders only Stalin (along with Chiang Kai-Shek) remained. Churchill had been replaced by Attlee, while Roosevelt's death had brought Harry S. Truman to the White House, and these new leaders now joined Stalin to discuss the perilous future of the world. Britain, Germany and France had been instrumental in causing two 'hot' wars which helped shape the twentieth century, yet they merely provided the stage for the Cold War. The principal actors in international affairs were now the Soviet Union and the United States, the former denied the secrets of 'the Bomb' and excluded from the (exclusively) American occupation of Japan.

The origins of the Cold War followed fast in the footsteps of the Second World War. It was not an 'inevitable' development any more than the Second World War was the 'inevitable' consequence of the First, although it is difficult to see how East–West relations could have been anything other than troubled. The two world wars of the twentieth century began within 25 years of one another, and if the Cold War is included, Europe endured over 54 years of 'world war' in the twentieth century. But historians have, on the whole, eschewed the temptation to treat the two world wars as sequential chapters in one story.

The two world wars were different in their causes, origins and consequences. Kaiser Wilhelm II represented 'traditional' authority and policies, like the Romanovs of Russia and Habsburgs in Austria: Adolf Hitler's 'expansionism' was rooted in National Socialist thought, a

Plate 9.8 Meeting of the Big Three at the Teheran Summit, December 1943.
Stalin, Roosevelt and Churchill, flanked by Foreign Minister Vlachyslav Molotov (at Stalin's right shoulder) and Foreign Secretary Anthony Eden (at Churchill's left). The Teheran Conference demonstrated how the balance of global power was shifting away from Britain and towards the Soviet Union, with American power pre-eminent.

confused but heady ideology, ushering in what Winston Churchill called 'a new Dark Age, made more sinister, and perhaps more protracted, by the lights of perverted science'. Although the origins of the Second World War can be fully understood only if the diplomacy of other countries, besides Germany, is taken into account, German diplomacy can only be understood if National Socialist ideology, strategy and economics are brought into the picture. Hitler's foreign policy sprang from more than a desire to overturn the 'shame' of Versailles.

The Second World War proved not to be complete in itself. Post-1945 history, very different from the history of the interwar years, is inextricably related to the history of what happened between 1939–45. There was no peace settlement as there had been in 1919, nor was there any sense even of the provisional assurance of peace, despite the conditional surrender of the main defeated powers – Germany, Japan and Italy – and the creation of a new United Nations organization with far more power at its disposal than the old League of Nations. Significantly it was to have its headquarters not in Europe but in New York. In the postwar world, the word 'global' was to acquire new significance – global issues, global problems and, not least, global weapons which presented 'mankind' (a term increasingly in use) with a new set of choices and calculations about 'balance', deterrence, terror and power.

References

1.   Quoted in R. J. Overy, *War and Economy in the Third Reich* (Oxford, 1994) p. 185.
2.   Quoted in R. J. Overy, *The Road to War* (1989) p. 45
3.   R. Dell, *The Geneva Racket* (1941) p. 8.
4.   D. C. Watt, *How War Came* (1989) p. 536.
5.   W. S. Churchill, *The Second World War: The Grand Alliance*, vol. III (1951) p. 308.
6.   W. S. Churchill, *The Second World War: The Hinge of Fate*, vol. IV (1951) p. 343.
7.   K. S. Karol, *Solik: Life in the Soviet Union, 1939–1946* (1986) p. 76.
8.   M. von der Grün, *Wie war das eigentlich? Kindheit und Jungend im Dritten Reich* (Darmstadt, 1981) pp. 236–7.
9.   W. Bergenruen, 'An die Völker der Erde', in W. Rose (ed.), *Modern German Lyric Verse*, 1986–1955 (Oxford, 1960) p. 185.

Chapter 10

Freezing and Thawing in Postwar Europe, 1945–1989

For the people of Moscow peace officially began at 2 a.m. on the morning of 8 May 1945 when a salvo of a thousand guns was sounded. Some citizens cheered while others sobbed, recalling the loved ones who would never return. In London's Trafalgar Square crowds lit fireworks, sang songs and embraced, and beneath the Arc de Triomphe General de Gaulle solemnly saluted the tomb of the unknown soldier before euphoric men and women swept away the barriers surrounding the tomb in enthusiastic celebration. In Germany, by contrast, news of the defeat was met in dumb, apathetic silence, despite Allied fears that zealous young soldiers would be reluctant to surrender arms.

For all of Europe, however, it did not take long for the pleasure of victory to be replaced by sobering recognition of the price to be paid by victors and vanquished alike. 'This noble continent', Winston Churchill proclaimed in neutral Switzerland in 1946, contained 'a vast quivering mass of tormented, hungry, care-worn and bewildered human beings' gaping at the ruins of their cities and scanning 'the dark horizons for the approach of some new peril, tyranny or terror'.

The damage of war

The Second World War had far outstripped its predecessor in the loss of life and property. This time, Britain and France had suffered less than in the First World War, with 260,000 and 620,000 victims respectively, but in central and eastern Europe the loss of life had been enormous. Civilian deaths far outnumbered those of military personnel. Soviet losses were estimated at 20 million lives, while relative death tolls in Poland, Yugoslavia and Germany were even higher. Poland had sacrificed over six million men and women, Yugoslavia had sacrificed 1.7 million and Germany more than five million men and women. More than half of all livestock in Poland and Yugoslavia was destroyed and eastern Europe's transportation network lay in ruins. Looting by the retreating Nazis and advancing Red Army also cost eastern Europe dear.

The total size of German looting was estimated at around $20–25 billion, while Soviet looting, under the guise of 'justifiable reparations', was especially ruthless in European territories which had been allied to the Axis powers – Bulgaria, Hungary and Romania. It was Soviet-occupied East Germany, however, which suffered the most. As Charles Kindleberger, an American economist working for the reparations commission, recalled, while 'the United States was feeding its zone, and the British were feeding their zone as best they could. . . . [The] Russians were looting their zone. It was really like a cow with the mouth in one zone and the udder in the other.'

There was also physical destruction on a breathtaking scale. A mobile, mechanized war had been fought across Poland, Yugoslavia, Russia, Greece, Italy, northern France, Belgium, the Netherlands and Germany, and heavy bombing had brought immense damage to almost every major European conurbation. Cities like Coventry, Rotterdam and Warsaw had only one commodity in plentiful supply in 1945: rubble, the piles of which could be measured in acres or mountains, and buried beneath the rubble were homes, schools, churches, hospitals, factories, shops and stations. For those living in the cities, eking out an existence amidst severe food and clothing shortages, the peace first brought further misery before it alleviated conditions. For many, the lack of adequate shelter was the greatest hardship of all. In Düsseldorf, for example, it was estimated that 93 per cent of dwellings were uninhabitable and Europe's urban housing shortage became acute with the approach of winter.

A river of refugees

Around 50 million people had been expelled from their homes by the advancing armies, particularly those of the Soviet Union, and the search for shelter quickly entailed the greatest migration Europe had known for 1,500 years. Refugees fled in many directions, although the predominant flow was from east to west. Prisoners and forced labour seized by the National Socialists also began to stream from Germany once hostilities ceased. This group were known as Displaced Persons (DPs), waiting to be repatriated or to be given an immigration permit to begin a new life overseas.

According to Allied estimates there were at least 25 million DPs from all over Europe in 1945, with the largest groups coming from the Soviet Union, France, Poland, the Netherlands, Belgium, Italy and Yugoslavia. Their shelter was often temporary and primitive, and their food supplies meagre; some DPs were even placed in Dachau, a former concentration camp converted to house refugees. 'Why is it I smell all the time, wherever

Plate 10.1   An open air meal for refugees. The Wickels family from Poland enjoy a respite at the Mercallo refugee camp in Piedmont, Italy. Father Wickel is on the extreme right. Alongside are his children – Otto, Anna and Irene. Refugees were scattered throughout Europe in 1945 and 1946.

I turn, the reek of the Displaced Persons' Camp?', asked English novelist Evelyn Waugh in his diary of November 1946.

For others, like ethnic Germans (*Volksdeutsche*) resident in eastern Europe since the thirteenth century, peace brought an end to a migration which had begun with a move to Germany in 1939–40, then on to Poland in 1941, only to be evacuated again once the Nazi dream of an eastern European empire evaporated in the face of the Red Army's advance. But the process of repatriation was not simple. Ukrainians and Latvians who had fought against the Red Army dared not return home (some were forced to go back anyway), and thousands of Jews sought to flee Europe, although the Jewish refugee ship, *Exodus*, laden with emaciated survivors of the death camps, ignominiously was unable to find safe harbour in Palestine or Europe.

Agreements signed between the Soviet Union and nations in Eastern Europe prompted further waves of migration, as regions like northern Czechoslovakia, southern Bohemia and Moravia, once inhabited by three million Sudeten Germans, were now populated by Czechs and Slovaks. In February 1946 Czechoslovakia and Hungary signed an agreement which sanctioned the compulsory transfer of 200,000 Magyars out of Czechoslovakia into Hungary and 200,000 Slovaks out of Hungary into Czechoslovakia. Particularly tragic was the fate of Poles living to the east of the Ribbentrop-Molotov line – the portion of Poland absorbed into the Soviet Union in 1939. Stalin made no secret of his intention to control this territory, and despite Churchill and Roosevelt's best efforts at Yalta to protect the four million Poles living there, Stalin forcibly resettled over two million of them into western Poland by 1950.

Added to the struggle for shelter came the struggle for food. In 1946 over 100 million people in Europe were still sustained by a diet of only 1,500 calories a day (a calorific level which would guarantee weight loss for healthy Europeans today), and only 900–1,000 calories were allocated to Germans within British and American zones of occupation. Food shortages continued long after the fighting had ceased as crops went unplanted, unharvested or undistributed, shortages which were greatly exacerbated by the terrible winter of 1946–47. It would take time for Europe's agriculture and industry to recover; even after the immediate physical shortages and transportation bottlenecks were cleared, Europe's overriding difficulty rapidly became earning sufficient foreign exchange to pay for food and other essential imports.

For the nations of Europe, which had long taken pride in their export industries, the war had caused substantial disruption. For fledgling postwar governments, troubled by inflation and widespread destruction, the need to revive international trade became imperative. As during the First World War, it was the American economy which had profited from Europe's warmongering. Britain's export trade in the aftermath of war, for example, had fallen to 25–30 per cent of its pre-war level and some countries in eastern Europe were unable to produce any exports at all.

The legacy of resistance and collaboration

In Germany, 1945 was marked as *Das Jahr Null* (the Year Zero) and the situation was critical: trains had ceased to run, banks were closed, there was no coal and hence no electric light, and there was little food. Europe was in no position to pay for its provisions, but Germans still needed to eat. Early relief efforts in Europe were managed by the United Nations Relief and Rehabilitation Administration (UNRAA), set up in 1943 to provide food, fuel, clothing, shelter and other basic necessities. But UNRRA quickly found its resources stretched. In August 1945 the Soviet Union applied for $700 million to launch relief operations, but had to be content with $250 million for the two devastated republics of Byelorussia and the Ukraine. At the height of its far-flung activities UNRAA, a product of wartime cooperation, employed around 25,000 people outside as well as inside Europe. But by 1947 Europe's inability to pay for its food was to provoke an international crisis which had important and far-reaching consequences for both diplomatic relations between European powers and for their links with the two 'superpowers' which now straddled the globe: the United States and the USSR.

In 1945 many well dressed and well fed American observers regarded European politicians and, indeed, European politics as morally bankrupt – a view shared by the Soviet Union. If the slaughter of the First World War had undermined Europe's confident belief in human progress, the Second World War eroded any vestiges of the implicit belief in Europe's moral superiority. In former German-occupied territories, the 'criminals' were the 'collaborationists', men and women who had worked for the Germans and their allies during the war: chief amongst them was Marshal Pétain, the 84-year-old 'supreme patriot' who assumed control of Vichy France and helped to create a corrupt, authoritarian state centred on his personal authority (official Vichy documents began: *Nous, Philippe Pétain, chef de l'État*).

The suspicion and iniquity which Vichy encouraged (so movingly recounted in François Maspero's novel *Cat's Grin*), had prompted around three to five million Frenchmen and women to denounce members of their town, village and even family. Now this was overtaken by a desire to punish the 'collaborators'. It is important not to exaggerate the degree of either collaboration or of resistance in France. While it is true that in some regions – notably the Dordogne – resistance leaders took matters into their own hands, the French liberation government sanctioned only 746 executions after trial. There were, however, around 9,000 summary executions – rumours at the time put the figure closer to 100,000.

Inside Germany the trials of Nazi war criminals, which began in November 1945, were of a different order. Intended as part of a de-Nazification process, the trials reminded all Europeans, not just the

Plate 10.2 The Nuremberg Trials, Summer 1945. Under the auspices of the
Nuremberg trials, the murder trial of the camp guards of the Bergen-Belsen
concentration camp was held in Court Room 30, Lindenstrasse in Lüneburg in
September 1945. The prosecution, conviction and hanging of notorious women
guards, like Juana Bormann (No.6), Elizabeth Volkenrath (No.7) and Herta Ehlert
(No.8), challenged contemporary sexual stereotyping which held that women were
normally incapable of violent and barbaric crime.

Germans, of the depths to which humanity could sink. Typical amongst the
prosecution evidence in Nuremberg were excerpts from SS General
Stroop's report on the razing of Warsaw:

> I . . . decided to destroy the entire Jewish residential area by setting every block
> on fire. . . . Not infrequently, the Jews stayed in the burning buildings until,
> because of the heat and the fear of being burned alive, they preferred to jump
> down from the upper stories. . . . With their bones broken, they still tried to crawl
> across the street into blocks of buildings which had not yet been set on fire.[1]

Many Germans felt shame, horror and anger when they contemplated their
former Nazi leaders, but they were also anxious to press on with the task
of reconstruction, and took little interest in the trials. Germany's stunned,
dazed population spent its days trying to find food, clothing, shelter, and
posting messages to bombed-out buildings in efforts to be reunited with
other family members. Reminders of Germany's inglorious past were
unwelcome: war veterans, especially the wounded, were unable to find
work when they returned home, while former concentration camp inmates
were shunned. Such bitter suspicion was not confined to local

communities. It found a parallel in the mounting ill will and division between East and West in international relations.

The origins of the Cold War: the view from the West, 1945–47

If the Cold War began with the deliberate Soviet decision to cut Europe in two, equally momentous was the decision by the Western powers to extend the division of Germany after 1945. The question of what to do with Germany had exercised the Americans, in particular, during the course of the war. Indeed, complaints were even voiced within Roosevelt's administration that too much attention was being devoted to planning for the peace, too little on waging the war. In 1944 the most influential proposal was that of Henry Morgenthau Jr, Secretary of State to the US Treasury, who proposed that the world impose a punitive peace on Germany: it should be turned into a 'pastoral' country, with industrial assets like the *Kohlenpot* (coalpot) of the Ruhr given to France.

This was the kind of retributive peace which dominated the Allies' seizure of reparations from Germany during the war to 'liberate' Europe, with France and the USSR especially keen to extract recompense for German aggression. Like Stalin's, General de Gaulle's strategy was designed to weaken Germany fundamentally by destroying all trace of centralized government, and he blocked attempts by the Allied council to treat Germany as whole. To some extent this reflected the different war experiences of France and the USSR compared with those of their 'Anglo-Saxon' allies, but it was also a product of French and Russian attitudes to German history and the rise of Nazism. Thus, the four zones of military occupation soon became four distinct political units, each reflecting the political identity of its occupier.

By the end of 1945 peace settlements which threatened to debilitate Germany had been abandoned in favour of policies which increasingly placed the British, American and French zones of Germany at the heart of western Europe's defence. Rather as in the 1930s, the capitalist governments of western Europe and the United States feared that economic deprivation, rather than direct Soviet aggression, would be sufficient to see all western Europe engulfed by communism. Their fears appeared to be supported by the early success of communist parties in France, Italy and Greece. Once the Allies, democratic and communist alike, had reeled in horror at the discovery of the concentration camps and were determined to enforce a policy of non-fraternization with the Germans. Now the need to manage Germany's mounting economic problems initiated a new response from the Western Allies.

While the State Department in Washington received exaggerated reports of the expansionist ambitions of the USSR – amongst the most famous and

Plate 10.3 German civilians at Buchenwald Concentration Camp, Summer 1945.
As part of the Allied effort to de-Nazify Germany, civilians from Weimar –
predominately women, as the men were still returning from the battle-front – were
escorted by military police to Buchenwald to get a taste of the magnitude of
Germany's war crimes. As they walked around the camp in hundreds, many wept
and some fainted at the sight of charred human remains and emaciated survivors.

influential being the so-called 'Long Telegram' of George Kennan, coun-
sellor to the US Embassy in Moscow – conditions within Europe continued to
deteriorate. Reconstruction loans granted by the new economic institutions
set up at Bretton Woods in 1945 – the International Monetary Fund and the
International Bank for Reconstruction and Development (the World Bank) –
proved hopelessly inadequate. UNRAA, too, was unable to satisfy Europe's
desperate need for dollars to buy food and other essentials and by the time
the foreign ministers of Germany's occupying powers met in March 1946,
the Anglo-Americans and the Soviets were beginning to evolve largely
incompatible plans. At this meeting, the disparate approaches of East and
West were obvious, especially since the USSR and USA had begun to
appeal directly to the German people for support against the other: the
USSR offering a workers' republic; the USA offering a federal, liberal
government to prepare for economic resuscitation.

It was in February 1946, too, that Churchill, in opposition, pre-empted the West's future hostility to the Soviet colossus, in his famous 'iron curtain' speech made in Fulton, Missouri:

> From Stettin in the Baltic to Trieste in the Adriatic, an iron curtain has descended across the continent. . . . [Moreover], in a great many countries, far from the Russian frontiers and throughout the world, Communist fifth columns are established and at work in complete unity and absolute obedience with the Communist centre.[2]

Churchill's words were condemned by Stalin in *Pravda* as a 'dangerous, calculated move' and his argument did not yet appeal to many Americans. There were many who suspected that Churchill's 'scaremongering' was born of Britain's desire to keep America involved in Europe. There were many in the US administration who still advocated sharing atomic technology with the Soviet Union, or who urged greater conciliation between East and West believing that the increase in international tension would harm world prosperity, and fearing that 'the tougher we get, the tougher the Soviets will get'. Typical was the influential journalist Walter Lippmann, who argued that the doomladen prophesies of Soviet expansionism were grossly exaggerated and that a political settlement for central and eastern Europe should be possible. In 1947 Lippmann's articles were published together in a book entitled *The Cold War* (September 1947), a term which quickly made its way into the world's political vocabulary.[3]

Throughout 1946, there was no further progress on the still unresolved issue of how to treat defeated Germany. For US Secretary of State James Byrnes, the one achievement of countless meetings with his Soviet counterpart, Molotov, was to establish that the latter thought American whisky as good as Russian vodka. The British Foreign Secretary, Ernest Bevin, too, had grown equally impatient with the Soviet Union. Much to the annoyance of the large British minority, which included many members of the Labour Party – who wanted a more independent, less pro-American-orientated policy – Bevin was determined to place the blame for dis-agreement on the Kremlin and, in a display of unity with the Conservative Party, he joined Churchill before Parliament in calling the Soviet Union the main obstacle to peace and stability.

The need to ameliorate conditions in Germany while at the same time lightening the aid burden on taxpayers in Britain, France and the United States was a further incentive to a speedy resolution of the German issue. Administering Germany in separate zones was costly and trade between the different zones was handled as if it were trade between different states. In June 1946 the Americans suggested that the other occupying forces merge the zonal economies, but only the British accepted and a joint administration of the two zones, dubbed 'Bizonia', was in place by the end of the year. Nonetheless, the drain on the British Treasury carried on. Britain continued, until March 1947, to honour its commitment to supply anti-communist rebels in Greece, but was also called upon to deal with troubles in India and Palestine

From 1945 until 1947 western European and American politicians were increasingly convinced that, in Kennan's words, the 'traditional and instinctive sense of Russian insecurity' made inevitable 'both Soviet domination of Eastern Europe and communist ambitions over the remainder of the world'. Yet few people in 1945 and 1946 recognized that the growing hostility between the East and West would generate a 'Cold War' which would envelop the globe for 45 years. When in September 1946 Byrnes announced that 'we favour the economic unification of Germany' and that if complete unification could not be secured, 'we shall do everything in our power to secure the maximum possible unification', this meant uniting the three western zones of Germany and creating a liberal democratic government in the image of the victorious western powers. In effect this permanently isolated the Soviet zone.

The view from the East, 1944–46

In the west it was the evolution of the desperate conditions inside Germany and mounting unease about Soviet intentions amongst the Western allies which increased the tension in East-West relations. In the East wartime developments helped Stalin's ambition to transform eastern Europe into a pro-communist security zone for the Soviet Union. For many people in Europe, communism was identified as a liberating, idealist creed, untainted by associations with the crisis of capitalism and liberal democracy in the 1930s, or with the barbarity of fascism in the 1940s. Indeed, many future communist leaders – like the German Erich Honecker (1971–89) and the Czech Gustáv Husák (1969–88) – had impressive anti-fascist credentials, having spent long years in fascist prisons. The extension of state control during the war also appeared to make communist-style government an appropriate choice for the massive effort of reconstruction which eastern Europe would need once the war was over.

Although the application of Stalin's policies in Europe appeared inconsistent, his aim was not. He was determined to establish as much of a security zone as possible for the USSR in eastern Europe without provoking America, giving the Soviet Union time to 'catch up' with its rival superpower. Stalin did not establish Soviet control in eastern Europe simply by right of conquest in 1945, but step by step, in response to political developments within each eastern European country and international events. By 1948 he was in exclusive control of most of eastern Europe.

When in the last year of the war armed communist partisans, supported by popular front political movements, appeared capable of bringing communist revolution to both eastern and western Europe, Stalin had responded with caution: he did not wish to alienate his western allies and urged communist partisans from the Balkans to France to abandon talk of popular communist governments 'from below', and instead accept proposals to join postwar coalition governments as partners, sometimes even junior partners. Communists in France, Italy and, with considerable reluctance, in Greece did as they were told. But there were limits to his influence, for already a popular communist revolution 'from below' in Yugoslavia, led by Tito, had gone too far for Stalin to stop.

Europe's experience of democratic government in the interwar period had been brief and desultory, but Stalin was by no means confident that all these nations would make a successful transition to communism. There was a clear distinction between countries like Poland, Romania and Bulgaria, which Stalin placed under effective Soviet control from the moment the Red Army crossed their borders, and countries like Hungary and Czechoslovakia where the Soviet Union was content, at first, to allow the communists to have influence (but not complete control) in coalition governments.

Once again, as in the nineteenth century and during the Russian Civil War, Poland threatened Russia's strategic plans. The Polish people presented a sizeable obstacle to Stalin's determined effort to guarantee Soviet security. Their historic hostility towards Russia, their vibrant Catholicism, the opinions expressed by their vociferous government in exile and the public knowledge that it was Soviet soldiers who had murdered 15,000 Polish officers in the Katyn forest in 1943 stood in the way. Even Poland's communists had a tradition of opposition to the Moscow line which first began with Rosa Luxemburg; and in July 1944 Moscow acted decisively to ensure that political developments in Poland fell in their favour. In July 1944 the Lublin Committee, a communist-dominated group of Polish leaders drawn from the Polish resistance movement and subsequently groomed in Moscow, was established in Warsaw as the government of Poland in order to frustrate the aspirations of the London Poles who had conducted the fight against the Germans from exile. But this was not enough to ensure Soviet control. Here, as in Bulgaria and Romania in 1945, the intervention of the Red Army was decisive.

In Czechoslovakia and Hungary, however, where at the end of the war the communists dominated the resistance movement and might have seized power immediately, there was a time-lapse before they took over. Stalin, Churchill and Roosevelt had agreed in 1943 that coalition governments should be established across Europe in the aftermath of war, and Stalin ordered Czech and Hungarian communists to participate in 'popular front' governments as he had ordered communists to do in the west. There was one important difference, however, in the instructions that he gave to communists in eastern Europe and their comrades in the west. In Czechoslovakia and Hungary communist militas were not disbanded

and they soon became the basis of communist army and security units. It was a further source of strength that they carefully took control of the powerful Interior Ministries.

Klement Gottwald, the Czechoslovakian communist leader, obediently followed Stalin's instructions. Far from immediately asserting control over the 'national revolutionary committees' which had sprung up across Czechoslovakia, he sought instead to broaden the membership of these committees in 1945, bringing in other political parties. Meanwhile, Edvard Beneš, the Czechoslovak leader who had been exiled in London during the Nazi occupation, continued to have an influential voice in Czechoslovakian politics. In May 1946 free elections were held and the communists won 38 per cent of the vote while the socialists secured a total of 51 per cent. This was a clear signal that the communists would not acquire decisive political power through the ballot box, but still under Gottwald, they did not push for power.

Hungary was more vulnerable to a communist take-over as a defeated Axis power, but even there Stalin acted swiftly in 1945 to stop Hungarian communists from openly proclaiming that the 'dictatorship of the proletariat' was nigh. So Hungary, too, had elections in 1945. The communists and socialists achieved similar levels of support, but when the peasant-dominated Smallholders Party secured 50 per cent of the vote for themselves, it was the Allies who made it clear that they preferred the stability offered by a coalition government. The communists were quick to seize the advantage and in 1946 secured control of the Interior Ministry and exploited the growing conflict between the left bloc of socialists and communists on the one hand and the Smallholders Party on the other. The result was that on New Year's Eve in 1946, the Smallholders Party resigned from government amid accusations that some of their senior leaders were involved in an extensive anti-republican conspiracy. Having attacked conservative and centrist political groups with charges of 'anti-Sovietism' and 'pro-fascism' and driven them from government by what the Hungarian communist leader, Mátyás Rákosi, later called 'salami tactics', it was now the turn of socialists to be cut off from power.

The same tactics had earlier been used in Bulgaria and Romania, where there were fewer reasons to move cautiously. The much proclaimed popular front governments of eastern Europe thus became caricatures of democracy – hiding behind their self-proclaimed status as 'People's Democracies' – as the communists exploited their control not only of the Interior Ministries, but of the machinery of propaganda.

Plate 10.4 Communists marching in Bulgaria. The transition of Eastern Europe to communism was most easily achieved in Bulgaria. People there were friendly towards Russia and had never declared war on the Soviet Union. There was indeed a strong sense of solidarity. Notice the two armed women marching in the front rank of the brigade: only in the Red Army did women bear arms.

The Marshall plan, 1947

Events in Western Europe encouraged Stalin to fortify the position of the communists in eastern Europe. By early 1947 the twin issues of a German peace treaty and economic unification became crucial as conditions across Europe continued to deteriorate. The winter of 1946–47, which had killed winter wheat and washed away resown seeds in the spring floods, seriously disrupted rail and road transport, affecting victors and vanquished alike. When the World Bank and International Monetary Fund opened their doors in the spring of 1947, it was France which quickly borrowed to the hilt from both institutions, although neither had been created for such an eventuality. In Germany miners in the Ruhr were so hungry that, in the cold, already dwindling levels of coal production further declined.

At the depth of the winter, in February 1947, the British, themselves among the sufferers, informed the United States that they could no longer continue to provide assistance to the Greek and Turkish governments and urged the American government to help. Desperate times required radical measures, and they seemed to come when President Truman announced (it became known as the 'Truman doctrine') that 'it must be the policy of the United States to support free peoples who are resisting attempted subjugation by armed minorities or by outside pressures. . . . If we falter in our leadership, we may endanger the peace of the world.' Washington was becoming convinced that the communist cancer was spreading, feeding on poverty and despair, and that America should act to 'contain' this menace.

The winter was over when, on 5 June 1947, a speech by Truman's Secretary of State, George Marshall, announced an extensive recovery plan to haul Europe to its feet. A massive aid package was offered to all European powers who were having great difficulty recovering from the war, particularly after the harsh winter of 1946–47. Congress and the American people gave the plan unprecedented support, although their approval was predicated, in part, on the fact that the Marshall plan embodied a longstanding tenet of American foreign policy: economic stability helps secure democracy. Self-interest also played its part. As both Truman and Marshall made clear, America's economic well-being was dependent upon the health of the European markets. The Marshall plan was a bold and imaginative declaration, far more than what an American economist, Charles Kindleberger, was to call an experiment costing $17 billion 'to test the theory about the relationships between economic dislocation and political behaviour'. Historians now argue that the confidence which Marshall aid injected into western Europe, and the impact of the Korean War (1950–53), were more significant to European recovery than simply the injection of American dollars.

The Soviet Union disliked both the character and the intent of the plan in 1947 and (as the West had calculated) refused to participate. Although the Eastern European countries were desperate for economic assistance and both Czechoslovakia and Poland quickly assented to Marshall aid, they were forced by the Soviet Union to withdraw. Relations worsened when Eastern bloc communists, along with communists from France and Italy who in their own countries had been marginalized from political power, were summoned to a meeting in Poland, where they were presented with the Kremlin's vision of a world which had 'repudiated the principles of international cooperation' and was now divided into two camps. In articulating this vision, the Soviets, of course, helped to make it a reality.

Czechoslovakia, 1948

Europe's future now hinged on Czechoslovakia, the only country in central Europe which at the end of 1947 had a genuine coalition government. To many people in the West it seemed like a bridge, democratic but within the Russian security zone, but the democracy was not to last long. Disagreements between the socialists and communists had grown increasingly acrimonious throughout 1947 (tension was also rife among the communists); and in February 1948, in a bitter dispute over rates of pay for civil servants, ministers from the Slovak Democratic People's Party, the People's Party and the National Socialist Party all resigned from the government. It was a grave tactical error. The Communists promptly called a number of large public meetings and set up Action Committees across Czechoslovakia to demonstrate popular support for communism.

By March 1948, the cabinet was entirely Communist, apart from Jan Masaryk, Czechoslovakia's Foreign minister and son of the founding President of Czechoslovakia, and even this semblance of political diversity did not last long. On 10 March 1948 he and a cabinet colleague were found dead after an apparent 'fall' from a high window. The deaths shocked the West which immediately concluded that Masaryk had been pushed (the resonances of the 1648 defenestration of Habsburg officials in Prague offered tempting 'proof'), and furthered soured relations between East and West. In the aftermath of the coup all Czechoslovak political parties, including the Slovak Communist Party, were amalgamated within the Czech Communist Party. From February 1948 Czechoslovakia, like all the other countries of what was beginning to be thought of as an 'Eastern bloc', was now under one-party rule.

The Berlin blockade, 1948–49

Ideological difference was obvious in the new alignment, and the attempt to find practical, effective solutions to Europe's problems was made more difficult. Nowhere was this more apparent than over the question of

German currency reform in 1947–48. The western powers had delayed as long as possible over the issue of monetary reform, recognizing its powerful political and economic implications: a Western-supported currency introduced into the trizonal area would create a completely separate economy from that of the Soviet zone, simultaneously undermining the value of the currency in the eastern zone and, most important, contravening the agreement to treat all four German zones as a single economic unit. But with relations worsening between East and West, and with the imminent introduction of Marshall aid, something had to be done. It was sudden and in secret. A new German mark was printed and introduced into Trizonia without warning in June 1948.

The result was a dramatic escalation in Cold War tensions. On 23 June 1948, in protest at what amounted to the creation of 'West' Germany, the Soviets began to blockade Berlin, a city which was divided into four occupied zones but which lay deep within the Soviet zone. Stalin's action was typically ham-fisted. Rather than make the West more conciliatory, Stalin's blockade only served to convince those who had doubted alarmist prophesies of Soviet expansion and to hasten the creation of a West German Federal Republic. In a dramatic and resolute initiative, the Allies airlifted supplies to over two million stranded Berliners until May 1949 when the Soviet Union called off its blockade. British Air Commodore Fred Rainsford reflected on the irony of the operation: 'it was very odd that people like myself, who had been bombing Berlin a few years earlier, should now be intent . . . on keeping it alive'.

An end to diversity: eastern Europe, 1948–50

Stalin's vicelike grip over eastern Europe tightened as relations between East and West deteriorated, and in 1948 the Cold War received new impetus from an unexpected quarter – the growing rift between Stalin and Tito. Until January 1948 Belgrade and Moscow had enjoyed good relations, although Stalin had disagreed with Tito's strategy of advancing communism 'from below' with widespread, popular support. The new Communist Information Bureau (Cominform), established in September 1947 and designed to aid communism in eastern Europe and to impose some kind of ideological uniformity on the region, had its headquarters in Belgrade. Yugoslavia had pressed full ahead with the implementation of a Soviet-style economy, collectivizing agriculture as early as July 1946, and introducing its First Five Year Plan in April 1947. Throughout 1947 Tito actively promoted communism in eastern Europe, including Greece, and bolstered his reputation further with a number of commercial treaties with Bulgaria, Hungary and Romania, raising the stakes in January 1948 by stationing Yugoslav troops in Albania to help defend Greek communist bases. He did this, however, without the approval of Stalin who increasingly perceived Tito's independence as a threat to his authority. Tito publicly proclaimed that he looked forward to the creation of a Balkan federation of 'free Balkan peoples'. Such ambition was too much for Stalin and he could tolerate Tito's independence no longer. As Tito told the British in 1950, 'the Russians are [not] prepared to accept anybody who is keeping a relationship with the other side . . . you have to be 100 per cent on their side'.

The consequences of the Tito-Stalin split were dramatic. The Soviet leader accused Tito and the Yugoslav Communist Party of operating semi-illegally, of failing to collectivize agriculture and, most significantly, of diminishing the status of the Communist Party. On 28 June 1948 Yugoslavia was expelled from the Cominform. Nor was that the end. By 1950 Stalin was contemplating a joint Soviet and eastern European military action against Yugoslavia. He knew that he could count on the 'bloc'. Major General Béla Király of the Hungarian Army made it clear, for example, that 'at the pleasure of Stalin, we would have marched against Yugoslavia'. The Yugoslavian republic was saved from this fate by the outbreak of the Korean War which diverted Stalin's attention to the most eastern tip of his empire.

For Tito, the outcome of the split was not all bad. He was able to press ahead with his conception of a planned economy and to improve Yugoslavian relations with the West, especially with the United States, and in July 1948 frozen Yugoslavian assets in America, including over $47 million in gold, were liberated. Yet the impact of the Tito-Stalin split was not confined to Soviet-Yugoslav relations. The allegations levelled against Tito were soon taken up elsewhere to ensure that communist parties would be loyal to Stalin. Allegations of 'Titoism' provided the grounds for purges which cost Władysław Gomułka his post as Communist Party leader in Poland, and in a spectacular show trial in Hungary, a former leader of the Hungarian Communist Party and cabinet minister, László Rajk, confessed to spying for the Nazis, the United States, Britain *and* Tito. He and his 'accomplices' were executed on 15 October 1949. Rajk's conviction subsequently became the justification for all Eastern European countries to break diplomatic relations with Yugoslavia.

In Czechoslovakia purges concentrated on suspected pro-Titoists and communists who had spent the war exiled in London. The trials quickly snowballed, culminating in the trial of the 'Moscow communist' and former party leader Rudolf Slánský in 1951 (the anti-semitic flavour of this purge reflected similar developments inside the USSR at this time), and in a sustained attack on the Catholic Church which was to span many years. In Albania and Bulgaria, by contrast, the determination of some communists to root out their pro-Tito comrades was not, on the whole, motivated by an unflinching loyalty to Stalin but by longstanding, ethnic and national rivalries.

Nationalism and communism, 1948–56

In July 1946 Albania and Yugoslavia had signed a treaty of friendship, cooperation and mutual aid which, in practice, made communist Albania a virtual satellite of its Yugoslav neighbour – Serbian was made compulsory in schools and Yugoslavian 'experts' were given key roles in the armed forces and government. It was not long, however, before the Albanians began to resent their vassal status, and Stalin's condemnation of Tito and the wave of 'anti-Titoist' purges provided an excellent opportunity for anti-Yugoslav Albanian communists, clustered around Enver Hoxha, to eliminate their pro-Yugoslavian comrades. Despite their 'internationalist' credentials, this dispute among Albania's communists was marked by all the historic enmity which had long characterized Serbian-Albanian relations. For Albanian communists hostile to Yugoslavia, it was very significant that the day of Yugoslavia's expulsion from the Comintern (28 June 1948) coincided with the feast day of St Vitus, patron saint of Serbia. Albania became the first Eastern European state to line up behind the Soviet Union in its crusade against Tito and its loyalty to Stalin was richly rewarded by the USSR: it received over $600 million in economic aid.

Some Bulgarian communists were also happy to turn against their Yugoslavian comrades in 1948. Bulgarian pride was wounded by the leading role taken by Yugoslavia's communists in the area and they were angered by their leadership's willingness to cede Bulgarian claims over Macedonia to Tito in his plans for a Balkan federation. After the Stalin-Tito split the anti-Serbian communists in Bulgaria seized the initiative. In December 1949 Traicho Kostov, a leading communist with well-known connections to the Yugoslavs, was executed (December 1949), and until the 1970s Bulgaria, unlike the sometimes wavering Albania, adopted a staunch pro-Soviet line which extended to contributing Bulgarian troops to the Soviet invasion of Czechoslovakia in 1968.

Communism did not banish or even repress nationalism in Eastern Europe for very long after the Second World War. Once the communist parties attempted to widen their appeal in the societies over which they governed, they resorted to traditional nationalist rhetoric. There was little attempt, for example, to protect ethnic minority rights to cultural and linguistic diversity within these multi-ethnic, communist republics. Even Yugoslavia, which had a reasonable record in protecting the linguistic rights of Hungarians, Albanians and Gypsies, had few qualms in quashing demands from Croatia for the right to a separate language status.

Stalinization, 1948–53

The witch-hunt for 'Titoists' in eastern Europe, like the blood letting which had accompanied collectivization and industrialization in the Soviet Union during the interwar period, helped now to accelerate the transition to a Stalinist political and economic system. Any pretence of democracy was abandoned as, in the haphazard and brutal style characteristic of Stalinism, the USSR imposed Soviet-style constitutions (which placed real power in the hands of the Politburo), and Soviet-style command economies on Poland, Czechoslovakia, Hungary, East Germany, Romania, Albania and Bulgaria. According to the principles of 'democratic centralism', the constitutions of eastern Europe established a strict hierarchy of Communist Party committees, soviets, bureaux, secretariats and congress, which were ultimately responsible to the Politburo, and established an invisible relationship between party and state. The lower bodies in this hierarchy 'elected' the higher ones, but, in turn, were compelled to obey the decisions taken by the higher bodies. This hierarchy explains the application of 'centralism', but what of the party's claim to democracy which was based on the assumption that communist society was free of 'class' or social conflict? The political leadership was even unwilling to permit the collection of economic or social data on income distribution, crime or social attitudes, affirming – logically if not truthfully – that since there were no conflicting interests the party leadership ruled in the interest of all.

In 1948 the limited nationalization of key industries which had taken place in the first years of communist rule was now replaced by sometimes idealistic, often irrational plans to complete the industrialization of eastern Europe. Private ownership was abolished and the ownership of the means of production rested with the communist state as the representative of the working class. 'Democratic centralism' thus sought to concentrate economic, as well as political, power in the hands of the state, a fusion which underlined the unquestioned authority of the party: there were no longer any businessmen or bankers or free trade unions to challenge the decisions of government. The party now claimed that it acted in the 'collective' interest. In practice, however, this was false, as the state primarily served the party, offering such 'perks' as better housing for its members and better education for their children.

In eastern Europe old ruling classes, shop-owners, businessmen and artisans were soon erased as a command economy was introduced into the Soviet puppet states. Interestingly, the pace of nationalization reflected the strength of indigenous communist parties. In Yugoslavia and Albania, where communist parties were in full control by 1945, and in Czechoslovakia's industrial heartland of Bohemia-Moravia, where the Communist Party was strong, the bulk of industry was nationalized by 1946. (By this date 82 per cent of Yugoslavian, 80 per cent of Czechoslovakian and 84 per cent of Albanian industries were in state hands.)

Nationalization in ex-enemy countries proceeded more slowly. In 1947 only 16 per cent of Bulgarian industry was under state control, while in Romania and Hungary the figures stood at 11 and 45 per cent respectively.

Of this group, Hungary's advanced level of industrialization and its legacy of state intervention eased its transition to full nationalization as the percentage of manual workers increased from 25 per cent to 50 per cent within 20 years. Private business was eliminated, and the state lavished its attention on extravagant projects to enhance the prestige of communism at home and abroad, like the new Hungarian steel town of Sztalinvaros.

By 1949 every eastern European country had its own version of GOSPLAN, a Soviet-style central planning office which professed its mission to rid the area of its ancient curse of technological backwardness. Despite these grand claims, the USSR also imposed a heavy burden of reparations upon its satellites. The burden of payments, mostly made up in deliveries of goods, fell upon Soviet-occupied Germany, Romania, Bulgaria and Hungary. The last of these, for example, supplied over 17 per cent of its very low national income in 1945–56 to the Soviet Union. These reparations payments (some of which were made to Czechoslovakia, Yugoslavia, Poland and Greece), undoubtedly impaired reconstruction and prolonged human suffering.

Industrialization, nonetheless, was rapid, partly spurred on by the outbreak of war in Korea, but it came at a high price. The safety of workers and the environment were treated with cavalier disregard as working-men and women discovered that the reality of the 'workers' state' was far removed from the Marxist rhetoric which accompanied its imposition. Freedom of movement and association were severely restricted and labour discipline was harsh. Although it was the spectacular show trials which captured public attention in eastern Europe, most of the prison population comprised blue- and white-collar workers arrested for infringements of labour discipline amid the welter of suspicion and intrigue which accompanied Stalinization.

As in the Soviet Union, it was the collectivization of agriculture far more than the Five Year Plans which provoked most popular discontent. The peasant was not just an important contributor to the economy of eastern Europe: as in the nineteenth century, there was a 'traditional peasant' ideal. Tilling the land had long remained at the centre of ethnic and national identity. Many of the indigenous communist parties, most notably in Romania, tried to turn a deaf ear to Moscow's entreaties for comprehensive collectivization, although there were benefits to be had from collectivizing 'dwarf' landholdings so that modern, efficient methods of farming could be used. By 1952 only Bulgaria could claim to have collectivized more than 50 per cent of arable land in the state sector. In Yugoslavia and Hungary only 25 per cent of land was collectivized, while in Romania the figure was as low as 15 per cent. After Stalin's death in 1953 collectivization was slowed or even temporarily halted across all of eastern Europe.

Again, as in the Soviet Union of the 1930s, education and Marxist culture were also placed high on the communist agenda, partly out of conviction, and partly to replace the indigenous culture the communists were doing their best to destroy. The Communist Party abolished all rival religious, social and political organizations. Religious observance was not completely banned, but the communists sought to 'depoliticize' it by controlling Churches' activities through Departments of Religious Affairs. Smaller religious groups, like Baptists and Methodists, suffered more than the larger Orthodox and Catholic Churches which continued to provide an important, alternative focus for social and political interaction.

On a more positive note, high school and university attendance doubled as the youth of eastern Europe was singled out for special attention. The school curriculum was modified to reflect the Soviet world view: history teachers were instructed to teach that the Second World War began with Operation Barbarossa. The fever of Stalinism also prompted some curious social experiments – such as rehousing the 'bourgeois' population of cities like Budapest and Prague in the countryside to provide accommodation for the new working class. To many, however, it seemed that the dictatorship of the Communist Party had simply been superimposed upon the dictatorship of the National Socialist Party. Typical was the experience of Josef Skvorecky, dissident Czech novelist and keen saxophonist. He recalled Soviet censorship of jazz:

> New little Goebbelses started working diligently in fields that had been cleared by the old demon. They had their own little Soviet bibles . . . their vocabulary was not very different from that of the Little Doctor, except that they were, if possible, even prouder of their ignorance.[4]

The death of Stalin and de-Stalinization, 1953–56

Until his death in 1953 Stalin continued to rule the Soviet Union with an iron hand, and celebrated his seventieth birthday in 1949 with extraordinary pomp and ceremony. Vociferous propaganda depicted him as a benevolent father figure, the 'Saviour' of the USSR. He was now very rarely seen in public – only glimpsed on top of the Lenin Mausoleum on national holidays – and had made his last public utterance in 1948, but his grip on power remained terrifyingly undiminished. Purges directed against the military and party members in the 1930s were replaced in the postwar period by an overt political anti-semitism. In January 1953, for instance, a large number of Jewish doctors in the employ of the Kremlin were arrested. Then on 5 March 1953 all fears of a renewed purge dramatically evaporated. Stalin was dead.

Stalin's death was followed by a period of collective leadership, at first under Georgi Malenkov, Lvarenti Beria and Nikita Khrushchev. By 1957 Khrushchev – the man who in 1954 had modified the powers of the security police (KGB) and who had brought previously uncultivated land under the Soviet plough (the 1954 'Virgin Lands' campaign) – had emerged as the new, undisputed leader of the USSR. Long before then, during his rise to the top, he had established a reputation for innovation and 'reformist' projects, especially with regard to agriculture. Already in 1950–51, for example, he proposed that the Communist Party establish *agrogorods* (agri-cities) in the countryside. The broad sweep and the impractical ambition of this plan were to characterize Khrushchev's years as Soviet leader.

Khrushchev's reputation as a 'reformer' helped him to secure his leadership position. He became famous, however, for his celebrated attack on Stalin during the 1956 Twentieth Party Congress, which condemned the old leader for, *inter alia*, using 'all conceivable methods to promote the glorification of his own person'. This attack on Stalin was primarily motivated by Khrushchev's desire to spur on the Soviet Union's cumbersome bureaucracy into supporting economic reform and to modify the prevailing political mood to one conducive to reform, but it had ramifications far beyond the boundaries of the USSR.

Stalin's death briefly raised hopes across eastern Europe that the pace and character of Stalinization would be modified. Nowhere was this more so than in East Germany, which had been systematically fleeced by the USSR for reparations since 1945 – on average more than 25 per cent of all income derived from industrial production went in reparations to the USSR. Within three months of Stalin's death, however, these hopes were hastily dashed by the imposition of higher production quotas (in effect, a wage cut) on East German workers.

On 17 June 1953 East Berlin workers downed tools in protest, and this demonstration spread like wildfire. Their numbers were soon swelled by workers from outside the city. Some even marched across from West Berlin to join them. This was an extraordinary demonstration of German workers' solidarity after, first, 12 years of Nazi, and then seven years of Soviet oppression. The East German state resorted to Red Army tanks to put down the demonstration and dozens of demonstrators were killed. Only a year earlier, Stalin had talked of the possibility of German reunification in exchange for a 'neutral Germany', but June 1953 effectively quashed any such proposals. The East Berlin workers' uprising had shown that Soviet control could be challenged, but not that it could be challenged successfully.

The problem for communist leaders in eastern Europe was that their slavish imitation of Stalin, which had once given their regimes a degree of legitimacy and security, became a liability once Khrushchev denounced him. Events in Poland and Hungary in 1956 provided an acute example of the limits of Soviet control over its satellites. That year the threat of unmanageable unrest in Poland persuaded the Russian Politburo to accept a Polish communist leader, Władsław Gomułka, whose loyalty appeared to be first to Poland and then to the USSR. Gomułka succeeded in loosening Moscow's stranglehold over Poland by reinstating workers' councils and securing some control over the deployment and command of Polish troops.

Plate 10.5 Hungarians burn a picture of Stalin, Budapest 1956. The varied ages and styles of dress of the group gathered around the burning poster illustrates the breadth of support for the Hungarian protest movement. For those who had enjoyed the loosening of Soviet control, the brutal reassertion of Soviet authority was a bitter blow. One immediate consequence was that at the 1956 Olympic games held in Australia no fewer than 45 members of the Hungarian Olympic team sought asylum abroad.

Yet he did not attempt to reform the character of communist government in Poland. His only aim was to modify Poland's strategic relations with the Soviet Union. The Stalinist style of government in Poland went unchallenged and Moscow recognized that there was little to be gained by full-scale intervention.

Developments in Hungary, by contrast, were treated with less leniency by the Kremlin because they threatened the essential character of the communist regime. After Stalin's death, political reform movements sprang into life across Hungary demanding improved living standards, an easing of collectivization and less secret police activity, and by November 1956 it had become clear to Moscow that the Hungarian communist Premier, Imre Nagy, was unable and unwilling to control this new, independent political life. Hated secret police officials were lynched and some army units were reported to be supporting demonstrations against the communist government. The Kremlin decided it must put down the unrest itself, a decision which was to compromise Khruschev's reformist credentials. Action followed quickly at a time when the West was divided by the Suez crisis. The Red Army amassed over 2,000 tanks inside Hungary – the same number deployed by Hitler in 1940 against France – and on 4 November Budapest was attacked. Within a week of increasingly articulate resistance the uprising had been quashed. Over 3,000 people were killed, 2,000 were later executed – some estimates suggest that between 25,000 and 50,000 Hungarians were killed – and over 20,000 fled abroad. Hungary's new Russian-appointed Premier, Janos Kádár, a communist who had himself experienced life in gaol, quickly reaffirmed Hungary's loyalty to Moscow and the Warsaw pact.

The brutal counter-revolutionary suppression of the Hungarian uprising stunned the world. It also damaged the reputation of Russian communists among their own comrades abroad in the East and West, despite the fact that in the aftermath of the bloodletting eastern European communist leaders showed a greater willingness to implement cautious reforms. Communist parties began to lose party members on a considerable scale in Europe, while communist governments elsewhere shuddered at the crude display of Russian strength. In the aftermath there was further strain on the already troubled relations between the communist Russian 'bear' and the communist Chinese 'tiger'.

The Cold War and the wider world, 1949–62

The origins of the Cold War were obviously in Europe, but it soon produced 'hot' wars elsewhere in the world. In Asia, for example, the British, French and Americans, already uneasy because of the long-feared communist victory in China, were appalled when communists from North Korea invaded South Korea (June 1950). The United Nations passed a resolution demanding the North Koreans' immediate withdrawal (the Soviet Union was boycotting the UN at the time). Soon afterwards a United Nations Command was set up under General Douglas MacArthur who was given orders to provide 'cover and support' for the South Koreans. In all, some 45 UN member states provided assistance of some kind, with the

USSR bitterly condemning their intervention. By July 1951 both sides began feeling their way to a truce, and it was a measure of the distrust which now permeated international relations that it took longer to sign a peace agreement than to wage war. It was only in 1955 that troops from the United States and China, which had joined the war on the side of North Korea, were finally withdrawn. By that time, intervention in Korea had stimulated the economic revival of the former adversary – Japan.

Some Cold War warriors, like the American Secretary of State, John Foster Dulles, talked 'of taking the offensive in the world struggle for freedom and for rolling back the engulfing tides of despotism'; others feared that localized wars would ultimately set the entire world ablaze. But the ethos of the Cold War meant that there could no longer be any localized defence structures: each 'small' conflict could bring the possibility of communist aggression. This conviction soon became appended to another new, simplistic theory of Cold War relations: the 'domino theory'. Expounded by the American President and former general, Dwight D. Eisenhower ('Ike'), to explain the dangers of allowing the communists any modicum of success, the theory claimed that if 'you have a row of dominos set up and you knock over the first one, what will happen to the last one is that it will certainly go over very quickly'. This became one of the guiding elements in American and western European foreign policy in south-east Asia, and provided the justification for superpower intervention around the globe.

The desire to 'contain' communism was complicated by the dissolution of Western overseas empires after the Second World War. The former colonies of Britain and France, in particular, decided for the most part not to attach themselves to either side in the Cold War, but instead to adopt a distinct, non-aligned position. The Indian Prime Minister, Jawaharlal Nehru, leader of one of the world's most populous states, took a leading role in the non-aligned movement, or 'third world' as it came to be known because it rejected the rigid Cold War division of the world split into two opposing ideological camps, which had little to do with its needs. At the same time the 'third world' leaders rejected neutrality as impractical (the Second World War illustrated the difficulty of containing war within national boundaries), and not necessarily appropriate to their requirements. Rather, they wanted to influence world politics and economics by their non-aligned position.

At first, the United States and the Soviet Union were cool towards this development, especially around the time of the Korean War, but they came to appreciate the value of a third voice, albeit not always in unison, in international affairs, especially as they were able to circumvent the non-alliance of some key states. In 1954, for example, Pakistan, Thailand and the Phillipines all concluded military agreements with the United States, while Afghanistan became the first non-communist country to receive Soviet aid. The Cold War increasingly penetrated into 'third world' countries. It was there, after Korea, that dangerous hot wars erupted in Vietnam (1965-1973) and in Angola (1975-1989), one of the richest countries in Africa. During the 1950s alone, financial aid and technical expertise were poured into Africa by both sides – around one billion dollars and 3,000 technical experts from 'the West' alone.

The new importance of Africa in international affairs was highlighted at the conference of non-aligned countries held in Bandung in April 1955 – a conference which had originally been designed to put Asia on the map. With Egypt, Libya, Sudan, Ethiopia, Liberia and Ghana represented amongst the 29 participants, the Bandung Conference became the prototype for future Afro-Asian solidarity in the 1960s and 1970s. The 'third world' had grown demonstrably larger. At Bandung, Russian and Chinese Marxist representations in favour of 'liberation' and 'equality' made a favourable impression on Asian and African delegates, especially when set against past imperialisms and the continued nationalism of the West. Bandung was more important, however, in that it established the basis for, and confidence in, Asian-African cooperation and laid the foundations for joint action at the United Nations, thus increasing Asian-African security and status in the world. Indeed, the increasing role of the non-aligned world in the dynamics of the Cold War was well illustrated during the deterioration of Chinese and Soviet relations which culminated in a bitter Sino-Soviet split by 1961. China's communist leader, Chairman Mao Zedong, began to press for the Soviet Union to use its military muscle to help their communist friends to power throughout the underprivileged world, but the Soviets were far less willing to engage in activities which threw up the possibility of open-ended conflict with the West.

Reforms in the Soviet Union, 1957–64

Combat in the Cold War was on a number of fronts – regional conflicts, the arms race, and the propaganda war – but in a war which saw no fighting in Europe, the underlying strength of the 'combatant' economies was crucial to determining its outcome. In the 1950s the economies of the United States and the western European bloc were undoubtedly stronger than their eastern bloc rivals, though it was the Soviet economy which appeared to be growing at the faster rate. As Alexei Adzhubey, Khrushchev's son-in-law, recalled, 'children were even called "Dogonyat-Peregonyat" – catch up and overtake'.

By the late 1950s, however, it was clear that official statistics in the USSR greatly overstated the growth of the Soviet economy. For one thing, communist statisticians did not recognize inflation in the USSR, although it consistently ran at around 3 per cent, and communist managers overestimated output on the plans to avoid punishment. Knowing that some reform was needed, Khrushchev sought to modify the economic system of the USSR so that individuals would be encouraged to work for themselves: he introduced new local and regional councils, brought new land into cultivation, and modified industrial output targets. He also planned to increase the supply of consumer goods, promising: 'give us time and we shall produce panties for your wives in colours which cannot be seen anywhere else'. He encouraged some political and public debate over economic reform, while insisting – in what was a difficult balancing act – that the Politburo should retain full authority over the Soviet Republics. Once again, attempts to reform Russia were more about modifying autocracy than introducing democracy.

At first all appeared to go well, but by the early 1960s the reforms had begun to falter: meat production began to fall, the autumn of 1962 brought a calamitous corn harvest, and heavy price increases for the workers followed. This, plus the Cuban missile crisis (1961), served to undermine Khrushchev's authority. To defuse domestic unrest, he energetically set about – or so he claimed – to promote an 'Administration Reorganization' in the USSR. But further changes to Soviet agriculture and the continued stagnation of Soviet industry spelled the end for Khrushchev. In what was to become a time honoured tradition (it befell President Gorbachev in August 1991), Khrushchev was removed from power while on holiday in 1964.

'Reform' communism in Eastern Europe, 1957–68

Khrushchev's economic reforms and the emerging split between the Soviet Union and China in 1960–61 sponsored change in the economic systems in the Eastern bloc. Yugoslavia's independent route had already embraced foreign aid, and in 1965 it received special drawing rights from the IMF which enabled it to develop its steel and refinery capacity, to introduce the market to price and distribute goods, and to cultivate a tourist industry. East Germany, in constant search of western European recognition, introduced limited economic reform and permitted the publication of long-banned books – Franz Kafka and T. S. Eliot were made available once more to an East German readership.

For Albania and Romania reform consisted of a radical change in their relationship with the USSR. Tiny Albania sided with China in the Sino-Soviet split (1961) and Romania, under the leadership of, first, Gheorge Gheorghiu-Dej and then Nicolae Ceauşescu, negotiated the withdrawal of Soviet troops from Albanian soil, remained neutral during the Sino-Soviet split, and cultivated economic contacts with western Europe. Poland and Bulgaria were largely out of step with this reformist trend, their tentative efforts at reform far surpassed by Hungary and Czechoslovakia.

Memories of 1956 determined that Hungary's reforms eschewed questions of political freedom and concentrated on economic issues. In

1968 the New Economic Mechanism was inaugurated which used the market to distribute goods and resources – it was dubbed 'goulash communism' – but GOSPLAN continued to have considerable influence on planning for the future. In the 1960s it was only in Czechoslovakia that pressures for economic reform emerged alongside a vibrant, popular movement for greater democracy. Aspirations for change flowered when Alexander Dubček took office, in March 1968, with promises of elections and economic reform. Under Dubček police surveillance and censorship almost disappeared, and the press was now filled with tales of torture in police cells and economic mismanagement. In a wave of reformist enthusiasm the newly liberated labour unions even offered unpaid work in 'Days for Dubček'.

This was too much for the USSR to swallow. Soviet troops, which had been on Warsaw pact 'manoeuvres' inside Czechoslovakia, accompanied by comrades from East Germany, Poland, Hungary and Bulgaria, invaded Czechoslovakia on 20 August 1968. Unlike the Soviet invasion of Hungary, there was little bloodshed in Czechoslovakia, although the psychological impact of Moscow's intervention remained profound. The 'Prague Spring', as this temporary thaw in USSR communist control over Czechoslovakia was called, quickly withered and died as Soviet tanks rolled into Prague.

The Cold War 'up in the air', 1957–69

The rise and fall of Khrushchev's buoyant confidence in the potential for reform within the eastern bloc mirrored developments in the Cold War. The USSR was the early leader in the 'race for space' – in 1957 the Soviet-launched *Sputnik* was the first artificial satellite in space, and four years later Yuri Gagarin became the first man to orbit the Earth. More menacingly, though equally astonishing for the West, was the USSR's launch of the first Inter-Continental Ballistic Missile (ICBM) in 1957. Such technological successes provoked a new phase of Western rearmament, with British, French and American governments investing heavily in nuclear technology.

In 1961 overt Cold War hostility returned to Europe when, to stem the endless flow of East Germans migrating westward, the Soviets and East Germans erected barriers around West Berlin to prevent movement between the western sectors and the areas outside. The Wall itself took months to build, and some East Berliners, desperate to escape, were willing to jump from high apartment blocks into the western sector. It was Churchill's 'iron curtain' brought to life. Indeed, the Berlin Wall quickly became a symbol of Soviet oppression throughout the world.

The Cuban crisis of the following year brought the world nearer to general war than at any time since 1945. Khrushchev later noted that 'there began to be a smell of burning in the air'. President John F. Kennedy had

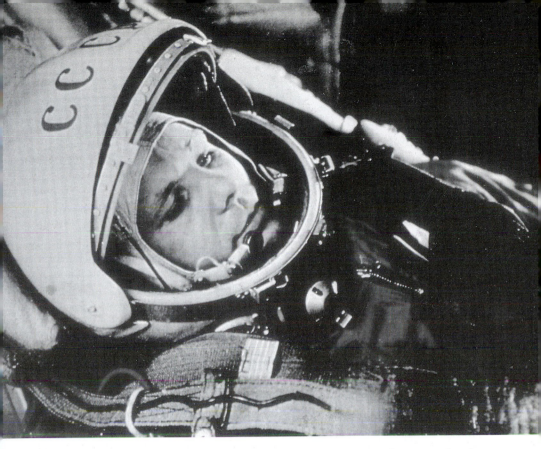

Plate 10.6 The first astronaut, Yuri Gagarin. On 12 April 1961 Gagarin completed the first manned orbit of the earth aboard *Vostok 1*. Flying at an altitude of 327 km and a maximum speed of 28,096 per hour, he was in flight for only 108 minutes before parachuting his craft down safely near the village of Smelovka in Saratov, USSR.

failed in his 1961 attempts to overthrow the left-wing government of Fidel Castro on the island of Cuba, and Khrushchev, seeing an opportunity to humiliate the young President, decided to build nuclear missile bases there. By blockading the delivery of the missiles to Cuba and standing firm, Kennedy forced Khrushchev to withdraw them, and subsequent years saw a gradual improvement in East-West relations, even though the threat of nuclear war remained. Since Hiroshima the spectre of the Bomb had hung over the world. Not only were scientists and defence ministries producing ever more numerous and ever more powerful nuclear weapons, but the potential, long-term effects of nuclear warfare, and indeed nuclear power, remained uncertain. There was a huge question mark – as well as an exclamation mark – in the mushroom cloud which represented a bomb that only the physicists could understand. After years of fearfully anticipating nuclear warfare, the world had stepped away from its brink in 1962.

The history of atomic and nuclear weapons in the postwar period illustrates the futility of American hopes in 1945 to keep this technology a secret. As J. Robert Oppenheimer, the American physicist involved in the Manhattan project wrote: 'You cannot keep the nature of the world a secret.' It took other powers increasingly less time to catch up on American weapon technology. The Soviet Union exploded its first atomic bomb in 1949 – four years after Hiroshima – but when, in 1952, the United States produced an even more terrifying nuclear weapon, the hydrogen bomb, the Soviets caught up within nine months.

By the 1960s nuclear technology was not confined to the superpowers – Britain was committed to nuclear weapons as early as 1947, France exploded its first nuclear weapon in 1960, China in 1964 – and, for this reason, it was now in the interests of both superpowers to control the indiscriminate spread of nuclear technology. In 1968 the United States and the Soviet Union signed a nuclear non-proliferation treaty, but the rapid advance of technology for mass destruction demanded continuing action and a year later, coincident with the beginning of Strategic Arms Limitation Talks (SALT) between the two military giants, negotiations began to prevent the deployment of weapons of mass destruction on the seabed.

In 1969 came an American triumph in space which symbolized the beginnings of the West's 'victory' over the East. On 21 July 1969, Neil Armstrong gave a tremendous boost to American claims to be the premier power in space by setting foot on the Moon. In economic and military terms, too, western Europe had developed a clear lead over the Eastern bloc. But it was a victory that had been won at a tremendous price. Growth in the Soviet economy was faltering under the strain of arms manufacture – for ordinary citizens hardships included insufficient housing and few consumer products – and, for both eastern and western Europe, military stockpiling had created the frightening strategy of 'mutually assured destruction' (MAD).

Stagnation and senility in the USSR, 1964–85

The Polish political philosopher Leszek Kolakowski once described reform communism as 'fried snowballs' – changing the temperature dissolves the substance – for if the planned economy and the role of the Communist Party were diminished by reform, then the system would no longer be communist. Events in the Soviet Union after Khrushchev's fall reflected Kolakowski's view. Even unambitious reform was rejected in favour of maintaining the status quo and of fortifying the role of the military in Soviet life. In 1964 there was, once again, no obvious successor to the Soviet leadership. Gradually, however, Leonid Brezhnev, just like Khrushchev before him, marginalized his rivals and appointed his own men, such as Yuri Andropov, into leading party positions.

After Brezhnev's appointment as General Secretary there was little political change in the Politburo. In his 18 years as leader, Brezhnev removed only nine individuals from the Politburo, whereas during the 'tempestuous' days of Khrushchev, 24 people were removed within nine years. Brezhnev's leadership brought no dramatic modifications, rather the slow, steady and inexorable slide towards stagnation and degeneration. His role was to undercut completely the sense of inward movement and expectant change which Khrushchev had, for a time, been able to communicate to the party and nation at large.

Under Brezhnev's rule the most important development was the continued growth of the USSR's military arsenals (the years 1965–75 witnessed one of the most substantial military build-ups in a country at peace in the twentieth century), and so, too, grew the perks and privileges showered upon party *apparatchiks*. Enhancing the authority and resources of the Soviet military brought the Soviet Union new assurance in its foreign policy, but the USSR's agricultural and industrial difficulties continued unresolved. Indeed, the Soviet military build-up only served to exacerbate the chronic imbalance between the Soviet Union's heavy industrial output and the output of consumer products (known within the Politburo as the A/B debate).

The monstrous bureaucratic and economic structures ostensibly created to benefit the working class, continued to oppress and exploit them. Ultimately, stagnation under Brezhnev and his short-lived successors (Yuri Andropov, who died in 1984, and Konstantin Chernenko who died in 1985) threatened the USSR as much as the failed reforms of Khrushchev. With the appointment of Mikhail Gorbachev as General Secretary of the Communist Party in 1985, the senile, the dying and the dead leadership of the preceding three Soviet leaders was replaced by the long awaited 'next' generation.

Gorbachev's 'Perestroika' and the crisis of communism

Gorbachev was cut from a cloth different from that of his predecessors. He had no memory of the purges and little of the war. He was well educated, interested in reform, able and young (only 49 years old when appointed to the Politburo), thus breaking the trend of the Brezhnev era which had been to replace old men with even older men. Gorbachev took pride in the achievements of the Soviet Union as a superpower, but expressed public concern that the slow-down in Soviet economic growth would mean that the USSR would no longer be a superpower in the year 2000. Such candour was unprecedented, and it was followed by Gorbachev's interpretation of the USSR's malaise: the key reason was the decline of discipline, order and morality. This in turn had permitted corruption, privilege, 'breaches of the law, bureaucratism, parasitism, drunkenness, prodigality, waste and other negative phenomena' to run rampant.

At first Gorbachev believed that it would be possible simply to eliminate these abuses and that the levels of production would subsequently climb. Unlike his predecessors, he was not afraid to expose the weaknesses of the USSR. Indeed, his policy of *Glasnost* (openness) encouraged others to do likewise, arguing 'we shall not go under since we are not afraid to discuss our weaknesses and will learn to overcome them'. Debate now opened on hitherto 'closed' issues, like the role of women, the environment (especially after disaster struck at the Chernobyl nuclear power station in Kiev on 26 April 1986), and the existence and levels of crime.

The second Russian word to capture Europe's imagination on both sides of the iron curtain was *Perestroika* (reform). But while Gorbachev had energetically begun to assert the need for major reform, no major economic changes were implemented. Ultimately, this proved his undoing. In 1986–87, for example, Moscow's economic ministries were reorganized, but economic policy governed by the 1986–90 Four Year Plan – it was to be the Union's last – still remained heavily centralized, with elementary incentives for workers to increase their output. By the following year, the Politburo frankly admitted to the Communist Party that the USSR's economic problems were far worse than had been feared. This news, rather than inspiring the party's reforming zeal, prompted increasing fragmentation within it. To the left were those who believed the pace of reform was too slow (among them was Boris Yeltsin, future President of Russia and the Commonwealth of Independent States), and to the right were those who became increasingly distrustful of Gorbachev and his reformist drive (this group included Egor Ligachev). By the summer of 1988, Yeltsin had been dismissed from the Politburo for his outspoken criticism of Gorbachev, while on the right of Soviet politics, Ligachev attempted to form a conservative alliance within the Politburo to block Gorbachev's policies.

Gorbachev was now under attack from all sides, and the June–July 1988 Special Party Congress saw the first open disagreements within the Communist Party since the 1920s. Meanwhile, tinkering with the command economy continued to yield barren results. At last, in January 1989, a major package of economic reforms were introduced, but to the peoples of the Soviet Republics it appeared that they would make things worse not better. Supplies of meat and dairy produce began to fall as farm labourers preferred to cultivate their own plots for produce they could sell at a substantial profit.

Arguably, Gorbachev's greatest domestic achievement was a political one: the land which had only ever enjoyed one democratic election (in November 1917) now called open elections. The 1989 election for the Congress of People's Deputies marked the beginning of this process. Although not truly democratic – 750 of the 2,250 seats were reserved for groups like the Communist Party and trade unions – it marked the dawn of democracy for the Soviet Republics and the beginning of the end for the Soviet regime. The pace of political change inside the Soviet Union grew ever quicker in 1990–91. In August 1991 an abortive coup by right-wing elements did little to enhance Gorbachev's dwindling popularity inside the faltering USSR, and on Christmas Day 1991 he resigned. The following day, what remained of the Soviet parliament dissolved the Soviet Union.

Eastern Europe: reform and decline, 1968–89

The symptoms of economic and political paralysis in the Soviet Union under Brezhnev and Gorbachev also infected eastern Europe. After 1968 religious and political freedoms were submerged once more beneath the apparatus of the Stalinist-style state. As in the USSR, the Communist Parties in eastern Europe continued to maintain a firm grip on power (despite rising, popular disillusionment) by encouraging and exploiting social inequalities. Ideology was betrayed as certain social groups, like skilled workers and 'card carrying' members of the intelligentsia, were given privileges. At the pinnacle of this social hierarchy were the *nomenklatura* ('loyal communists'), who were the backbone of the state. This pyramid of privilege, coupled with the Communist Party's monopoly on power (for no other political parties were allowed), its ideological control and strict codes of censorship for the media and education, all made opposition difficult; the methods of the state police ensured that it was dangerous too.

But gradually the need for economic reform came to subvert Moscow's claims to control eastern Europe. With the flowering of detente in the Cold War in the 1970s and the obvious paralysis of Comecon, eastern Europe increasingly imported western technology and capital. Hungary was at the forefront of this new wave of economic reforms, building on the changes implemented in the New Economic Mechanism to promote new economic contacts with the West: Hungary was made a member of GATT in 1973, received most-favoured-nation trading status from the USA in 1978 and joined the World Bank and the IMF in 1982.

Poland and Romania also advanced their commercial contacts with the West in favour of trade within the eastern bloc – for most of eastern Europe, membership of the Soviet bloc had been a persistent hindrance to trade and growth – and by 1974 half of Polish and Romanian trade was also with the West. Only Bulgaria baulked at diluting its links with the USSR and although Bulgarian communists cultivated trade with Middle Eastern and Mediterranean markets, they never weakened their economic links with the Soviet Union. In the short term this strategy paid off – Bulgaria was granted preferential access to Soviet credit and oil. In the long term, however, the uncompetitiveness and environmental destruction of Bulgarian industry fatally undermined the Communist Party in the 1980s.

Further fractures in the cohesion of the eastern bloc were apparent in the ethnic tensions within Yugoslavia and growing labour unrest in Poland. Yugoslavia was first and most radical in its attempts to modify the workings of the command economy, but by 1975 business enterprises had over 273 billion dinars worth of unpaid bills and owed the same in unpaid loans. In 1983 the IMF stepped in to solve Yugoslavia's mammoth debt problems with a substantial debt rescheduling package. Rampant inflation and labour unrest fuelled by it increased tensions between Croats and Serbs. In 1973 Croatian nationalists were put on trial, and in 1981, a year after the death of Tito, ethnic tensions between Albanians and Serbs in the Republic of Kosovo boiled over once more. Kosovo was placed under effective military rule and it appeared that Tito's dream of a united Yugoslavia had died along with him.

But it was in long-suffering Poland that the first substantial political challenge against the Communist Party came. The cause of Poland's economic malaise were much the same as Yugoslavia's: massive foreign debts, barely perceptible levels of growth, rising inflation and, perhaps most important, a clear disparity between the grand claims of their communist government to improve the living conditions of its workers and farmers and the grim reality. In 1980 demonstrations by industrial workers – an ominous development, for this group were the alleged 'vanguard' of the communist revolution – were organized by the trade union *Solidarnosc*, founded at the Lenin shipyard in Gdańsk and led by Lech Wałęsa. They threatened the Communist Party, but did not lever it from power. Instead, there followed a period of military dictatorship, although the pressure to reform the economy eventually prompted the legalization of *Solidarnosc* and the return of democracy to Poland. By the end of the 1980s it was not merely communism in Poland that was under threat, but the survival of the communist order in eastern Europe and the USSR.

The 'revolutions' of Eastern Europe, 1989

By 1989 the impetus for change had swept across all the Soviet satellites of eastern Europe. As the puppet governments began to unravel with surprising ease and speed, it was clear that the Kremlin had made a conscious decision to allow events to run their course without intervention. To the people of East Berlin, who warmly praised Gorbachev for this courageous decision, this Secretary General of the Communist Party did as much to ensure that the satellite system would dissolve peacefully in 1989 as his predecessor Stalin had done to impose brutally the system in 1945. As Gorbachev's Foreign Ministry spokesman, Gennadi Gerasimov, put it, the USSR now followed the 'Sinatra doctrine' in its relations with eastern Europe. They had to find their 'own way' out of their troubles.

Encouraged by Gorbachev, the communist parties in eastern Europe

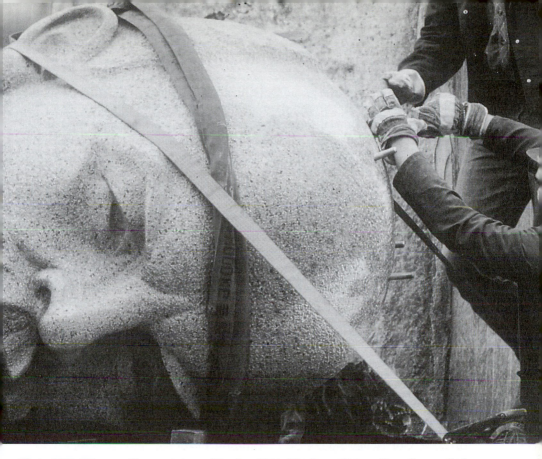

Plate 10.7 Dismantling a statue of Lenin, 1991. Work on dismantling the symbols of Soviet power began with the decreed end of the Soviet Union. Giant statues of Lenin were removed from public squares and parks. Place-names were also swept away in desire to return to the past: Leningrad reverted to St Petersburg, Gorky again became Nizhi-Novgorod, and Sverdlovsk was renamed Yekaterinburg (after Peter the Great's wife).

made earnest efforts at internal reform from 1988 until November 1989. The spell of fear cast by Stalin had been broken, and this was formally recognized in October 1989 when, as a 'fraternal' gesture of solidarity, the USSR formally renounced the 'Brezhnev Doctrine', which had been used to justify Soviet intervention in other communist countries. This brought the Cold War and Soviet domination of eastern Europe to an end. Already in August and September 1989, as the communist stranglehold over Czechoslovakia and Hungary loosened, thousands of young and professional people had begun to migrate to West Germany, their numbers soon swelled by East Germans, and with the effective creation of a single labour market between East and West Germany, the division of Germany and Europe was finally over. The Berlin Wall fell on 9 November 1989 and official German unification came on 3 October 1990.

The communist parties of central Europe appeared to surrender power with astonishing ease. The neutral stance of the Soviet Union had helped, but so, too, had widespread disillusionment with the 'moral' and 'economic' pledges of communism. Jealous eyes had been cast upon the economic achievements of their western European counterparts, and in the hope of good times ahead, communism was decisively rejected and centre-right governments installed. Further east, in Bulgaria and Romania, the transition was neither conclusive nor peaceful (in Romania there were over 1,000 deaths). The demand for independence also came from states within the Soviet Union, notably the Baltic states of Estonia, Lithuania and Latvia which had been absorbed into the Soviet Union in 1940. Even here, after some tough talking, Moscow was forced to relinquish control. As these regimes collapsed so too did the institutions of communism. First went Comecon, followed by the slow, painful demise of the Warsaw pact which was finally dissolved on 1 July 1991.

The relatively peaceful nature of these revolutions – in Czechoslovakia it was called the 'Velvet Revolution' – belied the painful and difficult path to democracy and prosperity which lay ahead. By 1991 the lavish claims of 'Cold War warriors' that the West had won the Cold War rang increasingly hollow as economic and political failures fuelled ethnic tensions which had been suppressed behind the iron curtain for 45 years. The ethnic violence which had erupted in the Soviet republics of Kazakhstan (December 1986), Armenia, Azerbaijan and Georgia (all in 1987), in the final years of the Soviet Union, were to rise to engulf Yugoslavia in 1991.

In 1987 Gorbachev spoke of a 'common European house' which was a single cultural and historic entity 'from the Atlantic to the Urals' (a similar sentiment was pinned to the collapsed Berlin Wall in 1989: 'Stalin is dead, Europe lives'). But in the years after 1989, the varied frameworks of west European cooperation, above all the European Union, which had identified their interests with those of Europe as a whole, were themselves to grow strained. To some people in Eastern Europe it seemed that the 'frying snowballs' had jumped out of the frying pan and into the fire.

References

1. International Military Tribunal, *Nuremberg: Trial of German Major War Criminals*, vol. 1 (1946) p. 67.
2. W. S. Churchill, *Triumph and Tragedy* (Boston, 1953) pp. 489–90. For discussion of the origins of the term 'iron curtain' see B. Bryson, *Made in America* (1994, 1995 edn) pp. 355–6.
3. In fact, the term 'Cold War' was first used by Herbert Bayard Swope in a speech written for American financier Bernard Baruch in 1947.
4. J. Skovrecky, *The Bass Saxophone* (1980) p. 15.

Chapter 11

Reconstructing Europe, 1945–1991

So long as eastern Europe ostensibly subscribed to Lenin's vision of workers' republics, called at first 'people's democracies', and so long as Soviet power held, the impetus to promote the integration of western Europe, exposed as it was to American political ideas, economic methods and culture on an unprecedented scale, was fed by the Cold War. An important group of allied countries – and it was to grow in size – soon recognized their ultimate dependence on one another and on the fate of West Germany, a conviction that was enhanced further by the disintegration of overseas empires. Indonesia was followed by India and Indochina, each with its own history. There was a sense of shared economic potential also, particularly after 1958.

Politics in Holland, Belgium, France, Portugal and Britain contrasted, but all were subject to similar pressures after 1945. Inside Europe the ring of neutral countries on its periphery stayed independent as the 'iron curtain' which now divided Europe deprived countries, like France and Germany, of their traditional spheres of interest in the East. At all times there was a strong desire amongst many politicians in continental western Europe to preserve and to assert 'European' values and interests, as distinct from those of the United States. Britain, however, which made much of its own values and interests, stressed its 'special relationship' with the United States even when the United States did not do so. Despite all the changes, particularly in attitudes towards capitalism, itself a developing *ism*, with the market, more often imperfect than perfect, at its core, the pattern was as complex in 1989 as it had been in 1945.

Britain's postwar consensus, 1945–51

Britain was the only major European power not to suffer defeat in the two world wars, and in 1945 it was hard to tar British democracy with the same discredited brush as democracy in France, Germany, Italy or Spain: the unwritten British constitution had proved more resilient than constitutions drawn up on the continent. There were parallels with 1815. The temper in many other societies was influenced by occupation as well as war, and, in the countries that Germany had occupied, by the memories of collaboration as well as resistance. There were stronger communist parties too than in Britain, each looking east as well as west.

In July 1945 the Labour Party won an historic, landslide election victory on a reform programme. It included comprehensive health and social security measures which had been developed in wartime after the Beveridge Report had appeared. There was also a commitment to provide greater housing and greater social equality and to nationalize coal and transport. Nonetheless, there were some voters in Britain, as elsewhere, who were disenchanted with politics and politicians. One voter, surveyed on the eve of the 1945 election, described politicians as 'a lot of old fish wives'.

From 1945 until the mid-1970s British 'fish wives', whether Conservative, Liberal or Labour, shared certain common, broad objectives relating to the role of government in society. All believed that governmental intervention would bring greater equality and wealth to the nation, and that there should be a 'welfare' not a 'night-watchman' state; and the perpetuation of this 'belief' (except on the extreme right) made for (limited) 'consensus politics' in Britain until the election of Margaret Thatcher in 1979. R. A. Butler, the 'architect of the new conservatism in the domestic field' and Chancellor of the Exchequer when the Conservatives were returned to power in 1951, proclaimed that Britain was to become 'one single society or community in which all careers will be open to talent'.

In 1945 Prime Minister Attlee's Labour government faced difficult tasks: the need to create a stable economic framework, to meet their election promises, and to revise Britain's relations with its empire. The greatest challenge was to create a welfare state within a bankrupt economy. In large part the challenge was met, although only by maintaining 'austerity' which lost votes. Within a year Labour had introduced 75 bills, a giant programme of nationalization (including the Bank of England, civil aviation, public transport, electricity and gas), and a far greater government commitment to providing social services. In 1946 the National Insurance Bill was passed insuring the nation's entire adult population in time of sickness, unemployment and retirement. In the same year, medical care was nationalized and the National Health Service quickly became the second largest item of government expenditure. It was a programme widely admired and emulated across western Europe, but it strained Britain's resources to the limit and posed problems for the future.

The winter of 1946–47 was an especially hard one for the British people. The economy proved resistant to recovery, rationing continued and even extended beyond its wartime range, and essentials, particularly coal, were in short supply. The problems at home reached their climax during the bitterest winter of the century when near arctic conditions covered the nation in snow and brought economic life to an almost complete halt. Britain was forced to secure another substantial loan from the United States and the Labour government was suddenly confronted with the harsh realities of Britain's economy: Chancellor Hugh Dalton saw ahead of him 'a looming shadow of catastrophe'. This domestic crisis also helped to exacerbate further the crisis for British authority overseas. Britain voluntarily withdrew from India (August 1947), as the Labour Party had long desired, and also, with no ideological complications, from armed intervention against the communists in Greece and Turkey (March 1947). It handed the thorny problem of an independent Jewish state in Palestine – the Labour Party were divided on this – back to the United Nations to resolve.

These changes in British foreign policy underlined the diminution of Britain's power relative to the new superpowers, but Britain still retained important interests in the Middle East, Africa and southeast Asia. The British were to play a main role in the escalation of the Cold War and the making of the Marshall plan, still hoping to retain a powerful voice in international affairs not only by cultivating their 'special relationship' with the United States but by strengthening ties with the Commonwealth. They also kept their own atomic weapons. As early as 1948, however, the problems of the British economy undermined the post-election optimism of 1945, and when in 1949 the pound was devalued (from $4.03 to $2.80 to the dollar) the relative decline of Britain's economy compared to the that of the United States was manifest. Nor was the United States sympathetic either to Britain's 'welfare state' or to its continuing Commonwealth involvement. Other European countries were viewed with some suspicion. Indeed in August 1950, Bevin told a United States representative that 'Britain was not part of Europe'.[1] Not everyone in Britain agreed.

Western Europe, 1945–57

Like Britain, France continued to parade the outward trappings of great power status through its seat on the National Security Council of the United Nations and the possession of its empire, but defeat, occupation and economic collapse pointed to the reality of French power in 1945. Industrial production was at one-third of pre-war levels and overseas trade was non-existent. After the short-lived leadership of Charles de Gaulle, which ended in January 1946, a tripartite coalition of Communists, Socialists and Christian Democrats (there was no 'Christian Democracy' in Britain) began to cooperate uneasily to create a constitutional framework for a new Fourth Republic. But within months economic paralysis, fears over the true intentions of the Communists, and constitutional disputes (exacerbated by de Gaulle's outbursts) proved too much for 'tripartism'. The Communist members of the cabinet were sacked abruptly by the Socialist Prime Minister, Paul Ramadier, in May 1947, and from 1947 until 1951 France once again experienced uneasy and transient cabinets formed by key individuals, among them Henri Queuille, Georges Bidault and René Pleven, who rotated in office. This was the same version of democracy which had characterized French politics of the interwar years, although Bidault's Christian Democracy was a new force.

For all this turmoil, the extension of state management into the economy and society brought dividends for many Frenchmen and women. The railway system recovered, as did the automobile industry, while the Monnet plan (1946) – so-named after Jean Monnet, head of the grandly named Plan for the Modernization and Equipment of France – eschewed widespread nationalization of industry, and set targets for key industries, namely steel, electricity, and cement. Supported by American loans, these helped to foster growth, as fashionable a word as 'planning', within the French economy. And while the crisis of French imperialism and the tensions of the Cold War continued to plague hopes for stable government in France, French reconciliation with West Germany and the creation of the European Economic Community in 1957 provided the basis for French domestic and foreign power in the final quarter of the twentieth century.

The conditions in Europe's smaller nations varied greatly after the war's end. Switzerland and Sweden, both neutral during the war, faced few recriminations, and did not need to worry about reconstruction, while Spain and, to a lesser extent Portugal, stubbornly resisting democracy, were generally ostracized until requirements of the Cold War determined a more cooperative western approach towards their (in some respects dissimilar) authoritarian dictatorships. The Benelux countries, devastated by occupation and the battle for liberation, struggled to revive. Rising inflation, a potent cause of instability in Europe after the First World War, was once again a danger to postwar recovery. In seeking to cope with this Belgium took the lead among former occupied nations, for in October 1944, even before the country had been liberated, Finance Minister Camille Gutt implemented drastic currency reform. The economy of the Netherlands was not as strong as that of its Belgian neighbour, but Gutt's currency reform in Belgium was emulated in the Lieftinck Reform (September 1945), supplemented by a policy of price control and continued rationing. Belgium faced other problems. Notwithstanding Gutt's success, there were signs of conflict between its French-speaking Walloons and the then more conservative Flemings which were to dominate much of its postwar history.

In the two defeated countries in the West, Italy and Germany, the speed and success with which democratic politics returned had depended on both the pace of the Allied invasion and the ability of the fascist state to withstand it. 'Normal' politics returned to southern Italy as the Allies pushed north, where the remains of the fascist state, once allied with Germany, now found its remaining territory invaded and occupied by it. Throughout 1944 Italian politics in the south were confused, with anti-fascist parties, each with a different champion among the Allies, unable to agree on how best to form a government and prepare for institutional change.

Democracy in Germany was first rekindled in free elections in the Bavarian village of Wohlmuttschüll in 1945, and by 1948 the western zones of Germany were ready to create a Parliamentary Council to draft a *Grundgesetz* (basic law) which was to remain a provisional constitution until Germany could be reunited. In the meantime, the FDR was ruled under a liberal democratic constitution – with substantial powers over cultural, educational and religious matters now decentralized from the *Reichstag* to Germany's states (*Länder*) represented in the *Landtag*. Many of Weimar's political parties, notably the SPD, re-formed for the Republic's first elections in August 1949.

In Italy, as in France, there was a weak postwar economy and a string of short-lived cabinets; in the aftermath of the defeat in war the Italian Communist Party (PCI), a strong force, argued that it would be impossible to effect a Marxist revolution in Italy because of the continued Allied presence (the Americans, in particular, sought to 'manipulate' Italian politics to contain the communists) and the lack of a revolutionary consciousness amongst the working class. The communists were to rue their mistake. The political opportunities of 1943–44 were not to come again. As Fausto Gullo, a PCI leader later recalled: 'we were all under the impression that the wind was blowing in our direction, and that therefore what was not achieved today, would be achieved tomorrow'.

On 2 June 1946 a new era of democratic politics began in Italy with elections to a new constituent assembly and a referendum on whether Italy should become a republic. The monarchy did not survive, although far from presenting a united picture, the referendum and the elections demonstrated the deep divisions among the anti-fascist parties as the new Republic was split into a conservative, monarchist south and a radical, republican north. The new Prime Minister was 62-year-old Alcide de Gasperi, the first Catholic politician to become Prime Minister of a united Italy. The new constitution, with its strong emphasis on regionalism as opposed to the centralism of the fascist state, was formally introduced on 1 January 1948 and de Gasperi, leader of the new Christian Democratic Party, was re-elected on a no-nonsense 'law and order' ticket.

It was the 'new right' – the Christian Democrats, led by Konrad Adenauer in Germany, de Gasperi in Italy and Georges Bidault in France – which pointed to the future for European politics, once again highlighting the difference between 'the continent' and Britain. Given the dominance of the Social Democratic Party in German politics after the First World War, many, especially its leader Kurt Schumacher, believed that it would again dominate democratic politics in Germany. But in 1949 the 70-year-old Adenauer, the former Mayor of Cologne and a veteran of centre politics in Weimar, became and then remained the Federal Republic's Chancellor for 14 years.

The charisma and political skills of 'old man' Adenauer helped to explain the unexpected success of the newly formed Christian Democratic Party. So, too, did the 'iron curtain' which divided German socialists and geographically separated the SPD from many of its former supporters in East Germany. But most important was the fact that many voters believed that the Church was the best protection against what was now perceived by many as the strongest threat to stability and security – communism. As one historian has put it, it was, 'perhaps not the rule of the Saints, but the rule of the Clericals.'[2] In de Gasperi's words, it was 'the sense of fraternity . . . the moving force of Christian civilization' (with a European base) which could reconcile human conflict. And while events in Czechoslovakia in 1948 confirmed the Christian Democrats' worst fears, there were signs in elections across western Europe that communism was a declining force.

In France and Greece communists, who had been hailed as heroes of the resistance, did not sustain their political influence for long. Once the war was over and 'normality' re-established on the left of European politics, traditional socialist parties simply resumed their previous dominance over the communists in France and the Netherlands. In Italy the communists only managed to retain political power by arranging a political pact with the new Christian Democrats, an alliance which robbed them of their working-class radicalism.

NATO, 1947–55

It was, as usual, western Europe's larger powers which thrashed out questions of financial and economic aid and defence with the United States. Countries as diverse as Greece, the Netherlands, Belgium, Norway, Denmark, and Turkey were more spectators than participants in the negotiations, but for these countries and for other European nations unoccupied by the Red Army, the transition to peace was an absorbing test. After March 1947 the United States was committed to preserving democracy in Greece and Turkey, although the popularity of the left continued to grow despite American disapproval.

The continued Red Army occupation of eastern Europe also made it clear that there would be no East-West cooperation over the issue of disarmament and this, coupled with international tension over Marshall aid and the Truman doctrine (see p. 390), made western European governments increasingly anxious to set up a formal defence structure to provide a secure environment in which European recovery could take place. Britain and France, in particular, wanted more than the vague

American pledge to help any country under threat in the Truman doctrine. The first important step in military cooperation came with the 1948 Treaty of Brussels between Britain, France and the Low Countries. Because of the number of its partners, it marked an advance in European cooperation, but its main focus, to thwart 'a renewal by Germany of aggressive policy', was outdated. Sweden also made strenuous efforts to establish a similar security pact between the Scandinavian powers, but its efforts came to naught after neutral Finland withdrew from negotiations for fear of triggering the ire of the Soviet Union and the United States refused to supply the Nordic alliance with weapons.

By the end of 1948 politicians, particularly in Britain and France, were calling for a military equivalent of the Marshall plan, and in 1949 they got what they wanted. In April of that year ten European powers joined the United States and Canada in signing the North Atlantic Treaty Organization (NATO) in Washington: Britain, France, the Benelux states, Italy, Denmark, Norway, Iceland and Portugal. Unlike in 1919, the United States was this time convinced that its national security was tightly bound with that of western Europe. In 1947 American Intelligence had concluded that the Soviet military threat to western Europe was insignificant, but by 1949 a more apprehensive assessment of Soviet military potential was made and the pattern of the Cold War 'engagement' and the future arms race was thus established. NATO was proclaimed as 'an armour not a lance, a shield but not a sword' to afford security for western Europe's reconstruction, and it was dedicated to the principles of the UN Charter. But NATO was regional, not global, in character and had substantial backing from the United States: the US Senate passed a vast programme of military aid to western Europe a day before news broke of the explosion of the first Soviet atomic bomb. Nuclear weapons were now the essence of military power. By 1950 American nuclear bombers were established in Britain, and by 1954, when NATO's military build-up had begun in earnest, nuclear missiles and artillery were based across continental western Europe.

With the arrival of Marshall aid, there were also more positive movements in a number of directions, most notably in the creation of a Benelux customs union (January 1948). This regional cooperation was soon mirrored by similar groupings of other European nations: thus, Sweden, Norway and Denmark formed a group to the North, and in the Mediterranean there were rumours that Greece and Turkey were planning to form a customs union. These associations, it was hoped, would promote domestic recovery and afford smaller European nations a stronger voice in shaping their future. The formation of groups to coordinate issues of trade, foreign policy and defence was an accelerating trend in western Europe in the later 1940s. However, while intra-European links grew stronger, Europe's former 'great' powers were also dissolving long-held imperial ties.

Map 11.1 The division of Europe in the Cold War

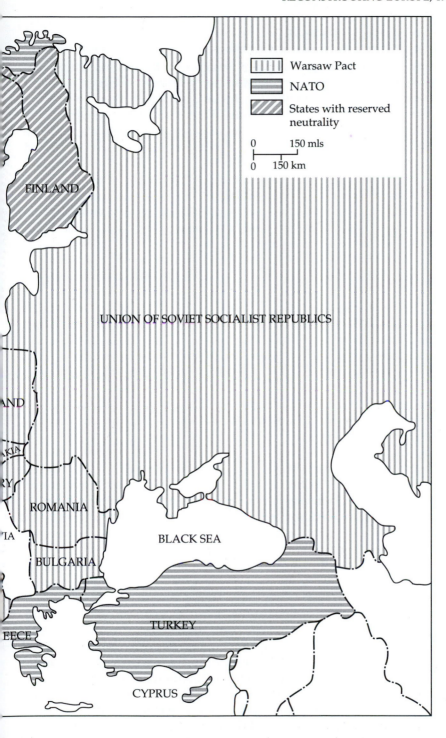

FINLAND

UNION OF SOVIET SOCIALIST REPUBLICS

Warsaw Pact

NATO

States with reserved neutrality

0   150 mls

0   150 km

ROMANIA

BLACK SEA

BULGARIA

TURKEY

CYPRUS

GREECE

Decolonization, 1946–62

The Second World War, global as it was in scale and its aftermath, contributed to a fundamental revision of relations between western Europe's imperial powers and the territories over which they held sway. The relative ease with which Britain and France ruled the waves in the nineteenth century now stood in dramatic contrast to their dependence upon America, and nowhere was the loss of power more clearly illustrated than in their imperial relations. Yet even before the Second World War had ended, there had been an Afro-Asian conference in Manchester, England, which drew up a declaration proclaiming that 'we are determined to be free. . . . We will make the world listen.' Among those present were Kwame Nkrumah, later Prime Minister and President of Ghana, and Jomo Kenyatta, future President of Kenya. This declaration, and others like it, reflected an idea which was widespread even during the war: that since the Second World War had been a truly global struggle, it would have global ramifications.

The Allies' wartime conferences were marked by protests against colonialism, especially on the part of the United States. Empire, according to its critics, was at best thought to be an archaic form of rule and at worst uneconomic and oppressive. It was at variance with the principles of self-determination first enunciated by President Wilson at Versailles and repeated by President Roosevelt in the 1941 Atlantic Charter. The Soviet Union, too, encouraged colonial struggles which its postwar propaganda was to describe as 'wars of liberation'. Ironically its own 'empire' was to collapse after briefer struggles of a totally different kind.

The transition to independence was traumatic for all involved, and in some countries it produced bitter violence and turmoil. In the Dutch territory of Indonesia, for example, when a new republic was proclaimed on 17 August 1945 the Dutch government found it impossible to accept it without making uneasy compromises. It was not until the late summer and early autumn of 1949 that agreements were reached which enabled Indonesian independence to become a fact by August 1950.

By March 1946 the British government had willingly rather than reluctantly recognized that India had to be granted total independence from the Crown. The transfer of power was complete by August 1947, although the process unleashed deep hatreds between Hindus and Moslems as two new countries emerged: India and Pakistan. Burma followed – choosing to stay outside the Commonwealth, unlike India, in January 1948. Closer to home, the Republic of Ireland Act was passed on 18 April 1949 (this was not true 'decolonization'), although the 'Six Counties' of Northern Ireland remained part of the Union. The 'Commonwealth' in Africa was to be 'liberated' later, usually by agreement, with the Gold Coast (Ghana) leading the way in 1957. The process of decolonization accelerated in east as well as west Africa during the 1960s. Meanwhile, South Africa, with an *Apartheid* philosophy of its own, withdrew from the Common- wealth in 1961.

France, like Britain, had begun to face some opposition to its colonial rule before the outbreak of war, but officials in Paris read these signs of protest as limited, and in 1945, now freed from German occupation, France was determined to retain significant parts of *France d'Outre-Mer*, the 'confetti' of the dispersed Empire of the French Republic, especially the territories of Indochina and, closer to home, Algeria. The consequent wars of decolonization were amongst the longest and most brutal of the decolonization era. In 1945 France immediately returned to Indochina (which had been abandoned by the French and occupied by the Japanese during the war), and was quickly involved in expensive political and military operations which lasted until 1954 – in time for a new crisis for French colonial authority in Algeria. In northern Vietnam, Ho Chi Min had established a 'free state' with a strong communist army, and France's struggle became yet another episode in the Cold War. Worse was to come for the *métropole* (the centre of the French Empire: Paris) with the challenge to imperial rule in Algeria. Summed up in the popular slogan, '*Algérie, c'est la France*', Algeria was considered an integral part of the Republic, a 'salt-water extension of France itself'.[3] It was only after ten years of protracted conflict, which even challenged political stability on the French mainland, that Algeria became a sovereign state on 1 July 1962.

Some historians have argued that European imperialism lived on after empire, with continuing economic ties between imperial territories and their former masters ('neo-colonialism') and with many people of the third world adopting 'western' forms of civilization enshrining traditional European values. The most obvious legacy was the resilience of the colonial 'languages', English and French being the most persistent, especially amongst the educated and powerful. Martiniquan-born author Frantz Fanon in his book *Peau noir, Masques blancs* ('Black Skin, White Masks'), argued that the use of the French language distorted indigenous culture – he called it 'the zebra striping of my mind'. More positive critiques of imperialism, on the other hand, stressed the educational and technological contribution made by the nineteenth-century conquerors. The first Prime Minister of India, for example, Jawaharlal Nehru, had been educated in England and inherited a relatively effective governmental structure from the Raj.

New appreciations of imperialism also led contemporary analysts to postulate that the Soviet Union, by annexing territories in eastern Europe, and the United States, by exploiting the dependence of western Europe and South America on American economic aid, took over the imperial mantle of the European powers. Indeed, some historians have argued that America's involvement in western European reconstruction amounted to 'empire by invitation'. There were other forces at work in western Europe, however, that contributed more to its recovery and led it into the most prosperous period in its history, sharply distinguishing it from the 'Soviet Empire'.

Economic miracles, 1949–68

The development of the Cold War, fast on the heels of the Second World War, had an important influence on the way Europe recovered. This time, the rejuvenation of Europe, after the first unsteady splutters in 1945–48, came quickly and durably, in a way that it had not done after 1919. By 1952 postwar reconstruction had largely been achieved, yet once property and goods lost through war had been restored, this did not mark the end of European industry's resurgent growth as it had done after the First World War. It was rather the beginning. Although the western Europeans and Americans were at odds over the former's desire to sustain higher levels of welfare provision than ever before – a goal which remained unaltered in the Christian Democrat and Conservative-dominated Europe of the 1950s – the Americans 'sold' western Europe the prospect of unprecedented levels of economic growth if Europeans would adhere to the governing principles of 'mass production, scientific management and productivity' in micro and macro levels of economic management. 'Productivity' was a watchword even in post-1945 Labour Britain, and during the 1950s the ethos of 'Americanization', which had begun to permeate Europe in the 1920s, now spread widely, with English as its language. The United States tried to make the old world new, and in an unprecedented international propaganda offensive, the USA was held up to Europe as an inspirational model for growth. The British author G. Hutton in his book entitled *We Too Can Prosper* (1949) explained why and how.

As in the interwar period, however, the Europeans took what they wanted from the American model and discarded the rest, although not without harsh words directed at the 'consumerism', popular culture and language of the Americans (once again, French intellectuals were the most vehement anti-Americans). Growth in the 1950s and 1960s was now faster in continental Europe (as in Japan) than in the United States, with growth rates of more than 4.4 to 5.5 per cent a year. The reasons behind this sustained growth are still controversial, but of crucial importance was the emergence of a mass consumer market which created higher living standards and prosperity for all those in work. There was also a move towards bigger units as the great corporation flourished, often as an international force. Meanwhile, trends established during the first half of the century continued: the numbers of farmers continued to dwindle (in Italy the proportion of workers employed in agriculture and fisheries fell from 43 per cent to 14 per cent) and the numbers of workers in the tertiary (service sector) began to expand rapidly.

A social consensus, sometimes also known as the postwar settlement, which had emerged across Europe also contributed towards economic growth, notably in Italy, France and Germany. Its terms differed across western Europe, but it usually involved acceptance of social reform and a recognition of workers' rights. Politically, it usually entailed support for alliance with the United States. In sharp contrast to the interwar years, western Europe's democratic governments were able to secure economic growth, greater cooperation between employers and employed, liberal political rights in a stable constitutional framework and, of course, peace within Europe.

Germany, 1949–68

The transformation of Germany in this period was undoubtedly the most dramatic example of a 'miracle'. While East Germany was being converted into a 'model' communist state, the Federal Republic of Germany (FDR) became the model of a modern capitalist liberal democracy. Under the leadership of Adenauer, the Republic, to the delight of the Americans and the disappointment of the British Labour Party, eschewed the nationalization of the German economy in favour of the 'social market'. Under the able direction of Economics Minister Ludwig Erhard, a strategy of low taxation, stable currency and liberal trade was followed. In consequence the Republic established favourable trading relations with northern, as well as with western, Europe, so that within a few years West Germany had become a major exporter of industrial goods within the expanding multilateral trading system of the West. In a transformation which became known as Germany's *Wirtschaftswunder* (Economic Miracle), Erhard nourished an unprecedented growth in West Germany's gross national product which rose from 98 to 162 points between 1949 and 1954.

The CDU coalition government also succeeded in creating industrial management structures which incorporated trade unions into a national wage-bargaining process and drew on workers' participation on the factory management boards of individual enterprises. In both East and West Germany, fundamentally different though the regimes were, the German industrial worker, exploited and marginalized in Hitler's social vision, was made central to Germany's reconstruction. As elsewhere in western Europe, the fruits of the new prosperity were not distributed evenly. War widows and pensioners, for example, fared less comfortably as Erhard's social market emphasized the role of workers and industrialists. Yet there was a sense of accomplishment and direction.

By the 1960s Germany had been plugged into the global system of banking and trade and had become both a formidable trading rival for Britain and France, and a serious competitor for the United States. Companies like Volkswagen cars, Bayer chemicals and Siemens electrics

Plate 11.1 Production lines at the Volkswagen factory in Wolfsburg, Lower Saxony, 1949. The 'Volkswagen' (Peoples' Car) was a potent symbol in Hitler's propaganda of a social revolution in Germany. Until 1945, despite all the razzmatazz, most of the money Germans put towards buying one was diverted to rearmament. But after the British forces of occupation relinquished control of the company in 1949, it became the first major company to be privatised by Erhard in 1957. Volkswagen had shed all its ideological associations with the Nazi era to become one of the world's most successful manufacturers.

stood amongst the top ten multinational corporations in the world, their success marking a long overdue victory for those Germans who had advocated an 'internationalist' economic policy in the interwar period but whose ideas had gone untried. West Germany's formidable economic success also restored a sense of confidence to the German people. Pension provision and the expansion of the network of social services continued to grow, unemployment stood at less than 1 per cent from 1961 to 1963, and to complement this economic and social achievement, Adenauer aspired to follow in Chancellor Stresemann's footsteps by working to reintegrate Germany into the international community by joining NATO and reaching a rapprochement with France.

In 1963 Adenauer was replaced by Erhard, and both he and his subsequent successors continued to use social market strategies to govern West Germany. When the SPD's Willie Brandt, an exile from Nazi Germany, became Foreign Minister in a Grand Coalition (CDU/CSU and SPD), in 1966, it was foreign policy, therefore, not domestic policy which was altered dramatically as Brandt established a new, more conciliatory *Ostpolitik* (Eastern Europe foreign policy) which marked West Germany's coming of age. Brandt hoped to advance relations between East and West Germany by a series of small steps – commentators in the Democratic Republic dubbed it 'aggression in carpet slippers' – and it was an initiative which he built upon during his tenure as Chancellor from 1969 until forced to resign in 1974, in the wake of revelations that a member of his personal staff was a communist spy. But despite intermittent spy scandals, the West German people now accepted East Germany as a separate entity. In Brandt's words there were 'two German states, one German nation', and this recognition brought the FDR new trading partners in Eastern Europe and a deeper sense of political stability and permanence.

Beginnings of a European Union, 1945–51

The evolution of the European Community (EC), as the various European collectives dominated by the European Economic Community (EEC) later came to be known, provided an important framework to ensure the FDR's commitment to West European, and not simply to German, prosperity and peace. Many different elements, political and economic, contributed to the creation of the EEC, its context set by international and domestic trends, by the prevailing balance of power and by economic and technical stability or change. So, too, did many personalities. The measures taken by, first, national politicians and later officials of the EEC acting in concert with national representatives often simply reshaped economic and social developments in western Europe which were sometimes independent of the EEC, but which nevertheless served to strengthen the power of the Community.

The idea of a European union had emerged long before 1945, long, indeed, before 1789, but it was only after the First World War – which had exposed the reality of European relations as one of bitter, bloody conflict – that a pan-European campaign began in earnest. The central European intellectual, the Hungarian Count Coundenhove-Kalergi, and the French Foreign Minister, Aristide Briand, were among the pioneers. During the Second World War Hitler sought to create some form of European union under German control, while the common experiences of resistance movements seeking to destroy him contributed in turn to a sense of common European identity across national frontiers.

The postwar debate over European integration was opened by Winston Churchill when, in a speech in Zürich in 1946, he proposed that a Council of Europe be established. It seemed as much a clarion call as his Fulton speech denouncing the 'iron curtain', and in a climate of rising tensions between the superpowers, his proposal was seized upon by aspirants hoping to create a 'third force' – a united Europe – to match the United States and the USSR. Churchill subsequently launched the 'United Europe Movement', while France established the 'Council for United Europe'. The shared sense of a 'European Movement' gathered momentum when the increasingly fashionable conviction spread that integration was a means to prosperity and security and an antidote to the demon of nationalism. Moreover, this approach attracted the warm support of the United States.

By the 1950s the 'European' debate was altered with the acceleration of the Cold War and the arrival of Marshall aid in Europe. The notion of Britain championing a European 'third force' now seemed hopelessly unrealistic in the face of Britain's near bankruptcy and the emergent divisions over the form a united Europe should take. It was now abundantly clear that the countries of eastern Europe, which had not been permitted to accept Marshall aid, would be unable to join such a union and that the institutions of a 'western' European community would advance the 'segregation' of Europe. At the time of the first Council of Europe, established in 1949 to explore the possibilities of European integration, only a minority of western European powers favoured a continental federation with a common parliament, cabinet and economic policy. Majority support rested with the notion of 'functional cooperation'. This was a pragmatic, evolutionary approach to cooperation by which integration could be pursued on areas on common economic interest – the production of coal, for example. It was not to last. Nor was the favoured approach of many Europeans, even in 1949, except as a first step.

For nations as diverse as Britain, Greece and Finland, the answer to European union in 1951 was already a resounding 'No'. The British Labour government soon lost interest in Europe in the face of the Christian-Democrat dominance in western European politics, Britain's imperial ties and the country's persistent economic problems which many feared would be exacerbated by a common market. Foreign Minister Ernest Bevin opted instead to cultivate a 'special relationship' with the United States. And when the 'European debate' shifted from political plans for a western European Union, towards suggestions for European economic co-operation, Britain still stood out. By contrast, the success of the OEEC, the European Payments Union (1950) to facilitate the transferability of currencies, and the creation of the Benelux Economic Union (Belgium, the Netherlands and Luxembourg), which aimed to free controls on 90 per cent of trade between the three countries, all pointed the way to the future. Italy, France and the Benelux states, in sharp contrast to Britain and

Denmark, sustained their enthusiasm for European cooperation as the old slogan of 'divide and conquer' gave way to 'unify and federate'.

France's commitment was especially important. In contrast to its interwar policy towards Germany, France was now determined that the Federal Republic should be integrated into western Europe. The French government's initiative was greatly assisted by Adenauer's staunch pro-West policies and by the warm support of the United States, anxious to create a strong and united western Europe, able to defend itself and avoid the misfortunes which engulfed Europe in the interwar years. It was the Frenchman, Jean Monnet, who focused the vision. Enlisting the support of the then French Foreign Minister, Robert Schuman, he proposed what to him was a first step, a European Coal and Steel Community (ECSC) dealing with commodities crucial for western European recovery and located in Europe's industrial heartland – the French province of Lorraine and the German Ruhr valley. The Schuman plan, as Monnet's scheme came to be known, offered an enticing mix of potential economic benefits, with the ultimate ideal of European integration founded on Franco-German cooperation.

The ECSC, formally created in Paris in 1951, was supported by the six European powers most committed to greater European cooperation: the Benelux countries, France, Germany and Italy. (Britain, Europe's most powerful nation, first rejected membership, then became an associate member in 1954.) The ECSC was an important innovation in the stimulation of coal and steel production – steel output increased by 50 per cent and industrial production expanded at twice the British rate during the ECSC's first five years. It was also a landmark in western European history, for the ECSC established the principle of supranational cooperation under which participating states had to cede authority to a European agency, restricted though it was to the production and sale of iron, coal and steel. A court to settle disputes amongst members was also set up along with an assembly which convened in the first European Council's Chamber in Strasbourg.

From 1958 to 1968 the economic resurgence of western Europe was particularly impressive within the European Community, and this success helped persuade countries of the Community's potential benefits. Britain had opted for looser co-operation afforded by the European Free Trade Association (EFTA), created in 1960 with Britain, Denmark, Norway, Sweden, Switzerland, Austria, Portugal, and later Finland and Iceland, as members. By 1960 western Europe's economy was booming. In that year alone it accounted for 58 per cent of world trade and for over two-thirds of the globe's GNP. Moreover, western Europe had also become the focus of the global security system (NATO), which grew to embrace Greece, Turkey (in 1952) and West Germany (in 1955), and which encouraged scientific cooperation, built underground pipelines to supply fuel in case of war and sought 'more and more to harmonize' the political views of members 'to create a sense of community.'[4]

Institutions of the Cold War

During the 1950s and 1960s, in both eastern and western Europe, the political and economic environment was stable for the first time in many decades, and hot wars outside Europe stimulated economic growth in the West. In consequence, despite the persistent fear that a 'Third World War' lay just around the corner, the division of Europe seemed to be set by an inexorable logic which made it difficult, in part given American policy, to erode the ideological differences between communists and non-communists. It was 'institutionalized' too by the growing numbers of organizations on either side of the 'iron curtain' designed to coordinate economic and military activities inside the two blocs. In the East there was the Cominform, the communist information bureau, interpreted by the West as a resurrection of the Comintern, dedicated to promoting Marxist revolution across the globe. In the West organizations of economic cooperation also advanced the segregation of Europe: the Bretton Woods institutions and, later, the EEC (see p. 435). It was in response to the creation and successful development in western Europe that the USSR established the Council for Mutual Economic Assistance (CMEA), or Comecon as it became known in the West (1949), to provide economic assistance to communist powers. Of course, the Soviet Union, unlike the United States, had no real aid to give, and in its early years Comecon, operating out of small, dingy offices in Moscow, concentrated instead on collecting reparations from East Germany, Romania and Bulgaria. After Stalin's death Comecon was remodeled to coordinate planning and production within the Soviet bloc as a whole, and it also took on some responsibilities for military coordination in the East until the inauguration of the Warsaw pact in May 1955.

The creation of military agencies, NATO and its Soviet equivalent, the Warsaw pact, formalized the military division of Europe between East and West. Founded in the year when Yugoslavia was reconciled with the Soviet Union in the wake of Khrushchev's visit to Belgrade in 1955 and his new foreign policy of 'co-existence' with the West, the Warsaw Pact largely reaffirmed the military status quo in eastern Europe. The Soviet Union continued to dominate the armed forces of the satellite countries – ostensibly they were there to discourage the imperialist West from invading – and the Pact was an attempt to integrate military command structures. It also lent a spurious legality to the Red Army's effective occupation of eastern Europe, for in the words of the Hungarian Prime Minister, András Hegedüs, its text gave 'at least in theory, an opportunity for the leaderships of these countries to take control of their armies'. Albania, Romania and Bulgaria did not have Soviet troops stationed on their soil, for their loyalty to the Soviet Union was unquestioned (though Albania was to drop out of the Warsaw pact in 1961). Yugoslavia, too, controlled its own military forces.

By 1960 Churchill's metaphoric iron curtain had become chillingly real as cultural and social contacts as well as diplomatic relations between East and West were infected by the suspicions and restrictions of the Cold War. It was during this period that a British woman exclaimed to a Czechoslovak visitor who had just flown to Britain, 'I didn't know that was possible . . . I didn't realize that 'planes could fly so high as to go over the iron curtain.' Yet, aside from the intrigue, popularized in novels like Graham Greene's *The Third Man*, the Cold War had a number of unexpected spin-offs. It provided a 'system' of sorts which maximized peace and stability and minimized the chance of war within Europe.

France, 1960–68

The new spirit of cooperation in western Europe was nowhere more clearly illustrated than in France, where internal developments fostered Franco–German reconciliation. Successive French governments, shaking off the uncertainty which had dogged their interwar performance, favoured the West German style social market over the large-scale nationalization of industry, and French industrialists and civil servants launched a drive for expansionist capitalism. Monnet's plan kick-started French economic growth which reached unprecedented heights when French productivity rose by 10.4 per cent between 1967 and 1968. The best indicator of this new found sense of purpose and optimism was the reversal of a trend which had plagued French confidence in economic and foreign policy matters since the late-nineteenth century: the country's birth rate began to rise dramatically. Throughout the 1950s the French birth rate was over 18 babies per 1,000 of the population; in the 1930s it had been 14.9 per 1,000.

As in Britain and Germany, this new prosperity was not distributed evenly throughout the nation, and it is important, therefore, not to exaggerate the sense of a permanent social equilibrium either in France or in western Europe as a whole during this period. *La France paysanne* (rural France) continued to decline as did the fortunes of small shopkeepers and artisans. And as elsewhere in western Europe, the prosperous new class in postwar France comprised the *cadres* (the executives or middle managers), who were particularly comfortably placed in years of economic boom. Regional differences persisted too, for as an exasperated de Gaulle once reflected 'How on earth does one govern a country which makes 265 different kinds of cheese?'

Political life in France reflected these mixed fortunes, riven as it was with instability and short-lived coalitions. This, plus the political crisis sparked by France's colonial struggle in Algeria, worked to return de Gaulle to power in 1958 after an absence of 12 years. He then set about devising a new constitution for France, and the Fifth Republic that he created was an attempt to foster greater mainstream loyalty, minimize the representation of small or extremist parties, and above all, to demonstrate that the French government now controlled parliament rather than vice versa. More remarkably, Algerian independence was conceded in the Evian agreements of 1962. By then the cost of Algerian 'freedom' was the death of 17,500 French people and over 200,000 Muslims.

From the start de Gaulle insisted on a strong hand in French foreign policy. In an effort to reassert French power after the loss of empire, he opened up closer relations with Russia, China and eastern Europe; the development of *Force de Frappe*, an independent nuclear deterrent, served to compensate the French military for their imperial losses. Although primarily motivated by the desire to liberate France from its recent role of victim by creating a strong, independent regime on the world stage, de Gaulle was also anxious to articulate and preserve European, as distinct from British and American, interests in the Cold War. Most dramatic was his announcement on 7 March 1966 that France, while remaining a signatory of the Atlantic Pact, was leaving NATO. The military alliance was thrown into turmoil. The Americans were particularly incensed as the French, along with the rest of the Brussels Pact, had been only too relieved to see the United States sign the Atlantic Treaty back in 1949. It was ironic, too, given de Gaulle's claim to champion European interests, that the NATO headquarters had to be moved from Fontainebleau to Brussels now that NATO forces were no longer welcome on French soil. But de Gaulle was a realist. He knew that ultimately western Europe needed the United States to counterbalance the USSR. He sought to maximize French independence without permanently alienating America, and he succeeded in returning authority to French foreign policy and a sense of pride to the French people.

Italy, 1951–65

Italy, too, enjoyed its own *miracolo economico* during these years. Despite constitutional weakness – some 48 different governments and 18 different premiers between 1945 and 1989 – there were unprecedented levels of economic growth in the mid-1950s and 1960s. Indeed, during this period of *'La Dolce Vita'* the Italian economy grew faster than any other major country in the world, including the USSR and Japan, with growth especially impressive in the production of automobiles (Fiat, Pirelli), office machinery (Olivetti) and electronics. The voracious growth of the Italian economy – in the 1950s and 1960s Italy's annual rate of growth was 5.7–5.8 per cent – was surprising perhaps, given Italy's poor economic record in the first half of the century when there was a chronic shortage of raw materials and a heavy dependence on food imports. Now the Italian people disproved critics who claimed that Italian economic growth could only be secured by cheap labour and showed themselves to be amongst the most hard-working and inventive peoples in Europe.

As in the remainder of western Europe, the state played an active role in generating economic growth, with 20–30 per cent of Italy's industry (including 60 per cent of all steel production) owned by the Italian state. Europe's burgeoning tourist industry in the first great age of civil aviation also played its part in firmly establishing prosperity in Italy. But, mimicking the trend elsewhere in western Europe, the wages and the standard of living in northern Italy comfortably equalled those of Europe's wealthiest regions, while the poor agricultural regions in the south became progressively more impoverished and substantial numbers of unemployed Sicilians set off to work as *Gastarbeiter* (guestworkers) in West Germany.

Britain, 1951–68

The one nation for which the postwar settlement did not bring an ebullient sense of national prosperity and confidence was Great Britain. When the Conservatives returned to power in 1951 with Winston Churchill as Britain's 76-year-old Premier, there was no strong sense of change. Nor was there any new commitment to the future. Indeed, there was little alteration to the Labour government's postwar settlement beyond the controversial denationalization of the iron and steel industries. The remainder of Labour's nationalization programme and the (largely uncontentious) welfare state remained intact. The Conservatives continued to hold the reigns of power from 1951 until 1964, with Anthony Eden succeeding Churchill in 1955, to be succeeded in turn by Harold Macmillan after a crisis which concerned not Europe but the Middle East. Despite Macmillan's sense that most people 'had never had it so good' – for levels of education, housing and health provision had all increased – the period was marked by '*la maladie anglaise*': self-doubt, sluggish economic growth (annual growth rates were amongst the lowest in West Europe at 2.7 per cent per annum), and a decline in international stature.

The Suez Crisis in 1956, which brought Macmillan to power, cruelly unmasked the reality of British power overseas. British governments had hoped that their claim to a 'special relationship' with the United States and their attachment to the Commonwealth would be sufficient to safeguard British interests in the Middle East and with it British world power status. Instead, the United States, the USSR and opposition parties at home were united in their condemnation of Britain and France's independent action in attacking Nasser's Egypt (with dubious contrasts being drawn with the appeasement of the 'dictators' in the 1930s). The decline of John Bull's influence abroad was clear and provoked a run on the pound sterling in November 1956, and Eden's resignation. When Britain decided to abandon the Suez campaign, it also alienated its Suez ally of France, at a crucial period in the evolution of the European Community.

The deep sense of national *malaise* which permeated Britain was compounded in the early 1960s by numerous scandals which rocked political and governmental life – the Vassall, Philby and Burgess spy scandals and the exposure of Secretary of State for War John Profumo in a sex case (March 1963). Still more serious, however, was continued sluggish economic growth. The British economy was afflicted by what became known as 'stop-go' economics (deflationary policies which, as soon as they were abandoned, were followed by inflation), with chronic symptoms of government overspending, and living on credit, involving regular, if unpredictable balance of payments crises.

Government policies did not help the British economy, but they were not the root of the economic problem. This lay deeper. Britain was now among the 'disadvantaged' as a result of having been the world's first industrial power, and of having been among the victors in two world wars which had destroyed British assets and generated substantial overseas debts. Even its old geographic assets now looked like disadvantages: its island status kept it apart from the centre of Europe; its high density of population involved government in the heavy economic costs of maintaining an efficient 'infrastructure'. During the 1960s Britain's most renowned export was pop music – The Beatles, The Rolling Stones and The Who were hugely successful groups overseas.

Britain's relative decline as a world power was a challenge that was to face it throughout the rest of the twentieth century. Historians have proposed numerous explanations for it, and debate still rages. The most telling interpretations centre on Britain's failure to invest sufficiently in its postwar manufacturing base, in its low level of investment in research and development relative to other European powers (as well as to the Japanese and Americans), in the negative influence of British trade unions on productivity levels, and in the 'amateurish', untrained calibre of British management. Some have argued that complacency was Britain's undoing. Unlike many countries in both western and eastern Europe, Britain did not ask the necessary questions of itself in the wake of the Second World War. It was not until the 1960s that institutions were questioned, and then only by the radical left. The serious questioning began in 1979.

It was during the controversial 1960s, when Germany and Italy increased their exports six times more quickly than Britain, that Harold Macmillan and his Labour successor, Harold Wilson, reluctantly reached the conclusion that trading with the Commonwealth and membership of the European Free Trade Association (EFTA) was no adequate alternative to membership of the EEC. And even then they both met with fierce opposition from inside their own parties.

Recovery in 'little' Europe

In the heady environment of capitalist boom, Britain's industrial rivals of the nineteenth century – France and Germany – now outstripped Britain's economic achievements, even though in both countries the radical left was stronger than in Britain. More humiliating, perhaps, was the unprecedented growth enjoyed by western Europe's smaller powers, including Sweden, the Netherlands, Austria and Belgium. According to the Belgian economic historian Herman Van Der Wee, the last of these, which had played an important part in early industrialization, developed a new style of mixed economy which promoted central consultation between various 'social partners' – bankers, employers' organizations and organized labour with cooperation between the latter two groups especially effective in creating an atmosphere of social peace that was highly conducive to economic recovery. Austria followed closely in the wake of Germany. Sweden and the Netherlands also enjoyed considerable export-led growth, particularly once exports to Germany were revived in 1949. Spain and Greece, on the other hand, began to make real economic progress at the beginning of the 1960s, with the tourist industry forging the way. Sunshine became a major economic asset, though the social costs of popular tourism were to be high.

The Treaty of Rome and after

Emboldened by their strengthening economies, the Netherlands, Belgium and Luxembourg – the most consistent northern advocates of greater European cooperation during the interwar period – launched a dramatic new initiative in 1955, led by Dutch Foreign Minister Johan Beyen. He argued that if the 'Europe of Six' was moving towards a common market through organizations like the ECSC, why not discuss the possibility of a European Common Market immediately? That same year the decision to explore this possibility was taken at Messina in Sicily, although the six member states of the ECSC proceeded with caution, with Britain watching from afar, confident that the common market scheme would collapse. Instead, by the 1957 treaties signed in Rome, the six had formed the European Atomic Energy Community (EURATOM) and the European Economic Community (EEC).

The EEC came into being on 1 January 1958. With its administrative centre in Brussels – a Commission with Vice-Presidents from each of the member states – the EEC seemed at first to lack much of the supranational authority enjoyed by the ECSC. By 1967, however, the EEC, EURATOM and the ECSC had merged together into a single European Commission. Large nations appointed two commissioners each, small nations one; and

Plate 11.2 The signing of the Treaty of Rome, 23 March 1957. Ministers from West Germany, France, Italy, Belgium, the Netherlands and Luxembourg gathered to sign the treaty which founded the European Economic Community. The same day, the world's press was treated to a different photo opportunity underlining British preoccupations: Prime Minister Harold Macmillan in Bermuda holding conference talks with the American President Dwight Eisenhower.

they in turn supervised a staff that by 1970 numbered more than 15,000 men and women. Political as well as economic authority came to the EEC by accretion. It soon acquired a European Court of Justice (with the important brief to ensure that Community law had 'equivalent' effect on all member states) and an elected European Parliament, although the latter had little control over the operations of the Commission (for example, it could not sack an individual commissioner).

The primary object of the EEC was to create a customs union with free and equal competition among its members. This would bring peace and prosperity to Europe and, for those who aspired to closer political union, it was hoped that greater economic cooperation would foster political unity in foreign, defence and social policies of the member states. A full customs union was in place by 1968, an expensive Common Agricultural Policy (CAP) had been devised and implemented to protect farmers in the member states, average GDP growth rates of 5 per cent per annum had been reached, and a five-fold increase in the volume of trade between EEC members had been achieved.

Impressed by such obvious success, Britain, having first sought to foster a looser form of European cooperation through EFTA, made its first application to join the EEC in 1961. But disputes with President de Gaulle over defence and foreign policy served to scupper both this request (finally rejected in 1963) and a further application under a new government in 1967. An exasperated American official complained at the time that de Gaulle was 'the most goddamn undealable-with human being that's ever existed'. However, de Gaulle's own government was challenged in 1968 following student demonstrations, and after his resignation in 1969 the important resolution to widen the Community was taken at the EEC's Hague Summit later that year. In the following year detailed talks on the enlargement of the Community began, with Britain, Eire, Denmark and Norway. Only the Norwegian people went on to reject proposed membership, as they were to do again years later in 1994.

Why had Britain's attitude changed? The decision to apply for membership tested the Labour Party more than the Conservative Party, for many feared that it would cost British jobs and that Christian-Democrat Europe would work to compromise socialist initiatives in Britain. By 1967, however, it was all too clear that not only was the British economy growing less quickly than its continental counterparts, but that the British Commonwealth, long thought of as 'an alternative to Europe', was itself in crisis over the question of Rhodesia, which had, for the first time, brought the British government into conflict with a white minority regime over the issue of independence. (It was also the first rebellion by a British dependency since the eighteenth century.) The leader of the Conservative opposition after 1964, Edward Heath, was a staunch pro-European, so that for Harold Wilson, sensitive to all currents of opinion, including business opinion, committing the Labour government to EEC membership would help steal Heath's electoral thunder. There was some urgency too in order to exert some influence over EEC policies, in particular CAP, which the British government considered to be poor economics and potentially damaging to the interests of British agriculture. Finally, Britain's potential participation in the EEC was warmly welcomed by the United States, while de Gaulle's veto itself encouraged popular enthusiasm to see it overturned. French *Grandeur* had to be confronted. This was an old task.

Into the sobering 'seventies', 1968–75

The political stability of the international system in postwar Europe until the early-1960s was remarkable when set against the first 45 years of the twentieth century. Yet it rested on assumptions which never went unchallenged. Nuclear deterrence, which kept the Cold War cold, always

LEAP FROG

Plate 11.3 Leap Frog, 1961. The hapless British Prime Minister Harold Macmillan appears set to overcome Luxembourg, Belgian, Italian, Dutch and German conditions for EEC membership, but de Gaulle's objections were insurmountable. In fact, much of the leg work for Britain's first application to the EEC was undertaken by Edward Heath, then Lord Privy Seal, who travelled over 100,000 miles in Europe in the bid to secure British membership.

had its critics and their numbers increased during the 1960s. The global picture also became more relevant as American and European pressure groups, often using militant tactics, demanded an end to the war in

Vietnam and the extension of civil rights for blacks (especially in the United States). Urban riots broke out on both sides of the Atlantic, triggered, in part, by the assassination of black civil rights activist Martin Luther King in April 1968, and the view, now widespread among the public and press, that the West could not win. (US strategists were surprised by a massive communist offensive in January 1968, this after the United States dropped more bomb tonnage on Vietnam between 1965 and 1967 than the Allies had dropped on the whole of Europe during the Second World War.)

In May 1968 in Europe, the universities were at the centre of demonstrations. France was brought to a virtual halt as students and young workers – angry at the 'hierarchical, authoritarian' methods of their professors and employers – joined the greatest general strike in European history: it involved nine million workers and lost 15 million working days. The year 1968 proved to be explosive not only in Paris, but in Germany (Frankfurt was the intellectual centre of the student revolt) and across the 'iron curtain' in Czechoslovakia (see above, p. 404). The convergence did not last, however. Society in the West was not much changed as a consequence of the demonstrations. Czechoslovakia was repressed.

The early resignation of de Gaulle was, however, a manifestation of change, while from the new left urban terrorist groups like the Red Army Faction in Germany set out to subvert the state. It, in turn, spawned new splinter groups like the German gang founded by Andreas Baader and Ulrike Meinhof which robbed banks and bombed military and civilian targets from 1970 until 1972. By 1975 most of the Baader-Meinhof gang had been tried at the specially-built Stammheim gaol and imprisoned, but their motivations and methods were echoed in the activities of the Italian Red Army Brigades. Culminating in the kidnapping and murder of the former Italian Prime Minister and leader of the Christian Democratic Party, Aldo Moro. These terrorized Italy from 1977 to 1980.

In the 1970s the certainty and confidence in the postwar settlement had all but disappeared. When President Nixon dramatically devalued the American dollar in 1971, it was clear that the American economy was in difficulties. Superpower status for the United States had come at a price and worse was to follow. In October 1973 war in the Middle East led to a quadrupling in oil prices which generated tremendous inflationary pressure throughout western Europe and quickly ate away at European growth, in both East and West. Western Europe now encountered a new economic phenomenon: 'stagflation' (unemployment – structural and cyclical – combined with high levels of inflation).

Economic dislocation brought political upheaval to western Europe during the 1970s, with West Germany and Austria faring better than Britain and France. Good labour relations between the government, employers and employees enabled the West German Socialist Chancellor, Helmut Schmidt, who succeeded Brandt in 1974, to keep wage demands

Plate 11.4 Popular protests on the streets of Lisbon, 26 April 1974. Here the crowd surrounded a tank carrying three former members of Portugal's hated security police (*Directorate General of Security*) attempting to escape from soldiers of the military junta which had just seized power. Their flight was in vain. All security police were subsequently rounded up by the military.

down and to control inflation. The same was not true of Britain, where Conservative Prime Minister Edward Heath fell in 1974 (there were two general elections that year) to be replaced first by an exhausted Harold Wilson and later by an equally beleaguered Labour Prime Minister, James Callaghan. In 1974 Heath had flirted briefly with the ideas of monetarists and free marketers, which were to dominate political life in varying degrees in the conservative, Christian Democratic-dominated western Europe of the 1980s. These ideas came to be associated with his successor as Conservative leader, Margaret Thatcher, who succeeded Callaghan as Prime Minister after the general election of 1979. It was Heath, however, pro-German in outlook, whose government took the decision to join the EEC in 1971. Britain was an uneasy member. Although membership was confirmed in a referendum in June 1975 (the majority was 67 per cent), there was little sense on the part of the public that substantial benefits had been gained.

By 1973 the EEC had already become the Europe of Nine, and it was to become the Europe of Twelve. It now held global economic importance comparable to the United States, accounting for more than 20 per cent of the world's trade, and its 320 million inhabitants were among the most prosperous in the world. The evolution of the EEC had proceeded on economic lines, but in October 1972 it had also resolved to pursue joint action on environmental, scientific and social issues, and soon these activities mushroomed.

It continued to be riven by disputes over CAP, fishing quotas and the allocation of the Regional Development Fund, and after 1973 the British government became the largest contributor to the Community's budget while benefiting little from CAP. Moreover, while widening the Community's political activities by making the European Parliament an elected body (1974), the evolution of a 'citizens' Europe' fell on fallow ground, and subsequent efforts to create monetary union floundered. So, too, did efforts to unify the Community's foreign policy.

Democracy in southern Europe, 1975–79

The economic crisis of the 1970s never seriously threatened democracy in western Europe. Indeed, for Spain and Portugal the 1970s marked the creation of liberal democracy after decades of authoritarian rule. Both countries had prospered during the 1960s, perhaps paradoxically, serving to undermine rather than to secure the continuation of General Franco's strongly authoritarian dictatorship beyond his death in 1975. As a result of economic expansion, new strata of technocrats and businessmen and women had emerged who were anxious to liberalize government and the economy. In his last years Franco attempted to pander to Spanish democrats without conceding real power, but after his death it became clear that Spain's new 37-year-old King Juan Carlos, nominated by Franco, and his chosen Prime Minister, Adolfo Suárez, were committed to bringing democratic government to Spain as rapidly as possible. The first democratic elections for 40 years were held on 15 June 1977.

Spain's transition to democracy was relatively orderly, despite an attempted military coup in 1980; Portugal's was not. In April 1974 a group of Army officers overthrew the dictatorship of Marcello Caetano (who had succeeded Salazar in 1968) and installed a junta under the presidency of General Antonio de Spinola, who soon lost power. The country was exhausted from a series of colonial wars in Africa, and from Portuguese politics oscillating between right and left in inconclusive elections and unstable coalition governments in 1976, 1977, 1978 and 1979. By the mid-1980s the worst was over, and in 1985 after further constitutional changes designed to reduce the role of government in industry and agriculture, the Socialist Dr Mario Soares became Portugal's first civilian Prime Minister in over 60 years in 1986.

Greece's fragile democracy, founded upon an unresolved civil war in 1946–49, began to crumble in 1967 when military officers staged a coup, and this was followed by attacks and counter-attacks from the left and right of Greek politics. By 1971 Greece was controlled by the dictatorship of a triumvirate of colonels who had taken control, but their bungling over the Cyprus question cost the colonels their power. After several years of constitutional upheaval in Greece, which saw the abolition of the monarchy, democracy was finally restabilized in the 1980s, greatly aided by an improvement in Greco-Turkish relations and, more important, by membership of the European Community in 1981. Spain and Portugal, too, benefited greatly from the political credibility, investment and aid which European membership brought after they joined in 1986.

Western Europe, 1979–89

Prospects were not auspicious for western Europe at the beginning of the 1980s, especially when, in the wake of the revolution in Iran in 1979 and war between Iran and Iraq, which began a year later, oil prices were hiked up again, bringing with it the renewed spectre of inflation and deep recession. There were threats too to heavy industrial capacity as Japan and the countries of the Pacific Rim took the lead in meeting world demand for new electronic products. France was fascinated by the new microchip technology and Germany profited from it, but in Britain there was a 'mismatch' between the available skills of its workforce and the demand for 'high-tech' products. Everywhere there was structural unemployment.

Adaptability was necessary in Europe's traditional heavy industries, and increasingly in industries like car and household goods manufacturing, where assembly line production was moving to more sophisticated forms of production, some based on robotics, the need for 'flexibility' raised important questions about 'redundancy' and the role of the state in the economy. Increasingly, monetarist and free-market economics began to influence the economic policies of Conservative and Christian Democrat governments, whose overriding objective was to reduce inflation. In Britain, which endured the most radical application of monetarist economics after 1979, hallowed policy objectives like full employment were discarded. In Germany, which was not immune to economic difficulties, Schmidt was replaced by Helmut Kohl in 1982. Both he and Margaret Thatcher were returned at subsequent elections – Thatcher in 1983 and the centre/right coalition under Chancellor Helmut Kohl in 1986. In the 1980s Thatcher even gave her name to an *ism*. Only in France did the left enjoy success with the election of François Mitterrand as the first Socialist President of the Fifth Republic. (However, his claim to extensive socialist credentials, like his symbolic role in the 1944 liberation of Paris by leading an armed assault on the *Commissariat général aux prisonniers de guerre*, rested uneasily with his rural, Catholic and conservative upbringing, and his employment and associations with the Vichy regime.) But, above all,

Mitterrand was the consummate politician, fighting four presidential elections and 23 other political seats at both national and local level in a political career which spanned 48 years (1947–95). In his writings Mitterrand described himself as a man of the past who made 'an enormous effort to leap into the present'. Yet his political career was characterized by ambiguity and the primacy of retaining political power over ideological positions (as well as great personal courage – he continued to serve as President after his terminal cancer was diagnosed and made public), making him very much a man of the 1980s.

By 1986 there had been some measure of economic recovery, induced less by government policy than by rearmament spending on the part of the United States, which under President Reagan ran a considerable deficit throughout this period. EEC trade increased again in a period of financial realignment and business mergers. The 'globalization' of the world's economy became a new buzz-word, with transnational corporations – increasingly deregulated and supported by information technology – crossing the boundaries of 'traditional' national economies and challenging the powers of government to shape economic policy.

It was continued fear of inflation and of unpredictable ramifications of international finance that helped to explain the appeal of the European Community's European Monetary System (EMS), which had been established in 1979 and which, after the report of the Commission's French President, Jacques Delors, in 1988, was to become the springboard for the full monetary union of the EC. Appointed in 1985, Delors, during his first two years as Commissioner, was extremely active, launching a number of cooperative initiatives with the French President until Mitterrand's power was curtailed by the election of a conservative government in 1986. A Socialist and a former Minister of Finance, he wanted to deepen the economic, social and political unity of Europe. Although he did not hold the fanatically federalist views ascribed to him by the British press, he was strongly in favour of the EC setting out social objectives.

The principal anchors of the EC system were the West German economy and the strong political partnership of France and Germany. Personalities were important, too, as cooperation between Paris and Bonn in Brussels was enhanced by the political friendship which developed between Kohl and Mitterrand, despite their differing political loyalties, through their strong commitment to the European ideal and their common provincial, Catholic backgrounds. In 1985 a majority of the Community's members committed their peoples to the Single European Act (Thatcher accepted it, although Britain and Denmark had a number of reservations) which, modifying some of the provisions of the Treaty of Rome, extended the legal authority of the EC into areas like the environment, technological cooperation and social policy. It was also decided to achieve a 'genuine common market' by 1992, with complete freedom of goods, capital and people across the Community. (This should have been achieved under the Treaty of Rome in 1970.)

Before recession dampened growth, the economic success of western Europe also made it an attractive, lucrative market for eastern Europe which Poland, Hungary, Romania and Yugoslavia had been determined to exploit. By the late 1970s, therefore, elements unknown in the Cold War order were already emerging. Eastern Europe now looked West, not East, for economic support but, with the 'deepening' of Community relations, western European countries continued to look largely to one another.

'Co-existence' in the Cold War, 1972–89

The mounting frustrations of eastern Europe, set against the apparent success of western European cooperation and integration, were made more acute by the now unbearable strain of maintaining the arms race in the Cold War. The stagnation which characterized life inside the Eastern bloc also began to affect the Cold War during the 1970s as the technical advances and growing economic strains on the superpowers had altered the character of the arms race. President Nixon became the first American president to recognize the communist government of China when he visited Beijing in 1972, and his efforts to secure a strategic arms limitation treaty with the Soviet Union (SALT I) ushered in a period of 'co-existence' between the two superpowers. The years of nuclear confrontation had fostered a kind of 'fearful intimacy' between the two powers, and increasingly they now recognized areas of common superpower interests. Notable among these was the desire to keep nuclear weapons out of the hands of other nations – the dangers of which had been little noticed during the 1950s and 1960s.

In the 1970s the Cold War had eased into static postures and a well-rehearsed routine, with the occasional adventure, such as the Soviet Union's invasion of Afghanistan in 1979. The arms race, with East and West vying for technological and numerical supremacy in weapons over the enemy, had become the principal means of sustaining the conflict. Yet huge arsenals of nuclear weapons meant that the Soviet Union's cherished 'buffer-zone' of eastern Europe was now irrelevant to Soviet defence needs. Western and eastern Europe no longer held centre stage in defence now that Intercontinental Ballistic Missiles (ICBMs) meant that the USA and the USSR could, in theory at least, wage war on each other's peoples directly. The USSR could bomb the USA without invading western Europe first.

In the later 1970s, however, the Cold War received renewed impetus from the limited success of the American President Jimmy Carter's attempts to secure greater commitment from Communist leaders to human rights in eastern Europe and the Soviet Union and of further technological advances in military equipment. Throughout the postwar period, the United States had enjoyed superior resources in weapons, while the Soviet Union had far greater conventional resources. In the event of a Soviet act of aggression, the President had only two options: bomb every target in the Soviet Union, or bomb every target in the Soviet Union except Moscow. The Kremlin had a similar nuclear 'strategy'. In the 1960s the West had tried to develop a more 'flexible response', but for most of the Cold War 'mutually assured destruction' had been enough to deter both sides. During the 1980s, first the United States and then the USSR ceased to enjoy an easy confidence in its inherited strategy.

Ronald Reagan, following his successful bid for the US Presidency in November 1979, endorsed the Strategic Defence Initiative (SDI) and this, alongside the deployment of Pershing II and Cruise missiles, revived the arms race. The stupendous cost of SDI and its implications for the American economy, as well as the design specifications of this allegedly defensive weaponry, all added an air of science fiction to a project which had been nicknamed 'Star Wars'. Western Europeans, by contrast, were quietly critical of the scheme – pacifist lobby groups, especially in West Germany, protested vehemently against this escalation of the arms race – and many were alarmed, too, by Reagan's crude, moralizing attacks against the USSR's 'evil empire'.

But tension in superpower relations began to dissipate in 1985 when Mikhail Gorbachev assumed the leadership of the Soviet Union. Convinced that the USSR needed, above all, to cut military expenditure, Gorbachev made a number of startling disarmament proposals. It was now clear that the USSR could no longer finance the Cold War; indeed, the demands of the arms race were to prove the undoing of the Soviet Union (some NATO 'Cold War warriors' claimed this had always been their intention). But the United States, too, was facing insolvency and the spectacle of homelessness and drug wars taking place around the corner from the White House increasingly made a mockery of America's superpower status. The historian Paul Kennedy thus found a ready audience in the East and West for his theory of 'imperial overstretch' – the overextension of national resources overseas prompting the dissolution of 'empire' and also decline at home.[5]

Towards a new Europe?

A commentator on West European politics writing in 1989, the year of great change in eastern Europe, could conclude that while the European Community had an 'untidy distribution of power' compared with 'existing federations', it already had 'many, though by no means all, of the attributes of a mature sovereign state'.[6] There was no intimation in this survey that countries outside the Twelve would soon become involved in seeking to join it or that Britain and Denmark would stand out against what seemed to be an inevitable trend towards greater federalism. The future appeared no more problematic than the past. An appeal by the American Secretary of

Plate 11.5 East Germans freely cross into the West, November 1989. The depth of popular dissatisfaction with communism became clear when Hungary, Poland and Czechoslovakia opened their frontiers with East Germany in November 1989. Within days of the announcements, 15,000 East Germans had fled their homes and sought asylum in West German embassies in Prague, Warsaw and Budapest. By the second week of November these refugees, as here on the border between Czechoslovakia and West Germany, were allowed to cross into the West. With the creation of a single labour market, East and West Germany were effectively re-united.

State, James Baker, in December 1989 (for a new relationship between the European Community and the United States) and an address to the European Parliament in the same month by the Soviet Foreign Minister Edvard Shevardnadze were taken as further evidence of the growing stature of the Community's institutions.

The subsequent sequence of events was determined less by the Community than by the disintegration of Communist Party control in the East, by the reunification of Germany, engineered by Chancellor Kohl, and by a change of leadership in Britain when Thatcher fell from power (though not influence) in 1990, to be succeeded by John Major. With the collapse of the Soviet Union, and the end of the Cold War, the politically-imposed geography of the European Community lost its rationale, and the countries of eastern Europe, isolated for so long behind the 'iron curtain', began to rebuild old links, drawn towards western Europe by a powerful economic and political attraction. Many of the eastern European countries, alongside neutral states like Austria and Finland, expressed their enthusiastic wish to join the European Community. Old questions were thus reopened: What is Europe? Does it incorporate Russia and all former Soviet Republics? Is Turkey part of Europe? How does Europe define itself in political, geographic, economic, cultural, linguistic and historical terms?

In retrospect, the history of Cold War Europe, perhaps paradoxically, boasted considerable achievements. It had overseen the most prosperous period in western European history and the truly novel integration of western Europe. This integration had taken shape in human, not simply economic terms. Western Europeans, especially the younger generations, were better informed about their European counterparts than ever before, and cross-border travel had increased immensely. In 1950 there were 25 million global cross-border tourist movements. By 1985 this figure had risen to 333 million, of which 45 per cent of tourist movements were within Europe. Added to this there had been a threefold increase in the number of foreign residents in Europe, and with it a cross-fertilization of culture, customs and knowledge, if seldom without strain.

In the wake of the Second World War, Europe – both East and West – had also experienced peace, though it had been maintained by a 'balance of terror' between two blocs, and the peoples of eastern Europe and the USSR had seemed no more than objects of curiosity for their more prosperous European cousins. Within western Europe there were regional variations, but the economic balance of power in Europe still centred on France and an ever more powerful, reunified Germany. Politics proved more complex after 1989 than was anticipated when the Wall fell, and what happened further east was to remain of crucial importance to Europe's peace and to the images of itself which it had fashioned since the Treaty of Rome.[7] With a new millenium in sight, images of Europe divereged as much as they had done in 1815, 1871, 1918 or 1945.

References

1. Quoted in J. Black, *Convergence or Divergence?* (1994) p. 243.
2. M. Clark, *Modern Italy, 1871–1982* (1984, 1990 edn) p. 325.

3. R. F. Betts, *France and Decolonisation, 1900–1960* (1991) p. 17.
4. E. Shuckburgh, *Aspects of NATO: Political Consultation* (Paris, May 1960) p. 1.
5. P. Kennedy, *The Rise and Fall of the Great Powers. Economic Change and Military Conflict* (1988) *passim.*
6. P. Ludlow, *The Annual Review of European Community Affairs*, vol. 1 (Centre for European Policy Studies, 1990) p. xv.
7. D. Reynolds, 'Thawing History: Europe in the 1990s and Pre-Cold War Patterns', *Political Quarterly*, no. 1 (1992) pp. 24–6.

Chapter 12

The Great Mutation? The End of History?

The need for perspective

This chapter, unlike the rest, has no dates attached to it. This is because the flow of history continues despite talk of its end. Each day news pours in, much of it instantly, much of it continuously, and in a 'media world' today and tomorrow count as much as yesterday ('tomorrow is already here'). At the end of each week, of each year and of each decade journalistic attempts are made to summarize it. There are also frequent public opinion polls and in Britain regular annual surveys of social trends and of underlying social attitudes. Such forms of accounting are as much part of the picture as the news itself. Indeed, the Second World War has been approached in terms of an audit, not a chronicle. The need for managerial accounting, public and private, was a major demand of the 1980s as productivity had been during the 1950s, not that it guaranteed good management.

It is difficult in such circumstances to secure any adequate sense of long-term perspective. There are some writers, moreover, notably the French Germanist and sociologist Jean Baudrillard, who argue that because of the endless media flow it is impossible to distinguish between 'social reality' and its simulation in the media, concluding that it will be impossible in future to recognize or differentiate a future period of time. History is reaching a 'vanishing point' in a surfeit of information about events, including distant events, that are too many to comprehend.[1] Meanwhile, the word 'vanishing' has acquired a double meaning. Ephemera (mobile telephone calls, fax messages), often dealing with important subjects, do not often make their way into the archives.

Already, before the full implications of a continuing communications revolution were apparent – and it is now based on highly sophisticated and versatile digital technology – the then President of the American Historical Association, Carl Bridenaugh, described recent history in 1962 as 'the great mutation', an image already used freely but appropriately when the

hydrogen bomb lay in reserve. It was used also in 1948 by the world historian W. H. McNeill when he referred to 'a general mutation in perception and in production as revolutionary as that when power shifted from hunting to farming' in the days before recorded history began. Spanning the centuries three years before Bridenaugh, the American anthropologist Margaret Mead claimed that 'the gulf separating 1965 from 1943' was 'as deep as the gulf that separated the men who became builders of cities from Stone Age men'.[2] Old values had crumbled as the processes of daily life had changed.

Such judgements must always be studied critically, not least statements which are made by historians, for there have been many sharp breaks in the past, produced not only by new human inventions but by plagues and famines (and these continue) and by earlier population movements. There have always been prophets, too, who have proclaimed the end of an old order and the beginning of a new age, not least just before and just after the First World War. There was a change, however, during the 1960s when the sense of one planet was strengthened – it was seen for the first time from space in 1969 – and when 'futurology' became more sophisticated than it ever had been before in history, with some of the prophets claiming to be social scientists. Models were devised, 'megatrends' were identified. Science and technology were directly related to human prospects. 'In the three short decades between now and the end of the millennium', Alvin Toffler warned in his best-seller *Future Shock* (1970) 'millions of psychologically normal people will experience an abrupt collision with the future.'[3]

Nevertheless, for all the power of technology and for all the sophistication of the 'advanced social sciences', the last decades of the twentieth century were characterized by many surprises, economic, political and cultural, demonstrating that it is easier to forecast the advance of science and technology than the future of the economy, of politics or of culture, all of which have become increasingly influenced by technology. In particular, the early collapse of the Soviet Union in 1989, the bicentenary year of the French Revolution, and with it the fall of the associated communist regimes of central and eastern Europe was seldom forecast. It seemed an 'unlikely' scenario to the authors of the illuminating *Europe 2000*, a cooperative study, launched by the European Cultural Foundation, which appeared in 1977; and it was only after it had happened that it was to be described by one writer, Francis Fukuyama, as 'the end of history'.[4]

The 'end of ideology' had been one of the key phrases of the 1960s,

---

Plate 12.1 Greenpeace activists abseil from the Arc de Triomphe in Paris, 1995.
Environmental protest groups, especially Greenpeace, proved particularly adept at presenting their case to the world's media as the battle to influence public opinion grew increasingly sophisticated and fierce. Here, they protest against renewed French nuclear testing in the Muraroa Atoll.

when there was talk of the convergence of conflicting political systems, and now, for Fukuyama, the victory of 'liberal democracy', for so he interpreted it, constituted 'the end point of man's ideological evolution' and 'the final form of human government'. With it, he claimed, the Hegelian and Marxist sense of history as one single and coherent process disappeared. It had been a product of European thought and experience.

So, too, were the events of 1989. As in 1848, some of the first disturbances in 1988 were manifest in Hungary, where the body of Imre Nagy, the leader of the 1956 anti-Russian uprising, was disinterred in April and given a hero's funeral. Already, in February, Soviet troops had pulled out of Afghanistan, and in March elections had been held which allowed an element of genuine free choice. In September the Hungarians opened their border to the West and East Germans flooded through at the rate of 200 an hour. In November the bulldozing of the wall separating the two Germanies – not only in Berlin but in the German countryside – changed German politics (and geography and economics) as much as the unification of Germany in 1870.

'End of history' or not – and Fukuyama did not invent the phrase – the echoes of history were loud through all these changes and were to grow louder in the daily flow of news. The collapse of the Soviet Union and with it of Marxism – or so many commentators as well as Fukuyama claimed – did not eliminate violence, international and domestic, from the world. Nor was 'liberal democracy' assured even in Europe. Anti-Semitism was not dead. Nor were racism and xenophobia. Marxism itself was alive and remained the operative ideology in China where Marxists adopted market models to fuel economic growth.

Fukuyama argued that because history – in the sense that he defined it – had ended, 'the world-wide ideological struggle that had called forth daring, courage, imagination and idealism' was over and would be 'replaced by economic calculation, the endless solving of technical problems, environmental concerns and the satisfaction of sophisticated consumer demands'. There would be 'neither art nor philosophy', just 'the perpetual caretaking of the museum of human history'.[5] Fukuyama had limited evidence, however, to support such a conclusion, and economic miscalculation alone continued to create human disasters, the consequences of which were unpredictable.

Technical problems were not all solved, and while they remained unsolved they produced different kinds of uncertainties. 'Environmental concerns' generated struggle: Greenpeace, founded in 1971, when a group of people hired a ship, not for the last time, to protest against nuclear tests in the Pacific, became increasingly active, and there were further environmental as well as human disasters. Not least, 'the satisfaction of sophisticated consumer demands', now described as consumerism, was compatible with a widening of economic inequalities, and in consequence free market economics, often entrapped in jargon, remained challengeable.

Plate 12.2 Cambridge scientists Francis Crick and James Watson, and a model of DNA, 1951. Their work on the structure of DNA, along with the research of Maurice Wilkins and Rosalind Franklin of Kings College London on x-ray crystalline studies, revealed the double-helix form of DNA and the genetic codes within. Crick, Watson and Wilkins shared the Nobel Prize for Physiology or Medicine in 1962. The fourth member of the quartet, Franklin, was excluded by her death from cancer in 1958.

If no new version of Marxism was advanced, in some countries, like Poland and Hungary, ex-Marxist ministers were returned to power through the ballot box. They were not 'finished'. More ominously, as on the eve of the First World War in 1914, Sarajevo once more hit the headlines. The ramifications of the collapse of an order were manifest in Serbia, Croatia and Bosnia, amalgamated in 1918 as parts of a Yugoslavia which no longer held together after 1992. Balkan nationalism remained a formidable force and there was no common European policy to cope with it.

The year 1989, therefore, for all its excitements, was not necessarily a good vantage point from which to survey past or future. Nor, indeed, is any single year, although an attractive attempt, one of several, to encapsulate the memory of 'our time' was made in 1977, the year of *Europe 2000*, when the first twin *Voyager* spacecraft left Cape Canaveral in Florida on a probe into the far reaches of outer space, carrying with it a record of a two-hour message from Planet Earth to other planets and stars within the galaxy. It included speeches in 60 languages and 116 pictures, giving details of the twentieth-century environment and of twentieth-century science (among them the discovery by J. D. Watson and F. H. Crick in 1953 of DNA, the genetic code) and of older cultural achievements from the nineteenth-century past (among them a page of Beethoven's sheet music).[6]

The sense of a century

As the end of the twentieth century – and with it, indeed, the millennium – drew nearer, efforts were made to see it as a whole and to give it a shape; and already historians began to speak of a 'short century' lasting from 1914 to 1989, just as they had earlier identified a 'long nineteenth century' lasting from 1815 to 1914. The Marxist historian Eric Hobsbawm, who in three volumes had charted world history since the French Revolution into the twentieth century, separated out three distinct periods within the 'short century' – the first from 1914 to 1945, a period of war and depression, following a *belle époque*; the second from 1960 to 1989, a period of unprecedented prosperity, particularly in Europe; and the third, since 1989, a period of unresolved uncertainties, 'an age of anxiety', including an economic 'recession' that during the mid-1980s brought to an end a brief but hectic boom. Britain, without 'feeling good', fared better than its European competitors.

The words 'great depression' remained reserved for the economic sequence which began with the Wall Street Crash of 1929, just as the words 'great war' remained reserved for the conflict that began in 1914. A key concept now was structural unemployment. How to deal with it was now conceived of as a difficult problem along with the reform of social security, made urgent as the population aged. The will to discover policies to phase 'welfare state' and to secure 'full employment' belonged to the postwar past. It lost its emotive power.

Such a historical schema focuses too much, perhaps, on the middle years, which like the middle years of the nineteenth century were years of undoubted economic advance, when the future offered still better to come. In social and political terms, however, they saw many shifts of mood and preoccupation. It was to be claimed in retrospect – before 1989 – that the 'Cold War' was best interpreted as the 'long peace', but before the fall of Khrushchev in 1964 there was an element of obvious unpredictability in the international scene, and although under his successor Leonid Brezhnev, who reigned rather than ruled, there was 'order', the order masked much else: it was in Brezhnev's personal office that the fateful decision to invade Afghanistan was taken on 24 December 1979.

In Western Europe, where the economy was stronger than ever before, there were mixed moods. As the contemporary historian David Thomson put it in 1966, 'the supreme question confronting Europeans was whether . . . traditional resilience and . . . material advantages could be so combined, using intelligence and wisdom, to relegate Europe's internal contrasts and divisions to the function of cultural diversification and enrichment of life, rather than to an intensifying of war-like jealousies and hatreds. Forces both of cohesion and of disunity still coexisted in a precarious balance'.[7] Eleven years later *Europe 2000* began with the words 'Europe has no idea where it is going but it is going there fast' and stressed the word 'anxiety', 'anxiety about the future, anxiety about the unknown'. A study of Europe embarked upon in the United States in 1964 had stressed one particular aspect of change. 'Europe is not entirely the mistress in her own house. What the United States and the Soviet Union elect to do in the next ten years will influence Europe, and there is only a limited sense in which Europe can determine these actions.'[8]

In each of the three subdivisions of the century, if we divide it in that way – and it has recently been called a 'dark century' – there have been both obvious anxieties and precarious balances – even in the brightly lit *belle époque* of the early century when the aristocracy glittered while the power of money was blatantly displayed. A generation later, the English poet of the 1930s W. H. Auden chose 'The Age of Anxiety' as the title of one of his poems, and during the 1930s there were many grounds for anxiety both for decadent sections of the aristocracy and for respectable sections of the working class.[9] Hobsbawm has chosen as the title for his latest volume on the years 1914–51 'The Age of Extremes', but during the years before 1914 there were obvious 'extremes' in European experience, as there were to be in the 1920s and 1930s to which at the time the label 'postwar' was attached. Among the privileged there was a nostalgic longing for the years before 1914 ('normalcy'): among 'the masses', a word often used patronizingly, there were great varieties of experience and reaction. There was also a relentless awareness of precarious domestic and international security, attenuated by belief in a better (or greater) future ahead; 'better' in the 'democracies', 'greater' in Germany, Italy and the other 'fascist' countries, the 'have-not' countries as they were called. Shadows of the last war criss-crossed ominously with the shadows of the next.

It required rearmament and war to dispose of mass unemployment. It required war, too, to create a new apparatus for safeguarding peace. The League of Nations had collapsed before 1939: the United Nations Organization, created in 1945, with its headquarters not in Geneva but in New York, was to face its biggest crises 50 years later. The one most publicized international crisis of the 'middle years' was centred not on Europe but on Cuba. So, too, was the most significant war – in Vietnam.

As in all schemes of periodization by century or by decade, it is possible to trace continuities across the divides. Thus, despite the breaks in historical continuities associated with two world wars, there were obvious continuities between the 1890s and the 1940s, bridging what Margaret Mead described as 'the deep gulf'. Technical development continued to follow logically in the wake of the spread of electrical power, of mobile transportation, and of 'mass communication'. The economic geography of the world did not then change drastically in its patterns of industry and trade. Nor did 'geopolitics', except (and it was a significant exception) through the rise of air power. The rule of empire, if challenged, persisted, and have-not countries without empires demanded a share in the imperial process. Social development continued to pivot on the developing relationship between 'masses' and 'minorities', of which there were many different kinds. The latter now included what had come to be called elites, among them specialized elites of 'experts', 'meritocracies' who owed little to birth.

The word 'elite' was first used in its current sense by the Italian sociologist Vilfredo Pareto in the first decade of the century, and it became as much of a key word as the word 'masses' with which it was originally bracketed. Pareto was an economist as well as a sociologist, but he did not examine one other feature of twentieth-century change – a continuing (but not continuous) rise in consumer incomes, a precondition of 'consumerism', despite unprecedented economic depression. It was Britain's Minister of Food during the Second World War, Lord Woolton, appointed in 1940, a retailer by occupation and later Minister of Reconstruction, who talked most of the luxuries of yesterday becoming the necessities of today.

A society which was increasingly 'consumer-orientated' depended increasingly on 'mass production', the production of the assembly line, the system pioneered before 1910 (though not invented) by the American automobile manufacturer Henry Ford who significantly gave his name to an *ism*. During the 1930s the great cinema comedian Charlie Chaplin, operating from the centre of 'mass entertainment', Hollywood, had depicted assembly lines unforgettably in a film significantly called *Modern Times*. (He also figured in the film *The Great Dictator*.) 'Consumerism' only turned into an *ism* a generation later – during the 1960s when 'Fordism' was already beginning to look out-of-date in an age of 'automation': robots were about to make their way into history in automobile factories like the

Plate 12.3 Charles Chaplin and Chester Conklin in *Modern Times*, **1936.** This film classic presented the modern world of mass production and time management as a mechanized nightmare which dehumanizes man and destroys social harmony.

great Fiat plant in Turin. In each phase in the history of production the ultimate appeal to the consumer depended on 'mass persuasion' – the 'arts' of advertising – and advertising of 'branded goods' had begun to flourish as early as the 1890s.[10]

Advertising, too, had its inherent logic, ensuring that within the longer movements of speeded-up time there were shorter up-and-down movements of the 'roller coaster' of fashion. Indeed, fashion was an essential facet of the process of mass persuasion which became part of the political process also. Wherever it was used, it made for some confusion. What some people thought of as 'fads' – radio, for example, in the 1920s, developed for the home before the 'talkies' took over the cinemas – were new features of life which would remain dominant until new technologies emerged. More than entertainment was usually involved. News was presented in the cinema ('newsreels') as well as in the home, and in the 'age of television', which grew out of the 'age of broadcasting', whatever people's political loyalties had been hitherto they were now subject to image refashioning. The 1960s was the crucial decade when fashion – in clothes (for example, jeans), in food (including 'new foods' and 'fast food'), in drink (more wine), in travel (including air travel) and in education (more universities) – became a main preoccupation of the media. In the same decade the presentation of politics, including the politics of protest, was speeded up.

Until the 1960s there were continuities in conceptions of contemporary culture, linking it with the historic past before 1914, although Nazism and Fascism inaugurated a new and more terrifying *Kulturkampf*. The great names of 'high culture', collected from different historical periods, still stood out in all countries, east and west, and schoolchildren everywhere were expected to know at least the names of writers like Homer, Dante, Shakespeare, Cervantes, Molière, Hugo and Goethe. Knowledge of painters and sculptors was less common, and although the audience for music expanded significantly (thanks to radio and gramophone technology) this was still 'the age of the book'. For that reason alone, it was cultural treason when in the name of 'Action against the Un-German Spirit' students at the University of Berlin in May 1933 hurled into a bonfire books that seemed to subvert that spirit.

There had been intimations even of this kind of behaviour in pre-1914 popular anti-Semitism, but now it was to be extended into other forms of ideological terror, ending with the burning not of books but of people. By the end of Hitler's 'Holocaust' six million Jews had been systematically murdered – with the help of doctors and 'scientists' as well as politicians and bureaucrats. The twentieth-century process was traced meticulously by Hannah Arendt in 1951, where in a great study of 'totalitarianism' she insisted a generation before Fukuyama that 'every end in history necessarily contains a new beginning'.

'Modern' and 'post-modern'

By the 1960s in all parts of Europe, including post-Nazi Germany, literary 'modernism', a many-sided product of nineteenth-century revolt, had been assimilated into the taught canon, with a number of writers being

Plate 12.4 Book burning in the Operaplatz Berlin, May 1933. Books were burnt in many German university towns. Golo Mann, the German historian and son of Thomas Mann, managed to save his father's works from the bonfire in Berlin, although those of his uncle Heinrich and brother Klaus were burned. Inspired by the party's call 'Burn whatever weakens you', Mann noted that 'the undertaking was entirely student inspired, an imitation of the Wartburg Festival of 1817, when the Napoleonic Code and other "un-German works" had been burned'.

identified as makers of a 'modern movement', powerful enough to have survived both the First World War, which deflected it but did not stem its vitality, and the rise and fall of Nazism. In parallel, the role of new *avant-gardes* – groups of writers prepared to shock, not to please – had been accepted by many devotees of 'high culture'. Not all the key figures in the literary and artistic *avant gardes*, many of whom had been active before 1914, had been politically to the left. T. S. Eliot, whose poem *The Waste*

Land (1922) became a major modern text, was a conservative. Ezra Pound lived throughout the war in Mussolini's Italy.

'Modernism', a vague term, like 'modernity', which was applied to all the arts, proved vague enough to encompass aspects of Nazi art and of Fascist architecture in Italy. In literature it set the horizons for what have been called the 'rebellious imperatives' of the continuing search for the self, a search which had been actively pursued by the romantics, yet it could also encompass 'classical' rejections of romanticism. It fostered experiment with form – in art and in music too – reaching its climax in literature in Joyce's *Finnegan's Wake*, published in 1939, a dream recounted in layers of wordplay: Joyce's *Ulysses* (1922) had for long taken its place in the modern canon. New language, new syntax and new rhythms were demanded and provided, and 'other cultures' were tapped as well as the culture of 'the West'. In pictorial art, where all kinds of materials were used as well as paint and canvas, they had already ranged before 1914 to Japan, Polynesia and Africa. In music jazz made its way into Europe from the black world via the United States during the 1920s.

The Nazis attacked with equal bitterness jazz and the atonal music of Arnold Schoenberg and Alban Berg, while themselves venerating Wagner who in his lifetime had been hailed as the greatest of all modernists. And while they banned the music of Gustav Mahler and burned the novels of Thomas Mann along with those of Franz Kafka, the plays of Bertold Brecht and the works of Albert Einstein and Sigmund Freud, from time to time they looked back to Nietzsche, prophet of the 'modern European mind'. Many of the greatest figures in German 'modernism' fled from their own country (and later from Austria) during the 1930s in an exodus ('diaspora') which in all carried to other lands half a million Jews, among them Schoenberg, Brecht, Mann, Einstein and Freud. The fact that the exiles included scientists as well as writers and musicians was itself revealing: Nazi 'anti-intellectualism' tapped a variety of different sources. 'Our national policies will not be revoked or modified even for scientists', Hitler had told a scientist who dared to protest as early as 1933. 'If the dismissal of Jewish scientists means the annihilation of contemporary German science, then we shall do without science for a few years.'

In the Soviet Union, where socialism was thought of as a science, no-one would ever have made such a statement. Yet versions of science which seemed to threaten state ideology were usually not tolerated in Moscow either. Nor was there any willingness to appreciate 'modern' tastes that were deemed, however absurdly, to be *bourgeois* – from 'impressionism' in painting to musical 'atonality'. Freud was anathema. Biology was less safe than physics. Even linguistics was not safe. After an initial phase of cultural experiment and innovation following the Revolution, much of it exciting, the Stalinist regime severely censored 'Western modernism' as a whole. A modern musician like Dmitri Shostakovich was never allowed to develop his music freely: his opera *Lady Macbeth of Mtsensk* (1930–32) had been dismissed as both 'formalistic' and 'decadent', although he regained favour in 1937 with his *Fifth Symphony*.

When the Soviet Union was at war with Germany from 1941 to 1945, Shostakovich's *Seventh Symphony* ('the Leningrad') was warmly welcomed in Britain, which now made much of cultural relationships between Russia and the West. There was an audience, too, for Maxim Gorky, who after a spell in exile had become first President of the Soviet Writers' Union. He was now read along with Dostoevsky and Tolstoy. Meanwhile, selected English 'classics' were published in cheap editions in the Soviet Union, as after the war were gramophone records of the great European composers of the past.

Such purposive 'cultural diffusion', associated as it was with a successful battle for literacy, represented a continuation of nineteenth-century aspirations as did much else in twentieth-century 'modernization'.[11] Yet the breakthrough from the past in the arts and in the physical sciences had come in the name of 'modernity' in the decade before 1914 and was continued during and after the end of the First World War. In 1916 in neutral Zurich, the city where James Joyce lived and died (and where Lenin lived in exile), the artistic and literary movement Dada, consciously international, set out from a cafe base to deflate everything that was inherited from the past. It embraced the slogan of the Russian anarchist Mikhail Bakunin: 'destruction is also creation'.

In the wake of Dada, surrealist artists set out in the following decade to bring to the page or to the canvas the forces of the subconscious which had been hitherto suppressed. The *ism* 'surrealism' had been coined by Apollinaire in 1917 and its disciples were guided in Paris (the word 'leader' was avoided) by André Breton who dreamed of a 'congress of intellectuals' that would 'distil and unify the essential principles of modernism'. The Spaniard Salvador Dali, who joined the Paris group in 1929, was disdained by Breton, but became the best-known of the surrealists, following a bizarre and totally unplanned career. He was to paint a *Last Supper* and a portrait of Queen Elizabeth II. A German surrealist, Max Ernst, pursued a very different path, moving through cubism, Dada and *collage*, the employment of a variety of glued-on scraps of other materials, like newspapers, cloth and string, in the search to realize 'painting beyond painting', 'visual poetry'. In 1941 he migrated to the United States, which was to become the centre of late-twentieth-century abstract expressionism. The human figure was expelled from the canvas.

The writing of the history of twentieth-century art has depended much on the use of labels, like 'surrealism' and 'expressionism', not the first *ism* to have been invented by its critics. Nonetheless, different painters followed their own course, sometimes drawing up common manifestos, selling through the same dealer and, whatever their 'school', exploring new techniques like *collage*. One of the great pioneers of cubism, Pablo Picasso, whose paintings went through many phases, passed into general history

with his Spanish Civil War painting 'Guernica' (1937), which depicted the destruction from the air of the Basque capital, Bilbao, and after 1945 with his 'doves of peace' which became the emblems of supporters of nuclear disarmament on both sides of the 'iron curtain'.

Influenced during the 1930s by what seemed to be ideological struggles, like the Spanish Civil War, and during the 1950s by the Cold War, artists, writers and musicians retained a sense of 'modernity' through into the late 1950s and early 1960s when the sense of the new was again reshaped. By then, dealers in and spokesmen for 'modernity' had acquired some of the trappings of an 'Establishment' in the educational, museums and arts world of 'the West', but 'modern' artists, writers and musicians, over-dependant on agents, still stood self-consciously in what the American literary critic Lionel Trilling called an 'adversary position', hostile to 'modern *bourgeois* society'. They were opposed, therefore, both to 'mass culture', which – particularly in change – seemed always to threaten it, and to 'middle-brow' culture, which seemed to represent the worst of all compromises. Those modernists who were favourable to communism, if often critical of the Soviet Union, could extol 'the masses' while treating 'mass culture' as a form of manipulative contamination. Conservatives – and liberals – felt threatened by mass pressures, sharing the view expressed in 1930 by the Spaniard Ortega y Gasset that 'the mass crushes beneath it everything that is different, everything that is excellent, individual, qualified and serious'.

During the immediate postwar years, when the regularities of daily life had broken up, the most fashionable, if short-lived, philosophy in continental Europe was 'existentialism', another *ism* that was repudiated by some of the philosophers from whom it derived. It focused on immediate human choices and on their impact on other human existences. Its main literary spokesman was Jean-Paul Sartre, French philosopher, essayist and playwright. The roots of existentialist philosophy, however, lay in pre-war Germany – and in nineteenth-century thought. The Danish Christian philosopher Soren Kierkegaard, different though he was from the Marxist Sartre, was back in fashion after 1945. The mood shifted, however, as the war receded. What did not recede was the threat of the Bomb which itself carried with it a terrifying choice. Either/or. In fact, it proved prudent to hold the Bomb, not to make use of it.

The shift in moods and styles during the late 1950s and the early 1960s was often associated at the time with talk of 'generation gaps'. In fact, differences of outlook within generations were as obvious as differences

---

Plate 12.5 *Guernica* **by Pablo Picasso, 1937.** Prepared for the Paris International Exposition of 1937, the painting was inspired by the bombing of Guernica, the ancient capital of the Basques in northern Spain. The painting's angular, distorted figures do not recreate the event, but seek in the series of powerful images, to evoke the agony of total war.

between generations. More significant were the influences originating in great cities, among them 'swinging London' and 'anti-conventional' Amsterdam and Copenhagen, and in universities, which were growing in numbers and in size. There was as much talk in the 1960s and 1970s of 'exploding' cities, however, as of 'swinging London' as cities, too, grew in size and the numbers of large cities increased. The same adjectives were sometimes attached to universities, where there were militant student movements in the late 1960s and 1970s which spread from one university to another, with Paris and Frankfurt as centres of action.

Shifts in values were so great during the late 1960s that Peter Drucker, a shrewd observer of changes in the world of business, could write an influential book in 1969 called *The Age of Discontinuity*. It was during the 1960s also that a cluster of adjectives and *isms* beginning with *post-* began to be identified, among them 'post-industrial' and, most general, 'post-modern', a term that was applied to art and architecture before it was applied to society. Both terms suggested that the kind of adversarial social system which took shape in the last decades of the eighteenth century under the influence of two revolutions – the making of which was described in Chapter 1 of this book – had drawn to a close. Drucker himself had used the word 'post-modern' in his *Landmarks for Tomorrow* (1957) which he subtitled 'a report on the new post-modern world'. In a 1965 edition he observed that 'at some unmarked point during the last twenty years we imperceptibly moved out of the Modern Age and into a new as yet nameless one'.[12]

For hostile critics the *post* terms include '*post mortem*'. There had always been a strand of cultural pessimism in the twentieth century, represented among historians by the German Oswald Spengler, whose *Der Untergang des Abendlandes* ('The Decline of the West') had appeared in 1918. For Spengler, indeed – and he was pessimistic about life as well as about culture – history was moving into its 'final stage' long before Fukuyama wrote of its end. And when another equally ambitious historian, Arnold Toynbee, surveying as Spengler did a global range of 'civilizations', used the word 'post-modern' in 1974, along with the word 'post-Christian', he too pointed to 'breakdown and disintegration'.

Pessimists were brushed aside, however, during the late-1960s by post-modern prophets who celebrated a liberation from 'modernism', reacting sharply against '*Bauhaus*' styles which, originating in 1919 with Walter Gropius (born in Berlin but exiled to the United States), had been carried across the Atlantic. Some architects and critics had assumed that the victory of functional modern architecture represented in the work of German-born Ludwig Mies Van der Rohe and Swiss-born Charles-Edouard Le Corbusier was final and universal. It was not, although it was difficult to find any other label for their successors than 'post-modern'. The adjective was used also in relation to religion and, (if in brackets), in relation to science: in his *The Broken Image* (1964) Floyd Matson referred to the 'modern [or post-modern] image of the scientist as actor, as "participant observer" rather than detached spectator'. In literature brackets might have been used also: in painting and in building in particular, in an essay of 1970 some figures previously thought of as 'modern', like Joyce, were now given a post- modern label.

In 1983 the Italian novelist and essayist Umberto Eco, who followed every cultural trend, traced the process which linked 'modern' and 'post-modern' in an illuminating *Postscript to the Name of the Rose*:

> The moment comes when the *avant-garde* (the modern) can go no further . . .
> The post-modern reply to the modern consists of recognizing that the past, since it cannot really be destroyed, because its destruction leads to silence, must be revisited but with irony, not innocently.

Eco's brilliant novel *The Name of the Rose*, translated into most European languages, was set in the Middle Ages.

Even such an orientation, however, was not completely new. The word *ricorso* was old, and there had already been more than one twentieth-century return to the Middle Ages just as there had been a nineteenth-century return. One medieval historian turned contemporary historian, Geoffrey Barraclough, suggested as early as 1955 that there were features of twentieth-century society that could be better understood in the light of medieval than of nineteenth-century history, while in 1978 Barbara Tuchman, who had written in depth of military blunders perpetrated during the First World War, called her study of the horrors of the fourteenth century *A Distant Mirror*, suggesting that the personalities, problems and events of that century clearly illuminate the twentieth century, a century of concentration camps and of curious cults and in its last phases of corruption and crime.

Ten discontinuities

It became common during the 1960s, when more social critics were looking ahead than looking backwards, to identify at least ten discontinuities between the nineteenth and twentieth centuries. Some still stand out in new post-1989 perspectives.

(1) Decolonization and the pressures of a politically independent but still largely economically dependent 'third world' (a new term of French origin, *le Tiers monde*), transformed the map. Large parts of that world had no written history, but burst into late-twentieth-century history through Africa as well as through Asia, as European empires disintegrated. Within that world, which was always more varied than it seemed on the surface, there have subsequently been wide varieties of experience. Different groups of countries have separated themselves out, with some countries, like 'Pacific Rim' South Korea, challenging

Europe economically. It is now impossible adequately to treat history as 'Eurocentric' as it still was in the late-1950s.

(2) Pressures from within 'the first world' (an unarticulated concept) of hitherto deprived or suppressed minorities altered the styles and content of politics. Some were prepared to use the ballot box and the machinery of the 'welfare state', also a new term in the postwar world: others relied on action outside parliaments – strikes and demonstrations. Poverty was not abolished during the boom years of the mid-century, and some regions of Europe had income (and amenity) levels far below those of the most favoured. Poverty was interpreted differently, however, usually relatively, as general living standards rose. Welfare objectives were not abandoned, particularly by the European Community, which set them out in charter form, but during the 1980s both the finances and the administration of 'welfare states' and the side range of 'welfare benefits', including pensions, were subjected to increasing criticism and in Britain, where the term 'welfare state' was first used, to erosion. It opted out of much that other European countries agreed upon in a new expression of divergence. Cutting of taxes had become a major object of policy – along with control of inflation. Yet other countries moved along this path. 'Privatization' schemes were carried through both in the West and after 1989 in the East with as much rigour as 'nationalization' schemes had been carried out almost 50 years before. Meanwhile, and it became an essential part of the picture, some private multinational companies had income greater than that of most 'sovereign states'.

(3) The drive for 'women's liberation', not new but never before so explicit or so direct, intensified after 1960. 'Feminists' like Simone de Beauvoir, a close associate of Sartre, probed hidden assumptions about gender in books like *The Second Sex* (1949), and in the name of 'consciousness raising' changed ways of thinking about 'gender' as it had operated in the past as well as about how it should operate in the future. Just as significant in practice, however, was the increasing volume and range of women's work, full-time and part-time, beginning in service occupations, like banking, but notable too in professions like the law: it carried with it changes in family roles and, indeed – along with other changes, including contraception and abortion – in the constitution of the family itself. What kind of a unit the family was – and could and should be – became a matter of political argument.

(4) The growth in the 1960s of what was already beginning to be thought of, again in the United States, as a radically new 'information society' (the labels have subsequently multiplied) had global as well as European implications. The word 'electronics' was itself new in the 1940s, and the subsequent convergence of computing with solid-state electronics through the invention in the 1960s of the integrated circuit pushed forward what in the 1980s, after a further advance in

Plate 12.6 The Live Aid concert, 13 July 1985. Transmitted simultaneously in both Europe and the United States, the concert to raise money for famine stricken Africa was the biggest live event in the history of rock and roll. On stage, a guards band plays the British National Anthem just before the concert opened with the rock band Status Quo playing their anthem, 'Rockin' All Over the World'.

technology, became known as 'a digital revolution'. 'Information', a European Commission Green Paper published in 1984 began, 'is a decisive, perhaps the only decisive factor in European unification'.

(5) Different national attitudes towards communications development persisted, but there were signs in all countries of basic shifts in values associated with changing balances of work and leisure. In the first instance these accompanied increases in disposable incomes for the young and for the unskilled. Later they increased work redundancies and created structural unemployment. Along with value shifts – the term 'spare time' passed out of the language – went basic changes in the organization of leisure, for example of both amateur and professional sports. In the 1960s the word 'sport' increasingly began to be used in the singular and, accompanied by commercialization, became a major ingredient in the content of old and new media, among which television, the most leisure-time consuming, created most controversy, whatever the public or private frameworks of ownership and control.

(6) The erosion of the distinctions between 'high culture' and 'mass culture', never universally accepted, was reflected not only on the

screen but on canvas in 'pop art', a product, like 'op-art' of the late-1950s and early-1960s, and, above all, in sound. Even in eastern Europe 'pop music' had a powerful appeal during the 1970s and 1980s. As the agency business thrived, there were new links between performers and advertisers. The study of the media and of 'popular culture' became a university subject in parts of western Europe. So, too, did the study of 'sub-cultures', particularly those of 'youth'. The word 'lifestyle' became fashionable.

(7)   In western Europe 'counter-cultures' or 'alternative cultures' emerged, involving not only retreats into 'inner space', many drug-assisted, but new attitudes towards sex and violence. The number of people deemed 'misfits' rose during the 1980s. Most thought of themselves not as 'misfits' but as 'travellers' prepared to alienate others as they had been alienated themselves. Some developed forms of 'new age' religion. By the 1980s bookshops had sizeable sections devoted to 'the occult', sometimes placed side by side with equally sizeable sections on business and management. At home it was possible with the internet to explore 'cyberspace'.

(8)   A highly planned (and costly) movement into outer space began in rivalry between the United States and the Soviet Union – and left the rest of Europe largely behind. It was to end in the 1990s with joint American-Russian cooperation. By then the sky was full of satellites traversing the Earth's orbit. An 11-nation European Space Agency, set up in 1975 to carry forward the earlier programmes of the European Space Research Organization, begun in 1962, had its headquarters in Paris, its technical centre in Holland, and its operations centre at Darmstadt in Germany. Another European scientific venture was the European Organization for Nuclear Research, set up in 1954 with its centre straddling the French-Swiss border near Geneva.

(9)   Despite or because of the Bomb, advances in quantum physics seemed less exciting from the 1950s onwards than advances in molecular biology, which raised new issues concerning life and death. So, too, did increased longevity, associated with developments in medicine and (not least) in surgery (replacements and transplants). In relation to these issues and environmental issues identified by ecologists there were, however, somewhat similar reactions, some 'doomsday-like' or apocalyptic, to those associated earlier with the Bomb. The year 1970 stands out as a landmark in the history of threatened ecosystems – a new emphasis on the environment became 'more than a phrase' – and the first World Conference on the Human Environment was held in Stockholm in 1972. The word 'bio-society' was coined in 1977 by FAST (Forecasting and Assessment in Science and Technology), a European body: its purpose was to create 'a society based on the conscious management of self-organizing systems for the sustenance and enrichment of human life and purposes'. There was more than a touch

of Euro-rhetoric in such pronouncements which followed in the wake of the work of the Club of Rome, a voluntary organization which produced a controversial computer-based model, *Limits to Growth*, in 1972.

(10) The last discontinuity, however, directly concerned people, not resources. As western Europe revived economically, and before it became computerized, countries became heavily dependent on immigration from outside their territories. Some immigration (for example that of Turkish and other male workers – *Gastarbeiter*, 'Guest workers' – employed in Germany) began as seasonal: others, like Caribbean and Asian immigration into Britain from its old Empire, was from the start more long-term. The *Gastarbeiter* had lower wages, little job security and no civic rights: the numbers and citizenship qualifications of British immigrants were restricted by government. In the middle years of the century it was Switzerland, however, not the bigger countries, which had the highest proportion of immigrant workers.

There were many inter-relationships, logical and chronological, between these ten discontinuities. Decades were given individual profiles, but no decade was self-contained and no decade lacked contradictions as well as continuities. Immigration issues had been raised during the first decade of the century. The Bomb had been the ultimate product of a revolution in nuclear physics that was one of the most remarkable intellectual achievements of the early-twentieth century – the dissolution of 'classical' Newtonian physics in the decade before 1914. (Einstein published five key papers in 1905, one of them setting out his special theory of relativity.) By 1925 A. N. Whitehead, a brilliant observer of what was happening not only in physics but in other sciences and in the arts, could conclude that 'the stable foundations of physics' had completely 'broken up'. 'The old foundations of scientific thought are becoming unintelligible. Time, space, matter, material, ether, electricity, mechanism, organism, configuration, structure, pattern, function, all require reinterpretation.' Quantum physics, which developed later, rested on what Werner Heisenberg described in 1927 in mathematical terms as a principle of 'uncertainty'.

The 'uncertainty' which physicists now identified was increasingly plain in the political world of the 1960s, while economies boomed. Nor did it diminish when economies slumped in the uneasy 1970s, when politicians were forced to confront the economic realities of an 'energy crisis' long in the making. Economics now seemed more relevant than sociology, but there were sharp divisions between economists and few insights concerning how to relate economics to other 'social sciences'. During the 1980s politicians in countries as different as Thatcher's Britain and Gorbachev's Soviet Union sought radical answers to old problems. The phrase 'enterprise culture' was coined in the short-lived boom in Britain from 1984 to 1987 which popularized the term, but the decade ended in the economic recession which severely hit both Germany and France and socialist Spain. By the late 1980s Britain had lost much of its industrial base, but as the issues shifted, British attitudes towards Europe and its future were increasingly caught up in distant history just as much as Irish politics were before a 'peace process' began belatedly during the 1990s.

Such entanglements were not exceptional. In the countries of central and eastern Europe many aspects of politics were explicable only in terms of the history of the Ottoman Empire. So, too, before 1989, was the sequence of international terrorist incidents, only the most dramatic of which, like hijacking, hit the headlines. Their numbers rose almost continuously from 125 in 1968 to 831 in 1987. Yet behind almost every one of them there was a historical legacy. The cause that moved many terrorists had its origins in Palestine, which had been made a British mandate after the First World War and which became the home of the new state of Israel after the Second World War. Another cause had its origins in Algeria. Europe's internal sources of terrorism included one of the oldest populations in Europe, the Basques.

In the case of technology, which some of the terrorists learned to use, there were continuities also, although new technology, the fourth discontinuity, always served in Toffler's phrase as 'the great growling engine of change', ushering in a 'third age' the contemplation of which pushed many of its critics into 'new age' philosophies. The continuities, less discussed, affected both processes and imaginative impact. There had to be an electrical revolution before there could be a dazzling world of electronic circuitry, and it had been during the first years of the electrical revolution before 1900, when electricity was a 'mystery', that its imaginative impact was as great as that of the steam engine a century earlier. During the 1890s the Marquess of Salisbury anticipated the language of the Canadian Marshall McLuhan, one of the key figures in the 1960s, when he extolled the electrical revolution, drawing analogies with the nervous system and foreseeing new patterns of human response to instant communication. It was Salisbury, too, fascinated by global communications technology, who for quite different reasons signed the alliance with Japan in 1901 which marked the end of the long period when Britain would sign alliances with no-one, little foreseeing that it would be Japan that during the 'age of discontinuity' would create one of the largest electronic industries in the world.

Japanese transistor radios, cheap and portable, were being used throughout the world during the 1960s, indispensable instruments (before satellites) of an international revolution both in news delivery (including propaganda) and in popular musical culture. The indispensable tool, the transistor, invented in 1948 – followed by integrated circuitry – made it possible to compress all kinds of electrical equipment, not least digital electronic computers, into smaller and smaller space. The journey into outer space thereby became possible. It was not until the 1960s, however, after the Russian *Sputnik* had appeared in the skies in 1957, that aeroplanes, which had first been flown before 1914, really began substantially to influence the operations of the world economy. The pioneer of rocketry had been a Russian, Konstantin Tsiolhovski, who was born in 1857 and who lived long enough (until 1935) to serve the Bolshevik regime.

The first aeroplanes to break the sound barrier were military – and countries engaged in the heavy 'defence' expenditures of the Cold War determined the scale of late-twentieth-century technology. The term 'Big Science' was coined in the United States.[13] France, however, responded after de Gaulle to the calls of 'the computer age', having joined the British before de Gaulle in 1953 (at a great research cost) in the Concorde project which immediately met with opposition from conservationists. In the remarkable expansion of passenger traffic it was the United States aircraft industry, however, which led the way – with 'jumbo jets' that from 1970 linked continents. Meanwhile, automobile traffic on the roads, changing all the historic relationships between homes and workplaces and facilities for leisure, and choking historic towns and cities while opening up the countryside, increased faster than any predictions had suggested, transforming the appearance of the environment. European geography changed radically as a new and expensive infrastructure was created, with France and Britain being directly linked – by rail tunnel – for the first time since the Ice Age.[14]

Changes in communications, particularly tourism and the advent and spread of television during the 1950s and 1960s, were among the factors at work in eroding the distinctions between 'high culture' and 'mass culture'. Yet educational expansion, particularly in higher education, which had preceded technological change, was a necessary precondition as it was of an 'information society' which depended on the acquisition of new skills. Education, including 'continuing education', opened new means of access to 'knowledge' to large numbers of people from different social strata: there were many western European countries where the number of university students more than doubled during the 1960s, and many where the annual rate of increase in annual national expenditure on education exceeded the growth rate in the gross national product. In eastern Europe, too, educational expenditures were high, although the content was carefully controlled. The precise relationship between educational expenditures and innovation in industry and business was, however, never clear. Nor was the relationship between the level of 'research and development' and gross national income.

'Knowledge', which writers like Drucker considered the base for the effective management of increasingly complex societies, was in the West the source of most criticisms of society. From the 1960s onwards there were opponents of the 'whole system', with the word 'system', the unifying notion of 'operational research' and systems analysis, taking on new undertones. One of the key phrases of the 1960s – 'the capitalist, military, industrial system' or 'complex' – was popularized in the United States, where the 'system' was strongest and most challenged, but one of its leading 'new left' popularizers, Herbert Marcuse, came from Europe, a representative of the Frankfurt *Institut für Sozialforschung* (Institute for Social Research) which had been exiled *en bloc* from pre-war Germany. Marcuse, like the leader of the Frankfurt School, Theodor W. Adorno, criticized repression in the Soviet Union also, so that there was a lead-up to the events of 1989 in the 'capitalist' West, where Margaret Thatcher also claimed to have influenced the course of events in the East through 'selling' the merits of the free market.

How little was 'settled' in 1989 was demonstrated forcefully three years later – and further west – near the start of the new *fin de siècle* 1990s. The Treaty of Maastricht, agreed upon in December 1991, opened with the words 'By This Treaty, the High Contracting Parties establish amongst themselves a European Union', and later in the text it was stated that the Union had been 'concluded for an unlimited period'. Nonetheless there were at least as many question marks as there had been during the 1960s. Denmark held a referendum and did not ratify the Treaty until a second referendum had been carried through; France ratified it by the smallest margin; Britain prevaricated before Parliament ratified it by the slenderest margin. Meanwhile, an old question was revived. 'What is Europe?' Austria, Sweden and Finland joined in a new expanded Union; Norway chose after a referendum to stay out; eastern Europe was not admitted, nor was Turkey. There was still a regional as well as a national map of Europe in the early 1990s, and for all the continuing talk of a 'post-industrial society' there were still some regions in Europe which had been barely industrialized. The title of the successor to the scholarly *Daedalus* 1964 survey of Europe, published a generation later in 1994, was 'Europe Through a Glass Darkly'.[15]

References

1. See M. Poster (ed.), *Jean Baudrillard, Selected Writings* (1988).
2. For the American context see E. N. Saveth (ed.), *American History and the Social Sciences* (1964).
3. A. Toffler, *Future Shock* (1970), especially ch. 17, 'Coping with Tomorrow'. Toffler refers sideways to Margaret Mead.
4. Fukuyama's article 'The End of History' in *The National Interest* (1989) was written before the fall of the Wall. His book *The End of History and the Last Man* followed and appeared in a Penguin edition in Britain in 1992. For earlier description and discussion of the end of history, see L. Niethammer, *Post-histoire: Has History Come to an End?* (1993).
5. Ibid.
6. For the discovery of the genetic code, see J. D. Watson, *The Double Helix* (1968).

7. D. Thomson, *Europe Since Napoleon* (1966 edn) p. 946.

8. Edition entitled 'A New Europe?', in *Daedalus* (Winter 1964). See also M. Camps, *European Unification in the Sixties* (1967).

9. The same title was chosen in 1995 by Mark Galeotti for his study of security and politics in Soviet and post-Soviet Russia covering the years after 1979.

10. See G. Cross, *Time and Money: the Making of Consumer Culture* (1993).

11. The word 'modernization' was often used as uncritically as the word 'modern' to describe the impact of 'the West' on the non-European world. See, for example, I. R. Sinai, *The Challenge of Modernisation* (New York, 1964).

12. For a brief account of Peter Drucker's writings, which began with his stimulating *The End of Economic Man* (1939), see J. J. Tarrant, *Drucker* (New York, 1976).

13. See D. de Solla Price, *Little Science, Big Science* (1963); and I. Spiegel-Rösing and D. de Solla Price, *Science, Technology and Society. A Cross Disciplinary Perspective* (1977).

14. For the Tunnel in historical perspective, see D. Abel, *Channel Underground* (1961) and for perceptive discussions of issues related to it, see ex-Ambassador Nicholas Henderson, *Channels and Tunnels: Reflections on Britain and Abroad* (1987).

15. See also editions entitled 'Old Faiths and New Doubts: the European Predicament', *Daedalus* (Spring 1979) and 'Eastern Europe ... Central Europe ... Europe.', *Daedalus* (Winter 1990).

Bibliographical Essay*

The long period covered in this volume has stimulated an immense amount of writing at all levels, much of it American. It reflects changes in the approach to history as well as in the accumulation of documentary and other evidence, visual and statistical. Much of the most searching interpretation is to be found in historical periodicals, many of them deliberately 'revisionist' in character. There are also, however, several series of useful paperbacks, for example, *Documents and Debates* (general editor, John Wroughton) and *Lancaster Pamphlets* (generals editors, E. J. Evans and P. D. King) which cover topics like *Bismarck and German Unification* (D. Hargreaves, 1991) and *The Unification of Italy* (J. Gooch, 1986).

The best general introduction remains D. Thomson, *Europe Since Napoleon* (1957) which was revised in 1966 before its author's death. Its select bibliography is out of date, however, and much revisionist interpretation now has to be taken fully into account. Compare from the same period G. Barraclough, *An Introduction to Contemporary History* (1964).

For the period before this volume begins see its companion volume, H. G. Koenigsberger, *Early Modern Europe, 1500–1789* (1987) and W. Doyle, *The Old European Order, 1660–1800* (1978). For the world setting, which has changed dramatically in the twentieth century, see J. M. Roberts, *The Pelican History of the World* (1980). For links with the twentieth century see W. R. Keylor, *The Twentieth-Century World: An International History* (1984). P. Kennedy examines the changing determinants in *The Rise and Fall of the Great Powers, Economic Change and Military Conflict from 1500 to 2000* (1988). See also A. W. Woodruff, *Impact of Western Man: A Study of Europe's Role in the World Economy* (1967).

E. J. Hobsbawm has written an impressive trilogy on 'the long nineteenth century' with revealing titles that reflect his approach: *The Age of Revolution, 1789–1848* (1962); *The Age of Capital, 1848–1875* (1975); *The Age of Empire* (1987). The trilogy has been followed (after the world had developed differently from what Hobsbawm anticipated) by his *The Age of Extremes* (1994). For more pluralistic interpretations by different authors see A. Briggs (ed.), *The Nineteenth Century* (1970) and P. Flora *et al.*, *State, Economy and Society in Western Europe, 1815–1975* (1983). For religion see H. McLeod, *Religion and the People of Western Europe, 1789–1970* (1981).

*Reader should note that in all cases the place of publication is London unless otherwise stated.

474

Different countries have followed their own paths, and although there is a considerable literature on Germany's 'special way' (*Sonderweg*), it is clear that Britain, France and Italy followed 'special ways' also. See M. Fulbrook (ed.), *National Histories and European History* (1993). The implications for Germany are considered, but not settled, in D. Blackbourn and G. Eley, *The Peculiarities of German History: Bourgeois Society and Politics in Nineteenth-Century Germany* (1984) and R. J. Evans, *Rethinking German History: Nineteenth-Century Germany and the Origins of the Third Reich* (1987).

For individual countries see A. Briggs, *The Age of Improvement* (1979 edn); N. McCord, *British History, 1815–1906* (1991); H. Perkin, *The Origins of Modern English Society, 1780–1880* (1969); R. F. Foster *Modern Ireland* (1988); W. Carr, *A History of Germany, 1815–1985* (3rd edn, 1987); C. A. Macartney, *The Habsburg Empire, 1790–1815* (1969 edn); R. A. Kann, *The Multinational Empire* (1950); D. Mack Smith, *The Making of Modern Italy* (1968); R. Carr, *Spain 1808–1939* (1966); R. Magraw, *France, 1815–1914: The Bourgeois Century* (1983); L. Kochan and M. Abraham, *The Making of Modern Russia* (1983 edn); J. K. Kerry, *A History of Scandinavia* (1979); D. Kirby, *The Baltic World, 1772–1993* (1995); N. Davies, *Heart of Europe: A Short History of Poland* (1986); and B. Jelavich, *The Establishment of the Balkan National States, 1804–1920* (1977).

There is a useful Open University course *What is Europe?* (AD 280) which has been produced by a course team drawn from different European countries. Volume I of the course material is called *The History of the Idea of Europe*, and the other three volumes are *Aspects of European Cultural Diversity*, *European Democratic Culture* and *Europe and the Wider World*. See also E. Bruley and E. H. Dance, *A History of Europe?* (1960); J-B. Duroselle, *Europe, A History of its Peoples* (English translation, 1990); D. Heater, *The Idea of European Unity* (1992); and H. Brugmans, *Europe: A Leap in the Dark* (1985).

For regions within Europe see C. Harvie, *The Rise of Regional Europe* (1994) and R. Schulze (ed.), *Structural Change in Early-Industrialized Regions* (1993). There are many detailed studies of particular regions. See also H. C. Meyer, *Mitteleuropa in German Thought and Action* (1955).

L. Snyder, *Fifty Major Documents of the Nineteenth Century* (1955) is a useful brief collection of texts. See also R. R. Mowat, *Select Treaties and Documents, 1815–1916* (1932). For geography turn to *The Penguin Atlas of Recent History: Europe Since 1815* (1986) and for statistics to B. R. Mitchell, *European Historical Statistics, 1750–1970* (1978).

On population see L. Kosinski, *The Population of Europe* (1970) and W. R. Lee (ed.), *European Demography and Economic Growth* (1979); D. V. Glass and D. E. C. Eversley (eds), *Population and Social Change* (1965); and D. V. Glass and R. Revelle (eds), *Population and Social Change* (1972). Compare E. A. Wrigley and R. Schofield, *The Population History of England* (1981) and E. Hofsten, *Swedish Population History, Main Trends from 1750 to 1970* (1976). See also P. Hall, *The World Cities* (1966).

For migration see L. P. Moch, *Moving Europeans: Migration in Western Europe since 1650* (1993); C. G. Pooley and I. D. Whyte, *Migrant: Emigrants and Immigrants, a Social History of Migration* (1991); and for one special group of migrants E. H. Carr, *The Romantic Exiles* (1933). See also B. Porter, *The Refugee Question in Mid-Victorian Politics* (1979).

For an overview of the changing role of women, recently a much examined subject, see B. S. Anderson and J. P. Zinsser, *A History of Their Own: Women in*

Europe from Prehistory to the Present (1988); A. Myrdal, *Nation and Family* (1968); J. Scott, *Women, Work and Family* (1978); and L. Tilly and T. McBride, *The Domestic Revolution: The Modernisation of Household Service in England and France, 1820–1920* (1976). For youth see J. R. Gillis, *Youth and History: Tradition and Change in European Age Relations, 1770 to the Present* (1974).

Chapter 1: Revolution and Empire: Experience and Impact, 1789–1815

The best recent British study of the French Revolution is by W. Doyle, *The Oxford History of the French Revolution* (1989). There is a useful and brief survey of the often controversial issues raised before and during the revolutionary sequence began by G. Lewis in *The French Revolution: Rethinking the Debate* (1993). Both books include bibliographies. C. Jones, *The Longman Companion to the French Revolution* (1989) provides a massive but manageable chronicle. For the most recent interpretation of the Revolution see the four volumes of *The French Revolution and the Creation of Modern Political Culture*, vol. I (1987) and vol. IV (1994) edited by K. Baker, vol. II (1988) by C. Lucas, and vol. III (1989) by F. Furet and M. Ozouf. See also R. Cobb, *The People's Armies* (1987), and P. Jones, *The Peasantry in the French Revolution* (1988). The most exciting book to appear in the bicentennial year of the Revolution was S. Schama, *Citizens* (1989).

P. D. Sutherland, *France, 1789–1815, Revolution and Counter- Revolution* (1985) carries the story further intelligently and critically through the rise and fall of Napoleon. It includes a valuable bibliography. So too does P. McPhee, *A Social History of France, 1780–1880* (1992).

The best life of Napoleon is by G. Lefebvre, in English translation in two volumes (1969). P. Geyl, *Napoleon, For and Against* (1963) covers the arguments surrounding him at different times then and since. M. G. Hutt (ed.), *Napoleon* (1972) presents a collection of illuminating documents. See also J. Godechet, B. F. Hyslop and D. L. Dowd, *The Napoleonic Era in Europe* (1971). On Napoleon's wars see M. Glover, *The Napoleonic Wars: An Illustrated History, 1792–1815* (1979); G. Best, *War and Society in Revolutionary Europe, 1770–1870* (1982); D. Chandler, *The Campaigns of Napoleon* (1966); and G. Rothenberg, *The Art of Warfare in the Age of Napoleon* (1978).

Industrial change is covered in different countries in two volumes of the Fontana *Economic History of Europe*, edited by C. M. Cipolla – vol. 3, *The Industrial Revolution* (1973) and vol. 4 *The Emergence of Industrial Societies* (1973). D. S. Landes, *The Unbound Prometheus: Technological Change and Industrial Development in Western Europe from 1750 to the Present* (1969) is an invaluable and highly stimulating survey. See also T. Kemp, *Industrialization in Nineteenth Century Europe* (1969); C. Trebilcock, *The Industrialisation of the Continental Powers, 1780–1914* (1981); S. Pollard, *Peaceful Conquest, The Industrialisation of Europe, 1760–1970* (1981) and *The Integration of the European Economy since 1815* (1981); and A. S. Milward and S. B. Saul, *The Economic Development of the Economies of Continental Europe, 1780–1870* (1973). See also G. Gerschenkron, *Economic Backwardness in Historical Perspective* (1962).

For Britain see P. Matthias, *The First Industrial Nation: An Economic History of*

Britain, 1700–1914 (1969) and the still fascinating older French book by P. Mantoux, *The Industrial Revolution of the Eighteenth Century* (English translation, 1928).

For more recent studies of the cultural implications of industrialization see A. Briggs, *Ironbridge to Crystal Palace: Impact and Images of the Industrial Revolution* (1979) and *The Power of Steam* (1982). An earlier work of considerable historiographical importance, profusely illustrated, is S. Giedion, *Mechanisation Takes Command* (1948). For distinctive aspects of the cultural history of the French Revolution see F. Kennedy, *A Cultural History of the French Revolution* (1989); M. Carlson, *The Theatre of the French Revolution* (1966); M. Ozouf, *Festivals and the French Revolution* (1988); and A. Ribeiro, *Fashion in the French Revolution* (1966).

Comparative history is treated in J. Black, *Convergence or Divergence?* (1994), G. A. Williams, *Artisans and Sans Culottes* (1968) and P. O. Brien and C. Keydor, *Economic Growth in Britain and France, 1780–1914* (1978). For comparative history over time see A. D. Harvey, *Collision of Empires: Britain in Three World Wars, 1793–1945* (1992).

Chapter 2: Order and Movement, 1815–1848

J. Droz, *Europe between Revolutions, 1815–1848* (1967) provides a brief introduction. See also A. Sked, *Europe's Balance of Power, 1815–1848* (1979); E. V. Gulik, *Europe's Classical Balance of Power* (1955); and P. Schroeder, *The Transformation of European Politics, 1763–1848* (1994). An older book by E. L. Woodward, *Three Studies in European Conservatism: Metternich, Guizot, the Catholic Church in the Nineteenth Century* (1929) is still worth reading. Compare the very different – not quite so old – book by H. Kissinger, *A World Restored: Metternich, Castlereagh and the Problems of Peace, 1812–1822* (1957), written before its author turned to diplomacy. For Metternich's personality and Austrian policies see E. Radvang, *Metternich's Projects for Reform in Austria* (1971) and A. Reinerman, *Austria and the Papacy*, 2 vols (1979, 1989).

For Germany see T. S. Hamerow, *Restoration, Revolution and Reaction: Economics and Politics in Restoration Germany (1815–1871)* (1958). For France see P. Pilbeam, *The French Revolution of 1830* (1971); D. Johnson, *Guizot* (1963); P. H. Hutton, *The Cult of the Revolutionary Tradition* (1981); M. Agulhon, *Marianne into Battle: Republican Imagery and Symbolism in France, 1789–1880* (1981); and F. L. J. Hemmings, *Culture and Society in France, 1789–1848* (1987). For Italy see K. R. Greenfield, *Economics and Liberalism in the Risorgimento: A Study of Nationalism in Lombardy, 1814–1848* (1934).

For nationalism as a force making for change see C. J. Hayes, *The Historical Evolution of Modern Nationalism* (1931), a dated but readable introduction to a complex subject; B. Anderson, *Imagined Communities: Reflections on the Origin and Spread of Nationalism* (1983); E. J. Hobsbawm, *Nations and Nationalism since 1780: Programme, Myth, Reality* (1990); J. Breuilly, *Nationalism and the State* (1985); A. D. Smith, *The Ethnic Origins of Nations* (1983); and, broad in its reference, E. Hobsbawm and T. Ranger (eds), *The Invention of Tradition* (1983).

For 'the city' see A. F. Weber, *The Growth of Cities* (1899); P. Hauser and L. Schnore (eds), *The Study of Urbanisation* (1965); E. Jones, *Towns and Cities* (1966); A. Briggs, *Victorian Cities* (1963); L. Chevalier, *Labouring Classes and Dangerous Classes in Paris During the First Half of the Nineteenth Century* (English translation, 1973); J.

M. Merriman, *The Margins of City Life: Exploration on the French Urban Frontier, 1815–1851* (1991); and W. Sharpe and L. Wallack, *Visions of the Modern City* (1983).

For the 'middle classes' see P. Pilbeam, *The Middle Classes in Europe, 1789–1914* (1990) and for labour D. Geary, *European Labour Protest, 1848–1939* (1981) which carries the story of socialism beyond the revolutions of 1848. See also A. Mitchell and I. Deak, *Everyman in Europe: The Industrial Centuries* (2nd edn, 1981). For the origins of socialism see G. D. H. Cole, *A History of Socialist Thought*, 4 vols (1953).

R. Clagg, *The Movement for Greek Independence* (1976) deals with one of the first European movements that inspired and made for change. For the revolutions of 1848 see R. Price, *The Revolutions of 1848* (1988); F. Fejtö, *The Opening of an Era, 1848* (1948); L. B. Namier, *1848: the Revolution of the Intellectuals* (1945), a brilliant essay which now dates; M. Traugott, *Armies of the Poor* (1985); R. Stadelmann, *Social and Political History of the German 1848 Revolution* (1975); W. H. Sewell, *Work and Revolution in France: The Language of Labor from the Old Regime to 1848* (1980); and P. Ginsberg, *Daniele Manin and the Venetian Revolution of 1948–9* (1979).

Chapter 3: Nation Building, 1848–1871

A valuable introduction to the diplomatic history of the period covered in this chapter and the next is A. J. P. Taylor, *The Struggle for Mastery in Europe, 1848–1914* (1954). The defeat of revolution and the development, by different means, of a new map of Europe is described in O. Pflanze, *Bismarck and the Development of Germany: the Period of Unification, 1815–1871* (1963).

For the Frankfurt Parliament see F. Eyck, *The Frankfurt Parliament, 1848–9* (1968) and for the European context W. E. Mosse, *The European Powers and the German Question, 1848–71* (1958). On the Crimean War and the 'destruction of the European Concert' see P. W. Schroeder, *Austria, Britain and the Crimean War* (1972). For two of the main contestants see O. Anderson, *A Liberal State at War, English Politics and Economics During the Crimean War* (1967) and J. S. Curtiss, *Russia's Crimean War* (1979). W. Baumgart, *The Peace of Paris* (1956) and W. E. Mosse, *The Rise and Fall of the Crimean System, 1855–1871* (1963) deal with the implications for the 'Concert of Europe'. See also W. N. Medlicott and D. K. Coveney (eds), *Bismarck and Europe* (1971); K. Bourne, *Victorian Foreign Policy, 1830–1902* (1970); and R. Hyam, *Britain's Imperial Century, 1815–1914* (1975).

For France see R. Price (ed.), *Revolution and Reaction, 1848 and the Second French Republic* (1975); P. McPhee, *A Social History of France, 1780–1880* (1992); and I. Collins (ed.), *Government and Society in France, 1814–1848* (1970). For the Second Empire see A. Plessis, *The Rise and Fall of the Second Empire, 1852–1871* (English translation, 1985); T. Zeldin, *France 1848–1945* (1973) and (ed.), *Conflicts in French Society: Anticlericalism, Education and Morals in the Nineteenth Century* (1970). There is a revealing detailed study by D. Pinkney, *Napoleon III and the Rebuilding of Paris* (1975).

For Italy, L. Riall, *The Italian Risorgimento, State, Society and National Unification* (1994) provides a useful chronology and sorts out the complexities of interpretation. See also H. Hearder, *Italy in the Age of the Risorgimento* (1983) and J. A. Davis and P. Ginsborg (eds), *Society and Politics in the Age of the Risorgimento* (1991); S. J. Woolf, *A History of Italy, 1700–1860, The Social Constraints of Political Change* (1979); and F. Coppa, *The Origins of the Italian Wars of Independence* (1992).

For three of the main figures in the mid-century story as seen by British historians, see A. J. P. Taylor, *Bismarck, the Man and the Statesman* (1955), D. Mack Smith, *Cavour* (1985), *Garibaldi* (1957) and *Cavour and Garibaldi, a Study of Political Conflict* (2nd edn, 1985) and for a British politician as seen by a British twentieth-century politician, see R. Jenkins, *Gladstone* (1995). The best biography of Bismarck (in translation in two volumes) is by L. Gall, *Bismarck: The White Revolutionary* (1990). See also F. Stern, *Gold and Iron: Bismarck, Bleichröder and the Building of the German Empire* (1971) and O. Chadwick, *The Popes and European Revolution* (1981).

Chapter 4: Rivalry and Interdependence, 1871–1914

For introductions to the period see J. Joll, *Europe since 1870* (1973); N. Stone, *Europe Transformed, 1878–1916* (1983); and C. L. Mowat (ed.), *The New Cambridge Modern History*, vol. XII (revised edn), *The Shifting Balance of World Forces* (1968). A classic American study focusing on diplomatic detail is W. L. Langer, *European Alliances and Entanglements, 1871–1890* (1950 edn). It was followed by his further study *The Diplomacy of Imperialism, 1890–1902* (1965 edn).

For contrasting perspectives see J. Bartlett, *The Global Conflict, 1880–1970: The International Rivalry of the Great Powers* (1984); D. Calleo, *The German Problem Reconsidered: Germany and the World Order, 1870 to the Present* (1978); G. F. Kennan, *The Decline of Bismarck's European Order: Franco-Russian Relations 1875–1890* (1979); F. R. Bridge, *Austro-Hungary and the Great Powers* (1990); M. Beloff, *Imperial Sunset* (1961); J. F. V. Keiger, *France and the Origins of the First World War* (1983); and R. Bosworth, *Italy, the Least of the Great Powers: Italian Foreign Policy before the First World War* (1979).

See also P. Kennedy, *The Rise of the Anglo-German Antagonism, 1860–1914* (1980) and B. Porter, *Britain, Europe and the World, 1850–1892, Delusions of Grandeur* (1983).

For imperial Germany compare H.-U. Wehler, *The German Empire, 1871–1914* (1985) and R. J. Evans (ed.), *Society and Politics in Wilhelmine Germany* (1978). See also R. J. Evans (ed.), *The German Working Class, 1888–1933* (1982) and *The German Bourgeoisie* (1991). For Wilhelm II see J. C. Röhl, *The Kaiser and his Court* (1995), and, dealing with questions of continuity, J. C. Röhl (ed.), *From Bismarck to Hitler: the Problem of Continuity in German History* (1970).

For Italy see C. Seton-Watson, *Italy from Liberalism to Fascism* (1967). For France see R. D. Anderson, *France, 1870–1914, Politics and Society* (1977); D. Thomson, *Democracy in France since 1870* (1969 edn); and J. McManners, *Church and State in France, 1870–1914* (1972). For Britain see H. Pelling, *Popular Politics and Society in Late-Victorian Britain* (1968).

For labour politics see J. Breuilly, *Labour and Liberalism in Nineteenth-Century Europe* (1992); E. H. Hunt, *British Labour History, 1815–1914* (1981); K. Burgess, *The Challenge of Labour: Shaping British Society, 1850–1930* (1980); H. Pelling, *Origins of the Labour Party* (1965); R. Morgan, *The German Social Democrats and the First International* (1965); S. Edwards, *The Paris Commune, 1871* (1971); C. E. Schorske, *German Social Democracy, 1905–1917* (1955); W. Guttsman, *The German Social Democratic Party, 1875–1933* (1981); and J. L. H. Keep, *The Rise of Social Democracy in Russia* (1963).

For the military base of the Empire see G. Craig, *The Politics of the Prussian Army, 1640–1945* (1955); M. Kitchen, *The German Officer Corps, 1890–1914* (1968); and, in translation, four volumes of G. Ritter's *The Sword and Sceptre: The Problem of Militarism in Germany* (1969). For educational systems see as a lead-in D. K. Müller, F. Ringer and B. Simon (eds), *The Rise of the Modern Educational System: Structural Change and Social Reproduction, 1870–1920* (1987).

For the power of colonial empires see D. Fieldhouse, *The Colonial Empires: A Comparative Study from the Eighteenth Century* (1966). The technological and economic implications are well dealt with by D. R. Headrich, *The Tools of Empire: Technology and European Imperialism in the Nineteenth Century* (1981). For the dissolution of old European empires see A. Sked, *The Decline and Fall of the Habsburg Empire, 1815–1918* (1989). For the Russian Empire see H. Seton-Watson, *The Decline of Imperial Russia* (1960); H. Rogge, *Russia in the Age of Modernisation and Revolution, 1881–1917* (1983); and H. Kohn, *Pan-Slavism* (1960); and for the Ottoman Empire see W. W. Haddad and W. L. Oshsenwold (eds), *Nationalism in a Non-National State: the Dissolution of the Ottoman Empire* (1977) and M. Kent (ed.), *The Great Powers and the End of the Ottoman Empire* (1984).

Attempts at reform in the Ottoman Empire are dealt with by R. H. Davison, *Reform in the Ottoman Empire, 1856–1876* (1963). See also D. Kushner, *The Rise of Turkish Nationalism, 1876–1903* (1977). For change in Russia see M. S. Miller, *The Economic Development of Russia, 1905–1914* (1926); W. L. Blackwell, *The Industrialisation of Russia: An Historical Perspective* (1970); and, for the fascinating comparison with Japan, C. E. Black *et al.*, *The Modernisation of Japan and Russia: A Comparative Study* (1975).

There is an enormous literature on the origins of the First World War, written at different times and from different angles. For a summary see J. Joll, *The Origins of the First World War* (1984). D. C. B. Lieven, *Russia and the Origins of the First World War* (1983) is a notable recent contribution. The role of Germany is discussed, with very different conclusions, in H. W. Koch (ed.), *The Origins of the First World War* (1982).

For 'plans' see G. Ritter, *The Schlieffen Plan* (1958); P. M. Kennedy (ed.), *The War Plans of the Great Powers, 1880–1914* (1979) and E. Miller (ed.), *Military Strategy and the Origins of the First World War* (1985).

For the last stages in the making of war, see V. Dediger, *The Road to Sarajevo* (1966).

Chapter 5: Classicism, Romanticism, Victorianism, Modernity

E. Weber (ed.), *Paths to the Present: Aspects of European Thought from Romanticism to Existentialism* (1960) provides an excellent, well-edited selection of documents. See also W. E. Houghton, *The Victorian Frame of Mind, 1830–1870* (1985), G. L. Mosse, *The Culture of Western Europe* (1963) and H. S. Hughes, *Consciousness and Society: The Reorientation of European Social Thought, 1890–1930* (1986 edn). For the lead into the twentieth century see S. Kern, *The Culture of Time and Space, 1880–1918* (1983).

Benedetto Croce's *History of Europe in the Nineteenth Century* (English translation, 1933), which provides the lead into this chapter, should be set within the framework of G. de Ruggiero, *The History of European Liberalism* (English translation, 1927). Compare J. Sheehan, *German Liberalism in the Nineteenth Century* (1978) and J. P. Parry, *Democracy and Religion: Gladstone and the Liberal Party* (1986). See also J. Gray, *Liberalism* (1986).

For 'romanticism' and 'classicism', including 'neoclassicism', see the Royal Academy and Victoria and Albert Museum Catalogue, *The Age of Neo-Classicism* (1972); K. Clark, *The Gothic Revival* (1944); the classic study by M. Praz, *The Romantic Agony* (1933); the excellent brief introduction by L. R. Furst, *Romanticism* (1969); and A. K. Thorlby (ed.), *The Romantic Movement* (1966). For positivism see F. E. Manuel, *The Prophets of Paris* (1962).

P. Gay has written three huge volumes, each complete with impressive bibliographical notes, *The Bourgeois Experience: Victoria to Freud – The Education of the Senses* (1984); *The Tender Passion* (1986) and *The Cultivation of Hatred* (1993). They reach down to 1914. See also his *Freud, A Life for Our Times* (1988). Compare A. Copley, *Sexual Moralities in France, 1780–1980, New Ideas on the Family, Divorce and Homosexuality* (1989).

Out of a huge literature on Darwin start with G. de Beer, *Charles Darwin* (1963) and L. Eiseley, *Darwin's Century* (1958). For its context and its implications see J. W. Burrow, *Evolution and Society* (1966), which focuses on England; L. L. Clark, *Social Darwinism in France* (1984); and A. Kelly, *The Descent of Darwinism: The Popularisation of Darwin in Germany, 1860–1914* (1981).

For technology see N. Rosenberg, *Perspectives on Technology* (1976); M. Kranzberg and C. W. Pursell (eds), *Technology in Western Civilisation* (1967); J. Beniger, *The Control Revolution: Technological and Economic Origins of the Information Society* (1986); M. Pearton, *The Knowledgeable State: Diplomacy, War and Technology since 1830* (1982); I. F. Clarke, *The Pattern of Expectation, 1644–2001* (1979); P. Anderson, *The Printed Image and the Transformation of Popular Culture, 1790–1860* (1991); and T. P. Hughes, *Networks of Power, Electrification in Western Society, 1880–1930* (1983).

For communications see M. Robbins, *The Railway Age* (1970); N. Faith, *The World of Railways* (1990); P. O'Brien, *Railways and the Economic Development of Western Europe, 1830–1914* (1983); J. Kieve, *The Electric Telegraph: A Social and Economic History* (1973); H. Perkin, *The Age of the Automobile* (1976); J. M. Laux, *The French Automobile Industry to 1914* (1976); H. O. Duncan, *The World on Wheels* (1926); C. E. Foyle, *A Short History of the World's Shipping Industry* (1933); C. Gibbs-Smith, *The Invention of the Aeroplane, 1799–1809* (1966); and, critical and constructive, D. Edgerton, *England and the Aeroplane* (1991). See also I. de Sola Poole (ed.), *The Social Impact of the Telephone* (1977); W. P. Joly, *Marconi* (1972); and R. N. Vyvyan, *Marconi and Wireless* (1974).

For the organizational shells within which technology and communications developed see W. Sombart, *The Quintessence of Capitalism* (1915); L. Hannah, *The Rise of the Corporate Economy* (1976); S. Rolfe, *The International Corporation* (1969); M. Wilkins, *The Emergence of Multi-national Enterprise* (1970); and A. Reichova, M. Lévy-Leboyer and H. Nussbaum (eds), *Multinational Enterprise in Historical Perspective* (1986). For links between economics and politics see J. A. Schumpeter, *Capitalism, Socialism and Democracy* (1943).

For the late-nineteenth century and early-twentieth century city see A. Sutcliffe (ed.), *Metropolis, 1890–1960* (1984). R. J. Evans, *Death in Hamburg: Society and Politics in the Cholera Years, 1830–1870* is a brilliant detailed study.

For *fin de siècle* perspectives see K. W. Swart, *The Sense of Decadence in Nineteenth*

Century France (1964); F. Stern, *The Politics of Cultural Despair* (1961); and M. Teich and R. Porter (eds), *Fin de siècle and its Legacy* (1990). A brilliant study is C. E. Schorske, *Fin de Siècle Vienna: Politics and Culture* (1980). Compare H. Jackson, *The Eighteen Nineties* (1913). See also P. Pulzer, *The Rise of Political Anti-Semitism in Germany and Austria* (1963). For Nietzsche see W. Kaufmann, *Nietzsche* (1950). For anarchists see J. Joll, *The Anarchists* (1964).

The psychology of 'the masses' was a familiar topic in the late century. See G. Le Bon, *The Crowd: A Study of the Popular Mind* (1903). G. Lichtheim, *Marxism: An Historical and Cultural Study* (1961) is one of the many books that notes Marxist appeals to 'the masses'. The word 'mass' had a wider application too through changes in production, retailing, consumption and culture. See W. H. Fraser, *The Coming of the Mass Market, 1850–1914* (1981). For the early department store M. Muller, *The Bon Marché: Bourgeois Culture and the Development of the Department Store, 1869–1920* (1981) raises interesting questions. So too does R. Williams, *Dream Worlds: Mass Consumption in Late-Nineteenth Century France* (1982). See also A. Briggs, *Victorian Things* (1988). For 'mass leisure' see J. Walvin, *Leisure and Society, 1830–1950* (1978) and P. J. Graham and H. Weberhorst (eds), *The Modern Olympics* (1976).

The development of journalism, 'a window on the world', is well traced in R. Pound and G. Harmsworth, *Northcliffe* (1959); L. Brown, *Victorian News and Newspapers* (1985); A. J. Lee, *The Origins of the Popular Press in England, 1855–1914* (1976); and D. Read, *The Power of News: The History of Reuters* (1992).

For 'everyday life' and changing approaches to needs and wants (as expressed in food and drink) see J. Burnett, *Plenty and Want: A Social History of Diet in England from 1815 to the Present* (1966); S. Mennell, *All Manners of Food: Eating and Taste in England and France from the Middle Ages to the Present* (1985); R. E. F. Smith, *A Social and Economic History of Food and Drink in Russia* (1984); A. Corbain, *The Foul and the Fragrant* (English translation, 1986); and P. Goubart, *The Conquest of Water: The Advent of Health in the Industrial Age* (1989).

For art and design see M. Brion, *Art of the Romantic Era* (1966); Scottish National Gallery, *The Romantic Spirit in English Art, 1790–1990* (1995); P. Pool, *Impressionism* (1967); Metropolitan Museum of Art, *Impressionism, a Centenary Exhibition* (1974); J.- L. Daval, *Modern Art: The Decisive Years, 1884–1914* (1979); B. Denvir, *The Late-Victorians: Art, Design and Society* (1986); and R. D. Mandell, *Paris, 1900: The Great World's Fair* (1967).

For science see C. G. Bernhard, E. Crawford and P. Sorborn (eds), *Science, Technology and Society in the Time of Alfred Nobel* (1982). For medicine compare R. H. Skyrock, *The Development of Modern Medicine* (1947) and B. Inglis, *A History of Medicine* (1965).

Chapter 6: A European Civil War, 1914–1918

The key histories of the First World War are Liddell Hart's still authoritative, *History of the First World War* (1972), first published in 1934, Keith Robbins, *The First World War* (Oxford, 1984) and Norman Stone's study of *The Eastern Front, 1914–1917* (1975). The studies of J. Kocka, *Facing Total War* (Leamington Spa, 1984) and Marc Ferro's, *The Great War* (1973) translated respectively from German and French are also very useful, as is J. M. Bourne's *Britain and the Great War, 1914–1918* (1989). See also, M. Gilbert, *First World War* (1994) with a useful, but selective, bibliography.

For greater detail on international politics and economic history during the war see David Stevenson, *The First World War and International Politics* (1988); P. Einzig, *World Finance since 1914* (1935); Gerd Hardach, *The First World War, 1914–1918* (1987); and David Fromkin's *A Peace to End All Peace* (New York, 1989).

The impact of the war on society and literature has been dealt with by many writers in recent years. Some examples are Susan Pedersen, *Family, Dependence and the Origins of the Welfare State: Britain and France, 1919–1945* (Cambridge, 1993); Jay Winter, *The Experience of World War I* (1989); Richard Wall and Jay Winter (eds), *The Upheaval of War: Family, Work and Welfare in Europe, 1914–1918* (Cambridge, 1988); J. Williams, *The Home Fronts: Britain, France and Germany, 1914–1918* (1972); and Arthur Marwick, *War and Social Change in the Twentieth Century* (1974). Paul Fussell, *The Great War and Modern Memory* (1975) and Frank Field, *British and French Writers of the First World War* (1991) are amongst the best books on the history of soldiers and writers in the war. For women see Claire M. Tylee, *The Great War and Women's Consciousness: Images of Militarism and Womanhood in Women's Writings, 1914–1964* (1990); Jose Harris, *Private Lives, Public Spirit: A Social History of Britain, 1870–1914* (Oxford, 1993); and David Mitchell, *Women on the Warpath: The Story of Women in the First World War* (1966).

There is an enormous collection of memoirs on the First World War. James W. Gerard, *My Four Years in Germany* (1917); David Lloyd-George's voluminous six-volumed, *War Memoirs* (1933–36); and Vera Brittain's *Testament of Youth: An Autobiographical Study of the Years 1900–1925* (Glasgow, 1979); first published in 1923, are especially interesting. For a more recent survey of life at the battlefront see Tony Ashworth, *Trench Warfare, 1914–1918: The Live and Let Live System* (1980).

For greater detail on individual countries see Jean-Jacques Becker, *The Great War and the French People* (1985); F. Carsten, *Revolution in Central Europe* (1972); V. Berghan and M. Kitchen (eds), *Germany in the Age of Total War* (1981); J. Turner, *British Politics and the Great War* (1992); Richard Bosworth, *Italy and the Approach of the First World War* (1983); Jozsef Galantai, *Hungary in the First World War* (Budapest, 1989); and Norman Davies, *Heart of Europe: A Short History of Poland* (Oxford, 1984).

The literature on the Russian Revolution is also vast. The best of most recent studies is Richard Pipes, *The Russian Revolution 1899–1919* (1990), while Sheila Fitzpatrick's *The Russian Revolution, 1917–1922* (Oxford, 1982) remains an excellent introduction.

Chapter 7: A New Order? 1919–1929

The most recent accounts of the Paris Peace Conference include Alan Sharp's, *The Versailles Settlement* (1991); E. Goldstein, *Winning the Peace. British Diplomatic Strategy, Peace Planning, and the Paris Peace Conference 1916–1920* (Oxford, 1991) and Lloyd Ambrosius, *Wilsonian Statecraft: Theory and Practice of Liberal Internationalism During World War I* (Wilmington, 1991). For contemporary accounts see Harold Nicolson, *Peacemaking, 1919* (1933); Francesco Nitti's, *Peaceless Europe* (1922); and John Maynard-Keynes, *The Economic Consequences of the Peace* (1919). On the question of German guilt see A. Lentin, *Lloyd George, Woodrow Wilson and the Guilt of Germany* (Leicester, 1984). Bruce Kent takes up the issue of war debts and reparations in *The Spoils of War: The Politics, Economics and Diplomacy of Reparations, 1918–1932* (Oxford, 1989).

Sally Marks offers the best, short survey of European diplomacy in this period in *The Illusion of Peace: International Relations in Europe, 1918–1933* (1976). Derek H. Aldcroft, *From Versailles to Wall Street* (1977) and Roger Munting and B. A. Holderness, *Crisis, Recovery and War: An Economic History of Continental Europe, 1918–1945* (1991) examines the economics.

Most histories of the Russian Revolution cover the Civil War, but for greater detail see Evan Mawdsley, *The Russian Civil War* (1987). Alec Nove, *An Economic History of the USSR* (3rd edn, 1982) gives an interesting account of the Soviet Union's economic development while Martin McCauley offers a stimulating, documentary account of the war and how it changed the party in *The Russian Revolution and the Soviet State, 1917–1921* (1975).

The literature on eastern Europe during this period in English is scant in comparison to that of its western counterpart. For the best examples see Robin Okey, *Eastern Europe, 1740–1985* (1982); Antony Polonsky, *The Little Dictators: the History of Eastern Europe since 1918* (1975); and, still most thorough, C. A. Macartney, *Independent Eastern Europe: A History* (1962). Thomas Masaryk in his *The Making of a State: Memories and Observations 1914–1918* (1927) gives an interesting, if lengthy, biographical account of the period.

Charles Maier, *Recasting Bourgeois Europe: Stabilisation of France, Germany and Italy after World War I* (Princeton, 1975), offers the best comparative perspective on postwar stabilization. For individual nations see, on Britain, Charles L. Mowat's *Britain Between the Wars, 1918–1940* (1955, 5th edn, 1987); David Reynolds, *Britannia Overruled: British Policy and World Power in the Twentieth Century* (1991); and, on the sunset and sunrise of British economy, *The Development of the British Economy, 1914–1990* by Sidney Pollard (1962, 4th edn, 1992). For stimulating and recent accounts of British and French colonial relations during this period see P. J. Cain and A. G. Hopkins, *British Imperialism: Crisis and Deconstruction 1914–1990* (1993), and Raymond Betts, *France and Decolonisation, 1900–1960* (1991).

The history of the French economic crises of the 1920s is more accessible in English than its political history. The best of the former is Stephen A. Schuker, *The End of French Predominance in Europe: The Financial Crisis of 1924 and the Adoption of the Dawes Plan* (Chapel Hill, 1976). For foreign policy consult J. Jacobsen, *Locarno Diplomacy: Germany and the West, 1925–1929* (Princeton, 1972). The best English introduction to French politics is James McMillan's *Twentieth Century France: Politics and Society* (1985 and 1992). For details of the emergence of the French right wing see Robert Soucy, *French Fascism: the First Wave, 1924–1933* (1986).

Dennis Mack Smith's *Mussolini* (1981), and Adrian Lyttelton's *The Seizure of Power: Fascism in Italy, 1919–1929* (1973 and 1987), offer stimulating accounts of Italian politics. On Italian fascism's intellectual origins see A. James Gregor, *Young Mussolini and the Intellectual Origins of Fascism* (Berkeley, 1979). The most commanding Italian history of the period is Renzo De Felice, *Mussolini il fascista* (1968). On Spain see Gerald Brenan's still useful *The Spanish Labyrinth: An Account of the Social and Political Background to the Civil War* (Cambridge, 1949 and 1950). The prolific output of Raymond Carr and Paul Preston on Spain includes Carr's *The Civil War in Spain, 1936–1939* (1986) and Preston's *The Coming of the Spanish Civil War* (1978).

The literature of Weimar Germany is voluminous. Richard Bessel, *Germany after the First World War* (Oxford, 1993); John Hiden, *The Weimar Republic* (1984); Detlev

Peukert's similarly titled *The Weimar Republic: The Crisis of Classical Modernity* (1991); Richard Bessel and E. J. Feuchwanger (eds), *Social Change and Political Development in Weimar Germany* (1981), are among the best. For greater detail on Germany's hyper-inflationary crisis see Gerald Feldman (ed.), *The Great Disorder: Politics, Economics and Society in the German Inflation* (Oxford, 1993), and on culture Peter Gay's entertaining, *Weimar Culture: The Outsiders as Insiders* (1968).

Chapter 8: Guns and Butter, 1929–1939

Charles Kindleberger's *The World in Depression, 1929–39* (Harmondsworth, 1987) is still the best, most accessible, account of the depression. Although dated, the account of H. W. Arndt, *The Economic Lessons of the 1930s* (1944) remains useful. Karl Brunner (ed.), *The Great Depression Revisited* (The Hague, 1981) and William Ashworth, *A Short History of the International Economy since 1850* (3rd edn, 1975) offer a global perspective, while Barry Eichengreen, *Golden Fetters: The Gold Standard and the Great Depression, 1919–1939* (New York, 1992) and Ian Drummond, *The Gold Standard and the International Monetary System, 1900–1939* (1987) detail the operation of the gold standard.

Martin Kitchen, *Europe Between the Wars* (1990) gives the best comparative political analysis of Europe in this period. Still useful, too, are Joseph Schumpeter, *Capitalism, Socialism and Democracy* (7th edn, 1987) and E. H. Carr, *International Relations between the Two World Wars* (1947). Steven Salter and John Stevenson, *The Working Class and Politics in Europe and America, 1929–1945* (1990) offer interesting accounts of the social and political impact of the crisis on Europe's working class. Unfortunately, no extensive comparative study of the middle class is yet available.

The depression also triggered debate about greater European unity. For the origins of the EU see P. M. R. Stirk (ed.), *European Unity in the Context of the Interwar Period* (1989). For the history of individual countries during the depression consult Charles L. Mowat, *Britain Between the Wars 1918–1940* (1955); Keith Robbins, *The Eclipse of a Great Power. Modern Britain. 1870–1975* (1983); and J. Stevenson and C. Cook, *The Slump: Society and Politics during the Depression* (1977).

The literature of the collapse of Weimar is vast. A good starting point is Ian Kershaw (ed.), *Weimar: Why Did German Democracy Fail?* (1990). The literature on interwar France is slight by comparison, but important new additions are Julian Jackson, *The Politics of Depression in France, 1932–1936* (Cambridge, 1985) and by the same author *The Popular Front in France* (Cambridge 1989); and Eugene Weber's insightful *The Hollow Years: France in the 1930s* (New York, 1994). See Kenneth Mouré, *Managing the Franc Poincaré* for an important new account of French economic policy during this period. Detailed monographs on eastern Europe during the depression are still scant. Those available include, F. L. Carsten, *The First Austrian Republic, 1918–1938* (1986); Hans Rogger and Eugen Weber (eds), *The European Right. A Historical Profile* (Berkeley, 1966); and Owen Rutter, *Regent of Hungary. The Authorized Life of Nicholas Horthy* (1938). For a summary of recent scholarship see Michael Kaser's edited volumes *The Economic History of Eastern Europe, 1919–1975* (Oxford, 1986).

Gerald Brenan's *The Spanish Labyrinth* (Cambridge, 1943) is a dated but fascinating explanation of the background to the Spanish Civil War, as is Franz Borkenau's eye-witness account of the war in *The Spanish Cockpit* (1937 and 1986).

More recent books include Raymond Carr, *The Spanish Tragedy* (1986) and Ronald Fraser, *Blood of Spain. An Oral History of the Spanish Civil War* (1986). Important, too, is the first complete study of Franco by Paul Preston, *Franco. A Biography* (1994).

Comparative studies provide an interesting insight into European fascisms. For the best examples see Walter Laquer, *Fascism: A Reader's Guide* (1979); Ernst Nolte, *Three Faces of Fascism* (1965); and Roger Griffin, *The Nature of Fascism* (1991). For an illuminating contemporary documentation of the dominant ideologies see, Michael Oakeshott, *Social and Political Doctrines of Contemporary Europe* (1940). (For further suggestions see Chapter 7.) Scholarship on the theory and practice of Nazism, sometimes treated as distinct from European fascism, is needless to say, voluminous. Ian Kershaw provides an invaluable aid to the historiographical disputes in *The Nazi Dictatorship* (3rd edn, 1993). Jeremy Noakes and Geoffrey Pridham offer documents and commentary in *Nazism, 1919–1945: A Documentary Reader* (Exeter, 1984). Karl Bracher, *The German Dictatorship* (1971) is a valuable account, as are those of Joachim Fest, *The Face of the Third Reich* (Harmondsworth, 1972), Fritz Stern, *The Politics of Cultural Despair: A study in Germanic Ideology* (California, 1961); Detler Peukert, *Inside Nazi Germany. Conformity, Opposition and Racism in Everyday Life* (1982, 1987) and, more recently, Micheal Burleigh and Wolfgang Wippermann, *The Racial State: Germany, 1933–1945* (Cambridge, 1991). Richard Overy offers an excellent study of *The Nazi Economic Recovery, 1932–1938* (1986). The now classic study by Eberhard Jäckel, on *Hitler's Worldview. A Blueprint for Power* (Cambridge, Massachusetts , 1972) is a fascinating exploration of Hitler's ideas.

Ian Kershaw's *Hitler* (1991) and Alan Bullock's study of *Hitler and Stalin: Parallel Lives* (1991) are the most recent biographies of *Der Führer*. New archival materials from the former Soviet Union have also prompted a number of revised studies on Stalinism. Amongst the best are Roy Medvedev, *Let History Judge: The Origins and Consequences of Stalinism* (New York, 1989); Robert C. Tucker, *Stalin in Power. The Revolution from Above, 1928–1941* (1991); Chris Ward, *Stalin's Russia* (1993); and Robert Conquest *The Great Terror* (1990).

Chapter 9: From European to World War, 1933–1945

The fiftieth anniversary of the outbreak of the war prompted the publication of a number of new studies on the Second World War. Donald Watt, *How War Came* (1989) and Richard Overy, *The Road to War* (1989) are the best. Esmonde Robertson and Robert Boyce (eds), *The Paths to War* (1987) and Gordon Martel, *The Origins of the Second World War Reconsidered* (1986) offer interesting perspectives on recent historiographical debates and A. J. P. Taylor's controversial *The Origins of the Second World War* (1961) remains an excellent read.

For an economic perspective on Britain's 'appeasement' of Hitler see George Peden, *British Rearmament and The Treasury, 1932–1939* (Edinburgh, 1979). France's dilemma is well illustrated by Anthony Adamthwaithe, *France and the Coming of the Second World War* (1977) and David Reynolds gives a fascinating account of Britain's increasing dependence on the United States in *Britannia Overruled* (1990).

For the story of *Mussolini's Early Diplomacy* see the book by Robert Cassels (Princeton, 1970). MacGregor Knox, *Mussolini Unleashed* (Cambridge, 1982) provides valuable insight into Italy's imperial ambitions while Jonathan Steinberg, *All or*

Nothing. The Axis and the Holocaust, 1941–1943 (1990) addresses a neglected area of Axis relations. Paul Ginsbourg, *A History of Contemporary Italy. Society and Politics, 1943–1988* (1990) tells of Italy under Allied occupation.

John Keegan, *The Second World War* (1989) and Martin Kitchen, *The World In Flames* (1990) are concise, well-written accounts of the war, as is the account of Martin Gilbert, *The Second World War* (1989). Peter Calvocoressi, Guy Wint and John Pritchard have updated their thorough treatment in *Total War* (2 vols, 2nd edn, 1989) and, alongside Gerhard L. Weinberg's magisterial, *A World at Arms. A Global History of World War II* (Cambridge, 1994) emphasize the global character of the war. Richard Overy explores the essential interaction of strategy and economics to explain *Why the Allies Won* (1995).

Michael Balfour, *Propaganda in War, 1939–1945* (1979) and Marlis G. Steinert, *Hitler's War and the Germans. Public Mood and Attitude during the Second World War* (Ohio, 1977) provide details as to propaganda efforts of the main belligerent. James D. Wilkinson's study of *The Intellectual Resistance in Europe* is an important contribution to the study of wartime resistance and art. In contrast Paul Fussell, *Wartime* (Oxford, 1989) writes of the experience of soldiers and families in the war. For a cartoonist's eye view, Roy Douglas, *The World War, 1939–1945: The Cartoonist's Vision* (1990). For radio see A. Briggs, *The War of Words* (1970).

For an insight into life under occupation and the social cost of the war see: Werner Ring's *Life With the Enemy* (1982); Michael Marrus, *The Holocaust in History* (1988); Arno Mayer, *Why the Heavens did not Darken* (1990); and Arthur Marwick (ed.), *War and Social Change* (1988). *The Berlin Diaries of Marie 'Missie' Vassiltchikov* (1985) provide an unusual, well-written insight into life in Nazi Germany and the officer's plot against Hitler. The role of women in the war is explored by an ever growing number of authors. See Penny Summerfield, *Women Workers in the Second World War* (1984); Mary Buckley, *Women and Ideology in the Soviet Union* (1989); and Dorothy Sheridan (ed.), *Wartime Women* (1990). See also Susan Briggs, *Keep Smiling Through* (1975).

Chapter 10: Freezing and Thawing in Postwar Europe, 1945–1989

Anna Bramwell (ed.), *Refugees in the Age of Total War* (1988); Christian von Krockow, *Hour of the Women* (1992) – a compelling account of life in defeated Prussia – and Josef Skvorecky, *The Cowards* (Prague, 1958; London, 1968) offer contrasting impressions of life in eastern Europe after the war's end. For greater detail on the treatment of Germany see: Anne Deighton, *The Impossible Peace: Britain, the Division of Germany and the Origins of the Cold War* (Oxford, 1990); D. L. Bark and D. R. Gress, *A History of West Germany*, 2 vols (Oxford, 1989). Nicholas Pronay and Keith Wilson offer an interesting analysis on the 're-education' of Germany in *The Political Re-Education of Germany and her Allies after World War II* (1985). For bibliographical suggestions on western Europe's economic, social and political reconstruction see Chapter 11.

The literature on the Cold War is vast, offering a variety of interpretations as to its origins, course, and, more recently, its conclusion. Compare Herbert Feis, *From Trust to Terror* (New York, 1970); Robert James Maddox, *The New Left and the Origins of the Cold War* (Princeton, 1973); John Lewis Gaddis, *The United States and the Origins of the Cold War, 1941–1947* (New York, 1972); and James L. Gormly, *From*

Potsdam to the Cold War: Big Three Diplomacy, 1945–1947 (Wilmington, Delaware, 1990). Gabriel Partos's recent publication makes lively use of interviews conducted since the iron curtain fell in *The World that Came in From the Cold* (1993).

For an account of life in the USSR before reform see: Richard Pipes, *Russia under the Old Regime* (1974); Carl Linden, *Khrushchev and the Soviet Leadership: With an Epilogue on Gorbachev* (1966 and 1990); Geoffrey Hosking, *The Awakening of the Soviet Union* (1990); David Lane, *Soviet Economy and Society* (Oxford, 1985); and Mary McCauley, *Politics and the Soviet Union* (1977). Gorbachev's attempts at reform and the consequences of his failure are still being digested by political commentators and historians. For appraisals of Gorbachev before and after the collapse of the Soviet Union consult Martin McCauley (ed.), *The Soviet Union Under Gorbachev* (1987); Seweryn Bialer (ed.), *Politics, Society, Nationality inside the USSR* (1990) Richard Sakwa, *Gorbachev and his Reforms, 1985–1990* (1991). Jon Bloomfield's two works *Perestroika and the Re-making of Socialism* (1989) and *The Soviet Revolution* (1990); David Lane, *Soviet Society under Perestroika* (1990); and for an insight into the impact of 'openness' on Soviet culture, Alex Nove, *Glasnost in Action: Cultural Renaissance in Russia* (1989). Geoffrey Hosking, Jonathon Avis and Peter Duncan, *The Road to Post-Communism* (1992) offer illuminating commentary on life in the Commonwealth of Independent Republics.

The fall of the iron curtain has also allowed historians access to new documentary evidence on the history of eastern Europe, enabling scholars to add details where before there was often conjecture. The best histories of eastern Europe still include works written before 1989, see: George Schopflin, *Politics in Eastern Europe* (1981); Stephen White, John Gardner and George Schopflin, *Communist Political Systems: An Introduction* (1982); Joseph Rothschild, *Return to Diversity: A Political History of East Central Europe* (Oxford, 1989); Robin Okey, *Eastern Europe, 1740–1985* (1982); Michael Roskin, *The Rebirth of Eastern Europe* (Eaglewood Cliffs, NJ, 1991); and Geoffrey Swain and Nigel Swain, *Eastern Europe Since 1945* (1993).

For greater detail on individual countries see Jörg Hoensch, *A History of Modern Hungary, 1867–1986* (1988); Christopher Cviic, *Remaking the Balkans* (1991) on Yugoslavia; Henry Ashby Turner Jr, *The Two Germanies since 1945* (1987) and Michael Balfour, *Germany: the Tides of Power* (1992); and Norman Davies, *Heart of Europe: A Short History of Poland* (Oxford, 1984). For an eye-witness account of the dramatic events of 1989 see Timothy Garton Ash, *We the People: The Revolution of '89 Witnessed in Warsaw, Budapest, Berlin and Prague* (1990).

Chapter 11: Reconstructing Europe, 1945–1991

Western Europe's reconstruction has been the subject of a number of excellent books in recent years. Michael Hogan, *The Marshall Plan. America, Britain and the Reconstruction of Western Europe, 1947–52* (Cambridge, 1987) and Alan Milward, *The Reconstruction of Western Europe, 1945–1951* (1984) offer contrasting accounts of the impact of Marshall aid on European reconstruction. Charles Maier (ed.), *The Marshall Plan and Germany. West German Development within the Framework of the European Recovery Programme* (New York, 1991) and David Ellwood, *Rebuilding Europe. Western Europe, America and Postwar Reconstruction* (1992) are also important introductions to the subject.

For a comparative perspective on western Europe's subsequent political history see: Derek W. Urwin, *Western Europe since 1945: A Political History* (1968, 4th edn 1989); Walter Laquer, *Europe Since Hitler. The Rebirth of Europe* (1970, revised 1982); John W. Young, *Cold War Europe. A Political History, 1945–1989* (1991).

Most books on postwar Europe touch on western Europe's economic recovery, but for greater detail consult Angus Maddison, *Economic Growth in the West: Comparative Experience in Europe and North America* (1964); Charles Kindleberger, *The Financial History of Western Europe* (1984); Derek H. Aldcroft, *The European Economy, 1914–1980* (1978); and Herman Van Der Wee, *Prosperity and Upheaval. The World Economy, 1945–1980* (1986). For a thorough, recent survey of the European economy consult Andre Boltho (ed.), *The European Economy. Growth and Crisis* (Oxford, 1982 and 1991).

Research by historians and sociologists into the consequences of western Europe's 'economic miracles' for class relations in the postwar period lies behind Anthony Carew, *Labour under the Marshall Plan* (Manchester, 1987); Howard Machin (ed.), *National Communism in Western Europe: A Third Way to Socialism?* (1983); and Peter Weiler, *British Labour and the Cold War* (Stanford, 1988). William Paterson has edited a number of books on this subject, including *Social Democracy in Post-war Europe* (1974).

For a broader exploration of the relationship between the state and capitalism consult Andrew Shonfeld, *Modern Capitalism* (Oxford, 1965); R. Kuisel, *Capitalism and the State in Modern France* (Cambridge, 1981); M. L. Smith and Peter M. R. Stirk, *Making the New Europe. European Unity and World War Two* (1991); and Peter Hall, *Governing the Economy: The Politics of State Intervention in Britain and France* (Cambridge, 1986). For further details on individual nations see: Alan Ginsborg, *A History of Contemporary Italy. Society and Politics, 1943–1988* (1990); Michael Balfour, *Germany: the Tides of Power* (1992); Raymond Carr and Jaun Pablo Fusi, *Spain. Dictatorship to Democracy* (1979, 2nd edn, 1991); and Peter Hennessy, *Never Again. Britain 1945–1951* (1992).

The literature on the European Community grows ever larger. Amongst the best are works by William Wallace, including *The Transformation of Western Europe* (1990) and his edited collection, *The Dynamics of European Integration* (1991). Also useful are Derek W. Urwin, *The Community of Europe. A History of European Integration Since 1945* (1991) and Stephen George, *Politics and Policy in the European Community* (Oxford, 1985). For empires see M. Doyle, *Empires* (1988).

Chapter 12: The Great Mutation? The End of History?

Most of the key texts are referred to – and cited – in the text of this chapter. The literature concerning it is massive. In particular, see S. Freud, *Civilisation and its Discontents* (1929); U. Apollonio, *Futurist Manifestos* (1973); J. Ortega y Gasset, *The Revolt of the Masses* (1930); H. Arendt, *The Origins of Totalitarianism* (1951); J. Ellul, *The Technological Society* (English translation, 1969); S. Giner, *Mass Society* (1976); P. Slater, *Origins and Significance of the Frankfurt School* (1971); N. Wiener, *The Human Use of Human Beings: Cybernetics and Society* (1954); A. Toffler, *Future Shock* (1970) and *The Third Wave* (1980); and S. Nora and A. Minc, *The Computerization of Society* (1980).

For 'the end of ideology' see D. Bell's book with that title (1960) and for 'the end of history' F. Fukuyama, *The End of History and the Last Man* (1989). See also D. Bell, *The Cultural Contradictions of Capitalism* (1976); T. Roszak, *The Making of a Counter Culture* (1970); D. Kumar, *Prophecy and Progress: The Sociology of Industrial and Post-Industrial Society* (1978); D. Harvey, *The Condition of Postmodernity: an Enquiry into the Origins of Cultural Change* (Oxford, 1989); and S. Connor, *Postmodernist Culture* (1989).

For capitalism – and the economic background of change – see A. Shonfield, *Modern Capitalism: The Changing Balance of Public and Private Power* (1965); J. R. Gillingham, *Coal, Steel and the Rebirth of Europe, 1945–1955* (1991); H. van der Wee, *Property and Upheaval: the World Economy, 1945–1980* (1986); F. Hirsch, *The Social Limits of Growth* (1976) and, with particular reference to technology, the *Fast Report: Eurofutures, the Challenges of Innovation* (1984). For links with politics see D. Brinkley and C. Hackett, *Jean Monnet and the Path to European Unity* (1991); *Europe 2000* (1977); S. Berger (ed.), *Organising Interests in Western Europe: Pluralism, Corporatism, and the Transformation of Politics* (1981); W. N. Lindberg, *The Political Dynamics of European Integration* (1963); A. S. Milward, *The European Rescue of the Nation State* (1992); and E. Gellner, *Nations and Nationalism* (1983).

There have been many books dealing with the rise of 'consumerism' and its various modes of expression, particularly American. See G. Cross, *Time and Money: The Making of Consumer Culture* (1993) which includes a useful bibliography; S. Ewen, *Captains of Consciousness: Advertising and the Social Roots of Consumer Culture* (1976); R. Willett, *The Americanization of Germany, 1945–1949* (1992); R. F. Krisel, *Seducing the French: the Dilemma of Americanization* (1990); H. Lefebvre, *Everyday Life in the Modern World* (English translation, 1979); and J. Grimwood, *Photohistory of the 20th Century* (1986).

For art see *Post-Impressionism* (Royal Academy, 1979–80); E. F. Fry, *Cubism* (1966); H. Richter, *Dada* (1965); B. Hinz, *Art and the Third Reich* (1979); P. Gay, *Weimar Culture* (1968); *Art and Power, Europe Under the Dictators, 1930–45* (Hayward Gallery, 1995); L. H. Nicholas, *The Rape of Europe* (1994); and L. R. Lippard, *Pop Art* (1966). See also B. Hillier, *The Style of the Century* (1983).

For the media see A. Smith, *The Shadow in the Cave* (1973); D. Dayan and E. Katz, *Media Events: The Live Broadcasting of History* (1992); A. Smith (ed.), *Television: An International History* (1995); and G. J. Mulgan, *Communication and Control* (1991). *Film, an International History of the Medium* (1995).

For science see G. Holton, *The Twentieth Century Sciences: Studies in the Biography of Ideas* (1972) and R. Mendelsohn, *Science and Western Domination* (1974).

For population see E. S. Woytinsky, *World Population and Production* (1953) and R. W. Hiorns (ed.), *Demographic Patterns in Developed Societies* (1980); for migration C. G. Pooley and I. D. Whyte, *Migrants, Emigrants and Immigrants: A Social History of Migration* (1991); and for cities P. Hall, *The World Cities* (1966) and M. Dogan and J. D. Kasarda, *The Metropolis Era*, 2 vols (1988).

Index